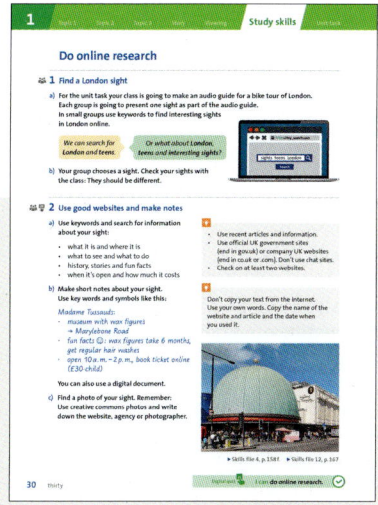
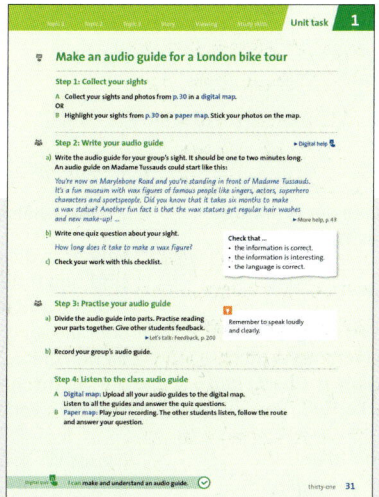
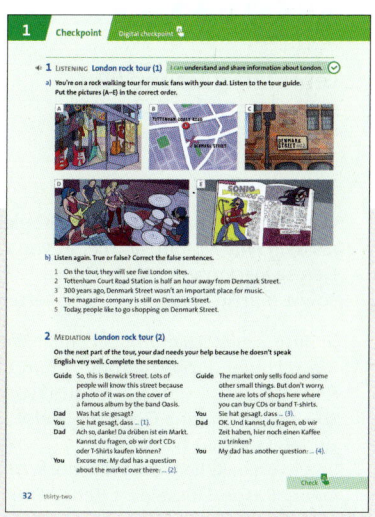

Lern- und Arbeitstechniken

Auf der *Study skills*-Seite übst du wichtige Lern- und Arbeitstechniken, z. B. wie du online recherchieren und die Ergebnisse notieren kannst.

Eine Aufgabe am Unit-Ende

In der *Unit task* erstellst du ein größeres Produkt, z. B. einen Audioguide. Dabei wendest du das Gelernte aus der Unit an.

Im *Checkpoint* wiederholst du

Hier überprüfst du, wie gut du die Lernziele der Unit schon erreicht hast.

Im Anschluss findest du ein *Text file* mit interessanten Texten zum Thema der Unit.

Diese Verweise führen dich in die *Diff bank* am Ende der Unit

▶ More help	▶ Parallel exercise	▶ More practice	▶ Challenge
Hilfen zu den Aufgaben	einfachere Variante einer Übung	weitere Übungen	weitere Übungen mit höherem Schwierigkeitsgrad

Diese Lernangebote findest du im hinteren Teil des Buches

▶ Skills file	▶ Language file	▶ Wordbank
eine Übersicht über die Lern- und Arbeitstechniken	die wichtigsten Sprachregeln	zusätzliche Wörter zu bestimmten Themen
Let's talk	**Vocabulary**	**Dictionary**
Redewendungen nach wichtigen Themen und Situationen geordnet	eine Liste der neuen Vokabeln einer Unit mit hilfreichen Tipps	alphabetische Wörterlisten zum Nachschlagen (Englisch – Deutsch)

lighthouse 3

Lehrkräftefassung Plus

Die **Unterrichtsvorschläge** und **Kopiervorlagen** der *Lehrkräftefassung Plus* wurden erarbeitet von Anke Barth, Plauen und Denise Heckmann, Hannover
sowie Martin Bastkowski, Schellerten *(Vorwort)*

in Zusammenarbeit mit der Englischredaktion
Klaus Unger (Projektleitung), Jenny Dames (verantwortliche Redakteurin), Chiara Castellano *(Vorwort, Glossar, Checkpoint-Lösungen)*, Brianna Gorman, Chelsea Ledvinka-Heß *(Vorwort)* und Julian Theo Wacker
sowie Anke Kellerhoff, Wilnsdorf *(Unit 2, Unit 4)* und
Georg Raspe, Düsseldorf *(Lehrkräftefassung, Lösungen)*

Schulbuch (978-3-06-036542-5)

Im Auftrag des Verlages herausgegeben von
Martin Bastkowski, Schellerten;
Sonja Mahne, Basel; Ulrike Rath, Aachen;
Berit Schaarschmidt, Aschaffenburg

Erarbeitet von
Rebecca Robb Benne, Kopenhagen;
Zoe Thorne, Royston
sowie Jennifer O'Hagan, Bristol und
Chris Maxwell, Berlin *(Checkpoints)*
und Ursula Fleischhauer, Hannover *(Vocabulary)*

Vocabulary, Dictionary
Ingrid Raspe, Düsseldorf

Beratende Mitwirkung
Anke Barth, Plauen; Peer Brändel, Gütersloh;
Claudia Görner, Maxdorf; Denise Heckmann, Hannover;
Stefan Herzberg, Berlin; Lara Jano, Rottweil;
Jimmy Miller, Berlin; Christoph Ullrich, Lemgo sowie
Vertr.-Prof. Dr. Christian Ludwig, Berlin;
Prof. Dr. Michaela Sambanis, Berlin

Medienmanagement
Silke Kirchhoff

Illustrationen
Harald Ardeias, Schelklingen; Irina Zinner, Hamburg

Fotos
Chocolate Films, London

Umschlaggestaltung
Rosendahl, Berlin

Layoutkonzept
Klein & Halm, Berlin

Layout und technische Umsetzung
Ungermeyer, Berlin *(Schulbuch)*;
Klein & Halm Grafikdesign, Berlin *(Lehrkräftefassung Plus)*;
MatMil & Kollegen, Kynšperk nad Ohří *(Kopiervorlagen)*

Druck
AZ Druck und Datentechnik GmbH, Kempten

PEFC-zertifiziert
Dieses Produkt stammt aus nachhaltig bewirtschafteten Wäldern und kontrollierten Quellen
PEFC/04-31-2260 www.pefc.de

www.cornelsen.de

Soweit in diesem Lehrwerk Personen fotografisch abgebildet sind und ihnen von der Redaktion fiktive Namen, Berufe, Dialoge und Ähnliches zugeordnet
oder diese Personen in bestimmte Kontexte gesetzt werden, dienen diese Zuordnungen und Darstellungen ausschließlich der Veranschaulichung und dem
besseren Verständnis des Buchinhaltes.

Dieses Werk berücksichtigt die Regeln der reformierten Rechtschreibung und Zeichensetzung.

Die Webseiten Dritter, deren Internetadressen in diesem Lehrwerk angegeben sind, wurden vor Drucklegung sorgfältig geprüft. Der Verlag übernimmt keine Gewähr für die Aktualität und den Inhalt dieser Seiten oder solcher, die mit ihnen verlinkt sind.

Alle Drucke dieser Auflage sind inhaltlich unverändert und können im Unterricht nebeneinander verwendet werden.

Die *Cornelsen Lernen App* ist eine fakultative Ergänzung zu *Lighthouse*, die die inhaltliche Arbeit begleitet und unterstützt. Als solche unterliegt sie nicht der Genehmigungspflicht.

© 2024 Cornelsen Verlag GmbH, Mecklenburgische Str. 53, 14197 Berlin

Das Werk und seine Teile sind urheberrechtlich geschützt. Jede Nutzung in anderen als den gesetzlich zugelassenen Fällen bedarf der vorherigen schriftlichen Einwilligung des Verlages.

Hinweis zu §§ 60a, 60b UrhG: Weder das Werk noch seine Teile dürfen ohne eine solche Einwilligung an Schulen oder in Unterrichts- und Lehrmedien
(§ 60b Abs. 3 UrhG) vervielfältigt, insbesondere kopiert oder eingescannt, verbreitet oder in ein Netzwerk eingestellt oder sonst öffentlich zugänglich gemacht oder wiedergegeben werden.
Dies gilt auch für Intranets von Schulen und anderen Bildungseinrichtungen.

1. Auflage, 1. Druck 2024

ISBN 9783060365463

lighthouse 3

Cornelsen

Inhalt

Legende — II

So funktioniert die *Lehrkräftefassung Plus* — III–IV

Vorwort *Lehrkräftefassung Plus* — V–XXIV

1. Das neue *Lighthouse* — V
2. Kommunikatives Handeln — V
3. Grammatik-Vermittlung — VII
4. Bewegtes Lernen — IX
5. Differenzierung / *Diff bank* — XI
6. Individualisierung — XIII
7. Lern- und Arbeitsheft — XV
8. *My task / Unit task* — XVII
9. Hybrides Arbeiten — XIX
10. Medien- und Aufgabenvielfalt — XXI
11. Lernstrategien — XXIII
12. *Global goals* — XXV

Begleitmedienübersicht — XXVII–XXVIII

Lehrkräftefassung mit didaktischen Kommentaren — 4–280

Quellenverzeichnisse

Lehrkräftefassung Plus — I
Schulbuch — 276–279

Anhänge zur *Lehrkräftefassung Plus* — 281–356

Lösungsbeispiele — 281–303
Methodisch-didaktisches Glossar — 304–328
Kopiervorlagen — 329–356

Quellenverzeichnis der Lehrkräftefassung Plus
Legende, S. II (Pearl): Cornelsen/Chocolate Films.

So funktioniert die Lehrkräftefassung Plus, S. III Lily: Cornelsen/Anja Poehlmann ; Ali: Cornelsen/Chocolate Films; A: mauritius images/alamy stock photo/dov makabaw; B: mauritius images/Novarc Images; C: stock.adobe.com/sborisov; **S. IV** D: Panther Media GmbH/Lucy Clark; E: dpa Picture-Alliance/robertharding; F: stock.adobe.com/Photocreo Bednarek.

Vorwort, S. VI: oben (Kleines Portrait von Dylan): Cornelsen/Chocolate Films; Collage: Cornelsen/Person re.: Chocolate Films, Wagen + Hintergrund: mauritius images/PHILIP SMITH/Alamy; **S. VIII** Fotos: 1: Aldo Kane; 2: Shutterstock.com/Dario Verdugo; 3: Shutterstock.com/HPH Image Library; **S. X** Shutterstock.com/sitthiphong; **S. XIV** oben li. (A–F): Cornelsen/Harald Ardeias, oben re.: Shutterstock.com/tommaso79; unten (Unit Plan): Foto 1.: mauritius images/Novarc Images, Foto 2.: mauritius images/Simon Belcher; Lighthouse Logo (Leuchtturm): Cornelsen/Inhouse/Bernd Lehmann; **S. XVI** li. oben + li. unten (S. 10): Flaggen: Shutterstock.com/SLdesign; Karte: stock.adobe.com/lesniewski; re. oben + re. unten (S. 11): Cornelsen/Chocolate Films; **S. XVIII** oben: Cornelsen/Laptop: Shutterstock.com/Passatic, Bildschirm-Illustration: Shutterstock.com/I000s_pixels; unten (Museum): ImagoStock&People GmbH/Mark Beto; **S. XX** Illustration (Aufstehen): Shutterstock.com/Net Vector; **S. XXII** oben (Nessie): Imago Stock & People GmbH/imagebroker/RolandxMarske; Mitte (Filmstills aus „The Coach"): Interfilm Berlin Management; **S. XXIV** Fotos oben: Fotos: 1: Aldo Kane; 2: Shutterstock.com/Dario Verdugo; 3: Shutterstock.com/HPH Image Library; Foto unten: Shutterstock.com/VH-studio; **S. XXVI** oben (SDG wheel): courtesy of the UNITED NATIONS/Department of Global Communications (https://www.un.org/sustainabledevelopment/ The content of this publication has not been approved by the United Nations and does not reflect the views of the United Nations or its officials or Member States.); Foto: mauritius images/alamy stock photo/Dmytro Zinkevych; Mitte (Rosie's fashion quiz): stock.adobe.com/eireenz; unten: stock.adobe.com/Soloviova Liudmyla.

Lösungsbeispiele, S. 285 (Ausschnitt Karte Hyde Park): Cornelsen/Carlos Borrell Eiköter.

Legende

Symbole und Markierungen in der *Lehrkräftefassung Plus*

last	Lernwortschatz (produktiv zu lernen)
°complete	situativer Wortschatz (nicht produktiv zu lernen)
⁺hotel	Wort, dessen Bedeutung sich erschließen lässt
you needn't	neue grammatische Strukturen
4 b) Yes, he did.	Lösungen zu geschlossenen Aufgabenformaten
1 a) Lösungsbsp. S. 281	Verweis auf Lösungsbeispiele (s. S. 281–303)
▶ Box: Voc., p. 208	Verweis auf Merkboxen im *Vocabulary*
Pearl	Auf den Abbildungen sind jeweils die Namen (ggf. mit Aussprachehinweisen) der wichtigen Personen angegeben.
Llandudno² 2 [lænˈdɪdnəʊ]	Aussprachehinweis bei Eigennamen und schwierigen Wörtern
🔊 1.1	CD- und Tracknummern aller für das SB aufgenommenen Hörtexte/Buchtexte
graue Schrift	fakultative Angebote

Schwerpunkte des sprachlichen *Skills*-Trainings

🎧 Listening   💬 Speaking   📖 Reading   ✏ Writing   ⇄ Mediation   MK Medienkompetenz inkl. Viewing

Verweise

▶ Bus stop	Verweis auf Einträge im methodisch-didaktischen Glossar (S. 304–328)
▶ KV 0.1	Verweis auf eine Kopiervorlage im Anhang der *Lehrkräftefassung Plus* (S. 329–356)
▶ Wordbank 1, S. 186	Verweis auf eine unterstützende *Wordbank* mit Seitenangabe
▶ Good to know, S. 11	Verweis auf eine *Good to know*-Box mit Seitenangabe
▶ Tippbox, S. 28	Verweis auf eine Tippbox mit Seitenangabe
▶ SF 1, S. 155	Verweis auf das *Skills file* im Anhang des SB (S. 154–168)
▶ LF 1, S. 169	Verweis auf das *Language file* im Anhang des SB (S. 169–183)

Abkürzungen

AA	Arbeitsanweisung		KV	Kopiervorlage(n) (s. Anhang S. 329–356)
App	Cornelsen Lernen App		L	Lehrkraft
Ausw.	Auswertung		MH	More help
Ch	Challenge		MP	More practice
DIFF	Extra-Differenzierung		PA	Partnerarbeit
EA	Einzelarbeit		S	Schüler/-in(nen)
Ex	Exercise		SB	Schulbuch
GA	Gruppenarbeit		Sich.	Sicherung
GSE	Grundschulenglisch		TA	Tafelanschrieb
HA	Hausaufgabe		UMA	Unterrichtsmanager Plus
INKL	Lern- und Arbeitsheft für Lernende mit erhöhtem Förderbedarf		WB	Workbook

So funktioniert die *Lehrkräftefassung Plus*

Unit-Übersicht:
- enthält Informationen zur **Storyline**, zu den neuen **Strukturen** sowie zum **Viewing** jeder Unit und nennt die **Unit task**

1

Unit-Übersicht

Storyline: Lily ist nach London gezogen. In dieser Unit werden Sehenswürdigkeiten, bekannte Plätze und Attraktionen in London vorgestellt. S lernen Pearl und Ali kennen, die gemeinsam mit Lily verschiedene Unternehmungen in London machen. Dabei nutzen sie öffentliche Verkehrsmittel. In der Story geht Lily verloren. Pearl und Ali machen sich auf die Suche nach ihr …
Strukturen: *(revision)* the will-future (S. 17) • conditional sentences type 1 (S. 19) • *(revision)* simple past (S. 25)
Viewing: eine virtuelle Tour durch London (S. 21) • gemeinnützige Projekte auf Londons Straßen (S. 29)
Unit task: einen Audioguide schreiben und aufnehmen

Handreichungen

Kommentierungen:
- methodisch-didaktische Hinweise zu jeder Aufgabe
- übersichtlich und schnell erschließbar in der Randspalte neben der jeweiligen Schulbuchseite

Unit 1 Einstieg:
- (SB zu) ▶Brainstorming: L aktiviert das Vorwissen der S über London:
  L: *What do you already know about London? Which famous sights and places do you know?*
- L sammelt Fakten in einer ▶Mindmap (auf einem großen Bogen Papier oder digital), die im Laufe der Unit weiter ergänzt werden kann.
- S übertragen die Mindmap in ihr Heft.

Ex 1 Einstieg:
- (SB auf) L zeigt Foto von Lily (UMA):
  L: *Do you remember Lily? She's new in London.*

Erarbeitung:
a) Lesen der AA, S beschreiben die Fotos in PA (UMA), ▶SF 11, S. 166.
- Alternative: ▶Picture duet zur Bildbeschreibung

b) S notieren die fünf Orte aus der Box untereinander ins Heft.
- 1. Hören gemäß AA
- Ausw.: ▶Meldekette, L/S notiert die Lösungen an der Tafel.

c) 2. Hören gemäß AA, S ergänzen ihre Einträge für jeden Ort im Heft.
- ☒ Lernstärkere S notieren weitere Informationen.
- Ausw.: ▶Meldekette
- S vergleichen ihre Lösungen/Notizen im Plenum, ggf. 3. Hören.

Differenzierungsangebote und Zusätze:
- Differenzierungsvorschläge für lernstärkere (☒) oder lernschwächere (☒) S bzw. *Early finisher* in grauer Schrift (optional)
- Alternativvorschläge und Zusätze ebenfalls in grauer Schrift

Glossar und Kopiervorlagen:
- gut sichtbare Verweise auf das umfangreiche methodisch-didaktische Glossar und eine Vielzahl an Kopiervorlagen

Unit 1
London: City life

🎧 **1** LISTENING **Your London, my London**

💬 a) BEFORE YOU LISTEN Lily has just moved to London. She's talking to her new friend Ali about London °sights. Look at the photos (A–F). What can you see?

🔊 b) Listen and match the places in the box to the photos.
1.3
🔊 c) Listen again. Who talks about each place, Lily (L) or Ali (A)? ☒ Take notes about each place.

Big Ben: L (at the Houses of Parliament)

1 a) Lösungsbsp. S. 282
▶ Skills file 11, p. 166

Big Ben • London Eye • South Bank • Leake Street Tunnel • +Orbit Slide • Camden Market

1 b) A South Bank • B Camden Market • C Big Ben • D Orbit Slide • E Leake Street Tunnel • F London Eye

1 c) Lösungsbsp. S. 282

14 fourteen

Lighthouse (General Edition) Band 3 Lehrkräftefassung Plus (9783060365463), S. 14–1

Inhalt:
- bietet eine Übersicht über **Lernschwerpunkt**, **Kompetenzen**, **Strukturen** und **Redemittel** jeder Doppelseite

Vorbereitung:
- listet das benötigte **Material**, den Einsatz der **Kopiervorlagen**, den ungefähren **Zeitbedarf** und die **Begleitmedien** auf
- nennt eine **Minimalversion**, wenn einzelne Aufgaben, z. B. bei Zeitmangel, ausgelassen werden können

1

Lead-in Inhalt

Lernschwerpunkt: Informationen über London verstehen
Kompetenzen: Listening Gespräche über Sehenswürdigkeiten in London verstehen und Bilder richtig zuordnen • Speaking sich über Londoner Sehenswürdigkeiten austauschen
Redemittel: London sights • I think … looks the most interesting because …

Vorbereitung

Material: Einstieg großer Papierbogen oder digitale Tafel • Ex 1 UMA, UMA/CD/App
Zeitbedarf: ca. 1 Std.
Minimalversion: Ex 1c) auslassen
Begleitmedien: WB (S. 18), App (Digital quiz), INKL (S. 14–15), DIFF (1.1), Unit plans (Unit 1)

Lehrkräftefassung

Markierungen und Symbole:
- Deutlich markiert sind neuer Wortschatz, neue Strukturen, Vokabelboxen und Aussprachehinweise.
- Symbole neben den Aufgabennummern zeigen, welche Kompetenz geübt wird.
- Lautsprechersymbol und Tracknummer bei Hörverstehensaufgaben

Lösungen und Lösungsbeispiele:
- befinden sich in einem blauen Kasten direkt neben der Aufgabe
- ausführlichere Lösungsbeispiele s. S. 281–303

Eingerahmte Verweise:
- deutlich hervorgehobene Verweise auf zusätzliche Angebote der *Diff bank* (*More practice*, *More help*, *Parallel exercise* und *Challenge*) und des Schulbuch-Anhangs (*Skills files*, *Language files* und *Wordbanks*)

Nach dieser Unit kann ich …
- Informationen über London verstehen und wiedergeben
- über Verkehrsmittel in London reden
- eine Tour planen
- das Leben in der Großstadt und in meiner Gegend beschreiben
- online recherchieren

Unit task
- einen Audioguide für London erstellen

Nach dieser Unit …
- L bespricht mit S die Lernziele der Unit (s. links) und kündigt die *Unit task* an.
- Am Ende der Unit überprüfen S das Erreichen der Ziele mithilfe des *Checkpoint* (S. 32–35) bzw. gemeinsam im Plenum.

Ex 2 Einstieg:
- (SB zu) ▸ Vokabelarbeit: L gibt Anweisung zum Einsatz/Führen des *Vocab file* im Schuljahr.
- L legt die Regeln für den Einsatz der ▸ Vokabeltafel fest.
- S übertragen den neuen Wortschatz selbständig.

Erarbeitung:
a) (SB auf) L präsentiert eine Vorlage für die *London page* des *Vocab file* als TA u. klärt im Plenum die AA.
- L od. freiwillige/-r S führen ein Bsp. an der Tafel vor (▸ Semantisierung).
- S arbeiten gemäß AA.
- **Sich.:** ▸ Five-minute teacher, S/L sichern die Wörter u. ihre Bedeutungen an der Tafel, anschl. ▸ Lautschulung.

b) gemäß AA in PA
- **Alternative:** ▸ Milling around
- **Ausw.:** S präsentieren zu zweit ihre Favoriten im Plenum.
- **Sich.:** L festigt den neuen Wortschatz von S. 14–15 (z. B. durch ▸ Vokabelrennen).
- **Zusatz:** Gemeinsam sammeln S die *activities*, die im *Lead-in* vorgestellt werden (z. B. *go shopping, ride a big slide*) und üben sie dann mithilfe eines ▸ Menschen-Memo.

Come to this sculpture if you love fast slides.

†Have a look at the graffiti in this tunnel.

A ride on this big wheel is great fun!

2 SPEAKING Visiting London

2 a) Riesenrad • Imbissstand • Graffitiwand • Parlament • Fahrt • Skulptur • Rutsche • Turm • Tunnel

a) WORDS Start a London page in your VOCAB FILE. Work out the meanings of the words in the box and add them. Use the pictures and words from other languages to help you.

▸ Skills file 1 + 2, p. 155 f.

big wheel • food stall • graffiti wall • parliament • ride • sculpture • slide • tower • tunnel

b) Tell a partner which place in 1 looks the most interesting to you.
I think … looks the most interesting (because it's … / because I like … / because you can … there).

2 b) individuelle Lösungen

▸ Workbook, p. 18

Digital quiz I can understand and share information about London.

fifteen 15

Vorwort

1 Das neue *Lighthouse*

Mit dem neuen *Lighthouse* wird ein differenziertes Lernen und lebendiges Unterrichten durch lebensnahe Themen und multimediales Üben ermöglicht. Dabei liegt ein umfassendes Differenzierungskonzept für Lernende an differenzierenden Schulformen und Orientierungsstufen seit Klasse 5 vor. Speziell mit der Lehrkräftefassung Plus möchten wir Ihnen als Lehrkräften zudem eine effektive Entlastung bei der Unterrichtsvorbereitung und -durchführung an die Hand geben.

Im folgenden Vorwort finden Sie zu den Grundsätzen und zentralen Charakteristika des neuen *Lighthouse* konkrete Beispiele und Erklärungen.

2 Kommunikatives Handeln

Zielsetzung des Englischunterrichts

Das neue *Lighthouse* leistet einen essenziellen Beitrag, um die zentrale Zielsetzung des Englischunterrichts zu erfüllen, nämlich die Schülerinnen und Schüler zu befähigen, inhaltlich-sprachlich sowie kulturell adäquat in Realsituationen zu handeln.

Dazu werden im Verlauf der Schuljahre konsekutiv die drei Handlungsebenen der Rezeption, Produktion sowie Interaktion, flankierend mit den Bereich der Sprachlernkompetenz, der Sprachbewusstheit sowie der fremdsprachlichen digitalen Kompetenz geschult und anhand zahlreicher Aufgaben und Übungen trainiert.

Um dies erfolgreich umzusetzen, benötigen die Lernenden zum einen kommunikative Fertigkeiten, also Sprechen, Schreiben und Sprachmittlung als produktive Fertigkeiten, sowie Hör-/Seh- und Leseverstehen als rezeptive Fertigkeiten. Zum anderen benötigen sie sprachliche Mittel, wie Grammatik, Wortschatz, Aussprache etc., die als Vehikel zur Umsetzung der kommunikativen Fertigkeiten dienen.

Des Weiteren müssen auch interkulturelle Kompetenzen (z. B. kulturelle Aspekte) sowie Methodenkompetenzen (Lernstrategien, Mediennutzung etc.) vorhanden sein, um die Zielsetzung zu erfüllen. Die zahlreichen kommunikativen Aufgaben in *Lighthouse* leisten hierfür einen wichtigen Beitrag.

Kommunikative Ausrichtung der Aufgaben

Die Übungen und Aufgaben in *Lighthouse* basieren auf modernen fachdidaktischen Modellen und aktuellen Leitprinzipien. Das sind z. B. das Prinzip des Übens (d. h. die Integration inhalts- und sprachbezogener Übungssituationen) und das Prinzip der Authentizität (d. h. die Einbindung alltagsnaher Themen und Kommunikationsszenarien). Hinzu kommen die Merkmale guten Englischunterrichts, die konsequent im Schulbuch eingebettet sind:
- hoher Grad an *Scaffolding*
- effektive Mediennutzung
- Fokus auf die Lernenden
- thematische Behandlung von bedeutungsvollen Inhalten
- die Umsetzung kommunikativer Szenarien.

Das Beispiel rechts unten von Aufgabe 4 *How adventurous are you?* zeigt, wie viele Merkmale guten Englischunterrichts in einer Aufgabe platziert werden können. Mit *I can talk about adventures and interests* liegt ein für die Schüler und Schülerinnen authentisches, bedeutungsvolles und realitätsnahes Thema vor. Daneben ist die Aufgabe kommunikativ in eine Konversation im *Double Circle* eingebettet und wird durch zahlreiche *Scaffolding*-Elemente (in diesem Fall Vorschläge für Aktivitäten) unterstützt. Des Weiteren zielt die Aufgabe darauf ab, die grammatische Struktur des *Present perfects* anzuwenden. Die Lernenden werden so befähigt, sich kommunikativ und unter Anwendung einer bestimmten grammatischen Struktur über ein Thema auszutauschen. Darüber hinaus erfahren sie anhand der sprachlichen Mittel auch eine echte Sprachprogression.

Die kommunikative Ausrichtung der Aufgaben gilt nicht nur für die produktiven Fertigkeiten (Sprechen, Schreiben), sondern auch für rezeptive Fertigkeiten (Hör- und Leseverstehen). Anhand der *story Looking good* in Unit 4 bauen die Lernenden sukzessive ihre Lesefertigkeit auf. Dabei nutzt *Lighthouse* das fachdidaktische Modell der *pre-/while-/post*-Phasen.

Zunächst stellen die Lernenden anhand des Titels sowie der Fotos Vermutungen zum Inhalt der *story* an. In klaren Leseaufgaben und unter Anwendung von Lesestrategien (Skimming) überprüfen die Lernenden ihre Vermutungen aus 1a) (1b) und beantworten, nach erneutem Lesen, *True/False* Fragen zur *story* (2). So wird niedrigschwellig das Leseverstehen in der *while*-Phase aufgebaut. Die *post*-Phase in Nr. 3 animiert die Lernenden, eine eigene Meinung zu bilden sowie eine persönliche Präferenz zu äußern.

Mit diesem Modell erfährt der Englischunterricht eine klare und logisch aufgebaute Schrittigkeit mit einem im Mittelpunkt stehenden *skills*-Fokus (hier: Leseverstehen).

Looking good

1 READING The camera never lies, right?

a) BEFORE YOU READ Look at the title of the story and the photos. What do you think the story is about?

I think that Dylan / Owen is going to … Maybe …

> When you **skim** a text, you read quickly to get the main ideas. You don't have to understand every word.

b) Now skim the story. Were you right?
▶ Skills file 9, p. 164

'Thanks for helping me with my bio, Dylan!' typed Owen. He used the social network a few times a week now.
'You're welcome!' wrote Dylan. 'It's great
5 that we can use this to talk to our German exchange partners before they come to Llandudno next week. My partner Saskia is sooooooo cool!'

Owen also enjoyed chatting online to his
10 exchange partner Tom as well as his friends at school. But he noticed that sometimes Dylan wrote strange things on the site.

Dylan
Love our new family car 😂!
#LiveFast
SaskiM and 97 others liked this

'Dylan's family doesn't have a new car,' he thought when he saw his latest post.
15 'That's a photo from when we went to the Llandudno Transport Festival last week. But maybe he's just joking.'

The next day at school, Owen heard Dylan talking to some people in their class.
20 'You know that photo I posted of me playing my new song? It got a HUNDRED likes! And I've got lots of new followers now!'

At the weekend, Owen and Dylan went to the beach, but it wasn't like their normal
25 trips. Dylan wanted Owen to take lots of photos of him to post online.
'This is boring!' said Owen. 'Let's go swimming now.'
'Just one more,' said Dylan. 'The light is
30 really good now.'
'But I've taken at least twenty photos! Who cares what they look like – let's just have fun!'
'I've got lots of followers who need to see
35 what I'm doing and how cool I look.'
'You mean you want Saskia to see how cool you look,' said Owen.

On Monday, everyone was excited. The exchange class arrived today! Owen
40 looked at his phone. There was a new photo of Dylan – but he looked different. 'That's a photo from the beach last weekend, but he's changed it,' Owen thought. He was annoyed.

118 one hundred and eighteen

2 What happens in the story?

Read the story again. Are the sentences true or false? Correct the false sentences.

1 Dylan and Owen don't know who their exchange partners are before they arrive.
2 Owen likes using the social network.
3 Dylan's mum has a new fast car.
4 Dylan doesn't have many followers.
5 Dylan edits the photo that Owen took.
6 Owen posts a nice photo of Dylan.
7 Owen and Dylan are friends in the end.

3 DOUBLE CIRCLE Social media opinions

Think about questions 1–4 and make notes. Then talk to a partner about question 1. Talk about questions 2–4 with new partners.
▶ Skills file 5, p. 160

1 Do you use social media? Why (not)?
2 Which influencers do you know? What do you think about them?
3 Is it a good idea to edit photos to make them look better? Why (not)?
4 How do you feel when you see photos of people who look perfect online?

4 SPEAKING How adventurous are you?

a) Write five questions with *Have you ever …?* about outdoor activities.
Use the ideas in the box or your own ideas.
▶ Irregular verbs, p. 272 f.

> catch a fish • go to the mountains •
> climb a tree • jump from a cliff • ride a pony •
> go on a zip wire • sleep in a tent •
> sleep under the stars • swim in a lake or river

b) **DOUBLE CIRCLE** Ask and answer questions. Move on to a new partner after each question.

Have you ever been to the mountains?
– Yes, once / twice / lots of times. / Yes, when I was in … / No, I've never done that.

Lighthouse (General Edition) Band 3 (9783060365425), S. 118, 120 und 81

3 Grammatik-Vermittlung

Engage – Discover – Activate: Kommunikative Vermittlung grammatischer Phänomene

Die Vermittlungsform grammatischer Phänomene ist seit Jahrzehnten ein kontrovers diskutiertes Feld. Mittlerweile liegen zahlreiche Modelle mit unterschiedlich komplexen Phasierungen und Fokussierungen vor. Mit dem neuen *Lighthouse* offerieren wir mit *Engage – Discover – Activate* eine neue Grammatikkonzeption, die praktikabel, flexibel und kleinschrittig angewendet werden kann. Dabei steht vor allem eine kommunikativ-kontextuelle Einbettung des grammatischen Phänomens im Mittelpunkt.

In der **Engage**-Phase erfolgt zunächst eine inhaltliche Hinführung zum Thema. Anhand eines Inputs (z. B. Lied, Lesetext, Bild) wird eine Kontextualisierung hergestellt und eine inhaltliche Beschäftigung mit dem Input initiiert. Das grammatische Phänomen ist dabei bereits in den Input eingebettet, sodass die Schülerinnen und Schüler es bereits unbewusst kennenlernen.

In dem Beispiel rechts (Nr. 5 *Adventurer Aldo Kane*) besteht die thematische Kontextualisierung in einer Kurzbiografie des Abenteurers Aldo Kane. Das grammatische Phänomen des *present perfect* mit *since* und *for* ist in ein *Reading* eingebettet. Dabei arbeiten die Schülerinnen und Schüler zunächst inhaltlich (*focus on meaning*) mit dem Text, wie in Aufgabe 5b), 5c) und 5d) umgesetzt.

Mit Blick auf den Erwerb einer neuen grammatischen Struktur sollen die Lernenden die *target structure* auch bereits reproduktiv umsetzen (*reproducing chunks*). Das *present perfect* mit *since* und *for* wird in dieser Phase unbewusst angewendet, indem die Lernenden Aktivitäten aus dem Text herausarbeiten und eine Liste anfertigen (5c)) und mithilfe von Scaffolding in Partnerarbeit über die beeindruckendsten Aktivitäten sprechen (5d)). Damit ist die gesamte *Engage*-Phase primär inhaltlich ausgerichtet, beinhaltet aber bereits die angestrebte grammatische Struktur.

In der Folgephase **Discover** erfolgt ein klarer Fokus auf die *target structure* (in unserem Beispiel das *present perfect* mit *since* und *for*) und die Aspekte *form, function* und *use*. Diese werden von den Lernenden (selbst)gelenkt entdeckt oder von der Lehrkraft präsentiert. Dazu eignen sich u. a. auch Erklärfilme (wie hier in Aufgabe 6 angeboten) und sprachbewusste Aufgaben, wo die Lernenden sich die Regel für das Bilden des *present perfect* mit *since* und *for* selbst herleiten (Nr. 6a) und 6b)) und erkennen welche Zeitpunkte bzw. Zeiträume das *present perfect* mit *since* bzw. *for* erfordern (Nr. 6c)). Um die Sprachbewusstheit der Lernenden zusätzlich zu steigern, können in dieser Phase auch weitere Schritte zum Einsatz kommen, z. B. die Umsetzung von *grammar posters* oder *grammar cards*.

Mit **Activate** erfolgt nun die dritte Phase der Grammatikvermittlung. Diese teilt sich in rezeptiv-kommunikative und produktiv-kommunikative Aktivitäten ein. Die Ursache liegt darin, dass nach dem sprachlichen Fokus in der *Discover*-Phase kein zu schneller Übergang in die kommunikative Umsetzung erfolgen sollte. Daher liegt der Fokus zunächst auf dem rezeptiven Stärken der Sprachbewusstheit der Lernenden, beispielsweise durch das Beantworten von Fragen mit *since* und *for* nach einem vorgegebenen Muster (Nr. 7).

Am Ende des *Topic* erfolgt eine produktive Aktivität im Rahmen der *My task*, wo das *present perfect* mit *since* und *for* als *target structure* kontextualisiert und mit einem klaren *Outcome* (*Write a short biography of your partner*, s. Nr. 8) angewendet wird.

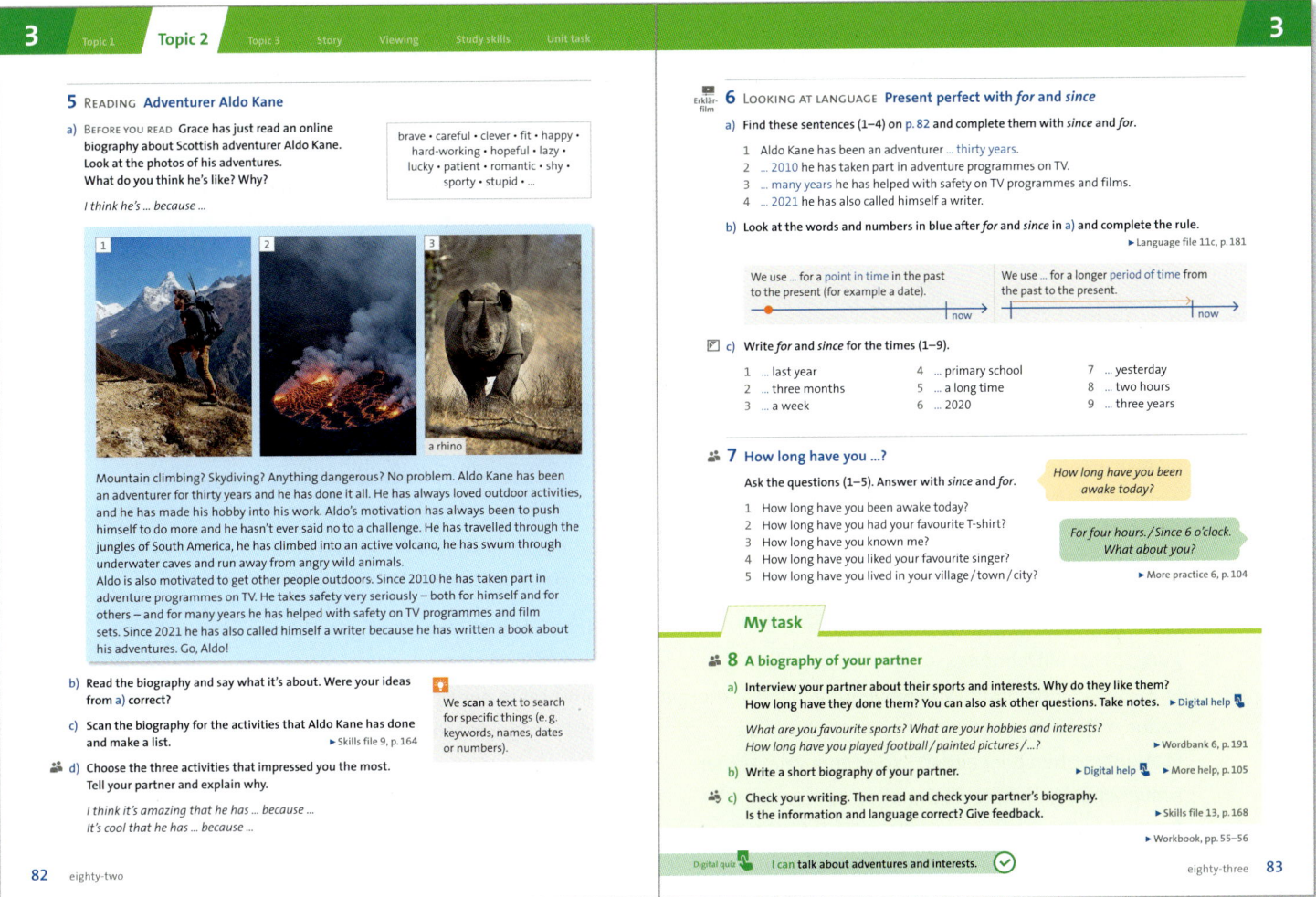

3 Topic 2

5 READING Adventurer Aldo Kane

a) BEFORE YOU READ Grace has just read an online biography about Scottish adventurer Aldo Kane. Look at the photos of his adventures. What do you think he's like? Why?

I think he's ... because ...

> brave • careful • clever • fit • happy • hard-working • hopeful • lazy • lucky • patient • romantic • shy • sporty • stupid • ...

a rhino

Mountain climbing? Skydiving? Anything dangerous? No problem. Aldo Kane has been an adventurer for thirty years and he has done it all. He has always loved outdoor activities, and he has made his hobby into his work. Aldo's motivation has always been to push himself to do more and he hasn't ever said no to a challenge. He has travelled through the jungles of South America, he has climbed into an active volcano, he has swum through underwater caves and run away from angry wild animals.
Aldo is also motivated to get other people outdoors. Since 2010 he has taken part in adventure programmes on TV. He takes safety very seriously – both for himself and for others – and for many years he has helped with safety on TV programmes and film sets. Since 2021 he has also called himself a writer because he has written a book about his adventures. Go, Aldo!

b) Read the biography and say what it's about. Were your ideas from a) correct?

c) Scan the biography for the activities that Aldo Kane has done and make a list. ▶ Skills file 9, p. 164

> We **scan** a text to search for specific things (e.g. keywords, names, dates or numbers).

d) Choose the three activities that impressed you the most. Tell your partner and explain why.

I think it's amazing that he has ... because ...
It's cool that he has ... because ...

6 LOOKING AT LANGUAGE Present perfect with *for* and *since*

a) Find these sentences (1–4) on p. 82 and complete them with *since* and *for*.

1. Aldo Kane has been an adventurer ... thirty years.
2. ... 2010 he has taken part in adventure programmes on TV.
3. ... many years he has helped with safety on TV programmes and films.
4. ... 2021 he has also called himself a writer.

b) Look at the words and numbers in blue after *for* and *since* in a) and complete the rule. ▶ Language file 11c, p. 181

> We use ... for a point in time in the past to the present (for example a date).
>
> We use ... for a longer period of time from the past to the present.

c) Write *for* and *since* for the times (1–9).

1. ... last year
2. ... three months
3. ... a week
4. ... primary school
5. ... a long time
6. ... 2020
7. ... yesterday
8. ... two hours
9. ... three years

7 How long have you ...?

Ask the questions (1–5). Answer with *since* and *for*.

1. How long have you been awake today?
2. How long have you had your favourite T-shirt?
3. How long have you known me?
4. How long have you liked your favourite singer?
5. How long have you lived in your village / town / city?

> How long have you been awake today?
>
> For four hours. / Since 6 o'clock. What about you?

▶ More practice 6, p. 104

My task

8 A biography of your partner

a) Interview your partner about their sports and interests. Why do they like them? How long have they done them? You can also ask other questions. Take notes. ▶ Digital help

What are your favourite sports? What are your hobbies and interests?
How long have you played football / painted pictures / ...? ▶ Wordbank 6, p. 191

b) Write a short biography of your partner. ▶ Digital help ▶ More help, p. 105

c) Check your writing. Then read and check your partner's biography. Is the information and language correct? Give feedback. ▶ Skills file 13, p. 168

▶ Workbook, pp. 55–56

Digital quiz • I can **talk about adventures and interests.**

Lighthouse (General Edition) Band 3 (9783060365425), S. 82–83

Vorwort

4 Bewegtes Lernen

Skills-Förderung durch Bewegungselemente – Verknüpfung von Bewegung und Sprache

Die zielführende Einbindung bewegungsreicher Aktivitäten offeriert ein enormes Potenzial zur Förderung verschiedener kommunikativer Fertigkeiten (Hör- und Leseverstehen, Sprechen, Schreiben etc.).

Zum einen steigert Bewegung die Lern-, Leistungs- und Konzentrationsfähigkeit der Lernenden und ermöglicht in diesem Zuge günstige Bedingungen für den Spracherwerb, z. B. durch die Reduzierung des Stress- und Angstgefühls. Zum anderen verbessern Bewegungselemente die Unterrichtsatmosphäre für alle Beteiligten, da Bewegung Spaß, Freude und das Lernen mit allen Sinnen befördert.

Generell kann zwischen zwei Formen der Lernbewegung unterschieden werden: lernbegleitend und lernerschließend. Lernbegleitende Aktivitäten umfassen z. B. Bewegungspausen (Dehnungs- und Lockerungsübungen) oder eine direkte Einbindung von Bewegung in der Lernorganisation, z. B. bei einer szenischen Darstellung, beim Stationenlernen oder einem Expertenpuzzle. Lernerschließende Aktivitäten beinhalten ein Lernen mit Bewegung. Das bekannteste Beispiel dafür ist die Erschließung unbekannter *lexical items* anhand von Gestik und Mimik.

Zielführende Bewegungsaktivitäten

Das neue *Lighthouse* bindet bewusst die o. g. positiven Aspekte des bewegten Lernens anhand zahlreicher bewegungsreicher Aktivitäten direkt in den Englischunterricht mit ein. Die Aufgabe *Classmate compliments* (Nr. 7) aus der Unit *Manchester: Who we are* bietet beispielsweise ein Bewegungselement an, nämlich das *Walk around*.

Die Aufgabe, bei der sich die Lernenden gegenseitig Komplimente machen, schafft für die Lernenden den Rahmen, sich produktiv in einem angstfreien Raum mit wechselnden Partnerinnen und Partnern im Rahmen des Themas *Confidence* auszutauschen, und zeichnet sich durch eine hohe Sprechaktivierung aus.

Mit der Aufgabe *Freeze!* (*More practice* 8) in der Unit 2 zu *Manchester: Who we are* erhalten die Lernenden die Möglichkeit, eine Szene aus der *story* in einem *freeze-frame* darzustellen. Die Schülerinnen und Schüler setzen dabei eine Szene ihrer Wahl in einem Standbild um und präsentieren das Ergebnis in der Klasse. Dabei sollen sie sich auch in die Charaktere hineinversetzen, sodass die Klasse Aussagen zu den Gefühlen der dargestellten Charaktere treffen kann. Damit erfährt der Englischunterricht eine deutliche dynamisch-räumliche Umwälzung des Inhalts der *story*.

Eine enorm hohe sprachliche Aktivierung wird durch die Aufgabe *Social media opinions* initiiert, hier eingebettet in der Unit 4 *Wales: Digital life*. Die Schülerinnen und Schüler machen sich Notizen zu vier Fragen und diskutieren diese anschließen mit zwei bis vier Mitschülern bzw. Mitschülerinnen in einem *Double circle*. Die Umsetzung dieser Aufgabe bietet zahlreiche Vorteile, u. a. eine entspannte Lernatmosphäre durch die persönliche Interaktion in Partnerarbeit, einen dynamischen kommunikativen Austausch sowie eine gezielte kritische Auseinandersetzung mit dem Unit-Thema.

7 SPEAKING Classmate compliments

a) Mei always ends her podcast with compliments. Her listeners send her anonymous compliments for their classmates.
Make a list of five to ten positive words or phrases to describe people in your class.

b) Tell your partner your ideas. Choose some of their ideas and add them to your list.

c) WALK AROUND Give each other compliments. Remember to say 'thank you' when you get a compliment!

   A Hi, Arlo. I think you're funny and I love your shoes.
   B Thanks, Suki! I want to tell you that you're great at football.
   A Thank you, that's nice of you.
   B You're welcome!

Here's a compliment for Ruby: You're a good leader. Maybe you'll be prime minister one day!

▶ Page 58

More practice 8 Freeze!

a) Choose a scene from the story. Talk about what happens in the scene and how the characters feel.

b) Show your group's scene as a freeze-frame. Other students say what the scene is, what's happening and how the characters feel.

3 DOUBLE CIRCLE Social media opinions

Think about questions 1–4 and make notes. Then talk to a partner about question 1.
Talk about questions 2–4 with new partners.
▶ Skills file 5, p. 160

1 Do you use social media? Why (not)?
2 Which influencers do you know? What do you think about them?
3 Is it a good idea to edit photos to make them look better? Why (not)?
4 How do you feel when you see photos of people who look perfect online?

Lighthouse (General Edition) Band 3 (9783060365425), S. 55, 73 und 120

Vorwort

5 Differenzierung / *Diff bank*

More help / More practice / Challenge / Parallel-Aufgaben

Das vielseitige und fundierte Differenzierungskonzept stellt eine der Säulen des neuen Lighthouse dar. Insgesamt liegen vier unterschiedliche Differenzierungsformen vor:

1. *More help*: Diese Differenzierungsform bietet den Lernenden eine zusätzliche Unterstützung zu den Aufgaben an.

Im Falle *von Make a difference* (siehe Beispiel rechts) erhalten die Lernenden zur erfolgreichen Umsetzung der Aufgabe z. B. *sentence starters* sowie Vorschläge und Ideen, die sie verwenden können. Damit erhalten insbesondere Lernschwächere ein hilfreiches *Scaffolding*.

2. *More practice*: Mit dieser zweiten Differenzierungsform wird es den Lernenden ermöglicht, weitere (teils vertiefende) Aufgaben zum Thema zu bearbeiten. Damit erfüllt sich ein Grundpfeiler des Englischunterrichts – das Prinzip des Übens. Innerhalb des *Topic* 2 aus Unit 1 haben sich die Schülerinnen und Schüler mit der Erschließung der Regel zur Bildung von *Conditional sentences type 1* beschäftigt und diese geübt. Mit *More practice* 3 können die Lernenden die erarbeitete Struktur vertiefend in einer weiteren Übung zu den *Conditional sentences type 1* anwenden.

3. *Challenge*: Das Differenzierungskonzept fördert nicht nur Leistungsschwächere (s. *More help*), sondern fordert auch Leistungsstärkere. Dafür fungieren die *Challenge*-Aufgaben, also weitere Übungen mit einem erhöhten Schwierigkeitsgrad.

Eingebettet im Thema *A different kind of tour* des *Topic* 2 befassen sich leistungsstärkere Schülerinnen und Schüler in der zugehörigen *Challenge*-Aufgabe 2 mit den *Conditional sentences type 1*. Ein höherer Schwierigkeitsgrad entsteht hier dadurch, dass die Lernenden das Verb in der richtigen Form sowohl im Haupt- als auch im Nebensatz einsetzen müssen.

Damit bietet *Lighthouse* die Möglichkeit, sich inhaltlich und sprachlich vertiefend mit dem Unterrichtsgegenstand auseinanderzusetzen.

4. Parallel-Aufgaben: Mit den Parallel-Aufgaben als vierte Differenzierungsform wird den Schülerinnen und Schülern die einfachere Variante einer Übung angeboten. Dies ist insbesondere sinnvoll, wenn z. B. der identische Input (wie bei einem Film) genutzt wird. Die Parallel-Aufgabe ist inhaltlich gleich, umfasst aber eine deutliche Reduzierung im Anspruch. Im Beispiel von *A virtual tour of London* ist die Ursprungsaufgabe eine Hörsehverstehensübung, bei der die Lernenden Richtungsanweisungen in einen Lückentext einsetzen müssen. Bei der Parallel-Aufgabe sind die einzusetzenden Richtungsanweisungen bereits in einem *Single-choice*-Format vorgegeben, sodass die Lernenden die korrekte Anweisung aus zwei möglichen Optionen auswählen können.

More help, More practice, Challenge und die Parallel-Aufgaben sind übersichtlich auf den *Diff bank*-Seiten platziert, die sich jeweils direkt im Anschluss an die Unit befinden und somit eine einschlägige thematische Einheit bilden.

Zuweisung von Aufgabenformaten (einfach / schwierig / Wahl)

Neben den vier Differenzierungsformen können die Aufgaben auch selbst ein unterschiedliches Anspruchsformat aufweisen: einfach ▯ (z. B. erhöhter Grad an *Scaffolding* oder Reduzierung der Teilaufgaben), schwierig ▯ (z. B. offene oder sprachlich vertiefende Aufgaben) und eine Wahlaufgabe ▯ (z. B. Wahl, welches Lernprodukt umgesetzt werden soll). So erkennen die Lernenden und Lehrkräfte sofort, auf welchem Niveau sie gerade arbeiten bzw. welche Aufgaben gezielt bestimmten Lernenden zugewiesen werden können.

► Page 29

More help 3 LIFE SKILLS **Make a difference!**

a) THINK Have you ever helped a friend, a grandparent or a neighbour? How?
Or do you know somebody who helps others?

went shopping at / for / in / with	my neighbour.
helped in the garden at	my grandma / grandpa.
explained a maths problem / homework / ... to	my friend.
downloaded an app for	my sports team / my club.
gave old clothes and toys to	a charity shop.
walked the dog / looked after a pet / ... for	my neighbourhood.
made a cake / soup / ... for	my park.
helped with the food at	a soup kitchen.
collected money at / for	my church / mosque / synagogue.
picked up rubbish at / in	

► Page 19

More practice 3 **Pearl's family's visit**

Complete the conditional sentences. Use the correct form of the simple present or the will-future.

1 If Pearl's cousins ... (be) late, they'll miss the train.
2 If they see some street musicians, they ... (listen) to the music.
3 If Aunt Vera ... (find) a nice souvenir, she'll buy it.
4 If the weather is good, Pearl's family ... (have) a picnic in the park.
5 If Uncle Roy loses his Travelcard, he ... (not be) happy!

Challenge 2 **My friend's visit to London**

Complete the conditional sentences about a future visit to London.
Use the correct form of the simple present or the will-future.

1 If my friend ... (go) to London, she ... (travel) on the underground.
2 If she ... (travel) on the underground, she ... (buy) a ticket.
3 If she ... (buy) a ticket, she ... (not have) much money to buy a nice souvenir.
4 If she ... (not buy) a nice souvenir, she ... (be) sad.
5 So I think she ... (walk) if she ... (go) to London because it's free!

► Page 21

Parallel exercise 7 VIEWING **A virtual tour of London**

b) Watch the video and choose the correct directions.

At Trafalgar Square (1) turn right at / go across the roundabout and (2) go down /
go straight over the road. Go straight on down Whitehall and take the (3) second / third street
on the (4) left / right. At the river (5) turn left / turn right and (6) go straight on / go across.

► Page 25

More practice 4 **Lily's blog**

Erklärfilm

REVISION **The simple past**
You use the simple past when you talk about the past.
• The simple past forms of regular verbs end in -ed: *I arrived in London yesterday.*
• Some verbs have irregular simple past forms: *I went to Camden Market. It was great!*
• Make questions with *did* and negatives with *didn't*: *Did you eat there? – No, I didn't.*
► Irregular verbs, p. 272 f.   ► Language file 4, p. 173 f.

Make a list with the positive and negative simple past forms in Lily's blog: *1) I went   2) ...*

Lighthouse (General Edition) Band 3 (9783060365425), S. 43, 41

6 Individualisierung

Arbeit mit dem *Checkpoint*

Mit den *Checkpoints* wird allen Schülerinnen und Schülern die Möglichkeit gegeben, sich einerseits selbst zu überprüfen und sich andererseits gezielt auf Tests oder Klassenarbeiten vorzubereiten.

Die strukturelle Grundlage für die Arbeit mit den *Checkpoints* stellen die *I can-statements* dar, die den Lernenden einen roten Faden bieten. Die *I can-statements* werden während der Unit behandelt und bilden bei den *Checkpoints* hilfreiche inhaltliche Eckpfeiler, zu denen verschiedene Aufgaben und Übungen bearbeitet werden müssen, z. B. *I can explain what's important to me, I can talk about fashion* oder *I can give advice (mustn't, have to, needn't, not be allowed to, should)*.

Die *Checkpoints* bieten den Lernenden eine ganze Palette an Aufgabenformaten zu verschiedenen sprachlichen Mitteln (*Words, Language*) oder kommunikativen Fertigkeiten (*Mediation, Speaking*) an. Damit werden bereits behandelte Themen und Aufgabenformate der Unit noch einmal zielführend umgewälzt und trainiert.

Aus methodischer Sicht hat die Lehrkraft verschiedene Möglichkeiten, die *Checkpoints* in den Englischunterricht einzubinden.

So können diese vier Seiten zum einen individuell in autonomen Arbeitsprozessen von den Lernenden bearbeitet werden. Eine beliebte Möglichkeit ist dabei die *Bus stop*-Methode, bei der die Lösungen der *Checkpoint*-Aufgaben an verschiedenen *Bus stops* zur selbstständigen Überprüfung ausgelegt werden. Die Lösungen finden Sie als KVs im Anhang dieses Buchs.

Zum anderen können die Übungen auch in dynamischer Form anhand von Partner- oder Gruppenarbeitsprozessen bearbeitet werden.

Das neue *Lighthouse* bietet zudem die Möglichkeit, alle Übungen des *Checkpoints* auch in digitaler Form zu bearbeiten. Der *Digital checkpoint* stellt hierbei eine digitale Alternative zum Schulbuch dar. Die Lernenden bearbeiten die Aufgaben in der *Cornelsen Lernen App* und erhalten dort ein sofortiges Feedback zu ihrer Leistung.

Die *Digital checkpoints* lassen sich darüber hinaus von der Lehrperson im UMA abrufen, sodass diese auch im Plenum bearbeitet oder als Beispiel präsentiert werden können.

Auch wenn die Schülerinnen und Schüler die Aufgaben nicht digital, sondern in ihrem Heft bearbeiten, können sie die *Cornelsen Lernen App* nutzen, um sich im *Check* die Lösungen zu den Aufgaben anzuschauen, sodass sie die Ergebnisse selbstständig überprüfen und ggf. korrigieren können.

Damit wird dem hybriden Gedanken des neuen *Lighthouse* Rechnung getragen.

Arbeit mit den *Unit plans*

Mit den *Unit plans*, die Sie im Unterrichtsmanager finden, haben Sie bei *Lighthouse* eine maßgeschneiderte Vorlage, mit der Sie Ihre Schülerinnen und Schülern zu mehr Lernautonomie anleiten und ihnen die Möglichkeit zu individualisierten Lernwegen geben können.

Die *Unit plans* sind so konzipiert, dass sie selbständige Lern- und Übungsphasen unterstützen, die sich in *whole class activities* einbetten. Entlang des roten Fadens der *I can-statements* werden die zu bearbeitenden Aufgaben aus dem Schulbuch und dem Workbook zusammengestellt. Die *Unit plans* beinhalten neben Hinweisen zu Niveaustufen und digitalen Angeboten (*Digital help, Digital quiz*) auch Vorschläge für die Sozialform, in der die jeweilige Aufgabe bearbeitet werden kann, sowie eine Vorlage zur Selbstkontrolle und Selbstevaluation und zum Feedback durch die Lehrkraft.

Abgerundet wird das Angebot der *Unit plans* durch eine Seite *Early finisher* mit Hinweisen zu vertiefenden Aufgaben und thematischen Wiederholungen, die im Sinne der Differenzierung genutzt werden kann.

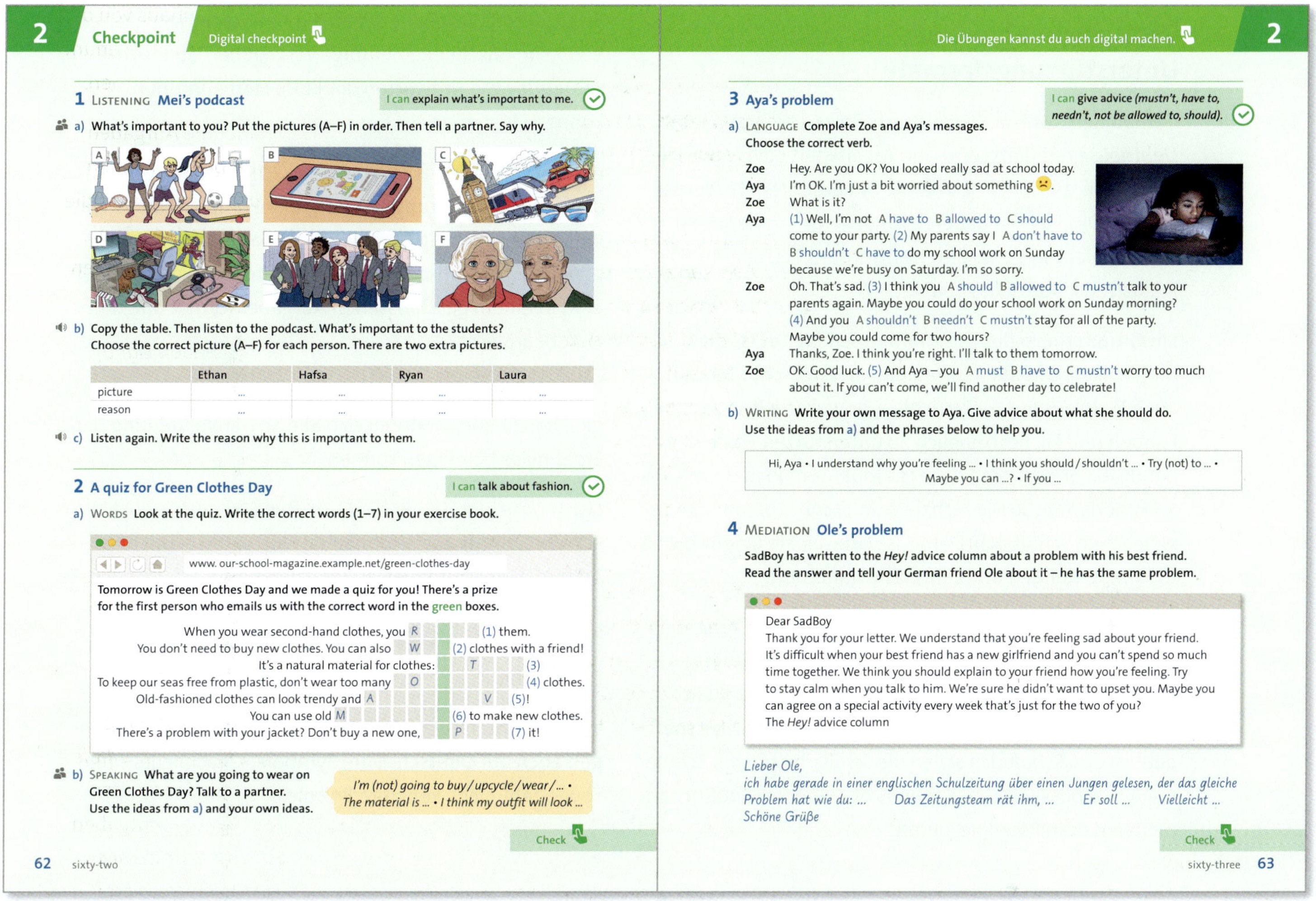

2 Checkpoint Digital checkpoint

1 LISTENING Mei's podcast
I can explain what's important to me.

a) What's important to you? Put the pictures (A–F) in order. Then tell a partner. Say why.

b) Copy the table. Then listen to the podcast. What's important to the students? Choose the correct picture (A–F) for each person. There are two extra pictures.

	Ethan	Hafsa	Ryan	Laura
picture	...	...	...	...
reason	...	...	...	...

c) Listen again. Write the reason why this is important to them.

2 A quiz for Green Clothes Day
I can talk about fashion.

a) WORDS Look at the quiz. Write the correct words (1–7) in your exercise book.

www.our-school-magazine.example.net/green-clothes-day

Tomorrow is Green Clothes Day and we made a quiz for you! There's a prize for the first person who emails us with the correct word in the green boxes.

- When you wear second-hand clothes, you R _ _ _ _ _ (1) them.
- You don't need to buy new clothes. You can also W _ _ _ (2) clothes with a friend!
- It's a natural material for clothes: T _ _ _ _ _ (3)
- To keep our seas free from plastic, don't wear too many O _ _ _ _ (4) clothes.
- Old-fashioned clothes can look trendy and A _ _ V _ (5)!
- You can use old M _ _ _ _ _ _ (6) to make new clothes.
- There's a problem with your jacket? Don't buy a new one, P _ _ _ _ (7) it!

b) SPEAKING What are you going to wear on Green Clothes Day? Talk to a partner. Use the ideas from a) and your own ideas.

I'm (not) going to buy / upcycle / wear / ... • The material is ... • I think my outfit will look ...

3 Aya's problem
I can give advice (mustn't, have to, needn't, not be allowed to, should).

a) LANGUAGE Complete Zoe and Aya's messages. Choose the correct verb.

Zoe Hey. Are you OK? You looked really sad at school today.
Aya I'm OK. I'm just a bit worried about something 🙁.
Zoe What is it?
Aya (1) Well, I'm not A have to B allowed to C should come to your party. (2) My parents say I A don't have to B shouldn't C have to do my school work on Sunday because we're busy on Saturday. I'm so sorry.
Zoe Oh. That's sad. (3) I think you A should B allowed to C mustn't talk to your parents again. Maybe you could do your school work on Sunday morning? (4) And you A shouldn't B needn't C mustn't stay for all of the party. Maybe you could come for two hours?
Aya Thanks, Zoe. I think you're right. I'll talk to them tomorrow.
Zoe OK. Good luck. (5) And Aya – you A must B have to C mustn't worry too much about it. If you can't come, we'll find another day to celebrate!

b) WRITING Write your own message to Aya. Give advice about what she should do. Use the ideas from a) and the phrases below to help you.

Hi, Aya • I understand why you're feeling ... • I think you should / shouldn't ... • Try (not) to ... • Maybe you can ...? • If you ...

4 MEDIATION Ole's problem

SadBoy has written to the *Hey!* advice column about a problem with his best friend. Read the answer and tell your German friend Ole about it – he has the same problem.

Dear SadBoy
Thank you for your letter. We understand that you're feeling sad about your friend. It's difficult when your best friend has a new girlfriend and you can't spend so much time together. We think you should explain to your friend how you're feeling. Try to stay calm when you talk to him. We're sure he didn't want to upset you. Maybe you can agree on a special activity every week that's just for the two of you?
The *Hey!* advice column

Lieber Ole, ich habe gerade in einer englischen Schulzeitung über einen Jungen gelesen, der das gleiche Problem hat wie du: ...   Das Zeitungsteam rät ihm, ...   Er soll ...   Vielleicht ... Schöne Grüße

Lighthouse (General Edition) Band 3 (9783060365425), S. 62–63

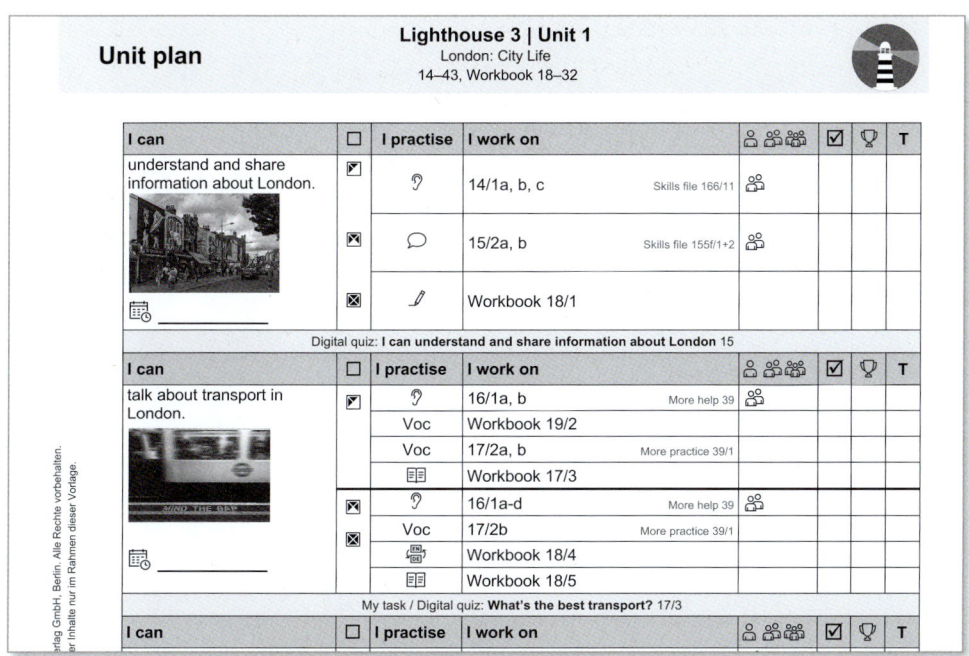

Lighthouse (General Edition) Unterrichtsmanager Plus (1100027746),
Unit Plan zu Unit 1, S. 1

Vorwort

7 Lern- und Arbeitsheft

Vereinfachungen und Unterstützungsformate

Gemäß dem Motto „Gemeinsam Ziele erreichen" bietet *Lighthouse* mit dem Lern- und Arbeitsheft eine Materialgrundlage speziell für Lernende mit erhöhtem Förderbedarf an. Das Heft ist dabei besonders für Schülerinnen und Schüler mit dem Förderschwerpunkt Lernen im inklusiven Unterricht geeignet.

Ein Grundprinzip des Lern- und Arbeitsheftes ist die Möglichkeit, mit allen Lernenden im Englischunterricht – auch im inklusiven Unterricht – parallel arbeiten zu können und sie bestmöglich zu unterstützen. Für einen parallelen Einsatz sind daher Layout, Aufgabennummerierung sowie Lernziele und *I can*-statements gleich zum Schulbuch. Damit ist eine leichte Orientierung für alle Lernenden und Lehrkräfte garantiert.

Das Lern- und Arbeitsheft enthält vereinfachte Aufgaben und Übungen, die direkt im Heft bearbeitet werden können. Am Beispiel von *Hello! Where we're from* wird exemplarisch der Unterschied zum Lern- und Arbeitsheft deutlich. Im Schulbuch sollen die Schülerinnen und Schüler anhand eines Hörsehverstehens Aussagen zu Großbritannien und Irland komplettieren.

Im Lern- und Arbeitsheft sind die Antwortmöglichkeiten bereits in falscher Reihenfolge vorgegeben, sodass die Lernenden die Antworten direkt im Heft zuordnen können (*Matching*).

Auch im Bereich des Sprechens (s. 2 *Hello!*) erfolgt eine deutliche Reduzierung der Aufgabenkomplexität. So wird im Lern- und Arbeitsheft in 2b) auf das Nennen der genauen geografischen Lage verzichtet und Aufgabe 2c) wird in einem geschlossenen Aufgabenformat direkt im Heft bearbeitet.

Dennoch befinden sich alle Lernenden inhaltlich auf der gleichen Ebene, wodurch sich alle an der Vorstellung der Ergebnisse beteiligen können.

Lighthouse bietet über die *Cornelsen Lernen App* zusätzlich den Zugriff auf vereinfachte Hörtexte an, um den Anspruch der Aufgaben zu reduzieren und Erfolgserlebnisse für die Lernenden mit Förderbedarf zu ermöglichen. Die ergänzenden Medien auf der App umfassen z. B. auch Erklärfilme.

Weitere Unterstützungselemente sind Aufgabenstellungen auch auf Deutsch, klare Symbole, sprachliche Hilfen sowie zahlreiche konkrete Beispiele.

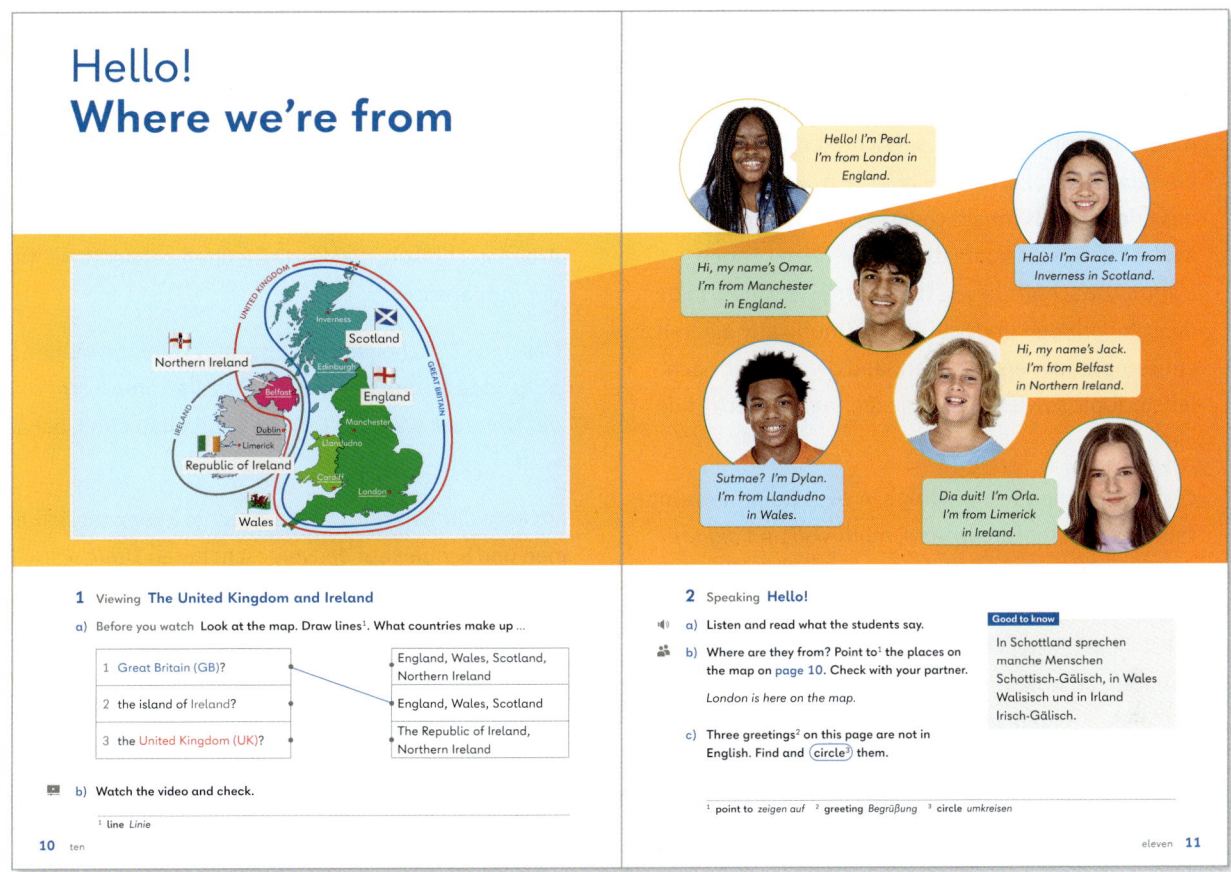

Lighthouse Lern- und Arbeitsheft für Lernende mit erhöhtem Förderbedarf Band 3 (9783060346158), S. 10–11

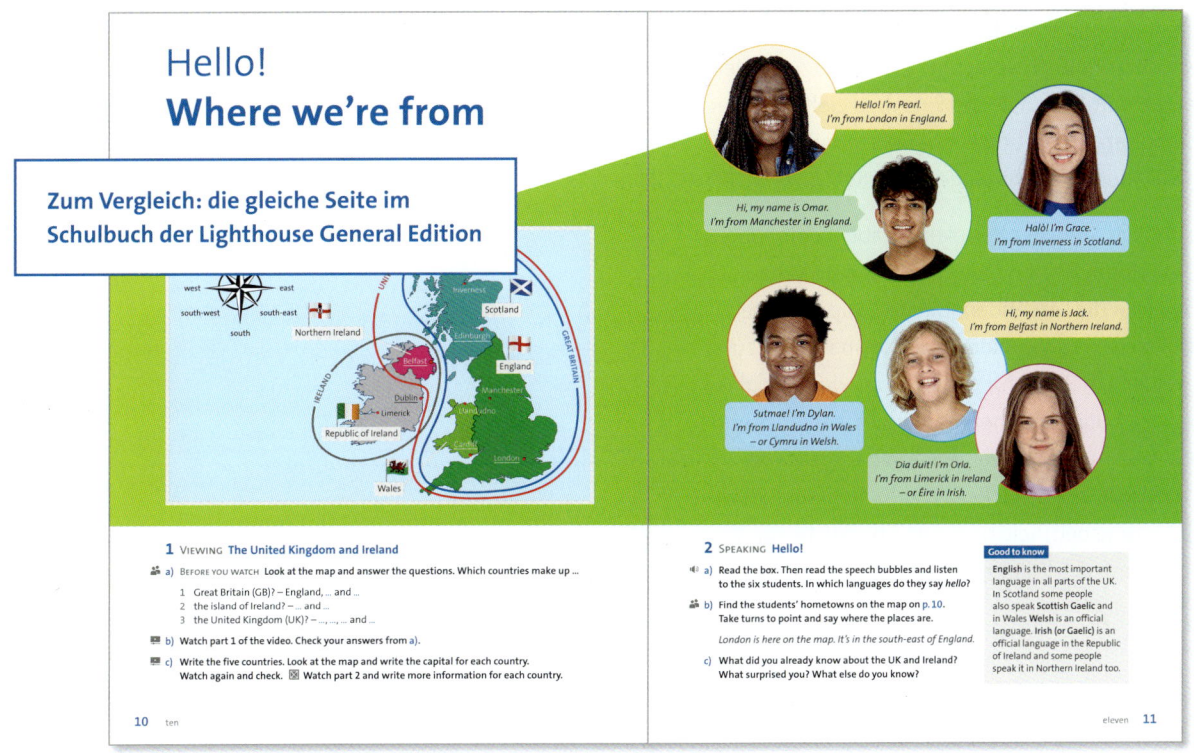

Zum Vergleich: die gleiche Seite im Schulbuch der Lighthouse General Edition

Lighthouse (General Edition) Band 3 (9783060365425), S. 10–11

Vorwort

8 My task / Unit task

Outcome-Orientierung

Das finale Lernprodukt (*Outcome*) spielt in einem modern-kommunikativ ausgerichteten Englischunterricht eine zentrale Rolle. Hierbei zeigt sich, ob die Lernenden das Erlernte (aus inhaltlicher oder sprachlicher Sicht) auch situativ und kontextuell anwenden können. *Lighthouse* schafft bewusst mehrere Szenarien, in denen die Schülerinnen und Schüler kommunikativ agieren und ein Lernprodukt erstellen: anhand der *My task* nach jedem Topic sowie der komplexen *Unit task* am Ende einer Unit.

Generell können Lernprodukte in vier Kategorien eingeteilt werden: *spoken*, *written*, *multi-skill* und *digital outcomes*. Die *Unit tasks* greifen diese vier Kategorien verteilt über alle Units des Schulbuches auf, um möglichst viele Lerntypen einzubinden und eine hohe Variation an Aufgabenformaten zu offerieren. Die Lernenden zeigen als summative Leistung bei der *Unit task* auf, was sie bisher in dieser Unit gelernt haben.

Das hier abgebildete Beispiel der *Unit task* zu *Make an audio guide for a London bike tour* zeigt die typische kleinschrittige Struktur auf.

In einzelnen *Steps* erarbeiten die Lernenden Schritt für Schritt die einzelnen Aufgaben, um am Ende als Lernprodukt einen Audioguide für eine Fahrradtour durch London zu erstellen. Aufgrund eines klaren kommunikativen Ergebnisses, der inhaltlich-sprachlichen Umsetzung, der interaktiven Gestaltung sowie des Einsatzes zielführender Medien beinhalten die *Unit tasks* unübersehbare Elemente von TSLT (*Task-Supported Language Teaching*).

Die insgesamt vier *Steps* der Beispielaufgabe rechts führen sukzessive zu einem finalen *Outcome*. Auf dem Weg dorthin recherchieren die Lernenden (hier in Gruppenarbeit) Sehenswürdigkeiten sowie Bilder und Informationen zu diesen, schreiben ein Skript für den Audioguide, üben das Einsprechen des Audios und nehmen dieses abschließend für die Klasse auf. Alle *Steps* werden durch *Scaffolding*-Elemente flankiert, z. B. *More help, Digital help* und *Study skills* sowie Lösungsbeispiele und eine Checkliste zur Selbstüberprüfung des Ergebnisses in *Step* 2.

Vorbereitende Lern- und Arbeitstechniken (*Study skills*)

Um ein produktives Lernprodukt erfolgreich umzusetzen, bedarf es neben den inhaltlichen und sprachlichen Vorkenntnissen aus der Unit auch gezielter Lern- und Arbeitstechniken, die den Lernenden bei der Bewältigung der Aufgabe helfen.

Das neue *Lighthouse* bietet vor jeder *Unit task* eine *Study skills* Seite an, auf der eine für das *Outcome* (Lernprodukt) der *Unit task* wichtige Lern- und Arbeitstechnik behandelt wird.

Im Falle der Beispiel-*Unit task* rechts lernen die Schülerinnen und Schüler auf der vorgeschalteten *Study skills*-Seite, wie Informationen im Internet recherchiert werden, was bei der Quellenwahl zu beachten ist und wie die recherchierten Informationen festgehalten werden können. Damit wird eine zentrale Grundlage geschaffen, den Anforderungen der *Unit task* gerecht zu werden. Die *Study skills*-Seite zur Internetrecherche schult die Lernenden, wie sie Informationen zu Sehenswürdigkeiten in London im Internet suchen (Nr. 1 u. 2a)), diese in Notizen festhalten (Nr. 2b)) und Bilder zu den Sehenswürdigkeiten finden (Nr. 2c)).

Mit dieser Vorbereitung sind die Lernenden nun gut gewappnet, erfolgreich die *Unit task* zu bewältigen.

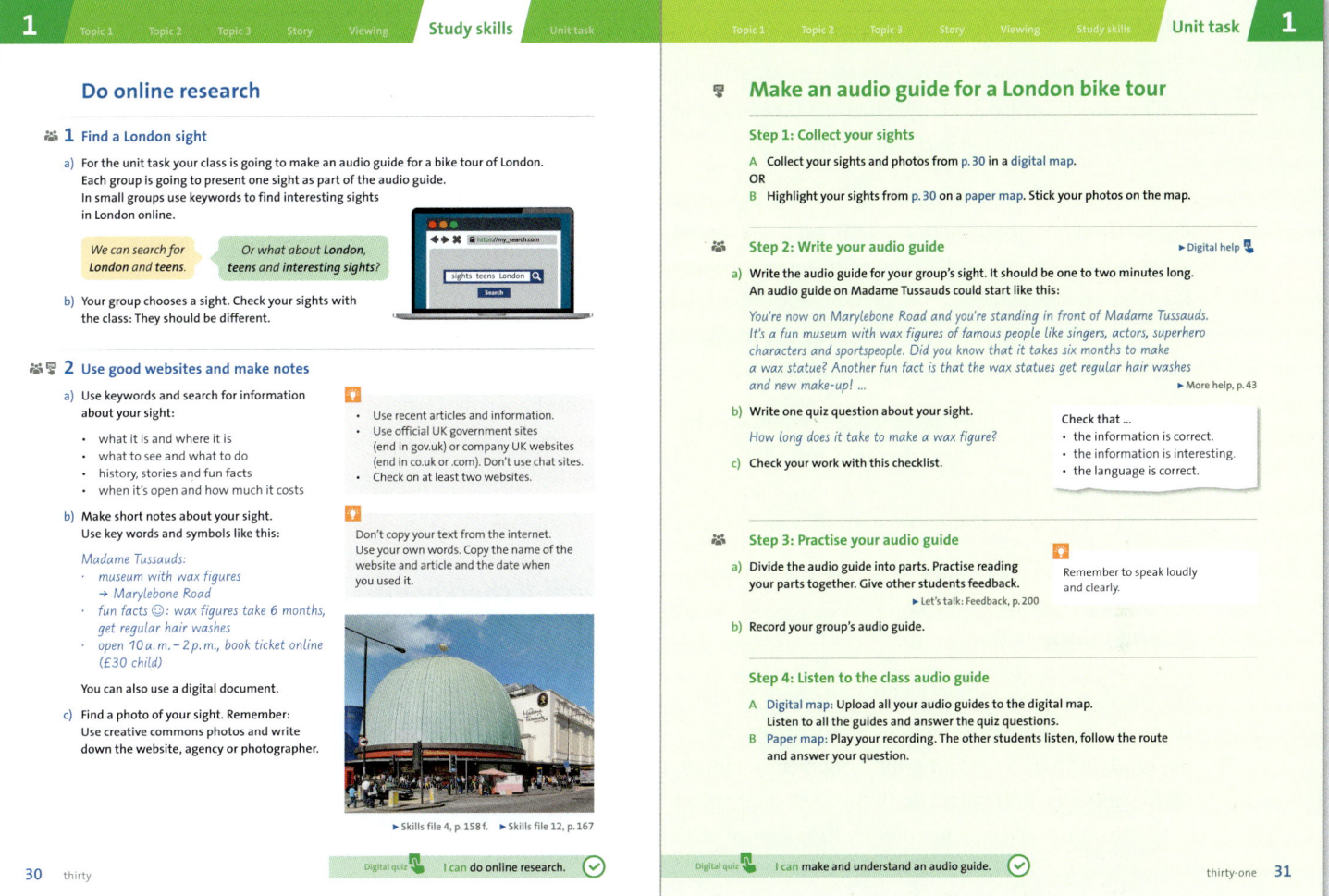

Vorwort

9 Hybrides Arbeiten

Allgemeines

Das neue *Lighthouse* bietet flexible digitale Möglichkeiten, den Unterricht sowie das Englischlernen für Schülerinnen und Schüler intuitiv und leicht zu unterstützen.

Dafür stehen die Anwendungen *Digital help*, *Digital quiz*, *Digital checkpoint* und *Check* zur Verfügung, die unabhängig von der Ausstattung der Schule im Sinne des neuen Hybridkonzeptes eingesetzt werden können. Dabei gilt bei der optionalen und kostenlosen Nutzung grundsätzlich das Motto: „Ein großes Plus, aber kein Muss."

Der Zugang verläuft über die *Cornelsen Lernen App*, bei der man sich zunächst registriert und anschließend das hybride Materialpaket zu *Lighthouse* auswählen kann. Über die Eingabe der Seitenzahl gelangt man direkt zu den digitalen Inhalten.

Digital help

Die Applikation *Digital help* ist ein zentraler hybrider Bestandteil, um allen Lernenden Unterstützung bei der erfolgreichen Umsetzung von Aufgaben zu bieten. Dazu gehören z. B. ergänzende Tipps, Ideen oder sprachliche Mittel, die in jedem der drei *Topics* in den einzelnen *Units* sowie bei den komplexeren Lernaufgaben der *My task* und *Unit task* zu finden sind.

Beim rechten Beispiel aus Band 1, eingebettet in die Aufgabe *My home*, sollen die Lernenden über ihr eigenes Zuhause bzw. Traumzuhause an einen Freund / eine Freundin schreiben. Dies steht im Einklang mit den klar strukturierten *I can-statements*, in diesem Falle *I can describe my room*. Somit fungiert *Digital help* immer als feste Unterstützungskomponente für das Erreichen der *I can-statements*. Beim rechten Beispiel haben die Lernenden bei eventuellen Schwierigkeiten nun die Möglichkeit, digitale Unterstützung zu erhalten. Dafür können sie eine Audioerklärung der Aufgabe erhalten, sprachlich-inhaltliche Starthilfen nutzen oder eine Erinnerung in Form einer Checkliste (ob sie an alle Punkte gedacht haben) verwenden. Damit können alle in ihrem Tempo lernen. *Digital help* beinhaltet somit eine vielseitige mediale Ergänzung und Unterstützung (Audios, Videos, Erklärfilme) für den Englischunterricht.

Digital quiz

Die Vielfalt des Englischunterrichts beinhaltet auch, eine hohe Abwechslung für die Lernenden zu ermöglichen. Das *Digital quiz* als spielerische Applikation leistet hierfür einen zentralen Beitrag. Innerhalb der einzelnen *Topics*, *Stories*, *Study skills* und *Unit tasks* erhalten die Schülerinnen und Schüler immer wieder die Möglichkeit, das Gelernte in Form motivierender digitaler Quizaufgaben anzuwenden. Dazu dienen Aufgabenformate wie z. B. *Put the words in the right order* oder *Memory*.

Dabei haben die Lernenden nicht nur Erfolgserlebnisse, sondern sehen gleichzeitig ihren Lernfortschritt. Ein Feedbacksystem (z. B. positive Kommentare durch die Leitfigur) schafft zusätzliche Motivation.

Digital checkpoint

Im Sinne der hybriden Ausrichtung des neuen *Lighthouse* stehen am Ende jeder Unit sowohl ein analoger *Checkpoint* im Schulbuch als auch ein digitaler *Checkpoint* in der *Cornelsen Lernen App* zur Verfügung. Für beide Versionen gilt, dass bisher erworbene Kompetenzen und sprachliche Mittel in Form eines *self-assessment* direkt angewendet werden können. Beim *Digital checkpoint* erhalten die Lernenden nach der Bearbeitung sofort eine Rückmeldung, wie viele Aufgaben richtig beantwortet wurden, und somit eine transparente Übersicht über den aktuellen Lernstand.

Check

Mithilfe des *Check* in der *Cornelsen Lernen App* können die Schülerinnen und Schüler nach der Bearbeitung der *Checkpoints* im Schulbuch ihre Lösungen selbständig überprüfen. Dazu rufen sie in der *Cornelsen Lernen App* die entsprechende Seite im Schulbuch auf und klicken auf den *Check* mit der Lösung zur jeweiligen Aufgabe.

Digital help

Digital quiz

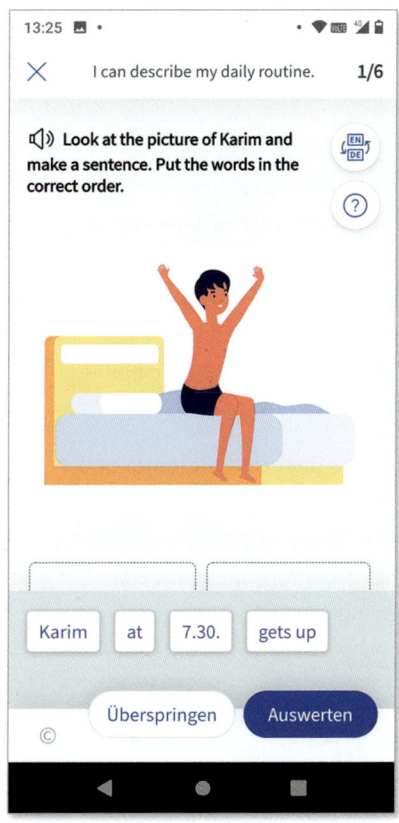

Digital checkpoint

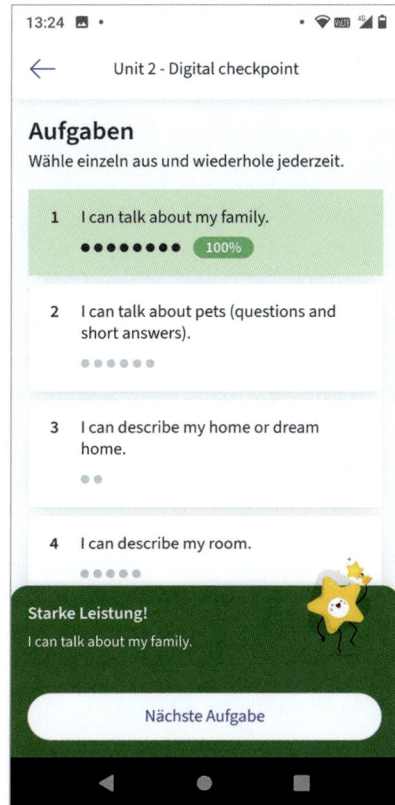

Check

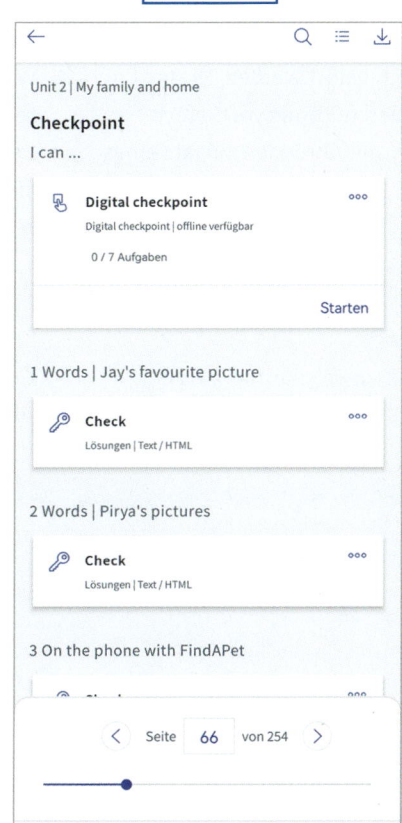

Lighthouse (General Edition) Band 1 Hybrides Material Paket Cornelsen Lernen App (220058915)

Vorwort

10 Medien- und Aufgabenvielfalt

Unterschiedliche Zugänge für die Vielzahl an Lernenden

Englischunterricht bedeutet Vielfalt und vor allem die Einbindung der vielseitigen und interessanten Typen von Lernenden. Um so viele Schülerinnen und Schüler wie möglich zu erreichen, sollte der Englischunterricht im Verlauf der einzelnen Units bezüglich des Einsatzes von Medien, Aufgaben und Methoden balanciert und variantenreich gestaltet sein. Das neue *Lighthouse* bietet dafür die richtige Grundlage.

Von Bildimpulsen und Videoclips über *chat messages* und *mind maps* zu *questionnaires* und Liedern: die Buchseiten von *Lighthouse* offerieren eine ganze Palette an verschiedenen Medieninputs und Aufgabenformaten, um eine spannende Variation in den Englischunterricht zu bringen.

So befasst sich im Beispiel rechts die Aufgabe *The legend of the Loch Ness monster* (Nr. 1) mit dem Stellen und Beantworten von Fragen zu zwei Artikeln. Partner A liest in diesem Fall den Artikel *The mystery of Nessie*, während Partner B den Artikel *Hunting for Nessie* auf den *Diff bank*-Seiten liest. Die beiden Lernenden stellen sich anschließend gegenseitig den jeweils unbekannten Artikel vor. Nur gemeinsam anhand der beiden Artikel kann die Aufgabe erfolgreich gelöst werden. Dieses Aufgabenformat zeigt die Verknüpfung von Sprachprogression, Spaß und dem zielführenden Einsatz eines Medieninputs.

Insgesamt berücksichtigt das neue *Lighthouse* die Vielzahl an Lerntypen durch eine Methoden-, Aufgaben- und Themenvielfalt:

- intrapersonelle Angebote für individuelles Arbeiten
- interpersonelle Angebote für die Zusammenarbeit mit anderen Lernenden
- musikalische Angebote
- visuelle Angebote, z. B. durch die Beschreibung von Bildern oder das Anschauen von Videos wie im Beispiel rechts in Aufgabe 2 *What happens*
- logisch-mathematische Angebote, indem z. B. Informationen im Sinne einer *Info-gap activity* herausgefunden werden müssen, siehe z. B. *The legend of the Loch Ness monster*

Weiterhin werden die Lernenden anhand variantenreicher Aufgabenstellungen befähigt, sich inhaltlich und sprachlich mit dem Unterrichtsgegenstand auseinanderzusetzen. Beispiele dafür sind *Listen and repeat, give advice, read the biography, watch the video, make a mind map, do the role-play, search online, compare, put the events in the correct order* etc.

In diesem Zuge offeriert *Lighthouse* auch eine Wahldifferenzierung bei möglichen *outcomes* (Lernprodukten). Wie das Beispiel von Aufgabe 4 *'Green' clothes* rechts zeigt, können die Schülerinnen und Schüler zwischen zwei verschiedenen Lernprodukten wählen und somit ihren persönlichen Präferenzen und Interessen Ausdruck geben.

Scary Scotland

1 READING The legend of the Loch Ness monster

a) BEFORE YOU READ Grace and Rhona are at the first place on their trip: Loch Ness. What do you know about 'Nessie'? The title of this exercise and the photo in the article below can help you.

Good to know
There are a lot of legends and scary stories from Scotland. They include monsters, ghosts and mermaids or mermen.

Nessie is a … It lives … It looks like …

b) **Partner B:** Look at p. 100.
Partner A: Read the article. What's it about? Choose the best main idea (A–C).

A There's something big in the loch, but nobody knows what it is.
B There's a monster in the loch with a long neck.
C There aren't any big creatures in the loch.

The mystery of Nessie

Does a monster live in the deep water of Loch Ness? A lot of people think that the Loch Ness monster is real and have lovingly named it Nessie.
In 1934 a photographer took a photo of the creature. It seemed to have a long neck and a small head like a snake. After the photo, people went out on the loch in boats to try and see the monster. Unfortunately they didn't find anything, but Loch Ness is very big: 23 miles long and 88 feet deep! In 1977 Nessie appeared in another photo: The monster looked like the 1934 photo, so a lot of people thought there was definitely a monster in the loch.
Later scientists used sonar equipment to try and discover the monster. They didn't find Nessie, but the equipment discovered several large living creatures.

c) **Partner A and partner B:** Read your article again. Write the reason for your choice in b).

d) Tell your partner what your article is about.

The main idea of my article is that … It says …

Good to know
one mile = 1.6 kilometres
one foot = 30.48 centimetres

2 VIEWING What happens

a) Watch the film. Were some of your ideas from 1 in the film?

b) Put the events in the correct order.
Then watch the video again and check.

1e, 2 …

a There's a problem with one of the car's tyres.
b A coach with an England flag goes past.
c Something happens at the service station and David's dad is angry.
d David's dad decides that they can go on the coach.
e In the car, David and his dad talk about the trip.
f David gets on the coach alone and a fan stops David's dad.
g An England fan from the coach says that David and his dad can trave…

My task

4 'Green' clothes ▶ Digital help

a) YOU CHOOSE Do task **A** or **B**.

A Make a poster with your top five tips for green clothes. Rosie's quiz and the words in the box can help you.
▶ More help, p. 70

(don't) buy • give • repair • swap • throw away • wash • wear • …

B Design a piece of green clothing and draw a picture. Think about the material, what it looks like and why it's better for the planet than other clothes.
▶ Wordbank 3, p. 188

b) Present your poster or your design to the class.

These are our top five tips for … We think people should …
This is our design for … It's a … It's better for the planet because …

Lighthouse (General Edition) Band 3 (9783060365425), S. 76, 59 und 47

11 Lernstrategien

Planung, Steuerung und Reflexion des Lernprozesses

Das neue *Lighthouse* ermöglicht den Lernenden verstärkt, ihr eigenes Lernen und ihren Lernfortschritt strategisch und zielgerichtet zu gestalten. Dazu werden zahlreiche Lernstrategien kontextbezogen direkt in die Aufgabenstellungen integriert und aufgebaut. Die Schülerinnen und Schüler lernen, die Aufgaben erfolgreich zu bewältigen, indem sie ihre eigenen Handlungen und den Bearbeitungsprozess bewusst reflektieren sowie Pläne und Techniken entwickeln, kurzum: Lernstrategien anwenden.

Die Bandbreite der Lernstrategien ist enorm. Sie reichen von Meta-Lernstrategien, die den eigenen Lernprozess steuern (z. B. der *Unit-Plan*), über Kommunikationsstrategien zur Aufrechterhaltung monologischer oder dialogischer Sprechhandlungen bis hin zu Text- und Informationsgewinnungsstrategien (z. B. Erklärvideos, Wörterbücher, Umgang mit Lesetexten etc.). Insbesondere in lexikalischer Hinsicht sind Gedächtnis- und Ordnungsstrategien unabdingbar, die dazu führen, sprachliche Strukturen sinnvoll zu speichern (z. B. Mindmaps).

Das neue *Lighthouse* greift die Vielfalt der Lernstrategien kontinuierlich auf und ermöglicht es den Lernenden, die dafür notwendigen Fertigkeiten kleinschrittig zu erwerben.

Die Aufgabe *Adventurer Aldo Kane* greift die Strategie der Text- und Informationsgewinnung kontextbezogen auf. Die Schülerinnen und Schüler lernen, wie ein Textinput mittels *Scanning* gezielt durchsucht werden kann und erfahren somit Strategien der gezielten Informationssuche.

Ein zentrales Ziel des Englischunterrichts ist die inhaltlich und sprachlich adäquate Umsetzung von Kommunikationssituationen durch die Lernenden. Die dafür notwendigen Kommunikationsstrategien werden anhand verschiedener Szenarien gezielt eingeübt. In der *Unit task* zu *Have a discussion* üben die Lernenden schrittweise das Führen einer erfolgreichen Diskussion und wenden dabei Strategien wie das Finden von Argumenten, *Buying time* oder das Geben von Feedback konkret an.

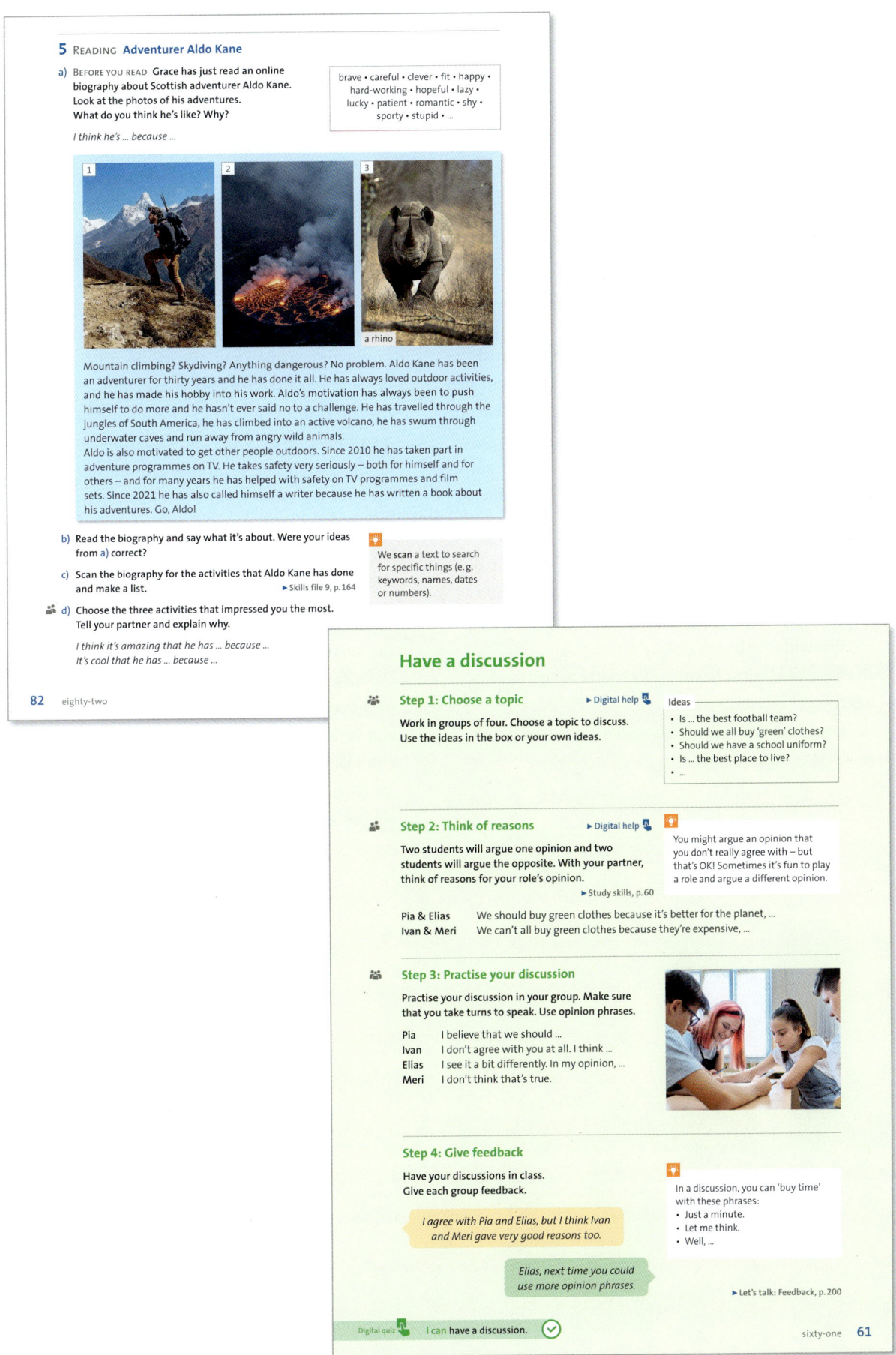

Lighthouse (General Edition) Band 3 (9783060365425), S. 82, 61

XXIV

12 *Global goals*

Verantwortung und Bewusstsein für ein globales Verständnis entwickeln und umsetzen

Ein großes Anliegen des neuen *Lighthouse* ist es, auch global diskutierte und gesellschaftlich relevante Aspekte aufzugreifen. In einer Welt, in der Ereignisse wie der *Earth Overshoot Day*, der Umgang mit Rohstoffen etc. auch für unsere Schülerinnen und Schüler immer näher und präsenter werden, ermöglicht *Lighthouse*, sich auch im Englischunterricht mit diesen Themen zu beschäftigen. Die eigens dafür vorgesehene Kategorie der *Global goals* (GG) bietet eine Bandbreite an Themen, um sich den 17 nachhaltigen Entwicklungszielen der UN schrittweise anzunähern und damit ein gesellschaftliches Bewusstsein zu schaffen.

Die *Global goals* greifen drei Zieldimensionen auf, die auch im *Lighthouse* sukzessive angestoßen werden:
1. Erkennen: Aneignung von Wissen über weltweit existierende Probleme und Syndrome,
2. Bewerten: kritische und reflektierte Auseinandersetzung,
3. Handeln: Finden von Lösungsansätzen und deren selbstständige Umsetzung.

In der Aufgabenstellung *Green cities* erkennen die Lernenden positive und zu verbessernde Umweltmaßnahmen und ordnen diese tabellarisch richtig zu. Anschließend schreiben sie ihre eigene Wohnumgebung für eine Website auf und bewerten deren Umweltgehalt in Form einer Kurzbeschreibung. Damit greift die Aufgabe das *Global goal* 11, *Sustainable cities and communities*, auf.

In einem weiteren Beispiel beschäftigen sich die Schülerinnen und Schüler mit einem Thema, das einen unmittelbaren Lebensbezug aufgreift: *Think before you buy*. Im Rahmen eines Quiz für eine Schulzeitschrift lösen die Lernenden ein Quiz und lernen spielerisch die Problematik von *fast fashion* kennen. Auch in dieser Aufgabe wird die zweite Zieldimension der Bewertungsebene aufgegriffen, indem die eigene Haltung in 3c) thematisiert wird. Die gesamte Aufgabe ist eingebettet in das *Global goal* 12, *Responsible consumption and production*.

Die Verknüpfung der digitalen Medienwelt mit den *Global goals* wird in der Aufgabe *Good health and well-being*, dem *Global goal* 3, thematisiert. Ausgehend von einem Hörverstehen setzen sich die Lernenden mit einer Gesundheits-App auseinander und diskutieren Möglichkeiten, die eigene (mentale) Gesundheit zu verbessern.

3 GLOBAL GOALS Green cities

a) At Rap Club, the three friends see a poster. Read it and then put the words and phrases in the box under the correct headings for green cities. ☒ Add more ideas.

More ...	Less / Fewer ...
bike lanes	air pollution

air pollution • bike lanes • clean transport • green energy • green spaces and parks • lakes • plastic • recycling • rubbish • second-hand shops • traffic • trees

Make your city greener!

'Green cities' is one of the 17 global goals
Leaders from 193 countries agreed on the goals in 2015. They want to make the world a better place and we want to help!

What you can do
You can join one of our groups to make your city or area greener. You can also write to us and tell us how green your area is: kylo@globalgreencities.example.org

b) Compare your ideas.

c) WRITING Write a short description of your area for *globalgreencities.org*. Use words from a).

*Dear Kylo
I live in ... It's a small / big town / ...
... is / isn't a big problem.
There's lots of rubbish. / There isn't much ...
There are lots of parks / ...
There aren't any ...
A lot of people use / recycle / ...
I think my area is quite / really / not very green.
Best wishes ...*

3 GLOBAL GOALS Think before you buy

a) Rosie thinks fashion isn't very good for the planet. She made a quiz for the school magazine. Can you guess the answers?

Rosie's fashion quiz

1. How many new pieces of clothing do businesses make for each person in the world each year?
   A 4 B 14 C 24

2. What percentage of clothes do we recycle into new clothes?
   A 1% B 10% C 30%

3. How many litres of water does it take to make one pair of jeans?
   A 500 B about 1,000 C nearly 4,000

4. Which material loses small bits of plastic when you wash it?
   A polyester B cotton C silk

5. What's fast fashion?
   A clothes that you can wear for a long time
   B trendy, cheap clothes that go out of style quickly
   C the coolest brands

b) Check your answers on p. 68.

c) What do you think is interesting, surprising or terrible? What can we do?

*I think it's interesting / surprising / terrible that ...   I didn't know that ...
We can buy / repair / wash / ...   Why don't we reuse / upcycle / ...?*

2 GLOBAL GOALS Good health and well-being

🔊 a) Listen to the second part of Flynn's interview and complete the sentences.

1. Zenn is a ... app.
2. It helps Flynn to feel ...
3. Only ... can read his diary on Zenn.
4. Clok is a ... app.
5. It works with Flynn's ...
6. Dylan also ... Clok.

b) Tell a partner which app you think is more useful and why.

*I think ... is more useful because you can ...
I think both apps are ...*

c) What do you do to improve your health and well-being? Tell your partner.

▶ Workbook, p. 72

Lighthouse (General Edition) Band 3 (9783060365425), S. 23, 47 und 114

Für Schülerinnen und Schüler

Schulbuch

Empowered by *Lighthouse*! Dreifachdifferenzierung mit zusätzlichen Angeboten: *More help* (sprachliche und inhaltliche Hilfen) – *More practice* (Vertiefung und quantitative Differenzierung) – *Challenge* (weiterführende Angebote mit höherem Anspruchsniveau)

App-Inhalte

Ergänzung des gedruckten Schulbuchs, des Workbooks und des Lern- und Arbeitsheftes durch optionale digitale Angebote, sowie alle Audios und Videos – bequem über die *Cornelsen Lernen App* nutzbar

Schulbuch als E-Book mit Medien

Das Schulbuch als E-Book unterstützt Lernende mit vielen digitalen Funktionen und enthält seitengenau platzierte Medien, auf die direkt aus dem E-Book heraus jederzeit unkompliziert zugegriffen werden kann.

Lern- und Arbeitsheft

Begleitend zu allen Ausgaben von *Lighthouse*, besonders geeignet für Lernende mit erhöhtem Förderbedarf im inklusiven Unterricht – auch erhältlich als E-Book mit Medien

Workbook

Perfekt geeignet zum selbstständigen Lernen, Vorbereiten von Klassenarbeiten und intensiven Training des Hörverstehens

Wordmaster und Grammarmaster

Mit dem **Wordmaster** wird der Wortschatz in immer neuen Zusammenhängen anhand verschiedener Methoden trainiert.
Mit dem **Grammarmaster** werden grammatikalische Strukturen individuell und selbstständig mithilfe vertiefender Übungen nachhaltig gesichert.

Lektüre

Die Lektüre *A Cardiff Chase – Lesespaß mit Rätseln* erscheint begleitend zu allen Ausgaben von *Lighthouse* und kann Unit 4 des Schulbuchs ersetzen.

Vokabeltaschenbuch

Das handliche Buch im Taschenformat zur Wiederholung des Vokabulars aus dem Schulbuch

Klassenarbeitstrainer

Abwechslungsreiche Übungen zum Wiederholen und Vertiefen – perfekt zur Vorbereitung von Klassenarbeiten

Vokabeltrainer phase6

Mit der Vokabeltrainer-App von phase6 werden die Vokabeln aus dem Schulbuch wiederholt – bestens geeignet zum gezielten Lernen für Tests und Klassenarbeiten.

ChatClass

Einfaches, individuelles Sprech- Grammatik- und Vokabeltraining per intuitiver Smartphone-App

Lighthouse (General Edition)
Band 3 (9783060365425)

Für Lehrkräfte

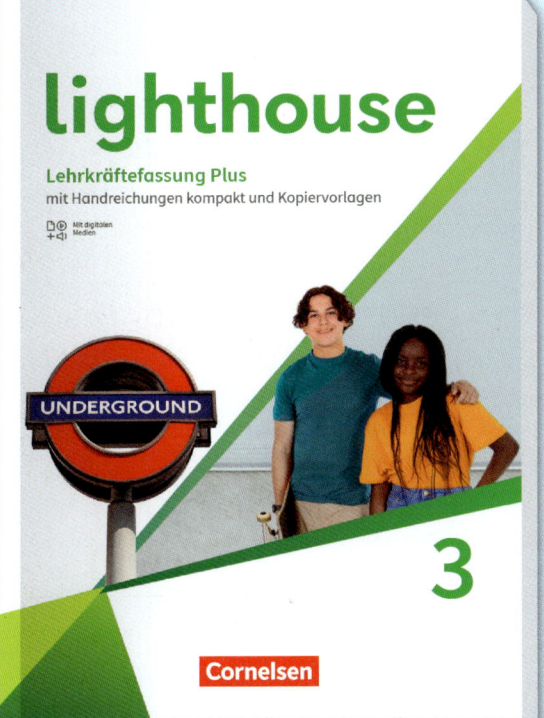

Lighthouse (General Edition)
Band 3 (9783060365463)

Workbook als Lehrkräftefassung
Das Workbook in der Lehrkräftefassung mit eingedruckten Lösungen

Extra-Differenzierung
Das Rundum-sorglos-Paket zum Fördern und Fordern – passend zu allen Ausgaben von *Lighthouse*

Video-DVD
Die Filmepisoden bieten passgenau und begleitend zu allen Ausgaben von *Lighthouse* authentische Materialien zum Training des Hörsehverstehens.

Audio-CDs
Enthalten alle längeren Textabschnitte, Hörtexte der Listening-Aufgaben und Songs aus dem Schulbuch und dem Workbook.

Diagnose und Fördern
Online-Anwendung zum schnellen und unkomplizierten Erheben des Lernstands Ihrer Lerngruppe sowie passende Lernmaterialien zum Fördern und Fordern

Vorschläge zur Leistungsmessung
Die Leistungsmessungsvorschläge unterstützen bei der Erstellung von differenzierenden Klassenarbeiten.

Lobaufkleber
Farbenfrohe „Well done!"-Lobsticker für Lernende

Schulbuch als Lehrkräftefassung Plus
Das Schulbuch in der Lehrkräftefassung mit einer kompakten Handreichung und Unterrichtskommentaren direkt an der Doppelseite

Unterrichtsmanager Plus
Vereint das digitale Schulbuch mit den umfangreichen Begleitmaterialien in einem Produkt und enthält neben den Lehrkräftefassungen des Schulbuchs alle Audios und Videos sowie ein umfangreiches Angebot weiterer Materialien – die ideale Unterstützung bei der Vorbereitung und Durchführung von Unterricht.

Lern- und Arbeitsheft als Lehrkräftefassung
Das Lern- und Arbeitsheft begleitend zu allen Ausgaben von *Lighthouse* in der Fassung für Lehrkräfte mit eingedruckten Lösungen und Markierung von neuem Wortschatz sowie Audio-CD.

ChatClass
Mit dem Dashboard für Lehrkräfte jederzeit die Lernaktivitäten der Lernenden einfach und gezielt steuern sowie individuelles Feedback geben

Inhalt

	I can …	Kompetenzen	Sprachliche Mittel	Seite
Hello! **Where we're from**				
	… talk about the UK and Ireland.	R Einer Karte Informationen entnehmen V/IC Einen Film über das UK und Irland verstehen R/L/S Sprachen und Akzente kennenlernen S Bilder beschreiben L Informationen über die Herkunftsorte der Schulbuchcharaktere verstehen R Einen Text über den Brexit verstehen	Voc the UK and Ireland · In the north / south / … of … · On the right / left of the picture … · In the middle of the picture … · In the foreground / background …	10
Unit 1 **London: City life**				
Lead-in	… understand and share information about London.	L Gespräche über Sehenswürdigkeiten in London verstehen S Sich über London und seine Sehenswürdigkeiten austauschen	Voc London sights · I think … looks the most interesting because …	14
Topic 1 Out and about in London	… talk about transport in London.	L/S Ein Gespräch über Verkehrsmittel in London verstehen und über den öffentlichen Nahverkehr sprechen My task Einer Tabelle Informationen entnehmen und geeignete Transportmittel finden	Voc travel and transport · How long does it take by …? · How much is the journey by …? · opposites: the fastest – the slowest G the will-future (revision)	16
Topic 2 A different kind of tour	… plan a tour.	R/S Flyern über Touren durch London Informationen entnehmen und sich über Aktivitäten in London austauschen M Bei einer Stadtführung ins Deutsche und Englische sprachmitteln V Einem Film über London Informationen entnehmen und wiedergeben My task Eine (virtuelle) Tour durch London gestalten	Voc prepositions of place and direction · Go straight on … · Take the first street on the left. · If you go/turn …, you'll arrive at the … · feedback phrases G conditional sentences type 1	18
Topic 3 Living in London	… describe life in cities and in my area.	L/S Einen Rap über London verstehen · Vor- und Nachteile des Großstadtlebens diskutieren R/GG/IC Ein Poster über nachhaltige Orte verstehen W Beschreiben, wie nachhaltig die eigene Region ist L Einem Bestelldialog in einem Café folgen S Essen bestellen (Rollenspiel) My task Einen Blogeintrag über eigene Aktivitäten schreiben	Voc words and phrases for green cities · food and drinks · free-time activities · feedback phrases · adjectives (-less/-ful) G simple past (revision)	22
Story Where is Lily?	… follow and discuss the events in a story.	R/W/S Den Spuren der Protagonisten in einer Geschichte folgen L/S Sich über ein mögliches Ende austauschen	Voc places in London · First they went to … · Then they went to … · Finally …	26
Viewing On the streets of London		V/IC Filmszenen verstehen S/LS Über Hilfe für andere sprechen	Voc helping other people · ideas to help	29

4 four

	I can …	Kompetenzen	Sprachliche Mittel	Seite
Study skills Do online research	… do online research.	**MK** Online recherchieren und Notizen machen	**Voc** keywords and fun facts about London sights	30
Unit task Make an audio guide for a London bike tour	… make and understand an audio guide.	**W/MK** Einen Audioguide schreiben und vertonen **L** Audioguides hören und verstehen **S** Feedback geben	**Voc** sights and activities · feedback phrases	31
Checkpoint	Kompetenzen und sprachliche Mittel (Unit 1) üben, Lernfortschritte erkennen			32
Text file	United – a magazine for young people across the UK: Multicultural London			36
Diff bank	Partner B, Parallel exercises, More help, More practice, Challenge			38

Unit 2 Manchester: Who we are

L Listening · **R** Reading · **S** Speaking · **W** Writing · **M** Mediation · **V** Viewing · **IC** Intercultural competence · **MK** Medienkompetenz · **LS** Life skills · **GG** Global goals · **Voc** Vocabulary · **G** Grammar

	I can …	Kompetenzen	Sprachliche Mittel	Seite
Lead-in	… explain what's important to me.	**L/IC** Einem Interview Informationen entnehmen **S** Darüber sprechen, was einem wichtig ist	**Voc** important things · That is/isn't really important to me.	44
Topic 1 Manchester fashion	… talk about fashion.	**R** Einem Artikel über Mode Wortschatz entnehmen **S** Über Shopping und Mode reden **R/S/GG** Ein Quiz über nachhaltige Mode lösen und besprechen **My task** (Ein Poster über) nachhaltige Kleidung gestalten und präsentieren	**Voc** clothes and fashion · opposites: tight – baggy · comparing outfits · discussion phrases · green fashion **G** comparisons (revision)	46
Topic 2 Family, friendship and love	… give advice.	**R/M** Eine Kolumne in einer Schulzeitung verstehen und Informationen ins Deutsche sprachmitteln **R/L/S** Leserbriefe, einen Dialog über persönliche Probleme und Ratschläge verstehen und sich darüber austauschen **My task** Einen Leserbrief beantworten und Feedback geben	**Voc** problems and feelings · giving advice: should – shouldn't · possible situations: may, could, might · feedback phrases · singular 'they' **G** modal verbs: must – mustn't, (don't) have to, needn't, be allowed to	48
Topic 3 Confidence	… talk about confidence.	**L/R** Vorbilder: einem Podcast und einem Artikel Informationen entnehmen **L/S** Sich über einen Song austauschen **V** Confidence tips verstehen **S** Komplimente machen und annehmen **My task** Ein Rollenspiel über Selbstbewusstsein schreiben und aufführen	**Voc** role models · confidence tips · compliments, advice · feedback phrases **G** reflexive pronouns and each other	52
Story A Manchester match	… discuss a conflict in a story.	**R/IC** Eine Geschichte über einen Konflikt verstehen **S/LS** Über den Umgang mit Konflikten sprechen **W** Ein eigenes Ende der Geschichte schreiben	**Voc** football · feelings · dealing with conflicts · discussion phrases	56

five 5

Inhalt

	I can ...	Kompetenzen	Sprachliche Mittel	Seite
Viewing Coach		V/IC Filmszenen verstehen	Voc *feelings · conflicts*	59
Study skills Explain your opinion	... give and explain my opinion.	Redemittel zur Meinungsäußerung sammeln und einordnen · Seine Meinung äußern und begründen	Voc *agreeing and disagreeing · I don't agree with you at all. · I completely agree.*	60
Unit task Have a discussion	... have a discussion.	S Pro und Kontra eines Themas überlegen und diskutieren · Feedback geben	Voc *opinion phrases · feedback phrases · phrases for 'buying time'*	61
Checkpoint	Kompetenzen und sprachliche Mittel (Unit 2) üben, Lernfortschritte erkennen			62
Text file	United – a magazine for young people across the UK: Manchester: the music capital			66
Diff bank	Partner B, More help, More practice, Challenge			68

Unit 3
Scotland: Adventure

	I can ...	Kompetenzen	Sprachliche Mittel	Seite
Lead-in	... talk about Scotland.	R/S/IC Einer Unterhaltung über eine Klassenfahrt Informationen entnehmen · Über schottische Fotos sprechen	Voc *describing places*	74
Topic 1 Scary Scotland	... understand stories and legends.	R/S Die Sage von Loch Ness verstehen und diskutieren R/M Eine deutsche Sage ins Englische sprachmitteln L/W Geistergeschichten hören und besprechen My task Einen Geist erschaffen und ein Poster dazu erstellen	Voc *ghost stories and legends · describing actions · opinion phrases* G *adverbs of manner (revision)*	76
Topic 2 Adventure sports	... talk about adventures and interests.	L/S Einen Dialog über sportliche Aktivitäten verstehen und besprechen R Einen Text über einen Abenteurer verstehen · Lesetechniken anwenden My task Eine kurze Biografie verfassen	Voc *free-time activities and adventures · describing people* G *present perfect (revision) · present perfect (for, since)*	80
Topic 3 In nature	... talk about nature.	S/GG Über Naturschutz sprechen L/IC/S Einen traditionellen schottischen Song verstehen und darüber sprechen My task Über den Stellenwert von Natur diskutieren	Voc *protecting nature · things in nature · Nature is important because ...*	84
Story A mountain adventure	... discuss good and bad choices in a story.	R Die Aussage einer Geschichte verstehen W Sätze gut verbinden S/LS Was man aus Fehlern lernen kann	Voc *linking words and phrases: in the end, so, then · saying sorry*	86
Viewing A road trip		V/IC Filmszenen verstehen S Über Unternehmungen in Schottland sprechen	Voc *ways to travel · sightseeing · activities*	89
Study skills Collect and structue ideas	... structure ideas for a story.	Ideen für eine Abenteuergeschichte sammeln und in einer Mindmap sortieren	Voc *places · people · events*	90

6 six

	I can ...	Kompetenzen	Sprachliche Mittel	Seite
Unit task Write a short adventure story	... write a short adventure story.	Seine Abenteuergeschichte planen **W** Eine *adventure story* schreiben **S** Feedback geben	**Voc** *adventures and places · feedback phrases*	91
Checkpoint	Kompetenzen und sprachliche Mittel (Unit 3) üben, Lernfortschritte erkennen			92
Text file	United – a magazine for young people across the UK: Amazing activities in Glasgow · Scottish traditions			96
Diff bank	Partner B, Parallel exercises, More help, More practice, Challenge			100

Unit 4
Wales: Digital life

L Listening · **R** Reading · **S** Speaking · **W** Writing · **M** Mediation · **V** Viewing · **IC** Intercultural competence · **MK** Medienkompetenz · **LS** Life skills · **GG** Global goals · **Voc** Vocabulary · **G** Grammar

	I can ...	Kompetenzen	Sprachliche Mittel	Seite
Lead-in	... understand information about Wales.	**R/S/IC** Ein Quiz über Wales lösen **L/IC** Einem Dialog Informationen über Wales entnehmen **S** Sich über Sehenswertes in der eigenen Region austauschen	**Voc** *places in Wales and in my area*	106
Topic 1 Welcome to Wales	... talk about Wales.	**R** Einem Dialog Informationen über einen Schüleraustausch entnehmen **L/S** Einen Song verstehen und seine Meinung dazu äußern **My task** Eine Sprachnachricht über Wales aufnehmen	**Voc** *places in Wales · songs and music · opinion phrases* **G** *possessive pronouns*	108
Topic 2 Life with and without technology	... give simple instructions.	**V/IC** Einem Film Informationen über das Leben in Wales 1927 entnehmen **S** Den Alltag damals und heute vergleichen · Sich über Technologie im Alltag austauschen **R/S** Ein Telefonat führen **L** Einem Gespräch entnehmen, wie man ein Video bearbeitet **M** Eine Gebrauchsanweisung ins Deutsche sprachmitteln **W** Eine technische Anleitung schreiben **My task** Eigene Anweisungen geben	**Voc** *life in the past and today · clothes words · technologies · telephone phrases · editing videos · understanding and giving tech instructions* **G** *going to-future (revision)*	110
Topic 3 Social media	... talk about the good and bad sides of social media.	**L** Interviews zur Nutzung von Social Media und Apps verstehen **S** Über die eigene Nutzung von Social Media und Apps sprechen · Hilfe anbieten, erbitten und annehmen **L/S/GG** Über Gesundheitsapps sprechen **W** Eine *bio* erstellen **R** Fakt und Meinung in Artikeln erkennen **My task** Kurzvorträge über Vor- und Nachteile von Social Media vorbereiten	**Voc** *describing social media apps · online activities · rules and habits · offering, asking for and accepting help · definitions · opinion phrases · feedback phrases* **G** *relative clauses*	114
Story Looking good	... talk about truth and lies on social media.	**R** Eine Geschichte über das Posten von Fotos und daraus entstehende Konflikte verstehen **S/LS/MK** Sich über Bildbearbeitung und ihre Wirkung austauschen	**Voc** *fake photos · clothes · make-up*	118

seven 7

Inhalt

	I can ...	Kompetenzen	Sprachliche Mittel	Seite
Viewing Sophie's cosplay costume		**V** Filmszenen verstehen **S** Über die Überwindung von Schwierigkeiten sprechen	**Voc** *cosplay · making a costume*	121
Study skills Make a talk flow	... make a talk flow.	Sprechkarten für einen Vortrag ordnen · Unbekannte Wörter erklären · Redewendungen für einen flüssigen Vortrag nutzen	**Voc** *sequencers: first, second, ... · phrases for buying time: Well, just a minute, ... · definitions*	122
Unit task Give a short talk about social media	... give a short talk.	**S/W/MK** Sich Gedanken zur eigenen Mediennutzung machen · Sprechkarten vorbereiten **S** Den Vortrag einüben und halten · Feedback geben	**Voc** *use of social media and the internet · sequencers · feedback phrases*	123
Checkpoint	Kompetenzen und sprachliche Mittel (Unit 4) üben, Lernfortschritte erkennen			124
Text file	United – a magazine for young people across the UK: My reading tip: A scary rescue			128
Diff bank	Partner B, Parallel exercises, More help, More practice, Challenge			132

Unit 5 OPTIONAL
Two Irelands: Together

L Listening · **R** Reading · **S** Speaking · **W** Writing · **M** Mediation · **V** Viewing · **IC** Intercultural competence · **MK** Medienkompetenz · **LS** Life skills · **GG** Global goals · **Voc** Vocabulary · **G** Grammar

	I can ...	Kompetenzen	Sprachliche Mittel	Seite
Lead-in	... talk about Ireland and Northern Ireland.	**L/R** Sprachnachrichten Informationen über Irland und Nordirland entnehmen **S** Fotos beschreiben	**Voc** *places and people*	138
Topic 1 A trip to Belfast	... plan and talk about a trip.	**S/IC** Über Reisen ins Ausland sprechen **L/IC** Einen Dialog über eine Reise verstehen **R/IC** Einer Website und einer Broschüre Informationen entnehmen **My task** Ein Rollenspiel am Empfang eines B & B aufführen	**Voc** *travel, passports and money · at a B&B*	140
Topic 2 In Belfast	... talk and write about Belfast.	**R/IC** Einer Broschüre Informationen über Belfast entnehmen **L** Ein Gespräch über die Tagesplanung verstehen **M** Fragen zu einer Buchung sprachmitteln **My task** Eine Nachricht mit Informationen über Belfast schreiben	**Voc** *activities and sights in Belfast · making a reservation*	142
Story Dance drama	... complete a story.	**R/L** Eine Geschichte über einen Tanzwettbewerb verstehen **S** Über das Verhalten der Protagonisten diskutieren **S/W** Eine Geschichte fortführen	**Voc** *feelings · fairness · discussion and feedback phrases*	144
Viewing Tina times two		**V/IC** Filmszenen verstehen **S/LS** Über Ängste und Mut sprechen	**Voc** *family · hopes and dreams · being scared/brave*	147
Checkpoint	Kompetenzen und sprachliche Mittel (Unit 5) üben, Lernfortschritte erkennen			148

8 eight

	I can ...	Kompetenzen	Sprachliche Mittel	Seite
Text file		United – a magazine for young people across the UK: The Titanic brothers · Finn McCool		150
Diff bank		Partner B, More help, More practice		152

> Die Angebote des Schulbuchs sind nicht obligatorisch abzuarbeiten.
> Die Auswahl der Übungen und Übungsteile richtet sich
> nach den Schwerpunkten des schulinternen Curriculums.

Anhang

Skills file		154
SF 1 Vokabeln lernen	155	
SF 2 Unbekannte Wörter erschließen	156	
SF 3 Im Wörterbuch nachschlagen	157	
SF 4 Im Internet recherchieren	158	
SF 5 Die eigene Meinung äußern	160	
SF 6 Eine Geschichte planen	161	
SF 7 Einen Kurzvortrag halten	162	
SF 8 Hörtexte verstehen	163	
SF 9 Lesetexte verstehen	164	
SF 10 Mediation	165	
SF 11 Bilder beschreiben	166	
SF 12 Texte markieren und Notizen erstellen	167	
SF 13 Texte überprüfen und verbessern	168	

Language file		169
LF 1 Die Wortstellung (Revision)	169	
LF 2 Die einfache Gegenwart (Revision)	170	
LF 3 Die Verlaufsform der Gegenwart (Revision)	172	
LF 4 Die einfache Vergangenheit (Revision)	173	
LF 5 Die Zukunft mit *will* (Revision)	174	
LF 6 Bedingungssätze Typ 1	175	
LF 7 Die Steigerung der Adjektive	175	
LF 8 Modale Hilfsverben	176	
LF 9 Reflexivpronomen	178	
LF 10 Adverbien der Art und Weise	178	
LF 11 Das *present perfect*	180	
LF 12 Possessivbegleiter und -pronomen	181	
LF 13 Die Zukunft mit *going to*	182	
LF 14 Relativsätze	183	
Grammatical terms	184	
Wichtige Schreibregeln im Englischen	185	

	Seite
Wordbanks (nach Themen sortierter Wortschatz, z. B. Sport, Gefühle, Natur, Technik etc.)	186
Let's talk (Redewendungen für wichtige Situationen, z. B. Diskussionen, Feedback geben, *Classroom English* etc.)	195
The English alphabet, English sounds	202
English numbers	203
Vocabulary (Lernwortschatz Unit für Unit)	204
English-German Dictionary (alphabetisch geordnetes Wörterverzeichnis Englisch-Deutsch)	245
Irregular verbs	272
Ähnliche Wörter im Englischen und Deutschen	274
Typical tasks (Übersicht über häufige Arbeitsanweisungen)	275
Quellenverzeichnis	276
Continents, countries and regions	280

Hello!

Übersicht

Storyline: Großbritannien und Irland werden vorgestellt. Die Lernenden erfahren etwas über Jugendliche aus verschiedenen Orten auf den beiden Inseln, ihre Sprachen und besondere Sehenswürdigkeiten. Sie erhalten geopolitische und historische Informationen über Großbritannien und Irland.
Viewing: geopolitische Informationen zum UK und zu Irland (S. 10)

Hello! Einstieg:
- (SB zu) ▶ Brainstorming:
  L: *This year we're going to learn a lot about the United Kingdom and Ireland. What do you already know about the people, sports, traditions etc.?*
- L nutzt Bildimpulse oder Realien, um das Vorwissen der S zu aktivieren, z. B. Tee, Bilder von Fußballteams, Bands.
- S antworten und L hilft ggf. mit sprachlichen Mitteln.

Ex 1 Einstieg:
- (SB zu) L zeigt die Karte von S. 10 (UMA) u. aktiviert das Vorwissen der S:
  L: *What can you see? What do you already know?* (L notiert Antworten der S als TA.)

Erarbeitung:
a) (SB auf) S arbeiten weiter gemäß AA in PA mit der Karte (UMA) u. ggf. ▶ KV 0.1 (Ex 1a).
- **Ausw.:** s. b)

b) 1. **Sehen** von *part 1*: S überpüfen ihre Antworten von a).
- **Ausw.:** Vergleich im Plenum

c) L gestaltet eine Tabelle als TA (Vorlage s. ▶ KV 0.1 (Ex 1d).
- S übertragen Tabelle in ihr Heft od. nutzen ▶ KV 0.1 (Ex 1d) u. ergänzen sie mithilfe der Karte.
- **Ausw.:** 2. **Sehen** u. Vergleichen im Plenum
- ☒ 1. **Sehen** von *part 2*: S ergänzen ihre Tabelle (s. ▶ KV 0.1 (Ex 1d).
- **Ausw.:** S präsentieren ihre Ergebnisse im Plenum od. in Kleingruppen (s. ▶ KV 0.1 (Ex 1e,f).

Hello!
Where we're from

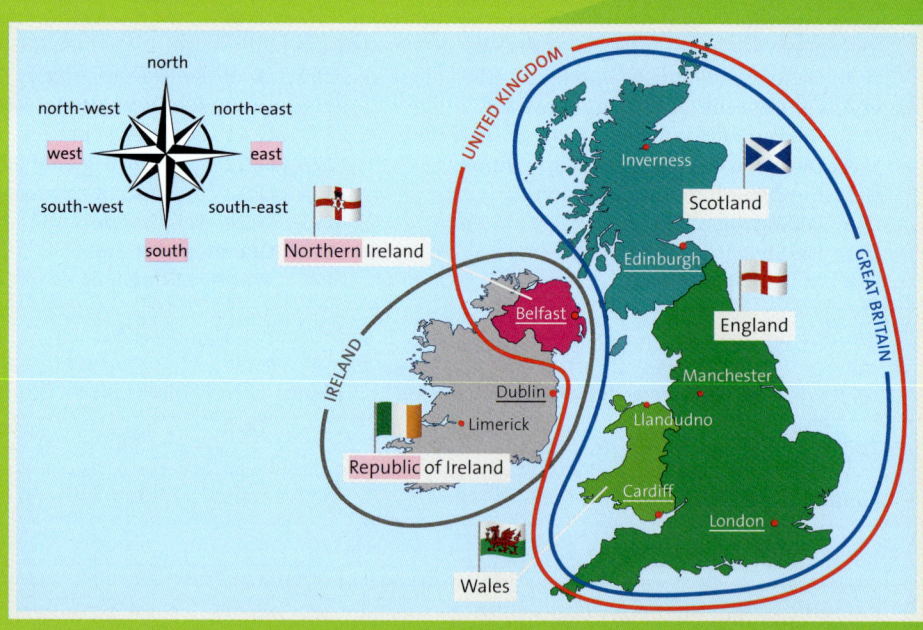

1 VIEWING The United Kingdom and Ireland

a) BEFORE YOU WATCH Look at the map and answer the questions. Which countries °make up …
1. Great Britain (GB)? – England, … and …
2. the island of Ireland? – … and …
3. the United Kingdom (UK)? – …, …, … and …

> **1 a)** 1 *England*, Wales and Scotland • **2** Northern Ireland and the Republic of Ireland • **3** England, Wales, Scotland and Northern Ireland

b) Watch part 1 of the video. Check your answers from a).

c) Write the five countries. Look at the map and write the capital for each country. Watch again and check. ☒ Watch part 2 and write more information for each country.

> **1 c)** Lösung S. 281

Hello!

Intro Inhalt

Lernschwerpunkt: *UK* und *Ireland*
Kompetenzen: Reading einer Karte Informationen entnehmen • Viewing / Intercultural competence einen Film über UK und Irland verstehen • Reading/Listening/Speaking verschiedene Sprachen und Akzente kennenlernen • Speaking Austausch über Fakten zum UK und zu Irland
Redemittel: *the UK and Ireland* • *in the north/south/... of ...*

Vorbereitung

Material: Einstieg Bilder und/oder Realien (*Life in Britain*) • Ex 1 Karte von UK und Irland (UMA), UMA/DVD/App, ▶ KV 0.1: Where we're from (Klassensatz) • Ex 2 UMA, UMA/CD/App, Karte von UK und Irland (UMA)
Zeitbedarf: ca. 1–2 Std.
Minimalversion: Ex 2c) auslassen
Begleitmedien: INKL (S. 10–11), Unit plans (Hello!)

2 a) **Pearl, Omar, Jack** English • **Grace** Scottish Gaelic • **Dylan** Welsh • **Orla** Irish/Gaelic

💬 **2 SPEAKING Hello!**

🔊 a) Read the box. Then read the °**speech bubbles** and listen
1.1 to the six students. In which languages do they say *hello*?

👥 b) Find the students' °**hometowns** on the map on p. 10.
Take turns to °**point** and say where the places are.

London is here on the map. It's in the south-east of England.

c) What did you already know about the UK and Ireland?
What surprised you? What else do you know?

| 2 b) Lösung S. 281 | 2 c) individuelle Lösungen |

1 [səˈmaɪ]   2 [lænˈdɪdnəʊ]   3 [ˈkʌmri]   4 [dʒɪə ˈxɔɪtʃ]   5 [ˈeːrjə]

Good to know

English is the most important language in all parts of the UK. In Scotland some people also speak **Scottish Gaelic** and in Wales **Welsh** is an official language. **Irish (or Gaelic)** is an official language in the Republic of Ireland and some people speak it in Northern Ireland too.

Ex 2 Einstieg:
- (SB auf) L leitet ein:
  L: *Let's find out more about the different languages in Ireland and the UK.*

Erarbeitung:
a) gemeinsames Lesen von
  ▶ Good to know, S. 11
- L schreibt die vier Sprachen an die Tafel und sichert die Aussprache (▶ Lautschulung).
  L: *Let's meet some people from the UK and Ireland.*
- L zeigt die sechs Teens von S. 11 (UMA):
  L: *They all say 'Hello' but which languages do they speak?*
- **1. Lesen/Hören** der Sprechblasen (▶ Mitleseverfahren)
- **Ausw.:** S schreiben die Namen und die Begrüßung unter die jeweilige Sprache (TA).
- **2. Lesen:** S lesen die Begrüßungen laut vor (▶ Lautschulung).

b) gemäß AA in PA
- **Ausw.:** Einzelne S-Paare präsentieren Ergebnisse im Plenum (Karte über UMA).

c) gemäß AA (▶ Think-Pair-Share)
- 🖼 L/S nutzen die Ergebnisse des Einstiegs (S. 10).
- **Ausw.:** im Plenum (TA)

- **Zusatz:**
  L: *In what languages can you say 'Hello'?*
  S: *I can say 'Hello' in Spanish. It's 'Hola' ...*
- L gibt ggf. sprachliche Hilfen (Nationalitäten, Sprachen).
- Klasse erstellt ein Plakat mit verschiedensprachigen Begrüßungen und Herkunftsländern (▶ English corner).

Hello!

Intro   Inhalt

Lernschwerpunkt: Sehenswürdigkeiten in Großbritannien und Irland kennenlernen
Kompetenzen: Speaking Bilder beschreiben • Listening einem Gespräch Informationen zu den Herkunftsorten der Schulbuchcharaktere entnehmen • Reading einen Text über den Brexit verstehen
Redemittel: *on the right/left of the picture … • in the middle of the picture … • in the foreground/background … • there is/are …*

Ex 3 Einstieg:
- (SB zu) L zeigt Foto einer bekannten britischen Sehenswürdigkeit mithilfe der ▶Gucklochmethode:
  L: *What can you see?* (S stellen Vermutungen an.)
- L präsentiert zur Auflösung das gesamte Bild u. leitet über:
  L: *Let's find some more interesting places in the UK.*

Erarbeitung:
a) (SB auf) L zeigt die Fotos von S. 12–13 (UMA). Klären der AA: L demonstriert ein Bsp. mit S, anschließend gemäß AA in PA (▶Partner talk).
- **Ausw.:** S beschreiben im Plenum ein Bild u. Klasse errät: S: *It's picture …*

b) L gestaltet Tabelle als TA:

| name | photo | notes |

- S übertragen die Tabelle in ihr Heft. L/S ergänzt im Plenum u. Heft die 1. Spalte (*names*).
- S ergänzen beim **1. Hören** die 2. Spalte (*photo*).
- **Ausw.:** ▶Five-minute teacher: S ergänzt die Tabelle (als TA).

c) ▶Klären der AA: S sollen sich beim Hören Stichpunkte machen (▶Note-taking).
- S ergänzen die 3. Spalte (*notes*) beim **2. Hören**.
- S überprüfen ihre Ergebnisse beim **3. Hören**.

d) gemäß AA in PA (▶Partner check), schriftl. in Tabelle
- **Ausw.:** ▶Meldekette
  S1: *What can you say about Pearl's place?*
  S2: *There's …*

Visit this beautiful city and meet friendly people.

Listen to bagpipes near a loch or in town.

See skyscrapers and other amazing modern buildings.

3 LISTENING Where we live

a) BEFORE YOU LISTEN Look at the photos (A–F). What can you see? Use the phrases in the box.
▶ Skills file 11, p. 166

> On the right / left of the picture … •
> In the middle of the picture … •
> In the foreground / background …

1.2 b) Write the names of the students from p. 11. Listen and °match the photos to the students.
Pearl: C, Omar: …

c) Listen again and take notes about each place.

d) °Compare with a partner. Add or correct information.

3 a) Lösungsbsp. S. 281
3 b) Pearl C • Omar F • Grace B • Dylan D • Jack E • Orla A
3 c) Lösungsbsp. S. 282
3 d) individuelle Lösungen

12 twelve

Hello!

Intro **Vorbereitung**

Material: Ex 3 Bild einer bekannten britischen Sehenswürdigkeit, Blatt Papier mit Loch, Dokumentenkamera, UMA/CD/App • **Ex 4** digitale Endgeräte für Recherchen, Umrisskarte von Europa (Klassensatz), ggf. Präsentationssoftware
Zeitbedarf: ca. 1–2 Std.
Begleitmedien: WB (S. 16–17), App (Digital quiz), INKL (S. 12–13), DIFF (0.1)

D
Visit Conwy Castle, one of many castles in this area.

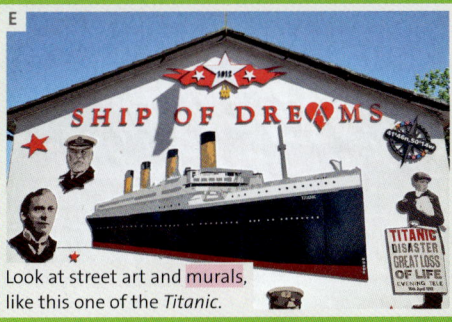
E
Look at street art and murals, like this one of the *Titanic*.

F
Experience the city on a boat trip on the canals.

4 1 The Republic of Ireland • 2 Scotland

📖 **4** READING °**Brexit**

An important event changed life in the UK. Read about it in the box and answer the questions:

1 Which of the countries below is still in the EU?
2 Which country would like to be in the EU?

| England | Wales | Scotland |
| Northern Ireland | The Republic of Ireland |

Digital quiz I can **talk about the UK and Ireland**.

Good to know

In 2020, the UK left the European Union (EU) after 47 years. We call this 'Brexit'. The vote was very close (leave: 51.9%, remain: 48.1%) and a lot of people were unhappy about the result. Most Scottish people voted to remain in the EU. Now a lot of Scottish people would like to leave the UK, become an independent country and join the EU again.
The Republic of Ireland is still in the EU.

▶ Workbook, pp. 16–17

thirteen 13

Ex 4 Einstieg:
- (SB zu) L notiert als TA: *BREXIT* (▶ stummer Impuls). S reagieren spontan. L unterstützt durch Fragen:
  L: *What does 'Brexit' mean?*
  S: *The UK has left the EU.*
  (TA: *Britain* + *exit* from the EU = *Brexit*)
- **Hinweis:** L führt vorab die ▶ English-only-Karte ein. Der Einsatz der Karte sollte ein festes Ritual jeder Stunde sein.

Erarbeitung:
- (SB auf) gemeinsames Lesen von ▶ Good to know, S. 13
- anschließend gemäß AA
- **Ausw.:** im Plenum

- **Zusatz:** Bei vorhandenem Interesse und Zeit recherchieren S weiter zum Thema Brexit und EU (auch in Verbindung mit anderen Fächern wie z. B. Geografie oder Geschichte):
- Zum Brexit: Was hat sich für die Menschen im UK geändert, was für die EU-Bürger/-innen, z. B. beim Reisen.
- S sammeln ihre Informationen z. B. auf Postern / digital und präsentieren sie in Kurzvorträgen im Plenum.
(▶ One-minute presentation)
- Zur EU: S recherchieren im Internet und listen die Mitgliedsländer der EU auf, deren Hauptstädte und seit wann sie Mitglieder der EU sind.
- S markieren diese Länder auf einer Umrisskarte von Europa und stellen die Länderinfos im Plenum vor.

1

Unit-Übersicht

Storyline: Lily ist nach London gezogen. In dieser Unit werden Sehenswürdigkeiten, bekannte Plätze und Attraktionen in London vorgestellt. S lernen Pearl und Ali kennen, die gemeinsam mit Lily verschiedene Unternehmungen in London machen. Dabei nutzen sie öffentliche Verkehrsmittel. In der Story geht Lily verloren. Pearl und Ali machen sich auf die Suche nach ihr …
Strukturen: *(revision) the will-future* (S. 17) • *conditional sentences type 1* (S. 19) • *(revision) simple past* (S. 25)
Viewing: eine virtuelle Tour durch London (S. 21) • gemeinnützige Projekte auf Londons Straßen (S. 29)
Unit task: einen Audioguide schreiben und aufnehmen

Unit 1 Einstieg:
- (SB zu) ▶ Brainstorming: L aktiviert das Vorwissen der S über London:
  L: *What do you already know about London? Which famous sights and places do you know?*
- L sammelt Fakten in einer ▶ Mindmap (auf einem großen Bogen Papier oder digital), die im Laufe der Unit weiter ergänzt werden kann.
- S übertragen die Mindmap in ihr Heft.

Ex 1 Einstieg:
- (SB auf) L zeigt Foto von Lily (UMA):
  L: *Do you remember Lily? She's new in London.*

Erarbeitung:
a) Lesen der AA, S beschreiben die Fotos in PA (UMA),
  ▶ SF 11, S. 166.
- **Alternative:** ▶ Picture duet zur Bildbeschreibung

b) S notieren die fünf Orte aus der Box untereinander ins Heft.
- 1. Hören gemäß AA
- **Ausw.:** ▶ Meldekette, L/S notiert die Lösungen an der Tafel.

c) 2. Hören gemäß AA, S ergänzen ihre Einträge für jeden Ort im Heft.
- ☒ Lernstärkere S notieren weitere Informationen.
- **Ausw.:** ▶ Meldekette
- S vergleichen ihre Lösungen/ Notizen im Plenum, ggf. 3. Hören.

Unit 1
London: City life

Watch musicians and acrobats.

Go shopping and eat amazing food here.

See this popular tower at the Houses of Parliament.

1 LISTENING Your London, my London

a) BEFORE YOU LISTEN Lily has just moved to London. She's talking to her new friend Ali about London °sights. Look at the photos (A–F). What can you see?

b) Listen and match the places in the box to the photos.

c) Listen again. Who talks about each place, Lily (L) or Ali (A)? ☒ Take notes about each place.

Big Ben: L (at the Houses of Parliament)

1 c) Lösungsbsp. S. 282

| 1 a) Lösungsbsp. S. 282 |
| ▶ Skills file 11, p. 166 |

Big Ben • London Eye • South Bank • Leake Street Tunnel • ⁺Orbit Slide • Camden Market

1 b) A South Bank • B Camden Market • C Big Ben • D Orbit Slide • E Leake Street Tunnel • F London Eye

14 fourteen

1

Lead-in **Inhalt**	**Vorbereitung**
Lernschwerpunkt: Informationen über London verstehen	**Material:** Einstieg großer Papierbogen oder digitale Tafel • Ex 1 UMA, UMA/CD/App
Kompetenzen: Listening Gespräche über Sehenswürdigkeiten in London verstehen und Bilder richtig zuordnen • Speaking sich über Londoner Sehenswürdigkeiten austauschen	**Zeitbedarf:** ca. 1 Std.
	Minimalversion: Ex 1c) auslassen
Redemittel: London sights • I think … looks the most interesting because …	**Begleitmedien:** WB (S. 18), App (Digital quiz), INKL (S. 14–15), DIFF (1.1), Unit plans (Unit 1)

Nach dieser Unit kann ich …
- Informationen über London verstehen und wiedergeben
- über Verkehrsmittel in London reden
- eine Tour planen
- das Leben in der Großstadt und in meiner Gegend beschreiben
- online recherchieren

Unit task
- einen Audioguide für London erstellen

Nach dieser Unit …
- L bespricht mit S die Lernziele der Unit (s. links) und kündigt die *Unit task* an.
- Am Ende der Unit überprüfen S das Erreichen der Ziele mithilfe des *Checkpoint* (S. 32–35) bzw. gemeinsam im Plenum.

Ex 2 Einstieg:
- (SB zu) ▶Vokabelarbeit: L gibt Anweisung zum Einsatz/Führen des *Vocab file* im Schuljahr.
- L legt die Regeln für den Einsatz der ▶Vokabeltafel fest.
- S übertragen den neuen Wortschatz selbständig.

Erarbeitung:
a) (SB auf) L präsentiert eine Vorlage für die *London page* des *Vocab file* als TA u. klärt im Plenum die AA.
- L od. freiwillige/-r S führen ein Bsp. an der Tafel vor (▶Semantisierung).
- S arbeiten gemäß AA.
- Sich.: ▶Five-minute teacher, S/L sichern die Wörter u. ihre Bedeutungen an der Tafel, anschl. ▶Lautschulung.

b) gemäß AA in PA
- Alternative: ▶Milling around
- Ausw.: S präsentieren zu zweit ihre Favoriten im Plenum.
- Sich.: L festigt den neuen Wortschatz von S. 14–15 (z. B. durch ▶Vokabelrennen).

D — Come to this sculpture if you love fast slides.

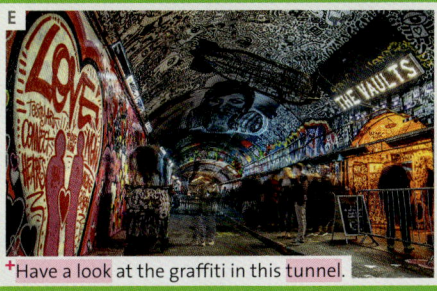

E — ⁺Have a look at the graffiti in this tunnel.

F — A ride on this big wheel is great fun!

2 SPEAKING Visiting London

2 a) Riesenrad • Imbissstand • Graffitiwand • Parlament • Fahrt • Skulptur • Rutsche • Turm • Tunnel

a) WORDS Start a London page in your VOCAB FILE. Work out the meanings of the words in the box and add them. Use the pictures and words from other languages to help you.
▶ Skills file 1 + 2, p. 155 f.

big wheel • food stall • graffiti wall • parliament • ride • sculpture • slide • tower • tunnel

b) Tell a partner which place in 1 looks the most interesting to you.
2 b) individuelle Lösungen

I think … looks the most interesting (because it's … / because I like … / because you can … there).

▶ Workbook, p. 18

 I can understand and share information about London.

- **Zusatz:** Gemeinsam sammeln S die *activities*, die im *Lead-in* vorgestellt werden (z. B. *go shopping, ride a big slide*) und üben sie dann mithilfe eines ▶Menschen-Memo.

fifteen 15

1

Topic 1 Inhalt

Lernschwerpunkt: etwas über die öffentlichen Verkehrsmittel in London und der eigenen Region erfahren
Kompetenzen: Listening Statements zu einem Hörtext auf ihren Wahrheitsgehalt überprüfen und korrigieren • Speaking Fotos interpretieren • in PA darüber sprechen, welche öffentlichen Verkehrsmittel man nutzt und wie häufig • in PA Preise und Fahrtzeiten unterschiedlicher Verkehrsmittel in London besprechen • Reading matching von Bildern und Wörtern
Strukturen: *(revision)* the will-future
Redemittel: travel and transport • How long does it take by ...? • How much is the journey by ...? • time and money words • opposites: the fastest – the slowest

---

Ex 1 Einstieg:
- (SB zu) *Warm Up*: L aktiviert das *will-future* mit vorbereiteten ▶ Swap cards (▶ KV 1.1 A+B) als Vorentlastung für a) (▶ Grammatikwiederholung).
- **Alternative:** ▶ Gucklochmethode: L zeigt das verdeckte Foto von S. 16 o. rechts (Ali u. Pearl in *King's Cross*) (UMA). L: *What can you see? What is it?* (S spekulieren, bis L das ganze Foto zeigt.) S: *It's Ali and Pearl! They're in a train station ...*

Erarbeitung:
a) (SB auf) L zeigt die Fotos von S. 16 (UMA). S beschreiben die Fotos, ggf. im ▶ Picture duet.
- gemeinsames Lesen der AA, ▶ SF 8, S. 163
- Bearbeitung gemäß AA
- S antworten: *I think Ali and Pearl will ... / They'll ...*
- ✉ Schwächere S nutzen ein ▶ Scaffolding (TA) und wdh. das *will-future* ggf. hier schon mithilfe von ▶ LF 5, S. 174.

b) **1. Hören** gemäß AA
- **Ausw.:** erst ▶ Partner check, dann im Plenum

c) S lesen die Sätze und notieren die Zahlen 1–8 in ihr Heft.
- S notieren die Antworten (T/F) gemäß AA beim **2. Hören** und korrigieren die falschen Sätze.
- **Ausw.:** ▶ Meldekette

d) (SB zu) ▶ Five-finger brainstorming: S nennen fünf Wörter zu *public transport*.
- (SB auf) PA gemäß AA
- ✉ More Help, S. 39
- **Ausw.:** S-Paare präsentieren ihre Ergebnisse im Plenum.

| 1 | **Topic 1** | Topic 2 | Topic 3 | Story | Viewing | Study skills | Unit task |

Out and about in London

🎧 **1 LISTENING A trip to Camden Market**

💬 a) BEFORE YOU LISTEN Ali and his friend Pearl are waiting for Lily at King's Cross Station to go to Camden Market. Look at the photos (A–C). Say what you think they'll do there.   ▶ Skills file 8, p. 163

> **1 a)** They'll go shopping, buy cheap clothes. • They'll go to the food stalls, have some cake. • They'll listen to street music.

Ali   Pearl

A

B

C

> **1 b)** They talk about what they can do at Camden Market, how to get there (bus or tube), tickets, how to get to the platform.

🔊 1.4 b) Listen to the °conversation. What do Ali, Pearl and Lily talk about? Compare your answers.

🔊 c) Listen again. True or false? Correct the false sentences.

1 They won't go by bus because of the traffic.
2 It's three stops to Camden Town.
3 They'll change at the next station.
4 Lily doesn't need a ticket because she has a Travelcard.
5 It will be busy on the tube.
6 They'll take the escalator down to the platform.
7 They have to wait a long time for the train.
8 There's an announcement about the next stop.

💬 d) Talk about transport in your area.   **1 c)** Lösung S. 282

1 Is there an underground in your area?
   🟢 **Yes** How often do you use it? What's it like?
   🔴 **No** Have you ever travelled on an underground? If yes, where? How was it?
2 What public transport (bus, tram, ...) do you use in your local area and why? ▶ More help, p. 39

> **Good to know**
> Londoners call the underground the 'tube'. It's the oldest underground in the world – parts of it are from 1863! Today it has modern stations with Wi-Fi.

1 d) individuelle Lösungen

16 sixteen

1

Topic 1 Vorbereitung

Material: Ex 1 vorbereitete *Swap cards* (bekannte Verben) oder ▶ KV 1.1 A+B: SWAP CARDS Verbs, UMA/Dokumentenkamera, ggf. ein Blatt Papier mit Loch, UMA, UMA/CD/App • Ex 2 UMA, von L vorbereitete Wortkarten mit den Begriffen von Ex 2a) • Ex 3 von L recherchierte Bilder/Fotos von öffentlichen Verkehrsmitteln, UMA
Zeitbedarf: ca. 2 Std.
Minimalversion: Ex 3c) auslassen
Begleitmedien: WB (S. 19–20), App (Digital quiz), INKL (S. 16–17), DIFF (1.2)

1

2 WORDS Transport

2 a) 1 g • 2 c • 3 e • 4 h • 5 a • 6 d • 7 b • 8 f

a) Match the words (1–8) to the correct pictures (a–h). Then add them to your VOCAB FILE.

1 lift
2 direct
3 stop
4 (to) change
5 escalator
6 Travelcard
7 traffic
8 platform

  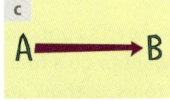 
a b c d

 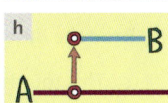
e f g h

b) °Complete the conversation with words from a).

Ali	It will be our … (1) soon. OK, let's get off.
Lily	That was really fast!
Pearl	It is when the train is … (2). But not when you … (3) to a different line. You often walk a long time to the … (4) for your next train!
Ali	OK, let's go up the … (5). There isn't a … (6) at this station.
Pearl	Do you have your … (7), Lily? Remember, you'll need it when we go out.
Lily	Yes, I have it. … °Wow, it's busy here! Look at all those taxis and buses!
Ali	Yes, there's always lots of … (8).

Good to know

The red London buses are often double-deckers and many are electric. You can use an app to hire a bike all over London. Or you can take a special London taxi – a black cab.

REVISION The will-future: ▶ Language file 5, p. 174 ▶ More practice 1, p. 39 ▶ Challenge 1, p. 40

2 b) 1 stop • 2 direct • 3 change • 4 platform • 5 escalator • 6 lift • 7 Travelcard • 8 traffic

My task

3 What's the best transport?

3 a,) b) Lösungsbsp. S. 282 f.

a) After Camden the three kids want to go shopping in Oxford Street.
Partner B: Look at p. 38.
Partner A: Answer partner B's questions.

b) Ask partner B about taxis, bikes and walking. Take notes.
How long does it take by taxi / by bike / if they walk?
How much is the journey by …?

c) °Decide which transport is:

3 c) Lösungsbsp. S. 283

the fastest ★ the slowest ★ the cheapest ★ the most expensive ★ the greenest ★ the healthiest ★ the most fun.

Camden Market to Oxford Street (3 km)		
	time	price
bus	16 min.	free for kids
tube	7 min.	90p
taxi	?	?
bike	?	?
walk	?	free

▶ Workbook, pp. 19–20

Digital quiz I can talk about transport in London.

seventeen 17

Ex 2 Einstieg:
- (SB zu) L zeigt die Bilder a–h (UMA):
L: *Where is it?*
S: *At a tube station …*

Erarbeitung:
a) (SB auf) L verteilt acht Wortkarten an freiwillige S:
L: *Match the word to the correct picture.*
- **Ausw.:** im Plenum mit ▶ Lautschulung
- **Sich.:** S notieren die Wörter ins *Vocab file*.

b) gemeinsames Lesen von
▶ Good to know, S. 17
- gemäß AA
- **Ausw.:** ▶ Meldekette
- *Revision* des *will-future*, s. ▶ LF 5, S. 174 u. ▶ More practice 1, S. 39 (zur Vorbereitung des *conditional 1* in Topic 2, S. 19)
- ☒ ▶ Challenge 1, S. 40

My task Ex 3 Einstieg:
- (SB zu) L zeigt Bilder von öffentl. Verkehrsmitteln:
L: *How do you and your friends get to school / the shops / … ?*
S: *I use the bus/train/… I walk.*
L: *How much is it?*
S: *It's free / … Euro/…*

Erarbeitung:
a) (SB auf) ▶ Klären der AA
- *Partner B* geht auf S. 38.
Partner A bleibt auf S. 17 u. beantwortet *B's* Fragen.

b) Gemäß AA: *Partner A* notiert *B's* Antworten ins Heft.
- **Ausw.:** im Plenum
- L ergänzt Tabelle als TA (UMA).

c) gemäß AA im Plenum
- **Ausw.:** Erfassen der Ergebnisse im Plenum (TA)

17

1

Topic 2 Inhalt

Lernschwerpunkt: verschiedene (touristische) Touren durch London kennenlernen und sich darüber austauschen
Kompetenzen: Reading einer Beschreibung zu einem Ausflug Informationen entnehmen und entsprechende Aussagen zuordnen • Speaking sich über (mögliche) Aktivitäten bei einem Ausflug nach London austauschen
Strukturen: conditional sentences type 1
Redemittel: sights of London

Ex 1 Einstieg:
- (SB zu) L zeigt Flyer oder Website einer *Hop on/ off*-Tour:
L: *Have you ever done such a city tour? If yes, did you like it?* (S antworten spontan.)

Erarbeitung:
a) (SB auf) S erfassen und notieren Ideen im ▶ Brainstorming.
- Ausw.: L sammelt S-Antworten im TA.

b) S lesen Sätze 1–6 vor.
- S lesen Texte in EA u. notieren die Zuordnungen im Heft.
- L klärt ggf. bei Bedarf unbekannten Wortschatz (▶ Semantisierung).
- Ausw.: ▶ Partner check, dann Plenum
- Zusatz: S lesen die Texte A–C laut vor.
- im Plenum: bei Bedarf weitere ▶ Semantisierung von Wortschatz und ▶ Lautschulung

c) gemäß AA in PA
- Ausw.: S-Paare präsentieren ihre Ergebnisse (mit Begründung) im Plenum.
- Alternative: L erfragt die Meinung der S im ▶ Meinungsbarometer: Der Raum wird in zwei Hälften unterteilt für *yes* und *no* (ggf. mit Symbolen kennzeichnen). L: *Do you like tour A?*
- S positionieren sich auf jeweils eine Seite und begründen ihre Meinung.
- Danach folgt je ein weiterer Durchgang mit *tour B* und *C*.

| 1 | Topic 1 | **Topic 2** | Topic 3 | Story | Viewing | Study skills | Unit task |

A different kind of tour

1 Reading Which tour?

a) Before you read Pearl's aunt, uncle and cousins are visiting from Manchester next week and want to do a tour of London. °Brainstorm different kinds of tours: boat tours, film tours, ... Think about transport and °themes.

1 a) Lösungsbsp. S. 283

b) Read the descriptions of the tours (A–C). Choose the correct tour for each sentence 1–6.

1 This tour is in the evening.
2 You can buy something on this tour.
3 You can see famous homes on this tour.
4 This tour is only on Saturdays and Sundays.
5 You must be brave to do this tour.
6 This tour uses an electric form of transport.

1 b) 1 B • 2 A • 3 C • 4 A • 5 B • 6 C

A Calling all music fans! Join our Rock Walking Tour to discover important London sites of music history. You'll visit Denmark Street, where many top rock bands and singers recorded their ⁺albums. Then we'll walk to Berwick¹ Street. People call it the Golden Mile because it has so many music shops – you can go shopping there. Then we'll have lunch at Hard Rock Cafe!

Weekends only
Meet at Tottenham Court Road Underground at 11 a.m.

B If you're scared of the dark, you won't like this tour! Join our Ghost Bus for a tour of the scariest and oldest places in London. Will you see the ghosts of young princes in the Tower of London? Are you brave enough to go into the London Dungeon? There's only one way to find out ...

Meet at the Ghost Bus stop at 9 p.m. ▶ Box: Voc., p. 208

C Discover traditional London sights, but not in a traditional way! Ride your own Segway as we show you the classic sights. See Buckingham Palace, where the royal family lives. Ride over the beautiful Tower Bridge over the river Thames. And visit the official home of the prime minister at 10 Downing Street!

2 p.m. every day except Mondays

c) Tell your partner which tour you want to do and why.
I want to do the ... tour because I'm interested in ... / I want to see ... / I want to travel ...

1 c) individuelle Lösungen

¹ [ˈberɪk]

▶ More practice 2, p. 40
▶ Workbook, p. 21

18 eighteen

Topic 2 Vorbereitung

Material: Ex 1 Flyer oder Website einer *Hop on/off*-Tour, ggf. Symbole für *yes* und *no* • Ex 2 UMA, UMA/App (Erklärfilm) • Ex 4 blanko Karteikarten (A7, Klassensatz) od. mit ▶ KV 1.2: GAME Quiz-quiz-swap vorbereitete Karteikarten (Klassensatz)
Zeitbedarf: ca. 2 Std.
Minimalversion: Ex 4 auslassen
Begleitmedien: WB (S. 21–22), App (Digital help), INKL (S. 18–19 f.)

1

2 LOOKING AT LANGUAGE Conditional sentences type 1

2 a) They chose Tour C.

a) Read what the tour guide said. Which tour from 1 did Pearl's family choose?

> If I push the handle, I'll go faster. Now you try.
> If you look to your left, you'll see the most beautiful building in London.
> If the king is at home today, there'll be a special flag on top of the building.
> If we have time, we'll visit the shop to buy ⁺souvenirs.
> If Tower Bridge is closed, we won't go that way.

b) Read the sentences in a) again and choose the correct words for the rule.

We use conditional sentences type 1 to talk about a possible condition and its result.
We make conditional sentences type 1 with:

if-clause (condition)	main clause (result)
If + simple present	will-future
If you like / 'll like history,	*you enjoy / 'll enjoy this tour!*

▶ Language file 6, p. 175

2 b) *If you like history, you'll enjoy this tour!*

3 What will we do if …?

3 1 d • 2 e • 3 a • 4 c • 5 b

Pearl is planning activities with her family after the tour.
Match the if-clauses (1–5) to the main clauses (a–e).

1 If Aunt Vera sees a famous person,
2 If it rains,
3 If my cousins go to Hamleys toy shop,
4 If we take the underground,
5 If it's too expensive,

a they'll buy too many toys.
b we won't go into the London Dungeon.
c we'll get there faster.
d she'll be so excited!
e I'll take them to a museum.

4 individuelle Lösungen

4 GAME Quiz-quiz-swap

a) Imagine you go to London. Write a verb on a card. Use the ideas in the box or your own ideas.

b) Find a partner and swap cards. Say:

> *If I go to London, I'll …*

Ideas
- bring (an umbrella / snacks / …)
- buy (a postcard / a T-shirt / …)
- eat (fish and chips / ice cream / …)
- travel (by bus / by underground / …)
- visit (the London Eye / a museum / …)
- …

Use the verb on your partner's card to finish the sentence.
Then it's your partner's turn.

c) Find new partners. Swap cards again and make new sentences. How many sentences can you make?

▶ More practice 3, p. 41   ▶ Challenge 2, p. 41
▶ Workbook, p. 22

nineteen 19

Ex 2 Erarbeitung:
a) (SB auf) **1. Lesen** gemäß AA
- **Ausw.:** im Plenum
- L zeigt Sätze von Ex 2a) (UMA).
- **2. Lesen:** Je zwei S lesen einen Satz vor: (S1: *if-clause* / S2: *main clause*) (▶ Meldekette).
- L markiert beide Teile als TA (mit unterschiedl. Farben).

b) Die markierten Sätze von a) bleiben für alle sichtbar.
- Gemäß AA, L semantisiert *possible condition*.
- **Ausw.:** im Plenum, L unterstreicht die richtigen Formen (Farben wie bei a)).
- **Sich.:** S übertragen die Übersicht in den Merkteil (▶ English folder) und schreiben die Sätze von a) dazu.
- ▶ LF 6, S. 175, Digital help u. Erklärfilm (App) zur Festigung

Ex 3 Erarbeitung:
- (SB auf) schriftlich gemäß AA
- **Ausw.:** ▶ Meldekette

Ex 4 Einstieg:
- (SB zu) L: *If you go to London, what will you do there?* (S antworten spontan.)

Erarbeitung:
a) (SB auf) gemeinsames Klären der AA des Spiels (s. a. b) + c)).
- S nutzen ▶ KV 1.2 od. schreiben ihre eigenen Verbkarten.

b) + c) gemäß AA z. B. im
- ▶ Milling around
- S nutzen bei Bedarf die ▶ Ideas-Box, S. 19.
- **Ausw.:** im Plenum
- ▶ More practice 3, S. 41,
- ▶ Challenge 2, S. 41

1

Topic 2 Inhalt

Lernschwerpunkt: weitere Touren durch London kennenlernen und eine eigene Tour erstellen
Kompetenzen: Speaking sich in PA über verschiedene Touren in London austauschen • Feedback geben • Mediation bei einer Stadtführung ins Deutsche und ins Englische sprachmitteln • Viewing einem Film über London Informationen entnehmen und wiedergeben • Writing/Reading eine virtuelle Tour planen und verstehen
Redemittel: travel and sightseeing • prepositions of places and directions • giving directions

---

Ex 5 Einstieg:
- (SB zu) L: *Do you remember any of the tours you can do in London?*
  S: *I remember the … tour.*

Erarbeitung:
a) + b) (SB auf) Gemäß AA in PA, *Partner B* arbeitet auf S. 38.
- *Partner A* u. *B* benötigen genügend Zeit für das Lesen der beiden Tour-Flyer.
- S machen sich beim Lesen Notizen (▶ Note-taking) und beantworten ggf. bereits dann die Fragen 1–6 (die Fragen sind identisch für beide Flyer).
- **Ausw.:** S-Paare präsentieren ihre Fragen und Antworten gemeinsam im Plenum.

Ex 6 Einstieg:
- (SB zu) L zeigt das Foto von Ex 6 (UMA).
- S-Paare beschreiben einander das Foto (▶ Picture duet).
- Zur Vorbereitung der ▶ Mediation können S ▶ SF 10, S. 165 lesen und vorab im Plenum besprechen.

Erarbeitung:
- (SB auf) Klären der AA (▶ Mediation)
- S ergänzen in Dreiergruppen (▶ Gruppenbildung) die fehlenden Passagen schriftlich im Heft.
- **Ausw.:** S-Gruppen präsentieren ihre Ergebnisse im Plenum (▶ Role-play).
- Lernschwächere S nutzen ▶ Cue cards für ihre Rollen.
- Stärkere S sprechen frei.

| 1 | Topic 1 | **Topic 2** | Topic 3 | Story | Viewing | Study skills | Unit task |

5 SPEAKING More tours   **5** Lösungsbsp. S. 283

a) Pearl told Lily about the tour and now she wants to do a special tour of London too.
Partner B: Look at p. 38.
Partner A: Ask partner B these questions about a special London tour.

1 What kind of tour is it?
2 How will I travel during the tour?
3 What will I see on the tour?
4 How much does the tour cost?
5 How can I book the tour?
6 Can you give me more information about the tour?

b) Now read the flyer about another London tour and answer partner B's questions.

Afternoon tea tour

Afternoon tea and London red buses are both traditionally English – so why don't you enjoy both at the same time? Sit on our bus and enjoy delicious sandwiches, cakes and tea while you see the top sights of London. If you like great food and interesting facts, you'll love this tour! You can listen to our audio guide as you watch the city through the windows. You'll see the London Eye, the Houses of Parliament, Buckingham Palace and many more places. Tours cost £25 per person and you can buy tickets online or from our kiosk.

6 MEDIATION St James's Park   **6** Lösungsbsp. S. 283

You're on a walking tour in St James's Park. Your mum needs your help because she doesn't speak English very well. Have a conversation with two partners. Then swap roles.

Guide	Here we are in St James's Park. It's not the biggest park in London, but I think it's the most beautiful.
Mum	Was hat er/sie gesagt?
You	Er/Sie hat gesagt, dass …
Mum	OK, aber kannst du fragen, was der größte Park in London ist?
You	Excuse me, my mum has a question: …
Guide	Great question! Well, the biggest park in central London is Hyde Park. In fact, over 40% of London is green space!
You	Er/Sie hat gesagt …
Guide	Now, if you look over the Blue Bridge, you'll see Buckingham Palace. It has 775 rooms.
Mum	Was sagt er/sie über den Palast?
You	…
Mum	Ach ja. Und kannst du fragen, was das für Vögel sind?
You	My mum has another question: …
Guide	Oh yes! We're lucky to see those birds! They're pelicans and they're very rare. Aren't they beautiful?
You	…

▶ Skills file 10, p. 165

20 twenty

Topic 2 Vorbereitung

Material: Ex 6 ggf. *Cue cards* • Ex 7 UMA, (digitale) Karte von *Central London* (mit Sehenswürdigkeiten) z. B. ▶ KV 1.3B: MY TASK London map, digitale Tafel, UMA/DVD/App • Ex 8 UMA, (digitale) Karte von *Central London* z. B. ▶ KV 1.3B: MY TASK London map (UMA/Klassensatz), digitale Endgeräte für S, ▶ KV 1.3A: MY TASK My virtual tour (Klassensatz), ggf. geeignete App/Website für virtuelle Stadttouren

Zeitbedarf: ca. 2 Std.

Minimalversion: Ex 7c) auslassen

Begleitmedien: WB (S. 23), App (Digital quiz), INKL (S. 20–21), DIFF (1.3)

---

7 VIEWING A virtual tour of London

a) BEFORE YOU WATCH Match the pictures (a–e) to the °directions (1–5).

1 Go straight on.
2 Turn left.
3 Turn right.
4 Go across the road.
5 Take the second road on the right.

7 a) 1 c • 2 e • 3 a • 4 b • 5 d

b) Watch the video and complete the directions.

At Trafalgar Square … (1) the roundabout and … (2) the road. Go straight on down Whitehall and take the … (3) street on the … (4). At the river … (5) and … (6).

▶ Parallel exercise, p. 41

c) Watch the video again and answer the questions. Give short answers.

1 What animal is at the bottom of Nelson's Column?
2 What's the name of the theatre on your right?
3 What time is the Changing of the Horse Guards?
4 What's Tattershall Castle?
5 How many capsules are there on the London Eye?
6 Where does the tour end?

7 c) 1 a lion • 2 Trafalgar Theatre • 3 10 or 11 o'clock • 4 a ship, now a restaurant • 5 32 • 6 Big Ben

Hey Grandma, I'm sorry you couldn't come to London with Aunt Vera. Cousin Leon +filmed a virtual tour for you instead while he was here!

7 b) 1 go across • 2 go straight over • 3 third • 4 left • 5 turn right • 6 go straight on

My task

8 My virtual tour

8 individuelle Lösungen   ▶ Digital help

a) Plan a walking tour of London with your partner. Look at a map and choose a start and an end. Start at Trafalgar Square, the London Eye, the Tower of London or Buckingham Palace. Then write directions. °Include some famous places and information about them.

Go straight on / across / along / past / …
Take the first / second / … street on the left / right.
If you go / turn …, you'll arrive at the … / you'll see a …

▶ Wordbank 1, p. 186

b) Do another pair's tour. Use a map or virtual tour app and °follow the directions. Which famous places do you 'see' on the tour?

c) Give feedback on the tour.

I thought the tour was clever / difficult / easy / fun / interesting / …

I liked seeing the …

▶ Workbook, p. 23

Digital quiz   I can **plan a tour**.

twenty-one 21

Ex 7 Einstieg:
- (SB zu) L zeigt das Handy-Display von S. 21 (UMA):
  L: *What can you see?*
  S: *I can see Pearl, the London Eye, a horse (and rider) …*
- S finden die *sights* auf einer (digitalen) Karte von *Central London* (z. B. ▶ KV 1.3B).

Erarbeitung:
a) (SB auf) gemäß AA
- Ausw.: ▶ Meldekette

b) S schreiben die Nrn. 1 bis 6 ins Heft und ergänzen die Antworten beim **1. Sehen**.
- ▶ Parallel ex, S. 41
- Ausw.: ▶ Partner check, dann im Plenum

c) Klären der AA, anschl. lesen S die Sätze 1–6 laut vor.
- S notieren die Antworten beim **2. Sehen** gemäß AA.
- Ausw.: ▶ Meldekette

My task Ex 8 Einstieg:
- (SB zu) S sammeln schon bekannte *London sights* von Unit 1, ggf. TA, L sichert ihre Aussprache (▶ Lautschulung).

Erarbeitung:
a) (SB auf) ▶ Klären der AA
- S nutzen ▶ KV 1.3A, u. ▶ KV 1.3B oder eine digitale Karte von *Central London* bzw. eine App/Website.
- L legt die Anzahl der *sights* für die Tour fest.

b) gemäß AA
- Ausw.: Sammeln der *sights*, die mit den Touren der S besichtigt werden (TA).

c) ▶ Feedback gemäß AA

1

Topic 3 Inhalt

Lernschwerpunkt: die Vor- und Nachteile des Lebens in einer Großstadt kennenlernen
Kompetenzen: *Listening* einem Rap Vor- und Nachteile des Großstadtlebens entnehmen • *Speaking* Vor- und Nachteile des Großstadtlebens diskutieren • *Reading* ein Poster über nachhaltige Orte verstehen • *Global goals / Writing* beschreiben, wie nachhaltig die eigene Region ist
Redemittel: *adjectives (-less/-ful)* • *city life* • *words and phrases for green cities*

Ex 1 Einstieg:
- (SB zu) TA: *My London*
  L: *What do you think you will hear in a song with this title?*
- L sammelt die Vermutungen als ▶ Ideenregen.

Erarbeitung:

a) ▶ Semantisierung von *against*
- PA gemäß AA, S-Paare übertragen die Tabelle ins Heft u. notieren dort ihre Argumente (*for/against*).
- Ausw.: S/L sichern Argumente in der Tabelle (als TA und im Heft) und übernehmen zusätzliche Ideen aus dem Einstieg.

b) 1. Hören: Klären der Globalverständnisfragen gemäß AA
- Ausw.: im Plenum

c) (SB auf) 2. Hören: Gemäß AA (▶ Mitleseverfahren), S suchen nach weiteren positiven und negativen Aspekten zum Leben in London u. ergänzen ihre Tabelle aus a).
- S markieren, welche ihrer eigenen Ideen in der Tabelle auch im Rap vorkommen.
- Ausw.: Ergänzung des TA aus a). S ergänzen ihre Tabellen im Heft.
- ☒ S ordnen die Bilder den Lyrics zu und begründen ihre Wahl.

d) S beantworten die Frage im Plenum od. im ▶ Milling around.
- S nutzen die ▶ Wordbank 2, S. 187 u. ggf. eigene, vorbereitete ▶ Cue cards.

| 1 | Topic 1 | Topic 2 | **Topic 3** | Story | Viewing | Study skills | Unit task |

Living in London

1 Song My London

> **1 a), c)** Lösungsbsp. S. 284

The next week, Pearl takes Ali and Lily to Rap Club to meet some friends and listen to some music.

a) BEFORE YOU LISTEN Find °reasons *for* and *against* living in a big city like London. Make notes.

for	against
exciting places, …	traffic, …

b) Listen to this rap. What's it about? Does the singer like London?
1.5

> **1 b)** It's about the singer's experience of London. He loves London.

My London

My London – it's not about the Tower or
the Dungeon or the big wheel –
my London's real,
it's something that you feel.
It's here I was born,
with all the traffic and the car °horns.
Capital L, with all the noises and the smells
and Big Ben's °bell goes bong,
can't stay away too long.
Don't get me wrong, we are strong,
°that's why I wrote this song. ▶ Box: Voc., p. 216
My London – sing it loud, I'm so proud!
My London – I don't care about the °crowds
or the grey clouds. My London, my London!

London is my city
and it's always °pretty busy,
on the walls we have graffiti
and the city's never °sleepy.
We have to help the homeless,
I know this.
Yeah, we have people on the street,
but we also have hip-hop °beats
and good things to eat.
I know it's not perfect,
but it's my favourite place on earth,
it's °worth it:
My London …

c) Listen to the rap again. Look at the photos and read the lyrics. Add other points to your notes in a).

d) What's the best and worst thing about cities for you? Tell the class.

▶ Wordbank 2, p. 187
▶ Workbook, p. 24

> **1 d)** individuelle Lösungen

Topic 3 Vorbereitung

Material: Ex 1 UMA/CD/App, ggf. *Cue cards* (Klassensatz) • Ex 2 ein bunter u. ein farbloser/durchsichtiger Gegenstand • Ex 3 UMA
Zeitbedarf: ca. 2 Std.
Minimalversion: Ex 1c), d) auslassen, Ex 3c) als HA
Begleitmedien: WB (S. 24–25), INKL (S. 24–25)

1

> 2 a) without a home • *-less* means *without*
> 2 b) full of colour • full of stress

2 Word building *-less* and *-ful*

a) Find the word *homeless* in the song. What does the word and the ending *-less* mean?

b) The opposite of the ending *-less* is the ending *-ful*. Lily thinks London is ⁺*colourful*, but also ⁺*stressful*. Explain what those words mean.

c) Look at Ali's tips for Lily. Use the words in °brackets to make a word with *-less* or *-ful*.
▶ Box: Voc., p. 211

1 Be (care...) when you cross the street because the traffic is crazy!
2 Ask people for directions: Londoners are usually very (help...).
3 Discover different parts of London. There are (end...) things to see.
4 Visit some of the London parks. They're really (peace...).
5 There are many (cloud...) days – it doesn't always rain.
But an umbrella is always a good idea!
6 Don't eat in tourist cafes. The food is expensive and often (taste...).
▶ Box: Voc., p. 211

Good to know
UK cars drive on the left side of the road. When you cross the street, remember to look right.

> 2 c) 1 careful • 2 helpful • 3 endless • 4 peaceful • 5 cloudless • 6 tasteless

3 Global goals Green cities

> 3 a) Lösungsbsp. S. 284

a) At Rap Club, the three friends see a poster. Read it and then put the words and phrases in the box under the correct headings for green cities. ☒ Add more ideas.
▶ Box: Voc., p. 212

More ...	Less / Fewer ...
bike lanes	air pollution

air pollution • bike lanes • clean transport • green energy • green spaces and parks • lakes • plastic • ⁺recycling • rubbish • second-hand shops • traffic • trees

Make your city greener!
'Green cities' is one of the 17 global goals Leaders from 193 countries agreed on the goals in 2015. They want to make the world a better place and we want to help!

What you can do
You can join one of our groups to make your city or area greener. You can also write to us and tell us how green your area is:
kylo@globalgreencities.example.org

b) Compare your ideas.

c) Writing Write a short description of your area for *globalgreencities.org*. Use words from a).

Dear Kylo
I live in ... It's a small / big town / ...
... is / isn't a big problem.
There's lots of rubbish. / There isn't much ...
There are lots of parks / ...
There aren't any ...
A lot of people use / ⁺recycle / ...
I think my area is quite / really / not very green.
Best wishes ...

▶ Workbook, p. 25

> 3 c) individuelle Lösungen

twenty-three 23

Ex 2 Einstieg:
- (SB zu) L zeigt ein buntes u. ein farbloses Objekt: L: *Look, I have two things: one is colourful and one colourless.*
- L notiert *colourful* und *colourless* als TA.

Erarbeitung:
a) (SB auf) gemäß AA, gemeinsame ▶ Semantisierung von *-less*
- **Ausw.:** im Plenum

b) gemeinsames Lesen der AA
- L notiert *stressful* unter *colourful* (s. **Einstieg**).
- Erarbeitung im Plenum
- L ergänzt TA mit Überschrift *Word building -less and -full*
- Vergleich mit deutschen Suffixen, z. B. *-los* u. *-voll*.
- **Sich.:** S übertragen TA in den Merkteil (▶ English folder).

c) gemäß AA in EA
- **Ausw.:** ▶ Five-minute teacher
- **Zusatz:** gemeinsames Lesen von ▶ Good to know, S. 23

Ex 3 Einstieg:
- (SB zu) L zeigt das Poster von Ex 3 (UMA): gemein. Lesen u. Klären von *global goals*. TA: *What can you do to make your city/village greener?*
- S sammeln Ideen mit ▶ Think-Pair-Share.

Erarbeitung:
a) (SB auf) S ergänzen die Tabelle schriftlich gemäß AA im Heft.
- ☒ Stärkere S ergänzen eigene Ideen.

b) gemäß AA in PA
- **Ausw.:** im Plenum

c) schriftlich gemäß AA
- **Ausw.:** im Plenum

23

1

Topic 3 Inhalt

Lernschwerpunkt: Essen in einem Café bestellen • einem Alltagsblog folgen
Kompetenzen: Listening einem Bestelldialog in einem Café folgen • Speaking Essen und Getränke bestellen (role-play) • über die eigenen Aktivitäten der vergangenen Tage sprechen • Reading einen Blog über ein Wochenende verstehen • Writing einen Blogeintrag über eigene Aktivitäten schreiben
Strukturen: (revision) simple past
Redemittel: food and drinks • freetime activities • feedback phrases

---

Ex 4 Einstieg:
- (SB zu) L leitet ein:
  L: *I'm going out to a new restaurant/cafe tonight. Look here what's on their menu …*
- L zeigt Bilder/Fotos von Ex 4 (▶Flashcards) und fragt S: *What is it?* – S antworten (▶Semantisierung des neuen Wortschatzes).
- L notiert Wörter als TA (▶Vokabeltafel) u. S üben die Aussprache (▶Lautschulung).

Erarbeitung:
a) (SB auf) L zeigt das *menu* von S. 24 (UMA) und liest AA vor.
- gemäß AA in PA
- Ausw.: S-Paare präsentieren Ergebnisse im Plenum.

b) Klären der AA
- S notieren die Zahlen beim **1. Hören**.
- Ausw.: ▶Partner check, dann im Plenum

c) S notieren die vollständigen Sätze in ihr Heft.
- Ausw.: S vergleichen die Ergebnisse beim **2. Hören**.

Ex 5 Einstieg:
- (SB zu) Wdh. des neuen Wortschatzes aus Ex 4 mithilfe von ▶Words in the Air.

Erarbeitung:
- (SB auf) Klären der AA (▶Role-play)
- L u. S demonstrieren einen Musterdialog.
- PA gemäß AA
- Ausw.: Präsentation der Dialoge im Plenum
- Bereitstellung der Requisiten (Speisekarte, Tisch, Stühle, …)

---

1 | Topic 1 | Topic 2 | **Topic 3** | Story | Viewing | Study skills | Unit task

4 LISTENING In a cafe   **4 a)** individuelle Lösungen

a) BEFORE YOU LISTEN After Rap Club, the three friends go to Ali's grandparents' cafe. Look at the menu and talk about it.

The ⁺kibbeh sound good.
I love … / I don't like … / I'm allergic to …

★ Menu ★

Drinks
1 Tap water   free
2 Sparkling water   £1.50
3 Soft drinks   £1.90
4 ⁺Mango milkshake   £2.60
5 Mint tea   £2.00
6 Coffee   £2.30

Lebanese small plates
7 ⁺Hummus (chickpea dip)   £5.75
8 ⁺Halloumi cheese with cucumber and olives   £6.25
9 Kibbeh (lamb ⁺meatballs)   £6.50
10 Spicy sausages with lemon   £6.50
11 ⁺Falafel with sesame sauce   £6.25
12 Chicken with spicy potatoes   £7.50
13 Bread   90p

b) 🔊 1.6 What food and drinks do the kids order? Listen and write the correct numbers from the menu.

drinks: …   food: …

4 b) drinks 1, 2, 4 • **food** 8, 10, 11, 13

c) Complete the phrases. Then listen again and check.

1 … I have a mango milkshake, please?
2 I'd … sparkling water, please.
3 … have number eleven, the falafel, please.
4 Can I have it … the sesame sauce?
5 Can you … me what halloumi cheese is?

4 c) 1 Could • **2** like • **3** I'll • **4** without • **5** tell

5 ROLE-PLAY Let's order!   **5** Lösungsbsp. S. 284

a) Partner A is the waiter. Partner B orders food and drinks from the menu in 4. Remember to say *please* and *thank you*. You can use °props like a menu and a screen.

Waiter	Are you ready to order?
	What would you like to drink?
You	…
Waiter	And to eat?
You	Can you tell me …
Waiter	…

You	…
Waiter	Anything else?
You	…
Waiter	So for drinks, that's … and for food, that's … Thank you.
You	…

b) Swap roles and do the role-play again.

24 twenty-four

1

Topic 3 Vorbereitung

Material: Ex 4 Fotos oder Flashcards (neuer Wortschatz von S. 24), UMA, UMA/CD/App • Ex 5 Requisiten für ein „Café" (z. B. Speisekarte, Tisch, Stühle)
Zeitbedarf: ca. 2 Std.
Minimalversion: Ex 5b) auslassen, Ex 7c) als HA
Begleitmedien: WB (S. 26), App (Digital help, Digital quiz), INKL (S. 22–23), DIFF (1.4)

1

6 Reading Lily's +blog

6 a) Lily writes about her new London life.

a) Read Lily's first blog post. What does she write about?

Did you eat Lebanese food in Brighton?

Yes, I did. But I didn't eat it very often. Hmm, maybe I should +blog about my London life for my old friends in Brighton?

www.lilysblog.example.com

Hi, everyone! My name is Lily. I'm new in London and I want to tell you about my new life here.

Last weekend I went to Camden Market with my new friends Ali and Pearl. I didn't buy anything, but I loved all the stalls and the canals there. After the market we hired bikes and cycled to Oxford Street. I love cycling! There were some amazing shops in Oxford Street and it was very busy.

Yesterday Pearl took us to Rap Club and we heard some cool music. After that we went to Ali's grandparents' cafe and ate some delicious Lebanese food. You can get food from all over the world in London.

I'm looking forward to next weekend. For my dad's birthday last month my mum bought him two tickets for a match at Wembley Stadium. Mum doesn't like football, so I can go with him. Yay!

Have a great week everyone!

REVISION The simple past: ▶ Language file 4, p. 173 f. ▶ More practice 4, p. 41

b) Think about your activities yesterday or last week. Then tell a partner.

Last weekend I went swimming with my best friend. ▶ More help, p. 42 ▶ More practice 5 + 6, p. 42

6 b) individuelle Lösungen

My task

7 My blog

7 individuelle Lösungen ▶ Digital help

a) Make notes for a new blog post about your activities in the last weeks. Use your ideas from 6 b).

b) Write your post. Lily's blog post can help you.
 • beginning: First introduce yourself like Lily.
 • middle: Use a new paragraph for each day or activity.
 • end: Finish with a message to your readers.

c) Check your post: °Make sure you °included all the points in b). Then check the language. ▶ Language file, p. 169 f. ▶ Dictionary, p. 245–271

d) Check a partner's blog post. Give feedback. ▶ Skills file 13, p. 168

e) °Rewrite your post after your partner's feedback.

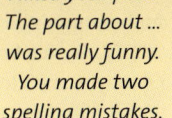

I liked your post. The part about … was really funny. You made two spelling mistakes.

▶ Workbook, p. 26

Digital quiz | I can describe life in cities and in my area.

twenty-five 25

Ex 6 Einstieg:
• (SB zu) S brainstormen *weekend activities* (▶ Five-finger brainstorming).
• L notiert Ideen als TA.

Erarbeitung:
a) (SB auf) S lesen Text in EA.
• **Ausw.:** im ▶ Partner check, dann im Plenum
• *Revision* s. ▶ LF 4, S. 173 f. u. ggf. ▶ Grammatikwiederholung (s. ▶ More practice 4, S. 41)

b) L leitet ▶ Think-Pair-Share an.
• S machen sich ggf. Notizen u. nutzen ▶ More help, S. 42.
• **Ausw.:** im Plenum

My task Ex 7 Einstieg:
• (SB zu) L notiert *My blog* (TA).
• S lesen ggf. *Lily's blog* (Ex 6a).

Erarbeitung:
a) (SB auf) S sammeln Ideen gemäß AA (▶ Note-making).
• **Ausw.:** Ideenliste als TA

b) gemeinsames Klären der AA
• S geben Beispiele für *beginning, middle* und *end*. L erstellt daraus ein ▶ Scaffolding als TA (im Plenum).
• S schreiben den Text in EA u. ggf. Digital help (App).

c) gemäß AA (▶ LF, S. 169 f.)
• S markieren ihre Abschnitte für *beginning, middle* u. *end* farbig.

d) gemäß AA (▶ SF 13, S. 168, ▶ Partner check, ▶ Feedback)

e) gemäß AA
• **Ausw.:** Präsentation im ▶ English corner, einzelne S stellen ihre Ergebnisse vor.
• anschl. Ablage im ▶ Dossier

25

1

Story Inhalt

Lernschwerpunkt: eine Geschichte über die Suche nach der verschwundenen Lily lesen
Kompetenzen: Reading Sehenswürdigkeiten (Fotos) auf einer Karte finden • Lesen der Geschichte • der Geschichte Informationen entnehmen • Auflisten der Handlungsorte in ihrer Reihenfolge im Text
Redemittel: *places in London*

Ex 1 Einstieg:
- (SB zu) L leitet ein:
  L: *What will happen if you don't come home after school?*
- S tauschen sich im ▶ Partner talk aus.
- 🗒 In schwachen Lerngruppen gibt L den Satzanfang vor (TA): *If I don't come home after school, my parents/friends/teachers/ ... will ...*
- Austausch im Plenum mit ▶ Meldekette. L sammelt wichtige Punkte und Vokabeln im TA.
- **Alternative:** (SB zu) L zeigt Titel der Story (UMA/TA) u. S äußern spontan Vermutungen, was passiert ist.

Erarbeitung:
- (SB auf) gemäß AA in EA
- **Ausw.:** L zeigt die Karte (UMA), S zeigen die Orte auf der Karte. L: *What do you think happened at these places?*
- S äußern Vermutungen, L sammelt diese ebenfalls im TA.

Ex 2 Einstieg:
- (SB auf) S liest AA vor.

Erarbeitung:
- **1. Lesen/Hören:** S lesen/hören die Story (▶ Mitleseverfahren) und sollen dabei noch keine Vokabeln nachschlagen oder erfragen.
- **Ausw.:** Sammeln und Vergleichen der Ortsliste im Plenum (TA).
- **Sich.:** S übertragen die korrigierte Liste auf einen Zettel oder ins Heft.
- Forts. s. S. 27

| 1 | Topic 1 | Topic 2 | Topic 3 | **Story** | Viewing | Study skills | Unit task |

Where is Lily?

💬 **1 BEFORE YOU READ Places in London**   **1** The places are marked with a star.

Look at the photos on pages 26–27. Find them on the map.

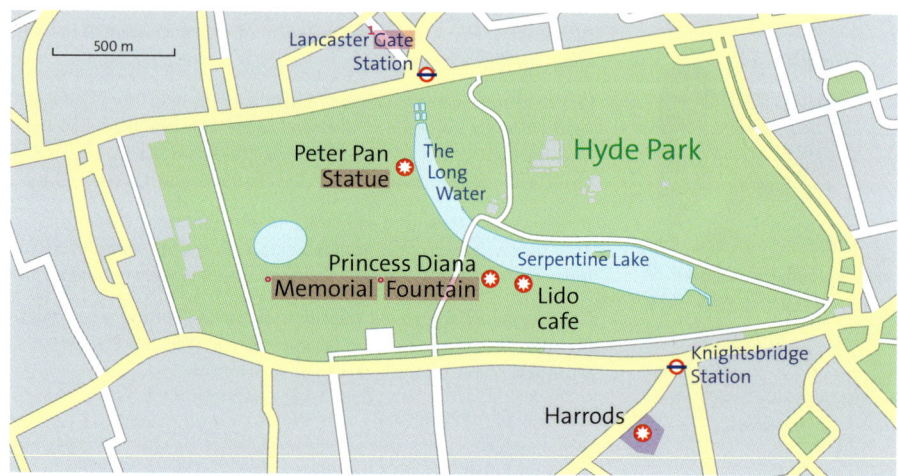

📖 **2 READING Let's find Lily**   **2** Lösung S. 284
▶ Skills file 9, p. 164

Read the story. Make a list of all the places that Pearl and Ali go to.

🔊 1.7

5.15 p.m. At Ali's flat
Pearl looked at Ali.
'That was Lily's dad on the phone. She didn't come home after school and she has °switched
5 off her phone – it goes to °voicemail. He asked if she was with us.'
'Hmm,' said Ali. 'She sent me some photos from Harrods right after school ... Look!'
'Harrods? The department store? Why was
10 she there? I mean, it sells everything, but it's super expensive!'
'She wanted to buy some special chocolates for her mum's birthday,' Ali explained.
'Ah, OK. So maybe her phone is dead now?
15 Or maybe she's lost. We should look for her.'
'What about our homework?' asked Ali.
'Lily is more important! Maybe she's in trouble.'

1 [ˈlæŋkəstə]

Harrods

26 twenty-six

1

Story Vorbereitung

Material: Ex 1 UMA • Ex 2 UMA/CD/App, ggf. Zettel (Klassensatz)
Zeitbedarf: ca. 2 Std. (inkl. S. 28)
Begleitmedien: INKL (S. 26–27)

5.30 p.m.
Pearl and Ali took the tube to Knightsbridge and walked to Harrods. 'If we ask the
20 doorkeeper, maybe he'll help us,' said Pearl. 'Excuse me, did you see this girl earlier?' She showed the doorkeeper a photo of Lily on her phone.
The doorkeeper shook his head. 'Sorry, we
25 have so many customers … Oh, wait a minute. Yes, I did. She had some cool red sunglasses. When she came out, she asked me for directions to Hyde Park.'

5.40 p.m.
30 Pearl and Ali walked towards Hyde Park. 'Why did Lily go to Hyde Park?' asked Pearl. 'I don't know,' answered Ali. 'Maybe she wanted to swim in the lake? I know Lily misses the sea and beach in Brighton.'
35 They asked at the Lido about Lily. 'No, sorry,' said the woman behind the desk. 'I haven't seen her. But you have to be sixteen to swim here. Maybe try the cafe.'

5.55 p.m.
40 There was no Lily at the cafe. But suddenly Pearl saw something. 'Those red sunglasses over there – they're Lily's! So she was here. But where is she now? I hope she's OK.'

Lido Cafe

'What else is near here?' asked Ali.
45 'Well, the Natural History Museum and the Science Museum are opposite Hyde Park,' Pearl said. 'But she won't go there because she doesn't like museums.' ▶ Box: Voc., p. 213
'OK. Let's walk across the grass,' suggested
50 Ali. 'Maybe we'll see her.'

6 p.m.
Suddenly Pearl remembered something. 'Look, here's Princess Diana's Memorial Fountain. It's a place to remember her life.
55 Lily's mum loved Princess Diana – °you know, King Charles's first wife. Maybe Lily wanted to take photos. Let's ask people.'
But nobody remembered Lily.

Princess Diana Memorial Fountain

'I'll ask that woman there. If she doesn't
60 know, we'll go home,' Pearl sighed. 'Yes, I remember her,' said the woman. 'She asked me the way to the +nearest tube station, so I gave her directions to Lancaster Gate. You just follow The Long Water that
65 way and go past the Peter Pan Statue.'

6.10 p.m.
Pearl and Ali said thank you and started to run. 'If we hurry, we'll see her!' The kids ran fast, but when they got to the
70 Peter Pan Statue, Pearl had a °pain in her side. 'Ow, I can't run any more,' she said. 'If you wait for me, we'll miss Lily. You run and I'll come after you.'

Peter Pan Statue

twenty-seven 27

Ex 2 (Forts. von S. 26)
- S vergleichen gemeinsam im Plenum den TA mit ihren Vermutungen zum Geschehen aus Ex 1: S/L streicht Falsches durch u. korrigiert/ergänzt ggf.
- 🔲 Schwächere S bearbeiten hier schon Ex 5, S. 28, gemäß AA (s. dort).
- **Ausw.:** im Plenum
- **2. Lesen:** S lesen die Story erneut, schlagen unbekannte Begriffe nach und notieren sie im *Vocab file*.
- S sammeln die neuen Vokabeln an der ▶ Vokabeltafel, ggf. ▶ Lautschulung.
- **Ausw.:** ▶ Five-minute teacher: S übernimmt Rolle von L an der Tafel und sammelt die Informationen über die verschiedenen Orte im Text (s. Liste). Ggf. zwei S einsetzen: S1 moderiert, S2 sammelt Infos an der Tafel.
- 🔲 für lernstärkere S: L: *Why do you think Lily went to these places?*
- S äußern Vermutungen (ggf. im ▶ Partner talk vorentlasten).
- 🔲 **Zusatz:** Lernstärkere S bzw. ▶ Early finishers können ein *Multiple Choice*-Quiz zu den Orten/Ereignissen der Story mit jeweils vier Antworten vorbereiten. L gibt Bsp. vor: *Harrods is …*
  a) *an expensive shop.*
  b) *a famous museum.*
  c) *an expensive cafe.*
  d) *a sports club.*
- **Ausw.:** Vorstellung der Quizze: S raten im ▶ Four corners-System.

27

1

Story **Inhalt**

Lernschwerpunkt: das Ende der Geschichte verstehen
Kompetenzen: Reading/Writing/Speaking den Spuren der Protagonisten einer Geschichte folgen • Listening dem Hörtext das Ende der Geschichte entnehmen • Reading unbekannte Worte erschließen
Redemittel: First they went to ... Then they went ... Finally ...

Vorbereitung

Material: Ex 3 UMA, ▶ KV Extra: Bus stop • Ex 4 UMA/CD/App
Zeitbedarf: ca. 2 Std. (inkl. S. 26–27)
Minimalversion: Ex 3b), Ex 5b) auslassen
Begleitmedien: App (Digital quiz), INKL (S. 28), DIFF (1.5)

Ex 3 Erarbeitung:
a) (SB auf) gemäß AA
- **Ausw.:** ▶ Five-minute teacher: S notiert an der Tafel die von Mit-S im Plenum beschriebene Route (*map* S. 26 über UMA).

b) gemäß AA
- **Ausw.:** ▶ Partner check am ▶ Bus stop. (▶ KV Extra)

Ex 4 Einstieg:
- (SB zu) ▶ Three truths, two lies zur Story

Erarbeitung:
a) (SB auf) PA gemäß AA
- **Ausw.:** L/S sammelt Ideen an der Tafel.

b) 1. Hören gemäß AA
- **Ausw.:** S beantworten Frage.
- ▶ Five-minute teacher: S sichtet u. korrigiert TA aus a) im Plenum, ergänzt Aspekte.

c) 2. Hören gemäß AA
- **Ausw.:** S raten Begriffe, lesen ▶ SF 2, S. 156.
- L sammelt richtige Antworten an ▶ Vokabeltafel.

d) **Ausw.:** Gemäß AA ergänzen S die Notizen im TA (s. a) u. b)).

Ex 5 Einstieg:
- (SB zu): L/S wdh. bekannte ▶ Worterschließungstechniken.

Erarbeitung:
a) (SB auf) S lesen ▶ Tippbox, S. 28 u. arbeiten gemäß AA (▶ SF 3, S. 157).
- **Ausw.:** wie Ex 2c)
- ggf. ▶ Semantisierung des Lernwortschatzes im Plenum

b) S diskutieren im ▶ Partner talk.
- **Ausw.:** gemeinsam im Plenum

| 1 | Topic 1 | Topic 2 | Topic 3 | **Story** | Viewing | Study skills | Unit task |

3 The route

3 a) Lösung S. 285

a) Look at the places in your list from 2. Read the story again and follow Pearl and Ali's route on the map on p. 26 with your °finger. Take turns to describe where they went.

> First/Then/Finally they went to ...

> Yes, they did. And after that .../ No, that's wrong. They went to ...

3 b) Lösung S. 285

b) Add another column to your list of places. Take notes about the clues or ideas that lead Pearl and Ali to the next place. Then compare with a partner.

The first clue was the photos from ...   Then ... helped them.

place	clue
at Ali's flat	Lily sent photos ...
Knightsbridge	...

4 LISTENING The ending

4 a) individuelle Lösungen

a) BEFORE YOU LISTEN What do you think happened next?
I think Ali found/didn't find ...   Maybe Lily went home/...

b) Listen to the end of the story. Did Ali find Lily?   **4 b)** Yes, he did.
1.8

c) Listen again. °Guess what these important words mean: **4 c)** Lösung S. 285
information board ★ path ★ ⁺key ring ★ park bench
▶ Skills file 2, p. 156

Ali

d) Together as a class make notes on the board about the main points of the ending.
4 d) Lösungsbsp. S. 285

5 Words in the story

a) Choose the correct meaning for the words in green.

1 When you switch off something (line 4), you
A make it start   B make it stop   C break it.

2 A department store (line 8) sells
A only food   B only clothes and shoes
C lots of different things.

3 A memorial (line 53) is a place to remember
A a dead person   B a famous living person   C a book character.

4 A fountain (line 54) is
A a big river   B a place with moving water   C a place where you can swim.

5 When you have a pain (line 70), it
A makes you laugh   B hurts   C feels strange.

Find the words in green in the story. Look at the words and sentences around that word and at the pictures. Similar words in German and other languages can also help you. You can check in the Dictionary (pages 245–271).

5 a) 1 B • 2 C • 3 A • 4 B • 5 B

▶ Skills file 3, p. 157

b) Have you ever been lost? Where were you? What did you do?
5 b) individuelle Lösungen

28   twenty-eight   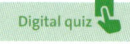 Digital quiz   I can follow and discuss the events in a story.

1

Viewing Inhalt

Lernschwerpunkt: Filmszenen zu einem sozialen Projekt verstehen
Kompetenzen: Viewing / Intercultural competence einem Video Informationen zum *volunteering* in London entnehmen • Speaking / Life skills über Hilfe für andere sprechen
Redemittel: *helping other people • ideas to help*

Vorbereitung

Material: Ex 2 UMA/DVD/App
Zeitbedarf: ca. 1 Std.
Minimalversion: Ex 3 auslassen
Begleitmedien: WB (S. 27), INKL (S. 29)

Topic 1 | Topic 2 | Topic 3 | Story | **Viewing** | Study skills | Unit task | **1**

On the streets of London

1 How can we make a difference?
   | **1 individuelle Lösungen**

BEFORE YOU WATCH Look at the title of this page. What do you think the video is about? What do you °expect to see in the video?

2 VIEWING Josh and Jade
   | **2 a)** The video is about Josh Coombes, a hairdresser. He and Jade help homeless people.

a) Watch the video °without the sound. Look at the pictures and the captions on the screen. What's the video about? How do Josh and Jade make a difference?

b) Copy the notes about Josh and Jade. Watch the video with the sound and complete them.

name: Josh
job: …
how he helps: …

name: Jade
job: …
how she helps: …

2 b) Lösungsbsp. S. 286

c) Watch the video again and complete the sentences.

1. Josh started his project 'Do something for nothing' in 20…
2. When they see his work, most of Josh's customers are …
3. Josh +uploads … and … photos of his customers.
4. Volunteering helps Josh and Jade … people and make …
5. A big part of their work in the community is … to people.
6. Josh says: You can say … and … and recognize that a homeless person is a person.
7. Helping people has made Josh …

2 c) 1 2015 • 2 happy • 3 before … after • 4 meet … friends • 5 talk • 6 hello … smile • 7 happy

3 LIFE SKILLS Make a difference!
   | **3 individuelle Lösungen**

a) THINK Have you ever helped a friend, a grandparent or a neighbour? How? Or do you know somebody who helps others?
   ▶ More help, p. 43

b) PAIR Tell a partner. Then together think of one more idea to help: for example, in a sports club, at a hospital or at an old people's home or at your °church, mosque or °synagogue.

c) SHARE Tell the class.

▶ Workbook, p. 27

twenty-nine **29**

Ex 1 Einstieg:
- (SB zu) ▶ Five-finger brainstorming im ▶ Milling around zum Thema *Problems in London (or other big cities)*

Erarbeitung:
- (SB auf) L semantisiert:
  L: *'Making a difference' here means helping someone.*
- gemäß AA in EA od. PA
- **Ausw.:** Im Plenum, L sammelt Vorschläge im TA.

Ex 2 Erarbeitung:
a) (SB auf) S liest AA vor.
   L: *Let's watch the video.*
- 1. Viewing gemäß AA ohne Ton
- **Ausw.:** S beantworten Fragen im Plenum und kommentieren ihre Aussagen im TA von Ex 1.
- S ergänzen Vermutungen zu dem, was sie hören werden.

b) gemäß AA, 2. Viewing
- **Ausw.:** ▶ Five-minute teacher: S notiert die Lösungen (TA).

c) 3. Viewing gemäß AA
- **Ausw.:** ▶ Meldekette

Ex 3 Einstieg:
- (SB zu) kurzes ▶ Blitzlicht mit Reaktionen der S:
  L: *What do you think about Josh and Jade's idea?*

Erarbeitung:
a) (SB auf) ▶ Think-Pair-Share gemäß AA, S notieren Ideen in EA (▶ More help, S. 43).

b) Gemäß AA im ▶ Partner talk, S-Paare notieren ihre Ideen.

c) **Ausw.:** gemäß AA im Plenum

- **Zusatz:** ein Projekt auswählen u. mit der Klasse durchführen

29

1

Study skills Inhalt

Lernschwerpunkt: online recherchieren
Kompetenzen: Medienkompetenz online recherchieren • Reading englischen Webseiten Informationen zu einer Sehenswürdigkeit entnehmen • Writing Notizen machen
Redemittel: *keywords and fun facts about London sights*

Vorbereitung

Material: Ex 1 digitale Endgeräte mit Internetzugang • Ex 2 digitale Endgeräte mit Internetzugang, Textverarbeitungsprogramm, Zettel (Klassensatz), ggf. Drucker
Zeitbedarf: ca. 2 Std.
Begleitmedien: App (Digital quiz), INKL (S. 30), DIFF (1.6)

Ex 1 Einstieg:
- (SB zu) ▶ Five-finger brainstorming zu *London sights*.
- 📧 L sichert die *sights* als Liste (TA).

Erarbeitung:
a) (SB auf) ▶ Klären der AA, gemäß AA suchen S online nach interessanten *sights*.
- L gibt Zeitrahmen vor.
- **Ausw.:** im Plenum als TA

b) gemäß AA
- **Ausw.:** im Plenum, als Liste

Ex 2 Einstieg:
- (SB auf) Klären der AA u. Lesen der ▶ Tippboxen, S. 30 u. ▶ SF 4, S. 158 f.
- Ggf. thematisiert L schon hier Quellenangaben u. creative commons (s. c)).
- **Hinweis:** L/S können geeignete Kindersuchmaschinen nutzen.

Erarbeitung:
a) S recherchieren in GA gemäß AA, s. a. ▶ SF 12, S. 167.
- 📧 In schwächeren Gruppen gibt L ggf. ein Raster für die Erstellung der *notes* vor, s. Vorlage ▶ SF 12, S. 167.

b) S sammeln ihre Notizen gemäß AA in einem (digitalen) Dokument od. auf Zetteln (s. a. ▶ SF 12, S. 167).

c) S suchen nach Fotos gemäß AA u. kopieren diese ins digitale Dokument od. drucken sie aus.
- S notieren die Quellenangaben gemäß AA.
- **Sich.:** S-Gruppen sichern ihre Ergebnisse für die *Unit task*.

30

---

1 | Topic 1 | Topic 2 | Topic 3 | Story | Viewing | **Study skills** | Unit task

Do online research

💬 👥 **1 Find a London sight**   **1** individuelle Lösungen

a) For the unit °task your class is going to make an audio guide for a bike tour of London. Each group is going to present one sight as part of the audio guide.
In small groups use keywords to find interesting sights in London online.

> We can search for **London** and ⁺**teens**.

> Or what about **London**, **teens** and **interesting sights**?

b) Your group chooses a sight. Check your sights with the class: They should be different.

---

2 Use good websites and make notes   **2** individuelle Lösungen

a) Use keywords and search for information about your sight:
- what it is and where it is
- what to see and what to do
- history, stories and fun facts
- when it's open and how much it costs

💡 ▶ Box: Voc., p. 215
- Use recent articles and information.
- Use official UK government sites (end in gov.uk) or company UK websites (end in co.uk or .com). Don't use chat sites.
- Check on at least two websites.

b) Make short notes about your sight. Use key words and °symbols like this:

Madame Tussauds:[1]
- museum with wax figures → Marylebone[2] Road
- fun facts ☺: wax figures take 6 months, get regular hair washes
- open 10 a.m. – 2 p.m., book ticket online (£30 child)

💡 Don't copy your text from the internet. Use your own words. Copy the name of the website and article and the date when you used it.

You can also use a °digital °document.

c) Find a photo of your sight. Remember: Use °creative commons photos and write down the website, °agency or photographer.

▶ Skills file 4, p. 158 f.   ▶ Skills file 12, p. 167

1 [təˈsɔːdz]   2 [ˈmærələbən]

30   thirty

Digital quiz 👆   I can do online research.

1

Unit task **Inhalt**

Lernschwerpunkt: einen Audioguide über Londons Sehenswürdigkeiten erstellen
Kompetenzen: Writing/Medienkompetenz einen Audioguide schreiben u. vertonen • Listening andere Audioguides hören und verstehen • Speaking Feedback geben
Redemittel: *sights and activities* • *feedback phrases*

Vorbereitung

Material: Step 1 ggf. von L recherchierter Londoner Audioguide, Zugang zu einer digitalen Karte von *Central London*, UMA, ▶ KV 1.3B: MY TASK London map (ggf. Klassensatz) • **Step 3** Aufnahmegeräte
Zeitbedarf: ca. 4 Std.
Begleitmedien: App (Digital help, Digital quiz), INKL (S. 31)

Topic 1 Topic 2 Topic 3 Story Viewing Study skills **Unit task** **1**

Make an audio guide for a London bike tour

Step 1: Collect your sights   **Unit task** individuelle Lösungen

A Collect your sights and photos from p. 30 in a digital map.
OR
B Highlight your sights from p. 30 on a paper map. °Stick your photos on the map.

Step 2: Write your audio guide   ▶ Digital help

a) Write the audio guide for your group's sight. It should be one to two minutes long. An audio guide on Madame Tussauds could start like this:

You're now on Marylebone Road and you're standing in front of Madame Tussauds. It's a fun museum with wax figures of famous people like singers, actors, superhero characters and sportspeople. Did you know that it takes six months to make a wax statue? Another fun fact is that the wax statues get regular hair washes and new make-up! ...

▶ More help, p. 43

b) Write one quiz question about your sight.
How long does it take to make a wax figure?

c) Check your work with this checklist.

Check that ...
- the information is correct.
- the information is interesting.
- the language is correct.

Step 3: Practise your audio guide

a) °Divide the audio guide into parts. Practise reading your parts together. Give other students feedback.

Remember to speak loudly and clearly.

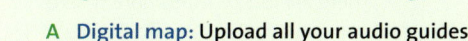

b) Record your group's audio guide.

Step 4: Listen to the class audio guide

A Digital map: Upload all your audio guides to the digital map. Listen to all the guides and answer the quiz questions.
B Paper map: Play your recording. The other students listen, follow the route and answer your question.

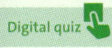 I can **make and understand an audio guide.**

thirty-one **31**

Unit task Einstieg:
- (SB zu) L spielt einen Ausschnitt aus einem Londoner Audioguide vor.
- S sammeln Kriterien für einen guten Audioguide (TA).

Step 1 Erarbeitung:
- (SB auf) S erhalten eine Karte von *Central London* (gedruckt, z. B. ▶ KV 1.3B od. digital/UMA).
- Gemäß AA markieren S ihre Sehenswürdigkeiten auf der Karte.

Step 2 Erarbeitung:
a) (SB auf) S schreiben ihren Text in GA gemäß AA.
- *Digital help* (App), ▶ More help, S. 43

b) gemäß AA

c) S prüfen ihren Text mit einem andersfarbigen Stift, damit die Korrekturen erkennbar sind.
- **Ausw.:** L prüft die überarbeiteten Texte u. gibt ggf. weiteres Feedback.

Step 3 Erarbeitung:
a) (SB auf) S-Gruppen teilen ihre Texte untereinander auf (ggf. farblich markieren).
- S üben das Lesen der Texte.
- ▶ Let's talk: Feedback, S. 200

b) S nutzen zur Aufnahme einen separaten Raum ohne Nebengeräusche (oder als HA).

Step 4 Erarbeitung:
- **Ausw.:** gemäß AA
- ▶ Four corners-Methode: Welches *sight* wollen S besuchen und warum.

31

1 Checkpoint Inhalt

Lernschwerpunkt: Kompetenzen und sprachliche Mittel üben, Lernfortschritte erkennen
Kompetenzen: Listening einem Audioguide Informationen entnehmen • Mediation bei einer Stadttour ins Deutsche und ins Englische sprachmitteln • Speaking einen Dialog zu geeigneten öffentlichen Verkehrsmitteln führen
Redemittel: *city tours • travel and transport*

Allgemeine Anmerkung:
Die Aufgaben auf den *Checkpoint*-Seiten dienen den S zur Überprüfung, ob sie die Lernziele *(I can …)* erreicht haben (s. Vorwort S. XIII f.). S schätzen ihr Können vor der Bearbeitung und nach der Besprechung der Lösungen ein. Bei Nutzung des *Digital checkpoint* (App) arbeiten die S selbstständig. Die Lösungen werden im Programm überprüft.
Check (App) enthält die Lösungen der SB-Checkpoints.

Ex 1 Einstieg:
- (SB auf) S lesen Lernziel *(I can …)*.
- Selbsteinschätzung z. B. mithilfe von ▶ Thumbs up

Erarbeitung:
a) Klären der AA
- 1. Hören gemäß AA in EA
- **Ausw.:** im Plenum

b) 2. Hören gemäß AA
- S notieren Antworten im Heft.
- **Ausw.:** ▶ Meldekette
- **Alternative** für a) + b):
  ▶ Bus Stop (▶ KV Extra):
  ▶ Partner check mithilfe von
  ▶ KV 1.4A

Ex 2 Einstieg:
- s. Ex 1 (Selbsteinschätzung)

Erarbeitung:
- (SB auf) Gemäß AA: S notieren vollständige Sätze (1–4) in ihr Heft.
- **Ausw.:** ▶ Meldekette
- **Alternative:** ▶ Bus Stop (▶ KV Extra): ▶ Partner check mithilfe von ▶ KV 1.4A
- erneute Selbsteinschätzung

32

---

1 Checkpoint Digital checkpoint

 1 LISTENING London rock tour (1)   I can understand and share information about London.

a) You're on a rock walking tour for music fans with your dad. Listen to the tour guide. Put the pictures (A–E) in the correct order.

> **1 a)** 1 C • 2 B • 3 D • 4 E • 5 A

 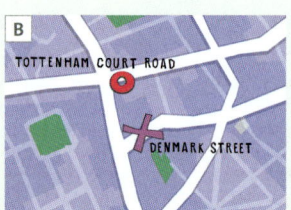 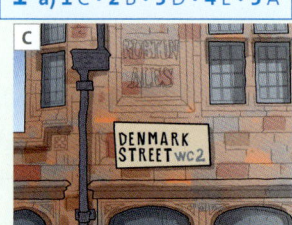

b) Listen again. True or false? Correct the false sentences.
1 On the tour, they will see five London sites.
2 Tottenham Court Road Station is half an hour away from Denmark Street.
3 300 years ago, Denmark Street wasn't an important place for music.
4 The magazine company is still on Denmark Street.
5 Today, people like to go shopping on Denmark Street.

> **1 b)** 1 false (*three*) • 2 false (*a few minutes*) • 3 true • 4 false (*until 1964*) • 5 true

2 MEDIATION London rock tour (2)

On the next part of the tour, your dad needs your help because he doesn't speak English very well. Complete the sentences.

> **2** Lösungsbsp. S. 286

Guide	So, this is Berwick Street. Lots of people will know this street because a photo of it was on the °cover of a famous album by the band Oasis.
Dad	Was hat sie gesagt?
You	Sie hat gesagt, dass … (1).
Dad	Ach so, danke! Da drüben ist ein Markt. Kannst du fragen, ob wir dort CDs oder T-Shirts kaufen können?
You	Excuse me. My dad has a question about the market over there: … (2).
Guide	The market only sells food and some other small things. But don't worry, there are lots of shops here where you can buy CDs or band T-shirts.
You	Sie hat gesagt, dass … (3).
Dad	OK. Und kannst du fragen, ob wir Zeit haben, hier noch einen Kaffee zu trinken?
You	My dad has another question: … (4).

Check

32 thirty-two

1

Checkpoint Vorbereitung

Material: alle Aufgaben ▶ KV Extra: Bus stop, ▶ KV 1.4A: Checkpoint answers, App (Check) • Ex 1 UMA/CD/App • Ex 3 vorbereitete *Cue cards* (Klassensatz)
Zeitbedarf: ca. 1 Std.
Minimalversion: Auswahl der Aufgaben erfolgt aufgrund der zu überprüfenden Lernziele
Begleitmedien: App (Digital checkpoint), INKL (S. 32–33)

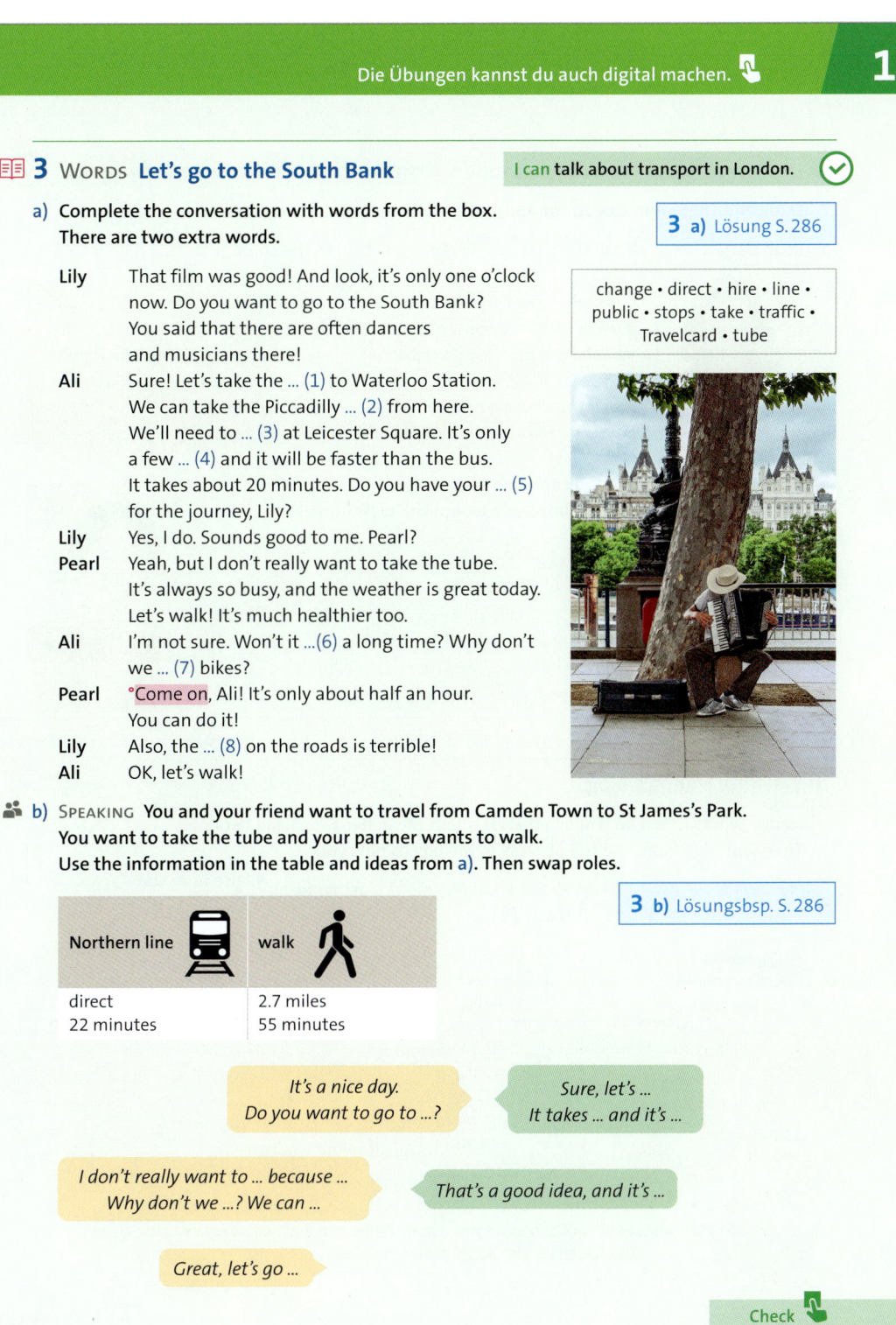

Ex 3 Einstieg:
- s. Ex 1 (Selbsteinschätzung)

Erarbeitung:
a) (SB auf) Gemäß AA in EA: S notieren Lösungen im Heft.
- **Ausw.:** ▶ Partner check, dann im Plenum
- **Alternative:** ▶ Bus Stop (▶ KV Extra): ▶ Partner check mithilfe von ▶ KV 1.4A
- ✉ **Zusatz:** S lesen den Dialog in verteilten Rollen (als Vorbereitung auf b) in schwächeren Gruppen).

b) Klären der AA im Plenum
- In PA: mündlich gemäß AA (mit ▶ English-only-Karte)
- **Ausw.:** Im Plenum, einzelne S-Paare präsentieren ihre Dialoge.
- erneute Selbsteinschätzung
- **Zusatz:** Neue S-Paare bilden sich (▶ Gruppenbildung) und gestalten einen weiteren Dialog mit geänderten Vorgaben (L teilt vorbereitete ▶ Cue cards aus.).

1

Checkpoint Inhalt

Lernschwerpunkt: Kompetenzen und sprachliche Mittel üben, Lernfortschritte erkennen
Kompetenzen: *Writing* einen Blogeintrag schreiben • *Reading* Aussagen zu einer Geschichte ordnen • *Speaking* sich in PA zu einer peinlichen Situation austauschen • *Study skills* online recherchieren
Strukturen: *conditional sentences type 1*
Redemittel: *city words • opinion phrases*

Ex 4 Einstieg:
- s. **Ex. 1** (Selbsteinschätzung)
- ▶ Bei schwacher Selbsteinschätzung zeigt L erneut den Erklärfilm zum *conditional sentence type 1* von S. 175 (UMA/App).

Erarbeitung:

a) (SB auf) S liest den Einstiegssatz vor.
- gemäß AA in EA
- ▶ S schreiben vollständige Sätze ins Heft.
- **Ausw.:** ▶ Five-minute teacher

b) Klären der AA
- S schreiben vollständige Sätze in ihr Heft.
- **Ausw.:** ▶ Partner check, dann im Plenum
- **Alternative** für a) + b):
  ▶ Bus Stop (▶ KV Extra):
  S vergleichen ihr Lösungen mithilfe von ▶ KV 1.4B.
- erneute Selbsteinschätzung

Ex 5 Einstieg:
- s. Ex 1 (Selbsteinschätzung)

Erarbeitung:
- (SB auf) S lesen AA und die sprachlichen Mittel in den Kästen.
- S arbeiten gemäß AA in EA und achten dabei auf die Trennung der Teile (Absätze).
- **Ausw.:** ▶ Bus Stop (▶ KV Extra):
  ▶ Partner check mithilfe von
  ▶ KV 1.4B: S vergleichen ihre Ergebnisse und verbessern sich ggf. gegenseitig.
- erneute Selbsteinschätzung
- **Zusatz:** Präsentation der Texte im ▶ English corner
- S geben einander ▶ Feedback (▶ Gallery walk).

---

1 Checkpoint Digital checkpoint

4 LANGUAGE Ideas for a day in London
I can plan a tour (conditional sentences type 1). ✓

Darja and Theo want to visit London and are planning what to do there.

4 a) 1 f • 2 a • 3 e • 4 c • 5 d • 6 b

a) Read Darja's ideas. Match the sentence beginnings (1–6) to the endings (a–f).

1 If we go on the London Eye,
2 If we go to Camden Market,
3 We'll have a picnic in the park
4 Maybe we'll see the King
5 And if the King isn't there,
6 If we visit the London Dungeon,

a we'll find nice presents.
b maybe we'll see a ghost!
c if we go to Buckingham Palace!
d we'll still wave at the Palace.
e if it's sunny.
f we'll see lots of the city.

b) Read Theo's ideas. Copy and complete the sentences.
Use the correct form of the simple present or the will-future.

1 If you … (go) to the Dungeon, I … (stay) outside!
2 If we … (stop) at Hyde Park, we … (see) the Princess Diana Memorial.
3 If it … (not be) sunny, we … (find) a nice cafe.
4 If we … (not go) on the London Eye, we … (have) more money for presents.
5 We … (see) some street art if we … (visit) Leake Street Tunnel.
6 We … (not get) tired if we … (travel) by tube.

4 b) 1 go … 'll stay • 2 stop … 'll see • 3 isn't … 'll find • 4 don't go … 'll have • 5 'll see … visit • 6 won't get … travel

5 WRITING Hanna's blog
I can describe life in cities and in my area. ✓

Hanna wants to tell her English friends about life in her area. Read her notes.
Then write her blog. Use the phrases in the box to help you.

5 Lösungsbsp. S. 286

Hi, everybody! I want to tell you about my life in Dortmund. …

beginning:
- Dortmund
- big city
- west Germany
- famous football team

middle:
⊕ big park, great places to go shopping, nice zoo
⊖ lots of traffic, air pollution, expensive cost of living

end:
- ask a question
- say something nice

I want to tell you about … • There are some great things about my city, like … •
But there are also some problems, like …

Check

1

Checkpoint Vorbereitung

Material: alle Aufgaben ▶ KV Extra: Bus stop, ▶ KV 1.4B: Checkpoint answers, App (Check) • Ex 4 UMA/App (Erklärfilm) • Ex 7 UMA/App

Zeitbedarf: ca. 2 Std.

Minimalversion: Auswahl der Aufgaben erfolgt aufgrund der zu überprüfenden Lernziele

Begleitmedien: App (Digital checkpoint), INKL (S. 33)

Die Übungen kannst du auch digital machen.   **1**

6 READING At Leake Street Tunnel

I can follow and discuss the events in a story. ✓

'Hey, Ali, sorry I'm late,' said Lily.
'No problem! That's a big bag – did you go shopping?'
Lily laughed. 'No, these are my art things.
5 Look, I have some paper and lots of pencils.'
'Cool! But you know this is a graffiti wall?' asked Ali. 'People don't use pencils and paper here!'
'Oh yeah, I know. But maybe it will give me
10 some ideas for my own art.'
'True!' said Ali. 'Let's go in.'
'Wow, this place is amazing,' said Lily. She couldn't see any walls at all, just art!
'Lily, I need to go outside to call my mum.
15 I'll find you in five or ten minutes, OK?' asked Ali. 'Sure!' said Lily.

When Ali went back into the tunnel, he was surprised. On Lily's paper there was a beautiful picture of a sunset
20 on a beach.
'Lily, this is so good!' said Ali.
'Oh, you're back. Do you think so? I'm not sure. It's just an idea.' Lily was a bit embarrassed.
25 Suddenly they heard someone speak.
'I'm sure it's a good picture! Sorry, I'm Zach. I come here every weekend. So are you going to paint this on the tunnel?'
'°Erm, I don't know how to do that,'
30 said Lily.
'If you come back next week, I'll show you!' smiled Zach.

6 a) 3 • 5 • 2 • 1 • 4 • 6

a) Read the story. Put the events in the correct order.
1 Lily drew a great picture.
2 Ali left the tunnel for a phone call.
3 Lily and Ali met outside the tunnel.
4 Two people liked Lily's picture.
5 Lily showed Ali her art equipment.
6 Zach asked about Lily's plan for the picture.

Lily

b) Complete Lily's message to her friend Sunita.
Hey, Sunita! You won't believe what happened today! I went to …   **6 b)** Lösungsbsp. S. 286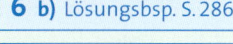

c) SPEAKING Why did Lily feel embarrassed? Discuss with a partner.   **6 c)** Lösungsbsp. S. 286

7 STUDY SKILLS London on a rainy day

I can do online research. ✓

You're in London, but the weather is bad. Search for a place or activity online.
Copy and complete the table with your place or activity.

keywords	websites	notes
London + … + …	1. … .com 2.	– place: … near … – tickets: £ … – open: … – fun facts: …

7 Lösungsbsp. S. 286

Check

thirty-five **35**

Ex 6 Einstieg:
• s. Ex. 1 (Selbsteinschätzung)

Erarbeitung:
a) (SB auf) S lesen den Text leise oder laut (▶ Buzz reading).
• Bearbeitung gemäß AA in EA, S notieren die Reihenfolge der Sätze im Heft.
• **Ausw.:** ▶ Bus Stop (▶ KV Extra): S vergleichen ihr Lösungen mithilfe von ▶ KV 1.4B.
• **Alternative:** ▶ Five-minute teacher

b) gemäß AA in EA
• S schreiben einen Text ins Heft.
• **Ausw.:** ▶ Bus Stop (▶ KV Extra): S vergleichen ihr Lösungen mithilfe von ▶ KV 1.4B.
• **Alternative:** ▶ Partner check, dann im Plenum

c) gemäß AA in PA
• **Ausw.:** S-Paare präsentieren ihre Ergebnisse im Plenum.
• erneute Selbsteinschätzung

Ex 7 Einstieg:
• s. Ex 1 (Selbsteinschätzung)

Erarbeitung:
• (SB auf) L klärt AA u. sammelt mit den S geeignete (Kinder-) Suchmaschinen (TA).
• gemäß AA: S recherchieren online u. ergänzen die Tabelle im Heft.
• **Ausw.:** S präsentieren ihre Tabellen im Plenum.
• **Alternative:** ▶ Partner check am ▶ Bus Stop (▶ KV Extra): S vergleichen ihr Lösungen mithilfe von ▶ KV 1.4B.
• erneute Selbsteinschätzung
• **Zusatz:** ▶ Meinungsbarometer zu den *activities* u. *places*, S begründen ihre Meinung.

35

1
OPTIONAL

Text file Inhalt

Lernschwerpunkt: Fakten über London kennenlernen
Kompetenzen: Reading Informationen aus einem Artikel erfassen
Redemittel: *multicultural London • languages and cultures*

Allgemeine Anmerkung:
Die Bearbeitung der *Text file*-Seiten ist optional. Die Seiten können zur Differenzierung und als Zusatzangebot genutzt werden, z. B. für ▶ Early finishers und lernstärkere S. Die Seiten dienen aber auch als Abwechslung für die gesamte Klasse. Die Aufgaben können wahlweise bearbeitet werden. S wählen selbst, an welchen Stellen sie sich produktiv einbringen können/wollen. Ggf. gibt L eine Minimalvorgabe für ein eingeführtes Portfolio (▶ Dossier).

Multicultural London Einstieg:
- (SB zu) L leitet ein:
  L: *Guess – how many different languages do all the people in this class speak?*
- Gemeinsame Sammlung, L sichert (TA, ggf. ▶ Vokabeltafel).

Erarbeitung:
- (SB auf) S lesen den Text in EA und schlagen unbekannte Worte ggf. selbst nach.
- S zählen die Anzahl an Sprachen in London auf der Karte.
- **Ausw.:** Vergleich mit der Anzahl der Sprachen in der eigenen (Wohn-)Gegend.
  L: *What could happen if people speak different languages?*
  (S antworten spontan.)
  L: *Zania has a great idea. What is it?*
- S lesen das Gedicht und beantworten die Frage.
- **Ausw.:** im ▶ Partner talk:
  L: *Do you like the poem? Why? / Why not?*

---

1 Text file
OPTIONAL

United[1]

A magazine for young people across the UK

Which languages do people speak in your area? Which languages do you speak at home?

Multicultural London by Pearl Cole

I love that people in my city come from all over the world! Did you know that kids in London schools speak over 300 languages? My best friends speak Arabic, Bengali (the language of Bangladesh) and Romanian.

Check out this map of London! →

Read my favourite poem about London! A London girl called Zaina wrote it when she was twelve. I like the poem because it talks about how we're all in the same °situation: It isn't important where we come from or what language we speak. We all have problems ('wear and tear'[2]) and we all have dreams – this is the language that we all speak!

Map of London with main second languages

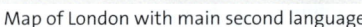
Datenquelle: Office for National Statistics in London: https://www.ons.gov.uk/dataset/TS024/editions/2021/versions/1#version-history

All in this together by Zaina (12)

Once I walked down the lane
and I heard somebody say:
I am Chinese, Japanese, German,
 Spanish, French.
But it doesn't matter[3] who you are
or what language you speak!

We are all in this together,
every wear and tear and dream.
It doesn't matter what your culture is
or if you're old or young.

Everybody can speak this language,
old or young or smart or not.
If we smile and laugh and love each other
it's clear what we're going to say.

We are all in this together,
doesn't matter who you are,
doesn't matter what you speak or say,
if you laugh or cry or love or play ...

Once I walked down the lane
and I heard somebody say:
We are all in this together,
every wear and tear and dream.

[1] **united** vereinigt, verbunden   [2] **wear and tear** Abnutzung, Verschleiß   [3] **it doesn't matter** es spielt keine Rolle

36 thirty-six

1 OPTIONAL

Text file Vorbereitung

Material: alle Texte zweisprachiges Wörterbuch (Klassensatz), UMA
Zeitbedarf: abhängig davon, welche Texte bearbeitet werden
Minimalversion: Alle Beiträge sind optionale Zusatzbeiträge.
Begleitmedien: INKL (S. 34–35)

1 OPTIONAL

Let me tell you more about …
London's multicultural communities

In 1948 my great-grandparents[1] came from Jamaica to the UK to work. Jamaica was still under British rule, and Britain needed workers. My great-grandfather was a train driver on the underground and my great-grandmother was a nurse. My dad says that their lives were difficult and racism was much worse back then. But they worked hard, so that their children could have better lives. I'm so proud of them! This is my family eating my grandmother's famous jerk chicken[2]!

My friend Fahra lives in London's East End near Brick Lane. Her grandparents came from Bangladesh to work as doctors. A lot of other Bangladeshi people came to work in clothes factories[3]. There's a big British Bangladeshi community near Brick Lane and there are lots of curry houses, markets and cool second-hand shops. You can also see amazing street art. Once a year there's a famous celebration with a big parade. I always enjoy going there with Fahra.

Don't miss Chinatown in London's West End. The first Chinese people in the UK were °sailors. Later a lot of Chinese people came to work in Chinese restaurants. I love Chinese food! Today's Chinatown began to grow in the 1970s, but Chinese Londoners live and work all over the city now – e. g. in offices or as managers. Sometimes I come here with my friend Bao. There are great shops and restaurants, lanterns[4] and lots of Chinese signs. I always take °awesome pictures there!

My neighbour Zuzia is from Poland. She came to London with her family because her dad got work as a builder and now he has his own business. A lot of Polish people came to live in the UK after Poland joined the EU in 2004! This is Zuzia's mum's Polish food shop. You can buy really good pierogi[5] here. Zuzia says that after Brexit, some Polish people didn't feel welcome any more and left the UK, but many people °decided to stay here.

[1] **great-grandparents** *Urgroßeltern* [2] **jerk chicken** *gewürztes, gegrilltes Huhn* [3] **factory** *die Fabrik*
[4] **lantern** *die Laterne* [5] **pierog** *die Pirogge (Teigtasche)*

thirty-seven **37**

London's Multicultural communities Einstieg:

- (SB zu) S aktivieren Vorwissen: L: *London is a multicultural city. Which communities can you find in London?*
- ▶Milling around, S antworten spontan (▶Five-finger brainstorming).

Erarbeitung:

- L zeigt die vier Fotos (UMA), Text bleibt abgedeckt. S vermuten in PA, zu welcher *community* das jeweilige Bild gehören könnte, und notieren ihre Vermutungen.
- (SB auf) S-Paare teilen sich die Texte auf und jede/-r Partner/-in liest jeweils zwei Texte.
- S notieren ggf. unbekannte Vokabeln u. schlagen diese nach.
- **Ausw.:** In PA: S-Paare klären, ob ihre Vermutungen richtig waren und geben mind. drei weitere Informationen zu der jeweiligen *community*.
- S befragen sich gegenseitig zu den Texten (PA oder GA).

- 🗹 **Zusatz:** In PA entwerfen S ein kurzes Quiz zu den vier Texten. Im Plenum stellen sich die S-Paare gegenseitig ihre Quiz-Fragen.

- ⊠ **Zusatz:** Stärkere S/S-Paare bzw. ▶Early Finishers schreiben einen eigenen Informationstext zu einer *community*, z. B. aus der eigenen Umgebung und präsentieren diesen in der Klasse.

37

1

Partner page Inhalt

Lernschwerpunkt: zusätzliche Übungen, Differenzierungs- und Hilfsangebote
Kompetenzen: Speaking in PA Dauer, Preise und Nutzung von Verkehrsmitteln erfragen • in PA Fragen beantworten
Redemittel: travel and transport • time and money words

Vorbereitung

Material: Ex 3 UMA
Zeitbedarf: abhängig davon, welche PA-Aufgaben durchgeführt werden

Allgemeine Anmerkung:
- *Partner page* enthält die Informationen für *Partner B* (▶ Info-gap activity). Die didaktischen Hinweise für die Aufgaben befinden sich im vorderen Teil der Unit bei *Partner A*.
- *Diff bank*: s. Vorwort S. XI f.

My task Ex 3 Einstieg:
- (SB zu) s. Einstieg Ex 3, S. 17

Erarbeitung:
a) (SB auf) ▶ Klären der AA
- *Partner B* bleibt auf S. 38, *Partner A* auf S. 17.

b) Gemäß AA, *Partner B* notiert *A's* Antworten ins Heft.
- **Ausw.:** als TA (UMA), s. S. 17

Ex 5 Einstieg:
- (SB zu) s. Einstieg Ex 5, S. 20

Erarbeitung:
a) + b) (SB auf) Gemäß AA in PA, *Partner A* arbeitet auf S. 20.
- *Partner A* u. *B* benötigen genügend Zeit für das Lesen der beiden Tour-Flyer.
- S machen sich beim Lesen Notizen (▶ Note-taking) und beantworten ggf. bereits dann die Fragen 1–6 (die Fragen sind identisch für beide Flyer).
- **Ausw.:** S-Paare präsentieren ihre Fragen und Antworten gemeinsam im Plenum.

---

1 Partner page

Partner page

▶ Page 17

3 MY TASK What's the best transport? **3** Lösungsbsp. S. 282

a) After Camden the three kids want to go shopping in Oxford Street.
Partner B: Ask partner A about buses, the tube and walking. Take notes.

How long does it take by bus / tube?
How much is the journey by … / if they walk?

b) **Partner B:** Look at the information. Answer partner A's questions.

Camden Market to Oxford Street (3 km)		
	time	price
bus	?	?
tube	?	?
taxi	6 min.	£10
bike	13–17 min.	£1.65 for 30 min.
walk	36 min.	?

▶ Page 20

5 SPEAKING More tours **5** Lösungsbsp. S. 283

a) Pearl told Lily about the tour and now she wants to do a special tour of London too.
Partner B: Read the flyer about a special London tour and answer partner A's questions.

Street art tour
London is an amazing place to see street art, from the world-famous Banksy to new artists. We have two tours, one on Brick Lane and one in Shoreditch. During the walking tour, we'll show you the best street art and if you're lucky, you'll see some graffiti artists at work! After the tour you can eat at one of the many Indian and Bangladeshi restaurants in the area. Tours are free, but you can tip your guide. Call or text the number below to book.

b) Now ask partner A these questions about another London tour.

1. What kind of tour is it?
2. How will I travel during the tour?
3. What will I see on the tour?
4. How much does the tour cost?
5. How can I book the tour?
6. Can you give me more information about the tour?

38 thirty-eight

1

Diff bank **Inhalt**	**Vorbereitung**
Lernschwerpunkt: zusätzliche Übungen, Differenzierungs- und Hilfsangebote	**Material:** MP 1 UMA/App (Erklärfilm), ▶ KV Extra: Bus stop
Kompetenzen: Speaking Partner/-in dazu befragen, welche öffentlichen Verkehrsmittel er/sie nutzt oder genutzt hat	**Zeitbedarf:** abhängig davon, welche Aufgaben bearbeitet werden
Strukturen: *(revision) the will-future:* Aussagesätze	**Minimalversion:** *More practice*-Aufgaben sind stets Zusatzaufgaben.
Redemittel: *travel and transport*	

Diff bank 1

Diff bank

▶ Page 16

 **More help** 1 LISTENING **A trip to Camden Market**

d) Talk about transport in your area.

1 d) individuelle Lösungen

1 Is there an underground in your area?

Yes
How often do you use it?
I often / sometimes / never use it. I use it every day / three times a week / …
What's it like?
It's cheap / easy to use / modern / old / …

No
Have you ever travelled on an underground? If yes, where?
I travelled on the underground in Berlin / …
How was it?
It was busy / easy to use / expensive / …

2 What public transport do you use in your local area and why?

I usually travel by bike / bus / the local train / tram / …
The stop is near my home. / I can be independent. / I can travel to school with my friends. / …

▶ Page 17

 More practice 1 **On the way to Camden Market**

REVISION **The will-future**
1 You use the will-future to talk about predictions or actions in the future:
How will we get to Camden? The train will be here soon. It won't be late.
Use the short form *'ll* after pronouns (*I, you, …*). Use *won't (= will not)* for the negative.
2 Use *I'll* or *We'll* when you decide suddenly: *Do you need a ticket? I'll get you one.*

▶ Language file 5, p. 174

Lily, Ali and Pearl are walking to the market. Complete their conversation with *will*, *'ll* or *won't* and the verb in brackets.

Ali There*'ll be* (1 be) lots of amazing stalls! You … (2 not want) to leave, Lily.
Pearl We … (3 show) you the canals near the market too. Maybe musicians … (4 play) there.
Lily Cool! I don't have a lot of money, so I … (5 not buy) much. I … (6 just / look) at everything and listen to the music.
Ali Me too! We … (7 go) to the food stalls, but it's hard not to buy anything! I … (8 take) you to my family's restaurant soon, Lily. We can eat there for free!

1 1 *'ll be* • 2 won't want • 3 'll show • 4 will play • 5 won't buy • 6 'll just look • 7 'll go • 8 'll take

thirty-nine **39**

MH 1 s. S. 16
- Diese Aufgabe bietet Unterstützung für lernschwächere S.

Erarbeitung:
d) (SB auf) PA gemäß AA mithilfe des ▶ Scaffolding
- **Ausw.:** s. S. 16

MP 1
- Diese Aufgabe bietet eine gute Möglichkeit zur Wiederholung des *will-future* in Vorbereitung auf die Vermittlung von *conditional sentences type 1*.

Erarbeitung:
- (SB auf) S lesen die Regelerklärung in der ▶ Grammatik-Box, S. 39.
- gemeinsame Verständnissicherung im Plenum
- Ggf. ergänzen/aktualisieren S den Eintrag zum *will-future* im Merkteil (▶ English folder).
- s. a. ▶ LF 5, S. 174 und Erklärfilm (UMA/App)
- S schreiben die vollständigen Sätze gemäß AA in ihr Heft.
- **Ausw.:** S suchen Partner/-in am ▶ Bus stop (▶ KV Extra) und vergleichen im ▶ Partner check.

1

Diff bank **Inhalt**

Lernschwerpunkt: zusätzliche Übungen, Differenzierungs- und Hilfsangebote
Kompetenzen: Writing Fragen zu einem zukünftigen Ereignis formulieren • Reading Beschreibungen von Sehenswürdigkeiten den richtigen Bildern zuordnen. • Viewing einem Film über London Informationen entnehmen und wiedergeben
Strukturen: *(revision) the will-future:* Fragen • *conditional sentence type 1:* Aussagesätze • *(revision) the simple past*
Redemittel: *planning a trip* • *sights of London* • *prepositions of places and directions* • *giving directions*

Challenge 1
- geeignet für lernstärkere S oder ▶ Early finishers

Erarbeitung:
- (SB auf) S schreiben die Fragen gemäß AA in ihr Heft.
- **Ausw.:** S suchen Partner/-in am ▶ Bus stop (▶ KV Extra) und vergleichen ihre Lösungen im ▶ Partner check.

MP 2 Einstieg:
- (SB zu) L zeigt Fotos von London mit bekannten Sehenswürdigkeiten (z. B. aus Unit 1, S. 14–15, UMA).
  L: *What sights of London do you know/remember?*

Erarbeitung:
a) (SB auf) Gemäß AA: S notieren die Antworten ins Heft.
- **Ausw.:** S vergleichen erst im ▶ Partner check, dann im Plenum.

b) selbstständige ▶ Semantisierung gemäß AA
- S übertragen die Wörter in ihr *Vocab File* (*London page*, s. Ex 2, S. 15, ▶ Vokabelarbeit)

- **Zusatz:** S lesen die Texte laut vor (▶ Lautschulung).

---

1 Diff bank

▶ **Page 17**

Challenge 1 Lily's questions

Write Lily's questions for Ali and Pearl.
Use *will* and the verbs in the box.

> be • buy • ~~do~~ • go • stay • travel

> **Ch 1** 1 *What will we do first?* • 2 Will there be a lot of people? • 3 Will you buy something, Pearl? • 4 How long will we stay at the market? • 5 Where will we go after the market? • 6 How will we travel to Oxford Street?

1 what / we / first? *What will we do first?* — We'll look at the clothes stalls.
2 there / a lot of people? — Yes, there will. There are always a lot of people!
3 you / something / Pearl? — No, I won't. I don't have much money.
4 how long / we / at the market? — One or two hours.
5 where / we / after the market? — Maybe we'll go shopping in Oxford Street.
6 how / we / to Oxford Street? — We can °decide that later.

▶ **Page 18**

More practice 2 London sights

> **2 a)** A London Dungeon • B Tower of London • C Buckingham Palace • D Tower Bridge

a) Match the sights to the photos (A–D). Then read the descriptions and check your answers.

> Buckingham Palace • London Dungeon • Tower Bridge • Tower of London

A This is a museum about the scary history of London. There are shows, rides and actors to frighten the visitors.

B This is a very old castle from 1708. It was a prison and some people think there are ghosts here. The royal family keeps their crowns and jewels safe here.

C This is the king's biggest home and it's where he meets the prime minister and other guests. The guards wear uniforms and special tall black hats.

D This is maybe the most beautiful bridge in London. You can walk, cycle or drive across it, and it can open when big ships need to go down the River Thames.

b) WORDS Work out the meanings of the words in blue and add them to your VOCAB FILE.

> **2 b) (to) frighten** Angst einjagen • **prison** Gefängnis • **crown** Krone • **jewels** Juwelen • **guard** Wache • **ship** Schiff

40 forty

Diff bank Vorbereitung

Material: Challenge 1 ▶ KV Extra: Bus stop • MP 2 UMA, Bilder von London (z. B. von S. 14–15) • Ex 7 UMA/DVD/App • MP 4 UMA, UMA/App (Erklärfilm)
Zeitbedarf: abhängig davon, welche Aufgaben bearbeitet werden
Minimalversion: *More practice*- und Challenge-Aufgaben sind stets Zusatzaufgaben.

▶ Page 19

3 1 are • 2 'll listen • 3 finds • 4 will have • 5 won't be

More practice 3 Pearl's family's visit

Complete the conditional sentences. Use the correct form of the simple present or the will-future.

1 If Pearl's cousins … (be) late, they'll miss the train.
2 If they see some street musicians, they … (listen) to the music.
3 If Aunt Vera … (find) a nice souvenir, she'll buy it.
4 If the weather is good, Pearl's family … (have) a picnic in the park.
5 If Uncle Roy loses his Travelcard, he … (not be) happy!

Challenge 2 My friend's visit to London

Complete the conditional sentences about a future visit to London. Use the correct form of the simple present or the will-future.

Ch 2 1 goes … 'll travel • 2 travels … 'll buy • 3 buys … won't have • 4 doesn't buy … 'll be • 6 'll walk … goes

1 If my friend … (go) to London, she … (travel) on the underground.
2 If she … (travel) on the underground, she … (buy) a ticket.
3 If she … (buy) a ticket, she … (not have) much money to buy a nice souvenir.
4 If she … (not buy) a nice souvenir, she … (be) sad.
5 So I think she … (walk) if she … (go) to London because it's free!

▶ Page 21

Parallel exercise 7 VIEWING A virtual tour of London

7 b) 1 go across • 2 go straight over • 3 third • 4 left • 5 turn right • 6 go straight on

b) Watch the video and choose the correct directions.

At Trafalgar Square (1) turn right at / go across the roundabout and (2) go down / go straight over the road. Go straight on down Whitehall and take the (3) second / third street on the (4) left / right. At the river (5) turn left / turn right and (6) go straight on / go across.

▶ Page 25

More practice 4 Lily's blog

4 1 went • 2 didn't buy • 3 loved • 4 hired • 5 cycled • 6 were • 7 was • 8 took • 9 heard • 10 went • 11 ate • 12 bought

Erklärfilm

REVISION The simple past
You use the simple past when you talk about the past.
• The simple past forms of regular verbs end in -ed: *I arrived in London yesterday.*
• Some verbs have irregular simple past forms: *I went to Camden Market. It was great!*
• Make questions with *did* and negatives with *didn't*: *Did you eat there? – No, I didn't.*

▶ Irregular verbs, p. 272 f. ▶ Language file 4, p. 173 f.

Make a list with the positive and negative simple past forms in Lily's blog: 1) I went 2) …

forty-one **41**

MP 3 Einstieg:
• (SB zu) L wdh. die Regel fürs *simple present* in 3. Ps. Sg.:
 L: *He, she, it …*
 S: *Das „s" muss mit.*
• ▶ LF 2, S. 170 (*simple present*)

Erarbeitung:
• (SB auf) gemäß AA in EA
• **Ausw.:** ▶ Partner check, dann im Plenum

Challenge 2 Erarbeitung:
• (SB auf) gemäß AA in EA
• **Ausw.:** ▶ Partner check, dann im Plenum

Parallel ex 7 s. S. 21
• Diese Aufgabe ist die leichtere Variante zu Ex 7b), S. 21 mit demselben Ergebnis.

MP 4
• S sollten diese Aufgabe direkt nach Ex 6a), S. 25 bearbeiten.

Erarbeitung:
• (SB auf) gemeinsames Lesen der Regel zum *simple past*
• s. a. ▶ LF 4, S. 173 f., Erklärfilm (UMA/App)
• L zeigt Text von Ex 6a), S. 25 (UMA); gemeinsames Finden der ersten Bsp. (Liste als TA).
• anschl. gemäß AA in EA
• **Ausw.:** ▶ Partner check, dann im Plenum (TA)
• **Zusatz:** *Find someone who …* (▶ Grammatikwiederholung) S erhalten eine KV mit ca. fünf Wochenendaktivitäten (z. B. *go to the cinema*) u. befragen sich gegenseitig: *Did you go to the cinema last weekend? Yes, I did. / No, I didn't.*

1

Diff bank Inhalt

Lernschwerpunkt: zusätzliche Übungen, Differenzierungs- und Hilfsangebote
Kompetenzen: Reading einen Blog über ein Wochenende verstehen • Writing einen Audioguide schreiben
Strukturen: *(revision) the simple past:* Aussagesätze und Fragen
Redemittel: *freetime activities • helping other people • ideas to help • sightseeing words*

MH 6 Erarbeitung: s. S. 25
- Diese Hilfe bietet sprachliche Mittel für lernschwächere S bei der Vorbereitung ihres mündlichen Austausches in PA, Ex 6b), S. 25.

MP 5 Einstieg:
- (SB zu) L zeigt das Foto vom Wembley Stadion (UMA):
  L: *Do you know this place? What can you do there?*
  S: *It's Wembley Stadium (in London). You can play football there.*

Erarbeitung:
- (SB auf) S schreiben die vollständigen Sätze ins Heft.
- **Ausw.:** ▶Partner check, dann im Plenum

MP 6 Einstieg:
- (SB zu) ggf. Wiederholung der Fragebildung im *simple past* (▶Grammatikwiederholung, s. Zusatz, MP 4, S. 41)

Erarbeitung:
- (SB auf) S schreiben die Fragen u. ihre Antworten im *simple past* gemäß AA ins Heft.
- **Ausw.:** ▶Meldekette
- **Alternative:** S befragen sich gegenseitig und notieren die Antworten (▶Milling around).
- **Ausw.:** S präsentieren ihre Ergebnisse im Plenum, ohne den Namen des/der befragten S zu nennen. Die Klasse errät den Namen mithilfe der Informationen.

---

1 Diff bank

▶Page 25

💬 **More help** **6** READING Lily's blog   **6 b)** individuelle Lösungen

👥 b) Think about your activities yesterday or last week. Then tell a partner.

Last week / Last weekend / Yesterday / …

	went	cycling / for a walk with my dog / shopping / swimming / …
	played	badminton / basketball / computer games / football / frisbee / …
	watched	a series / some sport / some videos / …
I	was	at a friend's house / on my phone / on my computer / out with friends / …
	made	a cake / ice cream / a picture / a °model / …
	did	my homework / an °experiment / my hair / …
	practised	the guitar / coding / English / …
	wrote	a story / messages to friends / …
	tidied my room / listened to music / read a book / took photos / drew a picture / …		

📖 **More practice 5** **Wembley Stadium**

5 1 opened • 2 happened • 3 didn't think •
4 didn't agree • 5 said • 6 cost

Complete the information about Wembley Stadium.
Use the simple past.

The old Wembley Stadium … (1 open) in 1923. England's famous win of the football °World Cup … (2 happen) here in 1966, but some people … (3 not think) the game was fair and … (4 not agree) with the result. London … (5 say) goodbye to the old stadium in 2003 and hello to the new one in 2007. The new stadium … (6 cost) £798 °million and with 90,000 seats it's the biggest in the UK.

✏️ **More practice 6** **Yesterday at school**

Write the questions about your last school day.
Then write answers for you.

1 what time / get up?
2 you / do / anything interesting or exciting at school?
3 eat / something nice for lunch?
4 what / do / after school?
5 you / have / a lot of homework?
6 when / you / go to bed?

6 Lösung und Lösungsbsp. S. 287

1

Diff bank Vorbereitung

Material: MP 5 UMA, ggf. selbst recherchiertes Foto vom Wembley Stadion • MH 3 UMA • MH Unit task UMA
Zeitbedarf: abhängig davon, welche Aufgaben bearbeitet werden
Minimalversion: *More practice*-Aufgaben sind stets Zusatzaufgaben

---

▶ Page 29

More help 3 LIFE SKILLS Make a difference!   3 individuelle Lösungen

a) THINK Have you ever helped a friend, a grandparent or a neighbour? How?
Or do you know somebody who helps others?

went shopping at / for / in / with	my neighbour.
helped in the garden at	my grandma / grandpa.
explained a maths problem / homework / ... to	my friend.
°downloaded an app for	my sports team / my club.
gave old clothes and toys to	a charity shop.
walked the dog / looked after a pet / ... for	my neighbourhood.
made a cake / soup / ... for	my park.
helped with the food at	a soup kitchen.
collected money at / for	my °church / mosque / °synagogue.
picked up rubbish at / in	

▶ Page 31

More help UNIT TASK Make an audio guide for a London bike tour, Step 2

a) Write the audio guide for your group's sight.
It should be one to two minutes long.
You can use these phrases.

You're now on ... Road / Street / ...
You're standing in front of ...
... has a long history.
You can see / hear / experience ...
Did you know that ...? / Not everybody knows that ...
A fun fact / story is ...
It's open from ... to ...
A ticket for a child costs ...
What are you waiting for? Visit now!

Unit task individuelle Lösungen

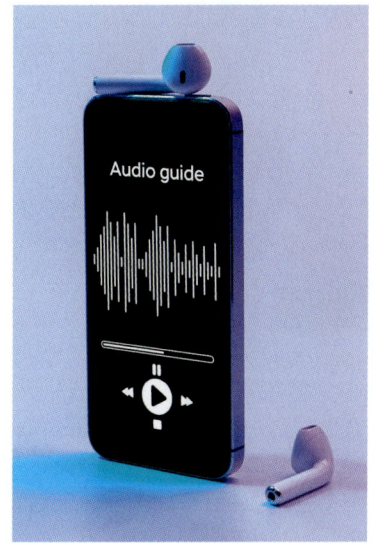

MH 3 s. S. 29
• Diese Aufgabe bietet sprachliche Mittel für lernschwächere S.

Erarbeitung:

a) S nutzen das ▶ Scaffolding in Phase *Think* (s. Ex 3a), S. 29) und machen sich Notizen zur Vorbereitung der Phase *Pair*.
• In schwächeren Lerngruppen sollten die sprachlichen Mittel für alle S nutzbar sein (TA/UMA).

MH Unit task s. S. 31
• Diese Aufgabe bietet sprachliche Mittel für lernschwächere S.

Erarbeitung:

a) S nutzen das ▶ Scaffolding zur Erstellung des Audioguides (s. Step 2, S. 31).
• In schwächeren Lerngruppen sollten die sprachlichen Mittel für alle S nutzbar sein (TA/UMA).

forty-three 43

2

Unit-Übersicht

Storyline: Omar und Rosie aus Manchester setzen sich für das Online-Magazin ihrer Schule mit dem Thema *Green fashion* auseinander. Sie bieten einen Kummerkasten in ihrem Magazin an. Rosie nimmt an einem Podcast zum Thema Selbstvertrauen teil. In der Story erlebt Omar einen unangenehmen Konflikt bei einem Fußballspiel.
Strukturen: *(revision) comparison of adjectives* (S. 46) • *modal verbs* (S. 49–51) • *reflexive pronouns* (S. 52)
Viewing: Video mit Tipps zu selbstbewusstem Auftreten (S. 54) • Film über einen Konflikt zwischen Fußballfans: Auf dem Weg zu einem Fußballspiel haben ein Vater und sein Sohn ein unangenehmes Erlebnis. (S. 59)
Unit task: an einer Diskussion teilnehmen

Unit 2 Einstieg:
- (SB zu) L zeigt Karte der Britischen Inseln, S. 10 (UMA). L: *Let's go to another place in the UK – to the city of Manchester. What do you know about this city?*
- L erfasst Ideen an der Tafel (ggf. mit Bildimpulsen helfen): *in the north of England, famous football team, …*

Ex 1 Einstieg:
- (SB zu) L zeigt die Fotos von Rosie und Omar (UMA). L: *Let's meet two students. They are students at Trafford Secondary School. Can you describe Rosie and Omar?*
- S beschreiben Rosie und Omar.
- L zeigt dann die komplette Abbildung von S. 44–45 (UMA). L: *What's this? What can you see in the pictures?* S: *It's a school / an online magazine. I can see …*

Erarbeitung:
a) (SB auf) Gemäß AA: S vergleichen in PA die Dinge, die Rosie und Omar wichtig sind.
- **Ausw.:** im Plenum, mit TA

b) Gemäß AA in arbeitsteiliger PA: Ein/-e S wählt Omar, der/die andere S wählt Rosie.
- S übertragen die Tabelle mit den Punkten 1–6 aus dem Online-Magazin ins Heft und ergänzen sie beim 1. Hören.

c) 2. **Hören** gemäß AA
- S berichten Partner/-in anschl. über ihre Person.
- **Ausw.:** im Plenum
- **Sich.** von neuem Wortschatz, mit ▶ Lautschulung

Unit 2
Manchester: Who we are

1 a) the same Family, friends and clothes are important to both of them. • different health, kindness, saving the planet, her phone / Manchester, football, fair play

1 LISTENING What's important to Rosie and Omar

a) BEFORE YOU LISTEN Look at the magazine and say what's important to Rosie and Omar. Say what's the same and what's different.

b) Choose Omar or Rosie and make a table for 1–6. Listen and add Omar or Rosie's reasons.

Omar	reasons	Rosie	reasons
1 his family	always support him	1 her health	has a disability

c) Listen again and check. Then tell your partner about Omar or Rosie. Say why.

Omar's family is important to him because they always … ▶ More practice 1, p. 68 ▶ Skills file 8, p. 163

1 b), c) Lösungsbsp. S. 287

44 forty-four

2

Lead-in Inhalt

Lernschwerpunkt: sagen, was einem wichtig ist
Kompetenzen: Listening einem Interview Informationen entnehmen • Speaking darüber sprechen, was einem wichtig ist
Redemittel: *important things* • *That is/isn't really important to me.*

Vorbereitung

Material: Unit-Einstieg UMA, ggf. von L recherchierte Bildimpulse zu Manchester • Ex 1 UMA, UMA/CD/App • Ex 2 ggf. Papier für Klassenplakat
Zeitbedarf: ca. 1–2 Std.
Minimalversion: Ex 2a) als Hausaufgabe vorbereiten lassen
Begleitmedien: WB (S. 34), App (Digital quiz), INKL (S. 44–45), DIFF (2.1), Unit plans (Unit 2)

Nach dieser Unit kann ich ...
- erklären, was mir wichtig ist
- über Mode und Umweltschutz reden
- Ratschläge geben
- über Selbstbewusstsein sprechen
- einen Konflikt besprechen
- meine Meinung äußern und begründen

Unit task
- an einer Diskussion teilnehmen

Nach dieser Unit ...
- L bespricht mit S die Lernziele der Unit (s. links) und kündigt die *Unit task* an.
- Am Ende der Unit überprüfen S das Erreichen der Ziele mithilfe des Checkpoint (S. 62–65) bzw. gemeinsam im Plenum.

Ex 2 Einstieg:
- (SB zu) L entwirft eine ▶ Mindmap zum Thema *What's important to people*.
- ▶ Brainstorming im Plenum: S ergänzen Ideen.
- ⊠ Lernstärkere S nennen auch jeweils mögliche Gründe.

Erarbeitung:
a) (SB auf) ▶ Think-pair-share
- *Think:* S notieren gemäß AA 4–6 Personen oder Dinge, die ihnen wichtig sind, jeweils mit Begründung.
- ⊡ Lernschwächere S finden sprachliche Mittel und Beispiele in ▶ More help, S. 69.

b) *Pair:* S besprechen in PA ihre Listen, finden Gemeinsamkeiten und Unterschiede.

c) *Share:* S-Paare präsentieren Ergebnisse im Plenum.
- L weist vorab auf ▶ Scaffolding hin.
- **Alternative:** Zwei Paare bilden jeweils eine Vierergruppe und besprechen gemeinsam ihre Ergebnisse.
- **Zusatz:** In einer Diskussion im Plenum werden die Top Six der Klasse zu *What's important to us* erfasst und ggf. als Klassenplakat veröffentlicht (▶ English corner).

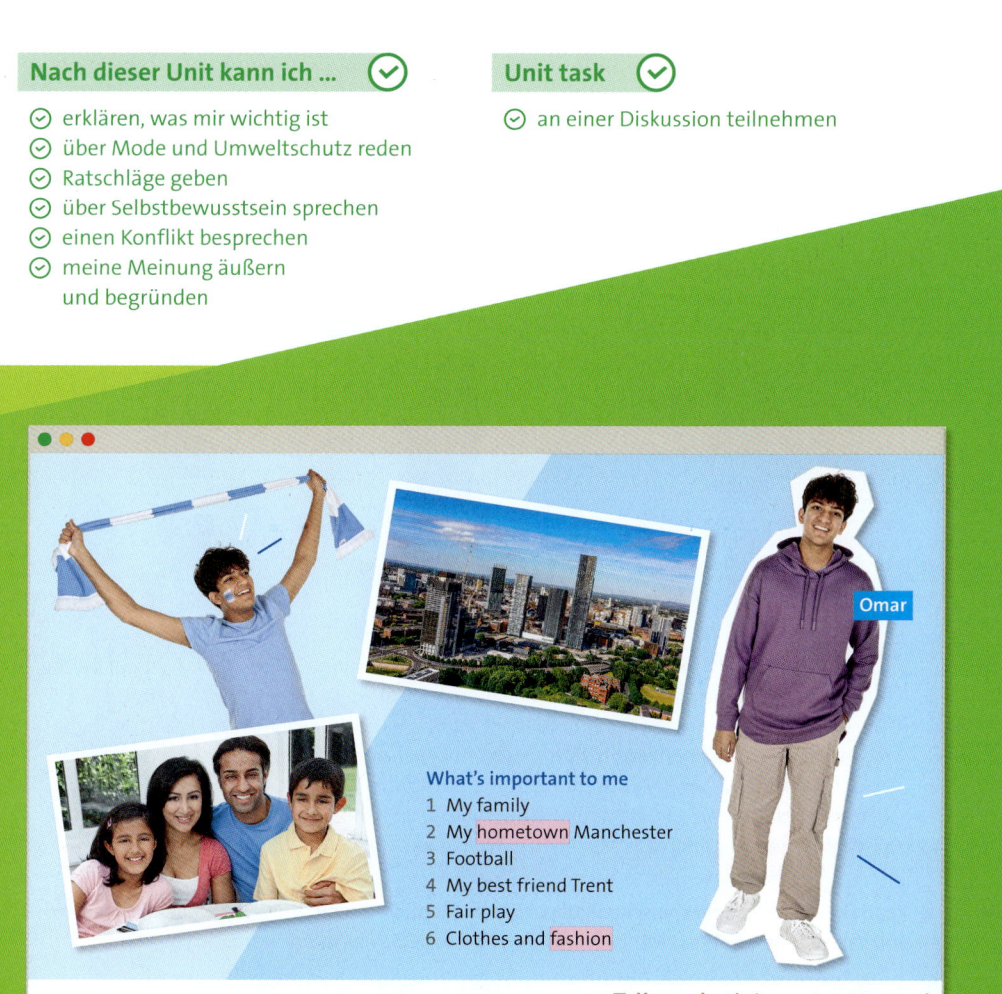

What's important to me
1 My family
2 My hometown Manchester
3 Football
4 My best friend Trent
5 Fair play
6 Clothes and fashion

Tell us what's important to you!

💬 **2** SPEAKING **What's important to you**

2 individuelle Lösungen

a) What's important to you? Make a list of four to six people or things. Think of reasons too.
▶ More help, p. 69

b) Tell a partner what people or things are important to you. Explain why.

c) Tell the class what's the same and what's different for you and your partner.
We both think ... is important.
I think ... is important, but Hanna thinks ...

▶ Workbook, p. 34

 Digital quiz | I can explain what's important to me. ✓

forty-five 45

45

2

Topic 1 Inhalt

Lernschwerpunkt: sich zu Mode äußern und ihren Einfluss auf die Umwelt erkennen
Kompetenzen: Reading einem Artikel über Mode Wortschatz entnehmen • Speaking Outfits miteinander vergleichen • sich äußern, welche Kleidung man kauft und wo • Reading/Speaking/Global goals ein Quiz über nachhaltige Mode lösen und besprechen • Writing ein Poster über nachhaltige Kleidung gestalten
Strukturen: *(revision)* comparison of adjectives
Redemittel: *clothes and fashion • adjectives to describe clothes • green fashion*

Ex 1 Einstieg:
- (SB zu) Wortschatz *clothes* wdh. mit ▶ Menschen-Memo.
- ☒ Lernstärkere S-Paare ergänzen ein Adjektiv, z. B. *a colourful skirt.*

Erarbeitung:
a) L zeigt Fotos von S. 46 (UMA) und vermittelt neuen Wortschatz, z. B.: *Look at the photos. These are trendy outfits. The girl's tights – what a colour! Do you like patterned clothes or do you prefer plain outfits? …*
- (SB auf) S lesen den Text und sammeln *clothes words* gemäß AA in PA.
- **Ausw.:** Im Plenum, L erstellt Liste als TA.
- **Sich.:** S übertragen Liste in ihr *Vocab file* (▶ English folder).

b) S notieren Adjektive gemäß AA in ihr *Vocab file*.
- **Sich.:** ▶ Five-minute teacher, Liste als TA
- **Alternative:** L präsentiert Text (UMA) und markiert Adjektive.

c) Gemäß AA, ▶ Scaffolding ggf. gemeinsam klären, dann PA.
- **Ausw.:** S-Paare präsentieren Ergebnisse im Plenum.
- Wdh. Steigerung der Adjektive: s. ▶ LF 7a + b, S. 175–176 und ▶ More practice 2, S. 69
- ☒ ▶ Challenge 1 + 2, S. 70

Ex 2 Einstieg:
- (SB zu) L: *Where can you buy clothes?* – S: *In a shop / online / in a second-hand shop / …*

Erarbeitung:
- (SB auf) gemäß AA in PA
- **Ausw.:** im Plenum

---

2 | Topic 1 | Topic 2 | Topic 3 | Story | Viewing | Study skills | Unit task

Manchester fashion

📖 **1 Words Clothes**

▶ Box: Voc., p. 216

Manchester fashion *by* Omar

Manchester has always been famous for clothes and fashion! So I decided to go out on the streets to find some great Manchester fashion. Look at these three attractive ⁺outfits. The dark blue blazer in the first photo looks really cool with the sunglasses and hat. Tight jeans like these are great, but I prefer baggy trousers. In the second photo, the girl's yellow ⁺tights look really ⁺trendy with the skirt and the light blue jacket, right? And who said patterned clothes are old-fashioned? The T-shirt in the third photo looks amazing with the plain white shorts. People in Manchester have great style! What do you think?

a) Read Omar's article for the school magazine and look at the pictures. Say what clothes you can see. What other clothes words do you know? Say as many words as you can.

b) In the article, find four pairs of opposites: *dark – …, tight – …, trendy – …, patterned – …* Write them in your VOCAB FILE and add other adjectives to describe clothes. ▶ Skills file 2, p. 156

c) Look at the pictures again. Compare the outfits and say if you like them.
*I think the clothes in picture … are trendier / more attractive / more colourful / … than …
The outfit in picture … isn't as cool / interesting / nice as the outfit in …
I think the outfit in picture … is the best / the coolest / the most attractive / ….*

REVISION Comparisons: ▶ Language file 7a + b, p. 175–176 | ▶ More practice 2, p. 69 | ▶ Challenge 1 + 2, p. 70

💬 **2 Speaking Buying clothes**

You have some money to buy some clothes. Think about style, colour and shops. Then tell a partner three things you'd like to buy.

I'd like to buy …   I'd like to shop in / at …

▶ Wordbank 3, p. 188
▶ Workbook, p. 35

46 forty-six

Lösungen:

1 a) 1 hat, blazer, T-shirt, jeans, sunglasses, shoes • 2 cap, jacket, skirt, tights, trainers • 3 T-shirt, shorts, shoes, chain, watch • *more:* trousers, boots, dress …

1 b) 1 dark – light • 2 tight – baggy • 3 trendy – old-fashioned • 4 patterned – plain

1 c) individuelle Lösungen

2 Lösungsbsp. S. 288

Topic 1 Vorbereitung

Material: Ex 1 ggf. von L vorbereitete Karteikarten (Wortschatz *clothes*) für Menschen-Memo, UMA • Ex 3 Blätter mit *agree/disagree/unsure* (ein Wort pro Blatt) • Ex 4 weiße Blätter für Poster (A4 oder A3, nach Bedarf)
Zeitbedarf: ca. 2 Std.
Minimalversion: Ex 3c) auslassen
Begleitmedien: WB (S. 35–36), App (Digital help, Digital quiz), INKL (S. 46–47), DIFF (2.2)

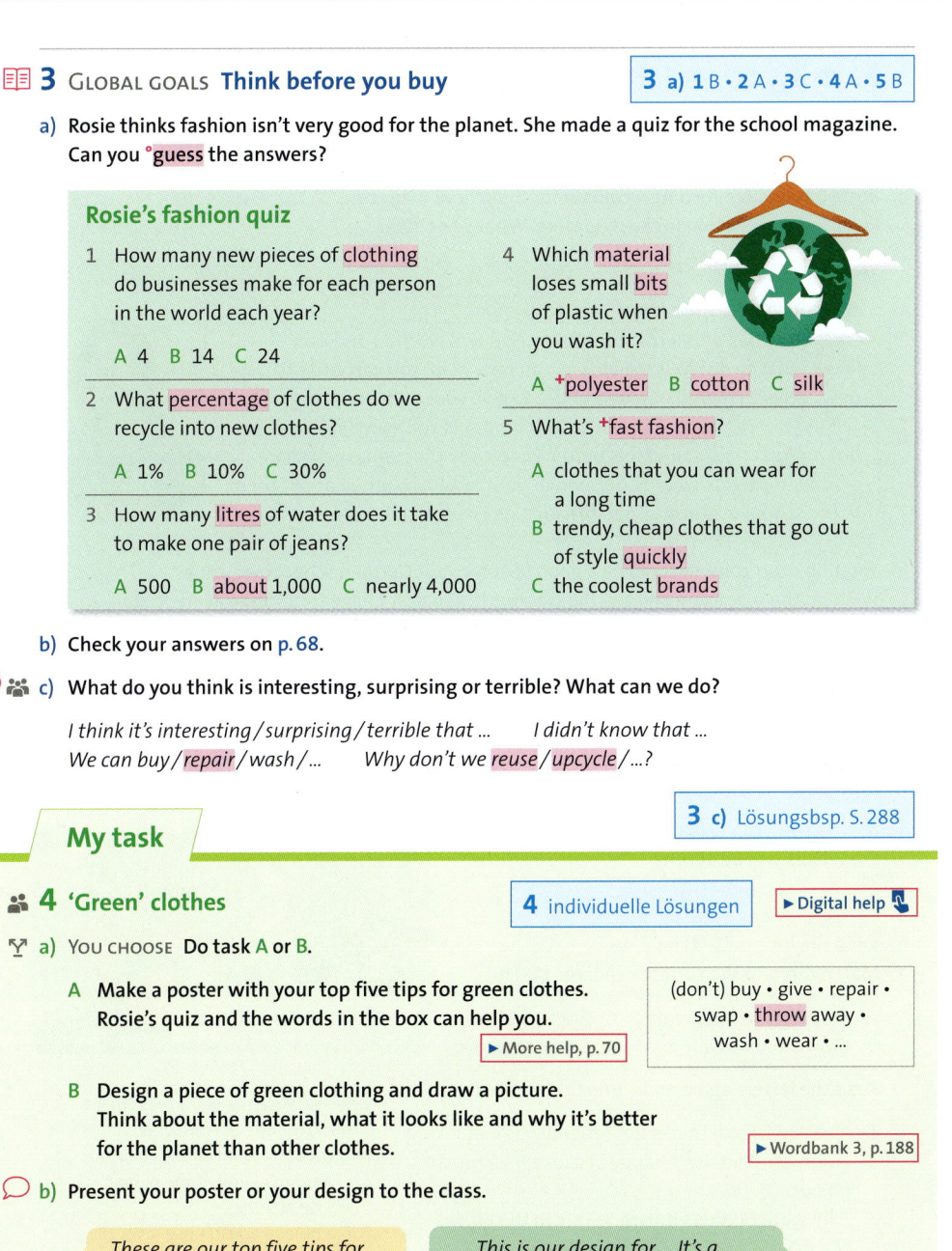

Ex 3 Einstieg:
- (SB zu) TA: *Fashion is good for our planet.*
- S positionieren sich nach ▶Meinungsbarometer (*agree/disagree/unsure*, ein Wort pro Blatt verteilt im Klassenraum) und begründen ihre Entscheidung.

Erarbeitung:
a) (SB auf) Klären der AA
- S lösen das Quiz, sie schlagen neuen Wortschatz im *Vocabulary*, S. 217–218 nach.

b) S prüfen Lösungen auf S. 68.
- **Ausw.:** L erfasst die Anzahl der richtigen Antworten mit ▶Thumbs up.

c) gemäß AA in GA
- **Ausw.:** Beispiele im Plenum

My task Ex 4 Einstieg:
- (SB zu) L: *How can you save the planet with your clothes?*
- Diskussion mit ▶Blitzlichtrunde
  S: *I can wear them longer, buy second hand, make my own clothes, …*
- L erfasst Ideen als TA.

Erarbeitung:
a) (SB auf) Klären der AA
- Gemäß AA: S-Paare entscheiden sich zwischen A und B, s. a. *Digital help* (App).
- Hilfen: s. ▶More help, S. 70 und ▶Wordbank 3, S. 188

b) S-Paare präsentieren Ergebnisse im Plenum.
- **Ausw.:** Klasse gibt ▶Feedback.
- **Alternative:** ▶Gallery walk
- **Zusatz:** Aushang der Ergebnisse im Klassenraum (▶English corner)

2

Topic 2 Inhalt

Lernschwerpunkt: in einem Online-Magazin über die Probleme junger Menschen lesen
Kompetenzen: Mediation eine Ankündigung im Online-Magazin verstehen und Informationen daraus ins Deutsche sprachmitteln • Reading Leserbriefe über persönliche Probleme verstehen
Strukturen: *modal verbs: must, mustn't, (don't) have to, needn't, (not) be allowed to*
Redemittel: *problems and feelings • singular 'they'*

Ex 1 Einstieg:
- (SB zu) L zeigt ggf. eigene Schulzeitung.
  L: *Do you know any other topics which are interesting for a school magazine?*
  S: *There can be articles about sport/hobbies/pets/…*

Erarbeitung:

a) (SB auf) L: *Let's find out about Rosie's idea for their school magazine.*
- S lesen Text gemäß AA und beantworten die Frage.
- Ausw.: im Plenum

b) Klären der AA
- S schreiben Nachricht gemäß AA ins Heft (▶ Mediation, s. a. ▶ SF 10, S. 165).
- Ausw.: ▶ Partner check, dann Plenum

Ex 2 Einstieg:
- (SB zu) L zeigt Bild von Ex 2 (UMA).
  L: *Who can you see?*
  S: *I can see two girls.*
  L: *Do you think they're friends?*
- S positionieren sich mit ▶ Meinungsbarometer und begründen ihre Entscheidung.
  L: *If you have a problem with a friend, what can you do?*
- S nennen Ideen.
- L leitet ggf. über: *You can also write to an advice column.*

Erarbeitung:

a) (SB auf) L liest AA vor und S antworten.
  S: *The letters can be about friends, …*
- ⏯ Alternative: S notieren ihre Ideen auf ▶ KV 2.1 (Ex 1a).
- Ausw.: L erstellt Liste als TA.
- Forts. s. S. 49

---

2 | Topic 1 | **Topic 2** | Topic 3 | Story | Viewing | Study skills | Unit task

Family, friendship and love

1 a) Rosie's idea is a new advice column. Students can write letters and get advice if they have a problem.

↔ **1 MEDIATION Rosie's idea**

a) Rosie has an idea for a new column for the school magazine.
Read the information in the magazine. What's her idea?

▶ Skills file 9, p. 164

A new column for *Hey!* ▶ Box: Voc., p. 219

Everybody has problems sometimes. You feel worried and don't know what to do. Well, we at *Hey!* can now help: You can write to our new ⁺advice column. You don't have to give your name or your class. Tell us your problem and we'll give you advice. You needn't take it – but it might help you to feel better. People say that when you share a problem, it gets smaller. So send us your letters by email or put them in the school magazine ⁺postbox outside the computer room.

Rosie

---

b) You think this column could be a good idea for your German school magazine.
Write to the magazine and tell them about it. You don't have to °include every °detail.

*Liebe Redaktion,
ich habe gerade in meinem Englischbuch etwas über eine Schülerzeitung gelesen.
Es geht um …   Manchmal …   Jetzt kann man …*

▶ Skills file 10, p. 165

1 b) Lösungsbsp. S. 288

2 READING Letters to the advice column

2 a) *friends*, family, school, love, bullying, …

a) BEFORE YOU READ What problems do you think the letters will be about?

friends, …

2 b) 1 C • 2 A • 3 D • 4 B

b) Read the letters (1–4) on p. 49.
Match them to the correct headings (A–D).

A Problems with parents   C Frenemies
B Worried about a friend   D Student in love

frenemies
She's mean!
I don't like her make-up.

c) Read the letters again and correct the sentences.

1 'Puzzled friend' thinks their friend was just joking.
2 'Angry student' isn't happy because they mustn't go out. ▶ Box: Voc., p. 219
3 'Shy student' finds it hard to talk to the girl in their class.
4 'BFF' thinks they can't do anything about their friend's situation.

▶ More practice 3, p. 71

We can use the word *they (them, their)* for **one** person when …
- we don't want to say *he* or *she*.
- we don't know if the person is a *he* or a *she*.
- a person doesn't use *he* or *she* because they don't identify as a boy or a girl.

2 c) Lösungsbsp. S. 288

48 forty-eight

Topic 2 Vorbereitung

Material: Ex 1 ggf. eigene Schulzeitung • Ex 2 UMA, ▶ KV 2.1: Letters to the advice column (Klassensatz) • Ex 3 beschriftete A4-Blätter (1 Puzzled friend, 2 Angry student, 3 Shy student, 4 BFF) für jeweils eine Ecke des Raumes, UMA/App (Erklärfilm), ▶ KV 2.1 (nach Bedarf), von L vorbereitete Swap cards (Klassensatz)
Zeitbedarf: ca. 1–2 Std.
Minimalversion: Ex 1b) als Hausaufgabe
Begleitmedien: WB (S. 37), INKL (S. 48–49)

Ex 2b) (Forts. von S. 48)
- S lesen die Briefe von S. 49 laut vor, dann gemäß AA in EA.
- ▶ **Alternative:** ▶ KV 2.1 (Ex 1b)
- **Ausw.:** ▶ Five-minute teacher

c) gemeinsames Lesen des Kastens unten auf S. 48 und ggf. Erläuterung mit TA
- Bearbeitung des ersten Beispiels im Plenum
- S schreiben korrigierten Satz ins Heft, dann weiter gemäß AA in EA.
- ▶ **Alternative:** ▶ KV 2.1 (Ex 1c)
- **Ausw.:** ▶ Partner check, dann Plenum

Ex 3 Einstieg:
- (SB zu) L heftet Schilder in vier Ecken des Raumes (1 Puzzled friend, 2 Angry student, 3 Shy student, 4 BFF) und fragt: *Do you remember: which letter are these sentences from?*
- L liest Sätze 1–6 aus Ex 3 nacheinander vor und S gehen in die jeweilige Ecke (▶ Four corners).

Erarbeitung:
- (SB auf) gemeinsames Lesen der AA u. der Fragen im Kasten
- S beantworten Fragen in EA.
- **Ausw.:** ▶ Meldekette, L notiert Antworten als TA.
- **Sich.:** S übertragen TA in den Merkteil (▶ English folder).
- ▶ **Alternative:** ▶ KV 2.1 (Ex 2)
- s. a. ▶ LF 8a + b, S. 176–177 und Erklärfilm (UMA/App)
- **Zusatz:** ▶ Swap cards: L bereitet Karten vor (z. B. *1 clean my room, 2 shout, …*). S bilden zu jeder Karte einen Satz mit einem passenden modalen Hilfsverb, z. B. *I have to clean my room every Saturday.*

---

www.hey-trafford-school.example.net/advice

1 Dear advice column
Last week I went to the bathroom at a friend's house and before I went back into his room, I heard him on the phone to another friend. He said I was **nerdy** and uncool. I felt really upset. But when I asked my friend about it, he **said sorry** and that he didn't mean it, it was just a joke. Now I don't know if I can **trust** him.
Puzzled friend 🤔

2 Dear advice column
My parents are really **strict** and I'm not **allowed** to do anything! I always have to tell them where I'm going and who with. I have to be back at 6 o'clock when I go out and I mustn't be late or I can't go out for a week. It's so unfair! And it's so embarrassing! What can I do? Please help!
Angry student 😠

3 Dear advice column
I **have a crush** on a girl in my class. She's really nice and clever and always positive. I'm quite shy and I sometimes find it hard to talk to other people. But I don't have to be funny or interesting with this girl – I can just be me with her. The problem is that she's a good friend and I don't want to lose her friendship. Should I tell her?
Shy student 🙂

4 Dear advice column
My friend's dad got married again a few months ago and I know my friend doesn't like her new ⁺**stepmother**. She was always really chatty and fun and now she's very quiet and sad. She says that she has to **deal** with this situation alone and that I needn't worry. But I'm really worried about her and I feel that I must do something to help.
BFF 🤗

3 LOOKING AT LANGUAGE *must, mustn't, (don't) have to, needn't, (not) be allowed to*

Look at the examples from the letters. Answer the questions in the box.

1. I have to be back at 6 o'clock when I go out.
2. I feel that I must do something to help.
3. And I mustn't be late.
4. I'm not allowed to do anything!
5. I don't have to be funny or interesting.
6. She says that I needn't worry.

Which verbs or phrases in blue mean …
1 *(ich) muss?*
2 *(ich) darf nicht?*
3 *(ich) muss nicht* or *(ich) brauche nicht?*
▶ Language file 8a + b, p. 176–177

3 1 have to, must • 2 mustn't, not be allowed to • 3 don't have to, needn't

▶ Workbook, p. 37

forty-nine 49

2

Topic 2 Inhalt

Lernschwerpunkt: sich zu Problemen junger Menschen verständigen und Ratschläge geben
Kompetenzen: Listening einen Dialog über persönliche Probleme und mögliche Ratschläge verstehen • Reading Antworten auf Leserbriefe verstehen • Speaking sich über Ratschläge austauschen und selbst Ratschläge geben • Writing einen Leserbrief beantworten und Ratschläge geben
Strukturen: *modal verbs: may, might, could; should/shouldn't*
Redemittel: *problems and feelings • giving advice • feedback phrases*

Ex 4 Einstieg:
- (SB zu) L verteilt Wortkarten mit den Verben aus dem Reservoir und notiert deutsche Bedeutungen als TA.
- S heften Karte zur Bedeutung.

Erarbeitung:
- (SB auf) Klären der AA
- Erster Satz gemeinsam im Plenum, S schreiben die vollständigen Sätze in ihr Heft.
- **Ausw.:** ▶ Partner check, dann Plenum
- **Zusatz:** S lesen den Dialog laut in verteilten Rollen.
- Vertiefung modale Hilfsverben: ▶ More practice 4, S. 71
- ✉ ▶ Challenge 3, S. 71 (Ersatzformen von *can* u. *must*)

Ex 5 Einstieg:
- (SB zu) L zeigt das Bild (UMA): *What does the picture tell you?*
- S äußern Vermutung mit ▶ Buzz group.

Erarbeitung:
a) (SB auf) AA klären.
- 📄 Brief 3 auf S. 49 noch einmal gemeinsam lesen.
- gemäß AA in PA
- **Ausw.:** im Plenum

b) 1. Hören: S beantworten Frage.

c) 2. Hören: S notieren *T/F* und korrigieren falsche Sätze.
- 📄 Schwächere S korrigieren die Sätze beim **3. Hören**.
- **Ausw.:** ▶ Meldekette

d) gemäß AA im Plenum
- gemeinsames Lesen der ▶ Grammatik-Box, S. 50
- **Sich.:** S übertragen Regel in den Merkteil (▶ English folder).
- ▶ LF 8d, S. 177 u.
- ▶ More practice 5, S. 72

2		Topic 1	**Topic 2**	Topic 3	Story	Viewing	Study skills	Unit task

📖 **4 Talking about the letters**

> **4** 1 allowed to • 2 have to / must • 3 don't have to / needn't •
> 4 mustn't • 5 don't have to / needn't • 6 have to / must

Complete Rosie and Omar's discussion about the letters.
Use the verbs in the box. Sometimes there are two answers.

> allowed to • don't have to • have to • must • mustn't • needn't

Rosie I understand the angry student in the second letter. I'm not … (1) come home late and it's so annoying.
Omar Yes, I know. That letter about the quiet, sad girl worries me. We … (2) help the writer.
Rosie Yes, I agree. It's good that Ms Hall will help us with this, so we … (3) answer the letters alone. We … (4) give people bad advice.
Omar Of course not. You … (5) worry, Rosie. I think Ms Hall will have some good ideas.
Rosie Yes, I'm sure she will. But first we … (6) talk about our ideas!

▶ More practice 4, p. 71   ▶ Challenge 3, p. 71

🎧 **5 LISTENING Crushes**

> **5 a)** 'Shy student' wants to know if they should tell a friend that they love her. • To 'have a crush on sb.' means you like them very much.

👥 **a)** BEFORE YOU LISTEN Rosie and Omar are now talking about the third letter on p. 49.
Do you remember: What was the letter about? What's a 'crush'?

5 b) Lösungsbsp. S. 288

🔊 **b)** Listen to Omar and Rosie. Do they think that it's easy or difficult to give advice? Why?
1.11

🔊 **c)** Listen again. True or false? Correct the false sentences.

5 c) Lösung S. 288

1 Rosie had a crush on somebody.
2 The story about Rosie's sister had a happy ending for her.
3 Rosie thinks that the two students could become more than friends.
4 Omar thinks that it might be embarrassing. ▶ Box: Voc., p. 220
5 The writer may never find out how the girl feels: Omar thinks that's OK.

d) What do you think could happen if 'Shy student' tells the girl about their crush?

I think 'Shy student' may / might / could …

▶ More practice 5, p. 72

5 d) Lösungsbsp. S. 288

> You know that we can use *may* and *could* in polite questions:
> *May I say something? Could you help me, please?*
>
> You can also use *may*, *could* and *might* to talk about possible situations:
> *It may work. It might be really embarrassing. The student could say nothing.*

▶ Language file 8d, p. 177

50 fifty

2

Topic 2 Vorbereitung

Material: Ex 4 von L vorbereitete Wortkarten mit Verben aus dem Reservoir • Ex 5 UMA, UMA/CD/App • Ex 6 beschriftete A4-Blätter (*1 Puzzled friend, 2 Angry student, 3 Shy student, 4 BFF*), *Right/wrong cards* (Klassensatz) • Ex 7 A4-Papier (Klassensatz), ▶ KV 2.2: Giving feedback (Part 1, Klassensatz), ggf. Smileys zum Bewerten (Klassensatz)
Zeitbedarf: ca. 2 Std.
Minimalversion: Ex 7a) als Hausaufgabe
Begleitmedien: WB (S. 37–39), App (Digital help, Digital quiz), INKL (S. 50–51), DIFF (2.3)

2

6 READING Answers from the advice column

6 a) A 4 • B 2

a) Read the two answers from *Hey!* below. Match them to the correct letters (1–4) on p. 49.

> Thank you for your letter. I think you're right that your friend might need your help. Often when we have a problem, we keep it inside because we feel embarrassed or ashamed. I think you should try to talk to your friend again. Ask her to talk to a teacher that she can trust. But you shouldn't make her do it if she doesn't want to do this. You can also ask a teacher or your parents for help. Thank you for being a good friend.
> Best wishes, The *Hey!* advice column
>
> **A**

> We understand that you're unhappy. But your parents love you and want to keep you safe. You should talk to your parents about how you feel. You shouldn't shout. Try to stay calm and explain why it's embarrassing for you. Maybe you can agree on one late night a week? If you text them while you're out or when you're on the way home, they'll probably feel better.
> Best wishes, The *Hey!* advice column
>
> **B**

b) Read the letters again. Say if you agree with the advice or not.

I think this is good/bad advice.

6 b), c) Lösungsbsp. S. 288

c) Give more or different advice.

You should call your friend's dad/… You shouldn't get angry/…

You can use *should* and *shouldn't* to give advice.

▶ Language file 8e, p. 177   ▶ More practice 6, p. 72

My task

7 a) Lösungsbsp. S. 289

7 Your advice

▶ Digital help

a) Choose one of the other two letters on p. 49.
Write a short letter with advice. Use *should* and *shouldn't*.
The letters in 6 a) can help you.   ▶ More help, p. 72

b) Swap letters with your partner, °underline any problems and give feedback.
- Does the letter have the right beginning and ending?
- Does your partner use *should* and *shouldn't*?
- Is the advice useful?   ▶ Let's talk: Feedback, p. 200

c) °Rewrite your letter for a GALLERY WALK. Choose the best advice.

7 b), c) individuelle Lösungen   ▶ Workbook, pp. 37–39

Digital quiz   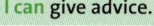 I can give advice.

fifty-one **51**

Ex 6 Einstieg:
- (SB zu) L heftet die Schilder von Ex 3, S. 49 an die Tafel (*1 Puzzled friend, 2 Angry student, 3 Shy student, 4 BFF*) und fragt: *Can you remember their problems in the letters?*
- L zeigt auf das jeweilige Schild und S antworten.

Erarbeitung:
a) (SB auf) gemäß AA in EA
- **Ausw.:** L zeigt auf Schild aus dem Einstieg, S reagieren mit ▶ Right/wrong cards.

b) gemäß AA in PA
- **Ausw.:** im Plenum
- ✉ S geben Begründung.

c) S nennen Ideen im Plenum.
- ⚑ Lernschwächere S machen sich vorab Notizen.
- **Ausw.:** L notiert Ideen als TA.
- **Sich.:** gemeinsames Lesen der ▶ Grammatik-Box, S. 51 und Übertragen in den Merkteil (▶ English folder)
- s. a. ▶ LF 8e, S. 177 und ▶ More practice 6, S. 72

My task Ex 7 Einstieg:
- (SB zu) TA: *Your advice*
- L nennt Lernziel der Aufgabe.

Erarbeitung:
a) (SB auf) S wählen Brief und schreiben Antwort gemäß AA.
- L verweist auch auf die Ideenliste aus Ex 6c).
- ⚑ ▶ More help, S. 72

b) gemäß AA in PA
- S nutzen ▶ KV 2.2 (Part 1).

c) S schreiben ihren Brief korrigiert noch einmal.
- **Ausw.:** ▶ Gallery walk (Bewertung z. B. mit Smileys)
- ▶ English corner

2

Topic 3 Inhalt

Lernschwerpunkt: einen Podcast und einen Artikel zum Thema Selbstvertrauen verstehen
Kompetenzen: Listening einem Podcast zum Thema Selbstvertrauen Informationen entnehmen • Reading einem Artikel über ein Vorbild Informationen entnehmen
Strukturen: *reflexive pronouns*
Redemittel: *confidence tips • role models*

Ex 1 Einstieg:
- (SB zu) TA: *CONFIDENCE* (Buchstaben senkrecht untereinander)
  L: *Make an acrostic with things you can do to make you feel confident. Examples: listen to musiC, join a fOotball team, daNce.* (L notiert die Beispiele.)
- S schreiben ein ▶ Acrostic.
- kurzer Vergleich im Plenum

Erarbeitung:

a) (SB auf) PA gemäß AA
- Ausw.: ▶ Blitzlichtrunde

b) S lesen AA und die Antwortmöglichkeiten.
- 1. Hören: S notieren richtige Lösungen im Heft.
- Ausw.: ▶ Five-minute teacher
- Zusatz: S kontrollieren, welche Ideen aus dem Akrostichon im Hörtext genannt werden.

Ex 2 Einstieg:
- direkter Anschluss an Ex 1

Erarbeitung:

a) (SB auf) S lesen die Sätze 1–7.
- 2. Hören: S ordnen die Reflexivpronomen aus dem Reservoir zu und notieren Lösung im Heft.
- Ausw.: ▶ Partner check, ggf. mit 3. Hören

b) S schreiben Tabelle gemäß AA in den Merkteil (▶ English folder) und füllen sie aus.
- Ausw.: ▶ Five-minute teacher: S fertigt TA mit Lösungen an (ggf. zwei S einsetzen, S1 schreibt, S2 führt das Gespräch).
- Zusatz: gemeinsames Lesen von ▶ LF 9, S. 178

c) gemäß AA im ▶ Think-Pair-Share

---

2 | Topic 1 | Topic 2 | **Topic 3** | Story | Viewing | Study skills | Unit task

Confidence

1 LISTENING Mei's school +radio podcast

1 a) individuelle Lösungen

a) BEFORE YOU LISTEN Do you listen to podcasts or radio shows? If you do, which topics? If you don't, why not? Tell a partner.

Mei is in year 12 at Rosie and Omar's school.

b) Listen to part 1 of Mei's podcast and choose the correct answers.

1 b) 1 C • 2 B • 3 C • 4 A

1 Mei always talks about   A school   B music   C teen problems   on her podcast.
2 When she was younger, Mei   A had lots of friends   B wasn't very confident   C was very happy.
3 Mei thinks that   A she's too young to help   B it's best to talk to a teacher   C she has good advice.   ▶ Box: Voc., p. 221
4 Mei says that it's important to be   A kind to yourself   B nice to others   C sporty.

2 a) 1 yourselves … itself • 2 each other • 3 myself • 4 yourself • 5 ourselves • 6 herself • 7 themselves

2 LOOKING AT LANGUAGE Reflexive pronouns and *each other*

a) Listen to the °whole podcast. Complete the phrases with the reflexive pronouns in the box and *each other*.

> herself • itself • myself •
> ourselves • themselves •
> yourself • yourselves

1 I hope that you'll all enjoy … and that the microphone won't switch … off.
2 The other students just talked to …
3 I didn't like … very much.
4 Be kind to …
5 It's normal that we lose confidence in …
6 Rosie has learned to be kind to …
7 I'll talk about how people give … confidence.

b) Copy and complete the tables with the reflexive pronouns in a).

I	myself	he	*himself*	we	ourselves
you	yourself	she	herself	you (all)	yourselves
		it	itself	they	themselves

c) Look at the sentences in a) again. Choose the correct pronoun for each picture.

They are looking at themselves / each other.

They are looking at themselves / each other.

2 c) A themselves • B each other

▶ Language file 9, p. 178

52 fifty-two

Topic 3 Vorbereitung

Material: Ex 1 ggf. Beispiele für Akrostichon vorbereiten, UMA/CD/App • Ex 2 UMA/CD/App
Zeitbedarf: ca. 2 Std.
Minimalversion: Ex 4a) auslassen
Begleitmedien: WB (S. 40–41), INKL (S. 52–53)

---

3 Confidence problems

3 1 themselves • 2 herself • 3 yourself … yourself • 4 each other

Read the sentences and choose the correct pronouns.

1. Mei wants her ⁺listeners to believe in himself / themselves.
2. She sometimes loses confidence in herself / myself.
3. But if you don't like ourselves / yourself, you can make yourself / itself feel bad.
4. That's why we all have to help each other / themselves.

▶ More practice 7, p. 73

4 READING A confidence role model

a) BEFORE YOU READ °Brainstorm confident people with your class. They could be famous or people from your personal life.

4 a) individuelle Lösungen

b) Mei and Rosie are talking about this article on the podcast. Read it and find three things in the text that Marcus Rashford is famous for.

Marcus Rashford: ⁺Champion of confidence

4 b) Lösung S. 289

Not only is Marcus Rashford a champion footballer, but he's a champion of the people too. He's a very successful player for Manchester United and as an activist, he helps poor children all over the UK to get free meals. He believes that we all need to support each other – just like a football team.

▶ Box: Voc., p. 221

Rashford is certainly keeping himself busy. He has also written two books about confidence: *You are a champion* and *You can do it*. In these books, he gives advice to young people to help them believe in themselves.

Rashford has experienced confidence problems in the past. When he missed a penalty in an important match, some people sent him horrible messages. It wasn't nice to read these nasty things about himself. But he had a lot of support too, and now he's more confident than ever. He says, 'Whenever I hear *no*, I ask myself *why not?*'.

Marcus, all your fans here in Manchester hope that you're proud of yourself – because we're proud of you!

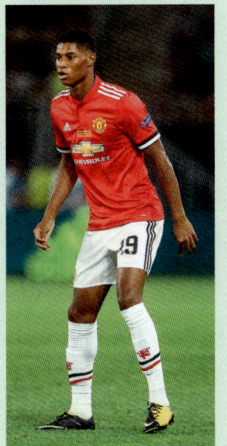

c) Read the article again. Are the °statements true, false or not in the text?

1. Marcus Rashford is only interested in sport.
2. He has scored more goals than any other player.
3. He fights against poverty.
4. He's also a writer.
5. Everyone supported him when he missed a penalty.
6. He wants to stay in Manchester.

4 c) 1 false • 2 not in the text • 3 true • 4 true • 5 false • 6 not in the text

▶ Workbook, pp. 40–41

fifty-three 53

Ex 3 Einstieg:
- (SB zu) ▶ Vokabelrennen zu den Reflexivpronomen aus Ex 2

Erarbeitung:
- (SB auf) gemäß AA ins Heft
- **Ausw.:** ▶ Meldekette
- weitere Übung zu den Reflexivpronomen:
  ▶ More practice 7, S. 73

Ex 4 Einstieg:
- (SB zu) ▶ Who is it? (kann ggf. auch schon mit a) verknüpft werden, indem L vorgibt, dass die gewählten Personen selbstbewusst sein müssen)

Erarbeitung:
a) (SB auf) gemäß AA, im Plenum
- **Sich.:** ▶ Five-minute teacher: S sammelt Ideen im TA.
b) Klären der AA, dann Lesen des Artikels in EA
- **Ausw.:** L: *So, what is Rashford famous for?*
- S nennen die drei Dinge. L: *Are there any words you don't understand?*
- S erfragen unbekannte Wörter, L ▶ semantisiert sie und sichert sie an der ▶ Vokabeltafel.
c) Gemäß AA, S notieren Antworten im Heft.
- **Ausw.:** ▶ Meldekette
- **Alternative:** ▶ Bewegtes Lernen: L liest die Aussagen vor, S stehen für *true* auf, hocken sich für *false* hin und bleiben für *not in the text* sitzen.
- ☒ **Zusatz:** Schnelle S wählen einen Star aus a) und nennen 2–3 Dinge, die sie/ihn selbstbewusst machen. Die anderen raten, um wen es sich handeln könnte.

2

Topic 3 Inhalt

Lernschwerpunkt: Tipps für mehr Selbstvertrauen verstehen und selbst Tipps geben
Kompetenzen: Listening das Thema eines Lieds verstehen • Viewing einem Video Tipps zu selbstbewusstem Auftreten entnehmen • Speaking Komplimente machen und annehmen • Writing/Speaking ein Rollenspiel über Selbstvertrauen schreiben und aufführen
Redemittel: *feelings* • *confidence tips* • *compliments, advice* • *feedback phrases*

Ex 5 Einstieg:
- (SB zu) TA: *Brave*
  L: *Today we will listen to a song called 'Brave'. What do you think you might hear?*
- S äußern Vermutungen, L sichert sie im TA.

Erarbeitung:
a) L zeigt Video gemäß AA.
- S beschreiben, wie sich die Tänzer/-innen im Video fühlen.
- s.a. ▶ Wordbank 4, S. 189
- Sich.: L notiert im TA.
- Zusatz: S beurteilen, ob Vermutungen aus dem Einstieg bestätigt werden können.

b) (SB auf) 1. Hören/Sehen: S wählen die passende Botschaft gemäß AA.
- Ausw.: im Plenum

c) PA gemäß AA
- Ausw.: im Plenum

Ex 6 Einstieg:
- (SB zu) ▶ Word race zum Thema *confidence* (z. B. *confidence tips, feelings, …*)

Erarbeitung:
a) (SB auf) AA und Beispiel lesen, dann PA gemäß AA
- Ausw.: ▶ Blitzlicht im Plenum

b) S schreiben Tabelle ins Heft.
- 1. Sehen: S tragen die Tipps in die Tabelle ein.
- Ausw.: im Plenum, mit TA

c) PA: S probieren Tipps im geschützten Raum und bewerten sie.
- Ausw.: ▶ Meldekette

d) gemäß AA
- Ausw.: Freiwillige S äußern Erfahrungen im ▶ Blitzlicht.

54

| 2 | Topic 1 | Topic 2 | **Topic 3** | Story | Viewing | Study skills | Unit task |

5 SONG *Brave*

5 a), c) Lösungsbsp. S. 289

a) BEFORE YOU LISTEN Find the music video for *Brave* by Sara Bareilles on the internet and watch the first minute with no sound. How do you think the dancers in the video feel? Discuss ideas with the class.
▶ Wordbank 4, p. 189

b) Now listen to the song. What's its message?

5 b) C

A I don't feel very confident.
B We should all be the same.
C You should believe in yourself.

c) Tell your partner what you think of the song and video. How do they make you feel?

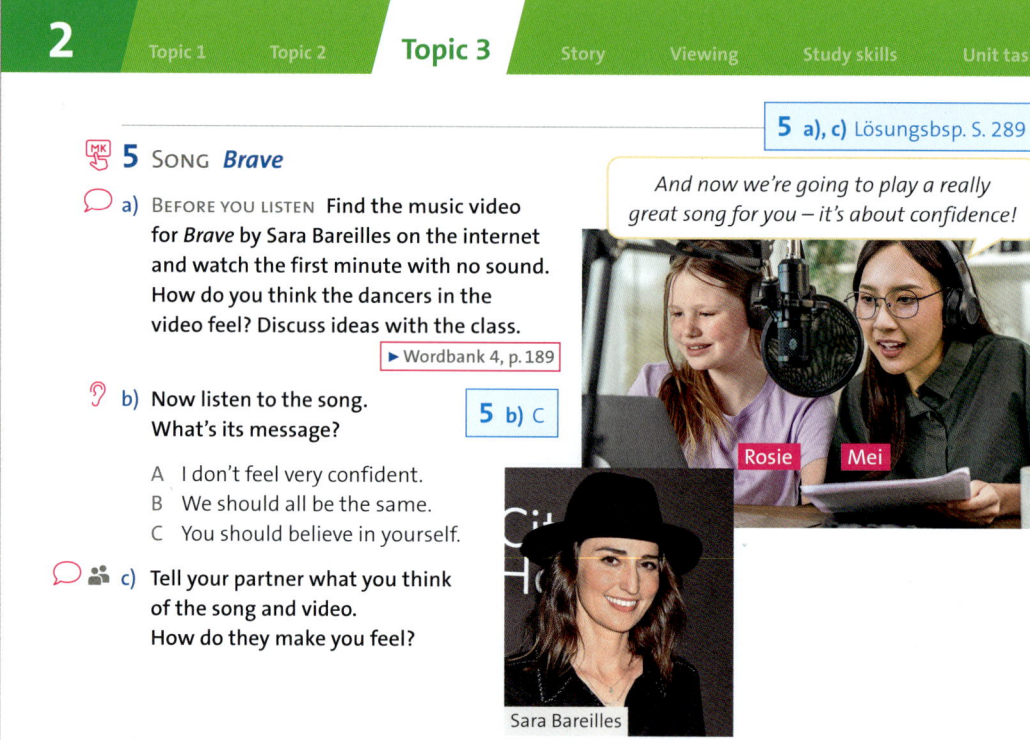

And now we're going to play a really great song for you – it's about confidence!

Rosie   Mei

Sara Bareilles

6 VIEWING **Ways to appear confident**

6 a), b) Lösungsbsp. S. 289

a) BEFORE YOU WATCH Later in the podcast, Mei °recommends a video with confidence tips. Think of some endings to this sentence with a partner.

I feel more confident when I wear my favourite clothes / when I'm with my best friend / when I do yoga / when …

b) Watch the video and take notes. What does Sammy say you should and shouldn't do?

You should …	You shouldn't …
stand up straight	slouch
…	…

Often if you try to appear confident, you feel more confident too!

c) Look at the tips in b) again and try some of them. How useful are the tips for you?
1 = not at all useful   4 = very useful

d) Sammy says you should stand up straight to feel more confident. As a class, stand in a power pose or superhero °pose for 30 seconds. Do you feel more confident?

6 c), d) individuelle Lösungen

54   fifty-four

Topic 3   Vorbereitung

Material: Ex 5 Video zum Lied *Brave* von Sara Bareilles, ggf. geeignete Technik zum Vorführen des Videos • Ex 6 UMA/DVD/App • Ex 8 ggf. Karteikarten o. Ä. für die *prompt cards* (Klassensatz) • ggf. Requisiten für das Rollenspiel (S können sie als HA mitbringen)
Zeitbedarf: ca. 2 Std.
Minimalversion: Ex 5 auslassen
Begleitmedien: WB (S. 42), App (Digital quiz), INKL (S. 54–55), DIFF (2.4)

2

7 SPEAKING Classmate compliments

a) Mei always ends her podcast with compliments. Her listeners send her °anonymous compliments for their classmates.
Make a list of five to ten positive words or phrases to describe people in your class.

b) Tell your partner your ideas. Choose some of their ideas and add them to your list.

c) WALK AROUND Give each other compliments. Remember to say 'thank you' when you get a compliment!

  A Hi, Arlo. I think you're funny and I love your shoes.
  B Thanks, Suki! I want to tell you that you're great at football.
  A Thank you, that's nice of you.
  B You're welcome!

> 7 a) kind, funny, nice, smart, good, clever, well-organized, attractive, …

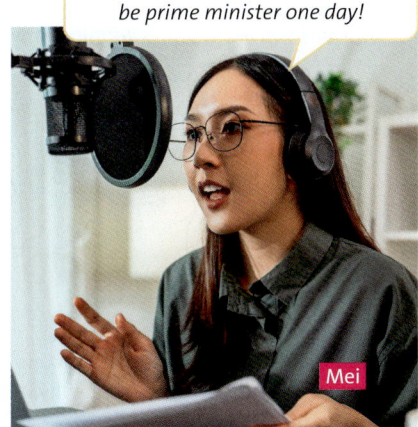

Here's a compliment for Ruby: You're a good leader. Maybe you'll be prime minister one day!

Mei

> 7 b), c) individuelle Lösungen

My task

8 Being confident

a) In groups of three, think of three to five tips for being more confident. The ideas in 6 b) can help you.

b) ROLE-PLAY Write a short role-play about meeting for the first time. It should have three parts:
  1 Student A meets student B. Student B is nervous and not very confident.
  2 Student C gives student B some tips for being confident. (Use *You should/shouldn't* …)
  3 Students A and B repeat the first part of the role-play. This time, student B uses the tips and is more confident.

c) Make cards with keywords to help you remember what you want to say.

d) Do your role-play for another group and listen to their role-play. Give each other compliments and advice.

You ⁺spoke clearly. / You gave some very useful tips. / …
Next time, you should add more tips / remember the words better / …

> 8 a) Wear your favourite clothes. • Smile. • Don't slouch. • Stand up straight. • …

> ▶ More help, p. 73

You should stand up straight.

> ▶ Let's talk: Feedback, p. 200
> ▶ Workbook, p. 42
> 8 b), c), d) individuelle Lösungen

Digital quiz   I can talk about confidence. ✓

fifty-five 55

Ex 7 Einstieg:
- (SB zu) ▶Word race zu diesen Kategorien: *describing a person, positive adjectives, skills, hobbies* (ggf. je zwei Beispiele vorbereiten)

Erarbeitung:

a) (SB auf) AA und Kompliment in der Sprechblase lesen.
- S erstellen Liste u. nutzen die Wörter aus dem Einstieg als Hilfe für ihre Komplimente.

b) Austausch in PA gemäß AA

c) gemeinsames Lesen der AA und des Beispieldialogs im Plenum
- Austausch der Komplimente im ▶Milling around
- **Ausw.:** Freiwillige S-Paare stellen Dialog im Plenum vor.

My task Ex 8 Einstieg:
- (SB zu) ▶Milling around: L nennt Gefühle (*nervous, shy, confident, happy, unhappy, …*).
- S stellen das jeweilige Gefühl schauspielerisch dar (oder begrüßen sich entsprechend).

Erarbeitung:

a) (SB auf) GA gemäß AA
- 🎬 L erinnert an **Ex 6b)**, S. 54.

b) GA gemäß AA
- 🎬 ▶More help, S. 73
- weitere Hinweise s. S. 73

c) S schreiben *prompt cards* gemäß AA und üben das Rollenspiel mehrmals.
- ⊠ Lernstärkere S versuchen das Rollenspiel ohne Text.

d) **Ausw.:** S spielen sich das Rollenspiel in Gruppen vor und geben sich Feedback.

55

2

Story Inhalt

Lernschwerpunkt: eine Geschichte über einen Konflikt bei einem Fußballspiel lesen
Kompetenzen: Speaking über Sportarten/Spiele und das Gewinnen sprechen • Reading der Geschichte Informationen zu den Charakteren und ihrem Konflikt entnehmen
Redemittel: *sports and games, football* • *dealing with conflicts*

Ex 1 Einstieg:
- (SB zu) L zeigt die Piktogramme aus Ex 1 (UMA). S benennen die Aktivitäten. L notiert (TA).
- Ggf. TA mit weiteren Aktivitäten ergänzen, die die S interessieren.

Erarbeitung:
- (SB auf) S tauschen sich gemäß AA aus (PA oder ▶ Milling around).
- Ausw.: ▶ Blitzlichtrunde

Ex 2 Einstieg:
- (SB zu) L: *Do you know any football teams in Manchester? What are their colours?*
- S nennen die Teams Manchester United (*red*) und Manchester City (*blue*).
- L hilft ggf. mit Bildimpulsen.
- L zeigt das Bild mit Omar, seiner Schwester und seinem Vater von S. 56 (UMA).
- S beschreiben das Bild und stellen Vermutungen an, was in der Geschichte passieren könnte.

Erarbeitung:
- GA: Gruppen bekommen den kopierten Text der Story in Schnipseln (Abschnitte: Z. 1–13, Z. 14–22, Z. 23–37, Z. 38–52 und Nachricht, Z. 53–65). Der letzte Abschnitt wird noch nicht mit ausgeteilt.
- S lesen die Textschnipsel in ihrer Gruppe und ordnen sie in der richtigen Reihenfolge.
- ⊠/⊡ Lernstärkere S können außerdem die Bilder den Textabschnitten zuordnen. Bei schwächeren Gruppen sollten sie mit vorgegeben sein.
- Forts. s. S. 57

---

2   Topic 1   Topic 2   Topic 3   **Story**   Viewing   Study skills   Unit task

A Manchester match

1 individuelle Lösungen

💬👥 **1 BEFORE YOU READ Sports and games**

Tell a partner about your favourite sports or games and why you like them. Is winning important to you?

My favourite sport / game is … because it's …
Winning is / isn't important to me.

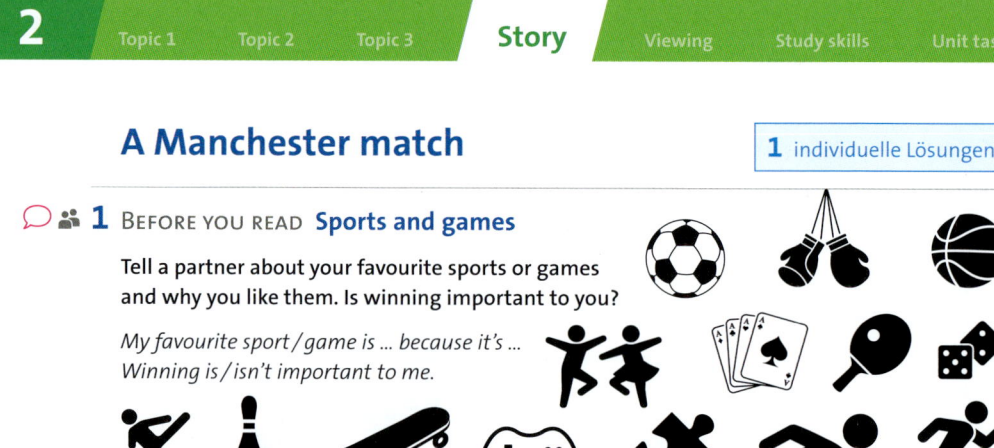

📖 **2 READING More than a game**

2 Lösungsbsp. S. 289

Read the story. Say who the characters in the story are and which team they support. Explain what the conflict is and why it happens.

Omar, his … and his … support …
Omar's best friend … and … support …
The conflict is between … and … because …

🔊 1.13

Omar[1] was so excited. The next day was the football match of the year between Manchester City and Manchester United. Omar, his dad and his sister had tickets
5 for the match.
'You know that Manchester City will win, right?' Omar said to his best friend Trent. Trent's older cousin Ollie was a Manchester United supporter and the two cousins
10 had tickets too. 'Do you want to change sides and support the best team?'
'No way,' laughed Trent. 'I want to see your face when Manchester United wins!'

Finally, it was the day of the match. Omar
15 put on his blue Manchester City football shirt and his scarf and smiled at himself in the mirror. He felt really happy.
'Come on,' said his sister. 'Stop admiring yourself! We shouldn't be late.' They took
20 the bus to the stadium and got in the queue with hundreds of other Manchester City supporters, all dressed in blue.

Trent   Omar

Omar's sister and dad   Omar

1 [ˈəʊmɑː]

Story Vorbereitung

Material: Ex 1 UMA • Ex 2 ggf. von L recherchierte Fotos der Trikots der beiden Fußballvereine aus Manchester, UMA, Kopien des Texts als Textpuzzle (Abschnitte siehe unten, eine Kopie pro Gruppe), ggf. auch Kopien der Bilder von S. 56–57
Zeitbedarf: ca. 1 Std.
Begleitmedien: INKL (S.56–57)

🎵 'We are City, super City, from Maine Road,' sang the fans and Omar sang with them.
25 🎵 'City, City, the best team in the land, in all the world.' The players came onto the pitch and the fans went crazy.
Omar's phone pinged. It was Trent.

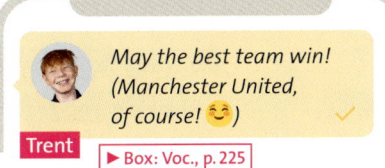

May the best team win! (Manchester United, of course! 😊)
Trent
▶ Box: Voc., p. 225

Omar read the message and laughed.
30 'In your dreams, Trent!' he thought.

At half-time there were no goals.
'I can't believe they missed those two chances,' Omar's dad said as they queued for a hot dog.
35 'They were +unlucky,' said Omar's sister. 'Just wait! The boys in blue will show them who are the best players.'

The next half was fast and exciting. The fans sang and Omar was so proud of his team.
40 But suddenly the players in red started running towards the goal, the Manchester City goalkeeper came out too far and the ball was in the net. 'Yes!' screamed the Manchester United fans. Omar, his sister
45 and his dad were silent. Omar was really disappointed. +Ping! Another text from Trent. Omar looked at the message, but then pushed his phone back in his pocket. He felt angry with Trent.
50 A few minutes later, Manchester City's best player hit the ball into the net. Omar cheered and texted Trent back.

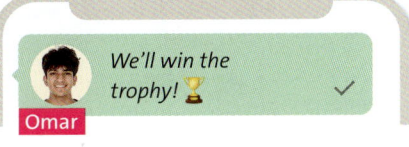

We'll win the trophy! 🏆
Omar

After 90 minutes the score was still 1-1, but there were three minutes of additional
55 time. Omar crossed his fingers in his pockets. Two minutes later Manchester City scored! Omar, his dad and his sister hugged each other and all around the stadium the Manchester City fans clapped and sang:
60 🎵 'This is the most amazing day: United lose, City hooray! For fans and team we win and play!' Omar got his phone to text Trent, but then he put it back. He knew how bad his friend
65 felt and he didn't want to be mean.

Omar and his family left the stadium. Outside, some unhappy Manchester United fans called the Manchester City fans nasty names and took their scarves. Omar's dad
70 told Omar and his sister not to look at them and just keep walking. But a little further on they saw Trent and his cousin Ollie. Trent looked down. Ollie didn't know Omar was Trent's friend. When he saw Omar and his
75 family, he smiled nastily and called them racist names. Then he pushed Omar's dad. Omar's dad tried to pull Omar away, but Omar stood in front of Trent and looked straight at him. 'Are you my friend or not?'
80 he asked. ▶ Box: Voc., p. 223

Omar — Olli — Trent

fifty-seven 57

Ex 2 (Forts. von S. 56)
- S stellen Vermutungen an, was nach dem Spiel passiert.
- (SB auf) **Ausw.:** S prüfen ihre Reihenfolge mit dem Originaltext und ändern ggf. die Reihenfolge ihrer Schnipsel.
- S bekommen den fehlenden letzten Textbaustein. Sie lesen das Ende und überprüfen ihre Vermutungen.
- S lesen die AA von Ex 2, S. 56.
- Sie lesen die Geschichte erneut und markieren auf ihrer Kopie die Antworten.
- S schlagen beim Lesen unbekannte Vokabeln im *Vocabulary* (S. 222–223) nach und notieren sie in ihrem *Vocab file*.
- **Ausw.:** ▶ Meldekette für die Aufgaben aus der AA. S nennen hierbei nicht nur die Antwort, sondern auch die zugehörigen Zeilenangaben. L kann die Stellen im UMA zeigen und markieren.
- L sammelt den neuen Wortschatz an der ▶ Vokabeltafel und übt ggf. die Aussprache (▶ Lautschulung).
- ☒ Zusatzaufgabe für lernstärkere S oder ▶ Early finishers: *Make a multiple-choice quiz about the story.*
- **Ausw.:** S stellen ihre Quizfragen, der Rest der Klasse rät.

57

2

Story Inhalt

Lernschwerpunkt: eine Geschichte über einen Konflikt verstehen und Lösungsvorschläge entwickeln
Kompetenzen: Reading dem Text Informationen entnehmen • Speaking / Life skills über den Umgang mit Konflikten sprechen • Writing eigenes Ende der Geschichte schreiben • Listening Ende der Geschichte hören
Redemittel: *dealing with conflicts • discussion phrases*

Vorbereitung

Material: Ex 3 ggf. UMA • Ex 5 UMA • Ex 6 UMA/CD/App
Zeitbedarf: ca. 1 Std.
Minimalversion: Ex 4 oder Ex 6a) auslassen
Begleitmedien: WB (S. 43), App (Digital quiz), INKL (S. 58), DIFF (2.5)

Ex 3 Einstieg:
- (SB zu) Falls nicht direkt im Anschluss an das Lesen: L zeigt noch einmal die Bilder der Story (UMA), S fassen zusammen, was passiert.

Erarbeitung:
- (SB auf) S notieren die korrekte Reihenfolge im Heft.
- **Ausw.:** ▶ Five-minute teacher

Ex 4 Erarbeitung:
- (SB auf) S lesen und besprechen die drei Antwortmöglichkeiten in PA.
- **Ausw.:** ▶ Four corners (hier nur drei Ecken): S entscheiden sich für A, B oder C.

Ex 5 Einstieg:
- (SB zu) L: *Have you ever been in a conflict? What did you do?*
- S berichten.

Erarbeitung:
a) (SB auf) S lesen AA und suchen dann in EA die Antworten im Text (mit Zeilenangaben).
  - **Ausw.:** S zeigen ihre Lösungen (UMA).
b) S diskutieren gemäß AA in PA.
  - **Ausw.:** ▶ Meldekette

Ex 6 Erarbeitung:
a) (SB auf) gemäß AA in PA
  - Lernschwächere S entwerfen stattdessen in PA oder GA ein Standbild.
  - **Ausw.:** Vorstellung einiger Enden im Plenum
b) (SB zu) S hören das Ende und beschreiben, was passiert.
  - **Ausw.:** S vergleichen im Plenum das Ende der Story mit ihren Ideen.

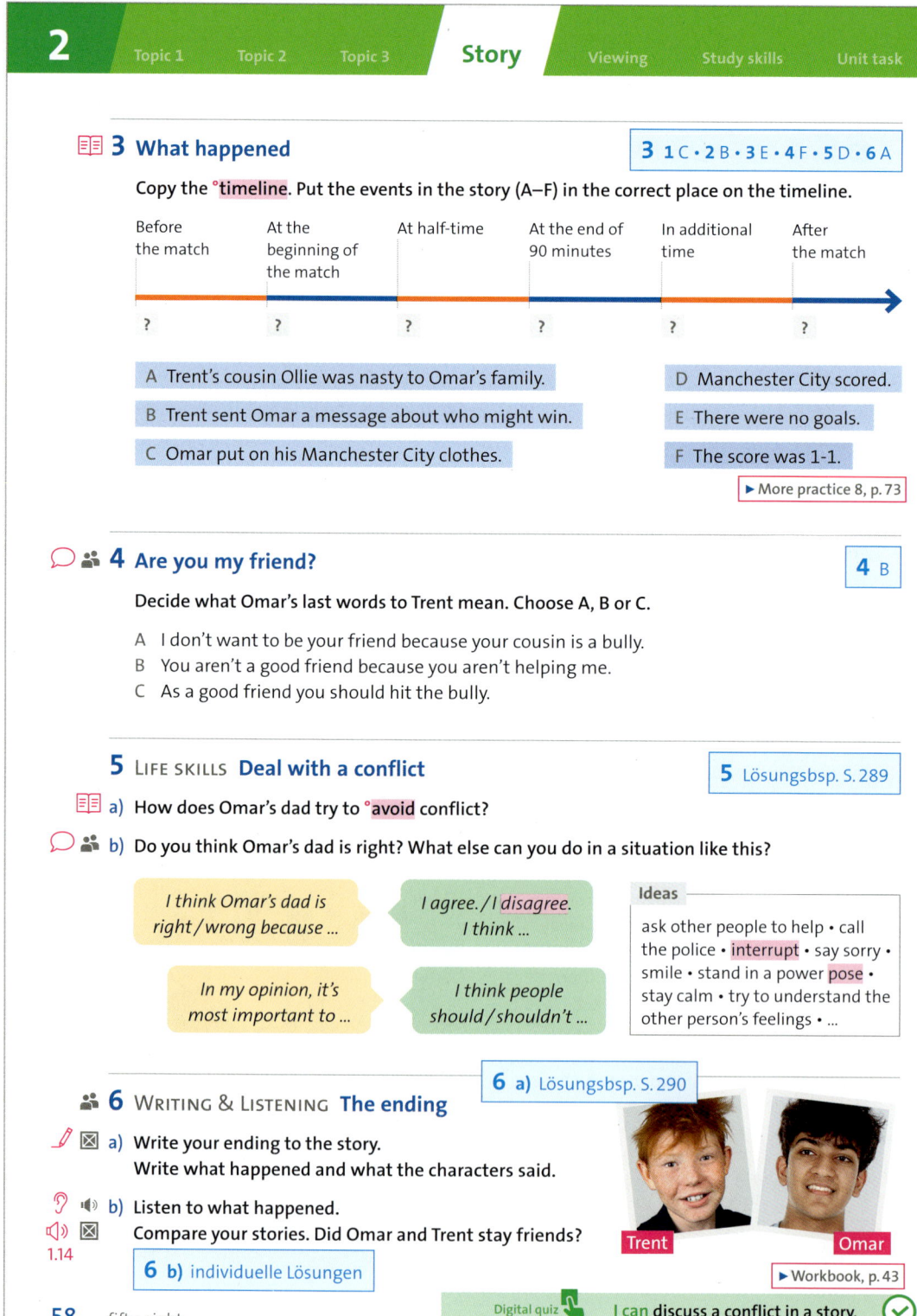

58

2

Viewing Inhalt

Lernschwerpunkt: Filmszenen zu einem Konflikt zwischen Fußballfans verstehen
Kompetenzen: Speaking anhand von Bildern Vermutungen über den Inhalt des Films anstellen • die eigene Meinung zum Film äußern • Viewing Filmszenen verstehen
Redemittel: *feelings • conflicts*

Vorbereitung

Material: Ex 1 UMA • Ex 2 UMA/DVD/App
Zeitbedarf: ca. 1 Std.
Minimalversion: Ex 3 auslassen
Begleitmedien: INKL (S. 59)

| Topic 1 | Topic 2 | Topic 3 | Story | **Viewing** | Study skills | Unit task | **2** |

Coach

1 Lösungsbsp. S. 290

1 On a trip

BEFORE YOU WATCH Look at the photos of David and his dad from the film. What do you think might happen in the film? The questions can help you.

1. Where are they going?
2. Why does David have an English flag?
3. Who is on the coach?
4. What happens to the car and what do they do?
5. Why does David's dad pull him away at the service station?

2 a) individuelle Lösungen

2 VIEWING What happens

a) Watch the film. Were some of your ideas from 1 in the film?

b) Put the events in the correct order. Then watch the video again and check.

1 e, 2 ...

a There's a problem with one of the car's tyres.
b A coach with an England flag goes past.
c Something happens at the service station and David's dad is angry.
d David's dad decides that they can go on the coach.
e In the car, David and his dad talk about the trip.
f David gets on the coach alone and a fan stops David's dad.
g An England fan from the coach says that David and his dad can travel with them.

2 b) 1 e • 2 b • 3 a • 4 g • 5 d • 6 c • 7 f

3 What do you think?

3 Lösungsbsp. S. 290

Talk about the questions.

1. Why was David's dad angry? What do you think happened at the service station?
2. Why did David change his mind and help his dad?
3. What did you think of the film? What was good and what was bad?

I liked the part when … / I didn't like the part when …

fifty-nine **59**

Ex 1 Einstieg:
- (SB zu) L zeigt die Bilder von S. 59 (UMA). S beschreiben sie.
- ⊠ S spielen ▶ Three truths, two lies bei der Bildbeschreibung.

Erarbeitung:
- (SB auf) Gemäß AA in PA: S stellen mithilfe der Fragen Vermutungen zur Handlung an.
- **Ausw.:** ▶ Five-minute teacher

Ex 2 Einstieg:
- (SB zu) ▶ Get-up game mit diesen Sätzen:
Get up if you have ever …
… gone to another country.
… got a very special birthday present.
… gone to a football match.
… got into a fight with your parents.

Erarbeitung:
a) (SB auf) 1. Sehen: gemäß AA
- **Ausw.:** ▶ Partner check

b) S bringen die Ereignisse in die richtige Reihenfolge und notieren sie im Heft.
- **2. Sehen:** S prüfen.
- **Ausw.:** ▶ Five-minute teacher

Ex 3 Einstieg:
- (SB zu) S schreiben je drei Quizfragen über den Film.
- ▶ Milling around: S stellen sich die Quizfragen und prüfen die Antworten.

Erarbeitung:
- (SB auf) S besprechen die Fragen in PA und notieren wichtige Punkte stichwortartig.
- ⊠ L geht umher u. unterstützt lernschwächere S mit Ideen.
- **Ausw.:** im Plenum

59

2

Study skills Inhalt

Lernschwerpunkt: seine Meinung äußern und begründen
Kompetenzen: Speaking/Writing seine Meinung ausdrücken, zustimmen und widersprechen • Study skills Redemittel zur Meinungsäußerung sammeln und einordnen
Redemittel: opinion phrases • agreeing and disagreeing

Vorbereitung

Zeitbedarf: ca. 1 Std.
Minimalversion: Ex 1c) u. 2b) auslassen
Begleitmedien: App (Digital quiz), INKL (S. 60), DIFF (2.6)

Ex 1 Einstieg:
- (SB zu) TA: Überschrift: *Explain your opinion,* dann Tabelle mit drei Spalten: *give your opinion, agree, disagree*
  L: *Today you will learn how to explain your opinion. Do you know any phrases yet?*
- S nennen ihnen bekannte Phrasen, L notiert sie im TA.

Erarbeitung:
a) (SB auf) PA gemäß AA
- **Ausw.:** Vergleich im Plenum

b) Lesen der AA. L: *Can we add anything to our list?* S nennen neue Phrasen, L ergänzt TA.
- **Sich.:** S übertragen den TA in ihr *Vocab file*.

c) EA: S schreiben neue Meinungen gemäß AA ins Heft.
- **Ausw.:** Austausch in PA

Ex 2 Erarbeitung:
a) (SB auf) gemäß AA
- **Ausw.:** ▶ Five-minute teacher

b) S schreiben Begründungen gemäß AA ins Heft.
- **Ausw.:** Vorstellung im Plenum

Ex 3 Erarbeitung:
- (SB auf) gemäß AA
- **Sich.:** TA aus Ex 1 ergänzen, ins *Vocab file* übertragen.

Ex 4 Einstieg:
- (SB zu) ▶ Vokabelrennen zu den Phrasen aus Ex 1 und Ex 3

Erarbeitung:
- (SB auf) ▶ Milling around gemäß AA
- **Ausw.:** ▶ Blitzlichtrunde mit einzelnen Meinungen
- s. a. ▶ SF 5, S. 160

---

2 | Topic 1 | Topic 2 | Topic 3 | Story | Viewing | **Study skills** | Unit task

Explain your opinion

💬 **1 Give your opinion**

👥 a) Tell a partner which opinions in the °speech bubbles (A–E) you agree with. How many opinions do you have °in common?

✏️ b) Opinion phrases can help you in a discussion. Find the five opinion phrases in the speech bubbles. Add them to your VOCAB FILE. ▶ Skills file 1, p. 155

I think, ...

💬👥 c) Change the underlined words and write new opinions. Then tell your partner.

A — *I think that football is the best sport.*
B — *In my opinion, pineapple on pizza is delicious.*
C — *If you ask me, snakes are scary.*
D — *I believe that we should learn coding at school.*
E — *I would say that fashion is stupid.*

1 a), c) individuelle Lösungen

1 b) I think • In my opinion • If you ask me • I believe • I would say

📖 **2 Give reasons**

a) Match the opinions in 1 (A–E) to the reasons below.
1 ... because they're fast and can be dangerous.
2 ... because it's both sweet and savoury.
3 ... because lots of people love it and it's exciting when the players score goals.
4 ... because it's expensive and clothes aren't important.
5 ... because it's a useful skill for the future and I like technology.

b) Think of reasons for your new opinions from 1c).

2 a) 1 C • 2 B • 3 A • 4 E • 5 D

2 b) individuelle Lösungen

📖 **3 Agree or disagree**

Order the phrases in the box along a line of °agreement.

1 (agree) ———— 6 (disagree)

Phrases
- I don't agree with you at all.
- I completely agree.
- Yes, you're so right.
- I don't think that's true.
- That's a good point.
- I see it a bit differently.

▶ Box: Voc., p. 224

3 I completely agree. • Yes, you're so right. • That's a good point. • I see it a bit differently • I don't think that's true. • I don't agree with you at all.

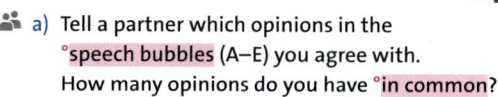

💬👥✉️ **4 WALK AROUND Quick opinions**

Your teacher says two things, for example 'cats and dogs'. Use the opinion phrases in 1 and tell different partners which you like better and why. Your partner agrees or disagrees and gives a reason. Remember to be polite!

In my opinion, dogs are better than cats because they're kind and friendly.
— I don't agree with you at all. I would say that cats are better because ...

4 individuelle Lösungen

▶ Skills file 5, p. 160

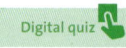 Digital quiz — I can give and explain my opinion.

2

Unit task Inhalt

Lernschwerpunkt: an einer Diskussion teilnehmen
Kompetenzen: Speaking Pro und Kontra eines Themas überlegen und diskutieren • Feedback geben
Redemittel: opinion phrases • feedback phrases • phrases for 'buying time'

Vorbereitung

Material: Einstieg UMA • Step 1 Karten für die Festlegung des Themas (möglichst so groß, dass man sie in Step 4 an die Tafel heften kann) • Step 3 ▶ KV 2.3: Discussion tickets (nach Bedarf) • Step 4 ▶ KV 2.2: Giving feedback (Part 2, Klassensatz)
Zeitbedarf: ca. 2 Std.
Begleitmedien: App (Digital help, Digital quiz), INKL (S. 61)

Topic 1   Topic 2   Topic 3   Story   Viewing   Study skills   **Unit task 2**

Have a discussion

Unit task individuelle Lösungen

Step 1: Choose a topic ▶ Digital help

Work in groups of four. Choose a topic to discuss. Use the ideas in the box or your own ideas.

Ideas
- Is … the best football team?
- Should we all buy 'green' clothes?
- Should we have a school uniform?
- Is … the best place to live?
- …

Step 2: Think of reasons ▶ Digital help

Two students will argue one opinion and two students will argue the opposite. With your partner, think of reasons for your role's opinion.

💡 You might **argue** an opinion that you don't really agree with – but that's OK! Sometimes it's fun to play a role and argue a different opinion.

▶ Study skills, p. 60

Pia & Elias	We should buy green clothes because it's better for the planet, …
Ivan & Meri	We can't all buy green clothes because they're expensive, …

Step 3: Practise your discussion

Practise your discussion in your group. °Make sure that you take turns to speak. Use opinion phrases.

Pia	I believe that we should …
Ivan	I don't agree with you at all. I think …
Elias	I see it a bit differently. In my opinion, …
Meri	I don't think that's true.

Step 4: Give feedback

Have your discussions in class.
Give each group feedback.

I agree with Pia and Elias, but I think Ivan and Meri gave very good reasons too.

Elias, next time you could use more opinion phrases.

💡 In a discussion, you can 'buy time' with these phrases:
- Just a minute.
- Let me think.
- Well, …

▶ Let's talk: Feedback, p. 200

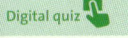 I can have a discussion.

sixty-one 61

Unit task Einstieg:
- (SB zu) ▶ Milling around wie in Ex 4, S. 60
- (SB auf) gemeinsames Klären der AA für alle Schritte, Lesen der ▶ Tippbox, S. 60, Step 2
- 📄 In schwachen Klassen die Themen für **Step 1** (s. Kasten) präsentieren (UMA).

Step 1 Erarbeitung:
- ▶ Gruppenbildung
- S suchen sich ein Thema aus, s. a. *Digital help* (App).
- S nutzen bei der Diskussion hierzu schon die Phrasen von S. 60 (*Vocab file*).
- **Ausw.:** S schreiben gewähltes Thema auf eine Karte.

Step 2 Erarbeitung:
- gemäß AA in PA, s. a. *Digital help* (App)
- S notieren Argumente im Heft.

Step 3 Erarbeitung:
- GA: S üben, ihre Argumente vorzubringen.
- **Hinweis:** ▶ Discussion tickets können für gleichmäßige Redeanteile u. die Verwendung aller Phrasen sorgen. Dazu verteilt L 4–5 Tickets der ▶ KV 2.3 an jedes S-Paar.

Step 4 Erarbeitung:
- Gruppen stellen ihre Diskussion im Plenum vor.
- **Ausw.:** S geben sich gegenseitig Feedback (s. ▶ KV 2.2 (Part 2)).
- **Hinweis:** Vor dem Vortrag die Feedbackkategorien unter den einzelnen Gruppen aufteilen, um die Verbindlichkeit und Beteiligung zu erhöhen.

2

Checkpoint Inhalt

Lernschwerpunkt: Kompetenzen und sprachliche Mittel üben, Lernfortschritte erkennen
Kompetenzen: Listening einem Podcast Informationen entnehmen • Speaking sich zum Thema nachhaltige Mode austauschen • Writing jemandem einen Rat geben • Mediation einen englischen Ratschlag auf Deutsch wiedergeben
Strukturen: modal verbs
Redemittel: important things • green fashion • giving advice

Allgemeine Anmerkung:
s. Unit 1, S. 32

Ex 1 Einstieg:
- (SB auf) Selbsteinschätzung zum Lernziel (▶ Thumbs up)

Erarbeitung:
a) PA: S finden Überschriften zu den Bildern A–F. L sammelt diese im TA (Hilfe für lernschwächere S).
- S bringen die Bilder in ihre persönliche Reihenfolge und notieren diese auf ▶ KV 2.4 (Ex 1a).
- PA: Austausch zur persönlichen Reihenfolge (mit Begründung)

b) S nutzen ▶ KV 2.4 (Ex 1b + c).
- 1. Hören: S füllen die erste Tabellenzeile aus.

c) 2. Hören: S notieren die Gründe aus dem Hörtext.
- Ausw.: ▶ Bus stop (▶ KV Extra): S vergleichen ihre Lösungen mithilfe von ▶ KV 2.5A.
- Alternative: ▶ Partner check mit 3. Hören
- erneute Selbsteinschätzung

Ex 2 Einstieg:
- (SB auf) Selbsteinschätzung s. Ex 1

Erarbeitung:
a) S lösen das Quiz auf ▶ KV 2.4 (Ex 2).
- Ausw.: ▶ Bus stop (▶ KV Extra): S vergleichen ihre Lösungen mithilfe von ▶ KV 2.5A.
- Alternative: Vergleich im Plenum (UMA)

b) PA gemäß AA
- Alternative: ▶ Double circle
- Ausw.: Beispiele im Plenum
- erneute Selbsteinschätzung

62

---

2 Checkpoint — Digital checkpoint

1 LISTENING Mei's podcast
I can explain what's important to me.

1 a) Lösungsbsp. S. 290

a) What's important to you? Put the pictures (A–F) °in order. Then tell a partner. Say why.

b) Copy the table. Then listen to the podcast. What's important to the students? Choose the correct picture (A–F) for each person. There are two extra pictures.
1.15

	Ethan[1]	Hafsa	Ryan	Laura
picture	D – home	A – hockey team	F – grandparents	C – travel
reason	...	...	...	...

c) Listen again. Write the reason why this is important to them.

1 c) Lösungsbsp. S. 290

2 A quiz for Green Clothes Day
I can talk about fashion.

a) WORDS Look at the quiz. Write the correct words (1–7) in your exercise book.

2 a) 1 reuse • 2 swap • 3 cotton • 4 polyester • 5 attractive • 6 material • 7 repair – upcycle

www.our-school-magazine.example.net/green-clothes-day

Tomorrow is Green Clothes Day and we made a quiz for you! There's a prize for the first person who emails us with the correct word in the green boxes.

When you wear second-hand clothes, you **R** ☐☐☐☐ (1) them.
You don't need to buy new clothes. You can also **W** ☐☐☐ (2) clothes with a friend!
It's a natural material for clothes: ☐☐**T**☐☐☐ (3)
To keep our seas free from plastic, don't wear too many ☐**O**☐☐☐☐☐☐☐ (4) clothes.
Old-fashioned clothes can look trendy and **A**☐☐☐☐☐☐**V**☐ (5)!
You can use old **M**☐☐☐☐☐☐☐ (6) to make new clothes.
There's a problem with your jacket? Don't buy a new one, ☐☐**P**☐☐☐ (7) it!

b) SPEAKING What are you going to wear on Green Clothes Day? Talk to a partner. Use the ideas from a) and your own ideas.

I'm (not) going to buy / upcycle / wear / … • The material is … • I think my outfit will look …

1 [ˈiːθən]

2 b) Lösungsbsp. S. 290

Check

sixty-two

2

Checkpoint Vorbereitung

Material: alle Aufgaben ▶ KV Extra: Bus stop, ▶ KV 2.5A: Checkpoint answers, App (Check) • Ex 1 UMA/CD/App, ▶ KV 2.4: Mei's podcast / A quiz for Green Clothes Day (Klassensatz) • Ex 2 ▶ KV 2.4, UMA • Ex 4 ggf. A5-Zettel oder Karteikarten für *Swap cards* (Klassensatz)
Zeitbedarf: ca. 1–2 Std.
Minimalversion: Auswahl der Aufgaben erfolgt entsprechend der zu überprüfenden Lernziele
Begleitmedien: App (Digital checkpoint), INKL (S. 62–63)

Die Übungen kannst du auch digital machen.

2

3 Aya's[1] problem

3 a) 1 B • 2 C • 3 A • 4 B • 5 C

I can give advice (mustn't, have to, needn't, not be allowed to, should). ✓

a) LANGUAGE Complete Zoe[2] and Aya's messages. Choose the correct verb.

Zoe Hey. Are you OK? You looked really sad at school today.
Aya I'm OK. I'm just a bit worried about something 🙁.
Zoe What is it?
Aya (1) Well, I'm not A have to B allowed to C should come to your party. (2) My parents say I A don't have to B shouldn't C have to do my school work on Sunday because we're busy on Saturday. I'm so sorry.
Zoe Oh. That's sad. (3) I think you A should B allowed to C mustn't talk to your parents again. Maybe you could do your school work on Sunday morning? (4) And you A shouldn't B needn't C mustn't stay for all of the party. Maybe you could come for two hours?
Aya Thanks, Zoe. I think you're right. I'll talk to them tomorrow.
Zoe OK. °Good luck. (5) And Aya – you A must B have to C mustn't worry too much about it. If you can't come, we'll find another day to celebrate!

b) WRITING Write your own message to Aya. Give advice about what she should do. Use the ideas from a) and the phrases below to help you.

3 b) Lösungsbsp. S. 290

> Hi, Aya • I understand why you're feeling … • I think you should / shouldn't … • Try (not) to … • Maybe you can …? • If you …

4 Lösungsbsp. S. 291

4 MEDIATION Ole's problem

SadBoy has written to the *Hey!* advice column about a problem with his best friend. Read the answer and tell your German friend Ole about it – he has the same problem.

> Dear SadBoy
> Thank you for your letter. We understand that you're feeling sad about your friend. It's difficult when your best friend has a new girlfriend and you can't spend so much time together. We think you should explain to your friend how you're feeling. Try to stay calm when you talk to him. We're sure he didn't want to upset you. Maybe you can agree on a special activity every week that's just for the two of you?
> The *Hey!* advice column

Lieber Ole,
ich habe gerade in einer englischen Schulzeitung über einen Jungen gelesen, der das gleiche Problem hat wie du: …   Das Zeitungsteam rät ihm, …   Er soll …   Vielleicht …
Schöne Grüße

1 [ˈaɪə] 2 [ˈzəʊi]

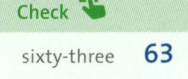
Check

sixty-three **63**

Ex 3 Einstieg:
- (SB auf) Selbsteinschätzung s. Ex 1
- ggf. ▶ Vokabelrennen zur Reaktivierung der modalen Hilfsverben aus der Aufgabe

Erarbeitung:
a) S schreiben Lösungen ins Heft.
- **Ausw.:** ▶ Bus stop (▶ KV Extra): S vergleichen ihre Lösungen mithilfe von ▶ KV 2.5A.

b) S schreiben eine eigene Nachricht gemäß AA.
- **Ausw.:** ▶ Partner check am ▶ Bus stop (▶ KV Extra): S vergleichen ihre Lösungen mithilfe von ▶ KV 2.5A.
- S geben sich Feedback zu ihrem Text.
- Zwei bis drei Arbeiten werden im Plenum vorgestellt.

Ex 4 Einstieg:
- (SB zu) S schreiben ein Problem auf einen Zettel oder eine Karte. Im ▶ Milling around nennen S ihr Problem, Partner/-in gibt Tipp, was sie tun könnten. Die Zettel werden als ▶ Swap cards genutzt.

Erarbeitung:
- (SB auf) S lesen den Brief.
- S verfassen eine Nachricht auf Deutsch gemäß AA.
- **Ausw.:** ▶ Partner check am ▶ Bus stop (▶ KV Extra): S vergleichen ihre Lösungen mithilfe von ▶ KV 2.5A.
- Ggf. ist es sinnvoll, im TA inhaltliche und formelle Kriterien für eine gute Lösung zu sammeln und diese für den ▶ Partner check zu nutzen.
- erneute Selbsteinschätzung

63

2

Checkpoint Inhalt

Lernschwerpunkt: Kompetenzen und sprachliche Mittel üben, Lernfortschritte erkennen
Kompetenzen: Speaking sich zum Thema Selbstvertrauen austauschen • Study skills Redemittel zur Meinungsäußerung verwenden • Reading einem Text über einen Konflikt Informationen entnehmen
Redemittel: confidence • opinion phrases • agreeing and disagreeing • dealing with conflicts

---

Ex 5 Einstieg:
- (SB auf) Selbsteinschätzung zum Lernziel (▶Thumbs up)
- ▶Milling around: L liest ein Wort aus dem Reservoir vor. S setzen es schauspielerisch um und begrüßen sich mit der jeweiligen Pose.

Erarbeitung:

a) + b) S machen sich Notizen gemäß AA.

c) Austausch zu a) u. b) in PA gemäß AA
- ✉ Lernstärkere S können die *opinion phrases* von S.60 nutzen, um den Lösungen des Partners / der Partnerin zuzustimmen oder zu widersprechen.
- **Ausw.:** Beispiele im Plenum
- erneute Selbsteinschätzung

Ex 6 Einstieg:
- (SB auf) Selbsteinschätzung s. Ex 5
- ▶Vokabelrennen zu den *opinion phrases* von S.60

Erarbeitung:

a) S übertragen Sätze mit jeweils einer *opinion phrase* ins Heft.
- ✉ Lernschwächere S können ihr *Vocab file* nutzen.

b) gemäß AA

c) S äußern und begründen ihre Meinung gemäß AA.
- **Ausw.:** ▶Partner check am ▶Bus stop (▶KV Extra): S vergleichen ihre Lösungen mithilfe von ▶KV 2.5B. Partner/-in achtet auf die Verwendung mehrerer unterschiedlicher Phrasen.
- erneute Selbsteinschätzung

64

---

2 Checkpoint   Digital checkpoint

5 a), b) Lösungsbsp. S. 291

💬 **5 SPEAKING Looking and feeling confident**   I can talk about confidence. ✓

✏ a) Look at the pictures (1–4): Who looks confident? Who doesn't look confident? Why? Make notes. Use the ideas in the box or your own ideas.

> look angry / happy / nervous / sad / … • look up • slouch • smile • stand up straight • …

b) When do you feel confident? Make notes.

▶ Skills file 12, p. 167

👥 c) Talk about the questions from a) and b) with a partner.

I think the boy / girl in picture 1 / 2 / … looks confident / doesn't look confident because …
I (don't) feel confident when I …

5 c) individuelle Lösungen

✏ **6 STUDY SKILLS An online °profile**   I can give and explain my opinion. ✓

a) Jack is giving his opinions on his online profile. Add opinion phrases to Jack's sentences.

If you ask me, dogs are the best because …

b) Do you agree or disagree with Jack's opinions? Use opinion phrases and give reasons.

I don't agree with Jack at all because …
In my opinion, …

💬 c) Give your opinion on the four questions below. Give reasons too.

- Cars or bikes?
- Books or TV shows?
- Saturdays or Sundays?
- Old-fashioned clothes or modern clothes?

Tell us what you prefer!
1. Cats or dogs?
   Dogs are the best because you can play games with them!
2. Cheese or chocolate?
   Chocolate is delicious because it's sweet.
3. Football or basketball?
   Football is better because you can play it anywhere.
4. Your phone or your computer?
   My computer is better because it's bigger.
5. The sun or the snow?
   The snow is really fun because you can °go skiing.

6 Lösungsbsp. S. 291   Check

64 sixty-four

Checkpoint Vorbereitung

Material: alle Aufgaben ▶ KV 2.5B: Checkpoint answers, App (Check) • Ex 6 + 7 ▶ KV Extra: Bus stop
Zeitbedarf: ca. 1–2 Std.
Minimalversion: Auswahl der Aufgaben erfolgt entsprechend der zu überprüfenden Lernziele
Begleitmedien: App (Digital checkpoint), INKL (S. 63)

Die Übungen kannst du auch digital machen.

7 READING The school fashion show

I can discuss a conflict in a story.

1 It was Monday lunchtime and Omar and Rosie were in the canteen. On the table in front of them was a piece of paper with lots of notes on it. In the middle of the paper
5 were the words: **Trafford School Green Fashion Show!** Rosie and Omar were excited about their project and had lots of ideas.

2 'So I think I will be the presenter. I can give a short °speech at the start of the
10 show. And you can sit at the front and take notes for the newspaper,' said Omar, smiling. 'OK, but … why don't you want to take notes?' asked Rosie.
'Oh, well, I thought it might be easier
15 for you. Because then you can sit down,' said Omar, looking at Rosie's legs.
'OK. I need to go to my next lesson now,' said Rosie.

3 After school, Omar's phone pinged.
20 It was a message from Rosie. 'Hi, Omar. I have thought about the show and I don't want to be part of it any more. Good luck with it. Rosie'
Omar couldn't believe it. That night he
25 didn't sleep at all because he had so many questions.

4 The next day, Omar saw Rosie before school. 'Rosie, wait,' he said. 'What's wrong? Have I upset you?'
30 'Yes, you have,' said Rosie. 'You didn't ask me what I wanted to do in the show, and you thought I couldn't do some things. You saw me as a disabled person, but you didn't see me as Rosie.'

35 5 After a long °pause, Omar started to speak. 'I'm so sorry Rosie. You're right, I didn't ask for your opinion. Can we meet at lunchtime to make a new plan? I can't do the show alone!'
40 'We can,' said Rosie, 'but this time we should both say what we want to do. And I'm going to be part of the show, not just watching it!'
'That's a good plan!' Omar said, smiling.

7 a) 1 C • 2 D • 3 F • 4 A • 5 E • extra B

a) Read the story. Match the paragraphs (1–5) to the correct headings (A–F). There's one extra heading.

A Rosie told Omar how she felt
B Rosie's mistake
C An exciting new project
D Omar's plan
E A different plan
F Omar was shocked

b) Correct the sentences. The mistakes are underlined.

1 Omar and Rosie were planning a <u>fast fashion show</u>.
2 Omar thought that Rosie should <u>be the presenter</u>.
3 In her text message, Rosie said that <u>she was excited about the show</u>.
4 Rosie was upset because Omar only thought about her <u>skills</u>.
5 Rosie <u>wanted to</u> watch the fashion show.

7 b) 1 green fashion show • 2 take notes • 3 she doesn't want to be part of the show • 4 disability / as disabled • 5 doesn't want to

c) Do you think Omar wanted to upset Rosie? Give reasons.

7 c) Lösungsbsp. S. 291

Check

sixty-five 65

Ex 7 Einstieg:
- (SB auf) Selbsteinschätzung s. Ex 5
- S sehen sich Überschrift, Lernziel und Foto an und formulieren eine Vermutung, was der Konflikt sein könnte.

Erarbeitung:
a) S ordnen die Überschriften den Absätzen zu.
- **Ausw.:** ▶ Partner check am ▶ Bus stop (▶ KV Extra): S vergleichen ihre Lösungen mithilfe von ▶ KV 2.5B.

b) S schreiben die korrigierten Sätze in ihr Heft.
- **Ausw.:** ▶ Partner check am ▶ Bus stop (▶ KV Extra): S vergleichen ihre Lösungen mithilfe von ▶ KV 2.5B.

c) S arbeiten mit Partner/-in aus b). S tauschen sich aus und nutzen dabei die *opinion phrases* (vgl. S. 60).
- Lernschwächere S nutzen ihre *Vocab file*-Einträge von S. 60, um ihre Meinung zu äußern.
- **Ausw.:** im Plenum
- **Zusatz:** Lernstärkere S oder ▶ Early finishers verfassen ▶ Three truths, two lies zum Text. Sie suchen Partner/-in am ▶ Bus stop und tauschen sich über die Wahrheiten und Lügen aus.
- erneute Selbsteinschätzung

2

OPTIONAL

Text file Inhalt

Lernschwerpunkt: Magazintexte zur Geschichte der Musik in Manchester lesen
Kompetenzen: Reading einen Artikel zur Musikgeschichte Manchesters verstehen • einem Zeitstrahl Informationen entnehmen • Listening Songs aus Manchester anhören und einen Favoriten wählen
Redemittel: Wortfeld *music*

Allgemeine Anmerkung:
s. Unit 1, S. 36

Manchester: the musical capital
Einstieg:
- (SB zu) ▶ Partner talk: *What kind of music do you like? Do you know any bands from the UK?*
- S suchen Partner/-in ggf. am ▶ Bus stop (▶ KV Extra).

Erarbeitung:
- (SB auf) S lesen den Artikel in EA und schlagen ggf. unbekannte Wörter nach.
- S formulieren 2–3 Fragen an den Text (entweder Unverstandenes oder Verständnisfragen für andere).
- **Ausw.:** ▶ Partner talk: S tauschen sich mit Partner/-in (ggf. am ▶ Bus stop) über ihre Fragen und mögliche Antworten aus.

Manchester's musical history
Einstieg:
- (SB zu) ▶ Brainstorming: S notieren verschiedene Musikstile auf einem Schmierblatt.
- S versuchen, die Musikrichtungen nach dem Alter zu ordnen.

Erarbeitung:
- (SB auf) S lesen den Zeitstrahl und vergleichen mit ihren Ideen aus dem Einstieg.
- **Zusatz:** ▶ Early finishers können im Internet recherchieren, falls sie weitere Stilrichtungen genannt haben, um diese zeitlich einzuordnen.

---

2 Text file
OPTIONAL

United

A magazine for young people across the UK

Manchester: the music capital *by Omar Roy*

Station Approach by the Manchester band **Elbow** is just one of many love songs for my city. And it's no surprise because Manchester is often called the music capital of the UK. We have more music venues[3] and concerts per person than any other city in the country!

Manchester has been an important place for music for a long time, and it's the home of some of the biggest bands of the last 60 years, across different genres of music.

Probably the most famous Manchester band of the time of Britpop in the 1990s was **Oasis**. Many people call their song *Don't Look Back In Anger*[4] the official song of Manchester. I really love this song!

Today, the city is still home to lots of different types of music – from pop boy band

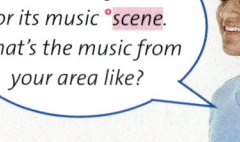

Manchester is famous for its music °scene. What's the music from your area like?

I never know what I want, but I know when I'm low[1] that I, I need to be in the town where they know what I'm like and don't mind.
(Station Approach[2] by Elbow)

Take That to rock band **The 1975**, and from rapper **Bugzy Malone** to the **Manchester Philharmonic Orchestra**.

And it's not just Manchester bands you can see here – our city welcomes[5] musicians from all over the world and it's one of the top places to play a concert. One million visitors come to the **Manchester Arena** every year. It's one of the biggest indoor music arenas in Europe!

If you don't mind Manchester's famous rain, then there are plenty of outdoor music festivals to visit too. For example, the **Sounds of the City Festival** takes place every summer

Manchester's musical history

The 1970s
The start of **punk rock** when people sang angry songs about things that were unfair in the world.

The 1980s
There were so many new rock and electro parties that many people called the city **Madchester** because of its rave and party culture!

---

[1] (to) **be low** *traurig sein* [2] **approach** *die Anfahrt (hier: zum Bahnhof)* [3] **venue** *der Veranstaltungsort*
[4] **anger** *der Ärger, die Wut* [5] (to) **welcome** *willkommen heißen*

66 sixty-six

66

2 OPTIONAL

Text file **Vorbereitung**

Material: Manchester: the musical capital ggf. ▶ KV Extra: Bus stop • Manchester's musical history ggf. digitale Geräte für eine Internetrecherche • Competition time! ggf. digitale Endgeräte für das Hören und Vorspielen der Lieder
Zeitbedarf: abhängig davon, welche Texte in welcher Tiefe bearbeitet werden
Minimalversion: Alle Texte sind optionale Zusatztexte.

---

2 OPTIONAL

at the **Castlefield Bowl**, an enormous outdoor theatre. You can see some of the most famous pop, rock and indie groups in the world there – and many local bands too, of course! I saw Bugzy Malone play there last year and it was amazing.

In their song *Manchester*, The Beautiful South sang:
'So convertibles[1] stay garage-bound[2],
save after-sun for later.
If rain makes Britain great,
then Manchester is greater!'

Well, there's certainly a lot of rain, but I think music makes Manchester the greatest!

The Beautiful South at the Sounds of the City Festival in Manchester

Competition time!

Manchester is famous for its many bands, old and new – but which is the best? Listen to these six songs from different times in the city's history and vote for your favourite! You can find them online.

1970s punk rock: **Love Will Tear Us Apart** by Joy Division	1980s Madchester: **Fools Gold** by The Stone Roses	1990s Britpop: **Don't Look Back In Anger** by Oasis
2000s Britpop: **Station Approach** by Elbow	2010s rap: **M.E.N** by Bugzy Malone	2020s pop rock: **Happiness** by The 1975

Tell us **which** song **you** like **best** and **why** !

The 1990s and 2000s
Manchester became famous around the world for its independent pop bands, called **Britpop**.

The 2010s
Manchester is one of the top places to visit for festivals and arena concerts with all kinds of music, including **rap**.

The 2020s
Pop, rock, metal, jazz, classical, alternative or indie – on every night of the week, Manchester will have a gig or concert for you!

[1] **convertible** *das Cabrio*   [2] **stay garage-bound** *in der Garage bleiben müssen*

sixty-seven **67**

Competition time! Erarbeitung:
- (SB auf) S lesen die Informationen zum Wettbewerb.
- L teilt S in Gruppen ein (falls als Differenzierung genutzt, können S auch alleine oder in PA arbeiten).
- S wählen einen der genannten Songs und bearbeiten diese Aufgaben:
  Find the song online and listen to it.
  (Talk to your partner about what you understood.)
  Find the lyrics to the song. Listen to the song again and read the lyrics.
  Look up unknown words. Then sum up what the song is about in one to two sentences.
  Pick your favourite lines of the lyrics and one minute of the song you like best.
  Prepare to present the song in class.
- **Ausw.:** S präsentieren ihren Songausschnitt im Plenum.
- S äußern ihre Meinung zum Song (ggf. mit Phrasen von S. 60, wenn schon bearbeitet).
- zum Schluss gemeinsames Abstimmen für den *class favourite*
- Der gewählte Song wird im Plenum komplett gehört.
- ✉ **Zusatz:** Die Ausschnitte aus den Songtexten auf S. 66–67 mit den S im Plenum diskutieren.

2

Diff bank Inhalt

Lernschwerpunkt: zusätzliche Übungen, Differenzierungs- und Hilfsangebote
Kompetenzen: Reading Fotos und Beschreibungen von Orten in und um Manchester einander zuordnen • Speaking sagen, welchen Ort man gerne sehen würde • darüber sprechen, was einem wichtig ist • die eigene Kleidung mit der Kleidung anderer Jugendlicher vergleichen
Strukturen: *(revision) comparison of adjectives*
Redemittel: *green fashion • important things • comparing outfits • adjectives to describe clothes*

Allgemeine Anmerkung:
s. Unit 1, S. 38

Ex 3 s. S. 47
Erarbeitung:
b) (SB auf) S prüfen ihre Antworten zum Quiz aus Ex 3, S. 47 mit diesen Lösungen.

MP 1 Einstieg:
- (SB zu) L zeigt die Bilder A–D (UMA).
  L: *What can you see in and around Manchester? Describe the pictures.*
  S: *I can see … / There is/are …*

Erarbeitung:
a) (SB auf) lautes Lesen der Texte (▶Buzz reading), anschließend gemäß AA in EA
- **Ausw.:** Bilder als TA (UMA), S schreiben entsprechende Zahl zum Bild.
b) gemäß AA in PA
- ☒ Lernstärkere S nennen zusätzlich eine Begründung.
- **Ausw.:** S-Paare präsentieren Ergebnisse im Plenum.
- **Alternative:** ▶Four corners: L verteilt Schilder mit den Buchstaben A–D im Raum (ein Buchstabe pro Karte).
- S oder S-Paare stellen sich zu dem Ort, den sie gerne sehen würden, und begründen ihre Entscheidung.

---

2 Diff bank

Diff bank

▶ Page 47

3 GLOBAL GOALS Think before you buy

b) Check your answers from p. 47.

1 B 14 (Remember: This is for each person in the world!)
2 A 1% (Recycling is using old clothes to make something new. Many people reuse clothes, but most clothes go in the bin.)
3 C nearly 4,000 (That's 4,000 one-litre bottles of water! Making new clothes uses 20% of the world's clean water each year.)
4 A polyester (Clothes produce 35% of the small bits of plastic in the world's seas.)
5 B trendy, cheap clothes that go out of style quickly

▶ Page 44

More practice 1 In and around Manchester

a) Omar loves Manchester! In the magazine he writes about four places. Read the descriptions (1–4) and match them to the photos (A–D).

1 The °National Football Museum is the coolest museum in Manchester. You can see famous football shirts and try to score goals. The building is cool too – it's really modern and has lots of windows.
2 I love the Trafford Centre. It's good for shopping, but also for bowling and watching films at the cinema.
3 Blackpool on the west coast is a great day trip from Manchester. You all know Blackpool Tower, right? It looks like the Eiffel Tower in Paris. I love the beach and the pier there too.
4 Another great day trip from Manchester is the Peak District. We visited a °cave there once. They switched all the lights off and it was so scary in the dark!

b) Which of these places would you like to see? Tell a partner.

1 a) 1 D • 2 A • 3 B • 4 C

1 b) individuelle Lösungen

68 sixty-eight

2

Diff bank **Vorbereitung**

Material: MP 1 UMA, vier Schilder (A4, ein Buchstabe A–D pro Blatt/Karte)
Zeitbedarf: abhängig davon, welche Aufgaben bearbeitet werden
Minimalversion: *More practice*-Aufgaben sind stets Zusatzaufgaben.

2

▶ Page 45

More help 2 SPEAKING **What's important to you**   **2 a)** individuelle Lösungen

a) What's important to you? Make a list of four to six people or things. Think of reasons too.

Being popular / sporty / …		it feels good / it makes me happy / …
How I look		it makes me confident / …
My bike / skateboard / …		it makes me independent / it's fun to ride / …
My hometown / village / …	is important to me because	it's a nice place / my friends live there / …
My pet		it's my best friend / it's really cute / …
School		I want a good job / I can meet my friends / …
My phone		it links me with the world / I can take photos / …
My friends / parents / …	are	they help me / we do fun things together / …

▶ Page 46

More practice 2 **Cool clothes**   **2 a)** 1 longer than • 2 taller than … as tall as • 3 older than • 4 more colourful than • 5 darker than • 6 the warmest … the sportiest

REVISION **Comparisons**

	adjective	comparative	superlative
short adjective	cool	cooler	the coolest
long adjective	colourful	more colourful	the most colourful
irregular adjective	good	better	the best
	bad	worse	the worst

To °compare two things, use the comparative + than: *Your trainers are cooler than my trainers.*
If two things are the same, use as … as: *Your trainers are as cool as my trainers.*
If two things aren't the same, use not as … as: *Your trainers aren't as cool as my trainers.*

▶ Language file 7a + b, p. 175–176

a) Look at the photo. Complete the sentences with comparatives or superlatives.
Sometimes you need to add *than* or *(not) as … as*.

1 The girls' hair is … (long) the boys' hair.
2 Eli is … (tall) Una. But Una is nearly … (tall) Eli.
3 Mila looks … (old) the others.
4 Luke's trainers are … (colourful) Mila's.
5 Luke's jacket is … (dark) Eli's T-shirt.
6 Eli has … (warm) outfit and Una has … (sporty).

b) Tell a partner about your clothes.

My clothes are (more) … than Eli's clothes.
My clothes are / aren't as … as Una's clothes.
I wear … too. / I don't wear …

2 b) individuelle Lösungen

MH 2 s. S. 45
• Diese Aufgabe bietet sprachliche Mittel sowie Ideen für lernschwächere S.

Erarbeitung:
a) (SB auf) gemäß AA, s. S. 45

MP 2
• Diese Aufgabe bietet eine gute Möglichkeit zur Wiederholung der Steigerung der Adjektive und der Vergleiche.
• s. a. ▶ Grammatikwiederholung

Einstieg:
• (SB zu) L: *Find five adjectives to describe your clothes.*
• S sammeln fünf Adjektive über ▶ Five-finger brainstorming.
• L sammelt im TA (▶ Vokabeltafel).

Erarbeitung:
a) (SB auf) S lesen die Regelerklärung in der ▶ Grammatik-Box, S. 69.
• gemeinsame Verständnissicherung im Plenum
• s. a. ▶ LF 7a + b, S. 175–176
• S bilden *comparative* und *superlative* der Adjektive des Einstiegs (▶ Vokabeltafel).
• S notieren Sätze ins Heft gemäß AA.
• **Ausw.:** ▶ Partner check, dann Plenum

b) gemäß AA in PA
• **Ausw.:** Einzelne S-Paare präsentieren Ergebnisse im Plenum.

sixty-nine **69**

69

2

Diff bank Inhalt

Lernschwerpunkt: zusätzliche Übungen, Differenzierungs- und Hilfsangebote
Kompetenzen: Writing Personen nach ihren Outfits vergleichen • Tipps für *green clothes* geben • Speaking eine Person beschreiben • sich über Regeln zu Hause austauschen
Strukturen: *(revision)* comparison of adjectives • modal verbs: must, mustn't, (don't) have to, needn't, (not) be allowed to; future and past forms
Redemittel: *comparing outfits* • *describing people (personality and feelings)* • *rules at home*

Challenge 1 Einstieg:
- (SB zu) L bittet drei S nach vorn.
  L: *Who is the tallest person?*
  S: *... is the tallest person.*
  L: *Who is shorter than ...?*
  S: *... is shorter than ...*

Erarbeitung:
- (SB auf) Klären der AA
- S notieren Sätze in ihr Heft.
- Ausw.: ▶Partner check, dann Plenum

Challenge 2
- Diese Aufgabe bietet eine Möglichkeit zur Vertiefung der Vergleiche (durch *and* verbundene Komparative).

Einstieg:
- (SB zu) ▶Brainstorming: S sammeln beliebige Adjektive.
- L erfasst Wörter in zwei Listen als TA und ergänzt am Ende die Überschriften *short adjectives* und *long adjectives*.

Erarbeitung:
- (SB auf) gemeinsames Lesen der ▶Grammatik-Box, S. 70 und Verständnissicherung
- s. a. ▶LF 7c, S. 176
- Adjektive aus dem Reservoir lesen und den Listen des Einstiegs zuordnen.
- Anschl. gemäß AA: S schreiben vollständige Sätze in ihr Heft.
- Ausw.: ▶Five-minute teacher

MH 4 s. S. 47
- Diese Aufgabe bietet sprachliche Mittel für schwächere S, die in Ex 4, S. 47 Wahlaufgabe A bearbeiten.

Erarbeitung:
a) (SB auf) gemäß AA, s. S. 47

---

2 Diff bank

▶ Page 46

Challenge 1 Three teens

Write as many sentences as you can to compare the kids in the picture.
Be careful with spelling.

Nia has the shortest trousers.
Her hair is ... than ...'s hair.
...

Ch 1 Lösungsbsp. S. 291

Challenge 2 More and more

Comparatives with *and*
- short adjective:
  Fast fashion is getting *cheaper and cheaper*. (= immer billiger)
- long adjective:
  Good clothes are becoming *more and more expensive*. (= immer teurer)

▶ Language file 7c, p. 176

Write comparatives with *and*. Choose adjectives from the box.

1 Over the years, jeans have become ... with both young and old people.
2 Tight jeans are getting ... and baggy jeans are getting ...!
3 What influencers wear has become ...
4 The fashion business is becoming ...
5 Luckily, to save our planet, clothes are getting ...
6 But good clothes are becoming ...

baggy • big • expensive • green • important • popular • tight

Ch 2 1 more and more popular • 2 tighter and tighter ... baggier and baggier • 3 more and more important • 4 bigger and bigger • 5 greener and greener • 6 more and more expensive

▶ Page 47

More help 4 MY TASK 'Green' clothes

a) Make a poster with your top five tips for green clothes. Rosie's quiz on p. 47 and the phrases below can help you.

	buy	cotton clothes / fewer clothes / fast fashion / polyester clothes / ...
	give	clothes to charity shops / clothes to your friends / ...
(Don't)	repair	your clothes when they need it / ...
	swap	clothes with your friends / clothes with your brothers or sisters / clothes at a swap party / ...
	wash	your clothes only when they're dirty / ...
	wear	your clothes until you grow out of them / second-hand clothes / ...

4 individuelle Lösungen

70 seventy

Diff bank Vorbereitung

Material: MP 3 ggf. UMA • Challenge 3 UMA
Zeitbedarf: abhängig davon, welche Aufgaben bearbeitet werden
Minimalversion: *More practice-* und *Challenge*-Aufgaben sind stets Zusatzaufgaben.

▶ Page 48

More practice 3 — Describing people

a) Look at the letters on p. 49 again. Collect words to describe people and their feelings in a mind map. You can add other words.

b) Describe somebody that you know.

My cousin is clever and also very helpful – she helps me with my homework.
Sometimes she gets upset because …   But usually she's very positive and funny.

3 a) Lösungsbsp. S. 291

Mindmap: describing people — feelings — upset; personality — funny

3 b) individuelle Lösungen

▶ Page 50

More practice 4 — At home

4 individuelle Lösungen

a) What rules do you have at home? Tell a partner. Use the ideas in the box or your own ideas. Use *must, have to, don't have to, needn't, mustn't*.

> babysit younger brothers or sisters • come home late • do chores • leave food on my plate • look after pets • play loud music • shout • take off my shoes when I come in • tell my parents where I am • use my phone at the dinner table

b) Tell the class one thing you and your partner both have to, don't have to or mustn't do.

Challenge 3 — My parents are strict

Ch 3 1 B • 2 C • 3 A • 4 A • 5 C

Modals and their substitutes
The modal verbs *can* and *must* only have a present form. To make future and past forms, we use substitutes like °*be able to*, *be allowed to* and *have to*.

can → *Somebody stole my bike. Luckily I was able to take the bus home.* (= ich konnte)
can → *I'll be allowed to go out tomorrow.* (= ich werde … dürfen)
must → *I had to look after my sister yesterday.* (= ich musste)

▶ Language file 8a–c, p. 176–177

Choose the correct form for each sentence. The time words can help you.

1. My parents are strict. I A can't B wasn't allowed to C had to go to a party **last weekend**.
2. If I don't do my homework, I A mustn't B will be allowed to C won't be allowed to go to the cinema **later**.
3. Before I played football **last Saturday**, I A had to B must C was allowed to tidy my room.
4. I'm having guitar lessons. I A will be able to B can C had to play in a concert **soon**.
5. I lost my phone **yesterday** and I A wasn't allowed to B can't C wasn't able to text my friends.

seventy-one

MP 3

- Diese Aufgabe sollte im Anschluss von Ex 2, S. 48 bearbeitet werden.

Einstieg:
- (SB zu) L: *Why do you like your friend?*
- S antworten, L erfasst Ideen in einer Liste (▶ Vokabeltafel).

Erarbeitung:
a) (SB auf) S erstellen ▶ Mindmap gemäß AA in ihrem Heft.
- **Ausw.:** L sammelt Antworten der S (UMA oder TA).

b) gemäß AA, mündl. in PA
- Lernschwächere S machen sich vorab Notizen.
- **Ausw.:** Einige S tragen ihre Ergebnisse im Plenum vor.

MP 4 Einstieg:
- (SB zu) TA: *Rules at home*
- Ideenfindung mit ▶ Five-finger brainstorming
- L erstellt Ideenliste als TA.

Erarbeitung:
a) (SB auf) Klären der AA, S lesen die Ideen im Reservoir.
- anschl. ▶ Think-Pair-Share
- *Think:* Sammeln der *rules* in EA
- *Pair:* S-Paare tauschen sich aus.

b) *Share:* S-Paare präsentieren ihre Ergebnisse im Plenum.

Challenge 3 Einstieg:
- (SB zu) Lesen der ▶ Grammatik-Box, S. 71 zu den Ersatzformen von *can* und *must* (UMA) und Verständnissicherung
- s. a. ▶ LF 8a–c, S. 176–177

Erarbeitung:
- (SB auf) gemäß AA in EA
- **Ausw.:** ▶ Meldekette

2

Diff bank **Inhalt**

Lernschwerpunkt: zusätzliche Übungen, Differenzierungs- und Hilfsangebote
Kompetenzen: Speaking/Writing Ratschläge geben • Speaking über eine Szene aus der Story und die Gefühle der Charaktere sprechen
Strukturen: *modal verbs: may, might, could; should/shouldn't* • *reflexive pronouns*
Redemittel: *problems and feelings* • *giving advice* • *confidence tips*

MP 5
- Diese Aufgabe bietet eine Möglichkeit zum Üben der modalen Hilfsverben *may, might, could*, vgl. Ex 5d), S. 50.

Einstieg:
- (SB zu) L zeigt Bild von MP 5 (UMA). L: *Look, there's Omar with his dad. What might he ask his dad?*
- S stellen Vermutungen an.

Erarbeitung:
- (SB auf) Gemäß AA, S schreiben vollständige Sätze ins Heft.
- **Ausw.:** S suchen Partner/-in am ▶Bus stop (▶KV Extra) und vergleichen im ▶Partner check.

MP 6
- Diese Aufgabe bietet eine Möglichkeit zum Üben von *should/shouldn't*, vgl. Ex 6c), S. 51.

Einstieg:
- (SB zu) TA: *should/shouldn't*
  L: *I'm hungry. What can I do?*
  S: *You should eat something.*
- L gibt ggf. weitere Beispiele: *I'm tired. / My car's broken. / …*

Erarbeitung:
a) (SB auf) gemäß AA in PA
- **Ausw.:** Beispiele im Plenum

b) gemäß AA
- **Ausw.:** im Plenum

MH 7 s. S. 51
- Diese Aufgabe bietet sprachliche Mittel für lernschwächere S.

Erarbeitung:
a) (SB auf) gemäß AA, s. S. 51

---

2 Diff bank

▶ Page 50

More practice 5 **What makes somebody attractive?**

Complete the conversation with *may, might* or *could* and a verb from the box.
There's more than one answer for each sentence.

~~ask~~ • be • get • make • say • sound

Omar *May I ask* (1) you a question, Dad?
Dad Sure, Omar!
Omar I know this … (2) strange, but what makes somebody attractive?
Dad Well, some people … (3) it's how a person looks. For other people, a person's personality … (4) them attractive – if somebody is kind or funny. Or it … (5) how a person makes you feel.
Omar Mm, OK, thanks, Dad. … I … (6) your opinion too, Mum?

> **5** 1 *May I ask* • 2 might sound • 3 could say • 4 might make • 5 might be • 6 May I get

▶ Page 51

More practice 6 **Help!**   6 a) Lösungsbsp. S. 292

This show is better!

a) Take turns to °read out a problem (1–6) and give advice with *should/shouldn't*.

1 Help! My cat can talk.
  You should go on a talk show.
2 Help! My mum is an alien.
3 Help! There's a lion in my garden.
4 Help! I have four legs.
5 Help! My ears have fallen off.
6 Help! My neighbours are vampires.

b) Think of two more problems for the class. Who can give the best advice?

> **6 b)** individuelle Lösungen

More help **7** MY TASK **Your advice**   7 a) Lösungsbsp. S. 289

a)		
	Thank you for	writing to the advice column / trusting us with your problem / your letter / …
	I/We understand	it's a difficult / embarrassing / … situation.
		why you're upset / why you're °unsure / why you need advice / …
	I/We think you should / shouldn't	be °afraid to talk to your friend / ask your friend to explain why it was a joke / tell them it made you feel bad / end the friendship / …
		ask her if you could be more than friends / tell her you don't want to lose her friendship / wait a few weeks / write her a letter / …

72 seventy-two

2

Diff bank **Vorbereitung**

Material: MP 5 UMA, ▶KV Extra: Bus stop • MP 7 ▶KV Extra: Bus stop • MH 8 ggf. Requisiten für das Theaterstück • MP 8 von L vorbereitete Karten mit Situationen aus der Story von S. 56–57
Zeitbedarf: abhängig davon, welche Aufgaben bearbeitet werden
Minimalversion: *More practice*-Aufgaben sind stets Zusatzaufgaben.

2

▶Page 53

More practice 7 **Looking after yourself**

Complete the advice. Use the words in the box.

> each other • himself • myself • ourselves • yourself • yourselves

It's important that you all take care of ... (1). We can't be really happy if we don't love ... (2). Of course, friends are important too, and good friends look after ... (3), but you should be just as kind to ... (4) as you are to your friends. My brother says something nice to ... (5) in the mirror every morning. And every day I go running after school to keep ... (6) happy and healthy.

7 **1** yourselves • **2** ourselves • **3** each other • **4** yourself • **5** himself • **6** myself

▶Page 55

More help **8** MY TASK **Being confident**

8 b) individuelle Lösungen

b)
1	**Student A:** Hello, nice to meet you! What's your name? How are you?	**Student B:** Hello. Erm, ... (name). Erm, ... OK.
2	**Student C:** You look quite nervous/shy/unhappy/... You don't look very confident/happy/... I have some tips for you:	
	You need to .../You should ... Why don't you ...? Next time, you could ...	ask questions/look at your partner/smile more/ speak clearly/speak loudly/stand up straight/ use full sentences/...
	Try not to .../You shouldn't ...	shout/slouch/speak too quickly/speak too quietly/...
	Student B: Thanks for your tips.	
3	**Student A:** Hello, nice to meet you! What's your name? My name is ... How are you?	**Student B:** Hello! Nice to meet you too! My name is ... What about you? I'm fine, thanks. And how are you?

▶Page 58

More practice 8 **Freeze!**

8 individuelle Lösungen

a) Choose a scene from the story. Talk about what happens in the scene and how the characters feel.

b) Show your group's scene as a freeze-frame. Other students say what the scene is, what's happening and how the characters feel.

seventy-three 73

MP 7 **Erarbeitung:**
- (SB auf) gemäß AA
- **Ausw.:** ▶Partner check am ▶Bus stop (▶KV Extra)
- ☒ **Zusatz:** *What do you do to look after yourself? Write three sentences.*

MH 8 s. S. 55
- Diese Hilfe kann für lernschwächere S oder als Ideensammlung für S genutzt werden, die Ex 8, S. 55 nicht ganz verstehen.
- **Hinweis:** Kleine Requisiten wie Schals, Mützen, Sonnenbrille bieten den S Rollenschutz und helfen ihnen, sich besser in eine Rolle einzufühlen. Die Requisiten können von den S als Hausaufgabe mitgebracht werden oder L bringt selbst einen kleinen Fundus mit.

Erarbeitung: s. S. 55

MP 8 **Einstieg:**
- (SB zu) ▶Milling around: L nennt Gefühle. S bewegen sich so durch den Raum, dass ihre Körpersprache das jeweilige Gefühl zeigt.

Erarbeitung:
a) (SB auf) GA: S wählen eine Szene aus der Story von S. 56–57, dann gemäß AA.
- 🖼 L stellt 5–7 Karten mit wichtigen Situationen aus der Geschichte zur Verfügung. S ziehen eine Karte und stellen die Situation dar.

b) Szene als ▶Freeze-frame einüben.
- **Ausw.:** Präsentation der Standbilder gemäß AA

73

3

Unit-Übersicht

Storyline: Grace und Rhona machen eine Klassenfahrt nach Schottland. Sie berichten über die Orte und ihre Erlebnisse. Dabei spielt der Naturschutz eine wichtige Rolle. Bei einer Bergwanderung stellt sich heraus, wie wichtig eine gute Vorbereitung ist.
Strukturen: *(revision) adverbs of manners* (S. 78) • *(revision) present perfect* (S. 81) • *present perfect with for and since* (S. 83)
Viewing: Film über einen *road trip* durch Schottland (S. 89)
Unit task: eine Abenteuergeschichte schreiben

Unit 3 Einstieg:
- (SB zu) L zeigt Karte des UK (UMA).
  L: *In the new unit we'll be in Scotland. Can you find it on the map?*
- **Alternative:** In Gruppen mit mehr Vorwissen spielen S ein (Online-)Quiz über Schottland.

Ex 1 Einstieg:
- (SB zu) L zeigt die Fotos von S. 74–75 (UMA). Den Seiten im Raum werden die Aussagen „true" and „false" zugeordnet. L macht *true/false statements* zu den Fotos:
  L: *Inverness is a small village. / People can visit Eilean Donan Castle.*
- S gehen zu den passenden Raumseiten.

Erarbeitung:
a) (SB auf) Gemäß AA als GA: S nutzen ihre Notizen aus Unit 1 (s. S. 10–13) u. ihr Vorwissen.
- **Ausw.:** Die Gruppen präsentieren im Plenum. L/S sichern die Ergebnisse als TA.

b) 1. Hören: gemäß AA
- **Ausw.:** ▶Meldekette

c) 2. Hören: gemäß AA in PA
- Als Vorbereitung notieren S die Namen der Orte in der korrekten Reihenfolge (s. b)) u. lassen rechts daneben Platz für die *notes* vom 2. Hören.

d) in PA gemäß AA
- **Ausw.:** ▶Meldekette: Je ein/-e S stellt eine Sehenswürdigkeit bzw. Aktivität vor.
- L notiert die wichtigen Informationen im TA.

Unit 3
Scotland: Adventure

Rhona | Grace

A — Inverness

B — Kayaking on the west coast

C — Eilean Donan[1] Castle, Dornie

1 LISTENING   A school trip in Scotland

a) BEFORE YOU LISTEN What do you remember or know about Scotland? Collect information. You can look back at pages 10–13.

2.1 b) Grace and her friend Rhona are talking about a school trip. Look at the photos and listen. Write the places or activities (A–F) in the order that you hear them.

c) Listen again and take notes about what Grace and Rhona say about the places and activities on the trip.

d) Swap information with your partner.

1 [ˌeɪlən ˈdɒnən]

1 a) Lösungsbsp. S. 292

1 b) D · A · F · C · B · E

1 c) Lösungsbsp. S. 292

74 seventy-four

3

Lead-in Inhalt

Lernschwerpunkt: Informationen zu verschiedenen Orten in Schottland erfassen
Kompetenzen: Listening Informationen zur Klassenfahrt von Grace und Rhona sowie zu beiden Charakteren entnehmen • Speaking Information zu Schottland sammeln • Fragen zu den Schottlandfotos beantworten
Redemittel: *describing places*

Vorbereitung

Material: Einstieg *UK map*, ggf. UMA, ggf. (Online-)Quiz zu Schottland • Ex 1 UMA, UMA/CD/App • Ex 2 ggf. vorbereitete Zettel, UMA
Zeitbedarf: ca. 1 Std.
Begleitmedien: WB (S. 50), App (Digital quiz), INKL (S. 72–73), DIFF (3.1), Unit plans (Unit 3)

Nach dieser Unit kann ich ...
- über Schottland reden
- Geschichten und Sagen verstehen
- über Abenteuer und Interessen sprechen
- über die Natur sprechen
- Entscheidungen in einer Geschichte besprechen
- Ideen für eine Geschichte gliedern

Unit task
- eine kurze Abenteuergeschichte schreiben

Shopping in Edinburgh[1]

Hiking on Ben Nevis

Loch Ness

💬 2 SPEAKING Pictures of Scotland

 2 individuelle Lösungen

a) Look at the photos again for one minute and °memorize them. Think about:
- where the picture is, what you can see in it and what the weather is like
- what the people are doing and what they're wearing or carrying

b) Close your books. Ask a partner three questions about the photos. Then answer their questions.

c) Ask and answer these questions. Give reasons for your answers.
1. Which place or activity in the photos looks the most interesting?
2. Do you like to go on trips or prefer to stay at home?

▶ More help, p. 100   ▶ More practice 1, p. 101   Workbook, p. 50

1 [ˈedɪnbərə]

 Digital quiz   I can **talk about Scotland.**

seventy-five **75**

Nach dieser Unit ...
- L bespricht mit S die Lernziele der Unit (s. links) und kündigt die *Unit task* an.
- Am Ende der Unit überprüfen die S das Erreichen der Ziele mithilfe des *Checkpoint* (S. 92–95) bzw. gemeinsam im Plenum.

Ex 2 Einstieg:
- (SB zu) S spielen ▶ Words in the air zum Thema Schottland.
- Schwächere S erhalten Begriffe auf vorbereiteten Zetteln.

Erarbeitung:
a) (SB auf) S lesen AA.
- S versuchen, sich so viel zu den Bildern einzuprägen, wie möglich.
- Schwächere S betrachten nur die Bilder auf einer der beiden Seiten.

b) (SB zu) gemäß AA in PA
- L notiert ggf. die Fragen von a) an der Tafel (UMA).
- S-Paare müssen sich dieselben Bilder angeschaut haben. L steuert ggf.
- **Ausw.:** ▶ Partner talk

c) (SB auf) S lesen AA und stellen sich in PA die Fragen (▶ Partner talk).
- ▶ More help, S. 100: sprachliche Hilfen, s. ▶ Scaffolding; ▶ More practice 1, S. 101
- **Ausw.:** Austausch im Plenum

- **Zusatz:** Für ▶ Early finisher: L: *Imagine you are on a class trip to Scotland too. Where would you like to go? Where not? Why? Talk to your partner.*

75

3

Topic 1 Inhalt

Lernschwerpunkt: verschiedene schottische Sagen verstehen
Kompetenzen: Reading in einer PA einem Text Informationen zu Nessie entnehmen • Speaking sich zur Legende von Nessie austauschen und die eigene Meinung vertreten • Mediation eine deutsche Sage ins Englische sprachmitteln
Redemittel: *ghost stories and legends • opinion phrases*

Ex 1 Einstieg:
- (SB zu) L: *Grace and Rhona are at their first stop: at Loch Ness. Let's find out more.*

Erarbeitung:
a) (SB auf) S lesen AA und ▶ Good to know, S. 76, Ex 1a) im Plenum.
- In PA: Austausch zum Vorwissen gemäß AA

b) Gemäß AA in PA: *Partner A* bleibt auf S. 76, *Partner B* arbeitet auf S. 100.
- *Partner A* liest den Text, die Infos in ▶ Good to know, S. 76, Ex 1b), schlägt unbekannte Wörter nach u. notiert sie im *Vocab file*.
- 🎬 Leitfragen für *Partner A*, die bei der Zusammenfassung der Texte in d) helfen (als TA):
  – What is Nessie?
  – When was Nessie first seen?
  – What was on the first photo?
  – What happened in 1977?
  – What did scientists learn about Loch Ness?
- für *Partner B*, s. S. 100

c) schriftl. in EA gemäß AA
- **Ausw.:** ▶ Partner check zu b) u. c): S treffen am ▶ Bus stop (▶ KV Extra) eine/-n Mit-S mit dem gleichen Text (Es gibt zwei verschiedene *Bus stops*.).

d) Gemäß AA, S-Paare (*Partner A u. B*) nutzen ihre Notizen aus b) u. c) u. geben sich gegenseitig den Inhalt ihres jeweiligen Texts wieder (▶ Partner talk).
- **Ausw.:** Freiwillige S-Paare präsentieren ihre jeweiligen Zusammenfassungen im Plenum.

---

3 Topic 1 | Topic 2 | Topic 3 | Story | Viewing | Study skills | Unit task

Scary Scotland

> **1 a)** Nessie is a monster. • It lives in Loch Ness. • It looks like a snake. It has a long neck. The story about Nessie is a legend.

1 READING The legend of the Loch Ness ⁺monster

a) BEFORE YOU READ Grace and Rhona are at the first place on their trip: Loch Ness. What do you know about 'Nessie'? The title of this exercise and the photo in the article below can help you.

Nessie is a …   It lives …   It looks like …

Good to know
There are a lot of legends and scary stories from Scotland. They include monsters, ghosts and mermaids or ⁺mermen.

b) **Partner B:** Look at p. 100.
Partner A: Read the article. What's it about? Choose the best main idea (A–C).

A There's something big in the loch, but nobody knows what it is.
B There's a monster in the loch with a long neck.
C There aren't any big creatures in the loch.

1 b) A

The mystery of Nessie

Does a monster live in the deep water of Loch Ness? A lot of people think that the Loch Ness monster is real and have lovingly ⁺named it Nessie. ▶ Box: Voc., p. 226
In 1934 a photographer took a photo of the creature. It seemed to have a long neck and a small head like a snake. After the photo, people went out on the loch in boats to try and see the monster. Unfortunately they didn't find anything, but Loch Ness is very big: 23 miles long and 88 feet deep! In 1977 Nessie appeared in another photo: The monster looked like the 1934 photo, so a lot of people thought there was definitely a monster in the loch.
Later scientists used sonar equipment to try and discover the monster. They didn't find Nessie, but the equipment discovered several large living creatures.

c) **Partner A and partner B:** Read your article again. Write the reason for your °choice in b).

d) Tell your partner what your article is about.

The main idea of my article is that …   It says …

Good to know
one mile = 1.6 kilometres
one foot = 30.48 centimetres

1 c), d) Lösungsbsp. S. 292 f.

76   seventy-six

Topic 1 Vorbereitung

Material: Ex 1 ▶ KV Extra: Bus stop • Ex 2 UMA, ggf. Notizzettel (Klassensatz), vorbereitete *Discussion tickets* (Klassensatz) (z. B. ▶ KV 2.3: Discussion tickets oder von S selbstgestaltete Karten) • Ex 3 ▶ KV 1.1 A+B: SWAP CARDS Verbs, zweisprachiges Wörterbuch (Klassensatz)
Zeitbedarf: 1–2 Std.
Minimalversion: Ex 2 direkt nach Ex 1 im Plenum durchführen, ohne *Think-Pair-Share*
Begleitmedien: WB (S. 51), INKL (S. 74–75)

---

2 SPEAKING My opinion about Nessie

2 b) Lösungsbsp. S. 293

a) THINK Think about the information in 1 from both articles. Do you think Nessie is real or not? Think of reasons and make notes. ▶ Skills file 12, p. 167

b) PAIR Tell your partner your opinion and give reasons.

In my opinion, it's just a story for tourists because …
I think there's something in the loch, but …
Yes, I think Nessie is real because …

c) SHARE What does the class think? How many students think Nessie is real?

2 a), c) individuelle Lösungen

'Waste of money, I've been here 200 years and never yet seen a monster.'
CartoonStock.com

3 MEDIATION The legend of Loreley

3 Lösungsbsp. S. 293

Grace wrote to her German friend Smilla about the trip to Loch Ness and the legend of the monster. Help Smilla write a message to Grace about a German legend.

Hi Grace!
Thanks for your message about the Loch Ness monster! I want to tell you about a German legend. A young woman called Loreley …

💡 A German-English dictionary can help you with new words. But only write the main ideas and don't translate every word. You can say things in different ways.
▶ Skills file 3, p. 157

▶ More help, p. 101   ▶ Skills file 10, p. 165

Die Legende der Loreley

Eine junge Frau, die Loreley hieß, liebte einen jungen Ritter von ganzem Herzen und wollte ihn heiraten. Am Tag ihrer Hochzeit wartete Loreley auf einem hohen Felsen am Rhein auf ihn. Jedes Mal, wenn sie ein Boot sah, dachte sie „Jetzt kommt er". Sie wartete und wartete, aber der Ritter kam nicht. Das brach ihr das Herz.

Von da an saß Loreley auf diesem Felsen. Sie bürstete ihr langes Haar, weinte und sang traurige Lieder mit ihrer wunderschönen Stimme. Jedes Mal, wenn ein Schiff vorbeikam, hatten die Seemänner nur Augen und Ohren für Loreley und ihre Lieder. Daher fuhren ihre Schiffe gegen die gefährlichen Felsen und sanken.

▶ Workbook, p. 51

seventy-seven 77

Ex 2 Einstieg:
- (SB zu) ▶ Stummer Impuls: L zeigt den Cartoon von Ex 2 (UMA). S reagieren spontan.

Erarbeitung:
a) (SB auf) ▶ Think-Pair-Share: klären der AA im Plenum
- EA: S notieren ihre Ideen in Stichworten im Heft oder auf Notizzetteln, s. ▶ SF 12, S. 167.

b) S tauschen sich gemäß AA in PA aus.
- L teilt ▶ Discussion tickets (z. B. ▶ KV 2.3) für diese Phase aus.

c) **Ausw.:** S äußern ihre Meinung, z. B. mittels ▶ Thumbs up.

Ex 3 Einstieg:
- (SB zu) *Warm-up*: Wdh. des *simple past* z. B. mithilfe der *Swap cards* von ▶ KV 1.1 A+B (▶ Grammatikwiederholung)

Erarbeitung:
- (SB auf) S lesen AA u. ▶ Tippbox, S. 77, s. a. ▶ SF 3, S. 157.
- In EA: S lesen den Text und schreiben Smillas Brief an Grace.
- s. a. ▶ More help, S. 101
- **Ausw.:** Im Plenum erarbeiten L u. S einen passenden Brief u. dabei Kriterien für eine gute Mediation (TA), ▶ SF 10, S. 165.
- ▶ Partner check: Mithilfe der Kriterien geben sich S gegenseitig ▶ Feedback.

- **Zusatz:** S recherchieren weitere Legenden z. B. aus der eigenen Gegend und schreiben englische Fassungen davon.
- Besonders motivierte Klassen bereiten einen englischen Märchenabend vor.

3

Topic 1 Inhalt

Lernschwerpunkt: verschiedene schottische Sagen verstehen
Kompetenzen: Listening einem Hörtext Informationen zu einer Geistergeschichte entnehmen • Writing eine lustige Geschichte mit Adverbien schreiben • eine furchterregende Kreatur beschreiben und ihre Hintergrundgeschichte erfinden
Strukturen: *(revision) adverbs of manner*
Redemittel: *describing actions • adjectives and adverbs*

Ex 4 Einstieg:
- (SB zu) L wdh. mit S, was ein Adjektiv ist und nennt 1–2 Bsp.
- ▶ Word race zu *adjectives*. TA mit Adj. für später sichern.

Erarbeitung:
a) (SB auf) PA gemäß AA, Foto S. 78 oben als Impuls (UMA).
- **Alternative:** in Kleingruppen (s. ▶ Gruppenbildung)

b) (SB auf) S betrachten das Bild (UMA) u. klären gemeinsam die AA, ggf. Höraufträge als TA.
- **1. Hören** gemäß AA
- **Ausw.:** S äußern ihre Meinung gemäß AA.
- **Zusatz:** Einsatz von ▶ Discussion tickets, s. ▶ KV 2.3 zum Steuern der Diskussion

c) **2. Hören** gemäß AA
- **Ausw.:** ▶ Meldekette

d) gemäß AA, ggf. **3. Hören**
- **Ausw.:** Vergleich der Bilder in PA

Ex 5 Einstieg:
- (SB zu) S stellen ihre Geister aus Ex 4 vor u. beschreiben sie. L kommentiert mit Adverbien: L: *This ghost is looking at us sadly …*

Erarbeitung:
a) (SB auf) L präsentiert Sätze 1–4 (UMA). S nennen die Adverbien, L unterstreicht sie.

b) gemäß AA
- **Sich.:** S notieren die Regel im Merkteil (▶ English folder).
- s. a. ▶ LF 10, S. 178, Erklärfilm (UMA/App)

---

3 | Topic 1 | Topic 2 | Topic 3 | Story | Viewing | Study skills | Unit task

4 LISTENING Scottish ghosts

4 a), b), d) individuelle Lösungen

a) BEFORE YOU LISTEN Tell your partner what scary stories, books, films or °series you know.

I know a scary story about a ghost in …
The film 'Nightbooks' is about a witch *and it has some really scary moments.*

▶ Wordbank 5, p. 190

b) Eilean Donan Castle is the next place on Grace and Rhona's school trip and a guide tells them about the castle ghost. Listen. Do you like the story? Why or why not? Tell the class.
2.2

It's a good story, but it isn't really scary.
I like the story because it's about soldiers *and history.*

4 c) Lösungsbsp. S. 293

Grace   Rhona

c) Listen again and take notes on the ghost:
1. why it is in the castle
2. what it looks like
3. what it does
4. what its name is

d) Draw the ghost. Then show your picture to a partner. Does °theirs look the same?

5 LOOKING AT LANGUAGE Adverbs of manner (°revision)

5 a) 1 carefully • 2 secretly • 3 sadly • 4 safely

a) Look at the sentences from the story about the castle ghost. Which words describe how people do something?

1. I'm going to tell you a story, so listen carefully.
2. A group planned secretly to kill the king.
3. He walks sadly around the castle.
4. He carries his head safely under his arm.

b) Now read the box. Then look at the sentences in a) again and complete the rule.

5 b) -ly

> Adjectives are words like careful, secret, sad or safe. They describe what something is like.
> Adverbs of manner describe how people do something or how something happens.
> To make most adverbs of manner, we add the ending … to the adjective.
> These adverbs have a different form: fast → fast, hard → hard, good → well.

▶ Language file 10, p. 178

78 seventy-eight

Topic 1 Vorbereitung

Material: Ex 4 UMA, UMA/CD/App, ggf. ▶ KV 2.3 Discussion tickets (Klassensatz) • Ex 5 UMA, UMA/App (Erklärfilm) • Ex 6 ▶ KV 1.1 A+B: SWAP CARDS Verbs (als vorbereiteter Klassensatz) od. eigene Verbkarten • Ex 8 Karteikarten (Klassensatz), Buchstabenkarten oder Zufallsgenerator für Buchstaben, ▶ KV 3.1: My scary creature (halber od. ganzer Klassensatz), Klebezettel (ca. 6–8 Stück pro S)
Zeitbedarf: ca. 2 Std.
Minimalversion: Ex 4d) und Ex 7 auslassen, Ex 8 als HA
Begleitmedien: WB (S. 52–53), App (Digital quiz, Digital help), INKL (S. 76–77), DIFF (3.2)

---

6 The Edinburgh Castle ghost

Complete the story in the pictures. ▶ Parallel exercise, p. 102
Make adverbs from the adjectives in the box.

surprising • good • hard • loud • sad • ⁺sudden

6 1 *surprisingly* • 2 *well* • 3 *loudly* • 4 *hard* • 5 *suddenly* • 6 *sadly*

A long time ago, ⁺workers *surprisingly* (1) found tunnels under Edinburgh Castle.

They wanted to make a map. So they asked a boy to help because he played the bagpipes … (2).

The boy walked down the tunnels and played his bagpipes … (3), so people could hear him.

Above ground, people listened … (4) and followed the music of the piper.

But then the bagpipes … (5) stopped. Nobody ever saw the boy again.

Today tourists often hear music from underground. Somebody is playing the bagpipes … (6).

7 A funny story

7 individuelle Lösungen

a) Read the example story. Then take turns to write one line of your story on a piece of paper. Fold the paper and give it to the next student.
▶ More help, p. 102

1. Joe the ghost met Suri the tourist at a castle.
2. He said angrily, 'I can't find my phone.'
3. She said politely, 'Where are the toilets?'
4. He laughed happily.
5. She sang badly.
6. In the end, they played badminton.

b) Open your paper and °read out the story.

▶ More practice 2, p. 102 ▶ More practice 3, p. 103 ▶ Challenge 1 + 2, p. 103

My task

8 My scary creature

8 individuelle Lösungen

a) Create a ghost or another scary creature and present it on a poster. ▶ Digital help

- Think of a good name.
- Describe what it looks like, what it does and how it does it.
- Write two or three sentences about the creature's story.

▶ Wordbank 5, p. 190

b) GALLERY WALK Walk around and look at the posters. Write °comments on °sticky notes.

▶ Workbook, pp. 52–53

Digital quiz I can understand stories and legends.

Ex 6 Einstieg:
- (SB auf) S formen die sieben Adjektive aus Ex 5 a) u. b) in Adverbien um (TA).
- S zieht eine Verbkarte (▶ KV 1.1 A+B) u. spielt pantomimisch das Verb mit einem Adverb vom TA vor. Mit-S versuchen Verb u. Adverb zu erraten.
- L korrigiert im ▶ Mothering.

Erarbeitung:
- gemäß AA
- ▶ Parallel ex, S. 102
- **Ausw.:** ▶ Five-minute teacher

Ex 7 Erarbeitung:
a) + b) (SB auf) L zeigt das Bsp. aus dem SB (UMA).
- Klären der AA (▶ Faltgeschichte)
- s. ▶ More help, S. 102
- ▶ More practice 2, S. 102,
- ▶ More practice 3, S. 103,
- ▶ Challenge 1 + 2, S. 103
- **Ausw.:** gemeinsam im Plenum

My task Ex 8 Einstieg:
- (SB zu) S spielen ▶ Bang zum Thema: *A scary creature*. S notieren auf jeder Karte zwei Worte (ein Nomen u. ein Adj. od. ein Verb u. ein Adv.).

Erarbeitung:
- Schwächere S notieren nur einzelne Wörter.
a) (SB auf) PA gemäß AA, S zeichnen ihre Kreatur auf ein Poster od. nutzen ▶ KV 3.1.
- **Zusatz:** S nutzen die im Einstieg gesammelten Phrasen.
- s. *Digital help* (App)
b) ▶ Feedback: ▶ Gallery walk gemäß AA. S schreiben ihr Feedback auf Klebezettel.
- **Ausw.:** S lesen ihr Feedback.

3

Topic 2 Inhalt

Lernschwerpunkt: Abenteuerreisen und Abenteuersportarten kennenlernen
Kompetenzen: Reading Bildern Informationen entnehmen • Listening verstehen, welche Sportarten Grace und Rhona bereits ausprobiert haben • Speaking sich über Outdoor-Aktivitäten austauschen, die man schon bzw. noch nicht gemacht hat • Writing einen Dialog mit dem *present perfect* befüllen
Strukturen: *(revision) the present perfect*
Redemittel: *free-time activities and adventures*

Ex 1 Einstieg:
- ✉ (SB zu) Wdh. des *present perfect*: L erklärt Regeln für ▶ Never have I ever u. S spielen 2–3 Runden in Gruppen à 4–5 S.
- L achtet auf die korrekte Verwendung des *present perfect*.

Erarbeitung:
a) (SB auf) S füllen die Tabelle gemäß AA aus (z. B. auf ▶ KV 3.2).
- s. a. ▶ SF 3, S. 157
- **Ausw.:** ▶ Five-minute teacher: S1 moderiert, S2 sichert im TA.

b) 1. Hören: gemäß AA
- ▶ SF 8, S. 163 (zur Vorbereitung aufs Hören)
- **Ausw.:** im Plenum

c) 2. Hören: S notieren die Aktivitäten gemäß AA (z. B. auf ▶ KV 3.2, c).
- **Ausw.:** L weist ausdrücklich auf die sprachlichen Hilfen hin.
- S tauschen sich in PA aus.
- **Sich.:** im Plenum, L achtet auf die Verwendung der Sätze aus der Hilfe im SB.

d) L beginnt ein Gespräch mit einem Beispielsatz aus d) und fragt stärkere S.
- S antworten und L korrigiert, wenn nötig (ca. 3–4 Beiträge).
- In PA od. ▶ Kugellager tauschen sich alle S mithilfe der sprachl. Hilfen gemäß AA aus.
- **Ausw.:** S berichten darüber, was sie über andere S erfahren haben. L gibt sprachl. Hilfen: TA: ... has / hasn't tried ... / ... would like to try ...
- L korrigiert im ▶ Mothering.

---

3   Topic 1   **Topic 2**   Topic 3   Story   Viewing   Study skills   Unit task

Adventure sports

1 LISTENING An adventure trip   **1 a)** Lösungsbsp. S. 293

a) BEFORE YOU LISTEN Look at the pictures (1–6) and the example in the table. Complete the table for the other pictures. You can use an online dictionary. Then talk about the pictures with a partner.

▶ Skills file 3, p. 157

Picture	Sport	Where you do this sport
1	cliff jumping	by the sea

Picture 1 / ... is ...   You can do that ...

1    **2**    **3**

4    **5**    **6**

🔊 2.3 b) Grace and Rhona are on the coach to the Adventure Centre. Listen and say why Rhona is worried.

1 b) Lösungsbsp. S. 293
▶ Skills file 8, p. 163

🔊 c) Listen again and take notes. Write which activities in a) the two girls have tried and which ones they haven't tried.
Then °compare with a partner.

1 c) Lösungsbsp. S. 293

Grace has tried ... / Grace hasn't tried ...   Rhona has tried ... / Rhona hasn't tried ...

💬 d) Tell a partner which activities you've already tried or which ones you'd like to try.

I've already tried ... How about you?

*I haven't tried ... yet. / I've tried ... too.
I'd like to try ..., but I don't want to try ...*

1 d) individuelle Lösungen   ▶ Workbook, p. 54

80   eighty

80

Topic 2 Vorbereitung

Material: Ex 1 Online-Wörterbuch, ▶ KV 3.2: Adventure sports (Klassensatz) • Ex 2 vorbereitete *Swap cards* mit unregelmäßigen Verben, z. B. ▶ KV 1.1 A+B: SWAP CARDS Verbs (Klassensatz), ▶ KV 3.3: Chant (Klassensatz), UMA/CD/App, UMA/App (Erklärfilm), UMA • Ex 4 UMA/CD/App, UMA
Zeitbedarf: ca. 2 Std.
Begleitmedien: WB (S. 54), INKL (S. 78–79)

---

2 LOOKING AT LANGUAGE The present perfect (revision)   2 a) have *or* has • -ed

a) Look at the examples from the °conversation between Grace and Rhona below.
Copy the rule in the box and complete it.

I've just read the programme and I've looked at all the activities again.
Have you ever been hiking? – No, I haven't. I've never been hiking.
Have you tried skiing yet? – No, my sister has been skiing, but I haven't tried that yet.
I've already tried ⁺snowboarding.

▶ Box: Voc., p. 233

1 We use the present perfect for an activity that
 • happened at an ⁺unknown time in the past
 • has already, just or not yet happened.

2 We also use the present perfect
 • to ask if somebody has ever done something (in their life)
 • to say that we have done something once, often or never (in our life).

We make the present perfect with ... or ... and the past participle.
Regular past participles *(looked, tried)* end in ... Sometimes the spelling changes.
Some past participles *(read, been)* are irregular. ▶ Irregular verbs, p. 272 f. ▶ Language file 11, p. 180

2.4

b) Listen and repeat the °chant. Then listen again, repeat and say the past participles.
2 b) Lösung S. 293 f.

3 Are you ready?   3 Lösung S. 294

Grace and Rhona are checking their equipment for a hiking trip.
Write their questions and answers in the present perfect.

Rhona *Have you packed* (1 you / pack) your rain jacket?
Grace Yes, I have. I ... (2 just / do) that.
Rhona ... (3 you / remember) your water bottle?
Grace Yes, I have. I ... (4 already / put) it in my rucksack. ... (5 Ms McKenzie / call) us yet?
Rhona No, she hasn't. But I ... (6 already / finish) my packing.
Grace You're so organized! ... (7 you / ever / forget) anything?
Rhona No, I haven't. I ... (8 never / forget) anything!

▶ More practice 4 + 5, p. 104

4 SPEAKING How adventurous are you?   4 a) Lösungsbsp. S. 294

a) Write five questions with *Have you ever ...?* about °outdoor activities.
Use the ideas in the box or your own ideas.

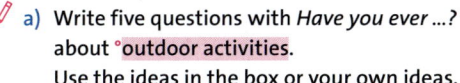

catch a fish • go to the mountains • climb a tree • jump from a cliff • ride a pony • go on a zip wire • sleep in a tent • sleep under the stars • swim in a lake or river

▶ Irregular verbs, p. 272 f.

b) DOUBLE CIRCLE Ask and answer questions. Move on to a new partner after each question.

Have you ever been to the mountains?   4 b) individuelle Lösungen
– Yes, once / twice / lots of times. / Yes, when I was in ... / No, I've never done that.

Ex 2 Einstieg:
• (SB zu) ▶ Swap cards mit unregelmäßigen Verben (▶ KV 1.1 A+B): S fragen sich gegenseitig.

Erarbeitung:
a) (SB auf) Klären der AA
• S schreiben die ▶ Grammatik-Box, S. 81 in ihren Merkteil (▶ English folder) ab, u. ergänzen die Regel.
• ▶ LF 11, S. 180, Erklärfilm (UMA/App)
• **Sich.:** im Plenum (UMA/TA), ggf. übersetzen der Regeln
• L sichert im TA (UMA).

b) 1. **Hören:** gemäß AA
• L klärt die Begriffe *echo verbs*, *sandwich verbs*, *cat verbs* und *chicken verbs* mit je 1–2 Bsp.
• ▶ KV 3.3: S lesen/hören den *chant* u. ergänzen das *past participle*.
• 2. **Hören:** S überprüfen ihre Verbformen.
• **Sich.:** TA mit dem Text (UMA)

Ex 3 Einstieg:
• (SB zu) ▶ Vokabelrennen mit den unregelmäßigen Verben

Erarbeitung:
• (SB auf) gemäß AA
• **Ausw.:** ▶ Five-minute teacher
• ▶ More practice 4 + 5, S. 104

Ex 4 Einstieg:
• (SB zu) S hören den *chant* aus Ex 2 (UMA) und sprechen das *past participle* mit.

Erarbeitung:
a) (SB auf) gemäß AA
• **Ausw.:** ▶ Partner check

b) S sprechen mehrere Beispieldialoge im Plenum, dann ▶ Double circle gemäß AA.

3

Topic 2 Inhalt

Lernschwerpunkt: eine Biografie lesen und selbst schreiben
Kompetenzen: *Reading* durch *Scanning* einer Kurzbiografie über den Abenteurer Aldo Kane Informationen zu seinem Leben sammeln • *Speaking* sich über Hobbys austauschen und sagen, wie lange man diese bereits macht • *Writing* eine Biografie über eine/-n Mit-S schreiben
Strukturen: *present perfect with for and since*
Redemittel: *describing people • sports, hobbies, interests • time phrases*

Ex 5 Einstieg:
- (SB zu) *Warm-up*: ▶ Bang mit Adjektiven. S schreiben ihr gesagtes Adjektiv auf eine Karte. Am Spielende werden alle Karten angepinnt.

Erarbeitung:

a) (SB auf) L zeigt die Bilder 1–3 (UMA).
L: *This is Aldo Kane. He is an adventurer from Scotland. What do you think he's like? Why?*
- S beschreiben Aldo mit den Adj. aus Reservoir u. Einstieg.
- Ausw.: ▶ Meldekette, L sammelt Ideen im TA.

b) S lesen den Text gemäß AA u. beantworten die Frage zum Globalverständnis (im Plenum).
- S prüfen ihre Ideen aus a).
L: *Are there any words you don't know?*
- S nennen unbekannte Wörter: ▶ Semantisieren u. Sammeln an der ▶ Vokabeltafel.
- Ausw.: gemäß AA im Plenum
- S streichen falsche Ideen aus dem TA aus a) und markieren bzw. ergänzen die richtigen.

c) gemeinsames Lesen der ▶ Tippbox, S. 82 zum *Scanning* (▶ Lesetechniken), ▶ SF 9, S. 164
- L gibt knappe Zeit vor: ca. 45 Sek., in denen S Notizen machen sollen.
- Ausw.: (SB zu) ▶ Meldekette zu den gefundenen Aktivitäten
- (SB auf) anschließend Abgleich mit dem Text u. ggf. Ergänzung

d) PA gemäß AA
- Ausw.: ▶ Blitzlichtrunde

| 3 | Topic 1 | **Topic 2** | Topic 3 | Story | Viewing | Study skills | Unit task |

5 READING Adventurer Aldo Kane

5 a), b), c) Lösungsbsp. S. 294

a) BEFORE YOU READ Grace has just read an online °biography about Scottish adventurer Aldo Kane. Look at the photos of his adventures. What do you think he's like? Why?

brave • careful • clever • fit • happy • hard-working • ⁺hopeful • lazy • lucky • patient • romantic • shy • sporty • stupid • …

I think he's … because …

a rhino

Mountain climbing? Skydiving? Anything dangerous? No problem. Aldo Kane has been an adventurer for thirty years and he has done it all. He has always loved outdoor activities, and he has made his hobby into his work. Aldo's motivation has always been to push himself to do more and he hasn't ever said no to a challenge. He has travelled through the jungles of South America, he has climbed into an active volcano, he has swum through underwater caves and run away from angry wild animals. ▶ Box: Voc., p. 229
Aldo is also motivated to get other people outdoors. Since 2010 he has taken part in adventure programmes on TV. He takes safety very seriously – both for himself and for others – and for many years he has helped with safety on TV programmes and film sets. Since 2021 he has also called himself a writer because he has written a book about his adventures. Go, Aldo!

b) Read the biography and say what it's about. Were your ideas from a) correct?

c) Scan the biography for the activities that Aldo Kane has done and make a list.
▶ Skills file 9, p. 164

💡 We scan a text to search for specific things (e.g. keywords, names, dates or numbers).

💬 **d)** Choose the three activities that °impressed you the most. Tell your partner and explain why.

5 d) individuelle Lösungen

I think it's amazing that he has … because …
It's cool that he has … because …

82 eighty-two

Topic 2 Vorbereitung

Material: Ex 5 Stoppuhr, weiße Karten (ca. drei pro S), ggf. UMA • Ex 6 UMA/App (Erklärfilm)
Zeitbedarf: ca. 3 Std.
Minimalversion: Ex 5d) auslassen
Begleitmedien: WB (S. 55–56), App (Digital quiz, Digital help), INKL (S. 80–81), DIFF (3.4)

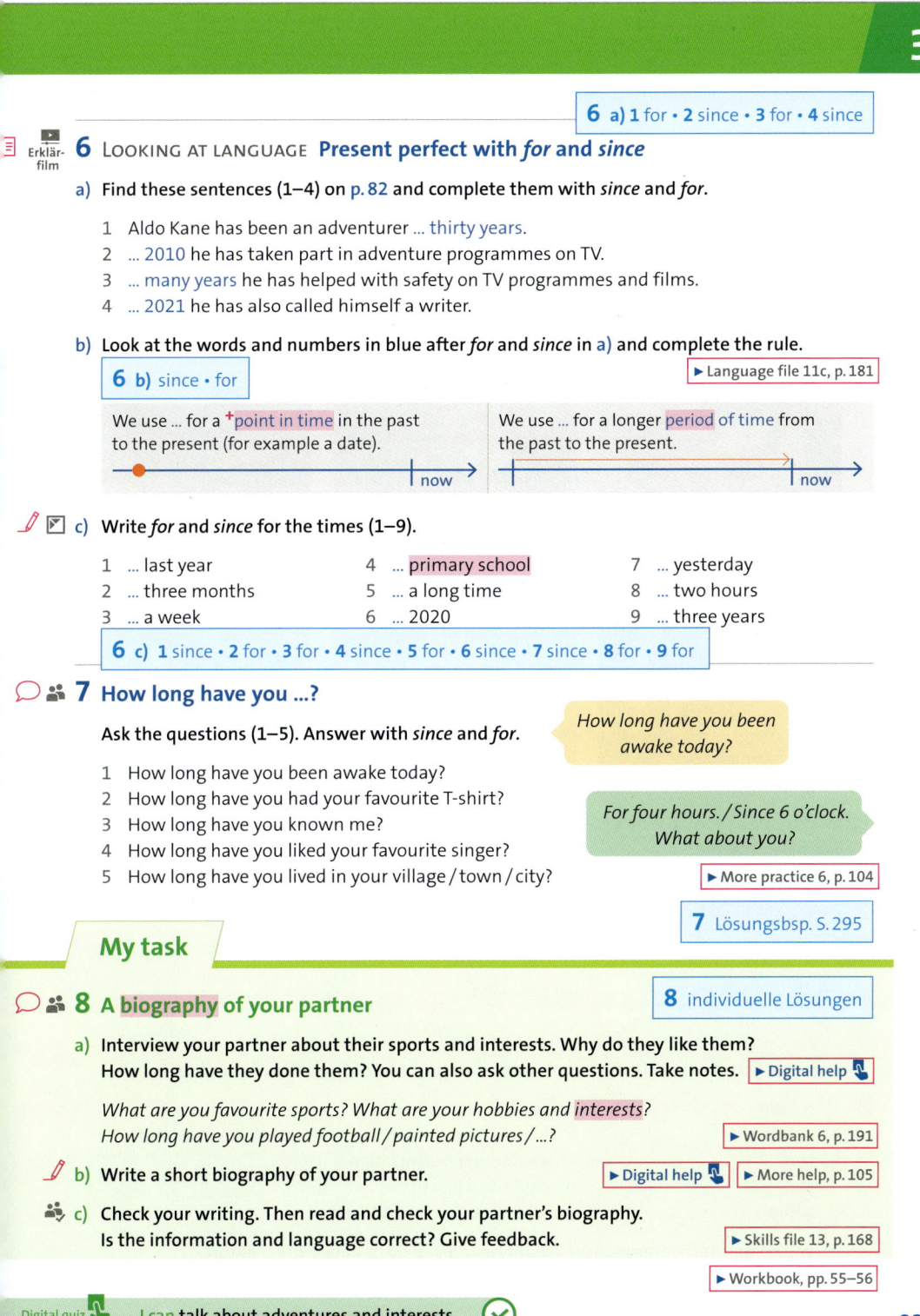

6 a) 1 for • 2 since • 3 for • 4 since

6 LOOKING AT LANGUAGE Present perfect with *for* and *since*

a) Find these sentences (1–4) on p. 82 and complete them with *since* and *for*.

1 Aldo Kane has been an adventurer ... thirty years.
2 ... 2010 he has taken part in adventure programmes on TV.
3 ... many years he has helped with safety on TV programmes and films.
4 ... 2021 he has also called himself a writer.

b) Look at the words and numbers in blue after *for* and *since* in a) and complete the rule.

6 b) since • for

▶ Language file 11c, p. 181

We use ... for a ⁺point in time in the past to the present (for example a date).
We use ... for a longer period of time from the past to the present.

c) Write *for* and *since* for the times (1–9).

1 ... last year 4 ... primary school 7 ... yesterday
2 ... three months 5 ... a long time 8 ... two hours
3 ... a week 6 ... 2020 9 ... three years

6 c) 1 since • 2 for • 3 for • 4 since • 5 for • 6 since • 7 since • 8 for • 9 for

7 How long have you ...?

Ask the questions (1–5). Answer with *since* and *for*.

1 How long have you been awake today?
2 How long have you had your favourite T-shirt?
3 How long have you known me?
4 How long have you liked your favourite singer?
5 How long have you lived in your village / town / city?

How long have you been awake today?

For four hours. / Since 6 o'clock. What about you?

▶ More practice 6, p. 104

7 Lösungsbsp. S. 295

My task

8 A biography of your partner

8 individuelle Lösungen

a) Interview your partner about their sports and interests. Why do they like them? How long have they done them? You can also ask other questions. Take notes. ▶ Digital help

What are you favourite sports? What are your hobbies and interests? How long have you played football / painted pictures /...?

▶ Wordbank 6, p. 191

b) Write a short biography of your partner. ▶ Digital help ▶ More help, p. 105

c) Check your writing. Then read and check your partner's biography. Is the information and language correct? Give feedback.

▶ Skills file 13, p. 168
▶ Workbook, pp. 55–56

Digital quiz — I can talk about adventures and interests.

eighty-three **83**

Ex 6 Einstieg:
- (SB zu) ▶ Never have I ever (ggf. mit Aktivitäten von Ex 5)

Erarbeitung:
a) (SB auf) Gemeinsames Lesen der AA: S übertragen Sätze 1–4 ins Heft u. vervollständigen sie.
- **Sich.:** im TA

b) Regelfindung gemäß AA, ggf. als ▶ Think-Pair-Share
- **Sich.:** TA der Regel, Ergänzung des Merkteils zum *present perfect* im ▶ English folder (s. Eintrag von Ex 2, S. 81)
- ▶ LF 11c, S. 181, Erklärfilm (UMA/App)

c) gemäß AA, schriftl. im Heft
- **Ausw.:** ▶ Five-minute teacher

Ex 7 Einstieg:
- (SB zu) L fragt Fragen ähnlich zur Aufgabe. S antworten.
- L prüft: verwenden S *for/since* korrekt? L korrigiert u. wdh. ggf. Regeln aus Ex 6.

Erarbeitung:
- (SB auf) ▶ Partner talk, s. AA
- **Ausw.:** ▶ Five-minute teacher
- ▶ More practice 6, S. 104

My task Ex 8 Einstieg:
- (SB auf) ▶ Semantisierung: *biography*

Erarbeitung:
a) PA gemäß AA, ▶ Note-taking

b) gemäß AA, s. *Digital help* (App)
- ▶ More help, S. 105

c) **Ausw.:** gemäß AA, ▶ Partner check, ▶ Feedback gemäß AA
- Ggf. überarbeiten S Text nach Feedback, ▶ SF 13, S. 168.

3

Topic 3 Inhalt

Lernschwerpunkt: über die Natur sprechen
Kompetenzen: Speaking über Naturschutz sprechen • sich zu einem Lied positionieren • über den Stellenwert von Natur diskutieren • Listening einen schottischen Song über Natur verstehen • Global goals Naturschutzprinzipien anhand von Bildern verstehen und beschreiben
Redemittel: *protecting nature • things in nature • nature is important because ….*

Ex 1 Einstieg:
- (SB zu) ▶Acrostic mit dem Wort *nature* erarbeiten (TA):
  L: *Which words can you find in 'nature'?*
  S: *nest, animal, tree, useful, rubbish, egg …*
  L: *Let's find out how to protect our nature.*

Erarbeitung:
a) (SB auf) S liest AA und Verben im Reservoir vor.
- ⊠ Bsp. im Plenum
- gemäß AA in PA
- **Ausw.:** L zeigt die Bilder (UMA).
- ▶Meinungsbarometer: L teilt Raum in zwei Hälften (*You should … / You shouldn't …*) und nennt nacheinander die Bildnrn. 1–6. S begeben sich jeweils auf eine Seite u. antworten im ganzen Satz, teilweise sind mehrere Antworten mögl..
- ⊠ S begründen ihre Entscheidung.

b) Klären der AA, L präsentiert die Mindmap (UMA).
- S erstellen eine ▶Mindmap für ihr *Vocab file*.
- **Ausw.:** ▶Partner check: S ergänzen weitere Wörter.
- **Sich.:** im Plenum (UMA/TA)
- s. a. ▶Wordbank 7, S. 192, ▶SF 1, S. 155

c) gemäß AA
- **Ausw.:** im Plenum

d) gemäß AA in PA
- **Ausw.:** im Plenum
- **Alternative:** ▶Speed dating: S diskutieren und präsentieren ihre Ergebnisse anschließend im Plenum. Die jeweiligen Partner/-innen korrigieren und ergänzen einander.

| 3 | Topic 1 | Topic 2 | **Topic 3** | Story | Viewing | Study skills | Unit task |

In nature

1 a) 1 *You* shouldn't feed *farm animals.* • 2 shouldn't leave • 3 should take • 4 should close • 5 shouldn't make • 6 shouldn't pick

💬 **1** GLOBAL GOALS Protect nature

👥 a) Before Grace and Rhona's class goes hiking, their °instructors give them some tips. Look at the pictures. What do you think the instructors say?

close • feed • go near • leave • make • pick • stay on • take • use

You should / shouldn't …

1
farm animals

2
paths

3
rubbish

4
gates

5
a fire

6
flowers and plants

✏ b) WORDS Make a mind map with words about nature in your VOCAB FILE. Start like this:

▶Wordbank 7, p. 192 ▶Skills file 1, p. 155

countryside — landscapes — nature — things in nature — tree
island — wild animals — farm animals — path
deer — dolphin — chicken — goat

1 b) Lösungsbsp. S. 295

💬 ⊠ c) Say what you can do at home to help protect nature. Match the parts of the phrases.

1 recycle   a an animal in danger
2 collect   b birds in your garden and on your balcony in winter
3 feed   c a volunteer organization
4 join   d paper and plastic
5 adopt   e rubbish in parks and forests

1 c) 1 d • 2 e • 3 b • 4 c • 5 a

👥 d) Do you do any of the things in c)? What else can you do to help protect nature?

1 d) individuelle Lösungen

▶Workbook, p. 57

Topic 3 Vorbereitung

Material: Ex 1 UMA • Ex 2 Realien (Blaubeeren und Heidekraut), UMA, UMA/CD/App, begonnene Mindmap von Ex 1b)
Zeitbedarf: 1–2 Std.
Minimalversion: Ex 1b) als HA, Ex 1d) auslassen
Begleitmedien: WB (S. 57–58), App (Digital quiz), INKL (S. 82–83), DIFF (3.5)

---

2 SONG The °Braes¹ of Balquhidder²

2 a) Blaubeeren/Heidelbeeren • Heide(kraut)

a) BEFORE YOU LISTEN Look at the plants in the pictures. What are their names in German?

blueberries

heather

Good to know
Scotland has lots of traditional songs. They're often about nature. The songs usually have some Scots words – like 'brae' (hill).

b) Listen to the song. A '°laddie' (boy) is asking a '°lassie' to go with him. What does 'lassie' mean?
▶ Skills file 2, p. 156
2 b) girl

c) Listen again and read the lyrics. Decide if the sentences are true or false and say why.
1 Fruit grows on the hills.
2 There are animals on the hills.
3 The laddie wants to take the lassie to a lake.
4 The laddie will sing a song about love.
2 c) Lösung S. 295

d) Find all the nature words in the song. Add new ones to your mind map in 1b).
2 d) Lösung S. 295

e) Tell a partner what you think of the song.
I like/don't like the song because …
I think that the music is beautiful/too slow/…
2 e) individuelle Lösungen

Will you go, lassie, go?
To the braes of Balquhidder
where the blueberries grow
around the °pretty purple heather.
Where the deer and rabbits play
all running together
through the long summer day
on the braes of Balquhidder.

I will find a pretty place
by the clear silver °fountain,
and around it I will put
all the flowers of the mountain.
If my lassie will go,
we will journey together,
and to her I will sing
of the hills and °sky and nature. …

My task

3 Nature and me
3 individuelle Lösungen

a) THINK Nature is important to the singer. How important is nature to you?

b) PAIR Tell a partner how important nature is to you.

I like doing outdoor sports/⁺camping/… in nature.
I think it's relaxing to be by a lake/in the countryside/…
I like to look at the stars/see wild animals/…
Nature is important because it gives us food/clean air/…

I don't like being in nature because there are lots of insects/…

c) SHARE Tell the class. Is nature important to most students?
▶ Wordbank 7, p. 192

1 [breɪz]   2 [bælˈwɪðə]
▶ Workbook, p. 58

Digital quiz I can **talk about nature.** ✓

eighty-five 85

Ex 2 Einstieg:
• (SB zu) L bringt Realien mit oder zeigt die Fotos (UMA). L: *Look, what grows in my garden. Do you know the names of these plants in German?*

Erarbeitung:
a) (SB auf) L semantisiert Wortschatz gemäß AA.
• Lesen von ▶ Good to know, S. 85
• Sich.: L schreibt die Wörter an die ▶ Vokabeltafel.

b) L/S liest die Frage vor. TA: *What does 'lassie' mean?*
• ▶ SF 2, S. 156, dann 1. Hören
• Ausw.: Im Plenum, L notiert Antwort als TA.

c) 2. Hören: gemäß AA
• Ausw.: ▶ Meldekette

d) schriftlich gemäß AA
• Ausw.: ▶ Partner check, dann im Plenum (UMA), S ergänzen ihre Mindmap.

e) PA gemäß AA
• Ausw.: ▶ Thumbs up im Plenum, freiw. S geben Begründung.

My task Ex 3 Einstieg:
• (SB zu) Aktivierung von Wortschatz zu *nature* mit ▶ Alphabet game

Erarbeitung:
a) (SB auf) Klären der AA
• ▶ Think-Pair-Share, gemäß AA

b) gemäß AA, ▶ English-only-Karte

c) S-Paare geben ihre Meinung im Plenum wieder, z. B. mithilfe von ▶ Wordbank 7, S. 192.
• Ausw.: im Plenum

3

Story Inhalt

Lernschwerpunkt: eine Abenteuergeschichte lesen
Kompetenzen: Speaking Brainstorming • Reading die Hauptaussage einer Geschichte verstehen
Redemittel: *should* • *outdoor, hiking, mountain rescue*

Ex 1 Einstieg:
- (SB zu) ▶ Gucklochmethode: L zeigt verdeckt ein Foto von Ben Nevis u. lässt die S raten. L/S ergänzt Infos über Schottlands höchsten Berg (TA).

Erarbeitung:

a) L zeigt das Bild von Ex 1a) (UMA).
L: *What should you do to prepare for hiking or mountain climbing?*
- S brainstormen Ideen gemäß AA, L hilft ggf. bei Vokabeln.
- **Ausw.:** im Plenum (TA)

b) (SB auf) S lesen/hören den Text (▶ Mitleseverfahren) in Stillarbeit. Sie dürfen noch keine Vokabeln nachschlagen.
- S erhalten je fünf Notizzettel für einen ▶ Question pot.
- S notieren Fragen zur Story, deren Antwort sie kennen auf je einem der Zettel und notieren die Antwort auf der Rückseite. Diese Fragen werden mit „Quiz" markiert.
- S schreiben für sie noch offene Fragen auf die restlichen Zettel (unbekannte Vokabeln, unverstandene Phrasen etc.). Diese Fragenkarten werden mit „?" markiert.
- ⧖ Die Zahl der Fragen kann variieren. Schwächere S können z. B. mehr offene Fragen aufschreiben und weniger Quizfragen.
- L sammelt die Zettel der S in einem ▶ Question pot.
- S bilden Vierergruppen.
- L mischt die Fragen im *Question pot* und teilt jeder Gruppe 20 Fragen aus.
- Forts. auf S. 87

| 3 | Topic 1 | Topic 2 | Topic 3 | **Story** | Viewing | Study skills | Unit task |

A mountain adventure

1 READING Preparing for an adventure

a) BEFORE YOU READ What should you do to prepare for hiking or mountain climbing? °Brainstorm ideas as a class. Look at Grace's rucksack to help you.

You should bring / check / remember / wear / …

1 a) individuelle Lösungen

1 b) You should always think carefully about your choices.

▶ More help, p. 105

b) Read the story. What's the main message of the story?

🔊 2.6

'I still can't believe you've never climbed Ben Nevis before!' said Grace.
Rhona laughed. Grace was always so dramatic! ▶ Box: Voc., p. 230
5 'I know, it's strange because I've always lived so close to the mountain,' said Rhona.
'But you know me – I'm not really a ⁺hiker.'
'Well, you'll love it,' said Grace. But Rhona wasn't so sure.

10 It was the last day of their trip and the whole class was on the coach to Ben Nevis. Mr McAlister, one of the teachers, walked along the coach, checking that everybody had the right equipment.
15 'Rhona, where are your walking boots? You shouldn't wear trainers today. I know we're taking the easy path, but it's still best to wear the right shoes.'
'Oh …,' Rhona's face was red.
20 'It's OK, Mr McAlister – my walking boots are with all the bags under the coach. I'll change when we get there.'

The teacher continued along the coach and Grace looked at Rhona.
25 'I didn't see you put any boots under the coach this morning.'
'I know … I don't have any. Walking boots are so expensive. And it's stupid to buy a pair when I'll never go hiking again!'

30 A few hours later, the class was halfway up the mountain. It wasn't as bad as Rhona thought, but Grace was bored. '°Ugh, there are too many people on this path and it's too easy – it's the path for °wee babies!
35 Come on, I know a shorter way. It's a bit more difficult, but the views are amazing and there aren't as many tourists. No one will know we're gone.'

Rhona was worried, but Grace pulled her
40 along a different path while Mr McAlister wasn't looking. She was right – it was very beautiful and not busy.

86 eighty-six

Story Vorbereitung

Material: Ex 1 Foto von Ben Nevis (von L recherchiert), UMA, UMA/CD/App, je fünf Notizzettel pro S, Körbchen o. Ä. für den *Question pot*
Zeitbedarf: ca. 2 Std.
Begleitmedien: INKL (S. 84–85)

However, when they got to a narrow ridge, Rhona stopped, suddenly scared. She could
45 see all the way down to the valley far below. One wrong step ...
'I can't do it,' Rhona started to cry. 'It's too high. I don't like heights!'
Grace tried to help her, but Rhona couldn't
50 speak and she started to get really scared.
Then Grace took Rhona's hands and looked into her eyes. 'Breathe slowly, like me. In ... out ... in ...'

Grace   Rhona

Eventually, Rhona calmed down. However,
55 as she walked on, she slipped on some rocks because her trainers weren't good enough for this path.
'Ow!' she cried. 'Oh, Grace, I've really hurt my ankle. I can't walk any more. We need to
60 call the others.'
'But what will I tell them? I don't know where we are. I think we're lost.'
Suddenly, Rhona remembered she had an app on her phone that could help.
65 'Mr McAlister told us to +download it – every place in the world has three words, so you can find out where you are.'
She quickly opened the app and checked the words for where they were:
70 snow.workroom.winds. Then Grace called Mr McAlister and explained, telling him the three words. 'Mountain Rescue are sending a helicopter now,' he said. 'Stay there – we'll find you with the app.'

75 As they waited, eating their snacks and feeling more and more scared, they started to argue.
'This is all your fault, Grace. Why did you decide to run off and take a stupid path
80 with loose rocks and narrow ridges?'
'Well, why did you wear trainers for climbing a mountain?'
'Hey, I didn't even want to climb this mountain!'
85 Finally, after what felt like hours, they heard a loud noise – the helicopter was here at last! They stood up and shouted, waving their hands. The ridge was too narrow for the helicopter to land, therefore the rescue
90 people lowered a paramedic on a rope and pulled the girls up. Rhona felt sick and her ankle hurt, but she remembered how Grace had helped her to breathe slowly.

Soon they were safely in the helicopter and
95 it began to fly away from the mountain. Grace and Rhona didn't say anything while the +rescuers checked Rhona's hurt ankle. They both felt tired, angry and embarrassed. Suddenly, both girls spoke at the same time:
100 'Grace ...'
'Rhona ...'
In the end, they both laughed. 'You go first, Grace,' said Rhona. 'What did you want to say?'

eighty-seven **87**

Ex 1 (Forts. von S. 86)
- S beantworten zunächst nur die Quizfragen. Hierzu liest ein/-e S die Frage vor, dann sucht die Gruppe im Text die Antwort.
- Anschließend prüfen sie, ob ihre Antwort mit der Lösung auf der Rückseite der Quizfrage übereinstimmt.
- Sind alle Quizfragen beantwortet, werden die Verständnisfragen geklärt. S suchen die Antworten im Text (ggf. arbeitsteilig) und notieren sie auf der Rückseite der jeweiligen Karte.
- S tauschen sich in der Gruppe nun auch über Vokabeln aus, schlagen diese nach u. übertragen sie ins *Vocab file*.
- Jede Gruppe stellt ihre Fragenkarten vor und nennt die Antwort auf die Fragen.
- Neue Vokabeln werden gemeinsam im TA gesichert u. ins *Vocab file* übertragen.
- Doppelte Karten können ggf. übersprungen werden.
- ▶Early finisher: Schnellere Gruppen wählen eine Szene aus der Story u. stellen sie in einem ▶Freeze-frame dar.
- ▶Early finishers stellen ihre *Freeze-frames* vor. Die Klasse rät, um welche Szene es sich handelt.
- **Ausw.:** L schreibt Frage zum Globalverständnis an die Tafel, s. S. 86, Ex 1b) (UMA): *What's the main message of the story?*
- S beantworten die Frage im Plenum, ggf. mit Begründung.
- s. a. ▶More help, S. 105

3

Story Inhalt

Lernschwerpunkt: aus Fehlern lernen
Kompetenzen: Reading falsche Entscheidungen in der Geschichte identifizieren • Speaking sich entschuldigen
Redemittel: *linking words and phrases* • *saying sorry*

Vorbereitung

Material: Ex 2 ggf. UMA/CD/App
Zeitbedarf: ca. 1 Std.
Minimalversion: Ex 4 und Ex 5 auslassen
Begleitmedien: App (Digital quiz), INKL (S. 86), DIFF (3.6)

Ex 2 Erarbeitung:
- (SB auf) L semantisiert *choice*.
- gemäß AA, ggf. ▶ Mitleseverfahren
- Ausw.: ▶ Blitzlichtrunde

Ex 3 Einstieg:
- (SB zu) ▶ Word race zu *linking words*

Erarbeitung:
- (SB auf) Lesen der ▶ Tippbox, S. 105, ▶ Semantisieren: *order*, *summary*, *contrast* und *result*.
- TA der Tabelle: L/S ordnet als Bsp. einige *linking words* zu.
- gemäß AA im Heft
- Ausw.: ▶ Five-minute teacher

Ex 4 Erarbeitung:
- gemäß AA
- 🔊 Semantisierung: *wherever*
- Ausw.: ▶ Meldekette

Ex 5 Einstieg:
- (SB auf) S lesen das Ende der Story (ab S. 87, Zeile 85 ff.).

Erarbeitung:
a) gemäß AA in EA
b) in PA gemäß AA
- Ausw.: S-Paare tragen einen ihrer Dialoge im Plenum vor.

Ex 6 Einstieg:
- (SB zu) ▶ Milling around zur Frage: *Have you ever made a bad choice? What was it?*

Erarbeitung:
a) (SB auf) gemäß AA
- Ausw.: ▶ Meldekette
b) Gemäß AA, S nutzen Ideen aus dem Einstieg.
- Ausw.: Im Plenum

---

3 | Topic 1 | Topic 2 | Topic 3 | **Story** | Viewing | Study skills | Unit task

📖 2 Good and bad choices **2 Lösungsbsp. S. 295**

Read the story again. What good and bad choices did each character make?

1 Grace helped …, but she …
2 Rhona used …, but she …

Rhona   Grace

📖 3 Linking words and phrases **3 Lösungsbsp. S. 295**

Copy and complete the table. Find linking words in the text for each list.

order	summary	contrast	result
then	in the end	but	so
…	…	…	…

💡 Remember: You can join sentences together with linking words to make the text more interesting.

▶ More practice 7, p. 105

📖 4 Where?

4 1 where • 2 wherever/everywhere • 3 everywhere/wherever • 4 everywhere/where/wherever • 5 where

Complete the sentences with the words from the box.

> everywhere • where • wherever

1 When you go hiking, make sure someone knows … you are.
2 There were tourists … the girls looked!
3 Rhona always takes her phone … she goes.
4 Grace takes notes on … she has hiked.
5 It's important to look … you are going, so you don't fall.

✏ 5 Saying sorry **5 a) Lösungsbsp. S. 295**

a) Write what you think Grace and Rhona say to each other at the end of the story.

I'm sorry, it was a bad idea to …
I'm sorry I forgot to … / I don't know why I …
That's OK. / Thank you for saying sorry.

👥 b) Read your partner's °conversation. Then choose one and read it out.

5 b) individuelle Lösungen

Grace   Rhona

6 a) Grace should stay with the class. Rhona should bring better shoes.

💬 6 LIFE SKILLS Learn from your mistakes

👥 a) Look at the bad choices in 2. What should each character do next time?
✖ b) Like Grace and Rhona, everybody makes mistakes. Think about a small mistake you or someone else made recently. What should you or they do next time?

6 b) individuelle Lösungen

88 eighty-eight   Digital quiz   I can discuss good and bad choices in a story.

3

Viewing Inhalt

Lernschwerpunkt: ein Video über einen Roadtrip durch Schottland verstehen
Kompetenzen: Speaking sich über unterschiedliche Reisearten austauschen • über Unternehmungen in Schottland sprechen • Viewing einem Film Informationen entnehmen
Redemittel: *ways to travel • sightseeing • activities*

Vorbereitung

Material: Ex 2 UMA/DVD/App • Ex 3 UMA
Zeitbedarf: ca. 1 Std.
Begleitmedien: WB (S. 59), INKL (S. 87)

Topic 1 | Topic 2 | Topic 3 | Story | **Viewing** | Study skills | Unit task | **3**

A road trip

1 Before you watch The best way to travel

a) What's your favourite way to travel and why? Tell your partner.

b) What's a road trip? Compare your answers.

> **1 a)** individuelle Lösungen
>
> **1 b)** A road trip is a holiday or a long trip you take by car.

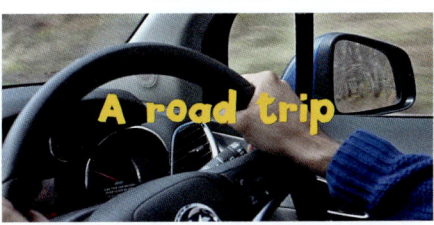

2 Viewing Sightseeing

a) Watch the video. Which of these things do Mon and George see on their road trip?

A a bridge	E a farm	H a city
B a valley	F a cow	I a lake
C a volcano	G a castle	J a cave
D a boat		

> **2 a)** A • B • D • G • H • I • J

b) Watch the video again and complete the sentences.

1 George has never …
2 Mon has always …
3 They haven't … today.
4 Mon and George have never …
5 They've already …

> **2 b) 1** driven on the left side of the road before. • **2** loved castles. • **3** seen any monsters • **4** seen so many beautiful natural places. • **5** got lots of ideas for their next vlog.

3 Scottish activities

a) Complete the sentences with the activities.

1 On the Isle of Skye[1], they don't … because …
2 At Loch Ness, they go …
3 At Dunrobin, they listen to …

> **3 a) 1** swim … the sea is cold. • **2** horse riding. • **3** bagpipes.

b) Which place in the video would you most like to visit and why? Tell your partner.

> **3 b)** individuelle Lösungen

1 [skaɪ]

▶ Workbook, p. 59

eighty-nine **89**

Ex 1 Einstieg:
- (SB zu) ▶ Give me five im ▶ Milling around (ohne Zettel, *items* an der Hand abzählen) zum Thema *Ways to travel* (TA)
- L sammelt die Begriffe im TA.

Erarbeitung:
a) (SB auf) S lesen die Frage und beantworten sie in PA.
- Ggf. TA mit Scaffolding: *I like travelling by … because …*
- **Ausw.:** ▶ Blitzlichtrunde im Plenum

b) S-Paare spekulieren gemäß AA.
- **Ausw.:** Vergleich im Plenum

Ex 2 Einstieg:
- (SB zu) L: *Today we're going to watch a video of a road trip through Scotland. Which things do you think you'll see? Write a list.*
- S erstellen eine Liste mit Dingen, die sie im Video erwarten (TA).

Erarbeitung:
a) (SB auf) S vergleichen ihre Liste mit den *items* aus a).
- ✉ S ergänzen ggf. einige *items* ihrer eigenen Liste.
- 1. Viewing: gemäß AA
- **Ausw.:** ▶ Meldekette

b) 2. Viewing: gemäß AA
- **Ausw.:** ▶ Five-minute teacher

Ex 3 Erarbeitung:
a) (SB auf) S ergänzen die Sätze gemäß AA.
- **Ausw.:** Im Plenum. L zeigt die Fotos (UMA).

b) PA gemäß AA
- **Ausw.:** ▶ Blitzlichtrunde im Plenum

3

Study skills Inhalt

Lernschwerpunkt: Ideen für eine Abenteuergeschichte strukturieren
Kompetenzen: Study skills Ideen in einer Mindmap sammeln und sortieren
Redemittel: places • people • events

Vorbereitung

Material: Ex 2 Schreibblätter (Klassensatz, ein Blatt pro S-Paar) • Ex 3 weiße Blätter für die Mindmap (Klassensatz), Stoppuhr o. Ä.
Zeitbedarf: ca. 1 Std.
Begleitmedien: App (Digital quiz), INKL (S. 88), DIFF (3.7)

Ex 1 Einstieg:
- (SB zu) L notiert *A short adventure story* (TA):
L: *Let's plan a story. What information do we need?*
S: *We need the time, place, people, objects, ….*

Erarbeitung:
- (SB auf) L liest AA vor.
- S lesen die Bsp., s. *ideas box*, ggf. ▶ Semantisierung.
L: *Do you know more places?*
- S antworten u. ergänzen (TA).
- Gemäß AA in PA: S-Paare entscheiden sich für eine gemeinsame *situation*.
- Ausw.: im Plenum

Ex 2 Erarbeitung:
a) (SB auf) gemäß AA in EA, aber zu zweit an einem Blatt.
b) gemäß AA (S-Paare wechseln.)
- L nutzt Stoppuhr o. Ä.
- Ausw.: S vergleichen im ▶ Partner talk.

Ex 3 Erarbeitung:
a) Gemäß AA: S1 wählt *people*, S2 *events*.
- S erstellen je eine ▶ Mindmap im Heft od. auf separaten Blättern in EA.
b) gemäß AA
- Ausw.: S vergleichen ihre Mindmaps im ▶ Partner talk.

Ex 4 Erarbeitung:
- Partner/-innen tauschen die Mindmaps und arbeiten gemäß AA in EA, s. a. ▶ SF 6, S. 161. Sie nutzen die Hilfen aus dem SB.
- Ausw.: S-Paare vervollständigen ihre zwei Mindmaps (▶ Partner talk).

90

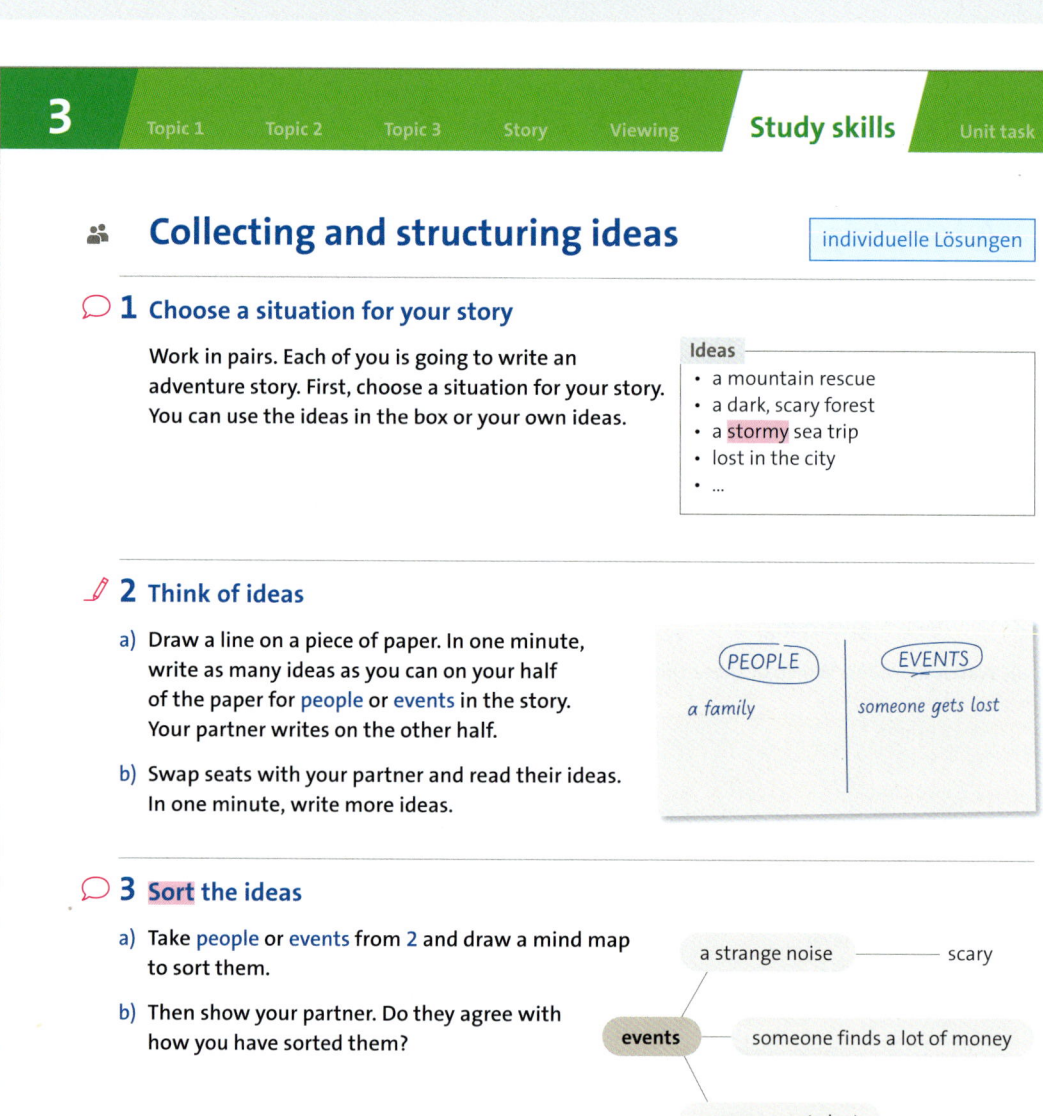

Unit task Inhalt

Lernschwerpunkt: eine Abenteuergeschichte schreiben
Kompetenzen: Media Skills Notizen erstellen und ordnen • Writing gemeinsam eine Abenteuergeschichte schreiben • Speaking Feedback geben
Redemittel: *useful phrases for writing a story • linking words • adventures and places*

Vorbereitung

Material: Step 1 Mindmaps von Ex 4, S. 90 • Step 2 ggf. Papierstreifen (mehrere pro S) • Steps 3–5 ggf. digitale Endgeräte u. Textverarbeitungsprogramme • Step 5 ggf. Klebezettel (Klassensatz)
Zeitbedarf: ca. 2 Std.
Minimalversion: Step 1 + Step 2 als vorbereitete HA
Begleitmedien: App (Digital quiz, Digital help), INKL (S. 89)

Topic 1 | Topic 2 | Topic 3 | Story | Viewing | Study skills | **Unit task 3**

Write a short adventure story

Unit task individuelle Lösungen

Step 1: Choose ideas for your story
▶ Digital help

Look at your mind maps from p. 90 and highlight or °underline the ideas you want to use. Your partner might choose the same or different ideas for their story.
▶ Skills file 6, p. 161

Step 2: Plan your story

a) Make short notes about your events and characters using your ideas from step 1. What are their names? How do they feel? …

b) Put the ideas in order and plan your story.

> Joe + Salim: go fishing →
> pack + go out in boat →
> get dark, Joe is scared →
> storm, Joe falls into water →
> Salim: pulls Joe into boat, calls 999 →
> lifeguard: rescues boys

Step 3: Write the story

Write your story and use the simple past. Make sure you have a beginning, a middle and an end.

💡 If you write your story digitally, you can use the ⁺spellchecker to make sure your spelling is correct.
▶ More help, p. 105

Step 4: Check and rewrite
▶ Digital help

a) Check your story with the checklist and make sure you have thought of everything.

b) Rewrite or °edit your story in a digital document or on a new piece of paper.

- Is there a beginning, a middle and an end?
- Have you used the simple past?
- Have you used linking words?
- Have you spelled everything correctly?
- Is the story exciting? Have you used adjectives and adverbs?

Step 5: Share your story

Read your partner's story or they can read it °aloud. Give feedback about the story and the language they have used. You can use °sticky notes or digital °comments.

*I think your story was very exciting.
You used lots of interesting vocabulary and linking words.
Next time, include a happy ending!*

▶ Let's talk: Feedback, p. 200

Digital quiz — I can write a short adventure story. ✓

ninety-one **91**

Unit task Einstieg:
- (SB auf) L bespricht mit S das Ziel der *Unit task* (*Write a short adventure story*) u. die *steps* 1–5 zum Erreichen des Ziels.

Step 1 Erarbeitung:
- gemäß AA, s. a. ▶ SF 6, S. 161
- S highlighten ihre Mindmaps ggf. mit unterschiedlichen Farben.

Step 2 Erarbeitung:
a) Klären der AA a) und b)
- S arbeiten gemäß AA (▶ Notemaking).
b) gemäß AA
- **Alternative:** S schreiben auf Papierstreifen u. ordnen diese.

Step 3 Erarbeitung:
- gemeinsames Lesen der AA und der ▶ Tippbox, S. 91
- S schreiben ihre Story auf Papier oder nutzen digitale Endgeräte.
- L unterstützt individuell.
- ▶ More help, S. 105

Step 4 Erarbeitung:
a) L zeigt Checkliste (UMA) u. S lesen vor, ggf. ▶ Semantisierung.
- S prüfen ihren Text gemäß AA.
b) gemäß AA auf Papier oder mit digitalen Endgeräten
- ▶ **Early finisher:** S illustrieren ihre Story.

Step 5 Erarbeitung:
- PA gemäß AA mit ▶ Feedback
- ▶ Let's talk: Feedback, S. 200
- **Ausw.:** im Plenum, anschließend im ▶ English corner od. an einer digitalen Pinwand

3

Checkpoint Inhalt

Lernschwerpunkt: Kompetenzen und sprachliche Mittel üben, Lernfortschritte erkennen
Kompetenzen: Speaking über eine Sehenswürdigkeit in Edinburgh sprechen • Listening eine Geschichte hören und Informationen erfassen • Reading Lückentexte grammatisch korrekt vervollständigen • Mediation Informationen aus einem deutschen Text ins Englische übertragen
Strukturen: adverbs of manners • present perfect with for and since
Redemittel: describing places • sightseeing • adventure

Allgemeine Anmerkung:
s. Unit 1, S. 32

Ex 1 Einstieg:
- (SB auf) Selbsteinschätzung zum Lernziel mit ▶Thumbs up

Erarbeitung:
- gemeinsames Klären der AA
- anschl. ▶Partner talk
- **Ausw.:** Einzelne S-Paare präsentieren ihre Ergebnisse im Plenum.
- **Alternative:** Am ▶Bus stop (▶KV Extra): S vergleichen ihre Ideen mit den Lösungsbsp. auf ▶KV 3.4A.
- erneute Selbsteinschätzung

Ex 2 Einstieg:
- s. Ex 1 (Selbsteinschätzung)

Erarbeitung:
a) 1. Hören: gemäß AA
- **Ausw.:** im Plenum

b) 2. Hören: gemäß AA
- S notieren vollständige Sätze in ihr Heft.
- ⬛ Schwächere S schreiben nur die gesuchten Wörter auf.
- **Ausw.:** ▶Meldekette

c) gemeinsames Lesen der AA
- kurze mdl. Wdh. der *adverbs of manner*
- ⬛ Schwächere S schauen sich den Erklärfilm von S. 178 an.
- S notieren die vollständigen Sätze gemäß AA in ihr Heft.
- ⬛ S schreiben nur die Wörter.
- **Ausw.:** ▶Five-minute teacher
- **Alternative:** Am ▶Bus stop (▶KV Extra): S vergleichen ihre Lösungen mithilfe von ▶KV 3.4A.
- erneute Selbsteinschätzung

---

3 Checkpoint Digital checkpoint

1 SPEAKING A day in Edinburgh

> I can talk about Scotland. ✓

You're planning a trip to Edinburgh with your Scottish friend. Look at the information on a °tourism website. Tell your friend which place you want to visit and why. You can use the phrases below to help you.

> **1** Lösungsbsp. S. 295

www.discover-Edinburgh.example.net

Edinburgh Castle
The perfect place to discover Scottish history and to enjoy amazing views of the city.

Open every day from 9.30 a.m.
Ticket: £19.50
Child ticket (°age 7–15): £11.40

Edinburgh Zoo
Calling all animal °lovers! Our zoo is home to over 2,500 animals from around the world.

Open every day from 10 a.m.
Ticket: £24.25
Child ticket (age 3–15): £15.25

I'd like to go to / visit ... • I'm really interested in / I love ... • I want to know more about / see / take ... • It's cheaper than ... • I don't want to go to ... because ...

2 LISTENING Grace's story

> I can understand stories and legends (adverbs of manner). ✓

  a) Listen to Grace's story. Which picture matches the story, A or B?
2.7

> **2 a)** B

b) Listen again. Complete the sentences with the correct word.

1 Culloden[1] is a ... near Inverness.
2 Nearly ... years ago, there was fighting.
3 1500 ... were killed there.
4 The ghosts come back every ...
5 One Scottish soldier walks through the fields ...
6 The ghosts come to Culloden on ... April.

> **2 b) 1** small village • **2** 300 • **3** soldiers • **4** year on the day of the battle. • **5** alone and wears tartan and looks sad. • **6** 16th

c) LANGUAGE Read what Grace's uncle said. Make the adjectives 1–6 into adverbs.

I went to Culloden last April. At first it was calm, but the ghosts appeared (1) sudden. They shouted (2) loud and ran (3) fast. One ghost was alone. He walked around (4) slow and (5) sad. I went back to my car (6) careful because I didn't want the ghosts to see me!

> **2 c) 1** suddenly • **2** loudly • **3** fast • **4** slowly • **5** sadly • **6** carefully

Check

92 ninety-two   1 [kəˈlɒdən]

3

Checkpoint Vorbereitung

Material: alle Aufgaben ▶ KV Extra: Bus stop, ▶ KV 3.4A: Checkpoint answers, App (Check) • **Ex 2** UMA/CD/App, UMA/App (Erklärfilm) • **Ex 3** *Right/wrong cards* in zwei Farben, als (Klassensatz), UMA/App (Erklärfilm) • **Ex 4** *online dictionary* od. App (*Vocabulary*)
Zeitbedarf: ca. 2 Std.
Minimalversion: Auswahl der Aufgaben erfolgt aufgrund der zu überprüfenden Lernziele
Begleitmedien: App (Digital Checkpoint), INKL (S. 90–91)

Die Übungen kannst du auch digital machen. 3

3 The adventure centre website

I can talk about adventures and interests (present perfect with *for* and *since*). ✓

a) LANGUAGE Read the interview on the adventure centre website. Complete the sentences with *since* or *for*. 1 ...

3 a)
1 for
2 since
3 for
4 since
5 for

www.adventure-centre-who-is-who.example.net

Hi Gemma[1], *tell us a bit about yourself.*
Hi everyone, I've been an °instructor here at the adventure centre ... (1) five years. My job is to teach °paddleboarding and skiing. It's my dream job – I love it!

And when did you learn to ski and to paddleboard?
Well I grew up near the sea, so I've paddleboarded ... (2) primary school.
I've skied ... (3) a long time too. I've taught skiing ... (4) 2019.

And what about your favourite place for an adventure?
That's easy: Scotland! I've lived here ... (5) many years and I'm still discovering amazing new places.

b) WORDS Complete the sentences with the correct words. 1 ...

b)
cliff
stormy
pack
outdoor

1 Learn more about exciting activities like _ _ _ _ _ f jumping!

2 The weather can be very _ t _ _ _ _. Bring rain clothes!

3 Click here for a full list of what things you need to p _ _ _.

4 In our centre you can take part in many _ u _ _ _ _ _ activities.

→ **4** MEDIATION **A German adventurer**   4 Lösungsbsp. S. 295

Your British friend Mark wants to find out about a German adventurer. Write a message to him about Rüdiger Nehberg.

Hi Mark, I want to tell you about ...

Rüdiger Nehberg (1935–2020) war Abenteurer und Aktivist. Ursprünglich wohnte er in Hamburg, wo er als Bäcker arbeitete. Im Laufe der Zeit interessierte er sich immer mehr für Reisen und Abenteuer. Er reiste in viele Länder, oft ohne Wasser, Essen oder sonstige Ausrüstung. Er arbeitete jahrelang, um Menschen überall auf der Welt zu unterstützen. Für diese Arbeit bekam er viele Preise.

1 [ˈdʒemə]

Check ⬇

ninety-three **93**

Ex 3 Einstieg:
- s. Ex 1 (Selbsteinschätzung)
- 📋 (SB zu) L schreibt *since* u. *for* in den zwei Farben der Karten (z. B. in Rot und Grün) an die Tafel.
- L erklärt den Einsatz der ▶ Right/wrong cards:
  L: *Take a red and a green card. Red means 'since' and green means 'for'.*
- kurze Wdh. mit Bsp. im Plenum (TA), Erklärfilm (UMA/App), ▶ LF 11c, S. 181
- L nennt *time words* (z. B. *yesterday, four weeks, ...*), S halten mit geschlossenen Augen die richtige Farbe hoch, z. B. *yesterday* – rote Karte.

Erarbeitung:
a) (SB auf) S notieren Lösungen.
- **Ausw.:** ▶ Bus stop (▶ KV Extra): S vergleichen ihre Lösungen mithilfe von ▶ KV 3.4A.

b) gemäß AA
- **Ausw.:** ▶ Bus stop (▶ KV Extra): S vergleichen ihre Lösungen mithilfe von ▶ KV 3.4A.
- **Alternative:** ▶ Five-minute teacher

Ex 4 Erarbeitung:
- (SB auf) Lesen der AA
- S lesen den dt. Text in EA und schreiben die Antwort an Mark in ihr Heft.
- 📋 Lernschwächere S nutzen die Wörtersuche in der App od. ein *online dictionary*.
- **Ausw.:** im Plenum
- **Alternative:** ▶ Bus stop (▶ KV Extra): S vergleichen ihre Lösungen mithilfe von ▶ KV 3.4A.
- erneute Selbsteinschätzung

93

3

Checkpoint Inhalt

Lernschwerpunkt: Kompetenzen und sprachliche Mittel üben, Lernfortschritte erkennen
Kompetenzen: Writing eine Nachricht an einen Freund / eine Freundin schreiben • Study skills Ideen in einer Mindmap anordnen • Reading eine Geschichte lesen und Details entnehmen
Redemittel: nature • adventure • free-time activities

Ex 5 Einstieg:
- (SB auf) S lesen das Lernziel (I can ...) vor.
- Selbsteinschätzung zum Lernziel mit ▶ Thumbs up
- 🖼 In lernschwächeren Gruppen zeigt L die Fotos A u. B (UMA): *What can you see?*
- S antworten u. L notiert bei Bedarf neue Vokabeln an der Tafel (▶ Vokabeltafel).

Erarbeitung:
- gemeinsames Lesen der AA
- L verweist aufs ▶ Scaffolding.
- S arbeiten schriftlich in EA.
- **Ausw.:** ▶ Partner check, dann im Plenum
- **Alternative:** ▶ Bus stop (▶ KV Extra): S vergleichen ihre Texte mit den Lösungsbeispielen von ▶ KV 3.4B.
- erneute Selbsteinschätzung

Ex 6 Einstieg:
- s. Ex 5 (Selbsteinschätzung)

Erarbeitung:
- gemeinsames Lesen der AA
- S übertragen die ▶ Mindmap ins Heft und ergänzen die Ideen gemäß AA.
- **Alternative:** S arbeiten digital und nutzen dabei eine geeignete App zur Erstellung der Mindmap.
- **Ausw.:** S präsentieren Ergebnisse im Plenum (UMA/Dokumentenkamera).
- **Alternative:** ▶ Bus stop (▶ KV Extra): S vergleichen ihre Lösungen mithilfe von ▶ KV 3.4B.
- erneute Selbsteinschätzung

---

3 Checkpoint Digital checkpoint

5 WRITING A message to a friend

I can talk about nature.

Imagine you're on a camping holiday in Scotland and you're staying near place A or B. Write a message to your friend Michelle. Tell her:
- what you can see and hear.
- what activities you're doing.
- if you like it there and why.

Write about 80 words. The phrases in the box can help you.

5 Lösungsbsp. S. 296

Dear Michelle,
I'm camping in Scotland at the moment. ...

> The area / landscape is ... • I can see lots of ... • Sometimes I can hear ... •
> Yesterday I went / saw / heard ... • I (don't) like it here because it's ...

A

B

6 STUDY SKILLS Ahmed's story

I can structure ideas for a story.

Read Ahmed's notes for his story.
Draw a mind map to sort his ideas.
Use the headings below.

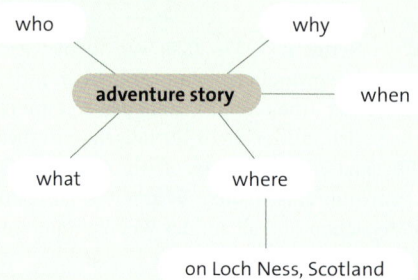

Adventure story: my ideas
- on Loch Ness, Scotland
- last summer
- two boys – James and Hussein
- school trip
- want to see the monster
- big storm
- lights on the boat stop working
- James – nervous, Hussein – brave
- James thinks he sees a big animal in the water, but it's very dark ...

6 Lösung S. 296

Check

94 ninety-four

3

Checkpoint Vorbereitung

Material: alle Aufgaben ▶KV Extra: Bus stop, ▶KV 3.4B: Checkpoint answers, App (Check) • Ex 5 UMA • Ex 6 Software/App zur Erstellung von Mindmaps, digitale Endgeräte, UMA/Dokumentenkamera • Ex 7 UMA
Zeitbedarf: ca. 2 Std.
Minimalversion: Auswahl der Aufgaben erfolgt aufgrund der zu überprüfenden Lernziele.
Begleitmedien: App (Digital Checkpoint)

Die Übungen kannst du auch digital machen. **3**

7 READING Kayaking on the river

I can discuss good and bad choices in a story. ✓

a) Read the story. What's it about? Choose the best main idea.

'Right, everyone,' said the °instructor, 'I have shown you how to use the boats safely. The last thing I want to talk about is the dry bag. This is where you need to put your important things so that they don't get wet. Great, everyone looks ready
5 now. Let's get onto the water. Just remember the number one rule: °Focus on the boat at all times. Any problems, call me!'

Grace and Rhona got into their kayak excitedly. 'This is amazing,' said Grace. 'Let's go faster!' Rhona laughed. It was a little bit scary at first, but after a few minutes she really
10 enjoyed going down the river with Grace.
'Let's take some photos,' said Grace. 'My parents will love to see us kayaking!'
'I'm not sure,' answered Rhona. 'My phone is in the dry bag. The instructor said we should leave our things in there.'
'That's true. But we can take it out for a minute and then put it in the bag again,'
15 said Grace. Rhona opened the bag very carefully and took out her phone.
'°Woah!' called Grace as the kayak stopped suddenly. 'I think there are some big rocks under our boat! Are you ok?'
'°Erm, yes, I'm OK ...,' said Rhona. 'But my phone isn't. It's in the water!'
'Oh no, I'm so sorry,' said Grace. 'The water isn't very deep here. I'll get out and find
20 your phone.'
'No, you stay in the boat,' said Rhona. 'I'm a stronger swimmer than you are. I'll get out and find the phone.'
Rhona climbed into the water confidently. 'I can see it,' she called, 'it's not far from the boat. I'll just ...,' Rhona suddenly looked worried.
25 'Rhona? Are you OK?' asked Grace. 'The ground here is really soft,' said Rhona. 'I – I can't lift up my foot! I think it's °stuck.'
'Stay there, and don't try to move,' said Grace. 'I can see the instructor. I'll ask him to come and help us.'

7 a) C

Grace and Rhona ...
A really enjoyed their kayaking adventure.
B found kayaking really difficult.
C made some mistakes while kayaking.

b) Complete the sentences with the correct name.

1 ... wanted to take photos.
2 ... took her phone out of the bag.
3 ... got out of the boat.
4 ... asked the instructor for help.

7 b) 1 Grace • 2 Rhona • 3 Rhona • 4 Grace

c) For each sentence from b) write 'good choice' or 'bad choice' and say why.

7 c) Lösungsbsp. S. 296

Check

ninety-five 95

Ex 7 Einstieg:
- s. Ex 5 (Selbsteinschätzung)
- (SB zu) L zeigt das Foto (UMA) mittels Gucklochmethode: L: *What/Who can you see? Where is it? ...*
- S antworten.

Erarbeitung:

a) + b) (SB auf) Klären der AA für beide Teilaufgaben
- S lesen den Text laut oder leise.
- Bearbeitung gemäß AA
- ☒ ▶Early finisher: Schnellere S bearbeiten selbstständig c).
- **Ausw.:** ▶Bus stop (▶KV Extra): S vergleichen ihre Lösungen mithilfe von ▶KV 3.4B.
- **Alternative:** ▶Meldekette
- erneute Selbsteinschätzung

c) Klären der AA
- S notieren die Antworten ins Heft.
- **Ausw.:** ▶Partner check, dann im Plenum
- **Alternative:** am ▶Bus stop (▶KV Extra): S vergleichen ihre Lösungen mithilfe von ▶KV 3.4B.
- erneute Selbsteinschätzung

95

3
OPTIONAL

Text file Inhalt

Lernschwerpunkt: verschiedene Informationen zu Aktivitäten in Glasgow verstehen
Kompetenzen: Reading einem Artikel Informationen zu Aktivitäten in Glasgow entnehmen

Allgemeine Anmerkung:
s. Unit 1, S. 36

Amazing activities in Glasgow
Einstieg:
- (SB auf) S lesen die Überschrift und betrachten die Fotos 1–6 (UMA). Die Texte werden noch nicht gelesen.
- S äußern Vermutungen dazu, was sie auf den Bildern sehen in PA (Partnersuche ggf. über ▶ Bus stop steuern).

Erarbeitung:
- **Hinweis:** Diese Erarbeitung kann L auch nutzen, um eine Sprechprüfung vorzubereiten.
- S lesen Texte zu jeweils drei Sehenswürdigkeiten.
- In PA tauschen S die Informationen zu den Sehenswürdigkeiten aus.
- S diskutieren (in PA od. im Plenum), welche Sehenswürdigkeit ihnen am besten gefällt, und begründen ihre Meinung (▶ SF 5, S. 160, ggf. ▶ Discussion tickets, z. B. ▶ KV 2.3).
- **Ausw.:** S einigen sich auf einen Kompromiss.
- S-Paare präsentieren ihre Wahl einer anderen Gruppe und begründen ihre Meinung.
- ☒ Zwei Gruppen stellen sich gegenseitig die Ergebnisse ihrer vorherigen Diskussion (in PA) vor. Anschließend müssen sie sich gemeinsam auf eine Aktivität einigen, die sie auf jeden Fall und auf eine, die sie auf keinen Fall durchführen möchten.
- Forts. auf S. 97

3
OPTIONAL

Text file

Do you want to visit Glasgow? Here are my top tips.

A magazine for young people across the UK

Amazing activities in Glasgow
by Angus Fraser

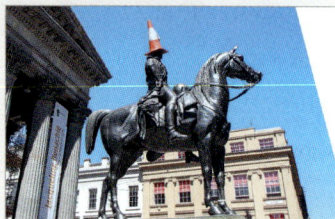

1 Take a selfie with the **Duke of Wellington Statue** in front of the Gallery of Modern Art. Glaswegians[1] are famous for their humour[2] and for years people have put traffic cones[3] on the Duke – and sometimes on his horse too! On Brexit Day in 2020, the Duke wore a cone with the colours of the EU flag because most Scottish people wanted to stay in the EU.

2 Enjoy a show at the **Britannia Panopticon**, the world's oldest music hall, where you can sing along[4] to traditional songs, watch silent films or see comedy[5] shows. In the past, music hall shows were very popular with working people. If people liked the show, they made a lot of noise with their feet – but if they didn't like the show, they threw old vegetables at the performers[6]!

3 Do a guided walk along the **River Clyde** and hear about its shipbuilding history. At one time, Glasgow built one fifth of all the world's ships! You can still see some of the old buildings from that time, but there are also some amazing modern buildings and bridges. You can also just have a picnic by the river and enjoy the view.

[1] **Glaswegian** *der Glasgower, die Glasgowerin*   [2] **humour** *der Humor*   [3] **traffic cone** *der Verkehrskegel*
[5] **(to) sing along** *mitsingen*   [6] **comedy** *die Komödie*   [7] **performer** *der Darsteller, die Darstellerin*

96 ninety-six

3
OPTIONAL

Text file Vorbereitung

Material: *Amazing activities in Glasgow* UMA, vorbereitete *Discussion tickets* (Klassensatz) (z. B. ▶ KV 2.3: Discussion tickets oder von S selbstgestaltete Karten), ggf. kleine Karteikarten als Quizkarten (Klassensatz)
Zeitbedarf: Abhängig davon, welche Texte bearbeitet werden
Minimalversion: Alle Beiträge sind optionale Zusatztexte.

Text file 3
OPTIONAL

Travel back *in* time !

4 In the past in the UK, there were police boxes on the street where you could get help. In Glasgow you can still see many of these on the streets, but they aren't police boxes any more – some sell drinks, ice cream or hot dogs. In *Doctor Who*, the famous British sci-fi series, the Doctor's time machine looks like a police box. It can travel to different places in the past and in the future. If you're a *Doctor Who* fan, you can do a tour of Glasgow's police boxes. Or just visit one and imagine you can travel in a time machine: Where would you like to go?

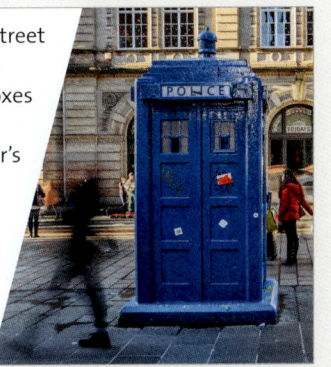

5 When you're on holiday you probably don't want to go to school. But a visit to the Scotland Street School Museum is really interesting – and it's free! A famous Scottish architect called Charles Rennie Mackintosh designed the beautiful building and until the 1970s it was a real school. Today you can see what school was like in Victorian[1] times, as well as in the 1950s and 1960s.

6 When it gets dark, do a scary ghost tour of the Necropolis[2], Glasgow's beautiful Victorian cemetery[3]. In this quiet place, listen to stories about the famous people in the cemetery (many of them shipbuilders) and learn about life in the past in Glasgow.

Would you go to *a* cemetery at *night* ?

---
[1] **Victorian** viktorianisch (Regierungszeit der Königin Viktoria, 1837–1901)   [2] **necropolis** die Totenstadt
[3] **cemetery** der Friedhof

Amazing activities in Glasgow
(Forts. von S. 96)

- **Alternative:** S lesen die sechs Texte in EA. Sie schlagen ggf. unbekannte Wörter selbst nach.
- S erstellen in EA *true / false / not in the text*-Statements zu den Texten (im Heft od. auf kleinen Karten).
- **Ausw.:** Am ▶ Bus stop: S lesen und beantworten die Quizfragen der Partnerin / des Partners (▶ Partner check).
- **Zusatz:** S recherchieren weitere Informationen zu einer der Aktivitäten (z. B. Ort, Preis, Öffnungszeiten, …) und stellen diese in der Klasse vor.

3 OPTIONAL

Text file Inhalt

Lernschwerpunkt: Überblick über verschiedene schottische Bräuche
Kompetenzen: Reading einem Text zu *Hogmanay* und *Burns Night* Informationen zu den jeweiligen Bräuchen entnehmen • mithilfe einer Anleitung einen traditionellen schottischen Tanz lernen • einem Rezept Informationen dazu entnehmen, wie man Shortbread backt.

Scottish Traditions Einstieg:

- (SB auf) L liest die folgenden Sätze vor (TA) u. S entscheiden, ob sie glauben, dass sie wahr oder falsch sind.
  - 'Hogamanay' is another word for Scottish Christmas.
  - Scottish New Year's Eve is celebrated for three days.
  - At midnight on New Year's Eve everybody sings 'Auld Lang Syne'.
  - First footing is a dance danced at Hogmanay.
  - At 'Burns Night', people meet and read poems to each other.

Erarbeitung:
- S lesen die Texte von S. 98 in EA u. suchen die Antworten auf die Statements aus dem Einstieg.
- **Ausw.:** L liest die Statements erneut vor, S berichtigen die falschen Aussagen.

Auld Lang Syne Erarbeitung:

- (SB auf) gemeinsames Hören des Songs *Auld Lang Syne* (▶ Mitleseverfahren) L: 'Auld lang syne' means 'a long time ago' in Scots. What could people want to remember on the last night of the year? What do you think?
- S äußern spontan Vermutungen.
- **Ausw.:** Klasse singt gemeinsam *Auld Lang Syne*.
- **Zusatz:** L zeigt der Klasse eine Videoaufnahme von *Auld Lang Syne* bei den *Last Night of the Proms* (BBC).
- Interessierte Klassen proben einen einen Auftritt und studieren trad. Lieder ein.

---

3 OPTIONAL

Text file

Scottish traditions
by Rhona Murray

Hogmanay

We have wonderful traditions in Scotland. You can try some of them at home or in class!

Hogmanay means *New Year's Eve* and we celebrate it from 31 December to 2 January. There are street parties, fireworks, music and concerts. It's amazing!

At midnight[1], people sing the famous song *Auld Lang Syne*[2]. The Scottish poet Robert Burns wrote the lyrics. In the song, old friends have a drink together and remember the past.

First footing is an old Hogmanay tradition when people visit friends and family after midnight. If the 'first foot' is a man with dark hair and a gift of coal, salt or shortbread, then the people in the house will be lucky that year.

Burns Night

Do you know what Burns Night is? It's on 25 January, the birthday of Robert Burns. On Burns Night people eat haggis. Today you can buy vegetarian haggis, but traditional haggis is made from the heart and other parts of a sheep, cooked in a sheep's stomach[6] with onions and spices.

People bring the haggis into the dining room to the sound of bagpipes and read a special Burns poem to the haggis. After the meal, there's music and dancing. At the end of the evening, people sing *Auld Lang Syne*.

🔊 2.8 *Auld Lang Syne*[1]

Should auld acquaintance[3] *be forgot
and never brought to mind*[4]*?
Should auld acquaintance be forgot
and days of auld lang syne?*

*For auld lang syne, my dear,
for auld lang syne
we'll take a cup of kindness*[5] *yet,
for auld lang syne.*

Sing *Auld Lang Syne* in class!

Would you like to try haggis?

---

[1] **midnight** *Mitternacht* [2] **auld lang syne** (Scots) = **old long since** *etwa: vor langer Zeit* [3] **acquaintance** *die Bekanntschaft* [4] **(to) bring to mind** *erinnern* [5] **(to) take a cup of kindness** *etwa: gemeinsam etwas trinken* [6] **stomach** *der Magen*

1 [ɔːld ˌlæŋ ˈzaɪn]

3 OPTIONAL

Text file Vorbereitung

Material: *Auld Lang Syne* UMA/CD/App, ggf. Video (online) von einer Aufführung von *Auld Lang Syne* bei den *Last Night of the Proms*-Konzerten (BBC) • *Ceilidh dancing* Internetzugang zum Recherchieren des *Ceilidh*-Tanzes (*Strip the willow*) und einer passenden Musik • *Shortbread: a recipe* ggf. Zugang zur Schulküche, Zutaten und Backutensilien (für die Klasse)
Zeitbedarf: Abhängig davon, welche Texte bearbeitet werden
Minimalversion: Alle Beiträge sind optionale Zusatztexte.
Begleitmedien: INKL (S. 92–93)

---

3 OPTIONAL

Try this in class. It's great fun!

Ceilidh dancing

A ceilidh ('kay-lee') is a traditional event with music and dancing. Look at the pictures and read the instructions or watch a video on the internet. (You can search for the dance 'Strip the Willow'.)

Girls and boys stand across from each other.

Boy 1 and Girl 1 link **right** arms and turn.

Girl 1 goes to Boy 2. Boy 1 goes to Girl 2. Both pairs link **left** arms and turn.

Boy 1 and Girl 1 link **right** arms again and turn.

Repeat all the way down to the end of the line: Girl 1 turns with all the boys and Boy 1 turns with all the girls.

Shortbread: a recipe

You need: 200 g butter, 100 g sugar, 300 g flour

| Heat[1] the oven to 160°C. | Put baking paper in a tin[2]. | Mix the butter and sugar. | Add the flour and mix. | Press the shortbread into the tin. |

| Make small holes[3] with a fork. | Bake for 25 minutes. | Cut the shortbread into 'fingers' in the tin. | Leave the shortbread to cool[4] in the tin. Enjoy! |

[1] (to) **heat** vorheizen [2] **tin** das Backblech [3] **hole** das Loch [4] (to) **cool** abkühlen

ninety-nine **99**

Ceilidh dancing Einstieg:
- (SB zu) L: *What do you think about dancing?*
- S tauschen sich im ▶ Milling around aus.

Erarbeitung:
- (SB auf) S lesen die Anweisungen für den Tanz.
- In PA bzw. Kleingruppen à mind. sechs üben S die Tanzschritte ein.
- Ggf. recherchieren L/S online ein passendes *Ceilidh*-Video bzw. einen Song (Name des Tanzes: *Strip the Willow*). (L gibt ein Zeitlimit vor.)
- **Ausw.:** S-Gruppen, die den Tanz bereits gut können, unterstützen bei Bedarf die anderen als „Experten".
- Klasse tanzt den Tanz zusammen zur ausgewählten Musik (ggf. wird dafür ein größerer Raum, z. B. die Turnhalle benötigt).
- **Zusatz:** S studieren weitere *Ceilidh*-Tänze ein.

Shortbread: a recipe
Erarbeitung:
- S lesen das Rezept.
- S backen das Rezept zu Hause oder in der Schulküche nach.
- **Ausw.:** gemeinsames Verkosten, ggf. Verkauf auf dem nächsten Schulbasar
- **Zusatz:** Die Klasse plant und veranstaltet einen *Ceilidh* oder einen schottischen Abend/Nachmittag in der Klasse.

3

Partner page / Diff bank — Inhalt

Lernschwerpunkt: zusätzliche Übungen, Differenzierungs- und Hilfsangebote
Kompetenzen: Reading Informationen über das Monster von Loch Ness entnehmen • Informationen zu Edinburgh und Glasgow verstehen • Mediation einen Brief über die Legende der Loreley verfassen
Redemittel: *tourist attractions* • *legends*

Allgemeine Anmerkung:
s. Unit 1, S. 38

Ex 1 Erarbeitung: s. a. S. 76
b) (SB auf) Gemäß AA in PA: *Partner A* bleibt auf S. 76, *Partner B* arbeitet auf S. 100.
- *Partner B* liest den Text u. ▶ Good to know, S. 76, Ex 1b).
- S schlagen unbekannte Wörter nach u. notieren sie im *Vocab file*.
- 🗹 Leitfragen für schwächere *Partners B*, die bei der Zusammenfassung der Texte in d) helfen, ggf. als TA:
  – What did Steve Feltham do in 1991?
  – What did people learn in 1994?
  – What does Steve think about the monster?
  – What do scientists say about Steve's idea?

MH 2 s. S. 75
- Diese Hilfe unterstützt schwächere S bei der Bildung grammatikalisch korrekter Sätze und liefert erste Ideen.

Erarbeitung:
c) (SB auf) Gemäß AA, L kann das ▶ Scaffolding ggf. über den UMA visualisieren.
- **Ausw.:** s. S. 75

---

3 Partner page / Diff bank

Partner page
▶ Page 76

1 READING The legend of the Loch Ness monster ｜ **1 b) C**

b) **Partner B:** Read the article. What is it about? Choose the best main idea (A–C).

A Loch Ness monster **hunter** Steve Feltham has seen Nessie.
B When people found out the 1934 photo wasn't real, they stopped believing in a monster.
C Nessie might be a very large **eel** – but nobody knows.

> **Hunting for Nessie**
>
> In 1991 Steve Feltham said goodbye to his girlfriend, his job and his life in south-west England and travelled over 450 miles to become a Loch Ness monster hunter. He moved to a home next to Loch Ness and now he looks for Nessie in the loch every day. In 1994 people discovered that the famous Nessie photo from 1934 was **fake**: It was a toy **submarine** with a fake monster head! But people continued to believe in the monster. Surprisingly, after over 30 years, Steve still hasn't seen Nessie. In his opinion, the monster might be a big **catfish**.
>
>
>
> **However**, in 2018 scientists collected DNA to find what creatures lived in the lake. Interestingly, there were no monsters or catfish – but lots of eels. **Therefore** some scientists think that Nessie may be a big eel. But another scientist says a 20-feet eel isn't possible. So it's still a mystery …

Diff bank
▶ Page 75

More help 2 SPEAKING Pictures of Scotland ｜ **2 c) individuelle Lösungen**

c) Ask and answer the questions. Give reasons for your answers.

1					
	I think	Inverness / kayaking / Eilean Donan Castle / shopping in Edinburgh / hiking on Ben Nevis / Loch Ness	looks the most exciting / fun / interesting / …	because I like	lakes / old places / the sea / shopping / small towns / water sports / walking / …
				because I'd like	to see a ghost / to see the Loch Ness monster / …

2		
I like going on trips / I prefer to stay at home	because	I like seeing new places / I like being outside / …
		I don't like travelling / it's nice to stay at home / …

3

Partner page / Diff bank Vorbereitung

Material: MH 2 ggf. UMA • MP 1 ▸ KV Extra: Bus stop • MH 3 persönliche Nachricht/E-Mail (Realien) als Vorlage
Zeitbedarf: abhängig davon, welche Aufgaben bearbeitet werden
Minimalversion: *More practice*-Aufgaben sind stets Zusatzaufgaben.

Diff bank 3

More practice 1 — **Glasgow and Edinburgh**   **1** individuelle Lösungen

Look at the photos. Read the information about Edinburgh and Glasgow. Which city would you like to visit and why? Tell your partner.

Activities for kids and teens in Edinburgh
- Climb Arthur's Seat, a hill which is °actually an old volcano.
- Visit the amazing castle on a rock above the city.
- Go on an underground tour through Edinburgh's tunnels.
- Watch the Royal Edinburgh °Military Tattoo – a great show with pipers, °drummers and singers!

Activities for kids and teens in Glasgow
- Go shopping in Buchanan Street with its busy shops, cafes and street artists.
- Visit the Science Centre, an amazing °interactive museum in a building like a °spaceship.
- See the Tall Ship outside the Riverside Museum and old cars, trams and Glasgow street scenes.
- Visit the Museum of °Piping if you love the bagpipes!

▸ Page 77

More help **3** MEDIATION **The legend of Loreley**   **3** Lösungsbsp. S. 293

Grace told her German friend Smilla about the trip to Loch Ness and the legend of the monster. Read the legend on p. 77 and help Smilla write a message to Grace about it.

Thanks for your message about the Loch Ness monster!
I want to tell you about a German legend. A young woman called Loreley ...

MP 1
- In dieser Aufgabe erhalten S weitere Informationen über Glasgow und Edinburgh.

Erarbeitung:
- In EA: S lesen die Texte u. betrachten die Bilder gemäß AA.
- S schlagen ggf. unbekannte Wörter im *Dictionary* (S. 245–271) nach.
- **Ausw.:** S arbeiten zu zweit am ▸ Bus stop (▸ KV Extra): Austausch in PA gemäß AA.
- **Alternative:** Falls die Aufgabe für ▸ Early finishers genutzt wird, können diese in der Klasse kurz die beiden Städte präsentieren (z. B. mit einer ▸ One-minute presentation).

MH 3 s. S. 77
- Diese Hilfe bietet schwächeren S Vokabeln, konjugierte Verben und Bildimpulse für die ▸ Mediation der Sage der Loreley.

Erarbeitung:
- gemäß AA
- Schwächere S arbeiten in PA.
- Ggf. benötigen S weitere Unterstützung beim Schreiben der Nachricht (passende Anrede, informeller Stil, Grußformeln etc.) Dies kann durch das gemeinsame Besprechen einer persönlichen Nachricht/E-Mail (Realien) in der Klasse noch einmal wiederholt werden.
- **Ausw.:** s. S. 77

one hundred and one 101

3

Diff bank — Inhalt

Lernschwerpunkt: zusätzliche Übungen, Differenzierungs- und Hilfsangebote
Kompetenzen: Writing eine Sage mit Adverbien ergänzen • eine lustige Geschichte schreiben • einen Dialog mit *state verbs* ergänzen • Vergleiche mit Adverbien schreiben • Speaking Sätze mit Adverbien ergänzen
Strukturen: *state verbs* • *comparison with adverbs*
Redemittel: *legends* • *adverbs* • *adjectives after state verbs*

Parallel ex 6 s. S. 79
- Diese Übung eignet sich für lernschwächere S, da sie die Adverbien nicht mehr zuordnen müssen.

Erarbeitung:
- s. S. 79

MH 7 s. S. 79
- Schwächere S nutzen das ▶ Scaffolding beim Schreiben ihrer ▶ Faltgeschichte.

Erarbeitung:
- (SB auf) L kann die Hilfen auch für alle vergrößert zeigen (UMA).
- 🖥 In schwächeren Klassen kann L die Hilfe zum Erklären der AA nutzen.
- **Ausw.:** s. S. 79

MP 2
- Mit dieser mündlichen Übung werden Adverbien geübt.

Erarbeitung:
a) (SB auf) in GA gemäß AA (▶ Gruppenbildung)
- Beispielsatz: *Rhona rides her bike _____ every day.*
- 🖥 L schreibt die Sätze an (TA).
- **Ausw.:** gemäß AA

b) + c) gemäß AA

---

3 Diff bank

▶ Page 79

Parallel exercise 6 The Edinburgh Castle ghost

6 1 surprisingly • 2 well • 3 loudly • 4 hard • 5 suddenly • 6 sadly

Complete the story in the pictures. Make adverbs from the adjective(s).

A long time ago, workers (surprising) ... found tunnels under Edinburgh Castle.

They wanted to make a map. So they asked a boy to help because he played the bagpipes (good) ...

The boy walked down the tunnels and played his bagpipes (loud) ..., so people could hear him.

Above ground, people listened (hard) ... and followed the music of the piper.

But then the bagpipes (sudden) ... stopped. Nobody ever saw the boy again.

Today tourists often hear music from underground. Somebody plays the bagpipes (sad) ...

More help 7 A funny story

7 individuelle Lösungen

a)

1	Vlad the vampire met / Mary the monster met / ...	Vera the teacher / Matt the shop assistant / ...	at a loch / at the station / at a cafe / at school / ...
2	He said	quietly / sadly / scarily / ...,	'It's hot.' / 'I feel ill.' / ...
3	She said	bravely / clearly / kindly / ...,	'Are you German?' / 'What time is dinner?' / ...
4	He	ran away / rode his bike / ...	annoyingly / crazily / rudely / ...
5	She	ate a sandwich / scored a goal / smiled / ...	excitedly / fast / well / ...
6	In the end, they	hugged / played cards / went to the cinema / ...	

More practice 2 The perfect minute

2 individuelle Lösungen

slowly

a) Work in groups. Your teacher says a sentence. Say as many adverbs as you can for the sentence in one minute. The adverbs must fit the sentences! One student °counts the adverbs.

b) Your teacher says a different sentence. Say more adverbs.

c) Which group said the most correct adverbs?

Diff bank Vorbereitung

Material: MH 7 ggf. UMA • MP 3 ggf. ▶ KV Extra: Bus stop • Challenge 1 UMA
Zeitbedarf: abhängig davon, welche Aufgaben bearbeitet werden
Minimalversion: *More practice-* und *Challenge*-Aufgaben sind stets Zusatzaufgaben.

More practice 3 — The Blue Men of the Minch

3 1 *secretly* • 2 *fast* • 3 *quietly* • 4 *loudly* • 5 *crazily* • 6 *cleverly*

clever • crazy • fast • loud • quiet • ~~secret~~

Complete the legend about mermen.
Use the adverb form of the adjectives in the box.

The Minch is a sea between the north-west of Scotland and islands called the Hebrides[1]. The Blue Men of the Minch have blue faces and bodies and they live *secretly* (1) in underwater caves. They can swim very ... (2). The Blue Men usually sleep ... (3) below the water, but when the weather is bad, they swim and play ... (4) like dolphins. They °cover boats with water and laugh ... (5) when the boats °sink. They shout poems at sailors and if the °sailors don't answer ... (6) with poems, then the Blue Men °attack their boat.

Challenge 1 — I feel ill

Ch 1 adjectives •
1 *seemed* • 2 *felt* • 3 *was* • 4 *looked* • 5 *sounded* • 6 *smelled*

Adjectives after state verbs
These verbs don't describe actions, they describe a °state (what somebody or something is like):
be • become • feel • look • seem • smell • sound • taste
Look at these examples and choose the correct word in the explanation below.
That food doesn't look *nice and it doesn't* smell *good! Ugh, it* tastes *terrible too!*
After verbs like *look*, *smell* and *taste*, we use **adjectives** / adverbs.

▶ Language file 10b, p. 179

Complete the sentences with a **state verb** from the box above in the simple past.

Rhona Do you feel OK? You *seemed* (1) scared when you came back from the toilets.
Grace I ... (2) fine, but then I met a woman in old-fashioned clothes. She ... (3) very strange. She ... (4) like a ghost. She spoke to me and she ... (5) sad. And she ... (6) horrible – like dead flowers. ... Ha, ha, Rhona, only joking!

Challenge 2 — I work harder than my friend

The comparison of adverbs
To compare adverbs, we use *-er* / *-est* or *more* / *the most*.
Look at the examples and complete the table.
My brother walks more quickly *than me. My mum walks* the most quickly *in our family.*
I work harder *than my friend Ari. But our friend Ozan works* the hardest*.*
My sister can swim better *than me. But my brother can swim* the best*.*

▶ Language file 10c, p. 179

	adverb	comparative	superlative
adverbs that end in *-ly*	quickly	more quickly	(the) most quickly
short adverbs	hard	harder	(the) hardest
irregular adverbs	well	better	(the) best

Compare yourself with family or friends as in the examples in the box.

1. speak English – well / badly
2. talk – quietly / loudly
3. eat – fast / slowly
4. write – carefully / messily
5. cycle – safely / dangerously
6. work – hard / lazily

Ch 2 individuelle Lösungen

1 [ˈhebrədiːz]

MP 3 Einstieg:
- (SB zu) ▶ Words in the air: Ein/-e S schreibt ein Adjektiv (des Reservoirs) in die Luft. Zweite/-r S rät das Wort und formt dann das Adverb.

Erarbeitung:
- S ordnen die Adverbien zu und schreiben sie korrekt ins Heft.
- **Ausw.:** ▶ Partner check, ggf. Partnersuche am ▶ Bus stop (▶ KV Extra).

Challenge 1
- Diese Aufgabe bietet sich für lernstärkere S an.

Erarbeitung:
- S lesen die ▶ Grammatik-Box, S. 103, Challenge 1 und schreiben die Regel in ihren Merkteil (▶ English folder).
- S können die *state verbs* in der Regel (im Merkteil) markieren, damit sie wissen, was sie im Dialog einsetzen sollen.
- **Ausw.:** Vergleich mit der Lösung (UMA) oder Überprüfung durch L.
- **Sich.:** ▶ LF 10b, S. 179

Challenge 2 Erarbeitung:
- S lesen die ▶ Grammatik-Box, S. 103, Challenge 2 und übertragen die Tabelle in ihren Merkteil (▶ English folder).
- S füllen die Tabelle aus u. ergänzen die weiteren Adverbien (1–6).
- **Sich.:** gemeinsam im Plenum
- ▶ LF 10c, S. 179
- Anschließend schreiben die S Vergleiche 1–6 gemäß AA ins Heft.
- **Ausw.:** ▶ Meldekette

3

Diff bank Inhalt

Lernschwerpunkt: zusätzliche Übungen, Differenzierungs- und Hilfsangebote
Kompetenzen: Speaking Unterschiede im Klassenraum beschreiben • Informationen erfragen und Gemeinsamkeiten finden • Writing eine Biografie über einen Partner oder eine Partnerin schreiben • eine Kurzgeschichte als Comic schreiben
Strukturen: *present perfect*
Redemittel: *linking words and phrases • adventures and activities*

MP 4 Einstieg:
- TA: *Have you ever …?*
- L teilt Verbkarten (▶ KV 1.1 A+B) aus (▶ Swap cards).
- ▶ Milling around:
  S1: *Have you ever gone hiking?*
  S2: *Yes, I have. / No, I haven't.*

Erarbeitung:
- (SB auf) S schreiben den Dialog ins Heft und ergänzen dabei das *present perfect*.
- **Ausw.:** ▶ Five-minute teacher

MP 5
- Dieses Spiel (▶ Kimspiel) kann auch in Folgestunden zur Übung, Festigung und Wiederholung des *present perfect* genutzt werden.

Erarbeitung:
a) – c) (SB auf) gemeinsames Lesen der AA
- Spiel gemäß AA
- Bei Bedarf nutzen S die sprachlichen Hilfen im Buch.

d) gemäß AA
- **Ausw.:** Ggf. Anzahl der Fragen zählen, die die S fürs Erraten gebraucht haben.

MP 6 Einstieg:
- (SB zu) ▶ Swap cards (z. B. ▶ KV 1.1 A+B) mit unregelmäßigen Verben: S fragen sich gegenseitig ab.

Erarbeitung:
a) – b) (SB auf) gemäß AA

c) Ggf. wdh. S vorab im Plenum das Stellen von Fragen im *present perfect* (s. sprachl. Hilfen im SB).
- ▶ Milling around gemäß AA
- **Ausw.:** im Plenum

104

---

3 Diff bank

▶ Page 81

4 **1** has just sent • **2** 've never liked • **3** 've never learned • **4** Have you ever had • **5** haven't had • **6** Have they already thrown • **7** 've won • **8** have lifted

More practice 4 **The °Highland Games**

Complete the conversation with the present perfect.

Rhona My mum … (1 *just / send*) me some pictures from the Highland Games. Look!
Grace I … (2 *never / like*) Scottish dancing and I … (3 *never / learn*) to dance well.
… (4 *you / ever / have*) lessons?
Rhona I … (5 *not have*) lessons, but you know I love dancing! I think Scottish dancing is great fun.
Grace Well, that's because you're a good dancer! I like the photo of the four guys in °kilts.
… (6 *they / already / throw*) the °caber¹?
Rhona I don't know. Maybe they … (7 *win*) and … (8 *lift*) the caber for a photo to celebrate. It looks very big!

a caber

More practice 5 **Spot the difference**   **5** individuelle Lösungen

a) Look carefully around the classroom. Look where people are sitting and where things are in the classroom.
b) Two or three students leave the classroom. One student in the classroom moves something or asks students to move.
c) The other students come back and ask questions about changes.

Have you moved the blue rucksack? – No, we haven't.
Have Lukas and Mateo swapped chairs? – Yes, they have.

d) Play again: This time different students go out and a different student changes something.

▶ Page 83

More practice 6 **Who is it?**   **6** individuelle Lösungen

a) On pieces of paper, write three sentences about you with *for* and *since*. Use the verbs in the box.

be • have • know • like • live • play • study • want

I've liked chocolate for a long time.   *I've had a dog since last year.*   …

b) °**Mix up** the pieces of paper and give them to different students.
c) WALK AROUND Ask questions to find the right students for your sentences.

Have you played badminton for two years? – Yes, I have. / No, I haven't.

1 [ˈkeɪbə]

104 one hundred and four

3

Diff bank Vorbereitung

Material: MP 4 vorbereitete Verbkarten (z. B. ▶ KV 1.1 A+B: SWAP CARDS Verbs für unregelmäßige Verben od. von L selbst erstellte Karten) • MP 6 ▶ KV 1.1 A+B: SWAP CARDS Verbs od. von L selbst erstellte Verbkarten (Klassensatz), Zettel im Klassensatz • MH 4 Step 3 ggf. digitale Endgeräte u. geeignete Programme für die Erstellung von *grafic novels / comics*
Zeitbedarf: abhängig davon, welche Aufgaben bearbeitet werden
Minimalversion: *More practice*-Aufgaben sind stets Zusatzaufgaben.

3

More help 8 MY TASK **A biography of your partner** | **8** individuelle Lösungen

b) Write a short biography of your partner. You can use the biography below and change the parts in blue or add new parts.

> **A biography of Sofia**
> Sofia is 13 years old. She's from Bochum and her favourite sport is football. She has played football for a long time. She likes football because it's exciting. She also likes °gymnastics. She has done gymnastics since 2016. Her main interest is painting. She has painted pictures since primary school. She likes it because it's relaxing.

▶ Page 86

More help 1 Preparing for an adventure | **1** b) B

b) Read the story. Choose the correct message of the story (A–C).
A If you're really brave, nothing bad can happen.
B You should always think carefully about your choices.
C Mountain climbing is too dangerous.

▶ Page 88

7 1 However • 2 then • 3 so • 4 finally • 5 in the end

More practice 7 Linking words and phrases

Complete the sentences with the words in the box.

finally • however • in the end • so • then

I went hiking once. … (1), the weather was bad. At first, it was sunny, but … (2) there was a big °rainstorm. I was cold, … (3) I put on a scarf. … (4), after an hour, the rain stopped, so I started walking again. But … (5), I think it was a good hike!

▶ Page 91

Unit task individuelle Lösungen

More help UNIT TASK **Write a short adventure story, Step 3**

You can write your story as a comic. Use two or three pictures for each part. Write a sentence under each picture. You can also add °speech bubbles.

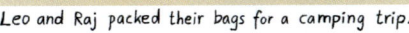
Leo and Raj packed their bags for a camping trip.   But Leo forgot to bring his phone charger!

one hundred and five **105**

MH 8 s. S. 83
• Diese Hilfe dient als Vorlage für lernschwächere S.

Erarbeitung:
b) s. S. 83

MH 1 s. S. 86
• Diese Aufgabe bietet Hilfe für lernschwächere Klassen.

Erarbeitung:
b) (SB auf) S lesen die Geschichte und arbeiten gemäß AA.
• **Ausw.:** im Plenum (s. S. 86)
• **Alternative:** ▶ Four corners: L bezeichnet drei Ecken im Raum mit A, B, C und S positionieren sich.

MP 7 Erarbeitung:
• (SB auf) S arbeiten schriftlich gemäß AA
• **Ausw.:** ▶ Five-minute teacher

MH Unit task s. S. 91
• Diese Hilfe bietet lernschwächeren S mehr Unterstützung beim Schreiben der *adventure story*.

Step 3 Erarbeitung:
• gemäß AA
• Die Anzahl der Bilder und Sprechblasen sollte von L vorgegeben werden.
• Beim Verwenden von digitalen Endgeräten können S geeignete Programme für die Erstellung von *graphic novels / comics* nutzen.

4

Unit-Übersicht

Storyline: Owen und Dylan planen Videos, um ihrer deutschen Austauschklasse Wales vorzustellen. Dabei setzen sie sich mit den Vor- und Nachteilen der sozialen Medien auseinander. In der Story nutzt Dylan Bildbearbeitung, um sich vor seiner Austauschpartnerin besser darzustellen, und verärgert damit seinen Freund Owen.
Strukturen: *possessive pronouns* (S. 108), *(revision) going to-future* (S. 111), *relative clauses* (S. 116), *contact clauses* (S. 137)
Viewing: Video über das Leben in Wales 1927 (S. 110) • Film über die Erstellung eines Cosplay-Kostüms (S. 121)
Unit task: einen kurzen Vortrag über soziale Medien halten

Unit 4 Einstieg:
- (SB zu) Mit einer walisischen Flagge und einer Umrisskarte des UK führt L in das Thema ein: *Look at the parts of the UK. What are their names?*
- S zeigen und antworten.
- L zeigt auf die Flagge: *The flag of which country is this?*
  S: *Wales.*
  L: *What do you know about Wales?*
- ▶ L erinnert an das Video von S. 10.
- S antworten.
- **Alternative:** ▶KV 4.1A (Ex 1): S stellen die Fragen im ▶Milling around. Um den Wettbewerbscharakter zu steigern, nutzt L ein akustisches Signal für eine zeitliche Begrenzung.
- **Ausw.:** S präsentieren ihre Ergebnisse im Plenum.

Ex 1 Einstieg:
- (SB zu) L zeigt die Bilder von S. 106 und Ex 1 (UMA): *What can you see in the pictures?*
- PA: S beschreiben die Bilder mit ▶Picture duet.

Erarbeitung:
a) (SB auf) AA lesen u. auch an die Infos von S. 10–13 erinnern (Fotos, Video, Hörtext).
- S notieren Informationen gemäß AA in PA.
- **Ausw.:** S präsentieren Ergebnisse im Plenum und L erstellt Liste als TA.
b) Klären der AA
- S notieren Antworten in EA.
- **Ausw.:** S vergleichen ihre Ergebnisse gemäß AA in PA.
- **Alternative:** ▶KV 4.1A (Ex 2): S markieren Antworten in EA.

Unit 4
Wales: Digital life

Owen   Dylan

A
Donkeys on Llandudno[1] beach

B
Wales uses green energy.

C
You'll see sheep everywhere!

1 READING & SPEAKING An online quiz about Wales   **1 a)** Lösungsbsp. S. 296

a) BEFORE YOU READ A German °exchange class is going to visit Dylan and Owen's school in Llandudno in Wales. Collect information about Llandudno and Wales. Look at the pictures on this page and the information on pages 10–13 to help you.

b) Dylan and Owen have made an online quiz about Wales for the German students (p. 107). Do you know or can you °guess any of the answers? Write your answers.

> I think question 1/2/... is A/B/C because ...

> Yes, I agree. / I'm not sure. It could be ...

1 b) 1 C • 2 B • 3 B • 4 A • 5 C • 6 C • 7 B

1 [lænˈdɪdnəʊ]

4

Lead-in Inhalt

Lernschwerpunkt: erste Informationen über Wales verstehen
Kompetenzen: Speaking sich über Wales austauschen • sich über Sehenswertes in der eigenen Region austauschen • Reading ein Quiz über Wales lösen • Listening einem Dialog Informationen über Wales entnehmen
Redemittel: *places in Wales and in my area*

Vorbereitung

Material: Unit-Einstieg Flagge von Wales u. Umrisskarte des UK, ▶ KV 4.1A: Wales (Klassensatz), akustisches Signal • Ex 1 UMA, ▶ KV 4.1A • Ex 2 UMA/CD/App, ▶ KV 4.1B: Wales
Zeitbedarf: ca. 1–2 Std.
Minimalversion: Ex 2c) als HA vorbereiten lassen
Begleitmedien: WB (S. 66), App (Digital quiz), INKL (S. 102–103), DIFF (4.1), Unit plans (Unit 4)

Nach dieser Unit kann ich …
- ein Quiz über Wales durchführen
- über Wales und meine Region sprechen
- einfache Anleitungen verstehen und geben
- über soziale Medien sprechen
- flüssig vortragen

Unit task
- einen kurzen Vortrag über soziale Medien halten

Nach dieser Unit …
- L bespricht mit S die Lernziele der Unit (links) und kündigt die *Unit task* an.
- Am Ende der Unit überprüfen S das Erreichen der Ziele mithilfe des Checkpoint (S. 124–127) bzw. gemeinsam im Plenum.

Ex 2 Einstieg:
- (SB zu) L schreibt den Begriff *voice-over* an die Tafel: *Dylan and Owen are recording a voice-over. Do you know what it is?*
- L hilft bei Begriffsklärung.

Erarbeitung:

a) (SB auf) S haben die Lösungen von Ex 1b) vor sich und vergleichen beim **1. Hören** gemäß AA.
- **Alternative:** ▶ KV 4.1B (Ex 3a)
- **Ausw.:** ▶ Meldekette, L erfasst S mit den meisten richtigen Antworten: *Stand up: Who has … right answers?* S stehen auf (mit einer richtigen Antwort beginnen und dann die Zahl bis sieben erhöhen).

b) Arbeitsteilige PA: S notieren Antworten gemäß AA beim **2. Hören** in ihr Heft.
- **Alternative:** ▶ KV 4.1B (Ex 3b): S ergänzen die Tabelle beim 2. Hören.
- **Ausw.:** ▶ Partner check, dann Plenum

c) Gemäß AA bereiten S eine ▶ One-minute presentation vor.
- **Alternative:** ▶ KV 4.1B (Ex 3c): S ergänzen die Mindmap.
- **Ausw.:** S präsentieren im Plenum.

Dylan and Owen's quiz about Wales

1. What's the Welsh word for Wales?
   A Ffrwyt   B Afon   C °Cymru¹
2. Who is the Prince of Wales? Prince …
   A Harry   B William   C George
3. What's on the Welsh flag?
   A a red lion   B a red dragon   C a red sheep
4. What's the national sport in Wales?
   A rugby   B football   C judo
5. How many million sheep live in Wales?
   A two   B five   C ten
6. What superhero has a large cave behind a waterfall in Wales?
   A Spiderman   B Superman   C Batman
7. What was Wales famous for in the past?
   A fishing   B coal mining   C shipbuilding

D People in Wales love this sport!

E A great place to visit

2 LISTENING Dylan and Owen's voice-over

3.1 a) The two boys are recording a voice-over for a video for the exchange class. Listen and check your quiz answers from 1b).   **2 b)** Lösungsbsp. S. 296

b) Listen again and take notes. Partner A: Listen for information about Dylan and Owen. Partner B: Listen for information about Llandudno and Wales. Then swap information.

   Partner A: *Dylan / Owen learns / plays / uses / …*
   Partner B: *In Llandudno / Wales there is / …   You can …*   ▶ More practice 1, p. 132

c) Talk about what places in your area you would show exchange students.   ▶ Wordbank 8, p. 193

   2 c) individuelle Lösungen
                                                                 1 [ˈkʌmri]   ▶ Workbook, p. 66

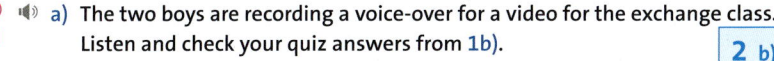
Digital quiz I can understand information about Wales.

one hundred and seven **107**

4

Topic 1 Inhalt

Lernschwerpunkt: Informationen und Meinungen über Wales erfahren und sich dazu äußern
Kompetenzen: Reading einem Dialog Informationen über einen Schüleraustausch entnehmen • Listening einen Song verstehen • Speaking seine Meinung zu einem Song äußern • eine Sprachnachricht über Wales aufnehmen
Strukturen: possessive pronouns
Redemittel: places in Wales • songs and music • opinion phrases

---

Ex 1 Einstieg:
- (SB zu) L: *You want to present your region. Which places would you choose?*
- S finden Ideen in ▶Buzz groups und präsentieren Ergebnisse. L: *Let's read what the students in Wales want to present.*

Erarbeitung:
- (SB auf) AA gemeinsam klären.
- S lesen den Dialog.
- S notieren Antworten.
- **Ausw.:** Für die erste Frage nennt L die Namen und S antworten mit ▶Right/wrong cards, für die zweite Frage antworten S und begründen ihre Wahl im Plenum.
- **Zusatz:** S lesen den Dialog in verteilten Rollen.
- ▶Good to know, S. 180: S lesen/ hören und sprechen das Wort nach (▶Lautschulung).

Ex 2 Einstieg:
- (SB zu) L bereitet Wortkarten mit Personalpronomen (*I, you, ...*) und Possessivbegleitern (*my, your, ...*) vor, S ordnen und heften die Karten als Tabelle an die Tafel.

Erarbeitung:
a) (SB auf) S arbeiten gemäß AA.
- **Ausw.:** L/S ergänzen Tabelle an der Tafel mit Wortkarten der Possessivpronomen (*mine, yours, ...*).
- **Sich.:** S übertragen Tabelle in den Merkteil (▶English folder).
- s. a. ▶LF 12, S. 181

b) gemäß AA
- **Ausw.:** ▶Meldekette
- zur Vertiefung:
  ▶More practice 2, S. 133

---

4 Topic 1

Welcome to Wales

1 Gwen, Samara and Louise, and Promit have finished their videos. • I think the roller coaster at the theme park sounds most interesting.

1 READING Talking about the class videos

Read the conversation. Who in Dylan and Owen's class has finished their videos? Which places in the videos sound most interesting to you?

▶ Box: Voc., p. 235

Dylan Hey, has anyone finished their video for the exchange class yet? Owen and I have nearly done ours. We just need to edit it.
Gwen Mine is finished. I went to Cardiff at the weekend with my family, so I filmed the castle, the beach, the shops, everything!
Owen Cool! I think Samara and Louise have finished theirs too. They filmed the pier and the beach in Llandudno.
Flynn °Yeah, and Promit showed me his video yesterday. He made his about the roller coaster at the GreenWood theme park! I still need to finish mine.
Dylan That park is really great! I hope the German class will like our videos.
Gwen Have you written a song for yours, Dylan?
Owen Yes, he has and it's amazing! You'll love it!
Dylan Aww, thanks Owen. I've just learned to use some new music software. I'm really proud of it, actually. I wrote the music and the lyrics and my sister sang it.

Good to know

Wales has one of the longest place names in the world: Llanfairpwllgwyngyllgogerychwyrn drobwllllantysiliogogogoch[1]
🔊 Listen. Can you repeat it? Say 'Llan-vire-poolI-guin-gill-go-ger-u-queern-drob-ooll-llandus-ilio-gogo-goch'.

🔊 3.2

2 LOOKING AT LANGUAGE Mine and yours

a) Find the possessive pronouns in the conversation in 1. Copy and complete the table.

b) We use possessive pronouns so we don't have to repeat the noun. Complete sentences 1–5 with possessive pronouns from the table.

2 b) 1 yours • 2 mine • 3 theirs • 4 hers • 5 his

I	my (video)	mine
you	your (video)	yours
he	his (video)	his
she	her (video)	hers
it	its (video)	its
we	our (video)	ours
they	their (video)	theirs

We're filming our favourite places in Wales for the exchange class. What's ... (1)? I think ... (2) is the beach because I love swimming. I asked all my friends about ... (3). Samara told me that ... (4) is the pier and Flynn said that ... (5) is the ski centre.

▶ Language file 12, p. 181   ▶ More practice 2, p. 133
▶ Workbook, p. 67

1 [ɬan vaɪrˌəpʊɫˌgwɪn gɪɬ go ˌger ə ˌχwərn ˌdro buɬ ˌɬan də ˌsɪl jo ˌgo go ˈgoːχ];
usually called: [ˌɬænvaɪrˌəpʊːɬˈgwɪŋgɪɬ]

4

Topic 1 Vorbereitung

Material: Ex 1 UMA/CD/App, *Right/wrong cards* (Klassensatz) • Ex 2 von L vorbereitete Wortkarten mit Personalpronomen, Possessivbegleitern und -pronomen • Ex 3 von L recherchiertes Foto einer Band / Song als Beispiel, UMA/CD/App • Ex 4 UMA, digitale Endgeräte zur Aufnahme der Sprachnachricht
Zeitbedarf: ca. 2 Std.
Minimalversion: Ex 2b) als HA, Sprachnachricht von Ex 4b) als HA aufnehmen
Begleitmedien: WB (S. 67–68), App (Digital help, Digital quiz), INKL (S. 104–105), DIFF (4.2)

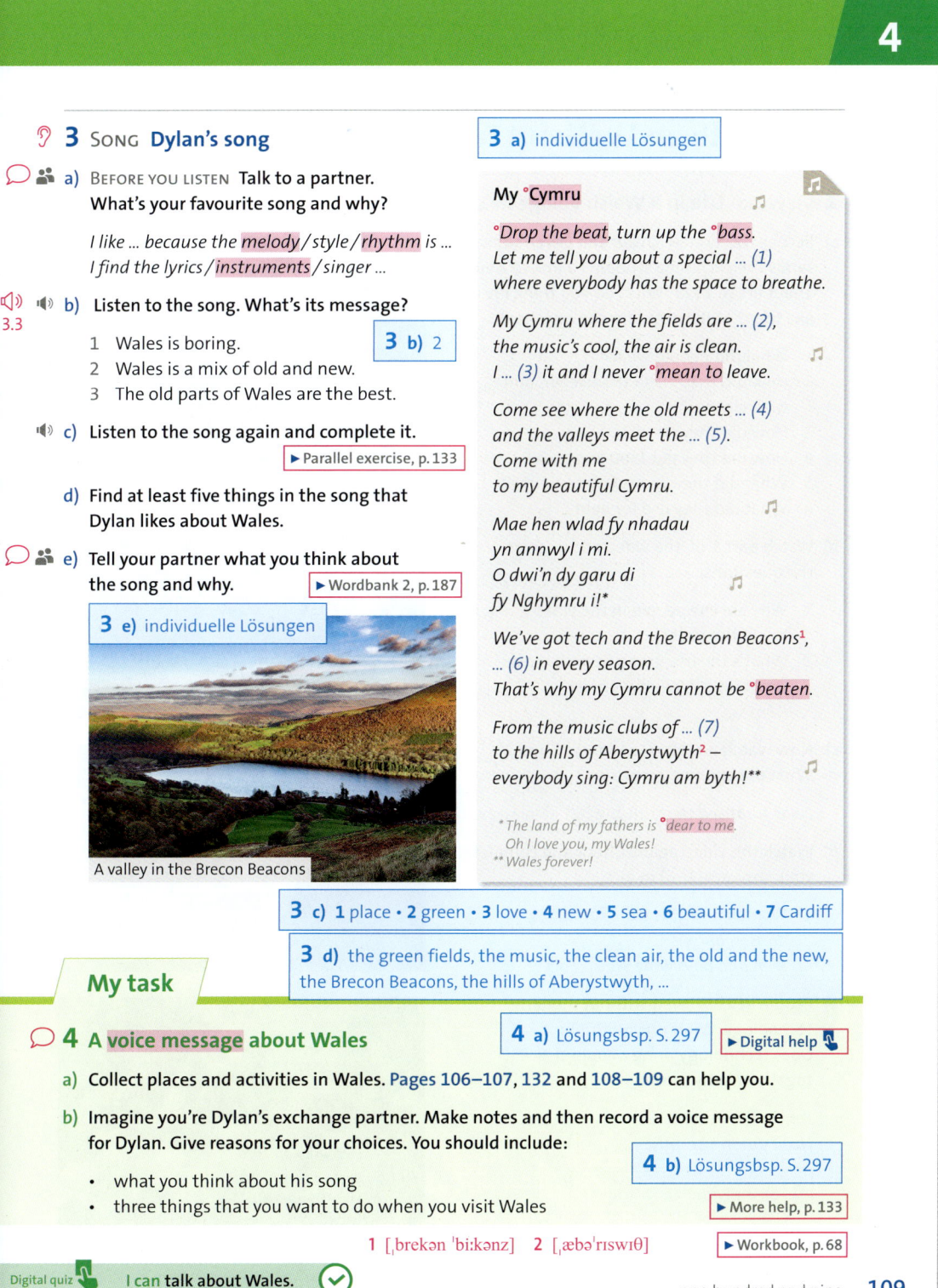

Ex 3 Einstieg:
- (SB zu) L zeigt Foto einer Band und/oder spielt ein Lied vor.
  L: *I like this song because …*

Erarbeitung:

a) AA u. ▶Scaffolding als TA
- S arbeiten in PA.
- **Ausw.:** Einzelne S-Paare präsentieren im Plenum.

b) L präsentiert AA und die drei Sätze als TA.
  L: *Let's listen to Dylan's song.*
- **1. Hören:** S wählen die passende Aussage.
- **Ausw.:** im Plenum

c) (SB auf) S notieren die Lösungen beim **2. Hören**.
- ▶Parallel ex, S. 133
- **Ausw.:** ▶Partner check, dann Plenum

d) S finden Antworten mit ▶Five-finger brainstorming.
- **Ausw.:** im Plenum, mit TA

e) Gemäß AA mit ▶Think-Pair-Share, S nutzen ▶Wordbank 2, S. 187.
- **Ausw.:** S-Paare präsentieren Ergebnisse im Plenum.

My task Ex 4 Einstieg:
- (SB zu) L zeigt Bilder der genannten Seiten (UMA): *What have you learned about these places?* S antworten.

Erarbeitung:

a) (SB auf) S sammeln Informationen gemäß AA in EA.

b) gemeinsames Klären der AA, ggf. mithilfe von *Digital help* (App) und ▶More help, S. 133
- S erarbeiten ihre Nachricht an Dylan und nehmen sie auf.
- **Ausw.:** im Plenum

4

Topic 2 Inhalt

Lernschwerpunkt: über das Leben in Wales früher und heute lernen und den Wandel der Technologie erkennen
Kompetenzen: Viewing einem Film Informationen über das Leben in Wales 1927 entnehmen • Speaking den Alltag damals und heute vergleichen • sich über Technologie im Haushalt austauschen • ein Telefonat führen • Reading einem Telefonat Informationen entnehmen
Strukturen: *(revision) going to-future*
Redemittel: *life in the past and today • technology at home • telephone phrases*

Ex 1 Einstieg:
- (SB zu) L zeigt ▶Flashcards mit elektrischen Geräten im Haushalt (z. B. Waschmaschine, Lampe, TV): *What do you use this gadget for at home? Mime it to the group.*
- S mimen die Tätigkeit, die Klasse errät das Gerät.
  L: *How was life without a washing machine / …?*
  S: *People had to wash by hand / …*
- L leitet über zum Thema: *Let's find out about life in the past.*

Erarbeitung:
a) (SB auf) S betrachten den Titel u. die Bilder und lesen die AA.
- S lesen die Fragen laut oder leise und notieren die Antworten zunächst in EA.
- **Ausw.:** ▶Partner check

b) S lesen die AA und die Fragen.
- 1. Sehen (Teil 1, bis 0:30): S notieren die Antworten.
- **Ausw.:** im Plenum

c) 2. Sehen (komplett): gemäß AA
- **Ausw.:** im Plenum

d) 3. Sehen (komplett): S-Paare vergleichen Antworten aus a).
- **Ausw.:** S-Paare präsentieren Ergebnisse im Plenum.

e) gemeinsames Lesen der AA
- L verteilt Moderationskarten, S-Paare notieren darauf Gründe für *yes* oder *no*.
- ▶More help, S. 134
- Karten an die Tafel heften (zwei Seiten, links: *Yes, it does because …*, rechts: *No, it doesn't because …*).
- **Ausw.:** ▶Meinungsbarometer, S begründen mit TA.

---

4 | Topic 1 | **Topic 2** | Topic 3 | Story | Viewing | Study skills | Unit task

Life with and without technology

1 VIEWING Life in a Welsh village in 1927

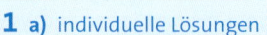
1 a) individuelle Lösungen

a) BEFORE YOU WATCH Dylan and Owen's class sends the exchange students a link to a video about life in 1927. What do you think life was like then? Make notes for the questions.

1 What did people wear?
2 How did they wash themselves and their clothes?
3 How did they travel?
4 How did they get food and cook?
5 What did they do in their free time?
6 What did they use for light?

b) Watch part 1 of the video and answer the questions. **1 b) Lösung S. 297**

1 Why are the people in the video going to live in the past?
2 What's the boy going to miss most?
3 What would you miss most?
 I'd miss …

c) Now watch all the video (parts 1 and 2). What did you find surprising?

I was surprised that … **1 c), d) Lösungsbsp. S. 297**

d) Watch the video again. Check and complete your answers (1–6) in a).

1 *Women and girls wore* cardigans, *dresses,* aprons, *…*
 Men and boys wore waistcoats, *…*

e) People in 1927 lived without modern technology. What do you think: Does technology bring people closer together? Why (not)?

Yes, it does because …
No, it doesn't because …. ▶More help, p. 134

1 e) individuelle Lösungen

▶Workbook, p. 69

110 one hundred and ten

Topic 2 Vorbereitung

Material: Ex 1 von L vorbereitete *Flashcards* mit elektronischen Geräten im Haushalt, UMA/DVD/App, Blanko-Moderationskarten (Klassensatz) • Ex 2 UMA, *English-only*-Karte • Ex 3 UMA/CD/App
Zeitbedarf: ca. 1–2 Std.
Begleitmedien: WB (S. 69), INKL (S. 106–107), DIFF (4.4)

---

2 SPEAKING An evening with or without technology?

2 a) Lösungsbsp. S. 297

a) Brainstorm free-time activities.

b) WALK AROUND Tell different partners what you're going to do this evening. Listen to them and take notes.

I'm going to do/go/listen to/make/play/watch/…
My family is going to …
My friends and I are going to …

2 b), c), d) individuelle Lösungen

▶ More help, p. 134

c) Tell the class about one partner.

Amira is going to do gymnastics.

d) How many students are going to use technology or °social media this evening?

REVISION The going to-future: ▶ Language file 13a + b, p. 182 | ▶ More practice 3, p. 134 | ▶ Challenge 1, p. 135

3 On the phone

3 a) Dylan and Owen are going to edit the video tomorrow after school at Owen's house.

a) Dylan and Owen want to finish their video. Read their phone conversation. What are they going to do, when and where? Don't worry about the missing parts.

Owen	Hi, Dylan. … (1)
Dylan	Great, thanks.
Owen	When are we going to edit the video?
Dylan	How about later after dinner? Are you free?
Owen	No, sorry, I'm going to watch a film with my brother. Mum and Dad are going to go out tonight. What about *(crrr)*?
Dylan	What? Sorry, … (2)
Owen	Can you hear me now? I said, 'What about tomorrow?'
Dylan	Yeah, that's cool. How about at *(crrr)* after *(crrr)*?
Owen	What? … (3)
Dylan	How about at your house after school?
Owen	Yes, that's fine.
Dylan	Oh, … (4), Owen. Can we use your computer? My ⁺tablet screen is broken.
Owen	Sure, no problem. Sorry, … (5) See you tomorrow!
Dylan	… (6)

Phrases
a Can you say that again, please?
b one more thing
c I can't hear you. You're breaking up.
d Bye!
e How are things?
f I have to go now.

3.4

b) Complete the phone call with the missing phrases (a–f) from the box. Then listen and check.

1e, 2 …

3 b) 1 e • 2 c • 3 a • 4 b • 5 f • 6 d

c) Read the complete phone call with a partner.

▶ More practice 4, p. 135

one hundred and eleven **111**

Ex 2 Einstieg:
- (SB zu) L zeigt die zwei unteren Bilder von S. 110 (UMA): *How did people in the past spend the evenings together?*
  S: *They talked/sang/…*

Erarbeitung:
a) (SB auf) gemäß AA
- **Ausw.:** L erfasst Bspe. als TA.

b) gemeinsames Lesen der AA
- ggf. Wiederholung des *going to-future*, s.
  ▶ Grammatikwiederholung u.
  ▶ LF 13a + b, S. 182
- L zeigt ▶ English-only-Karte.
- ▶ Milling around gemäß AA, S machen sich Notizen (▶ Note-taking).
- Lernschwächere S nutzen ▶ More help, S. 134.

c) **Ausw.** von b) im Plenum

d) L erfasst S mit *yes/no* über
  ▶ Meinungsbarometer.
- **Ausw.:** S geben weitere Informationen im Plenum.
- weitere Übungen zur Wdh. des *going to-future*:
  ▶ More practice 3, S. 134 u.
  ▶ Challenge 1, S. 135

Ex 3 Erarbeitung:
a) (SB auf) Klären der AA
- gemäß AA in EA
- **Ausw.:** im Plenum

b) S notieren die Lösungen.
- S vergleichen beim **1. Hören**.
- **Ausw.:** im Plenum
- ggf. **2. Hören**
- **Sich.:** S schreiben Wendungen ins *Vocab file*.

c) gemäß AA in PA
- **Ausw.:** S-Paare lesen Dialog laut vor.

111

4

Topic 2 | Inhalt

Lernschwerpunkt: Anweisungen geben und verstehen
Kompetenzen: Listening einem Gespräch entnehmen, wie man ein Video bearbeitet • Mediation eine Gebrauchsanweisung ins Deutsche sprachmitteln • Writing eine Anleitung für ein technisches Gerät oder eine App formulieren
Redemittel: *editing videos • understanding and giving tech instructions*

Ex 4 Einstieg:
- (SB zu) TA: *How to edit a video*
  L: *What do you need to make and edit videos?*
  S: *A computer, an app, …*
- L erstellt Liste an ▶ Vokabeltafel.

Erarbeitung:

a) (SB auf) gemäß AA in PA
- Alternative: ▶ KV 4.3 (Ex 1a)
- Ausw.: im Plenum

b) Klären der AA
- **1. Hören:** S notieren Lösungen.
- Alternative: ▶ KV 4.3 (Ex 1b)
- Ausw.: ▶ Partner check

c) S vergleichen die Reihenfolge der Bilder beim **2. Hören** und ordnen dann schriftlich die *instructions* zu.
- Alternative: ▶ KV 4.3 (Ex 1c)
- Ausw.: ▶ Five-minute teacher

d) gemäß AA in EA, ▶ Vokabelarbeit
- Alternative: ▶ KV 4.3 (Ex 1d)
- Ausw.: ▶ Partner check, dann Plenum

Ex 5 Einstieg:
- (SB zu) L zeigt Symbole von Ex 5a) (UMA): *Do you know any of these symbols?*

Erarbeitung:

a) (SB auf) S lesen die Verben im Reservoir, ▶ Semantisierung der neuen Vokabeln.
- L notiert Übersetzung an ▶ Vokabeltafel.
- S arbeiten gemäß AA in PA.
- Ausw.: im Plenum

b) S ergänzen ihre Liste im *Vocab file* gemäß AA.
- Ausw.: L erstellt Liste zum Vergleich als TA.

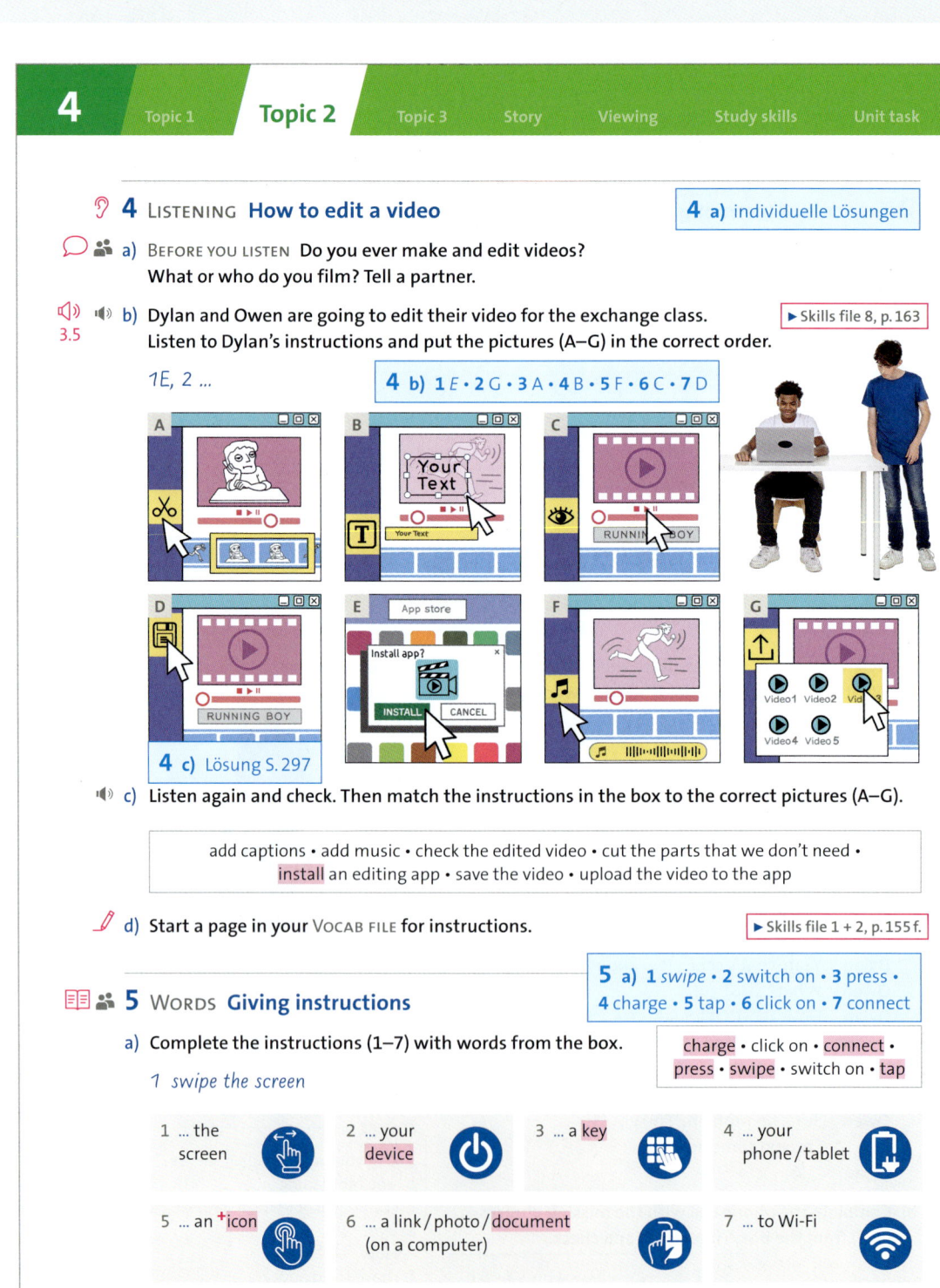

Topic 2 Vorbereitung

Material: Ex 4 UMA/CD/App, ▶KV 4.3: How to edit a video (Klassensatz) • Ex 5 UMA • Ex 6 UMA •
Ex 7 Beispiel eines Screenshots
Zeitbedarf: ca. 2 Std.
Minimalversion: Ex 5b) und Ex 7 als HA
Begleitmedien: WB (S. 70–71), App (Digital help, Digital quiz), INKL (S. 108–109), DIFF (4.4)

4

6 a) Lösungsbsp. S. 297

⇸ **6 MEDIATION Instructions**

a) **Partner B:** Look at p. 132.
Partner A: Partner B needs help with a new smartwatch. Explain instructions 1–5 in German. ▶Skills file 10, p. 165

1. Charge your smartwatch fully.
   Zuerst musst du …
2. Install the correct app for your phone.
3. Switch the watch on.
4. Tap to start and choose a language.
5. Open the app on your phone.

b) Now you need help. Listen to partner B's instructions. Ask what you do next and ask questions if you don't understand.

💡 Normally when you mediate, you explain the main ideas. But when you give instructions, it's important to be exact.

6 b) Lösungsbsp. S. 298

✏ **7 WRITING How to take and edit +screenshots**

Write six simple instructions for the pictures (1–6).
Use the verbs in the box and linking words to show the order.

7 Lösungsbsp. S. 298

click on (2 x) • copy •
edit • press • save

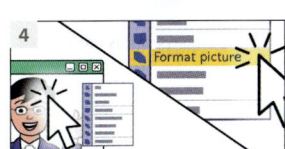

My task

👥 **8 Your instructions**

8 individuelle Lösungen

✏ a) Think of a digital device or an app that you often use. Write instructions how to use it.
   Use linking words to make the order clear.
   ▶Digital help ▶Wordbank 9, p. 194

💬 b) Read your instructions to a partner.
   Your partner listens and asks questions.
   Sorry, I don't understand that. Can you explain it again, please?

c) Swap roles.

▶More practice 5, p. 135
▶Workbook, p. 71

Digital quiz   I can give simple instructions. ✓

one hundred and thirteen **113**

Ex 6 Einstieg:
- (SB zu) L zeigt Bild von Ex 6 (UMA): *Describe the situation.*
  S: *A girl is helping her dad / explaining the watch / …*
  L: *Now imagine you have to help a friend with a new device.*

Erarbeitung:
a) + b) (SB auf) Klären der AA (▶Mediation)
- Gemäß AA in PA, *Partner B* arbeitet auf S. 132.
- 🔽 Lernschwächere S machen sich vorab Notizen.
- **Ausw.:** im Plenum

Ex 7 Einstieg:
- (SB zu) L zeigt Beispiel eines Screenshots: *Do you know how taking a picture from a screen is called?*
  S: *A screenshot.*

Erarbeitung:
- (SB auf) Lesen der AA
- 🔽 Für lernschwächere S erfasst L *linking words* als TA.
- S notieren die Sätze gemäß AA.
- **Ausw.:** ▶Partner check, dann Plenum (mit TA)

My task Ex 8 Einstieg:
- (SB zu) ▶Acrostic mit dem Wort *digital* an der Tafel erarbeiten: *Name any devices and apps that you use.*

Erarbeitung:
a) (SB auf) Klären der AA, L verweist auf ▶Wordbank 9, S. 194, dann Bearbeitung in EA.
- s. a. *Digital help* (App)
- 🔽 L prüft und unterstützt bei lernschwächeren S individuell.

b) + c) gemäß AA in PA
- **Ausw.:** ▶English corner, anschl. Ablage im ▶Dossier

113

4

Topic 3 Inhalt

Lernschwerpunkt: sich über die Nutzung von sozialen Medien und Gesundheitsapps austauschen
Kompetenzen: Listening ein Gespräch über die Nutzung von sozialen Medien und Apps verstehen • Speaking über die eigene Nutzung von sozialen Medien sprechen • über Gesundheitsapps sprechen • Hilfe anbieten, erbitten und annehmen • Reading einen Dialog lesen • Writing eine *bio* erstellen
Redemittel: social media apps • online activities • offering, asking for and accepting help

---

Ex 1 Einstieg:
- (SB zu) Frage als TA: *Do you use social media?*
- L teilt Raum in zwei Hälften (yes/no), S positionieren sich. L: *What do you use social media for?* S geben Beispiele.

Erarbeitung:
a) (SB auf) S nennen Beispiele, L erfasst Liste als TA gemäß AA.
- L erstellt ein Ranking: *Who uses …?* S melden sich und L notiert die Anzahl an die Tafel.
- Ausw.: Ein S fasst Ergebnisse zusammen: *… are the most popular social media apps.*

b) S lesen die *Debate club*-Ankündigung und die AA.
- 1. Hören: S notieren Lösungen.
- Ausw.: L erfasst die Lösungen mit ▶ Thumbs up.

c) 2. Hören: S notieren Lösungen.
- Ausw.: ▶ Meldekette, ggf. 3. Hören zum Überprüfen

d) gemäß AA in PA
- Ausw.: im Plenum

Ex 2 Einstieg:
- (SB zu) L zeigt/nennt einige Gesundheitsapps: *Do you know any of these apps? What are they for?* – S: *They help to keep fit/healthy, …*
- S nennen weitere Apps.

Erarbeitung:
a) (SB auf) 1. Hören gemäß AA
- Ausw.: ▶ Meldekette

b) gemäß AA in PA
- ggf. 2. Hören
- Ausw.: im Plenum

c) gemäß AA in PA
- Ausw.: S-Paare präsentieren Ergebnisse im Plenum.

114

| 4 | Topic 1 | Topic 2 | **Topic 3** | Story | Viewing | Study skills | Unit task |

Social media

1 a) individuelle Lösungen

1 LISTENING A **debate** about social media

1 b) 1 ☹ • 2 ☺☺ • 3 ☺ • 4 ☺☹

a) BEFORE YOU LISTEN What social media apps do you use? What are the most popular social media apps in the class?

b) [3.6] Look at the debate club poster. Dylan and Owen asked their friends about social media. Listen and decide if each person thinks social media is good (☺), bad (☹) or both (☺☹).

1 Samara   2 Promit   3 Gwen   4 Flynn

DEBATE CLUB
Tuesday at 12.30
in room 42

This week, our question is:
Is social media a good or bad thing for teens?

Dylan Jones **versus** Owen Thomas

c) WORDS Listen again and complete the phrases.

1 chat …
2 send (somebody) … messages
3 subscribe to … channels
4 forward a …
5 upload …
6 post …
7 … in touch
8 get a lot of …
9 … comments
10 un… (somebody)

▶ Box: Voc., p. 238

1 c) 1 online • 2 direct • 3 video • 4 link • 5 videos • 6 photos • 7 keep • 8 likes • 9 horrible • 10 follow

d) Tell a partner what you do or don't do on social media. Use the phrases in c).

I often / sometimes / never …
I'm not allowed to / I'm allowed to …

1 d) individuelle Lösungen

▶ More practice 6, p. 136

2 GLOBAL GOALS Good health and **well-being**

2 a) 1 well-being • 2 better • 3 Flynn • 4 fitness • 5 smartwatch • 6 has

a) [3.7] Listen to the second part of Flynn's interview and complete the sentences.

1 Zenn is a … app.
2 It helps Flynn to feel …
3 Only … can read his **diary** on Zenn.
4 Clok is a … app.
5 It works with Flynn's …
6 Dylan also … Clok.

b) Tell a partner which app you think is more useful and why.

2 b) Lösungsbsp. S. 298

I think … is more useful because you can …
I think both apps are …

c) What do you do to °improve your health and well-being? Tell your partner.

2 c) individuelle Lösungen

▶ Workbook, p. 72

114 one hundred and fourteen

Topic 3 Vorbereitung

Material: Ex 1 UMA/CD/App • Ex 2 UMA/CD/App, Apps für Gesundheit und Sport als Beispiele • Ex 3 ggf. UMA/CD/App • Ex 4 UMA, von L vorbereitete *bio* einer berühmten Person
Zeitbedarf: ca. 1–2 Std.
Minimalversion: Ex 3c) als HA, Ex 4 auslassen
Begleitmedien: WB (S. 72), INKL (S. 110–111)

4

3 SPEAKING Could you help me, please?

a) When did you last ask for or give help? Think about school, home, friends and hobbies. Tell a partner.   *3 a) individuelle Lösungen*

Last week, I asked for help with my homework.

b) Read the conversation and complete the sentence. 🔊 3.8

… is helping … to …

c) Copy and complete the table with the phrases in blue in the dialogue.   *3 b), c) Lösung S. 298*

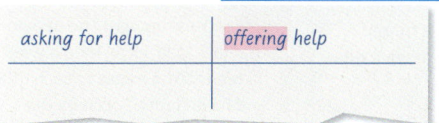

asking for help	offering help

d) WALK AROUND Make notes about things that you need or can help with. Then walk around and ask for or offer help. Use phrases from c).

I can help you with your maths homework if you like.

Yes, please. / No thanks. I'm OK. Shall I show you …?

3 d) individuelle Lösungen   ▶ More help, p. 136

Owen / **Dylan**

Dylan How can you talk about social media in the debate when you don't even use it, Owen?
Owen Hm, OK. Maybe I should try it. I'll text my mum to ask … Great, she said yes. But where do I start?
Dylan I can help you if you like.
Owen Yes, please! Could you help me make an account first?
Dylan Sure. Put in your information here. OK … Shall I upload a profile photo for you? Or do you want to do it?
Owen Can you do it, please? Look, this one is good.   ▶ Box: Voc., p. 239
Dylan No problem. There you go. Your account is private. Would you like me to make it public?
Owen No, thanks. That's too ⁺unsafe. And what should I put in my bio?
Dylan Just some facts about yourself and maybe a few ⁺emojis.

4 WRITING Owen's bio

4 a) 1 B – birthday • 2 E – home • 3 C – friends • 4 D – languages • 5 F – likes • 6 A – music

a) Match the emojis (A–F) to the information in Owen's bio (1–6). What does each emoji mean?

A 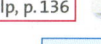 B   C

D  E  F

OwenT ⌄
1 12th June
2 Llandudno
3 Dylan, Samara and Flynn
4 English and Welsh (and a bit of German!)
5 singing, table tennis, going to the beach
6 pop, rock, rap – everything!

b) Write a bio for a famous person. Owen's bio can help you. °Guess who your partner's bio is for.

4 b) individuelle Lösungen

one hundred and fifteen **115**

Ex 3 Einstieg:
- (SB zu) L zeigt Handy: *Yesterday, I couldn't download an app. My friend helped me.*
- Überleitung zu Ex 3a): *When did you last ask for or give help?*

Erarbeitung:

a) (SB auf) Lesen der AA
- ▶ Partner talk gemäß AA
- 🗹 Lernschwächere S machen sich ggf. vorab Notizen.
- ☒ Lernstärkere S geben drei Beispiele.
- **Ausw.:** ▶ Meldekette

b) gemäß AA in EA
- **Ausw.:** im Plenum
- **Zusatz:** lautes Lesen des Dialogs in verteilten Rollen

c) S übertragen Tabelle gemäß AA ins Heft.
- 🗹 Bsp. gemeinsam erarbeiten.
- S ergänzen Tabelle in EA.
- **Ausw.:** ▶ Partner check, dann Plenum (mit TA)

d) ▶ Milling around gemäß AA
- 🗹 ▶ More help, S. 136
- **Ausw.:** Beispiele im Plenum

Ex 4 Einstieg:
- (SB zu) L zeigt Emojis aus Ex 4 (UMA): *Do you use emojis? What are your favourite ones?*

Erarbeitung:

a) (SB auf) gemäß AA
- **Ausw.:** im Plenum

b) ▶ Klären der AA
- L präsentiert *bio* als Beispiel.
- anschl. gemäß AA in EA
- **Ausw.:** ▶ Partner talk
- **Zusatz:** S erstellen eigene *bio*, anschließend errät Klasse in ▶ Gallery walk den Namen.

115

4

Topic 3 | Inhalt

Lernschwerpunkt: über Vor- und Nachteile von sozialen Medien sprechen
Kompetenzen: Reading Fakt und Meinung in Artikeln erkennen • Writing Kurzvorträge über Vor- und Nachteile von sozialen Medien vorbereiten
Strukturen: *relative clauses*
Redemittel: *definitions of social media words • opinion phrases • feedback phrases*

Ex 5 Einstieg:
- (SB zu) Satz als TA: *Every teenager uses social media.* L: *Do you think this is a fact or an opinion?* – ▶ Thumbs up
- ☒ Lernstärkere S begründen ihre Meinung.

Erarbeitung:
a) (SB auf) S lesen AA und diskutieren in ▶ Buzz groups.
- **Ausw.:** S nennen Beispiele und L erstellt Liste als TA.

b) gemäß AA in EA
- S erfragen unbekannten Wortschatz, L notiert an ▶ Vokabeltafel.
- **Ausw.:** L erfasst Lösung über Handzeichen der S, anschließend begründen S ihre Entscheidung.

c) S notieren Lösung gemäß AA.
- **Ausw.:** ▶ Meinungsbarometer, Raum in zwei Hälften (A/B)
- ☒ Lernstärkere S nennen Beispiele aus den Texten.
- s. a. ▶ SF 4, S. 158 f.

Ex 6 Einstieg:
- (SB auf) L: *Let's have a look at some phrases from these texts.*

Erarbeitung:
a) L zeigt die fünf Phrasen aus Ex 6a) (UMA/TA).
- gemäß AA
- **Ausw.:** L/S ergänzen Aussagen an der Tafel (UMA/TA).

b) L zeigt Regel (UMA/TA), dann gemäß AA.
- **Ausw.:** L/S ergänzen TA.
- **Sich.:** S übertragen den kompletten TA in den Merkteil (▶ English folder).
- s. a. ▶ LF 14, S. 183 und Erklärfilm (UMA/App)

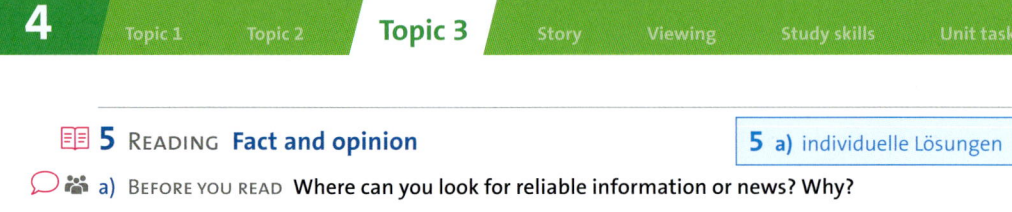

5 READING Fact and opinion   **5 a)** individuelle Lösungen

a) BEFORE YOU READ Where can you look for reliable information or news? Why?

b) Read the two texts. Which one has opinions and which has facts? Where are they from?

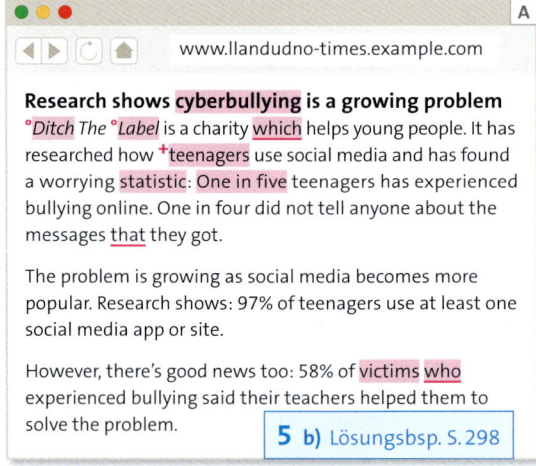

A www.llandudno-times.example.com

Research shows cyberbullying is a growing problem
°*Ditch The* °*Label* is a charity which helps young people. It has researched how ⁺teenagers use social media and has found a worrying statistic: One in five teenagers has experienced bullying online. One in four did not tell anyone about the messages that they got.

The problem is growing as social media becomes more popular. Research shows: 97% of teenagers use at least one social media app or site.

However, there's good news too: 58% of victims who experienced bullying said their teachers helped them to solve the problem.

5 b) Lösungsbsp. S. 298

B I HATE SOCIAL MEDIA!!!
We must stop social media! All the teens are using it and they're all bullying each other. Some boys who go to my daughter's school sent horrible messages to her. It happens to everyone, my daughter says. I can't believe we're letting this happen! The person that invented social media wanted all teens to be mean to each other and have fights. Social media is the worst thing EVER and we shouldn't let teens use it. Like and share if you agree!!! ▶ Box: Voc., p. 242

Datenquellen zu A: cybercrewuk und mayoclinic.org (siehe Quellenverzeichnis)

c) Match the sentences 1–6 to text A or B. Find examples in the texts.

1 It says where the information is from.
2 It talks about the writer's opinions.
3 It includes statistics.
4 It uses emotional language.
5 It says things that aren't true.
6 It looks at both sides of the problem.

5 c) 1 A • 2 B • 3 A • 4 B • 5 B • 6 A • examples S. 298

▶ Skills file 4, p. 158 f.

6 a) 1 which • 2 that • 3 who • 4 who • 5 that

6 LOOKING AT LANGUAGE Relative clauses

a) Read the texts in 5 again. Copy and complete the phrases.

1 a charity … helps young people
2 the messages … they got
3 58% of victims … experienced bullying
4 some boys … go to my daughter's school
5 the person … invented social media

b) Complete the rules.

> We use relative clauses to give more information about people or things.
> If you're talking about people, you use … or …
> If you're talking about things, you use … or …

▶ Language file 14, p. 183

6 b) who *or* that • which *or* that

▶ Workbook, p. 73

116 one hundred and sixteen

Topic 3 Vorbereitung

Material: Ex 6 UMA, UMA/App (Erklärfilm) • Ex 8 ggf. UMA, Blanko-Moderationskarten (nach Bedarf)
Zeitbedarf: ca. 1–2 Std.
Begleitmedien: WB (S. 73–74), App (Digital quiz), INKL (S. 112–113), DIFF (4.5)

---

7 What is it?

a) Match the beginnings and endings of the °definitions.

1. A social network is a site …
2. A bully is a person …
3. Cyberbullying is a type of bullying …
4. A follower is someone …
5. An emoji is a small digital picture …

a. that you use to show an idea or emotion.
b. who subscribes to your page or channel.
c. who is mean to other people.
d. that you use to talk to people online.
e. which happens online.

7 a) 1 d • 2 c • 3 e • 4 b • 5 a

b) Complete the definitions for these words with *who* or *which*.

1. A fact is something … is definitely true.
2. A victim is someone … experiences bullying.
3. A charity is an organization … helps people.
4. An influencer is someone … has lots of ⁺followers on social media.

7 b) 1 which • 2 who • 3 which • 4 who

💡 In English, we don't need a comma before *who*, *which* or *that* in this type of relative clause.

▶ More practice 7, p. 136 ▶ Challenge 2, p. 136 ▶ Challenge 3, p. 137

My task

8 WRITING Preparing for the debate

a) Help Dylan and Owen write their short talks for the first part of the debate.
Partner A: °Work on Dylan's argument: Social media is a good thing for teens.
Partner B: Work on Owen's argument: Social media is a bad thing for teens.
Write at least three good or bad things about social media. Give reasons.

*I believe that social media is a good / bad thing for teens because …
Social media also helps people …
I think one of the problems with social media is that …*

8 a) Lösungsbsp. S. 298

▶ More help, p. 137

b) Check your writing. Then read and check your partner's sentences:
- Is the language correct?
- Have they given reasons for each of their points? Give feedback.

*You gave some great reasons.
Next time, you could use more linking words.*

8 b) individuelle Lösungen

▶ Skills file 13, p. 168

▶ Workbook, p. 74

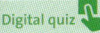 I can talk about the good and bad sides of social media.

one hundred and seventeen 117

Ex 7 Einstieg:
- (SB zu) ▶ Five-finger brainstorming: S nennen spontan fünf Wörter zum Thema *social media*.

Erarbeitung:
a) (SB auf) S lesen AA.
- erster Satz gemeinsam, dann schriftl. Bearbeitung gemäß AA
- **Ausw.:** ▶ Five-minute teacher

b) schriftl. Bearbeitung gemäß AA
- **Ausw.:** ▶ Meldekette
- ▶ More practice 7, S. 136 und ▶ Challenge 2, S. 136
- Aufgabe zu *contact clauses*: ▶ Challenge 3, S. 137

My task Ex 8 Einstieg:
- (SB zu) TA: *Preparing for the debate*. L nennt das Lernziel der Aufgabe und zeigt ggf. noch einmal die *Debate club*-Ankündigung von S. 114 (UMA).

Erarbeitung:
a) (SB auf) Lesen der AA
- Arbeitsteilige PA: S notieren jeweils mind. drei Dinge, die für bzw. gegen *social media* sprechen, und geben dazu eine Begründung.
- ▶ More help, S. 137

b) **Ausw.:** ▶ Partner check
- **Alternative:** TA: *social media* und zwei Spalten: *good thing for teens? / bad thing for teens?*. Partner A und B schreiben ihre Argumente auf Moderationskarten und prüfen die Korrektheit gemäß **Ex 8b)**. Anschl. Karten an die Tafel heften. Die Klasse positioniert sich zu den Argumenten und gibt ggf. noch Ergänzungen.

117

4

Story Inhalt

Lernschwerpunkt: eine Geschichte über das Posten von Fotos und daraus entstehende Konflikte verstehen
Kompetenzen: Reading / Study skills eine Geschichte überfliegen, um sich einen Überblick über den Inhalt zu verschaffen (*Skimming*)
Redemittel: *social media • friendship • fake photos*

Ex 1 Einstieg:
- (SB zu) ▶ Meinungsbarometer: L macht Aussagen, S positionieren sich dazu auf einer Linie. L fragt einzelne S nach einem Statement zu ihrer Position. Beispiele:
  – *Looks are important to me.*
  – *I upload pictures on social media.*
  – *When I take pictures, I like using filters.*
  – *I sometimes wish I could look like other people (on social media).*

Erarbeitung:
a) (SB auf) S betrachten die Bilder auf S. 118–119 und lesen die Überschrift gemäß AA.
- ▶ Partner talk: S stellen Vermutungen gemäß AA an.
- Ausw.: S nennen ihre Ideen im Plenum. L sichert sie im TA.

b) gemeinsames Lesen der ▶ Tippbox, S. 118 zum *Skimming*
- s. a. ▶ SF 9, S. 164
- S lesen Text leise in EA und finden heraus, ob ihre Vermutung stimmt (ggf. Zeitlimit vorgeben, damit S den Text tatsächlich nur überfliegen u. nicht im Detail lesen).
- Ausw.: Diskussion im Plenum dazu, welche Vermutungen korrekt waren. L ändert den TA aus a) entsprechend ab.
- S lesen/hören die Story im ▶ Mitleseverfahren.
- S erfragen unbekannte Vokabeln. L umschreibt Bedeutung auf Englisch und S erraten das deutsche Wort. L notiert die neuen Vokabeln an der ▶ Vokabeltafel.
- Forts. s. S. 119

118

---

4 | Topic 1 | Topic 2 | Topic 3 | **Story** | Viewing | Study skills | Unit task

Looking good

1 a) Lösungsbsp. S. 298
1 b) individuelle Lösungen

1 READING The camera never  right?

a) BEFORE YOU READ Look at the title of the story and the photos. What do you think the story is about?

I think that Dylan / Owen is going to …   Maybe …

When you skim a text, you read quickly to get the main ideas. You don't have to understand every word.

b) Now skim the story. Were you right? ▶ Skills file 9, p. 164

🔊 3.9

'Thanks for helping me with my bio, Dylan!' typed Owen. He used the social network a few times a week now.
'You're welcome!' wrote Dylan. 'It's great
5 that we can use this to talk to our German exchange partners before they come to Llandudno next week. My partner Saskia is sooooooo cool!'

Owen also enjoyed chatting online to his
10 exchange partner Tom as well as his friends at school. But he noticed that sometimes Dylan wrote strange things on the site.

Love our new family car 😂!
#LiveFast
SaskiM and **97 others** liked this

'Dylan's family doesn't have a new car,' he thought when he saw his latest post.
15 'That's a photo from when we went to the Llandudno Transport Festival last week. But maybe he's just joking.'

The next day at school, Owen heard Dylan talking to some people in their class.
20 'You know that photo I posted of me playing my new song? It got a HUNDRED likes! And I've got lots of new followers now!'

At the weekend, Owen and Dylan went to the beach, but it wasn't like their normal
25 trips. Dylan wanted Owen to take lots of photos of him to post online.
'This is boring!' said Owen. 'Let's go swimming now.'
'Just one more,' said Dylan. 'The light is
30 really good now.'
'But I've taken at least twenty photos! Who cares what they look like – let's just have fun!'
'I've got lots of followers who need to see
35 what I'm doing and how cool I look.'
'You mean you want Saskia to see how cool you look,' said Owen.

On Monday, everyone was excited. The exchange class arrived today! Owen
40 looked at his phone. There was a new photo of Dylan – but he looked different. 'That's a photo from the beach last weekend, but he's changed it,' Owen thought. He was annoyed.

118 one hundred and eighteen

Story Vorbereitung

Material: Ex 1 UMA/CD/App, ggf. Emoji-Sticker (nach Bedarf), digitale Endgeräte, ggf. digitale Pinnwand
Zeitbedarf: ca. 1–2 Std.
Begleitmedien: INKL (S. 114–115)

Dylan
Me at the beach 😎!
#BeachLover
131 liked this

Owen
The real Dylan 😄
#ScaredOfWater
32 comments

45 Just then he looked up and saw the coach with the German students arrive. Tom got off the coach and ran over to Owen, waving. 'Hi! It's so good to meet you!'

Then Owen saw Dylan go over to Saskia.
50 'It's great to meet you, Saskia!' he said.
'Dylan?' Saskia looked a bit surprised.
'You look different in your photos.'
'Erm, well, it's me', said Dylan.
They walked to the car where Dylan's mum
55 was waiting.
'Oh, you didn't bring your new car?' asked Saskia. Dylan looked embarrassed.

That evening, Owen thought about all of Dylan's photos and felt angry. 'If he thinks
60 he's an influencer, then let's show everyone the truth,' he thought. He posted a different photo of Dylan at the beach. Dylan didn't look quite as cool in this photo!

People quickly started to leave comments
65 and jokes under the photo. At first Owen thought that it was funny, but a few hours later there were lots of mean comments.

Owen deleted the photo. He felt terrible.

The next day, Owen saw Dylan and Saskia
70 in the school canteen. He walked over to Dylan and took a deep breath.
'Dylan, I'm sorry I posted that photo. It was mean. I guess I was jealous of you.'   ▶ Box: Voc., p. 240

'Thanks, Owen. You know, at first I was really
75 angry. But then I thought about it. It was stupid of me to post things that weren't real. I know I shouldn't worry about what other people think.'

Saskia turned and smiled at Dylan.
80 'You know, actually I prefer the second photo. It's more natural, and it's kind of funny!' Dylan smiled back at Saskia and for once, he didn't think about how he looked.

Saskia

Dylan

Ideen zur Weiterarbeit mit der Story (können auch nach Ex 2, S. 120 umgesetzt werden):

- erneutes Lesen der Geschichte bis Zeile 57
  L: *Imagine what would have happened if Dylan's mum had heard Saskia's comment about their car.*
- GA in Gruppen von 3–4 S: S entwickeln ein alternatives Ende, bei dem Dylans Mutter von Dylans Lügen erfährt, und schreiben einen kurzen Dialog dazu.
- **Ausw.:** S führen den Dialog im Plenum vor.
- S suchen im Text nach Informationen zu Saskia (Scanning, s. ▶ SF 9, S. 164):
  – *Scan the text and find out what Dylan thinks about Saskia based on her social media account.* (She is cool.)
  – *Scan the text again and find out what kind of photos Saskia prefers.* (She likes natural and funny photos.)
- daran anschl. Aufgabe:
  L: *Imagine Saskia and Dylan go to the beach together the next weekend. Write a post for Saskia or Dylan about their day at the beach. Also, take a picture to go with the post.*
- **Ausw.:** ▶ Gallery walk: L druckt die fertigen Posts aus und hängt sie auf. S kommentieren sie (ggf. mit Emoji-Stickern).
- **Alternative:** S können eine kostenlose digitale Pinnwand nutzen, um ihre Texte und Fotos geschützt hochzuladen und ggf. zu kommentieren.

4

Story Inhalt

Lernschwerpunkt: über Social-Media-Nutzung und nachbearbeitete Fotos reflektieren
Kompetenzen: Reading der Story Informationen entnehmen • Speaking eigene Meinung zur Social-Media-Nutzung äußern • Speaking / Life skills sich über Bildbearbeitung und ihre Wirkung austauschen
Redemittel: Wortfeld Bildbearbeitung

Vorbereitung

Material: Ex 2 UMA • Ex 3 ggf. ▶ KV 2.3: Discussion tickets (Klassensatz) • Ex 4 ggf. von L und S recherchierte Fotos von Influencern
Zeitbedarf: ca. 1–2 Std.
Minimalversion: Ex 4 auslassen
Begleitmedien: WB (S. 75), App (Digital quiz), INKL (S. 116), DIFF (4.6)

Ex 2 Einstieg:
- (SB zu) L zeigt Bilder von S. 118–119 (UMA), S wiederholen, was in der Geschichte passiert.

Erarbeitung:
- (SB auf, S. 118–119) Zwei Seiten des Raums werden je die Aussagen *true/false* zugeordnet.
- L/S liest Satz aus Ex 2 vor, S laufen zur passenden Seite.
- **Ausw.:** S berichten falsche Aussagen mündlich bzw. nennen Textstelle für richtige Aussage.

Ex 3 Einstieg:
- (SB zu) L wiederholt *opinion phrases* (ggf. mit ▶ KV 2.3, s. a. ▶ SF 5, S. 160 und S. 60).

Erarbeitung:
- (SB auf) S bereiten Notizen zu den Fragen im Heft vor.
- ▶ Double circle gemäß AA, ggf. Nutzung von ▶ KV 2.3.
- **Ausw.:** Vorstellung einzelner Meinungen im Plenum

Ex 4 Einstieg:
- (SB zu) L zeigt Bilder von Influencern oder Bilder von Dylan und Owen. L: *Are these pictures real? Why (not)?*

Erarbeitung:
- a) (SB auf) S ordnen die Begriffe gemäß AA zu.
- **Ausw.:** ▶ Five-minute teacher
- b) Diskussion gemäß AA im Plenum
- c) Bildsuche gemäß AA (ggf. HA)
- PA: S zeigen sich ihre Bilder und diskutieren gemäß AA.
- **Ausw.:** Vorstellung im Plenum

| 4 | Topic 1 | Topic 2 | Topic 3 | **Story** | Viewing | Study skills | Unit task |

2 What happens in the story?

Read the story again. Are the sentences true or false? Correct the false sentences.

1. Dylan and Owen don't know who their exchange partners are before they arrive.
2. Owen likes using the social network.
3. Dylan's mum has a new fast car.
4. Dylan doesn't have many followers.
5. Dylan edits the photo that Owen took.
6. Owen posts a nice photo of Dylan.
7. Owen and Dylan are friends in the end.

> **2** 1 false – they know their exchange partners • 2 true • 3 false – she doesn't have a new car • 4 false – he has lots of new followers • 5 true • 6 false – he posts a photo where Dylan doesn't look so cool • 7 true

3 DOUBLE CIRCLE Social media opinions

Think about questions 1–4 and make notes. Then talk to a partner about question 1. Talk about questions 2–4 with new partners.

1. Do you use social media? Why (not)?
2. Which influencers do you know? What do you think about them?
3. Is it a good idea to edit photos to make them look better? Why (not)?
4. How do you feel when you see photos of people who look perfect online?

> **3** individuelle Lösungen
> ▶ Skills file 5, p. 160

4 LIFE SKILLS Original or edited?

a) Influencers make themselves look good in their photos in different ways. Match the definitions (1–6) to the words (a–f).

1. the way that you stand or sit
2. a **tool** that changes the colour of a photo
3. what you wear
4. a tool that helps you change what's in the photo
5. something that you put on your face to look better
6. how light or dark it is in the photo

a filter
b lighting
c digital editing software
d pose
e clothes
f make-up

> **4 a)** 1 d • 2 a • 3 e • 4 c • 5 f • 6 b

b) Look at the two beach photos of Dylan on p. 119 again. Which things in a) do you think he used in the edited photo?

> **4 b)** filters, digital editing software, pose, clothes, lighting

c) Find a photo from an influencer that you know. How do you think they have changed the photo?

The influencer has used … to change the …
She has used … to make her hair/eyes/… look lighter/bigger/…
He has used … to look taller/stronger/…

> **4 c)** individuelle Lösungen
> ▶ Workbook, p. 75

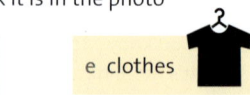 Digital quiz I can talk about truth and lies on social media.

120 one hundred and twenty

4

Viewing — Inhalt

Lernschwerpunkt: einem Film Informationen zur Erstellung eines Cosplay-Kostüms entnehmen
Kompetenzen: Viewing Filmszenen verstehen • Speaking über die Überwindung von Schwierigkeiten sprechen
Redemittel: cosplay • making a costume

Vorbereitung

Material: Ex 2 + 3 UMA/DVD/App
Zeitbedarf: ca. 1 Std.
Minimalversion: Ex 4 auslassen
Begleitmedien: INKL (S. 117)

| Topic 1 | Topic 2 | Topic 3 | Story | **Viewing** | Study skills | Unit task | **4** |

Sophie's ⁺cosplay costume

1 BEFORE YOU WATCH Cosplay

Read the information in the box. Which character would you choose for a cosplay costume and why? Tell a partner.

1 individuelle Lösungen

Good to know

'Cosplay' comes from 'costume' and 'play' and started in Japan. Fans make costumes of their favourite characters from video games, films, series or ⁺manga and take part in role-plays and competitions. They often meet and discuss their costumes on social media.

2 a) 1 Sophie designed the costume herself. It's a Twi'lek from 'Star Wars'. • 2 two weeks • 3 She likes learning new skills. • 4 She forgot to make a video.

2 VIEWING Sophie's costume

a) Sophie is a German ⁺vlogger. Watch the first part of the video and find out …

1. who designed Sophie's costume and what it is.
2. how long it took to make the costume.
3. why she made the costume.
4. what the problem was in Stuttgart.

b) Put the instructions for Sophie's costume in the correct order. Then watch the first part of the video again and check.

a Sew the costume.
b Design the costume.
c Put pink paint on your skin.
d Make the headpiece.
e Choose a character that you like.

2 b) e • b • a • d • c

3 1 true • 2 true • 3 false – this time she made a video •
4 false – she didn't win the competition • 5 true •
6 false – it was awesome!

3 VIEWING In °Cologne

Watch the second part of the video. True or false? Correct the false sentences.

1. Sophie went to a games event.
2. People took photos of Sophie.
3. Sophie forgot to make a video.
4. She won a costume competition.
5. She met people who have the same interests.
6. It was an embarrassing experience.

4 SPEAKING Making things work

'Nothing ever works on the first try – ever,' Sophie says. Have you ever had an experience like this? What did you do to make it work?

4 individuelle Lösungen

one hundred and twenty-one 121

Ex 1 Einstieg:
- (SB zu) L stellt Frage:
  L: *What's this called? It's an activity which has become popular because of anime. People dress up as their favourite character from a movie, a comic or a book.*
- S antworten.

Erarbeitung:
- (SB auf) ▶ Good to know, S. 121 lesen.
- Austausch im ▶ Milling around: Welchen Charakter würden S wählen und warum?
- **Ausw.:** Vorstellung im Plenum

Ex 2 Einstieg:
- (SB auf) L: *Most cosplayers design and make their own costumes. Let's find out how.*

Erarbeitung:
a) S lesen die Sätze 1–4.
- **1. Sehen** (Teil 1): S notieren Antworten stichwortartig im Heft.
- **Ausw.:** Vergleich im Plenum

b) gemäß AA im Anschluss an **1. Sehen**
- **Ausw.: 2. Sehen,** dann Vergleich im Plenum

Ex 3 Erarbeitung:
- (SB auf) S lesen die Sätze 1–6 und schreiben die Zahlen ins Heft.
- **1. Sehen** (Teil 2): S setzen Haken oder Kreuzchen.
- **Ausw.:** ▶ Five-minute teacher

Ex 4 Erarbeitung:
- (SB auf) Vorlesen des Zitats
- Austausch im ▶ Milling around
- **Ausw.:** ▶ Blitzlichtrunde im Plenum

121

4

Study skills — Inhalt

Lernschwerpunkt: Methoden für einen flüssigeren Vortrag kennenlernen
Kompetenzen: Speaking / Study skills einen Vortrag strukturieren • flüssigeres Sprechen und den Umgang mit Vokabelproblemen üben
Redemittel: *sequencers: first, second, …* • *phrases for buying time*

Vorbereitung

Material: Ex 1 UMA • Ex 3 UMA/CD/App, ggf. Karteikarten (nach Bedarf)
Zeitbedarf: ca. 1 Std.
Begleitmedien: App (Digital quiz), INKL (S. 118), DIFF (4.7)

Ex 1 Einstieg:
- (SB zu) L: *What makes a good talk?* S nennen Kriterien. L sammelt sie im TA.
- (SB auf) gemeinsames Lesen der ▶ Tippbox, S. 122 und ggf. Ergänzen des TA

Erarbeitung:
a) L: *First, let's take a look at how to structure your talk.*
- S lesen die Stichwortkarten und ordnen sie gemäß AA.
- **Ausw.:** ▶ Five-minute teacher: S sichert die Reihenfolge im TA (über UMA).

b) EA: S ordnen die Begriffe gemäß AA den Karten zu.
- ⊠ Lernstärkere S schreiben mit den Begriffen einen Satz, den Saskia sagen könnte.
- **Ausw.:** Vergleich im Plenum, Vorlesen der Sätze

Ex 2 Einstieg:
- (SB auf) L: *Next, let's see what you can do if you forget a word.*
- S nennen ihre Ideen.

Erarbeitung:
a) PA: S finden die korrekte Erklärung.
b) S lesen die ▶ Tippbox, S. 122 und erklären sich die Begriffe.
- **Ausw.:** S erklärt einen der Begriffe, die Klasse rät.

Ex 3 Erarbeitung:
- (SB auf) ▶ Semantisierung der Phrasen im Reservoir
- 1. **Hören** gemäß AA
- **Ausw.:** ▶ Meldekette
- ⊠ S notieren die Phrasen auf Karteikarten. ▶ One-minute presentation in PA: S nutzen die Karten statt Sprechpausen.

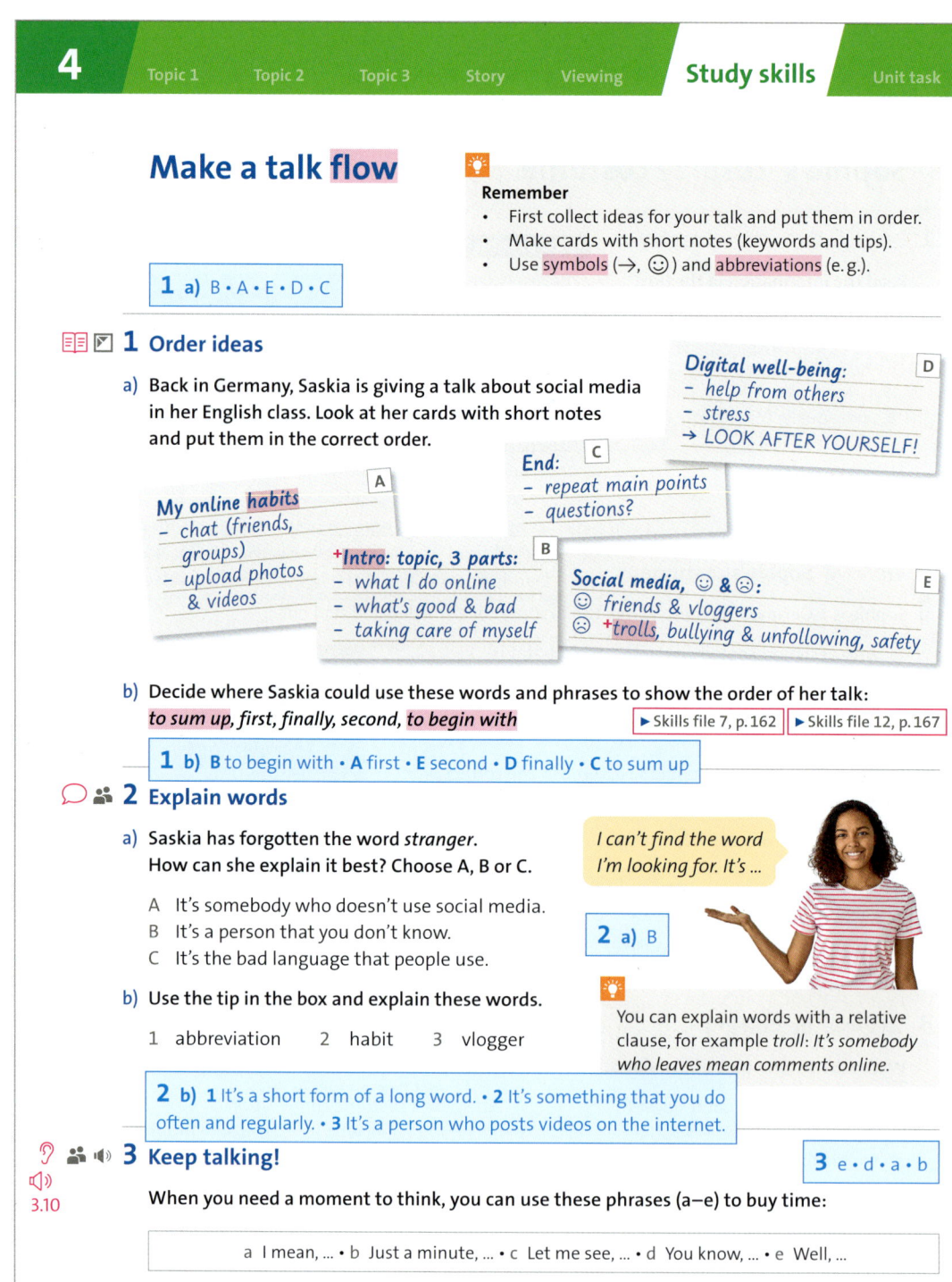

4

Unit task Inhalt

Lernschwerpunkt: einen Vortrag über soziale Medien halten
Kompetenzen: Speaking einen Vortrag einüben und halten • Study skills Note-making • einen Vortrag strukturieren
Redemittel: Wortfeld *social media*

Vorbereitung

Material: Step 2 Karteikarten, A4-Blätter (nach Bedarf) • Step 3 von S recherchierte und ausgedruckte Bilder, ggf. digitale Endgeräte zum Erstellen von Folien
Zeitbedarf: ca. 2 Std.
Minimalversion: Bilder für Step 3 als HA suchen lassen
Begleitmedien: App (Digital help, Digital quiz), INKL (S. 119)

Unit task 4 — Give a short talk about social media

Unit task individuelle Lösungen

Step 1: Make notes for your talk ▶ Digital help

You're going to give a short talk (two to three minutes) about your online and social media habits. Make notes to answer the questions (1–4).

1. What do you do online?
2. What are your favourite apps?
3. What do you think is good and bad about social media?
4. What do you do for your digital well-being?

Step 2: Make cards and order them

a) Think of a short introduction and ending.
b) Make cards with your ideas from Step 1 and 2a). Add words and phrases to order your ideas.
▶ Study skills 1b, p. 122

Step 3: Use photos and other images

Find images for your talk: photos, the covers of video games, °video clips and screenshots, … Make slides or °print out pictures that you can show.
▶ Skills file 4, p. 158–159

Use screenshots of your favourite apps and games. You can look at p. 113 for help.
Remember to use °creative commons photos and to give sources.

Step 4: Practise your talk

Practise your talk silently in class. Then practise it at home and record yourself. Explain new words or words that you have forgotten. Keep talking!
▶ Study skills 2+3, p. 122

Check how long your talk is:
Cut some points or add information.
Listen to difficult words in your app.

Step 5: Give your talk to a group

a) Give your talk to a group. The others listen and write three things:
▶ Skills file 7, p. 162

1. one good thing about the talk — *I really liked that you explained new words.*
2. one thing that could be better — *Next time, you should talk a bit more slowly.*
3. one question — *How often do you use social media?*

b) The students in your group give feedback and ask their questions.
▶ Let's talk: Feedback, p. 200

Digital quiz I can give a short talk.

one hundred and twenty-three **123**

Unit task Einstieg:
- (SB zu) gemeinsames Erstellen einer ▶ Mindmap mit Vokabeln zum Thema *social media*

Step 1 Erarbeitung:
- (SB auf) S notieren Antworten zu den Fragen gemäß AA.
- s. a. *Digital help* (App)
- **Ausw.:** ggf. Austausch von Ideen in PA (besonders für lernschwächere S)

Step 2 Erarbeitung:
a) + b) Gemäß AA, S orientieren sich an Ex 1, S. 122.
- ⊠ Lernschwächere S knicken ein Blatt in der Hälfte und schreiben den Text auf die eine Seite und die passenden Stichwörter auf die andere Seite.

Step 3 Erarbeitung:
- L wiederholt mit S, wie man Folien erstellt und Quellen angibt und wo man lizenzfreie Bilder findet.
- S erstellen ihre Folien bzw. Poster gemäß AA.

Step 4 Erarbeitung:
- ▶ Klären der AA. Gemeinsame Reflexion darüber, wie man gut übt und was dabei hilft.
- S üben ihren Vortrag als HA.

Step 5 Erarbeitung:
a) ▶ Gruppenbildung
- S halten ihren Vortrag vor der Gruppe. Mit-S machen Notizen gemäß AA.

b) ▶ Feedback gemäß AA
- **Ausw.:** S sagen, was sie beim nächsten Vortrag verbessern wollen.

4

Checkpoint Inhalt

Lernschwerpunkt: Kompetenzen und sprachliche Mittel üben, Lernfortschritte erkennen
Kompetenzen: Reading die Lesestrategie *Skimming* anwenden • einem Text Informationen entnehmen •
Mediation Informationen aus einer deutschen Nachricht auf Englisch wiedergeben
Redemittel: *places in Wales* • *technology* • *giving instructions*

Allgemeine Anmerkung:
s. Unit 1, S. 32

Ex 1 Einstieg:
- (SB auf) Selbsteinschätzung zum Lernziel mit ▶ Thumbs up

Erarbeitung:
a) S wiederholen die Bedeutung von *Skimming* (ggf. die ▶ Tippbox, S. 118 oder ▶ SF 9, S. 164 noch einmal lesen).
- S lesen und wählen eine Überschrift gemäß AA.

b) S lesen den Text und entscheiden gemäß AA. Sie korrigieren die falschen Aussagen.
- **Ausw.:** ▶ Bus stop (▶ KV Extra): S vergleichen ihre Lösungen mithilfe von ▶ KV 4.4A.
- **Alternative:** Um das *Scanning* (vgl. ▶ SF 9, S. 164) zu üben, kann die Klasse in Gruppen ein Wettlesen machen. Dabei liest ein/-e S die Aussagen 1–6 nacheinander vor und die anderen müssen möglichst schnell entscheiden, was die korrekte Lösung ist. Der/Die Gruppenleiter/-in prüft mit ▶ KV 4.4A und verteilt Punkte danach, wer am schnellsten die richtige Lösung gefunden hat.
- erneute Selbsteinschätzung

---

4 Checkpoint Digital checkpoint

1 READING A poster about Wales

I can understand information about Wales.

a) Owen and Dylan have made a poster for the exchange students.
Skim the texts and look at the photos. Choose the correct title (A–C) for their poster.

A Three free places to visit in Wales
B Three cool places for history fans
C The three best places for kids in Wales

> **1 a)** B

Conwy[1] Castle
This castle is over 700 years old. It has eight towers and only took four years to build. You can walk around the top of the walls and admire the town and river below. A family ticket costs £37.70. In summer it's open till 6 p.m. You should bring something to eat because there isn't a cafe in the castle.

Penrhyn[2] Castle
This castle is only about 200 years old and has a beautiful garden with views of Snowdonia national park. There are two cafes, shops and a train museum. There's also an old kitchen where you can see how people prepared food and ate their meals all those years ago. A family ticket costs £35 and the castle is open from 10 a.m. to 4 p.m. in summer.

Castell Dinas Brân[3]
You can't drive up to this castle – you can only get there on foot. It's high on a mountain, so you will have amazing views. The castle is nearly 800 years old, but there are only °ruins now. You'll need to wear good walking shoes and take a jacket because it's usually quite windy. You don't have to pay to visit this castle, but there are no shops, cafes or toilets.

b) Read the texts again. Are the sentences true (T) or false (F)? Correct the false sentences.

1 You can leave your car at Castell Dinas Brân.
2 All the castles have a cafe.
3 You get a good view from all of the castles.
4 Conwy Castle is the cheapest for families.
5 Two castles are over 700 years old.
6 You should visit Penrhyn castle if you're interested in the history of cooking.

> **1 b)** Lösungsbsp. S. 299

1 [ˈkɒnwi] **2** [ˈpenrɪn] **3** [ˌdiːnæs ˈbræn]

Check

4

Checkpoint Vorbereitung

Material: alle Aufgaben ▶ KV Extra: Bus stop, ▶ KV 4.4A: Checkpoint answers, App (Check)
Zeitbedarf: ca. 1 Std.
Minimalversion: Auswahl der Aufgaben erfolgt aufgrund der zu überprüfenden Lernziele
Begleitmedien: App (Digital checkpoint), INKL (S. 120–121)

Die Übungen kannst du auch digital machen. **4**

2 MEDIATION An email from Saskia
I can talk about Wales. ✓

Saskia is writing an email to her cousin Marie in Germany. Dylan wants to know what she's writing about. Read the email and then write Saskia's answers.

> Hi, Marie,
> ich bin gerade mit meiner Schulklasse in Wales. Wir sind in Llandudno – das ist eine kleine Stadt direkt am Meer. Es ist wirklich schön. Meine Gastfamilie ist nett. Mein Austauschpartner heißt Dylan. Wir werden uns Samstag ein Rugbyspiel anschauen, weil er und seine Eltern große Rugbyfans sind. Ich freue mich sehr auf das Spiel!
>
> Gestern waren wir auf der Seebrücke und haben Eis gegessen. Danach waren wir am Strand und haben mit Dylans Hund gespielt. Es ist aber ziemlich kalt und es regnet auch echt oft. Im Sommer ist es bestimmt besser.
>
> Bin Sonntag wieder zu Hause. Bis dann!

Dylan   What did you write about Llandudno?
Saskia I wrote that it's … (1).
Dylan   And what did you write about rugby?
Saskia I wrote that we … (2).
Dylan   And what's the smiley emoji for?
Saskia I'm … (3).
Dylan   Gestern – that means 'yesterday', right? What did you write about yesterday?
Saskia I wrote that we … (4).

2 Lösungsbsp. S. 299

3 WORDS Helping a neighbour
I can give simple instructions. ✓

Your neighbour has a new smartphone and doesn't speak German.
He asks you to help him take a photo and send it to his daughter.

Choose the correct words in the instructions.

1 First, make sure that you have a Wi-Fi A charger B connection C key.
2 Next, open the camera app and A take B make C do some photos.
3 Open your A messaging B voicemail C source app.
4 A Edit B Cut C Press the plus symbol and find your daughter's number.
5 A Upload B Tap C Subscribe the camera icon and then '°Gallery'.
6 Choose the A image B device C tool that you want to send.
7 Finally, write your A channel B diary C message and send it.
8 Don't worry. It's quite A jealous B simple C exact to send photos with your phone!

3 1 B • 2 A • 3 A • 4 C • 5 B • 6 A • 7 C • 8 B

Check

one hundred and twenty-five **125**

Ex 2 Einstieg:
- (SB auf) Selbsteinschätzung s. Ex 1
- 🔁 In schwächeren Klassen ggf. kurz wiederholen, was eine gute Sprachmittlung ausmacht (▶ Mediation).

Erarbeitung:
- S lesen den Text und schreiben die Informationen auf Englisch in ihr Heft.
- **Ausw.:** ▶ Partner check mit ▶ KV 4.4A
- Partner/-in prüft, dass nicht wortwörtlich übersetzt wurde und dass die Antworten keine überflüssigen Informationen enthalten.
- **Alternative:** ▶ Bus stop (▶ KV Extra): S vergleichen ihre Lösungen eigenständig mithilfe von ▶ KV 4.4A.
- erneute Selbsteinschätzung

Ex 3 Einstieg:
- (SB auf) Selbsteinschätzung s. Ex 1

Erarbeitung:
- S schreiben die Lösungen gemäß AA in ihr Heft.
- **Ausw.:** ▶ Bus stop (▶ KV Extra): S vergleichen ihre Lösungen mithilfe von ▶ KV 4.4A.
- **Alternative:** L teilt den Raum in drei Teile u. benennt sie mit A, B, C. L liest einen Satz mit den drei Optionen vor, S laufen zu dem für sie passenden Satzteil. Anschließend begründen sie ihre Wahl im Plenum.
- erneute Selbsteinschätzung

125

4

Checkpoint Inhalt

Lernschwerpunkt: Kompetenzen und sprachliche Mittel üben, Lernfortschritte erkennen
Kompetenzen: Listening einem Hörtext Informationen zu Lügen auf sozialen Medien entnehmen • Reading einen kurzen Vortrag verstehen • Speaking sich über positive und negative Erfahrungen mit sozialen Medien austauschen • unbekannte/vergessene Vokabeln umschreiben • Phrasen aus einem Vortrag richtig aussprechen
Strukturen: *relative clauses*
Redemittel: *social media • online activities • definitions*

Ex 4 Einstieg:
- (SB auf) Selbsteinschätzung zum Lernziel (z. B. mit ▶ Thumbs up)

Erarbeitung:
a) S schreiben die Sätze gemäß AA ins Heft und ergänzen sie.

b) S schätzen die Aussagen 1–7 gemäß AA ein und zeichnen die Smileys ins Heft.
- **Ausw.:** ▶ Bus stop (▶ KV Extra): S vergleichen ihre Lösungen zu a) und b) eigenständig mithilfe von ▶ KV 4.4B.

c) ▶ Partner talk gemäß AA
- **Alternative:** Austausch im ▶ Milling around. S können die *opinion phrases* von ▶ KV 2.3 (vgl. **Ex 3**, S. 120) nutzen, um ihre Meinung zu äußern.
- erneute Selbsteinschätzung

Ex 5 Einstieg:
- (SB auf) Selbsteinschätzung s. **Ex 4**

Erarbeitung:
a) 1. Hören: Gemäß AA, S notieren ihre Zuordnung im Heft.

b) 2. Hören: Gemäß AA, S ergänzen die Sätze im Heft.

c) S ordnen die Ratschläge gemäß AA im Heft zu.
- **Ausw.:** S suchen Partner/-in am ▶ Bus stop (▶ KV Extra): ▶ Partner check mit ▶ KV 4.4B.

d) Austausch in PA
- **Ausw.:** S teilen ihre Erfahrungen im Plenum.
- erneute Selbsteinschätzung

---

4 Checkpoint   Digital checkpoint

4 a) 1 which • 2 who • 3 which • 4 which • 5 who • 6 which • 7 who

4 LANGUAGE Life online – positive or negative?

I can talk about the good and bad sides of social media.

a) Copy and complete the sentences with *which* or *who*.

1 Cyberbullying is a problem … many people have experienced.
2 Older people … can't leave their houses can connect with friends on social media.
3 Some social media companies collect your personal °data … they sell to other companies.
4 Shops … use social media can sell their products to more people.
5 Lots of teenagers … use social media find friends with the same interests.
6 There are lots of news stories on social media … aren't true.
7 If you use social media, you can find friends … live in different countries.

4 b) 1 ☹ • 2 ☺ • 3 ☹ • 4 ☺ • 5 ☺ • 6 ☹ • 7 ☺

b) Which sentences are positive? Which are negative? Draw smileys (☺ or ☹).

c) SPEAKING What's your experience with social media? Give examples.

> My experience with social media is °mostly positive/negative because …

> I had a good/bad experience when …

> I don't use social media a lot because …

4 c) Lösungsbsp. S. 299

5 LISTENING Fake or real?

I can talk about truth and lies on social media.

a) Look at the photos and listen to four people talking about mistakes and lies on social media. What do they talk about? Match the people (1–4) to the photos (A–E). There's one extra photo.

1 Elsa   2 Hadi   3 Marie   4 Oskar

5 a) 1 E • 2 B • 3 A • 4 D

 A    B    C   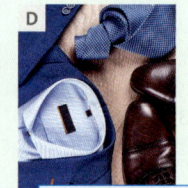 D    E

b) Listen again and complete the sentences.

1 Elsa's grandma fell in love with a man who only wanted …
2 The 'lion' near Berlin really was a …
3 The food at the restaurant in France was … and bad.
4 Oskar's dad bought some things which never …

5 b) 1 her money • 2 wild pig • 3 expensive • 4 arrived

c) Match the advice (1–4) to each person from a). Is it good or bad advice? Give reasons.

1 Don't date online – it usually ends badly.
2 Don't believe °reviews – they're all fake.
3 Never buy things online!
4 Be careful – some videos can be fake too!

d) SPEAKING Think of a story about truth and lies on social media. Tell a partner.

5 c), d) Lösungsbsp. S. 299

Check

126 one hundred and twenty-six

4

Checkpoint Vorbereitung

Material: alle Aufgaben ▸KV Extra: Bus stop, ▸KV 4.4B: Checkpoint answers, App (Check) • Ex 4 ggf. ▸KV 2.3: Discussion tickets (Klassensatz) • Ex 5 UMA/CD/App • Ex 6 ggf. Bildkarten für die Begriffserklärungen • Ex 7 UMA/CD/App
Zeitbedarf: ca. 1–2 Std.
Minimalversion: Auswahl der Aufgaben erfolgt aufgrund der zu überprüfenden Lernziele
Begleitmedien: App (Digital checkpoint), INKL (S. 121)

Die Übungen kannst du auch digital machen. **4**

> **6 a)** 1 C • 2 B • 3 E • 4 F • 5 A • 6 D

6 STUDY SKILLS **Describing a word that you forgot**   I can make a talk flow. ✓

a) If you forget a word in your talk, you can explain it to make your talk flow.
Match the explanations (1–6) to the words (A–F).

1 It's the opposite of 'follow'.
2 It's the short form of a word or phrase.
3 It's something that you do regularly.
4 It's somebody who gets bullied or hurt.
5 It's what happens when you don't contact somebody any more.
6 It's when you feel unhappy because somebody gets more than you.

A (to) lose touch
B an abbreviation
C (to) unfollow
D jealous
E a habit
F a victim

b) SPEAKING Now choose three words from the Dictionary (pages 254–271).
Explain the words to your partner. Can your partner guess the words?

> **6 b)** (*Bsp.*) It's a place where you can live and it's part of a bigger house. (flat)

7 STUDY SKILLS **Learning Welsh online**

a) Cody wants to give a short talk about learning Welsh.
Where in the talk (1–5) should he put the phrases A–E?

I'm going to talk to you this morning about learning Welsh online. I'm going to tell you about the course I did and then I'll tell you about some things I learned and what I thought about the course.

First, about the course: It's an online course. It's not very expensive. … (1). It's ten weeks long and it's great if you want to visit Wales and understand a little bit of the language. … (2). You get some exercises by email and there's an app you can use to practise speaking and listening. … (3)

Now, I'm going to tell you some things that I learned. … (4). 'Good morning' is 'bore da' and 'thank you very much' is 'diolch yn fawr iawn'. And in Welsh there's no word for 'no'. I think the course was good – it wasn't too easy and it wasn't too difficult. … (5).

To sum up, I think learning some Welsh before you travel to Wales is a good thing. It's quite a difficult language, but in ten weeks you can learn quite a lot.

A You know, it's amazing what you can do with a smartphone!

B Just a minute, I need to find my vocabulary list.

C I mean, it's polite to learn some words before you travel.

D Well, I didn't have any problems, but I'm quite good at languages.

E Let me see …, it costs 26 pounds.

3.12 b) Listen to Cody's talk and check your answers.

> **7 a), b)** 1 E • 2 C • 3 A • 4 B • 5 D

3.13 c) Listen carefully to sentences A–E and repeat them. Pay attention to the °intonation!

> **7 c)** individuelle Lösungen

Check

one hundred and twenty-seven **127**

Ex 6 Einstieg:
- (SB auf) Selbsteinschätzung s. Ex 4

Erarbeitung:
a) S ordnen die Erklärungen und Begriffe gemäß AA zu.

b) S schreiben Erklärungen gemäß AA.
- In schwächeren Gruppen kann L auch Begriffe über Bildkarten (z. B. aus einem Memo-Spiel) vorgeben.
- **Ausw.:** S suchen Partner/-in am ▸Bus stop (▸KV Extra): ▸Partner check mit ▸KV 4.4B für a), anschließend Austausch der Erklärungen.

Ex 7 Erarbeitung:
a) (SB auf) S lesen den Text in EA.
- S notieren im Heft, welche Phrase sie wo einsetzen würden.

b) 1. Hören: S prüfen ihre Antworten aus a).
- **Ausw.:** Vergleich im Plenum
- **Alternative:** ▸Bus stop (▸KV Extra): S vergleichen ihre Lösung mithilfe von ▸KV 4.4B.

c) 2. Hören: S üben die Aussprache gemäß AA, z. B. in PA mithilfe der App.
- **Ausw.:** Vortrag im Plenum
- erneute Selbsteinschätzung

127

4
OPTIONAL

Text file Inhalt

Lernschwerpunkt: das erste Kapitel einer Lektüre lesen, die in Wales spielt
Kompetenzen: Reading einen Text über einen Studenten verstehen, der in den Ferien in der walisischen Stadt Tref Môr als freiwilliger Helfer bei der Küstenwache arbeitet
Redemittel: *places in Wales • feelings • holidays • weather • rescue*

Allgemeine Anmerkung:
s. Unit 1, S. 36

My reading tip Einstieg:
- (SB zu) L schreibt Fragen an die Tafel: *What do you think about a day at the beach? Do you like swimming in the sea? Why (not)? Are there any dangers at the beach?*
- S diskutieren in Kleingruppen.

Erarbeitung:
- (SB auf) S lesen Owens *reading tip* sowie die Überschrift der Geschichte und betrachten das Bild auf S. 129.
- PA: S notieren drei Vermutungen, was in der Geschichte passieren könnte.
- 🔽 in schwächeren Klassen: kurze Wiederholung der Lesetechnik *Skimming* (s. ▶Tippbox, S. 118 oder ▶SF 9, S. 164)
- **1. Lesen:** S überfliegen die erste Seite der Geschichte (S. 128) und diskutieren anschließend, ob ihre Vermutungen korrekt waren.
- **2. Lesen:** S lesen erneut und notieren unbekannte Vokabeln.
- S erfragen die unbekannten Begriffe bei Partner/-in, diese/-r erklärt Begriffe, die ihm/ihr bekannt sind (wie in *Study skills*, Ex 2, S. 122).
- S teilen sich die unbekannten Begriffe auf und schlagen sie nach. Anschließend erklären sie sich gegenseitig die nachgeschlagenen Begriffe.
- S tragen die neuen Wörter in ihr *Vocab file* ein.
- Forts. s. S. 129

128

4
OPTIONAL

Text file

A magazine for young people across the UK

> I read an exciting story that takes place in Wales. This is the first chapter.

My reading tip *by Owen Thomas*

It's the summer holidays and Joe, a university student, has just started helping as a lifeboat volunteer. He's working with Ben and Jessie, who are both experienced volunteers, in the seaside town of Tref Môr in Wales. Today the team has to make one of the scariest rescues yet!

A scary rescue
(First chapter from the book *Rescued* by Christina de la Mare)

Joe was scared. The sky was a deep grey, the clouds looked full of rain, and the waves seemed too big and powerful for the small rescue boat. Every few seconds
5 a wave crashed into it, and covered the crew in cold sea water. But still the boat continued to move quickly across the surface[1], and flew over the water towards the two teenage boys.

10 It was Joe's second rescue, and although[2] he was with Ben and Jessie, two experienced lifeboat[3] volunteers, he was full of fear[4]. What had started out as a calm cloudy afternoon was now a storm.
15 And it was moving closer to the boat. Every twenty seconds or so there was a blinding[5] stroke of lightning[6] followed by loud thunder[7], and the crew had only minutes to save the boys. He could see
20 them now, their heads above the water, an arm waving. That was a good sign – a sign of life. But they had been alone in the water a long, long time.

Eventually the boat was close enough
25 to reach them. Jessie leaned over[8] and grabbed[9] the hand of the bigger boy. With Ben's help, she pulled him onto the boat. She quickly covered him in a blanket. But the other boy didn't look
30 good. His face was white, and it was taking all his energy not to sink below the surface of the water. Joe and Ben grabbed the boy under the arms and pulled. He slid on to the boat and lay on
35 its floor. Within seconds his eyes closed.

Joe looked at the boy. He didn't know what to do – all his training was just theory – this was *real*.

'Joe!' shouted Ben. 'Help me.' Quickly,
40 Joe came to his senses[10] and helped Ben cover the boy with a blanket. It was important to keep him awake. He might be in the boat, but he wasn't out of danger. Joe knew that the risks of
45 secondary drowning[11] were still there.

---

[1] **surface** *die Oberfläche* [2] **although** *obwohl* [3] **lifeboat** *das Rettungsboot* [4] **fear** *die Angst* [5] **blinding** *blendend*
[6] **stroke of lightning** *der Blitz* [7] **thunder** *der Donner* [8] **(to) lean over** *sich hinüberlehnen* [9] **(to) grab** *greifen*
[10] **(to) come to one's senses** *zur Besinnung kommen* [11] **secondary drowning** *das verzögerte Ertrinken*

128 one hundred and twenty-eight

Text file Vorbereitung

Material: My reading tip ggf. zwei bis drei Exemplare der Lektüre *Rescued* bereitstellen, digitale Endgeräte, ggf. digitale Pinnwand
Zeitbedarf: abhängig davon, in welcher Tiefe der Text bearbeitet wird
Minimalversion: Der Text ist ein optionaler Zusatzbeitrag.

Forts. von S. 128:
- S stellen Vermutungen an, wie es weitergehen könnte.
- **1. Lesen:** S überfliegen nun den zweiten Teil des Textes (S. 130) und prüfen ihre Vermutungen.
- **2. Lesen:** S lesen diesen Teil erneut und gehen bei unbekannten Begriffen analog zum Vorschlag auf S. 128 vor.
- analoges Verfahren für den letzten Teil der Geschichte
- ▶ Meinungsbarometer: L stellt Fragen, S positionieren sich dazu auf einer Linie und geben kurze Auskunft über den Grund für ihre Entscheidung.
  – *Did you like the story?*
  – *Would you like to be a volunteer on a life boat?*
  – *What Joe and his friends did was dangerous. Would you go out in a storm to save someone else's life?*
  – *Do you think Ben is angry at Joe? Why (not)?*
  – *Would you like to read the rest of the book?*

Ideen zur Weiterarbeit mit dem Text:
- Der Text ist ein Auszug aus einer Lektüre. Sollte diese nicht im Klassenverband gelesen werden, könnte L zwei bis drei Exemplare in der Klassenbücherei bereitstellen. Lernstärkere S könnten dann nach Belieben zu Hause oder nach Fertigstellung der Aufgaben in der Schule weiterlesen. Sie könnten ggf. einen kurzen Vortrag zum Buch vorbereiten oder ein *review* schreiben.
- Forts. s. S. 130

4 OPTIONAL

Text file Inhalt

Forts. von S. 128–129

Forts. von S. 129:

- S könnten den Text in Emojis darstellen. Hierzu überlegen sie sich die Gefühle von Joe im jeweiligen Absatz und suchen einen oder mehrere passende Emojis. Anschließend werden die Ergebnisse vorgestellt und S raten, auf welchen Teil des Textes sich die gewählten Emojis beziehen.
- ☒ Lernstärkere S überlegen sich auch die Gefühle der anderen Charaktere und stellen diese mit Emojis dar.

- S erstellen *Joe's social media post* über seine Aktion. Hierzu sollten sie auch ein passendes Bild heraussuchen. Fertige Ergebnisse werden ausgedruckt und aufgehängt oder auf einer digitalen Pinnwand hochgeladen (s. Kommentar auf S. 119). Anschließend können S die Beiträge gegenseitig kommentieren.

- S überlegen sich, was Joe mit seiner Familie im Sommerurlaub erlebt. Sie entwerfen ein kleines Rollenspiel zu einem weiteren Abenteuer von Joe.

- S schreiben einen Dialog zwischen Ben und Jessie, die sich am nächsten Tag ohne Joe treffen und über den Vorfall sprechen. S überlegen, wie die beiden sich fühlen und was Ben über Joe denkt.

- S erstellen in einer Kleingruppe ein Quiz zum Text, welches anschließend gemeinsam von der Klasse gespielt wird.

4 OPTIONAL — Text file

Even hours later it could happen to people who breathed in water. Together with Ben, he helped to hold[1] the boy between them. He rubbed[2] his shoulders
50 and talked to him until he opened his eyes again.

The other boy was speaking. His name was Harry, his friend was called Luke, and they were both 15. They had been at
55 the beach with their parents and gone swimming. 'Everything was fine at first,' he told them. 'But we swam too far out, and then we realized[3] that we couldn't get back to shore[4].' He was talking quickly
60 and his eyes were moving constantly, from Ben, to Joe, to the water and then to his friend Luke. 'But the weather changed so fast, and we got really scared!' Harry's eyes filled with tears[5]. 'Thanks
65 for saving us,' he said.

Joe smiled, but didn't know what to say. Jessie put an arm around the boy's shoulder. Joe looked down at Luke. Luke remained silent, and stared around him,
70 as if he couldn't understand where he was or how he had got there. By now, Joe was feeling better. But Luke's condition was worrying him. He could feel the boy shivering[6] underneath his blankets.
75 Joe looked for some colour in the boy's cheeks[7], but he remained as white as a sheet[8].

By the time the boat returned to shore, the storm was over. The boys' parents
80 were there, and their faces were full of worry. Behind them, Joe could see an ambulance was waiting, ready to take the boys to hospital.

The ambulance crew took over and
85 carried the boys into the ambulance. Joe, Jessie and Ben returned the boat to the lifeboat station and changed back into dry[9] clothes. Ben sat down to write a record of the rescue in the logbook[10].

90 'Do you need me to do anything?' Joe asked Ben.
'No thanks,' said Ben, without looking up.
'Umm, 'bye then,' said Joe. Ben said
95 nothing.
Joe's heart sank[11]. Maybe he had done really badly. He walked together with Jessie up the path towards the town. 'Don't look so worried, Joe,' said Jessie.
100 'You did really well.'

Tref Môr was a little seaside town[12] in south Wales, and it was Jessie's home, the place where she had lived all her life. Jessie was Joe's friend from university
105 and had a year of experience as a lifeboat volunteer. Thanks to Jessie, Joe was now volunteering at the Tref Môr lifeboat station too, and staying in a cottage[13] for the summer.

110 In Tref Môr, it was as if everything was normal. It was early afternoon, and people were shopping, drinking coffee, and chatting to friends, completely unaware of[14] the dramatic sea rescue.
115 Looking around him, Joe's feelings were mixed up: excitement, worry – even happiness. But he felt scared too.

---

[1] (to) **hold** *halten*   [2] (to) **rub** *reiben*   [3] (to) **realize** *sich klar werden*   [4] **shore** *die Küste*   [5] (to) **fill with tears** *sich mit Tränen füllen*   [6] (to) **shiver** *frösteln, schlottern*   [7] **cheek** *die Wange*   [8] **sheet** *das Laken*   [9] **dry** *trocken*   [10] **logbook** *das Logbuch*   [11] (to) **sink, sank, sunk** *sinken*   [12] **seaside town** *der Küstenort, der Badeort*   [13] **cottage** *das Häuschen*   [14] (to) **be unaware of sth.** *sich einer Sache nicht bewusst sein*

Text file Vorbereitung

Forts. von S. 128–129

Saving the two boys was maybe the best moment of his life! But at the same
120 time, it seemed as if he was still in the boat in the middle of the storm, and the boys were still in the water. And why could nobody see how he was feeling? He wondered if[1] he would feel like this
125 every time he did a rescue. He really hoped not. Jessie looked at him. 'I know what you're thinking,' she said, smiling. 'I promise you it gets easier.'

Together they continued through the
130 busy town. It was full of families and older couples[2] visiting for summer holidays, and teens enjoying the sea and sunshine. A long row[3] of hotels, cafes and restaurants lined[4] the beach, and
135 behind was a network of narrow streets. These were filled[5] with shops selling anything and everything from fishing equipment to jewellery[6]. At the centre was Tref Môr castle, built
140 hundreds of years before to protect Welsh shores from the enemy. And on the town's outskirts[7] stood rows of brightly coloured[8] cottages. Their windows were decorated with flowers
145 and their front doors opened directly onto the streets.

As Joe and Jessie turned into the road where he was staying, he saw a commotion[9]. His father's car was
150 there, and he suddenly remembered that his father and sister were arriving that day to spend the summer with him. One of the car doors was open, and he could see his sister Olive. She
155 was leaning out of it and vomiting[10] into the street. Car sick again, he thought, but his dad was doing nothing to help her. Instead, he was taking bags and cases out of the car. Joe sighed.
160 His father and sister had arrived, with their usual[11] drama and weird behaviour. The family summer had begun.

If you like the first chapter, read the rest of the story!

---

[1] (to) **wonder if** *sich fragen, ob* [2] **couple** *das Paar* [3] **row** *die Reihe* [4] (to) **line** *säumen, sich entlangziehen*
[5] (to) **be filled** *angefüllt sein* [6] **jewellery** *der Schmuck* [7] **outskirts** *die Außenbezirke* [8] **brightly coloured**
leuchtend bunt [9] **commotion** *die Unruhe, der Tumult* [10] (to) **vomit** *erbrechen, sich übergeben* [11] **usual** *üblich*

4

Partner page / Diff bank — Inhalt

Lernschwerpunkt: zusätzliche Übungen, Differenzierungs- und Hilfsangebote
Kompetenzen: Mediation eine Gebrauchsanweisung ins Deutsche sprachmitteln • Reading Texten über drei walisische Städte Informationen entnehmen • Listening einen Song verstehen • Speaking eine Sprachnachricht über Wales aufnehmen
Strukturen: possessive pronouns
Redemittel: understanding and giving tech instructions • places in Wales • songs and music

---

Allgemeine Anmerkung:
s. Unit 1, S. 38

Ex 6 Erarbeitung: s. S. 113
a) + b) Partner B gemäß AA

MP 1 Einstieg:
- (SB zu) L zeigt die drei Bilder aus MP 1 (UMA): *Which place do you like best and why?*
  S: *I like … because …*
  L: *Let's find out some more information about these places in Wales.*

Erarbeitung:
a) (SB auf) S übertragen die Tabelle in ihr Heft oder nutzen ►KV 4.2.
- Gemäß AA: S suchen in EA die drei Städte auf der Karte hinten im SB.
- **Alternative:** Karte präsentieren (UMA), S kommt nach vorn und zeigt den jeweiligen Ort.

b) S ergänzen die Tabelle in ihrem Heft oder auf ►KV 4.2 gemäß AA in EA.
- S können ►KV 4.2 nutzen, um in den Texten die wichtigen Informationen zu unterstreichen (evtl. in verschiedenen Farben).
- **Ausw.:** ►Partner check am ►Bus stop (►KV Extra)
- **Alternative:** ►Meldekette

---

4 Partner page / Diff bank

Partner page
▶ Page 113

6 MEDIATION Instructions 6 a) Lösungsbsp. S. 297

a) **Partner B:** You need help with a new smartwatch. Listen to partner A's instructions. Ask what you do next and ask questions if you don't understand.

b) **Partner B:** Now partner A needs help. Explain instructions 6–10 in German.

6 Set up the watch.   Als Nächstes musst du …
7 Read and agree to the terms. ▶ Box: Voc., p. 237
8 Tap the name of the watch on your phone.
9 Pair the phone with your watch. (Tap 'pair' on the phone.)
10 Connect your watch to Wi-Fi.

> Normally when you mediate, you explain the main ideas. But when you give instructions, it's important to be exact.

6 b) Lösungsbsp. S. 298

Diff bank
▶ Page 107

More practice 1 READING Three Welsh cities 1 Lösung S. 299

a) **BEFORE YOU READ** Copy the table. Find the three cities on the map on the last page of your book.

City	Where	About the city	Sights	Other information
Cardiff	south Wales	…	…	…
Swansea	…	…	…	…
Wrexham	…	…	…	…

b) Read about the three cities and complete the table.

Cardiff is the biggest city in Wales and its capital. In the city centre Cardiff Castle is popular. Watch rugby matches in the Principality Stadium and go to concerts in the amazing modern °Millennium Centre by the water.

Swansea is the second biggest Welsh city. It's a modern city with many parks. You can also have a picnic on one of the beautiful beaches just outside the city or visit the romantic Carreg Cennen[1] Castle.

Wrexham is a very old city. Its most famous sight is the Pontcysyllte[2] °Aqueduct. You can go across it in a boat. Wrexham's football club became famous when two Hollywood actors bought it.

1 [ˌkærəɡ ˈkænən]   2 [ˌpɒntkəˈsʌɬtə]

4

Diff bank Vorbereitung

Material: MP 1 UMA, ▶ KV 4.2: Three Welsh cities (nach Bedarf), ▶ KV Extra: Bus stop • MP 2 Gegenstand, z. B. Bleistift
Zeitbedarf: abhängig davon, welche Aufgaben bearbeitet werden
Minimalversion: *More practice*-Aufgaben sind stets Zusatzaufgaben.

Diff bank 4

▶ Page 108

More practice 2 Is this phone yours?

2 1 yours • 2 mine • 3 hers • 4 his • 5 ours • 6 mine

Complete the conversation with the possessive pronouns from p. 108.

Mr Price Somebody has forgotten their phone. It's on the desk over there. Owen, is it … (1)?
Owen No, I've got … (2) here. I'll ask Samara if it's … (3).
Dylan I think Samara has a white phone and this one is black. But Promit has a black phone, I think. Maybe it's … (4).
Louise No, Promit and I have the same kind of phone – … (5) are smaller than that one.
Mr Price Well, somebody must have forgotten it. I'll look at the screen photo to see if that helps. Oh, that's a picture of my family. Oops! It's actually … (6)!

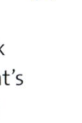

▶ Page 109

Parallel exercise 3 SONG Dylan's song

3 1 B • 2 A • 3 C • 4 A • 5 B • 6 C • 7 A

3.3 c) Listen to the song again and choose the correct words.

1 Let me tell you about a special A town B place C country.
2 My Cymru where the fields are A green B big C everywhere.
3 I A like B hate C love it and I never °mean to leave.
4 Come see where the old meets A new B modern C young …
5 … and the valleys meet the A beach B sea C °sky.
6 We've got tech and the Brecon Beacons, A wonderful B rainy C beautiful in every season.
7 From the music clubs of A Cardiff B Llandudno C Swansea to the hills of Aberystwyth – everybody sing: Cymru am byth!

More help 4 MY TASK A voice message about Wales

4 b) Lösungsbsp. S. 297

b) Imagine you're in the exchange class. Make notes and then record a voice message for Dylan. Give reasons for your choices. You should include:

• what you think about his song: *Hi, Dylan, thank you for the song! I think …*
• three things that you want to do when you visit Wales: *I'm looking forward to the visit …*

I'd like to	go to / see / visit	Cardiff / museums / the Batcave / the beach / the mountains / …
I really want to	go	hiking / shopping / swimming / …
Please can we	do	a town tour / lots of fun things / …
I hope we can	buy	clothes / souvenirs / …

MP 2

• Diese Aufgabe bietet eine Möglichkeit zum Üben der Possessivpronomen.

Einstieg:

• (SB zu) L zeigt einen Gegenstand, z. B. Bleistift: *Look, I've found a pencil.*
• L fragt eine/-n S: *Is it yours?* S: *No, it's not mine.*

Erarbeitung:

• (SB auf) gemäß AA schriftlich in EA
• S nummerieren ihre Lösungen im Heft.
• **Ausw.:** S lesen den Dialog in verteilten Rollen mit den Lösungen.

Parallel ex 3 s. S. 109

• Diese Aufgabe ist die einfachere Variante zu Ex 3c), S. 109 mit demselben Ergebnis.

Erarbeitung:

c) (SB auf) S nummerieren in ihr Heft und notieren die Lösungen beim **2. Hören**.
• **Ausw.:** ▶ Partner check, dann Plenum

MH 4 s. S. 109

• Diese Aufgabe bietet Ideen und sprachliche Mittel für lernschwächere S, die Unterstützung bei der Gestaltung der Nachricht benötigen.

Erarbeitung:

b) (SB auf) S nutzen die sprachlichen Mittel, um ihre Sprachnachricht vorzubereiten.

4

Diff bank Inhalt

Lernschwerpunkt: zusätzliche Übungen, Differenzierungs- und Hilfsangebote
Kompetenzen: *Speaking* sich über Technologie im Alltag austauschen • sich über Aktivitäten am Abend austauschen • über Pläne im Sommer sprechen • ein Telefonat zu Plänen am Wochenende führen • *Writing* Befehle für einen *digital assistant* formulieren
Strukturen: *(revision)* going to-future
Redemittel: *life in the past and today* • *telephone phrases* • *instructions*

MH 1 s. S. 110
- Diese Aufgabe bietet Ideen und sprachliche Mittel zur Bearbeitung von Ex 1e), S. 110.

Erarbeitung:
e) (SB auf) S nutzen die Redemittel zum Erstellen ihrer Moderationskarten.

MH 2 s. S. 111
- Diese Aufgabe bietet Ideen und sprachliche Mittel zur Bearbeitung von Ex 2b).

Erarbeitung:
b) (SB auf) S nutzen die Redemittel beim ▶ Milling around oder um sich vorab Notizen zu machen.

MP 3
- Diese Aufgabe bietet eine weitere Möglichkeit, das *going to-future* zu wiederholen.
- Die Aufgabe kann von lernschwächeren S bearbeitet werden, während lernstärkere S zur Vertiefung des *going to-future* **Challenge 1**, S. 135 bearbeiten.

Erarbeitung:
- (SB auf) gemeinsames Lesen der Regelerklärung in der ▶ Grammatik-Box, S. 134
- s. a. ▶ LF 13a + b, S. 182 und Erklärfilm (UMA/App)
- S-Paare arbeiten gemäß AA.
- **Ausw.:** Präsentation einzelner Beispiele im Plenum

---

4 Diff bank

▶ Page 110

More help 1 VIEWING Life in a Welsh village in 1927

1 e) individuelle Lösungen

e) What do you think: Does technology bring people closer together? Why (not)?

Yes, it does because … *Yes*
- you can talk to friends online.
- it's easy to meet new people with the same hobbies on social media.
- you can talk to people in different countries online.
- you can play online games together.
- you can share photos and videos.
- machines and cars can save us time.

No, it doesn't because … *No*
- often you spend more time with your phone than with your friends.
- people can be mean on social media.
- people °compare their lives on social media and get unhappy.
- it's more fun to walk to school with your friends than to go by car.
- candles are more romantic.

▶ Page 111

More help 2 SPEAKING An evening with or without technology?

2 b) individuelle Lösungen

b) WALK AROUND Tell different partners what you're going to do this evening.

I'm My family is My friends and I are	going to	do	gymnastics / homework / …
		go	shopping / to a club / to a friend's house / …
		listen to	a playlist / a podcast / music / …
		make	a cake / a video / pizza / …
		play	basketball / online games / video games / …
		watch	a video / TV / …

More practice 3 Summer plans

Erklärfilm

REVISION The going to-future
We use the *going to-future* to talk about plans in the future.
We often use time words like *soon, tomorrow, in the summer holidays, next year*.
We make the going to-future with *am / is / are + (not) going to + infinitive*.

My mum *is going to start* a new job tomorrow.
We're *going to have* an English test next week.
I'm *not going to do* anything special at the weekend.

▶ Language file 13a + b, p. 182

Tell a partner what you or your family are going to do in the summer.

We're going to stay in …   We aren't going to travel.
I'm going to do / go / have / make / play / visit / …

3 individuelle Lösungen

134 one hundred and thirty-four

Diff bank Vorbereitung

Material: MP 3 UMA/App (Erklärfilm) • MP 4 von L vorbereitete *telephone phrases* für Menschen-Memo (s. Kasten auf S. 111 u. S. 135), ggf. Trennwände für die Dialoge • MP 5 A4-Papier für die Poster (nach Bedarf)
Zeitbedarf: abhängig davon, welche Aufgaben bearbeitet werden
Minimalversion: *More practice-* und *Challenge-*Aufgaben sind stets Zusatzaufgaben.

Challenge 1 It's going to be fun! Ch 1 A • Lösung S. 300

The going to-future for predictions
Look at the examples and choose the correct explanation (**A** or **B**).

Dylan is excited about the exchange visit. It's going to be fun!
He's just looked at the weather app on his phone: It isn't going to rain today.
Look! They're going to have an accident!

We can use the going to-future when …
A we can see or are sure that something will happen soon.
B we don't know if something will happen later in the future.

▶ Language file 13c, p. 182

Look at the pictures. Write what you think is going to happen. Use the verbs in the box.

be late • not be happy • be sick • fall • not rain • not win

1
Dylan and Owen …

2
Oh no! Owen's phone …

3
Owen's parents …

4
Owen …

5
It …

6
Dylan …

More practice 4 Your phone call

a) Write a short phone call about your plans for the weekend. Use the phrases in the box.
b) Practise your phone call. Then read it to another pair.

Phrases
- Hi / Hello … How are things?
- Oh, one more thing: …
- I can't hear you. You're breaking up.
- Can you say that again, please?
- Sorry, I have to go now. Bye!

4 Lösungsbsp. S. 300

▶Page 113

More practice 5 Instructions for a digital assistant   5 Lösungsbsp. S. 300

a) Agree on a list of ten useful instructions for a digital assistant. You can choose your own name.
Hey Cortino, switch on the lights.
b) Try out your instructions with a real digital assistant or make a poster with your list.

Challenge 1 Erarbeitung:
- (SB auf) S lesen die ▶Grammatik-Box, S. 135 und finden den korrekten Merksatz.
- S schreiben die Sätze 1–6 gemäß AA in ihr Heft.
- **Ausw.:** ▶Partner check, dann ggf. Plenum

MP 4 Einstieg:
- (SB zu) L: *Can you remember any phrases for a phone call?*
- S nennen Beispiele und L erstellt Liste als TA.
- **Alternative:** ▶Menschen-Memo: L gibt Wendungen zum Thema Telefonieren vor.

Erarbeitung:
a) (SB auf) S gestalten einen Dialog gemäß AA in PA.
- L verweist auf Wendungen im Kasten.

b) gemäß AA
- **Ausw.:** im Plenum
- **Hinweis:** Eine Trennwand zwischen den S bietet eine authentische Situation, da die S sich beim Sprechen nicht sehen.

MP 5 Einstieg:
- (SB zu) L notiert These an die Tafel: *Digital assistants – useful or not?*
- S diskutieren in ▶Buzz groups.
- L erfasst Ideen in einer Pro- und Kontra-Tabelle.

Erarbeitung:
a) (SB auf) Klären der AA
- S-Gruppen notieren Ideen.
- **Ausw.:** im Plenum

b) gemäß AA
- **Ausw.:** ▶English corner

4

Diff bank Inhalt

Lernschwerpunkt: zusätzliche Übungen, Differenzierungs- und Hilfsangebote
Kompetenzen: Speaking Hilfe anbieten, erbitten und annehmen • Writing Definitionen schreiben • Vor- und Nachteile von sozialen Medien benennen
Strukturen: *relative clauses • contact clauses*
Redemittel: *online activities • offering, asking for and accepting help • definitions of social media words • use of social media*

MP 6 Einstieg:
- (SB zu) Wendungen von Ex 1c), S. 114 mithilfe von ▶Swap cards aktivieren: S erfragen deutsche Bedeutung (z. B. *What's 'forward a link' in German?*).

Erarbeitung:
- (SB auf) Klären der AA
- S schreiben die vollständigen Sätze in ihr Heft.
- **Ausw.:** ▶Meldekette

MH 3 s. S. 115
- Diese Aufgabe bietet sprachliche Mittel und zusätzliche Ideen für lernschwächere S.

Erarbeitung:
- **d)** (SB auf) S nutzen die Redemittel zum Anfertigen ihrer Notizen.

MP 7 Einstieg:
- (SB zu) L zeigt Bild von MP 7 (UMA): *What can you see in the picture? Can you name any devices?*

Erarbeitung:
- (SB auf) S arbeiten schriftlich gemäß AA.
- **Ausw.:** ▶Partner check, dann Plenum

Challenge 2
- In dieser Aufgabe geht es um Relativsätze. Sie eignet sich für stärkere Klassen/S.

Erarbeitung:
- **a)** (SB auf) Lesen der AA und des Beispiels
- schriftl. gemäß AA in EA
- **b)** Ausw. von a) im ▶Partner talk

---

4 Diff bank

▶Page 114

More practice 6   What do you do on social media?

Dylan is explaining to Owen how he uses social media. Choose the correct words and phrases from the box.

> forward the link • keep in touch • post • send • subscribe • unfollow • upload videos

I use it to ... (1) with my friends and family. My mum's family lives in Kenya, so they ... (2) photos of all my cousins. And I ... (3) to my uncle's video channel – he likes to ... (4) of his life in Nairobi. It's really cool. I'll ... (5) to you of his video about the music festival he played at last year! If you want to ... (6) me direct messages, then we need to follow each other because my account is private. I promise I won't ... (7) you!

> **6** 1 keep in touch • 2 post • 3 subscribe • 4 upload videos • 5 forward the link • 6 send • 7 unfollow

▶Page 115

More help 3   SPEAKING   Could you help me, please?

d) Make notes about things that you need or can help with.

> **3 d)** individuelle Lösungen

need / can help with	(maths) homework / spelling / a tech problem / an app / a problem / ...
show / teach	you / me how to dance / do tricks / draw / edit a video / make something / ...

▶Page 117

More practice 7   Tech °definitions

Complete the definitions. Use *who*, *which* or *that*.

1. smartphone (device): *A smartphone is a device that / which you can use to ...*
2. YouTuber (person): *A YouTuber is a ...*
3. smartwatch (device): *A smartwatch is a ...*
4. video channel (page): ...
5. developer (person): ...

> **7** Lösungsbsp. S. 300

Challenge 2   More definitions

a) Write definitions using relative clauses with *who*, *which* or *that*. Use the ideas in the box or your own ideas, but don't write the word.

> a keyboard • a mouse • a screenshot • your favourite app/site • your favourite influencer • ...

This is something that you can use to play music, so only you can hear it.

b) Look at your partner's definitions and guess what they're describing.

I think you're describing headphones. – That's right!

> **Ch 2** Lösungsbsp. S. 300

Diff bank Vorbereitung

Material: MP 6 von L vorbereitete *swap cards* mit den Wendungen von Ex 1c), S. 114 • MP 7 UMA
Zeitbedarf: abhängig davon, welche Aufgaben bearbeitet werden
Minimalversion: *More practice*-Aufgaben und *Challenge*-Aufgaben sind stets Zusatzaufgaben.

4

Challenge 3 The app I use the most

Contact clauses
In a relative clause, the relative pronouns *who*, *which* or *that* can be the subject or the object.

The student who/that won the debate is very clever. (who/that = subject)
The student (who/that) I met yesterday is new to the school. (who/that = object)

Look at these sentences and the ones above and complete the rule below.
The app which/that is best is also quite expensive.
The app (which/that) I use the most is a screen time app.

We can leave out *who*, *which* or *that* when it is …
A the subject.   **B** the object.

Ch 3 B

▶ Language file 14b, p. 183

a) Complete the sentences with *who*, *which* or *that*.

1 It's something … is a symbol of a country.
2 It's an animal … you often see in Wales.
3 It's the language … a lot of people speak in Wales.
4 It's a person … visits you from a school in a different country.
5 It's something … you use to write on a computer.
6 It's a short text … tells people about you on social media.
7 It's the name of the person … is the Prince of Wales.

Ch 3 a), b) 1 which/that • 2 (which/that) • 3 (which/that) • 4 who/that • 5 (which/that) • 6 which/that • 7 who/that

b) Look at the sentences in a). If the relative pronoun is the object, put it in (brackets).

c) What are the words for the definitions in a)?

Ch 3 c) 1 flag • 2 sheep • 3 Welsh • 4 exchange student • 5 keyboard • 6 bio • 7 William

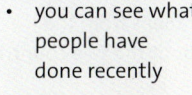 **8** MY TASK Preparing for the debate

a) Write at least three good or bad things about social media. Give reasons.
You can use these ideas.

8 a) Lösungsbsp. S. 298

- you can talk to your friends
- you can watch funny videos
- it feels good when people like your photos
- you can see what people have done recently

- sometimes people are mean online
- strangers can send you direct messages
- it can be dangerous
- people can unfollow you

one hundred and thirty-seven **137**

Challenge 3

- In dieser Aufgabe geht es um *contact clauses*. Die Aufgabe eignet sich für stärkere Klassen/S.

Erarbeitung:

a) (SB auf) S lesen die Sätze in der ▶ Grammatik-Box, S. 137 und erfassen die Regel.
- s. a. ▶ LF 14b, S. 183
- S notieren die vollständigen Sätze 1–7 mit den Relativpronomen.
- **Ausw.:** im Plenum

b) S markieren Relativpronomen als Subjekt oder Objekt farbig (Farben analog zur ▶ Grammatik-Box, S. 13).
- gemäß AA in EA
- **Ausw.:** im Plenum

c) gemäß AA
- **Ausw.:** ▶ Meldekette

MH 8 s. S. 117

- Diese Aufgabe bietet sprachliche Mittel und zusätzliche Ideen für lernschwächere S.

Erarbeitung:

a) (SB auf) S nutzen die Ideen, um ihre Argumente zu formulieren.

5

OPTIONAL

Unit-Übersicht

Storyline: Orla reist aus der Republik Irland nach Belfast (UK), um dort an einem Tanzwettbewerb teilzunehmen. In Belfast lernt sie Jack kennen, mit dem sie einen Nachmittag verbringt, bevor sie herausfindet, dass sie beim Tanzwettbewerb gegen ihn antreten muss.
Viewing: Ein Geburtstagswunsch geht unerwartet in Erfüllung. (S. 147)

Allgemeine Anmerkung:
Diese verkürzte Unit ist optional. Der neue Wortschatz ist fakultativ und wird in Band 4 nicht vorausgesetzt.

Unit 5 Einstieg:
- (SB auf) L: *Please describe the pictures to your partner. Make statements that are true and some that are false.*
- ▶ Three truths, two lies: S1 beschreibt Bilder, S2 rät u. berichtigt ggf.
  L: *Which of these places would you like to see?* (S antworten u. begründen ihre Aussage.)

Ex 1 Einstieg:
- (SB auf) L: *Our next unit will take us to Ireland. Where is Ireland on the map? What's special about Ireland?*
  (S nutzen UK-Karte im SB.)

Erarbeitung:
a) S sammeln ihr Vorwissen zu Irland gemäß AA (z. B. als TA).
- L od. freiwillige/-r S moderiert.
- S lesen ▶ Good to know, S. 138.
- S beschreiben, warum das Projekt durchgeführt wird und was das Ziel des Projekts ist.
- **Ausw.:** L sichert Infos im TA.

b) S lesen AA und notieren die Kategorien als Tabelle im Heft:

	Jack	Orla
city: …		
problems: …		
favourite: …		

1. Hören: S machen sich beim Hören Notizen (▶ Note-taking).
- **Ausw.:** Vergleich im Plenum
- **Sich.:** als TA

OPTIONAL

Unit 5
Two Irelands: Together

Jack

A
Belfast

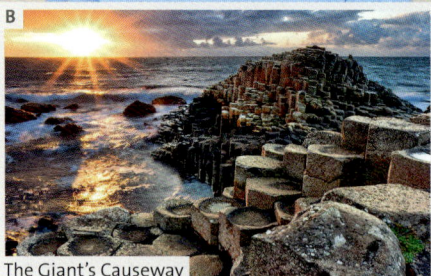

B
The Giant's Causeway

C
Belfast

1 LISTENING North & South Voices   **1 a) Lösungsbsp. S. 301**

a) BEFORE YOU LISTEN *North & South Voices* is a project to bring together teens from the Republic of Ireland and Northern Ireland. What can you remember about the two countries? Which one is part of the UK? Look back at pages 10–13 to help you.

3.14
3.15 b) Like lots of other teens in the project, Jack Wilson and Orla O'Brian recorded voice messages for the project. Listen and take notes for each person.   **1 b) Lösungsbsp. S. 301**

- city: …
- problems from the past: …
- favourite places: …

Good to know
The conflicts between °Catholics and °Protestants over British rule, called the °Troubles, led to years of fighting.

5

OPTIONAL

Lead-in Inhalt

Lernschwerpunkt: den historischen Konflikt zwischen Nordirland und der Republik Irland verstehen
Kompetenzen: Listening einem Hörtext Informationen über die zwei Charaktere, Nordirland sowie die Republik Irland entnehmen • Speaking Fotos beschreiben
Redemittel: *places and people*

Vorbereitung

Material: Ex 1 UMA/CD/App
Zeitbedarf: ca. 1 Std.
Begleitmedien: WB (S. 82), App (Digital quiz), INKL (S. 130–131), DIFF (5.1)

OPTIONAL

Nach dieser Unit kann ich ...

- über Irland und Nordirland sprechen
- eine Reise planen und darüber reden
- über Belfast sprechen und schreiben
- eine Geschichte über einen Wettbewerb zu Ende schreiben

Limerick

Dublin

Orla

Dublin

Nach dieser Unit ...
- L bespricht mit S die Lernziele der Unit (s. links).
- Am Ende der Unit überprüfen die S das Erreichen der Ziele mithilfe des *Checkpoint* (S. 148–149) bzw. gemeinsam im Plenum.

(Forts. von S. 138)

c) S lesen die Sätze 1–6.
- **2. Hören:** S entscheiden gemäß AA, welche Sätze wahr sind.
- **Ausw.:** ▶ Five-minute teacher

d) S schreiben die Bildunterschriften gemäß AA ins Heft.
- **Ausw.:** Vergleich in Gruppen (▶ Gruppenbildung), ggf. Wahl der besten Bildunterschrift
- **Zusatz:** In interessierten Gruppen recherchieren S in Kleingruppen od. PA weitere Informationen zu den Fotos. Die Gruppen/S-Paare präsentieren ihre Ergebnisse im Plenum (s. a. ▶ One-minute presentation) bzw. als Poster im ▶ English corner.

3.14
3.15

c) Listen again and find the three correct sentences.

1 Jack has to go through °checkpoints.
2 Jack's family is Protestant.
3 Only Northern Irish people can stay in Jack's family's °bed and breakfast.
4 Orla says she wants the two countries to be one country again.
5 Jack and Orla both live in cities with a river.
6 Orla °recommends a big event.

1 c) 2 · 5 · 6

d) Look at the photos (A–F) and write captions.

A) *Belfast: a sculpture in the city centre*

1 d) Lösungsbsp. S. 301

▶ More practice 1, p. 152
▶ Workbook, p. 82

Digital quiz I can talk about Ireland and Northern Ireland.

one hundred and thirty-nine **139**

139

5

OPTIONAL

Topic 1 Inhalt

Lernschwerpunkt: eine Reise planen und vorbereiten
Kompetenzen: Speaking / Intercultural competence sich über seinen Pass und seine Auslandserfahrungen austauschen • Informationen zu verschiedenen *Bed and Breakfasts* austauschen und die richtige Option für Orla und ihre Mutter finden • einen Dialog an einer Hotelrezeption nachstellen (*role-play*) • Listening einem Dialog zu Reisevorbereitungen Informationen entnehmen
Redemittel: *travel, passports and money* • *at a B&B*

Ex 1 Einstieg:
- (SB zu) ▶ Five-finger brainstorming im ▶ Milling around zu verschiedenen Ländern (ohne Papier, S merken sich ein Land pro Finger): *Which countries do you know?* (TA)
- Sammlung der Länder im TA

Erarbeitung:
- (SB auf) S lesen die Fragen und überlegen sich die Antworten.
- ▣ Schwächere S machen sich Notizen zu ihren Antworten.
- **Ausw.:** Austausch in PA oder im ▶ Milling around

Ex 2 Einstieg:
- (SB zu) L: *Imagine you want to go on holiday to a different country. What do you need to prepare?*
- S tauschen Ideen im ▶ Milling around aus. Anschließend: Sammeln der Ideen im Plenum.

Erarbeitung:
a) (SB auf) S lesen die Website gemäß AA und tauschen sich in PA zu den Fragen aus.
- **Ausw.:** Vergleich im Plenum

b) S lesen die Begriffe im Reservoir. L semantisiert ggf. unbekannte Begriffe.
- **1. Hören:** S wählen die passenden Begriffe aus und notieren sie im Heft.
- **Ausw.:** ▶ Meldekette

c) Lesen der ▶ Good to know Box, S. 140 und der Fragen.
- **2. Hören:** gemäß AA
- **Ausw.:** ▶ Meldekette

d) Stärkere S beantworten die Frage gemäß AA im Plenum.

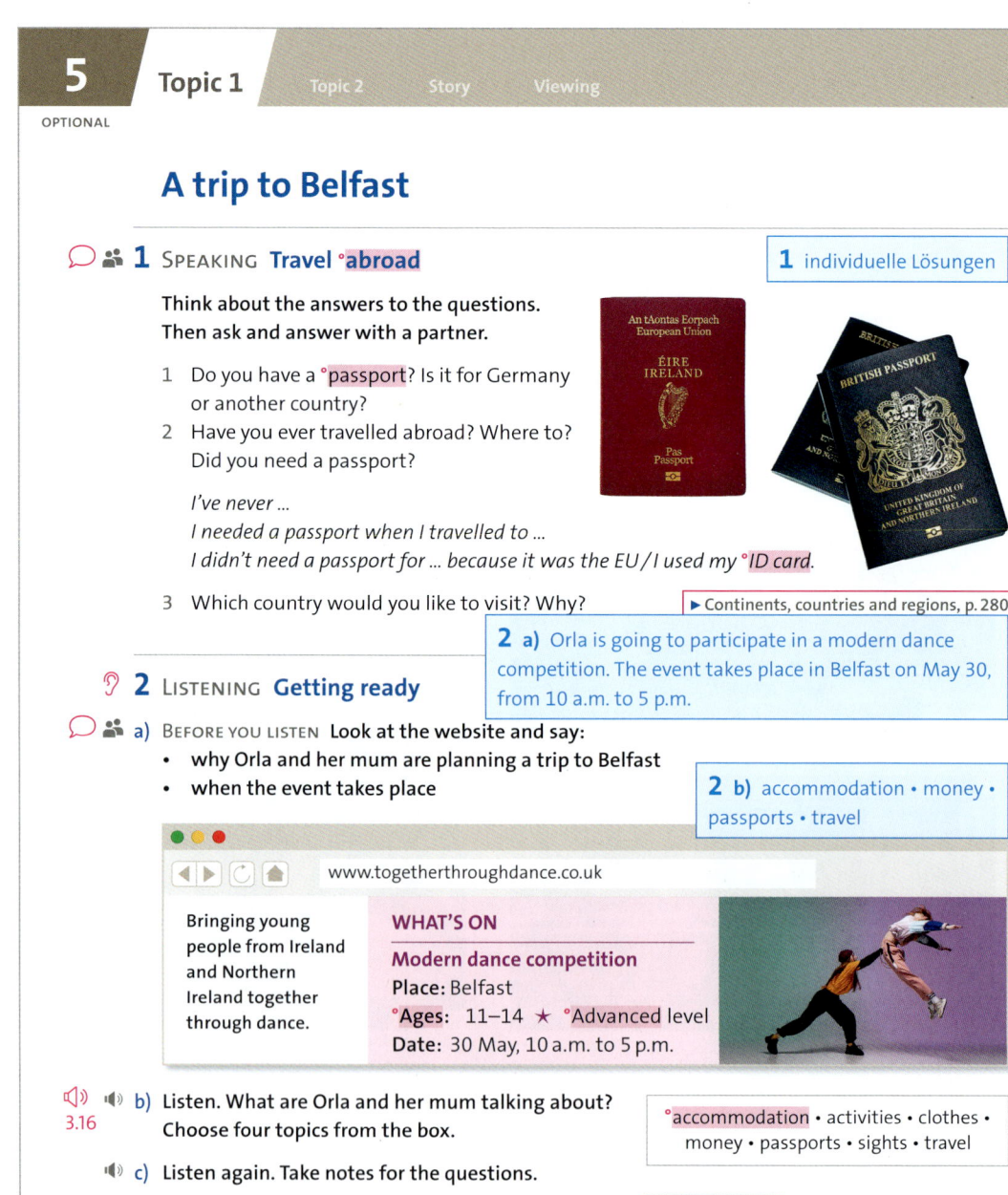

5 OPTIONAL

Topic 1 Vorbereitung

Material: Ex 2 UMA/CD/App • Ex 3 Bilder zur Semantisierung der neuen Begriffe • Ex 4 UMA, UMA/CD/App
Zeitbedarf: ca. 2 Std.
Minimalversion: Ex 1 auslassen
Begleitmedien: WB (S. 83), App (Digital quiz), INKL (S. 133), DIFF (5.2)

---

5 OPTIONAL

3 a), b) Lösung S. 301

3 SPEAKING Staying in Belfast

a) Partner B: Look at p. 152.
Partner A: Read the B&B description here. Then answer partner B's questions about *The Beyond B&B*.

b) Partner A: Ask partner B questions about *Ivy House B&B* and take notes.
1. how much?
2. rooms with °twin beds?
3. own bathroom?
4. Wi-Fi in the room?
5. a kettle in the room?
6. a °cooked breakfast?
7. other information?

c) Say which B&B you think is better for Orla and her mum. Why?

The Beyond B&B

You can find our family B&B in the centre of Belfast. Our comfortable rooms (£85) have double or twin beds, and all rooms have their own bathroom with a shower. Each room also has Wi-Fi, a TV and a kettle.

A full cooked breakfast with tea or coffee is included in the price, and we have vegetarian alternatives for our °guests.

We are here to help! If you have any questions, please send us an email.

3 c) Lösung S. 302

My task

4 At the B&B

4 a) 1 h • 2 d • 3 g • 4 c • 5 e • 6 f • 7 b • 8 a

🔊 3.17 a) Put the conversation in the correct order. Then listen and check. *1h, 2..., ...*

a Mum   Thank you.
b Earl   That's fine. Here's your key. Your room number is number 6, it's on the second floor. We don't have a lift. Oh, breakfast is from 7 to 10 o'clock. I hope you have a good stay!
c Mum   Caitlin and Orla O'Brian.
d Mum   Hello – yes, thanks. We've booked a twin room for three nights.
e Earl   Ah yes, the O'Brians. Could you complete this °form, please? And may I see some ID?
f Mum   Of course. ... Here you are.
g Earl   Right. Can you give me your names, please?
h Earl   Hello, welcome to Belfast! I'm Earl. Have you had a good trip?

b) ROLE-PLAY You're at the B&B. Change the words in blue in a) and do a role-play. You can add other questions and answers (for example, where the dining room is, what time °checkout is, ...).

4 b) individuelle Lösungen

▶ Workbook, p. 83

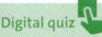 Digital quiz   I can plan and talk about a trip.

one hundred and forty-one **141**

Ex 3 Einstieg:
- (SB zu) ▶ Semantisierung der unbekannten Begriffe mit Bildern (z. B. *bath, twin beds, cooked breakfast*).
L: *When you're on holiday how important is it for you to have your own bathroom / special food?* (▶ Meinungsbarometer)

Erarbeitung:
a) *Partner A* liest den Text auf S. 141. *Partner B* bereitet die Fragen auf S. 152 vor.
- PA gemäß AA

b) PA gemäß AA: *Partner B* liest Text auf S. 152, *Partner A* fragt.
- **Ausw.:** s. c)

c) S entscheiden, welches B&B besser für Orla und ihre Mutter ist u. begründen ihre Wahl.
- **Ausw.:** Vergleich im Plenum.

My task Ex 4 Einstieg:
- (SB zu) L zeigt das Bild (UMA). S beschreiben es u. sagen, wen sie sehen und wo sich die Personen befinden.

Erarbeitung:
a) (SB auf) S lesen den Text u. notieren die Buchstaben in der richtigen Reihenfolge im Heft.
- S überprüfen sich beim **1. Hören** gemäß AA.
- **Ausw.:** ▶ Meldekette

b) Vorbereitung des eigenen ▶ Role-play gemäß AA
- S-Paare üben den Dialog in verteilten Rollen.
- ☒ Stärkere S-Paare fügen weitere Sätze hinzu.
- **Ausw.:** Freiwillige Gruppen führen ihren Dialog in der Klasse vor.

141

5

OPTIONAL

Topic 2 Inhalt

Lernschwerpunkt: Informationen zu Sehenswürdigkeiten und Aktivitäten in Belfast erfassen und eine Nachricht dazu schreiben

Kompetenzen: *Reading / Intercultural competence* einer Broschüre Informationen über Belfast entnehmen • *Listening* ein Gespräch über die Tagesplanung von Orla und ihrer Mutter verstehen • *Mediation* Fragen zu einer Buchung in einem B&B sprachmitteln • *Writing* eine E-Mail mit Informationen über Belfast schreiben

Redemittel: *activities and sights in Belfast • making a reservation*

Ex 1 Einstieg:
- (SB zu) L schreibt Belfast an (TA):
  L: *What do you know about this city?*
  S: *It's the capital of Northern Ireland. It's in the east of Northern Ireland. Orla and her mum are there.*
  L: *Let's have a look at some sights in Belfast.*

Erarbeitung:

a) L zeigt die Bilder 1–5 (UMA).
- L liest AA vor und heftet Wortkarten mit den Namen der Orte/Plätze an die Seitentafel.
- S ordnen gemäß AA in PA zu.
- Ausw.: L zeigt eine Wortkarte und S-Paare zeigen die Nummer des Bildes (Anzahl der Finger oder Zahlkarten). L heftet die Wortkarte zum korrekten Bild.

b) (SB auf) Lautes oder leises Lesen der Texte zu den Bildern
- S notieren die Lösungen gemäß AA in EA.
- Ausw.: ▶ Meldekette

- **Zusatz:** In GA (▶ Gruppenbildung) gestalten S einen ähnlichen Flyer über ihren Heimatort bzw. eine Stadt der Region mit mind. drei Fotos und kurzen Beschreibungen von Sehenswürdigkeiten.
- ☒ Lernstärkere S recherchieren zu mind. fünf Sehenswürdigkeiten.
- Ausw.: S-Gruppen präsentieren ihren Flyer in der Klasse (im ▶ English corner od. per Dokumentenkamera).

---

5   Topic 1   **Topic 2**   Story   Viewing

OPTIONAL

In Belfast

> **1 a)** 1 *the Murals* • 2 the Peace Walls • 3 Belfast Castle • 4 St George's Market • 5 the Titanic Belfast museum

1 READING   Sights in Belfast

a) BEFORE YOU READ   At breakfast, Orla and her mum are looking at a °brochure about Belfast sights. Match the photos to the names in the box.

> Belfast Castle • St George's Market • ~~the Murals~~ • the Peace Walls • the Titanic Belfast museum

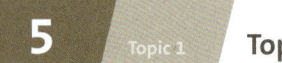
1 the Murals

See Belfast's amazing street art, which shows the Troubles and today's culture.

Do a special tour in a black cab and discover how Belfast was °divided during the Troubles.

See the wonderful views over the city from this famous old building in a beautiful park.

From Friday to Sunday, taste and buy food, find gifts, and listen to local musicians.

Find out about this famous ship from its °construction in Belfast to its unhappy end.

b) Read the brochure. Write the name of the place or places where you can …

1. enjoy visiting a green area.
2. discover more about a sad journey.
3. find out more about the conflict in Belfast.
4. eat and relax.
5. see where Belfast was divided.
6. experience part of Belfast's history.

> **1 b)** 1 Belfast Castle • 2 the Titanic Belfast museum • 3 the Peace Walls, the Murals • 4 St George's Market • 5 the Peace Walls • 6 the Peace Walls, the Murals, (Belfast Castle, the Titanic Belfast museum)

142   one hundred and forty-two

Topic 2 Vorbereitung

Material: Ex 1 UMA, Wortkarten mit den fünf Orten/Plätzen aus dem Reservoir, ggf. Zahlkarten (1–5) pro S-Paar, ggf. (touristische) Fotos/Bildmaterial z. B. des Heimatortes, Dokumentenkamera • **Ex 2** Wortkarten von Ex 1, UMA/CD/App • **Ex 4** UMA, ggf. weiße A4-Blätter für die Nachrichten (Klassensatz), ggf. ▶ KV 5.1 Belfast sights (Klassensatz)
Zeitbedarf: ca. 1–2 Std.
Minimalversion: Ex 3 auslassen
Begleitmedien: WB (S. 84), App (Digital quiz, Digital help), INKL (S. 132)

Ex 2 Einstieg: (SB zu)
- L verteilt Wortkarten aus Ex 1 im Raum: *Which place would you like to visit? Why?*
- S bewegen sich im Raum und wählen eine Sehenswürdigkeit.
- **Ausw.:** Ranking an der Tafel

Erarbeitung:
a) (SB auf) gemäß AA
- **Ausw.:** im Plenum

b) S erfassen die Lösungen beim **1. Hören** gemäß AA.
- 📝 S machen sich Notizen (▶Note-taking) beim **1. Hören**.
- **Ausw.:** im Plenum

c) S bereiten eine Tabelle vor:

place	Orla's opinion
the castle	…

- S ergänzen Tabelle gemäß AA beim **2. Hören**.
- **Ausw.:** ▶Partner check, dann im Plenum

Ex 3 Erarbeitung:
- (SB auf) schriftl. Bearbeitung gemäß AA (▶ SF 10, S. 165)
- **Ausw.:** ▶Five-minute teacher

My task Ex 4 Erarbeitung:
a) (SB auf) schriftl. gemäß AA, *Digital help* (App)
- **Alternative:** Einsatz von ▶KV 5.1 für a)–d)

b) gemäß AA schriftl. auf einem A4-Extrablatt. S nutzen sprachl. u. digitale Hilfen (App).

c) ▶Partner check gemäß AA
- S-Paare geben sich ▶Feedback.

d) gemäß AA
- **Ausw.:** ▶Gallery walk, Klasse erfasst die *top 3 activities*.

5
OPTIONAL

Story Inhalt

Lernschwerpunkt: eine Geschichte über einen Tanzwettbewerb verstehen
Kompetenzen: Speaking Vermutungen über die Handlung der Story äußern • Reading/Listening einer Geschichte Informationen zu den Charakteren und den Ereignissen entnehmen
Redemittel: *feelings • friendship • hobbies*

Ex 1 Einstieg:
- (SB zu) L teilt den Raum in zwei Teile und ordnet einer Seite die Aussage *true* und der anderen Seite die Aussage *false* zu.
- L macht Aussagen über Jack und Orla. S entscheiden, ob sie *true* or *false* sind, indem sie auf die jeweilige Seite laufen. Anschließend nehmen ausgewählte S Stellung zu ihrer Wahl.
  1. Jack is from Belfast. (t)
  2. Orla is from Belfast too. (f)
  3. Belfast is in Northern Ireland. (t)
  4. Orla has never left the Republic of Ireland before. (t)
  5. Jack and Orla take part in a programme to bring the two parts of Ireland closer together. (t)
  6. The programme they take part in is a film project. (f)
  7. Orla and her mum went to Belfast for the dance project. (t)
  8. Orla met Jack at the competition. (f)

Erarbeitung:
a) L zeigt die Fotos (UMA) und liest die Überschrift vor.
- S diskutieren Vermutungen in PA gemäß AA.
- **Ausw.:** Vergleich im Plenum (als TA sichern)

b) (SB auf) S lesen/hören den ersten Teil der Geschichte bis Zeile 40 (in Stillarbeit od. im ▶ Mitleseverfahren).
- Forts. von b) auf S. 145

---

5 OPTIONAL
Topic 1 | Topic 2 | **Story** | Viewing

Dance drama

1 READING What do you think?

1 a) Lösungsbsp. S. 302

a) BEFORE YOU READ Look at the title of the story and the pictures. Say what you think the story is about.

I think the story is about …
In the first / … picture, Jack / Orla looks …
Jack / Orla dances …

b) Read the story. Were your ideas from a) correct? Say who the main competitors are and add any information that you find out about them.

1 b) Lösungsbsp. S. 302

🔊 3.19

The next day Orla and her mum took a taxi to the dance competition. In the taxi Orla thought about the afternoon with Jack. They played crazy golf and then got ice cream and
5 hung out by the river. She had an amazing time. 'But it was just an afternoon,' thought Orla. 'We live in different cities – in different countries! I probably won't see him again.'

Orla went to the changing room to get ready.
10 'Hello,' she said to some other Irish girls who she knew. 'This is going to be an interesting day.' The °aim of the competition was to help keep peace between Ireland and Northern Ireland, but also to bring together boys and
15 girls in a mixed competition. Orla was curious to see how it would work.

As Orla thought about her °routines and went into the competition area, she walked into somebody. She looked up – it was Jack. They
20 looked at each other.

'Are you going to dance?' asked Orla in surprise.
'Yes, I am. Why didn't you say you were here for the competition?' asked Jack. He seemed
25 annoyed. 'I didn't want to talk about it,' said Orla. 'I get stressed before competitions. But you °didn't say anything either!' Jack looked embarrassed now.
'Other boys have bullied me because I like to
30 dance. I know it's stupid, but I just don't tell people now.'
'It is stupid,' said Orla kindly. 'You should be proud to be a dancer! … °Good luck, Jack!' Jack smiled. 'Thanks, Orla. You too!'
35 Orla went to sit with her mum and some other dancers. She asked if they knew Jack. 'He's good,' said a girl called Quinn who was from Dublin. 'Everybody thinks he will win.' 'No, he won't,' thought Orla. '*I'm going to be*
40 *the winner!*'

But after the first routine, Jack was in first place, Orla was second and a small boy from Belfast called Declan was third. In the freestyle dance next, Declan °did well.
45 'Northern Ireland is definitely going to °beat Ireland in this competition,' said Declan loudly. 'That isn't what this competition is about!' said Orla.

Jack | Orla

144 one hundred and forty-four

Story Vorbereitung

Material: Ex 1 UMA, UMA/CD/App
Zeitbedarf: ca. 1 Std.
Begleitmedien: INKL (S. 133)

Then it was Jack's turn. His dance was
50 amazing and he nearly got top marks –
but not quite. Orla was the last dancer. She
looked at the °scoreboard: She needed to
beat Jack, Declan and Quinn to get in the
first three – and beat Jack to win.

Jack

Orla

55 Orla was a little nervous now, but she
°performed her dance perfectly – until
suddenly there was a °flash of light from a
phone in the audience. It °confused her and
she missed a step.
60 'Come on, Orla!' she told herself angrily.
The audience cheered and clapped when
Orla finished her dance without any more
problems, but Orla was worried. Did the
°judges see the flash? Would they think about
65 that when they decided on her score? Or
would they just think that she wasn't good
enough to win?

2 Who and what?

2 1 B · 2 C · 3 B · 4 A · 5 C · 6 C

Read the story again and choose the correct answers.

1 Orla thinks that after their time together …
  A she is going to see Jack again.
  B another meeting with Jack won't happen.
  C she isn't interested in seeing Jack again.

2 Orla and Jack didn't tell each other about
being in the competition because …
  A they were both embarrassed.
  B Jack was nervous and Orla
    was embarrassed.
  C Jack was embarrassed and Orla
    was stressed.

3 Before the competition started, Orla was …
  A unhappy that Jack was there.
  B confident of winning.
  C nervous about losing.

4 Declan was …
  A unfriendly.
  B a bad dancer.
  C shy.

5 Orla missed a step because …
  A she forgot the steps.
  B she was nervous.
  C something happened in the audience.

6 At the end of the story …
  A the judges knew that Orla's mistake
    wasn't her fault.
  B Jack won.
  C we don't know what happened.

Ex 1 (Forts. von S. 144, b))
- ☒ Lernstärkere S überlegen, wie die Charaktere sich fühlen und belegen ihre Ideen mit Zeilenangaben.
- Gemäß AA prüfen S, ob ihre Vermutungen von a) sich bisher bestätigt haben. Sie sammeln Informationen über Orla, Jack und Declan schriftlich als *notes* im Heft.
- S lesen den Rest der Geschichte (ab Zeile 41) und prüfen wiederum, ob ihre ursprünglichen Vermutungen richtig waren. Sie ergänzen die Informationen über die drei Charaktere im Heft.
- ☒ Lernstärkere S überlegen, wie die Charaktere sich fühlen und belegen ihre Ideen mit Zeilenangaben.
- **Ausw.:** S nennen die Informationen im Plenum, L oder S sichert im TA.
- ☒ Vergleich zu den Gefühlen erfolgt ebenfalls im Plenum. L/S kann den vorhanden TA ergänzen.

Ex 2 Erarbeitung:
- (SB auf) gemäß AA
- **Alternative:** ▶ Four corners: Drei Raumecken wird je eine Antwortmöglichkeit (A, B, C) zugeteilt. L liest eine Aussage vor. Die S wählen die korrekte Aussage, indem sie in die entsprechende Ecke laufen.
- **Ausw.:** Vergleich der Lösungen im Plenum

5

OPTIONAL

Story Inhalt

Lernschwerpunkt: eine Geschichte passend zu Ende erzählen
Kompetenzen: Speaking Austausch der eigenen Meinungen zur Handlung • Writing eine Geschichte fortführen
Redemittel: fairness • discussion and feedback phrases

Vorbereitung

Material: Ex 5 UMA/CD/App
Zeitbedarf: ca. 1 Std.
Minimalversion: Ex 4 und Ex 5 auslassen, das Ende ggf. alleinstehend hören
Begleitmedien: WB (S. 85), App (Digital quiz), DIFF (5.3)

Ex 3 Erarbeitung:
- Hinweis: Falls Ex 3 nicht direkt im Anschluss an die Story durchgeführt wird, lässt L die Handlung von S wiederholend zusammenfassen.

a) (SB auf) ▶ Think-Pair-Share:
Fünf Min. in EA (*Think*): S beantworten die Fragen für sich u. machen sich ggf. Notizen. Sie können dabei den Text erneut lesen (S. 144–145).

b) (*Pair*) gemeinsames Lesen des ▶ Scaffolding
- Diskussion der Ergebnisse aus a) in PA gemäß AA

c) Ausw.: (*Share*) S äußern ihre Ideen im Plenum, L sammelt im TA.

Ex 4 Einstieg:
- (SB auf) Bei Bedarf wdh. S im Plenum zur Erinnerung das offene Ende der Geschichte (s. S. 145).

Erarbeitung:
a) Gemäß AA: S schreiben ein eigenes Ende der Geschichte ins Heft.

b) Ausw.: PA gemäß AA
- S unterstreichen gute Dinge (inhaltlich, sprachlich) grün (▶ Feedback).
- Freiwillige S stellen ihr Ende im Plenum vor.

Ex 5 Erarbeitung:
- direkt im Anschluss an 4b)

a) (SB auf) 1. Hören gemäß AA in PA

b) gemäß AA
- Ausw.: ▶ Blitzlichtrunde im Plenum

---

5 | Topic 1 | Topic 2 | **Story** | Viewing

OPTIONAL

3 By accident or °on purpose?   3 individuelle Lösungen

a) THINK Decide what you think happened. The questions can help you.

1. Did somebody just take a photo with flash? Or did somebody flash their phone light on purpose?
2. If it was on purpose, who was it and why?
3. How did the judges rate Orla's dance?
4. Who won?

b) PAIR Discuss your ideas with a partner.

I think it was an accident because …
If you ask me, it was on purpose because …
Maybe … did it because …
I think the judges decided to …
For me, the winner was …

c) SHARE Discuss your ideas with the class.

4 What did the judges decide?   4 individuelle Lösungen

a) Write an ending for the story. You can use your own ideas or another idea from 3.

The judges said / thought … They decided …
The winner was …
Orla / Jack felt …

b) Swap endings with a partner and comment on your partner's ending.

What a great ending! I love it!

I don't think this ending is fair, but your writing is good!

5 Another possible ending   5 individuelle Lösungen

3.20 a) Now listen to a possible ending. How is it different to yours? Talk to a partner.

The judges decided the same / differently.
The winner is different in this ending. In this ending … won, but in my ending …

b) How do you feel about the ending in a)?

I liked / didn't like this ending because …
I like my ending better!

▶ Workbook, p. 85

Digital quiz **I can complete a story.** ✓

146 one hundred and forty-six

146

5 OPTIONAL

Viewing Inhalt

Lernschwerpunkt: einen Film über ein Mädchen und ihre Doppelgängerin verstehen
Kompetenzen: Viewing / Intercultural competence Filmszenen verstehen • Speaking / Life skills über Wünsche, Ängste und Mut sprechen
Redemittel: family • hopes and dreams • being scared/brave

Vorbereitung

Material: Ex 2 und Ex 3 UMA/DVD/App
Zeitbedarf: ca. 1 Std.
Minimalversion: Ex 4 auslassen
Begleitmedien: INKL (S. 134)

Topic 1   Topic 2   Story   **Viewing**   5 OPTIONAL

Tina °times two

1 A wish | **1** individuelle Lösungen

BEFORE YOU WATCH Tina makes a special birthday wish in the video. What would you wish for? Tell the class.

I would wish for …

Tina

2 VIEWING 'I'm Tina too'

Watch the first part of the video and say if each sentence is true or false.

1. Tina doesn't like dancing.
2. Tina's parents don't listen to her.
3. Tina has a dance partner in her class.
4. Tina's parents forgot her birthday.
5. Tina 2 is a secret.
6. Tina 2 is more confident than Tina.

2
1 false
2 true
3 false
4 false
5 true
6 true

3 VIEWING 'I had the most absolutely amazing day today'

a) What do you think Tina 2 is going to do? Make predictions. ▶ More help, p. 153

3 a) individuelle Lösungen

b) Watch the second part of the video and take notes:

First Tina 2 …   **3 b)** Lösungsbsp. S. 303

c) Now think about the whole video. Match the events to Tina's feelings.

1. when she is dancing   a disappointed
2. when she first meets the boy   b angry
3. when she gets her birthday present   c shy
4. when she first meets Tina 2   d happy
5. when Tina 2 locks her in the wardrobe   e scared

3 c) 1 d • 2 c • 3 a • 4 e • 5 b

4 LIFE SKILLS 'Don't be scared, be °spectacular!'

a) How did Tina 2 change Tina?

She helped her to …   **4 a)** Lösungsbsp. S. 303

b) Tell your partner about a time when you were scared. How did you feel braver?   **4 b)** individuelle Lösungen

one hundred and forty-seven **147**

Ex 1 Einstieg:
- (SB zu) L: *Do you have a best friend? What should a good friend be like?* (S antworten spontan.)

Erarbeitung:
- (SB auf) S diskutieren Aufgabe zunächst in PA.
- **Ausw.:** ▶ Meldekette

Ex 2 Erarbeitung:
- (SB auf) S lesen die Sätze.
- **1. Sehen (1. Teil):** S entscheiden, ob die Aussagen wahr oder falsch sind u. schreiben die Antworten (t/f) ins Heft.
- ☒ S korrigieren falsche Sätze.
- **Ausw.:** ▶ Meldekette

Ex 3 Erarbeitung:
a) (SB auf) gemäß AA in PA
- ▶ More help, S. 153
- **Ausw.:** Austausch im Plenum

b) **1. Sehen (2. Teil):** ▶ Note-taking gemäß AA

c) Gemäß AA: S nutzen ihre Notizen aus b).
- **Ausw.:** 2. Sehen (1. u. 2. Teil) mit ▶ Partner check

Ex 4 Einstieg:
- (SB zu) L: *What do you think about the film? Why?*
- S tauschen sich im ▶ Milling around aus.

Erarbeitung:
a) (SB auf) gemäß AA in EA
- **Ausw.:** ▶ Meldekette

b) PA mit vertrauten Mit-S gemäß AA
- **Ausw.:** Freiwillge S stellen ihre Erlebnisse im Plenum vor.

5

OPTIONAL

Checkpoint Inhalt

Lernschwerpunkt: Kompetenzen und sprachliche Mittel üben, Lernfortschritte erkennen
Kompetenzen: *Mediation* Unterschiede zwischen Irland und Nordirland von einer Website ins Deutsche sprachmitteln • *Listening* einem Telefongespräch zu einer Hotelbuchung Informationen entnehmen • *Speaking* ein Telefongespräch zu einer Zimmerreservierung führen • *Reading* einem *online review* Informationen entnehmen • *Writing* einen eigenen *online review* schreiben
Redemittel: *phone call phrases* • *booking a room* • *holiday adventure* • *weather*

Allgemeine Anmerkung:
s. Unit 1, S. 32

Ex 1 Einstieg:
- (SB auf) S liest Lernziel vor.
- Selbsteinschätzung zum Lernziel mit ▶ Thumbs up

Erarbeitung:
- Mündl. gemäß AA, S nehmen sich selbst auf.
- **Ausw.:** ▶ Bus stop (▶ KV Extra): S vergleichen ihre Lösungen mithilfe von ▶ KV 5.2.
- **Alternative:** ▶ Partner check, dann Plenum
- erneute Selbsteinschätzung

Ex 2 Einstieg:
- (SB auf) s. Ex 1 (Selbsteinschätzung)
- L zeigt Bilder A–E (UMA): *Describe the pictures.* (z. B. als ▶ Picture duet)

Erarbeitung:
a) S notieren die Reihenfolge gemäß AA beim **1. Hören** in ihr Heft.
- **Ausw.:** ▶ Five-minute teacher
- **Alternative:** s. Ausw. bei **c)**

b) schriftl. gemäß AA in EA
- **Ausw.:** S überprüfen ihre Ergebnisse beim **2. Hören**, anschl. Plenum
- **Alternative:** s. Ausw. bei **c)**

c) gemäß AA in PA
- ☑/☒ L präsentiert einen Beispieldialog mit stärkerem/-er S.
- **Ausw.:** ▶ Bus stop (▶ KV Extra), S vergleichen ihre Lösungen mithilfe von ▶ KV 5.2.
- erneute Selbsteinschätzung
- **Zusatz:** ▶ Double circle (pro Durchgang eine Frage)

148

---

5 Checkpoint   Digital checkpoint

OPTIONAL

➔ **1** MEDIATION **Two countries**   *I can talk about Ireland and Northern Ireland.* ✓

Your dad wants to know about some differences between Ireland and Northern Ireland. You find this information online. Read it and tell your dad about the differences in German.
Start like this: *Es gibt viele Unterschiede zwischen Irland und Nordirland, z. B. ...*

1 Lösungsbsp. S. 303

www.twoirelands.example.com

Ireland and Northern Ireland: What's different and what's the same?
- If you want to buy something in Ireland, you pay in euros. It's in the EU. In Northern Ireland, you pay with pounds, like in England. Northern Ireland is part of the UK and it's not in the EU. But everybody in both countries can speak English – and everybody drinks tea!
- When you drive in Ireland, you will notice that the road signs show kilometres. In Northern Ireland, they use miles, not kilometres. In both countries you drive on the left – but be careful: A lot of roads are only big enough for one car!
- Lots of people in both countries are crazy about sport. Football is popular everywhere, but Gaelic football is more popular in Ireland than in Northern Ireland. It's different to regular football – there are 15 people in a team and it's like a mixture of football, rugby and basketball.
- The Irish flag is green, white and orange. In Northern Ireland, you will see the UK flag – the Union Jack, which is red, white and blue.

2 LISTENING & SPEAKING **Phoning a hotel**   *I can plan and talk about a trip.* ✓

🔊 3.21 **a)** Joe phones a hotel to book a room. Listen. Put the pictures (A–E) in the correct order.

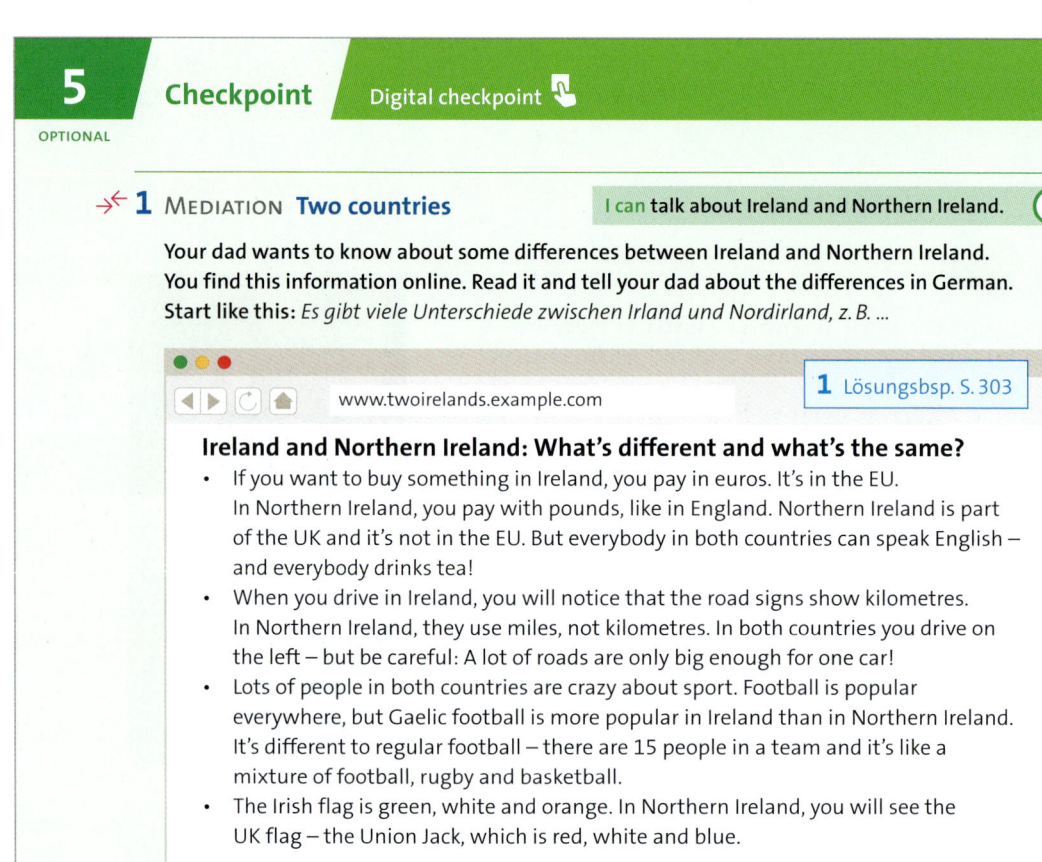

2 a) 1 C • 2 D • 3 E • 4 B • 5 A   **2 b)** 1 H • 2 J • 3 H • 4 J • 5 J • 6 H • 7 H • 8 H

🔊 **b)** Who asks what? Write H for hotel and J for Joe. Then listen again and check.

1. How can I help you?
2. Do you have a room free?
3. How many people is it for?
4. How much does it cost?
5. Is there a kettle / ... in the room?
6. Is there any other information you need?
7. Can I take your name, please?
8. What time will you arrive?

💬 **c)** SPEAKING Make a similar dialogue with a partner. Use the questions in **b)**.
Start like this: *Bay View hotel, good morning. How ...? – Hello, I need ...*

2 c) Lösungsbsp. S. 303

Check

148   one hundred and forty-eight

5
OPTIONAL

Checkpoint Vorbereitung

Material: alle Aufgaben ▶ KV Extra: Bus stop, ▶ KV 5.2: Checkpoint answers, App (Check) • Ex 1 geeignete Aufnahmegeräte • Ex 2 UMA/CD/App

Zeitbedarf: ca. 1–2 Std.

Minimalversion: Auswahl der Aufgaben erfolgt aufgrund der zu überprüfenden Lernziele

Begleitmedien: App (Digital Checkpoint), INKL (S. 135)

Die Übungen kannst du auch digital machen. 👆 **5** OPTIONAL

3 READING & WRITING Online °reviews

I can talk and write about Belfast. ✓

National Football Stadium, Windsor Park, Belfast (★★★★)

★★★★★ **29.7. Julie, Paris** I visited the stadium last week when I was on holiday with my cousins. The highlight was walking through the tunnel where the players walk before the match. The museum was really good too, and there were lots of °interactive games to play. There's a bus stop outside the stadium, but we drove there.

★★★★ **14.7. Frankie, Brighton** I'm not interested in football, but we came to this museum with our school class. It was actually really interesting. It was the first stadium that I've ever visited. The tour guide knew a lot of secret stories about the football teams and players and made it really interesting and funny. Unfortunately, the weather was terrible, but we still had fun.

★★★★★ **12.7. Jannick, Gelsenkirchen** I love visiting stadiums. I have visited a lot of stadiums in Germany – at home, in Hamburg and Berlin – but this stadium is much smaller. It wasn't busy at all and the tickets weren't expensive. There's a good shop too with a lot of football books and other souvenirs. I bought a T-shirt and some stickers. 5 stars from me.

> **3 a)** 1 F (with her cousins) • 2 F (by car) • 3 T • 4 F (liked) • 5 F (not many people) • 6 N

a) READING Read the online reviews about the football stadium in Belfast. Are the °statements true (T), false (F) or not in the text (N)? Correct the false statements.

1. Julie visited Belfast with her family.
2. Julie went to the stadium by bus.
3. Frankie isn't a football fan.
4. Frankie didn't like the tour guide.
5. There were too many people in the stadium for Jannick.
6. Jannick bought tickets for the stadium online.

b) WRITING You visited the Giant's Causeway near Belfast in your holidays. Now you want to write an online review about your experience.

1. Look at the notes that you made.
2. Read the reviews in a) again. What words and phrases can you use in a review about the Giant's Causeway? Write them down.
3. Now write your online review.

> **3 b)** Lösungsbsp. S. 303

☺ beautiful, views, tour guide ✓✓, free!
☹ very busy, windy and cold, cafe ££

Check 👆

one hundred and forty-nine **149**

Ex 3 Einstieg:
- Selbsteinschätzung s. Ex 1

Erarbeitung:

a) In EA: S lesen den Text still und notieren die Lösungen gemäß AA in ihr Heft.
- **Ausw.:** ▶ Bus stop (▶ KV Extra): S vergleichen ihre Lösungen mithilfe von ▶ KV 5.2.
- **Alternative:** ▶ Partner check, dann Plenum

b) S lesen AA und die *notes* zum Bild in EA.
- S bearbeiten die Schritte 1–3 gemäß AA in EA. L unterstützt bei Bedarf individuell.
- 🗨 gemeinsames ▶ Klären der AA.
- Schwächere S vergleichen ihre Ergebnisse von Schritt 2 im Plenum. L erfasst Ideen in einer Liste als TA.
- Abschließend bearbeiten S Schritt 3 gemäß AA in EA.
- **Ausw.:** ▶ Partner check: S vergleichen ihre Ergebnisse in PA und verbessern sich ggf. gegenseitig.
- **Alternative:** ▶ Bus stop (▶ KV Extra): S vergleichen ihre Ergebnisse mit dem Lösungsbeispiel von ▶ KV 5.2.
- erneute Selbsteinschätzung

149

5
OPTIONAL

Text file Inhalt

Lernschwerpunkt: weitere Hintergrundinformationen zur *Titanic* erhalten und eine Legende zum *Giant's Causeway* lesen
Kompetenzen: Reading Texten Informationen zur *Titanic* / der Geschichte des *Giant's Causeways* entnehmen

---

Allgemeine Anmerkung:
s. Unit 1, S. 36

The *Titanic* brothers Einstieg:
- (SB zu) L: *The famous ship, the Titanic, was built in Belfast. What do you know about the Titanic?*
- S sammeln Ideen im ▶ Think-Pair-Share, anschließend Sicherung im TA.
  L: *Let's see if your ideas are correct.*

Erarbeitung:
- (SB auf) S lesen den Text und prüfen, welche ihrer Ideen aus dem Einstieg sie mit dem Text belegen können, welche nicht im Text sind und welche falsch waren.
- S schreiben ▶ Three truths, two lies über den Text.
- 🔲 Schwächere S arbeiten in PA.
- **Ausw.:** Austausch im ▶ Milling around, S lesen ihre Sätze dem Partner / der Partnerin vor, diese/-r muss sie ggf. berichtigen.
- 🔲 Schwächere S, die in PA gearbeitet haben, gehen ggf. auch als Paar ins *Milling around*.
- ✖ S recherchieren weitere Informationen zur *Titanic* und stellen sie auf einem Poster vor. Ggf. ▶ Gallery walk oder Ausstellen im ▶ English corner.
- **Zusatz:** Die Klasse schaut den Film als Teil eines selbstorganisierten *English film club* an. Ggf. gestalten sie Filmposter u. Tickets.

150

5
OPTIONAL

Text file

A magazine for young people across the UK

The *Titanic* brothers by Pippa O'Donnell

The *Titanic* left England for New York City on 10 April 1912 on its first — and sadly its last — voyage[1]. The ship hit an iceberg[2], broke into two pieces and sank. The *Titanic* didn't have enough lifeboats[3] for everybody on the ship.

A rescue ship saved over 700 people. They included the Navratil brothers, Michel and Edmond, who were only two and three years old. The two boys were on the *Titanic* with their father who secretly took the boys from their mother in France. He wanted to start a new life in America and used a false name on their tickets.

I went to the Titanic Belfast museum and read about two little brothers who were on the ship. It's an amazing story!

After the accident, the boys' father put them lovingly in a lifeboat and said goodbye. The father died[4] on the ship — but his sons lived. However, the little boys didn't speak English and their false name made it difficult to find their mother. After their rescue, a kind woman from the ship took the boys to her home in New York and looked after them.

Luckily the story had a happy ending: The boys' mother saw a picture of them in a newspaper and she travelled to New York to be united[5] with her children.

Have you seen the film *Titanic*, which won eleven Oscars? In the film, Rose (Kate Winslet) is a rich[6] girl who has to marry a man that she doesn't love. Jack (Leonardo DiCaprio) is a poor artist who won his ticket in a card game. They meet and fall in love. Will they survive[7]?

Let us know what you think!

---
[1] **voyage** *die Reise* [2] **iceberg** *der Eisberg* [3] **lifeboat** *das Rettungsboot* [4] **(to) die** *sterben*
[5] **(to) be united** *vereint werden* [6] **rich** *reich* [7] **(to) survive** *überleben*

5 OPTIONAL

Text file — Vorbereitung

Material: The *Titanic* brothers ggf. blanko Poster (Klassensatz), ggf. Beamer, Spielfilm • **Finn McCool** von L recherchierte Bilder des *Giant's Causeway*, ggf. passende Requisiten für eine Aufführung
Zeitbedarf: Abhängig davon, welche Texte bearbeitet werden
Minimalversion: Alle Beiträge sind optionale Zusatztexte.

---

5 OPTIONAL

Finn McCool – a local legend by Jack Wilson

Maybe you can try my play in class! — Jack

Scene 1

Narrator¹: This is the story of Finn McCool and the Giant's Causeway². A long time ago, the people of Finn's village came to him with some terrible news.

Conor: Finn, my friend! Have you heard of Benandonner?

Finn: The Scottish giant³? Of course, why?

Conor: Well, he's scaring people in Scotland – he's stealing animals, breaking into houses and killing people. We've heard that he wants to come to Ireland next!

Finn: Then we must stop him!

Conor: Don't let him come here, Finn! He's the biggest giant in the world. Do you really think we can win?

Finn: Don't worry, I'm not scared of him! I'll build a bridge of rocks across the sea and stop him before he can come to Ireland.

Scene 2

Narrator: So Finn built his bridge and walked across it to Scotland. But when he saw Benandonner, the giant was much bigger than he thought!

Finn walks over the bridge and sees Benandonner throwing things. Finn is scared. He runs back to Ireland and his clever wife, Oonagh.

Finn: Oonagh! Conor was right – I can't fight him! How can we stop him?

Oonagh: I have an idea. Quick, put this blanket around you and lie down here. Pretend⁴ to be my baby!

Finn lies down and pretends to sleep. Oonagh sings to him.

Scene 3

Benandonner walks over the bridge to Ireland. He sees Oonagh and Finn.

Benandonner: You, woman! Tell me where Finn McCool is! I heard he wants to stop me. Ha! I'll kill him and everyone else in this village!

Oonagh: He has gone out for a walk and left me alone with our baby. You should run away before he comes back.

Benandonner: *(looking at Finn)* THIS is his baby? Then how big is the father?

Oonagh: Oh, much bigger than you! He'll eat you in one go⁵!

Benandonner: *(scared)* Oh no! I'm going back to Scotland! Don't let him come after me!

Benandonner runs away, then Oonagh and Finn laugh.

Narrator: So Benandonner ran back home to Scotland. As he ran, he threw the rocks into the sea, so that Finn couldn't follow him. You can still see the Giant's Causeway today and maybe you'll see Benandonner's footsteps⁶ in the rocks.

¹ **narrator** *der Erzähler, die Erzählerin*   ² **causeway** *der Damm, der erhöhte Fußweg*   ³ **giant** *der Riese, die Riesin*
⁴ **(to) pretend** *vortäuschen, so tun als ob*   ⁵ **in one go** *auf einen Streich*   ⁶ **footstep** *der Fußabdruck*

one hundred and fifty-one **151**

Finn McCool – a local legend

Einstieg:

- (SB zu) L zeigt Bilder vom *Giant's causeway*. S beschreiben die Bilder.
  L: *What's special about the stones at the Giant's Causeway?*
- S beschreiben die hexagonale Form der Steine. L ergänzt die geologischen Hintergründe (Lava aus Basalt erkaltet in hexagonalen Säulen).
  L: *Today, scientists know why the stones have these shapes. Hundreds of million years ago hot lava made of basalt (a special kind of very hard stone) cooled down and formed those columns. But there's a local legend in Northern Ireland about how these columns were formed. It's also the reason for the name 'Giant's Causeway'. Have you got ideas what could have happened?*
- L semantisiert den Begriff *causeway*. S stellen Vermutungen dazu auf, was in der Legende passiert.

Erarbeitung:

- (SB auf) Lesen des Texts in verteilten Rollen
- S prüfen, ob ihre Vermutungen zutreffen.
- **Ausw.:** S fassen die Geschichte im Plenum zusammen.
- ▶ Zusatz: S spielen das Stück in Kleingruppen mit verteilten Rollen nach (▶ Role-play).
- Ggf. führen sie das Stück beim nächsten Klassenfest auf.

151

5

Partner page / Diff bank — Inhalt

Lernschwerpunkt: zusätzliche Übungen, Differenzierungs- und Hilfsangebote
Kompetenzen: Speaking einen Dialog an einer Hotelrezeption nachstellen • einen Reiseplan präsentieren • Vermutungen äußern • Listening einem Podcast Jahreszahlen zu historischen Ereignissen entnehmen
Redemittel: booking a room • planning a trip

Allgemeine Anmerkung:
s. Unit 1, S. 38

Ex 3 Erarbeitung: s. S. 141
a) (SB auf) *Partner B* bereitet die Fragen von S. 152 vor.
• PA gemäß AA
• **Ausw.:** Findet erst im Anschluss an b) im Plenum statt, s. c) auf S. 141.

b) PA gemäß AA: *Partner B* liest Text auf S. 152, *Partner A* stellt die Fragen von S. 141.
• **Ausw.:** s. c) auf S. 141

MP 1 Einstieg:
• (SB zu) S wiederholen Jahreszahlen mithilfe von vorbereiteten ▶ Swap cards.
• ⌧ Schwächere S lesen vorab gemeinsam die ▶ Tippbox, S. 152.

Erarbeitung:
a) (SB auf) S lesen die AA und die Ereignisse laut oder leise.
• ggf. ▶ Semantisierung von unbekanntem Wortschatz
• S notieren a–g als Liste in ihr Heft und ergänzen die Jahreszahlen gemäß AA beim **1. Hören**.
• ⌧ ggf. 2. Hören

b) gemäß AA in PA (▶ Partner check)
• **Ausw.:** S präsentieren die Lösungen im Plenum, L od. freiwillige/-r S ergänzt die korrekten Jahreszahlen als TA.
• Ggf. übertragen die S (als HA) die gesamte *timeline* mit den korrekten Jahreszahlen ins Heft.

---

5 Partner page / Diff bank

Partner page
▶ Page 141

3 SPEAKING **Staying in Belfast**   **3** Lösung S. 301

a) **Partner B:** Ask partner A questions about *The Beyond B&B* and take notes.

1 how much?
2 rooms with twin beds?
3 own bathrooms?
4 Wi-Fi in the room?
5 a kettle in the room?
6 a cooked breakfast?
⌧ 7 other information?

b) **Partner B:** Read the description of *Ivy House B&B*. Then answer partner A's questions.

Our large double and twin rooms have their own bathroom with a °bath and °shower. There are free bottles of water in every room. Rooms are £95 including breakfast.

Guests can use Wi-Fi in all areas and relax in the garden. We also have a living room with a TV, books and games for our guests. Our breakfast °buffet includes °cereals, fruit, yoghurt, cheese and °cold °meats, and bread or °toast.

Diff bank
▶ Page 139

1 a) **a** 1175 • **b** 1919 • **c** 1921 • **d** 1968 • **e** 1972 • **f** 1998 • **g** 2020

More practice 1 LISTENING **Northern Ireland's history**

3.22 a) Listen to the podcast. Write the correct dates for the events (a–g) on the timeline in your exercise book.

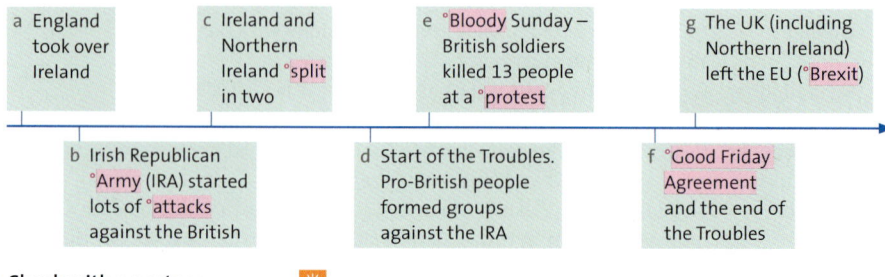

b) Check with a partner.

England took over Ireland in …

Remember: In English we usually say years as pairs of numbers.
19|60 = nineteen sixty   20|23 = twenty twenty-three

1 b) individuelle Lösungen

152   one hundred and fifty-two

5

Diff bank Vorbereitung

Material: MP 1 vorbereitete *Swap cards* mit Jahreszahlen (als Ziffern), UMA/CD/App • MP 3 *English-only*-Karte, weiße A3- oder A4-Blätter für die Gruppen zur Gestaltung des Posters, Klebezettel fürs Feedback (Klassensatz) • MH 3 UMA

Zeitbedarf: abhängig davon, welche Aufgaben bearbeitet werden

Minimalversion: *More practice*-Aufgaben sind stets Zusatzaufgaben.

5

▶ Page 143

2 1 museum • 2 skydiving • 3 ride • 4 waterpark • 5 crazy golf

More practice 2 **Fun activities in Belfast**

Read the conversation and put the words in the correct place.

crazy golf • museum • ride • skydiving • °waterpark

Jack We could go to the Science Centre. It's an interactive … (1).
Orla Erm, can we do something sporty?
Jack Well, there's an °indoor … (2) centre. It's really cool!
Orla Sounds cool, but I don't need a broken leg right now!
Jack Well, there's an exciting … (3) in a forest park. You go really fast down a hill in a little car.
Orla Maybe. What else is there?
Jack Hmm, what about going to a really good … (4)?
Orla That sounds great, but I don't have a swimsuit with me.
Jack Oh, that's a shame. Erm, I know. Let's play … (5).
Orla Isn't that for little kids?
Jack Not this place. It's called Lost City. You're in a rainforest and you have to find gold.
Orla Oh, that sounds fun, Jack! Let's do that!

More practice 3 **Planning a trip**

3 individuelle Lösungen

a) Your class is going on a trip to the UK or Ireland. In a group, decide where to go and how to get there (by ferry, bus, train, plane, …).
b) Now decide where to stay (at a B&B, a hotel, a youth hostel, a campsite, …).
c) What sights do you want to see? Think of ones in this book or °general sights (museums, parks, famous buildings, the beach, …).
d) Make a poster with your travel plan. Comment on other groups' plans.

*We're going to go on a trip to … and travel there by …
We're going to see / visit / stay at a … (because) …*

That sounds amazing / exciting / fun / interesting / …

▶ Page 147

3 a) individuelle Lösungen

More help **3** VIEWING 'I had the most absolutely amazing day today'

a) What do you think Tina 2 is going to do? Make predictions.

I think Tina 2 is going to	go	shopping / to the dance class / to the beach / …
	speak to	Tina's parents / the boy on the bike / Tina's teacher / …
	dance	in the street / on the hill / …
	buy / steal	clothes / food / a present / …
	eat	a cake / lots of sweets / …
	do	something funny / Tina's homework / …

one hundred and fifty-three **153**

MP 2 Erarbeitung:
- (SB auf) S nummerieren von 1–5 im Heft und ergänzen die Lösungen gemäß AA.
- **Ausw.:** ▶ Partner check mit gemeinsamem Lesen des Dialoges in verteilten Rollen

MP 3 Erarbeitung:
- (SB zu) L notiert *Planning a trip to the UK or Ireland* als TA und nennt das Lernziel der AA.
- Bildung von Dreiergruppen (▶ Gruppenbildung)
- (SB auf) gemeinsames Lesen und Klären der AA für a)–d)

a)–c) gemäß AA in GA
- **Alternative:** Jede/-r S einer Gruppe übernimmt eine Aufgabe und macht sich Notizen (▶ Note-making).
- **Ausw.:** S präsentieren ihre Ergebnisse und diskutieren in der Gruppe mit ▶ English-only-Karte.

d) gemäß AA in GA
- **Ausw.:** S-Gruppen präsentieren ihre Ergebnisse im Plenum.
- ▶ Gallery walk: S geben ▶ Feedback auf Klebezettel.
- Aufhängen im ▶ English corner

MH 3 s. S. 147
- Diese Aufgabe bietet zusätzliche sprachliche Mittel für lernschwächere S.

Erarbeitung:

a) (SB auf) L zeigt das ▶ Scaffolding mithilfe des UMA.
- S stellen in PA Vermutungen gemäß AA auf.
- **Ausw.:** Austausch im Plenum

153

Skills file

Auf den **Skills file**-Seiten findest du Methoden und Tipps, die dir helfen, z. B. Wortschatz zu lernen, Informationen zu sammeln, Texte zu überprüfen oder kleine Vorträge zu halten.

Inhalt

	Seite
SF 1 Vokabeln lernen	155
SF 2 Unbekannte Wörter erschließen	156
SF 3 Im Wörterbuch nachschlagen	157
SF 4 Im Internet recherchieren	158
SF 5 Die eigene Meinung äußern	160
SF 6 Eine Geschichte planen	161
SF 7 Einen Kurzvortrag halten	162
SF 8 Hörtexte verstehen	163
SF 9 Lesetexte verstehen	164
SF 10 Mediation	165
SF 11 Bilder beschreiben	166
SF 12 Texte markieren und Notizen erstellen	167
SF 13 Texte überprüfen und verbessern	168

Die mit diesem Symbol gekennzeichneten Abschnitte enthalten Hinweise und Tipps, die dir dabei helfen, elektronische Medien beim Englischlernen einzusetzen.

Erklärfilm: Dieses Symbol zeigt dir, dass du einen Erklärfilm zu diesem Thema in der App findest.

Lösungen der Merkaufgaben

SF 2, Merkaufgabe:
a) ähnliches Wort im Deutschen: Pyjama stammt aus dem Dari-Persischen (پای‌جامه pāy-jāmeh), wörtlich „Beinkleidung"
b) Wortfamilie und Wortbildungsgesetze: taste + Nachsilbe -ful: tasteful
c) Wortfamilie und Wortbildungsgesetze: (to) care + Nachsilbe -er: carer

SF 3, Merkaufgabe:
a) die Säule
b) die Spalte

SF 4, Merkaufgabe:
Nein: Dann musst du die Urheberinnen und Urheber der Bilder um Erlaubnis fragen oder eigene Bilder machen, wenn es keine *creative commons*-Bilder sind.

SF 5, Merkaufgabe:
Zehen: *They're part of my foot.*
Küche: *It's a room where you can cook and eat.*

SF 6, Merkaufgabe:
Weitere Bindewörter (*linking words*), die du schon kennst, sind z. B. *after that, and, because, but, or, so, soon, …*

SF 7, Merkaufgabe:
Mögliche Satzanfänge könnten z. B. sein: *I mean, …; Just a minute, …; Let me see, …; You know, …; Well, …*

SF 8, Merkaufgabe:
a) Allgemeine Dinge   b) Details

SF 9, Merkaufgabe:
Edinburgh Castle: £19.50, child ticket £11.40; Edinburgh Zoo: £24.25, child ticket £15.25

SF 10, Merkaufgabe:
b)

SF 11, Merkaufgabe:
a) *The person is playing the guitar.*

SF 1

Erklärfilm

Vokabeln lernen

▶ Unit 1 | p. 15   ▶ Unit 2 | p. 60
▶ Unit 3 | p. 84   ▶ Unit 4 | p. 112

Führe dein VOCAB FILE aus Klasse 5 und 6 weiter. Ergänze eine Spalte für Wörter aus anderen Sprachen, die du sprichst.

Neue Vokabeln lernst du am besten an einem ruhigen und aufgeräumten Platz, an dem du nicht abgelenkt wirst.

English	Deutsch	Türkçe
biscuit	Plätzchen	bisküvi

Wiederholen kannst du sie immer und überall. Für unterwegs kannst du sie dir aufs Handy sprechen oder per Vokabeltrainer-App üben. Je öfter du die Vokabeln wiederholst, desto besser wirst du sie dir merken können.

Wie merke ich mir neue Wörter besser?

Erstelle Wortfelder

- Ordne die Wörter unter einem Oberbegriff *(umbrella word)*. Du kannst eine Liste machen oder eine Mindmap anlegen, die du immer weiter ergänzt.

- Oder du arbeitest mit Karteikarten. Schreibe den Oberbegriff in Großbuchstaben auf die Vorderseite einer Karteikarte und die dazu passenden Wörter auf die Rückseite. Später kannst du neue Wörter ergänzen.

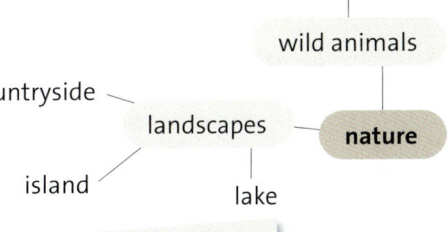

- Wenn Informationen sich in verschiedene Teile ordnen lassen, kannst du gut auch eine Tabelle anlegen, z. B. wenn du darüber reden möchtest, wann du etwas machst.

Sammle Gegensatzpaare und Wörter mit der gleichen Bedeutung

Sammle gegensätzliche Wörter und Wörter mit der gleichen Bedeutung, z. B. auf der letzten Seite deines VOCAB FILE.

friend	◀ ▶	enemy
young	◀ ▶	old
(to) remain	▶ ▶	(to) stay

Lerne *phrases* statt Einzelwörter

Phrases sind Ausdrücke, die aus mehreren Wörtern bestehen, z. B. *a bottle of water = eine Flasche Wasser*. Lerne also nicht *bottle* und *water* als Einzelwörter, sondern den ganzen Ausdruck: *a bottle of water*.

Checkliste Vokabeln lernen
- ✓ Lerne nur 5–10 Vokabeln auf einmal.
- ✓ Lerne jeden Tag 10 Minuten.
- ✓ Lerne zusammen mit Freunden.
- ✓ Lerne unterwegs mit einer Vokabeltrainer-App.
- ✓ Schreibe schwierige Wörter mehrmals auf.
- ✓ Sprich die Wörter und nimm dich mit dem Handy auf.

Merkaufgabe 1

Gehe dein VOCAB FILE aus Klasse 5 und 6 durch und erstelle eine Liste mit zwanzig bedeutungsgleichen Wörtern.

one hundred and fifty-five **155**

Skills file

SF 2

Unbekannte Wörter erschließen

▶ Unit 1 | p. 15, 28   ▶ Unit 2 | p. 46
▶ Unit 3 | p. 85   ▶ Unit 4 | p. 112

Du kannst englische Texte verstehen – auch wenn du nicht alle Wörter kennst. Diese Tipps helfen dir, die Bedeutung von Wörtern ohne Wörterbuch herauszufinden.

Bilder

Bilder zeigen oft Dinge in einem Text, für die du das englische Wort noch nicht kennst. Schaue sie deshalb genau an.

Till has left his key ring on the park bench at the end of the path.

Ähnliche Wörter im Deutschen oder in anderen Sprachen

Viele englische Wörter klingen ähnlich wie im Deutschen oder sie werden ähnlich geschrieben. Manche kennst du vielleicht aus anderen Sprachen und kannst sie auch daher verstehen.

🇬🇧 garage
🇩🇪 die Garage
🇫🇷 le garage
🇷🇺 гараж
🇹🇷 garaj

Wortfamilien und Wortbildungsregeln

Ein Wort gehört immer zu einer Wortfamilie, z. B. *friend*, *friendly*, *friendship*. Kennst du ein Wort aus der Wortfamilie und ein paar Regeln zur Wortbildung, kannst du die Bedeutung ableiten:

Vorsilben		
un-	Aus einem positiven Adjektiv wird ein negatives.	friendly → unfriendly
Nachsilben		
-er	Aus einem Tätigkeitsverb wird eine Person.	(to) support → supporter
-ful	Aus einem Nomen wird ein Adjektiv.	care → careful
-less	Aus einem Nomen wird ein Adjektiv.	cloud → cloudless
-ness	Aus einem Adjektiv wird ein Nomen.	fit → fitness

Kontext

Manchmal helfen dir die Wörter oder Sätze vor und nach dem neuen Wort dabei, es zu verstehen.

We made it to the station on time! The train departs in ten minutes from platform 3.

Merkaufgabe 2

Schaue dir die Wörter an. Mit welcher Strategie kannst du ihre Bedeutung herausfinden?

a) *pyjama*   b) *tasteful*   c) *carer*

(Die Lösung findest du auf Seite 154.)

SF 3

Im Wörterbuch nachschlagen

▶ Unit 1 | p. 28   ▶ Unit 3 | p. 77, 80

Wie finde ich Wörter und Ausdrücke im englisch-deutschen *Dictionary*?

Dein *Dictionary* hinten im Buch (S. 245–271) hilft dir, wenn du ein unbekanntes Wort nicht erschließen kannst. Du kannst aber auch ein (Online-)Wörterbuch verwenden. Beachte dabei folgende wichtige Dinge:

Die Wörter im Wörterbuch sind alphabetisch aufgelistet (j kommt vor k, ka vor ke, keb vor kee).

Der Haupteintrag (z. B. *name*) steht farbig und **fett** am Anfang. Daneben oder darunter findest du oft zusammengesetzte Wörter oder Redewendungen (z. B. *first name*).

Längere Ausdrücke findest du meist unter mehr als einem Stichwort, z. B. *first name* unter *first* und unter *name*.

Die Ziffern 1, 2 usw. zeigen, dass ein Wort mehrere Bedeutungen hat oder sogar als unterschiedliche Wortarten vorkommt. Lies also immer den ganzen Eintrag und entscheide dann, welche Bedeutung die richtige ist.

Du erfährst, wie das gesuchte Wort geschrieben und ausgesprochen wird. Schau dir für die Aussprache und Betonung die Lautschrift in den eckigen Klammern an.

▶ English sounds, p. 202

 In Online-Wörterbüchern stellst du nur die Suchrichtung (E–D oder D–E) ein und tippst dann das Wort ein. Durch einen Klick auf das Lautsprechersymbol kannst du dir ein Wort anhören.

Was muss ich bei einem deutsch-englischen Wörterbuch beachten?

Schlage bei Verben immer den Infinitiv (die Grundform) nach, also z. B. „singen" statt „gesungen".

Wenn ein Wort mehrere Übersetzungen hat, dann lies alle Einträge genau, um die passende Bedeutung zu finden.

> **Merkaufgabe 3**
>
> Was heißt *column* in diesen Sätzen?
>
> a) *One of the most famous columns in London is Nelson's Column.*
> b) *Make a table with five columns.*
>
> (Die Lösung findest du auf Seite 154.)

one hundred and fifty-seven   **157**

Skills file

SF 4

Im Internet recherchieren

▶ Unit 1 | p. 30   ▶ Unit 4 | p. 116

Im Internet kannst du dir schnell und einfach Informationen zu allen Themen besorgen. Mit ein paar Tricks behältst du trotz der Menge an Informationen den Überblick.

Benutze auch andere Quellen wie Bücher aus der Bücherei, Zeitungen und Magazine.

Suchen

- Überlege dir Suchbegriffe, die zu deinem Thema passen.
- Gib nicht nur einen Suchbegriff ein, sondern zwei oder mehrere. Du suchst z. B. Informationen zu Nessie. Wenn du nur *monster* eingibst, wirst du weniger Passendes finden, als wenn du *Scotland + Loch Ness + monster Nessie* eingibst.

Auswählen und prüfen

Beschäftige dich nur mit Webseiten, die wirklich zu deiner Aufgabe passen und glaubwürdig sind. Nicht alle Informationen, die du findest, sind wichtig und richtig. Prüfe sie also sorgfältig:

- Passen die Informationen zu deinem Thema? Sind sie wichtig? Um dir einen Eindruck zu verschaffen, überfliege die Seite und achte auf Überschriften und Bilder.

Unseriöse Quellen erkennst du z. B. an reißerischen oder unpassenden Überschriften, fehlenden Angaben zur Autorin oder zum Autor, fehlenden Belegen oder einem veralteten Datum.

- Sind die Informationen korrekt? Fakten sind gut, wenn sie wahr und überprüfbar sind. Es gibt aber auch gefälschte „Fakten" und Statistiken. Prüfe daher:
Woher stammt die Information? Ist es z. B. ein Online-Lexikon oder ein Chat-Forum? Achte auf die Endung der Internetadresse oder URL (http://www...), sie kann dir wichtige Hinweise geben:
.com bedeutet, es ist eine kommerzielle Webseite, die auch (versteckte) Werbung enthalten kann.
.gov weist auf eine offizielle Webseite der amerikanischen Regierung hin.
.uk bedeutet, dass es eine britische Seite ist.

Vorsicht bei Wikipedia. Das Online-Lexikon ist von freiwilligen Helfern geschrieben und kann Fehler enthalten.

- Verlasse dich nicht nur auf eine einzige Internetseite als Quelle, sondern ziehe zwei oder drei heran.
- Überprüfe, wer den Text verfasst hat. Verfolgt er oder sie ein bestimmtes Ziel? Ist die Person neutral und sachlich? Handelt es sich um Experten?

Es ist natürlich in Ordnung, eine eigene Meinung zu äußern oder die Meinung anderer Leute wiederzugeben, solange sie auf Fakten basiert und respektvoll vorgetragen wird.

Sichern

- Setze *bookmarks*, also Lesezeichen oder Favoriten, in deinem Browser, um die ausgewählten Seiten später schnell wieder aufzurufen.

- Wenn du Inhalte einer Webseite verwendest, nenne immer die Autorin oder den Autor der Seite und die dazugehörige Internetadresse, die du direkt in dein digitales Dokument hineinkopieren kannst. Schreibe auch das Datum dazu, wann du die Webseite zuletzt aufgerufen hast.

- Mache dir Notizen oder drucke wichtige Seiten sofort aus und markiere wichtige Textstellen. Schreibe die Texte nicht wörtlich ab – gib die Inhalte in deinen eigenen Worten wieder. Ordne deine Ergebnisse in deinem Heft oder in einem Dokument auf dem Rechner mit Überschriften oder sortiere sie in einer Mindmap.

- Wenn du Inhalte wörtlich übernehmen möchtest, kennzeichne sie durch Anführungszeichen als Zitat und nenne die Quelle, z. B. „*A lot of people think that the Loch Ness monster is real and have lovingly named it Nessie.*" (Loch Ness Times vom 11. 11. 2023)

Bookmarks setzt du so: Du navigierst im Browser zu der Webseite, die du zu einem Favoriten machen möchtest, und klickst dann, je nach Browser, im Menü auf „Favoriten" oder „Lesezeichen", gibst den Namen des Lesezeichens in die Adressleiste ein und bestätigst mit „↵".

Bilder verwenden

Wenn du ein Bild aus dem Internet verwendest, ist es wichtig, dass du die Quelle angibst, also den Ort, wo du das Bild gefunden hast. Dazu klickst du in deinen Suchergebnissen auf das Bild, das du nutzen möchtest, und gehst auf die eigentliche Seite, auf der es zu finden ist. Dann kopierst du die URL der Seite und setzt sie in deinem Dokument unter das Bild. Nenne auch die Fotografin oder den Fotografen, wenn du die Angabe findest. Am besten verwendest du eigene oder lizenzfreie Bilder *(creative commons)*.

Denke daran, dass eine Suchmaschine keine Quelle ist, d. h. du musst immer die Adresse der Webseite angeben, auf der das Bild tatsächlich steht.

Wenn du Fotos mit anderen Personen machst und verwendest, musst du diese Personen um Erlaubnis bitten.

Merkaufgabe 4

Wenn dein Poster oder deine Folien z. B. auf der Webseite deiner Schule stehen, also an die Öffentlichkeit kommen, darfst du dann Fotos aus dem Internet verwenden, ja oder nein?

(Die Lösung findest du auf Seite 154.)

Skills file

SF 5

Die eigene Meinung äußern

▶ Unit 2 | p. 60   ▶ Unit 4 | p. 120

Wie drücke ich aus, was ich denke?

Zu Beginn einer Diskussion sagst du, was du über ein Thema denkst. Dann begründest du deine Meinung.

> In my opinion, ...
> I think / believe that ...
> I would say that ...
> If you ask me ...

Wie frage ich nach der Meinung?

In Diskussionen geht es nicht nur um die eigene Meinung. Daher fragst du die anderen nach ihrer Meinung.

> What do you think?

Wie reagiere ich angemessen?

Gehe auf die Beiträge anderer ein und respektiere andere Meinungen. Sei auch bei Meinungsverschiedenheiten sachlich und höflich. Wenn du etwas nicht richtig gehört oder verstanden hast, bitte dein Gegenüber, es zu wiederholen oder langsamer zu sprechen:
Can you say that again, please?
Don't speak so fast, please.

> I (completely) agree.
> Yes, you're so right.
> That's a good point.

> I'm not sure here.
> I see it a bit differently.
> I don't think that's true.
> I don't agree with you (at all).

Was mache ich, wenn mir Wörter nicht einfallen?

Fehlt dir beim Sprechen ein Wort oder fällt es dir nicht ein, kannst du es umschreiben, z. B. durch einen Oberbegriff *(umbrella word)*, mit Wörtern, die eine ähnliche oder gleiche Bedeutung haben, oder mit gegensätzlichen Wörtern. Auch mit Relativsätzen kannst du Eigenschaften des gesuchten Begriffes erklären.

> It's a place where ...
> It's very similar to ...
> It's the opposite of ...
> It's somebody who ...

Füllwörter

Um ein Gespräch nicht stocken zu lassen, kannst du Füllwörter verwenden. Wenn du Zeit zum Nachdenken brauchst, kannst du diese mit *Let me see ...* oder *Well, ...* überbrücken.

> Well, ...
> Just a minute.
> Let me think.

Merkaufgabe 5

Überlege dir passende Umschreibungen für „Zehen" und „Küche".
(Die Lösung findest du auf Seite 154.)

SF 6

Eine Geschichte planen

▶ Unit 3 | p. 90, 91

Schritt 1: Ideen sammeln

Damit deine Geschichte verständlich und interessant wird, sammelst du zuerst wichtige Ideen und Wörter, z. B. in einer Liste oder einer Mindmap. Beantworte dafür die *wh*-Fragen: *Who? When? Where? What? Why? How?*

```
a strange noise ──→ scary
events ── someone finds a lot of money
         someone gets lost
```

Schritt 2: Die Geschichte strukturieren

Deine Geschichte ist viel besser zu verstehen, wenn du sie sinnvoll gliederst. Unterteile sie deshalb in:
- **Anfang** *(beginning)*: In einem einleitenden Satz beschreibst du die Ausgangssituation: den Schauplatz und die Personen.
- **Mittelteil** *(middle)*: Im Mittelteil beschreibst du die Handlung deiner Geschichte.
- **Schluss** *(end)*: Schließe deine Geschichte mit einem Happy End, einer Auflösung oder einer neuen Situation ab.

> Remember: Geschichten erzählst du im *simple past*.

Schritt 3: Einen Textentwurf erstellen

Möchtest du die Geschichte mündlich vortragen, mache dir nun Stichpunkte. Schreibe dafür wichtige Wörter auf Karteikarten und übe, sie frei sprechend vorzutragen.

Möchtest du die Geschichte aufschreiben, erstelle einen Textentwurf – auf einem Blatt Papier oder am Computer.

Überlege dir eine sinnvolle Reihenfolge und beginne bei neuen Punkten mit einer neuen Zeile, z. B. nach deiner Einleitung und vor deinem Schluss.

> *Joe and Salim wanted to go fishing.* →
> *They packed and went out in the boat.* →
> *It started to get dark and Joe was scared.* →
> *A storm started.*
> *Joe fell into the water.* →
> *Salim pulled Joe into the boat.* →
> *Salim called 999.* →
> *A lifeguard rescued Joe and Salim.*

Schritt 4: Deine Geschichte interessant klingen lassen

Deine Geschichte klingt interessanter, wenn du Adjektive verwendest, um Personen, Orte oder Dinge zu beschreiben. So kann sich dein Publikum deine Geschichte besser vorstellen. Verbinde deine Sätze mithilfe von Bindewörtern *(linking words)*, z. B. *eventually, first, finally, however, in the end, then, therefore*.

> Gute Adjektive für die Geschichte von Joe und Salim könnten zum Beispiel sein: *black, careful, cold, dark, exciting, extreme, hard, happy, helpful, horrible, scared, wild, ...*

> **Merkaufgabe 6**
> Fallen dir noch fünf weitere *linking words* ein, die nicht auf dieser Seite stehen?
> (Die Lösung findest du auf Seite 154.)

Skills file

SF 7

Einen Kurzvortrag halten

▶ Unit 4 | p. 122, 123

Um einen guten Kurzvortrag vor der Klasse halten zu können, musst du ihn gut vorbereiten und üben.

Meinen Kurzvortrag vorbereiten

- Nutze verschiedene Medien, um Informationen zu sammeln: Internet, Bücher, Zeitschriften, Zeitungen. Sammle und ordne deine Ideen.

- Ein Kurzvortrag sollte folgendermaßen aufgebaut sein:
  - **Einleitung:** Hier nennst du dein Thema.
  - **Hauptteil:** Nun nennst du deine Hauptpunkte. Dann erzählst du mehr zu jedem Punkt.
  - **Schluss:** Du fasst deine Hauptpunkte zusammen, bedankst dich fürs Zuhören und erkundigst dich, ob jemand Fragen hat.

> I'd like to talk about ...

> To begin with, I'd like to tell you about ...
> To sum up ...

> Thank you for listening.
> Do you have any questions?

- Veranschauliche deinen Vortrag mit einem Poster, Folien mit Bildern oder Gegenständen.

- Mache dir für die Präsentation kurze Notizen auf Karteikarten. Strukturiere deine Notizen genauso wie deine Präsentation. Hebe die wichtigsten Begriffe mit verschiedenen Farben hervor. Du kannst auch kleine Erinnerungen zum Ablauf deines Vortrags notieren.

▶ Skills file 12, p. 167

- Übe deinen Vortrag mehrmals vor dem Spiegel oder mit jemandem. Gebt euch gegenseitig Tipps, wie ihr euch verbessern könnt. Du kannst dich auch selbst mit dem Smartphone aufnehmen. Achte auf die Zeit.

Meinen Kurzvortrag halten

Überprüfe zu Beginn, ob alles vorbereitet ist. Dann schaue dein Publikum an und warte, bis es ruhig ist. Sprich langsam, laut und deutlich. Zeige während deines Vortrags auf Bilder oder dein Poster.

Merkaufgabe 7

Wenn dir etwas nicht einfällt und du Zeit zum Nachdenken benötigst, welche Satzanfänge kannst du dann verwenden, um Zeit zu gewinnen?

(Eine mögliche Lösung findest du auf Seite 154.)

Checkliste Computerpräsentation
- ✓ Wähle ein einfaches Folienlayout.
- ✓ Verwende eine Schriftgröße von mindestens 16 Punkt.
- ✓ Beschränke dich auf wenig Text.
- ✓ Wähle nur ein Bild pro Folie.
- ✓ Schreibe die Adresse der Internetseite dazu, von der du das Bild hast.

SF 8

Hörtexte verstehen

▶ Unit 1 | p. 16   ▶ Unit 2 | p. 44   ▶ Unit 3 | p. 80   ▶ Unit 4 | p. 112

Es kommt in der Begegnung mit dem Englischen sowohl im Alltag als auch im Unterricht darauf an zu verstehen, was gesagt wurde. Gesichtsausdruck und Körpersprache, die beim Verstehen helfen, fehlen meist bei Höraufgaben im Unterricht. Mit ein paar Tipps wird das Verstehen des Gehörten und das Lösen der Aufgaben dazu leichter.

> Nutze die zahlreichen Möglichkeiten, um englische Texte zu hören. Wähle etwas aus, was dir gefällt, z. B. dein Lieblingslied oder dein Lieblingsbuch als Hörbuch auf Englisch. Schaue Filme und Serien auf Englisch. Blende englische Untertitel ein, falls du Probleme beim Verstehen hast. Blende sie aus, wenn du dich sicherer fühlst oder eine Episode schon mehrfach gesehen hast.

Vor dem Hören

Lies dir die Aufgabenstellung genau durch und überlege, was du tun sollst. Finde die Schlüsselwörter in der Aufgabenstellung. Geht es um ein allgemeines Thema oder um Details? Stelle dir die Situation bzw. das Thema vor – was erwartest du? Welche Leute sind beteiligt? Was weißt du schon über das Thema und welche Wörter wären wohl typisch?

Beim Hören

Versuche, zunächst grob zu verstehen, worum es in dem Text geht. Konzentriere dich auf die Schlüsselwörter aus der Aufgabenstellung und achte auch auf Hintergrundgeräusche. Wenn du ein wichtiges Wort nicht verstehst, dann denke an die Situation, um die es geht. Manchmal können dir andere Wörter im Satz oder ähnliche Wörter im Deutschen oder in anderen Sprachen helfen.
Mache dir kurze Notizen. Bleib ruhig, wenn du beim ersten Mal nicht alles verstehst. Du hörst den Text meist zweimal.

> Die Aufgaben stehen in der Regel in der gleichen Reihenfolge, in der die Stellen, die du für die Lösung brauchst, im Hörtext vorkommen.

Nach dem Hören

Vervollständige deine Notizen sofort und vergleiche sie. Lies noch einmal genau durch, was du geschrieben hast. Passen deine Antworten zu den Fragen?
Konzentriere dich beim zweiten Hören auf das, was du beim ersten Mal nicht verstanden hast, und beantworte die Fragen.

▶ Skills file 12, p. 167

> Auch wenn du es nicht geschafft hast, alles aufzuschreiben, kannst du die Informationen noch aus deinem Gedächtnis abrufen.

Merkaufgabe 8

Welche dieser beiden Aufgaben fragt nach allgemeinen Dingen, welche nach Details?

a) *What topic do Ali and Pearl talk about?*
b) *What food and drinks do the kids order?*

(Die Lösung findest du auf Seite 154.)

Skills file

SF 9

Lesetexte verstehen
▶ Unit 1 | p. 26   ▶ Unit 2 | p. 48   ▶ Unit 3 | p. 82   ▶ Unit 4 | p. 118

In diesem Buch findest du viele verschiedene Texte, z. B. Artikel, Dialoge, Geschichten. Die folgenden Tipps helfen dir beim Verstehen der Texte und Lösen der Aufgaben.

Je mehr englische Texte du liest, desto größer wird dein Wortschatz und desto schneller und besser verstehst du Texte.

Vor dem Lesen

Schaue dir die Aufgaben zum Text an und achte auf Schlüsselwörter. Überlege dir, was du tun sollst und welche Lesestrategie gefordert ist.

Lesestrategien: *Skimming* und *Scanning*

Skimming und *Scanning* sind Lesestrategien, die dich bei bestimmten Fragestellungen unterstützen können.

Skimming hilft dir, einen schnellen Überblick über den Inhalt eines Textes zu bekommen. Dafür siehst du dir diese Dinge an:
- Überschrift und Zwischenüberschriften sowie Bilder und Bildunterschriften,
- den ersten Satz jedes Absatzes, der oft die Hauptidee des Absatzes enthält,
- den letzten Absatz des Textes, der oft eine Zusammenfassung des Textes enthält.

Du musst nicht jedes Wort in einem Text verstehen, um den Inhalt zu verstehen. Um einen schnellen Überblick über den Inhalt zu bekommen, überfliegst du den Text.

Scanning hilft dir, nach bestimmten Informationen zu suchen.
- Überlege dir Stichwörter. Suchst du z. B. Öffnungszeiten, könnten das Ziffern oder Wörter sein wie *open*, *hours*, *days*.
- Überfliege den Text und suche nach den Stichwörtern. Du kannst dabei mit dem Finger in einer „S-Form" über den Text gehen.
- Lies die Textstelle, die dein Stichwort enthält, um zu sehen, ob du dort die gesuchten Informationen findest. Wenn nicht, scanne weiter.

Merkaufgabe 9
Schaue dir die Webseite auf S. 92 zu Edinburgh an. Scanne die Informationen nach den Eintrittspreisen der Burg und des Zoos.
(Die Lösung findest du auf S. 154.)

Wenn du mit Texten im Internet arbeitest, kann dein Browser dir viel Arbeit abnehmen: Mit Strg+F (Cmd+F am Mac) kannst du nach deinen Stichworten suchen und nur die Textstellen lesen, in denen ein Stichwort markiert ist.

SF 10

Mediation

▶ Unit 1 | p. 20 ▶ Unit 2 | p. 48 ▶ Unit 3 | p. 77 ▶ Unit 4 | p. 113

In manchen Situationen musst du zwischen zwei Sprachen vermitteln, um Personen zu helfen, die wenig oder kein Englisch oder Deutsch können. Dies nennt man Sprachmittlung *(mediation)*. Du überträgst die wichtigsten Informationen von der einen Sprache in die andere, entweder mündlich oder schriftlich.

Gib nur die wichtigsten Informationen weiter

Lasse unwichtige Wörter und Satzteile weg und bilde kurze und einfache Sätze.

> Normalerweise gibst du nur den wesentlichen Inhalt wieder. Nur bei Gebrauchsanweisungen ist es wichtig, genau zu sein.

Keine Panik vor unbekannten Wörtern

Wenn du für jemandem z. B. während einer Stadtführung vermitteln oder einen englischen Artikel auf Deutsch erläutern möchtest, musst du nicht alle Details übersetzen. Deshalb ist es auch in Ordnung, wenn du nicht jedes Wort, sondern nur die zentrale Aussage verstehst. Wenn du ein Wort nicht kennst, versuche es mit anderen Wörtern zu umschreiben. Wenn dir zum Beispiel das englische Wort für „Onkel" nicht einfällt, kannst du auch sagen *my mum's / dad's brother*.

> **Checkliste Mediation**
> ✓ nur die wichtigen Infos weitergeben
> ✓ unbekannte Wörter umschreiben
> ✓ auf Pronomen achten: An wen wendest du dich?
> ✓ kulturelle Unterschiede bedenken

Achte in Gesprächen auf die Pronomen

Überlege immer, an wen du dich gerade wendest, und passe die Pronomen entsprechend an (siehe Foto).

Frage Sam doch mal, wie ihm sein Tag gefallen hat.

Did you enjoy your day?

Achte auf kulturelle Unterschiede

Überlege, was für dein Gegenüber wichtig ist, um die Situation und die Inhalte verstehen zu können.

Merkaufgabe 10

Du bist mit deiner Familie in Belfast und deine kleine Schwester möchte wissen, worum es auf dem Wandgemälde 1 auf S. 142 geht. Was sagst du ihr?
a) Hier geht es um Straßenkunst in Nordirland.
b) Es geht um Frieden und die Zukunft in Nordirland.
(Die Lösung findest du auf Seite 154.)

Skills file

SF 11

Bilder beschreiben

▶ Intro | p. 12   ▶ Unit 1 | p. 14   ▶ Unit 2 | p. 46

Wie gehe ich vor?

Wenn du ein Bild beschreiben möchtest, dann erwähne zuerst, was du beschreibst, z. B. ein Foto oder ein Poster, und die dargestellte Situation. Danach kümmerst du dich um die Details. Sage, wo sich was im Bild befindet. Wichtige Personen und Dinge befinden sich meist im Vordergrund.

> *I want to talk about this photo/poster/…*
> *It shows a group of people in the street.*

In the foreground/On the right I can see a boy with bagpipes.
In the middle I can see happy people.
On the left there is a man.

Beschreibe die Personen genauer, z. B. die Kleidung oder das Alter: *The piper is young. He is wearing a green top.*

Wer macht was?
The boy is playing the bagpipes. The people are dancing.
One man is clapping his hands.

Wenn du die Position von Dingen oder Menschen näher beschreiben willst, kannst du auch folgende Präpositionen verwenden:

Denke daran: Benutze immer das *present progressive*, wenn du beschreibst, was jemand in einem Bild macht. Andere Dinge im Bild kannst du mit *"You can see …"* oder *"There is/are …"* beschreiben.

behind • between • in front of • next to • over • under

The people are standing next to each other.

Am Ende deiner Beschreibung kannst du noch sagen, was du von der Abbildung hältst und warum:
I like/don't like this picture because …

Merkaufgabe 11

Suche dir ein Foto in Unit 1 und beschreibe es.
Welcher Satz wäre z. B. richtig für Foto C auf S. 16?

a) *The person is playing the guitar.*
b) *The person plays the guitar.*

(Die Lösung findest du auf Seite 154.)

SF 12

Texte markieren und Notizen erstellen

▶ Unit 1 | p. 30   ▶ Unit 2 | p. 64
▶ Unit 3 | p. 77   ▶ Unit 4 | p. 122

Oft ist es hilfreich, wenn du Wesentliches in Texten hervorhebst und dir Notizen machst, z. B. wenn du einen Kurzvortrag vorbereitest oder wenn du den Inhalt eines Textes zusammenfassen oder nacherzählen möchtest.

Textstellen markieren

Auf Kopien von Texten kannst du Informationen markieren, um sie hervorzuheben und einfacher wiederzufinden. Konzentriere dich dabei auf die Informationen, die du laut Aufgabe aus dem Text heraussuchen sollst, wie z. B. die fünf *wh*-Fragen. Markiere nur die wichtigsten Informationen. Oft reichen ein oder zwei Wörter in einem Satz. Zusätzlich kannst du dir zu dem Text auch Notizen machen.

Checkliste Text markieren
Du kannst die wichtigen Stellen
- ✓ mit Textmarker markieren
- ✓ unterstreichen
- ✓ umkreisen
- ✓ mit Symbolen und Abkürzungen markieren (?, !, →, ☺, ☹)
- ✓ durch Notizen am Rand hervorheben

Wie erstelle ich Notizen?

- Verwende für deine Notizen kleine Zettel oder Karteikarten.

- Du kannst deine Notizen z. B. in einer Tabelle sammeln, in der du *wh*-Fragewörter *(what, where, when, who, why, how)* als Überschriften verwendest. Eine solche Tabelle ist gut, wenn du Fragen zu einem (Hör-)Text beantwortest, weil sie sehr strukturiert ist.

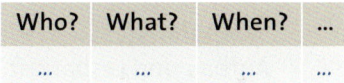

Who?	What?	When?	…
…	…	…	…

- Ein Notizzettel ist gut, wenn du möglichst frei sprechen möchtest, z. B. bei einem kleinen Vortrag.
Schreibe deine Notizen gleich in der Reihenfolge auf, in der du deine Gedanken vortragen möchtest. Strukturiere deine Notizen optisch, z. B. durch Überschriften und Absätze.

My London sight
- *what it is and where it is*
- *what to see and what to do*
- *history, stories and fun facts*
- *when it's open and how much it costs*

- Schreibe keine ganzen Sätze, sondern das, was für dich wichtig ist, in Stichpunkten auf *(keywords)*.
  – Schreibe Ziffern anstelle von Zahlwörtern, z. B. „15" statt „fifteen", und verwende Abkürzungen, z. B. „Aug" statt „August", „+" statt „and", „/" statt „or".
  – Verwende Symbole und Zeichnungen anstelle von Stichwörtern, z. B. Smileys für Gefühle, Flaggen für Länder, Strichzeichnungen für Personen usw.

Es gibt auch Apps, mit denen du deine Notizen anfertigen kannst, wenn es deine Eltern erlauben. Das bietet sich vor allem dann an, wenn du über einen längeren Zeitraum Notizen machst, die du bearbeiten und ergänzen möchtest, wie z. B. bei einem kleinen Projekt. Du kannst deine Notizen zu Hause am Computer anfangen und später auf dem Handy ergänzen.

Merkaufgabe 12

Probiere es gleich aus. Suche dir ein Wunschurlaubsziel für den nächsten Sommer und mache dir Notizen dazu.

one hundred and sixty-seven

Skills file

SF 13

Texte überprüfen und verbessern

▶ Unit 1 | p. 25 ▶ Unit 3 | p. 83
▶ Unit 4 | p. 117

Ein Text ist noch nicht fertig, wenn du ihn zu Ende geschrieben hast. Du solltest ihn noch mehrmals durchlesen bzw. in Partnerkorrektur durchlesen lassen und auf folgende Punkte achten:

Überprüfe und korrigiere deinen Text

Mache nach dem Schreiben eine kurze Pause. Dann fange an, den Text inhaltlich und sprachlich zu verbessern. Prüfe:
- Hast du irgendwo ein Wort vergessen?
- Sind die Sätze gut verständlich?
- Ist die Reihenfolge der Sätze sinnvoll?
- Hast du Absätze gemacht?
- Hast du *linking words* (Bindewörter) benutzt?
- Hast du Personen, Orte oder Dinge mithilfe von Adjektiven beschrieben?

Beim Korrekturlesen empfehlen sich mehrere Durchgänge, in denen du nacheinander auf folgende Dinge achtest:
- Sprache: Stimmen Rechtschreibung, Zeichensetzung, Grammatik?
- Aufbau und Lesbarkeit: Hat dein Text eine logische Struktur, ist er verständlich und liest sich flüssig?
- Ausdruck: Verwendest du eine abwechslungsreiche und lebendige Sprache und vermeidest Wiederholungen?
- Gestaltung: Benötigst du eine Überschrift? Hast du Abschnitte eingefügt? Hast du bei einem Brief oder einer E-Mail an Anrede und Schluss gedacht?
- typische Fehlerquellen wie …
  – Groß- und Kleinschreibung, denn im Englischen schreibt man fast alles klein.
  – die richtige Zeitform: Schreibst du über die Gegenwart? Oder über Dinge, die du regelmäßig machst? Dann brauchst du das *simple present* (I *often go* to the swimming pool.). Oder schreibst du über Sachen, die schon passiert sind? Dann brauchst du das *simple past* (*Yesterday* I *went* to the swimming pool.).

Checkliste typische Fehlerquellen
- ✓ Groß- und Kleinschreibung
- ✓ unregelmäßige Pluralformen *(child – children, man – men)*
- ✓ gleicher Klang, aber unterschiedliche Schreibweisen und Bedeutungen *(to – too – two, their – there – they're)*
- ✓ Präpositionen *(by train, in the picture, on the bus)*
- ✓ unregelmäßige Verben (siehe die Liste auf S. 272–273)
- ✓ Wörter mit stummen Buchstaben *(climb, know)*

▶ Wichtige Schreibregeln im Englischen, p. 185

Merkaufgabe 13

Probiere es gleich aus. Nimm dir einen englischen Text, den du in letzter Zeit geschrieben hast. Lies ihn dir zweimal durch und überprüfe ihn anhand der obigen Schritte.

Language file

Inhalt

		Seite
LF 1 (Rev)	Die Wortstellung	169
LF 2 (Rev)	Die einfache Gegenwart	170
LF 3 (Rev)	Die Verlaufsform der Gegenwart	172
LF 4 (Rev)	Die einfache Vergangenheit	173
LF 5 (Rev)	Die Zukunft mit *will*	174
LF 6	Bedingungssätze Typ 1	175
LF 7	Die Steigerung der Adjektive	175
LF 8	Modale Hilfsverben	176
LF 9	Reflexivpronomen	178
LF 10	Adverbien der Art und Weise	178
LF 11	Das *present perfect*	180
LF 12	Possessivbegleiter und Possessivpronomen	181
LF 13	Die Zukunft mit *going to*	182
LF 14	Relativsätze	183
	Grammatical terms	184
	Wichtige Schreibregeln im Englischen	185

Erklärfilm: Dieses Symbol zeigt dir, dass du einen Erklärfilm zu diesem Thema in der App findest.

LF 1 — Revision

Die Wortstellung *(Word order)*

a) **Orts- und Zeitangaben** *(Phrases of place and time)*

Time		Place or time
	Put the books	on the table.
	I'm very busy	today.
Yesterday	I was bored.	
Last year	we got married.	

		Place	Time
Orla came		here	on Friday.
My dad moved		to Dresden	in 2020.

Ortsangaben (*on the table, at school* usw.) stehen meist am Ende des Satzes (häufig nach Verb und Objekt).
Zeitangaben (*today, yesterday, at 2 o'clock* usw.) stehen ganz am Anfang oder ganz am Ende des Satzes.

Beim Zusammentreffen von Orts- und Zeitangaben in einem Satz gilt im Englischen die Regel: **O**rt vor **Z**eit.

b) **Häufigkeitsadverbien** *(Adverbs of frequency)*

	Frequency	
Pearl	always	goes out at weekends.
I	sometimes	feel unhappy.

Häufigkeitsadverbien (*always, often, sometimes, rarely, never* usw.) stehen im Englischen meist direkt vor dem Hauptverb (*go, feel* usw.).

one hundred and sixty-nine **169**

Language file

LF 2 Revision

Erklärfilm

Die einfache Gegenwart *(The simple present)*

I always get up at 7 o'clock.
Ich stehe immer um 7 Uhr auf.
My sister doesn't usually go to parties.
Meine Schwester geht normalerweise nicht auf Partys.
We all love Indian food.
Wir alle lieben indisches Essen.
Where do you live?
Wo wohnen Sie?

> Mit dem *simple present* sagst du, was oft, regelmäßig, jeden Tag oder auch selten oder nie geschieht oder was immer so ist (Dauerzustände).
>
> Oft findest du diese Signalwörter in Sätzen im *simple present*: *always*, *never*, *often*, *rarely*, *sometimes*, *usually*.

a) Bejahte Aussagesätze *(Positive statements)*

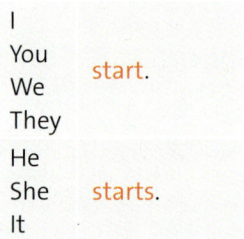

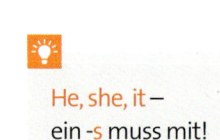
He, she, it – ein -s muss mit!

> Bei der 3. Person Singular (*he*, *she*, *it* oder *your dad*, *Lily* usw.) musst du immer ein *-s* ans Verb anhängen.
>
> ❗ Manchmal gibt es Besonderheiten, z. B.:
> do → does   tidy → tidies
> go → goes   wash → washes
> have → has   watch → watches

b) Verneinte Aussagesätze *(Negative statements)*

| I / You / We / They | don't start. |
| He / She / It | doesn't start. |

| We | don't do the shopping online. |
| Steve | doesn't do sports. |

> Aussagen im *simple present* musst du mit *don't* oder *doesn't* verneinen. Das Verb steht dann immer im Infinitiv (der Grundform): *He doesn't start*.
>
> ❗ Auch das Vollverb *do* („machen", „tun", „ausführen") verneint man im *simple present* mit *don't / doesn't*.

Rachel doesn't live here any more.

LF 2 Revision

c) Entscheidungsfragen und Kurzantworten *(Yes/No-questions and short answers)*

Do	I / you / we / they / your parents	like music?
Does	he / your dad / she / Lily / it	like music?

Bejahte Antwort	Verneinte Antwort
Yes, I do.	No, I don't.
Yes, you do.	No, you don't.
Yes, he/she/it does.	No, he/she/it doesn't.
Yes, we do.	No, we don't.
Yes, they do.	No, they don't.

Fragen, auf die man mit „Ja" oder „Nein" antworten kann, heißen Entscheidungsfragen. Sie beginnen mit *Do* oder *Does*.
Mit *I, you, we, they* verwendest du *Do*.
Mit *he, she, it* verwendest du *Does*.

Es ist unhöflich, auf Entscheidungsfragen nur mit *yes* oder *no* zu antworten. Besser ist eine Kurzantwort.

Do you like sauerkraut? — *Yes, I do.*

d) Fragen mit Fragewörtern *(Questions with question words)*

Where do the pets sleep?
Wo schlafen die Tiere?
Who does Luca love?
Wen liebt Luca?
What do you think?
Was meinst du?

Who loves Luca?
Wer liebt Luca?
What makes you sad?
Was macht dich traurig?

Auch Fragen mit Fragewörtern stellst du mit *do* oder *does*. Das Fragewort steht wie im Deutschen am Anfang.

! Wenn mit *Who* oder *What* nach dem Subjekt des Satzes gefragt wird, bildest du die Frage <u>ohne</u> *do/does*.

Why do you answer every question with another question, Ms Ratby? — *Do I?*

one hundred and seventy-one **171**

Language file

LF 3 Revision

Die Verlaufsform der Gegenwart *(The present progressive)*

I'm reading a comic.
Ich lese gerade einen Comic.
Dad is cooking dinner.
Papa macht gerade das Abendessen.
What are you doing at the moment?
Was machst du jetzt gerade?
I'm working.
Ich bin gerade am Arbeiten. /
Ich arbeite gerade.

Mit dem *present progressive* sagst du, was jemand jetzt gerade tut. Damit beschreibst du auch, was auf Bildern passiert.

Folgende Zeitangaben findest du oft in Sätzen im *present progressive*:
now, at the moment, today.

Im Deutschen sagst du meist „Ich bin gerade am / beim ..." oder „Ich ... gerade.".

a) **Bejahte und verneinte Aussagesätze** *(Positive and negative statements)*

Bejahte Aussagesätze	
I'm	
You're	
He's / She's / It's	working.
We're	
They're	

Verneinte Aussagesätze	
I'm not	
You aren't	
He / She / It isn't	working.
We aren't	
They aren't	

Das *present progressive* besteht aus zwei Teilen: Form von *be* + *ing*-Form des Verbs.

am ('m)	
are ('re)	
is ('s)	
Verneinung:	+ *ing*-Form des Verbs
am not ('m not)	
is not (isn't)	
are not (aren't)	

❗ Bei Verben, die auf *-e* enden, fällt das *-e* bei der *ing*-Form weg:
hav*e* → hav*ing*; mak*e* → mak*ing*;
giv*e* → giv*ing*

❗ Bei einigen Verben wird der letzte Buchstabe verdoppelt, z. B.:
pla*n* → pla*nn*ing; sto*p* → sto*pp*ing;
si*t* → si*tt*ing

I'm singing in the rain.

b) **Fragen und Antworten** *(Questions and answers)*

Am I	working?	No, you aren't.
Are you		Yes, I am.
Where is he	going?	Home.

In Fragen vertauscht man das Subjekt und *am / is / are*:
I am → *am I?*

LF 4 Revision

Die einfache Vergangenheit *(The simple past)*   ▶ Unit 1 | p. 25, 41

Yesterday Dad and I visited Grandma.
Gestern haben Papa und ich Oma besucht.
Last week I didn't have any homework.
Letzte Woche hatte ich keine Hausaufgaben auf.
Did you watch the fireworks last night?
Hast du gestern Abend das Feuerwerk gesehen?

Mit dem *simple past* sprichst du über Dinge, die in der Vergangenheit geschehen sind.

Du verwendest es oft mit Zeitangaben wie *yesterday, last week / last year / last summer, two weeks ago, in 2022*.

a) Bejahte Aussagesätze *(Positive statements)*

I / You He / She / It We / They	helped.

Die Vergangenheitsform der Verben ist für alle Personen gleich:
- Bei regelmäßigen Verben hängst du *-ed* an das Verb: *walk → walked*.
- Bei Verben, die auf *-e* enden, wird nur *-d* angehängt: *arrive → arrived*.
- Einige Konsonanten werden verdoppelt: *plan → planned; stop → stopped*.

🟥 Unregelmäßige Formen musst du lernen: *go → went; have → had; see → saw*.
Du kannst sie auf S. 272–273 nachschlagen.

I had a fight last night.

b) Verneinte Aussagesätze *(Negative statements)*

I / You He / She / It We / They	didn't help.

Wenn du sagen willst, dass etwas nicht geschah, setzt du *didn't* vor das Verb. Das Verb steht dann immer im Infinitiv (der Grundform), z. B. *help*, nicht *helped*.

c) Entscheidungsfragen und Kurzantworten *(Yes/No-questions and short answers)*

Did	I / you he / she / it we / they	help?	Yes, I did. Yes, she did. No, they didn't.

Entscheidungsfragen im *simple past* bildest du mit *Did* und dem Infinitiv (der Grundform) des Verbs, z. B. *help*, nicht *helped*.
Auch in Kurzantworten verwendest du *did* oder *didn't* (ohne folgenden Infinitiv).

one hundred and seventy-three **173**

Language file

LF 4 | Revision

d) Fragen mit Fragewörtern *(Questions with question words)*

What		she	watch?
When	did	it	finish?
Where		they	go?

Who said that?
Wer hat das gesagt?
What made you unhappy?
Was hat dich unglücklich gemacht?

Auch bei Fragen mit Fragewörtern verwendest du *did* und das Verb im Infinitiv, z. B. *watch, go,* nicht *watched, went*.

❗ Wenn mit *Who* oder *What* nach dem Subjekt des Satzes gefragt wird, bildest du die Frage <u>ohne</u> *did*.

LF 5 | Revision

Erklärfilm

Die Zukunft mit *will* (The will-future)

▶ Unit 1 | p. 17, 39

I think you'll have a great party.
Ich glaube, du wirst eine tolle Party haben.
Wait – I'll help you.
Warte – ich helfe dir.

Du verwendest das *will-future*
- für Dinge, die in der Zukunft vermutlich geschehen werden. Die Sätze beginnen oft mit *I think, maybe, I'm sure*.
- für spontane Entschlüsse und Hilfsangebote.

a) Bejahte und verneinte Aussagesätze *(Positive and negative statements)*

Bejahte Aussagesätze		
It	will ('ll)	be sunny tomorrow.

Verneinte Aussagesätze		
It	will not (won't)	be sunny tomorrow.

Du bildest das *will-future* mit *will* und dem Infinitiv (der Grundform) des Verbs.
Die Kurzform von *will* ist *'ll*.
Die Kurzform von *will not* ist *won't*.

I'll tidy my room later.

b) Fragen und Antworten *(Questions and answers)*

Will it be sunny?	Yes, it will.
	No, it won't.
What will the world look like in 100 years?	It will look quite different.

In Fragen vertauscht man das Subjekt und *will/won't*:
it will → will it?
it will not → will it not? / it won't → won't it?

LF 6

Bedingungssätze Typ 1 *(Conditional sentences type 1)* ▶ Unit 1 | p. 19

If you send me a message, I'll come.
Wenn du mir eine Nachricht schickst, komme ich.
If it rains tomorrow, we won't play football.
Wenn es morgen regnet, spielen wir nicht Fußball.

Mit Bedingungssätzen sagst du, was unter bestimmten Bedingungen geschehen wird.

Sie bestehen aus zwei Teilen:
- einem Nebensatz mit *if (if-clause)* im *simple present*, der die Bedingung nennt,
- einem Hauptsatz *(main clause)* mit *will*, *'ll* oder *won't*, der die Folge nennt.

We won't play football if it rains tomorrow.
Wir spielen nicht Fußball, wenn es morgen regnet.

Der *if*-Teil kann auch nach dem Hauptsatz stehen.

LF 7

Die Steigerung der Adjektive *(Comparison of adjectives)*

a) **Revision** Steigerung mit *-er / -est (Comparison with -er / -est)* ▶ Unit 2 | p. 46, 69

Ella is taller than Pete.
Ella ist größer als Pete.
The airport is busier during the holidays.
Der Flughafen ist in den Ferien stärker ausgelastet.

The biggest tree in the park is 90 years old.
Der größte Baum im Park ist 90 Jahre alt.
The earliest train leaves at 7 a.m.
Der früheste Zug fährt um 7 Uhr morgens.

Adjektive kann man steigern und in Vergleichen benutzen.
Bei einsilbigen Adjektiven und bei zweisilbigen Adjektiven, die auf *-y* enden, hängst du *-er / -est* an das Adjektiv:
- *tall → taller*
  (Komparativ = erste Steigerungsform)
- *tall → (the) tallest*
  (Superlativ = höchste Steigerungsform)

! Bei einigen Adjektiven musst du bei der Schreibung aufpassen (z. B. bei *big → bigger / biggest; hot → hotter / hottest* oder *busy → busier / busiest; early → earlier / earliest*).

The weather today is better than yesterday.
Das Wetter ist heute besser als gestern.
The worst part of the film was the ending.
Der schlimmste Teil des Films war das Ende.

! Beachte diese Ausnahmen:
good → better → (the) best
bad → worse → (the) worst

Language file

LF 7

b) `Revision` Steigerung mit *more / most* (Comparison with *more / most*) ▶ Unit 2 | p. 46, 69

Thea's job is more interesting than Leo's.
Theas Job ist interessanter als der von Leo.
The most expensive house in the world is Buckingham Palace.
Das teuerste Haus der Welt ist der Buckingham Palace.

Bei längeren (vor allem dreisilbigen) Adjektiven setzt man *more/most* vor das Adjektiv:
- *expensive* → *more expensive*
  (Komparativ = erste Steigerungsform)
- *interesting* → *most interesting*
  (Superlativ = höchste Steigerungsform)

c) `Challenge` Durch *and* verbundene Komparative *(Comparatives with* and*)* ▶ Unit 2 | p. 70

Our maths tests are getting harder and harder / more and more difficult.
Unsere Mathearbeiten werden immer schwieriger.

Zwei durch *and* verbundene Komparative entsprechen dem deutschen „immer schwieriger", „immer härter", „immer besser" usw.

LF 8

Modale Hilfsverben *(Modal verbs)*

Can you help me, please? – Yes, I can.
She must wait for the next bus.
He's ill and shouldn't go to school.

Can, could, must, needn't, may, might und *should* sind modale Hilfsverben. Sie haben nur <u>eine</u> Form und stehen mit dem Infinitiv (der Grundform) eines Verbs.

a) Erlaubnis, Verbot *(Permission, prohibition)* ▶ Unit 2 | p. 49, 71

Can I open the window?
Kann ich das Fenster aufmachen?
May / Could I have some more tea, please?
Könnte ich bitte noch etwas Tee haben?
Mum says I can't / mustn't go to the party.
Mama sagt, ich darf nicht zu der Party.
You aren't allowed to take photos here.
Sie dürfen hier keine Fotos machen.

`Challenge` I was allowed to stay up late last night. You'll be allowed to bring your own drinks to the concert tomorrow.

Mit *can* sagst du, was jemand tun darf. Wenn du sehr höflich fragen möchtest, ob du etwas tun darfst, verwendest du *may* oder *could*.
Um zu sagen, dass jemand etwas <u>nicht</u> tun darf, verwendest du *can't* oder *mustn't*.
Bei Erlaubnissen und Verboten kannst du auch *be (not) allowed to* verwenden.

Be (not) allowed to hat auch Vergangenheits- und Zukunftsformen.

176 one hundred and seventy-six

LF 8

b) Notwendigkeit, Zwang *(Necessity, compulsion)* ▶ Unit 2 | p. 49, 71

You must do your homework.
Du musst deine Hausaufgaben machen.
I have to go now, but I don't have to run.
Ich muss jetzt gehen, aber ich muss nicht rennen.
She needn't worry. Everything is OK.
Sie muss sich keine Sorgen machen. Es ist alles OK.

Challenge

He was so ill. We had to call the doctor.
You won't have to wait.

Mit *must* oder *have to* sagst du, was jemand tun muss.
Mit *don't/doesn't have to* oder *needn't* sagst du, was jemand nicht zu tun braucht.

Must I brush my teeth? — *No, you needn't.*

Have to hat auch Vergangenheits- und Zukunftsformen.

c) Fähigkeit *(Ability)* ▶ Unit 2 | p. 71

I can bake, but I can't cook.
Ich kann backen, aber ich kann nicht kochen.

Challenge

Is your grandpa able to speak English?
I was able to dance well when I was young.
We'll soon be able to speak Spanish.

Mit *can/can't* sagst du oft, was jemand tun oder nicht tun kann.

Mit *be (not) able to* kannst du ebenfalls über eine Fähigkeit sprechen. *Be (not) able to* hat auch Vergangenheits- und Zukunftsformen.

d) Möglichkeit *(Possibility)* ▶ Unit 2 | p. 50

It may rain.
Es könnte regnen. / Vielleicht regnet es.
They might get married soon.
Sie werden / könnten vielleicht bald heiraten.
This could be a possible solution.
Dies könnte eine mögliche Lösung sein.

Du kannst *may*, *might* und *could* auch verwenden, um zu vermuten, was möglich sein könnte.

e) Empfehlung, Rat *(Advice)* ▶ Unit 2 | p. 51

You should take your jacket – it's cold.
Du solltest deine Jacke mitnehmen …
You shouldn't eat so much sugar.
Du solltest nicht so viel Zucker essen.

Mit *should/shouldn't* rätst du jemandem, etwas zu tun oder nicht zu tun.

Language file

LF 9

Reflexivpronomen *(Reflexive pronouns)* ▶ Unit 2 | p. 52

a) Pronomen auf *-self / -selves* (Pronouns ending in *-self / -selves*)

He has cut himself.
Er hat sich geschnitten.
We can look after ourselves.
Wir können uns um uns selbst kümmern.

I wash myself.	We wash ourselves.
You wash yourself.	You wash yourselves.
He washes himself.	They wash themselves.
She washes herself.	
It washes itself.	

Reflexivpronomen enden auf *-self* oder *-selves*. Sie zeigen an, dass sich die Handlung auf die Person bezieht, die sie ausführt.
He washed the baby.   Er wusch das Baby.
He washed himself.   Er wusch sich selbst.
Merke dir diese Ausdrücke:
Help yourself.   Greif zu. / Bediene dich.
Enjoy yourself!   Viel Spaß!

b) *each other*

We often help each other.
Wir helfen uns oft (gegenseitig).

Each other entspricht „uns / euch / sich" im Sinne von „uns / euch / sich gegenseitig".

LF 10

Erklärfilm

Adverbien der Art und Weise *(Adverbs of manner)*

a) **Revision** Verwendung und Bildung *(Use and form)* ▶ Unit 3 | p. 78

Please speak slowly and clearly.
Bitte sprich langsam und deutlich.
Sarah ate her breakfast quickly.
Sarah aß ihr Frühstück schnell auf.

Adjektiv	Adverb	Adjektiv	Adverb
clear	clearly	angry	angrily
nervous	nervously	happy	happily
quick	quickly	full	fully

You speak English very well.
Du sprichst sehr gut Englisch.
Rhona worked hard.
Rhona hat hart gearbeitet.
Grace can run fast.
Grace kann schnell laufen.

Adverbien der Art und Weise beschreiben, wie man etwas tut oder wie etwas geschieht. Sie beschreiben also ein Verb. Vergleiche:

Adjektiv		Adverb
a careful driver	→	she drives carefully
a slow worker	→	he works slowly

Die meisten Adverbien bildet man durch Anfügen von *-ly* an ein Adjektiv.

❗ Manchmal gibt es Unregelmäßigkeiten bei der Schreibung (z. B. *angrily* oder *fully*).

❗ Beachte diese Ausnahmen:
- Das Adverb zu *good* ist *well*.
- Bei *hard* und *fast* sind Adjektiv und Adverb gleich.

178   one hundred and seventy-eight

LF 10

b) **Challenge** Adjektiv nach Zustandsverben *(Adjective after state verbs)* ▶ Unit 3 | p. 103

The driver was careful.
Die Fahrerin war vorsichtig.
Mmm! This tastes good!
Mmm! Das schmeckt gut!
I don't feel happy.
Ich fühle mich nicht glücklich.
This sounds nice.
Das klingt gut. / Das hört sich gut an.

Nach Verben, die einen Zustand oder eine Eigenschaft beschreiben („wie jemand oder etwas ist"), steht ein Adjektiv, kein Adverb. Solche Verben sind *be, become, feel* („sich fühlen"), *look* („aussehen"), *seem, smell, sound, taste*.

! Beachte:
Tätigkeit: Verb + Adverb
She looked at me angrily.
Sie sah mich wütend an.

Zustand: Verb + Adjektiv
She looked angry.
Sie sah wütend aus.

Mmm. This tastes good.
You cooked it so well.

c) **Challenge** Die Steigerung der Adverbien *(Comparison of adverbs)* ▶ Unit 3 | p. 103

Can you draw it more carefully?
Kannst du es genauer zeichnen?
Which bird sings (the) most beautifully?
Welcher Vogel singt am schönsten?

Adverbien kann man ebenso wie Adjektive steigern und in Vergleichen benutzen.
Bei *-ly*-Adverbien bildet man die erste Steigerungsform (Komparativ) mit *more* vor dem Adverb und die höchste Steigerungsform (Superlativ) mit *most* vor dem Adverb.

I can run faster than my brother.
Ich kann schneller laufen als mein Bruder.
Which animal runs (the) fastest?
Welches Tier läuft am schnellsten?

Bei kurzen (meist einsilbigen) Adverbien hängt man *-er* für den Komparativ und *-est* für den Superlativ an das Adverb.

Milena speaks English better than me.
Milena spricht besser Englisch als ich.

! Merke dir diese Ausnahmen:
- well → better → (the) best
- badly → worse → (the) worst

one hundred and seventy-nine

Language file

LF 11

Das *present perfect* *(The present perfect)*

I have never eaten sushi.
Ich habe noch nie Sushi gegessen.
Has Leo ever been to Rome?
Ist Leo schon mal in Rom gewesen? /
War Leo schon mal in Rom?

💡

Ivy has been to Rome.
Ivy ist schon mal in Rom gewesen
(und kennt die Stadt daher, aber sie ist
jetzt nicht dort).
Ivy has gone to Rome.
Ivy ist nach Rom gefahren (und ist
jetzt dort).

Mit dem *present perfect* sagst du, dass jemand etwas – irgendwann – in der Zeit bis jetzt gemacht oder nicht gemacht hat. Der genaue Zeitpunkt ist unwichtig oder unbekannt und wird nicht genannt.

Oft hat die Handlung Auswirkungen auf die Gegenwart.

Signalwörter: *already, just, ever, never, not yet, once, twice, lots of times*

a) **Revision** Bejahte und verneinte Aussagesätze *(Positive and negative statements)* ▶ Unit 3 | p. 81

Bejahte Aussagesätze

I / You / We / They	have ('ve) started early.
He / She / It	has ('s) started early.

Verneinte Aussagesätze

I / You / We / They	haven't started early.
He / She / It	hasn't started early.

Das *present perfect* besteht aus zwei Teilen:
have / has + *past participle*-Form des Verbs.

have ('ve) / has ('s) / Verneinung: have not (haven't) / has not (hasn't)	+ *past participle*

Wie bildest du das *past participle*?
• Bei regelmäßigen Verben hängst du *-ed* an das Verb: *walk → walked*.
• Bei Verben, die auf *-e* enden, wird nur *-d* angehängt: *arrive → arrived*.

❗ Unregelmäßige *past participle*-Formen musst du lernen, z. B.:
be → been   do → done   eat → eaten
go → gone   have → had   see → seen
Du kannst sie in der dritten Spalte der *List of irregular verbs* auf S. 272–273 nachschlagen.

I've learned so much this year.

LF 11

b) Revision — Fragen und Antworten *(Questions and answers)* ▶ Unit 3 | p. 81

Has it started yet?	Yes, it has. / No, it hasn't.
Where has he been?	At school.

In Fragen vertauscht man das Subjekt und *have/has*:
it has → has it?

c) Das *present perfect* mit *since* oder *for* *(The present perfect with since or for)* ▶ Unit 3 | p. 83

We have lived in this flat since 2023.
Wir wohnen seit 2023 in dieser Wohnung.
Ella has been in our class for two months.
Ella ist seit zwei Monaten in unserer Klasse.

Mit dem *present perfect* sagst du auch, wie lange etwas schon andauert. Dann verwendest du:
- *since* zur Angabe eines Zeitpunkts: *since* 3 o'clock, *since* May.
- *for* zur Angabe eines Zeitraums: *for* ten weeks, *for* two days.

I've had this phone for 20 years.

LF 12

Possessivbegleiter und Possessivpronomen
(Possessive determiners and possessive pronouns) ▶ Unit 4 | p. 108

This is my phone. It's mine.
Das ist mein Handy. Es ist meins. / Es gehört mir.
I think it's her bike. It's hers.
Ich glaube, es ist ihr Fahrrad. Es ist ihrs.
I've found this book. Is it yours?
Ich habe dieses Buch gefunden. Ist es deins?

mit Nomen	ohne Nomen
my game	mine
your game	yours
his / her / its game	his / hers / its
our game	ours
your game	yours
their game	theirs

Possessivbegleiter und Possessivpronomen zeigen an, wem etwas gehört.

It's mine.

Die Possessivbegleiter *my*, *your*, *his*, *her*, *its*, *our*, *their* werden vor einem Nomen (z. B. *game*) gebraucht.

Die Possessivpronomen *mine*, *yours*, *his*, *hers*, *its*, *ours*, *theirs* stehen allein, ohne Nomen.

Language file

LF 13

Erklärfilm

Die Zukunft mit *going to* (The going to-future)

We're going to have a picnic on Sunday.
Wir haben vor, am Sonntag zu picknicken.
Are you going to come to the party?
Wirst du zur Party kommen?

> Mit *going to* … sagst du, was du vorhast oder planst.
>
> *Going to* hat hier nichts mit dem deutschen „gehen" zu tun, sondern bedeutet „werden" oder „wollen".

a) Revision — Bejahte und verneinte Aussagesätze (Positive and negative statements) ▶ Unit 4 | p. 134

Bejahte Aussagesätze

I'm		
You're		
He's / She's / It's	going to	ask.
We're		
They're		

Verneinte Aussagesätze

I'm not		
You aren't		
He / She / It isn't	going to	ask.
We aren't		
They aren't		

> Das *going to*-future besteht aus drei Teilen: Form von *be* + *going to* + Verb.
>
> | am ('m) / are ('re) / is ('s) Verneinung: am not ('m not) / is not (isn't) / are not (aren't) | + *going to* | + Verb |
>
> Das Verb bleibt immer im Infinitiv:
> *I'm going to watch a video.*
>
> ❗ Nicht: *I'm going to watching a video.*

b) Revision — Fragen und Antworten (Questions and answers) ▶ Unit 4 | p. 111, 134

| Are you | going to | ask? | No, I'm not. |
| Where is he | going to | live? | In York. |

> In Fragen vertauscht man das Subjekt und *am / is / are*:
> *you are going to → are you going to?*

c) Challenge — Vorhersagen mit *going to* (Predictions with *going to*) ▶ Unit 4 | p. 135

Look at all this traffic. We're going to be late.
… Wir werden zu spät kommen.
I'm so excited. It's going to be fun.
… Das wird ein Spaß.
The sky is clear. It isn't going to rain today.
… Es wird heute nicht regnen.

> Mit *going to* … kannst du auch sagen, was wahrscheinlich bald passieren wird.

LF 14

Relativsätze *(Relative clauses)*

a) Relativpronomen *(Relative pronouns)* ▶ Unit 4 | p. 116

Are you the boy *who* won first prize?
Bist du der Junge, der den ersten Preis gewonnen hat?
This is the girl *who* we met yesterday.
Das ist das Mädchen, das wir gestern getroffen haben.

I know a shop *which* sells really cool shoes.
Ich kenne einen Laden, der richtig coole Schuhe verkauft.
The game *which* you gave me is great.
Das Spiel, das du mir geschenkt hast, ist toll.

This is the girl *that* I told you about.
Das ist das Mädchen, von dem ich dir erzählt habe.
The phone *that* she uses is new.
Das Handy, das sie benutzt, ist neu.

> Mit Relativsätzen kannst du zusätzliche Informationen über eine Person oder eine Sache geben. Sie werden in der Regel durch die Relativpronomen *who*, *which* oder *that* eingeleitet:
> - Für Personen verwendest du *who*.
> - Für Dinge benutzt du *which*.
> - Das Relativpronomen *that* kann für Personen und Dinge stehen.
> - Bei Tieren verwendest du *which* oder *that*. Nur für Tiere mit Namen (z. B. Haustiere) verwendest du *who*.
>
> Die meisten englischen Relativsätze werden **nicht** durch **ein Komma** vor *who*, *which*, *that* abgetrennt, anders als im Deutschen. Man nennt sie *defining relative clauses* (bestimmende Relativsätze).

b) `Challenge` **Relativsätze ohne Relativpronomen** *(Contact clauses)* ▶ Unit 4 | p. 137

This is the girl *we met yesterday*.
The game *you gave me* is great.
This is the girl *I told you about*.
The phone *she uses* is new.

This is the girl who phoned yesterday.
Wenn das Relativpronomen direkt vor dem Verb steht, dann ist es Subjekt und darf nicht weggelassen werden.

> Das Relativpronomen kann als Subjekt oder Objekt des Relativsatzes stehen:
> Subjekt: *the boy who asked* → *he* asked
> der Junge, der fragte
> Objekt: *the boy (who) I asked* → *I asked him*
> der Junge, den ich fragte
>
> Wenn das Relativpronomen nicht Subjekt, sondern Objekt ist, kann man es weglassen. (Im Deutschen ist das nicht möglich.) Relativsätze ohne Relativpronomen nennt man *contact clauses*.

This is Rita, the rat who won the marathon. It's the third marathon she has run.

Language file

Grammatical terms *(Grammatische Fachbegriffe in diesem Buch)*

adjective	das Adjektiv	old, good, popular
adverb of frequency	das Häufigkeitsadverb	often, always, sometimes, rarely, never
adverb of manner	das Adverb der Art und Weise	well, carefully, quietly, angrily
article	der Artikel	**a**/**the** book, **an**/**the** apple
comparative	der Komparativ	older, better, more popular
comparison	die Steigerung	old – older – (the) oldest
conditional sentence	der Bedingungssatz	If it's rainy, I'll stay at home.
contact clause	der Relativsatz ohne Relativpronomen	a boy I know; things we eat
going to-future	das Futur mit *going to*	I'm going to eat …; We're going to watch …
if-clause	der Nebensatz mit *if*	If it rains, …
infinitive	der Infinitiv (Grundform)	(to) do, (to) go, (to) love
irregular adjective / adverb / verb	das unregelmäßige Adjektiv / Adverb / Verb	adjective: bad – **worse** – **worst**; adverb: good – **well**; verb: (to) do – **did** – **done**
long form	die Langform	I am, we do not, you are
main clause	der Hauptsatz	If it rains, **I won't go out**.
modal verb	das modale Hilfsverb	can, must, shouldn't
negative	die verneinte Form	**don't** go, **can't** go, **aren't** going, **hasn't** gone
noun	das Nomen / Substantiv	friend, car, competition
object	das Objekt	I like **cats**.
past participle	das Partizip Perfekt (3. Form)	loved, eaten, seen, done, gone
personal pronoun	das Personalpronomen	I, you, he, she, it, we, they
plural	der Plural, die Mehrzahl	book**s**, child**ren**, potato**es**, stor**ies**
possessive determiner	der Possessivbegleiter	my, your, his, her, its, our, their
possessive pronoun	das Possessivpronomen	mine, yours, his, hers, ours, theirs
preposition	die Präposition	**in** the house, **on** the desk, **near** the river
present perfect	das Perfekt	He has gone.; Have you seen?
present progressive	die Verlaufsform der Gegenwart	I'm speak**ing**, she's look**ing**, we're talk**ing**, they **are**n't listen**ing**
reflexive pronoun	das Reflexivpronomen	myself, yourself, ourselves
regular verb	das regelmäßige Verb	(to) move – moved – moved
relative clause	der Relativsatz	someone **who loves**, a shop **which sells**
relative pronoun	das Relativpronomen	who, which, that
short answer	die Kurzantwort	Yes, I do. / No, I'm not. / Yes, she does.
short form	die Kurzform	I**'m**, we **don't**, you**'re**
simple past	die einfache Vergangenheit	it was; I went; he talked
simple present	die einfache Gegenwart	it is; I go; he talks
singular	der Singular, die Einzahl	book, child, potato, story
state verb	das Zustandsverb	(to) be, (to) become, (to) feel, (to) look, (to) seem, (to) smell, (to) sound, (to) taste
statement	der Aussage(satz)	I like oranges. I don't like bananas.

subject	das Subjekt	**They** eat dinner.; **The cat** is cute.
substitute	die Ersatzform	He **was able to** run. Will you **be allowed to** ...?
superlative	der Superlativ	(the) oldest, (the) best, (the) most popular
tense	die Zeitform	present progressive, simple past, future
verb	das Verb	(to) go, (to) do, (to) have, (to) think, (to) love
wh-question	die Frage mit Fragewort	What's this? Who are you?
will-future	das Futur mit *will*	Noah **will** phone, you'**ll** see, he **won't** buy
word order	die Wortstellung	subject – verb – object: We know them.
yes/no-question	die Entscheidungsfrage	Are you OK?; Will she go?; Did it go well?

Wichtige Schreibregeln im Englischen

Groß- und Kleinschreibung
Im Englischen wird fast alles kleingeschrieben. Merke dir nur diese Ausnahmen:
- das Wort *I* (ich)
- Monatsnamen *(January, February, ...)*
- Wochentage *(Monday, Tuesday, ...)*
- Eigennamen und geografische Namen *(Tom, Lisa, London, ...)*
- Länder, deren Bewohner und Bewohnerinnen, Sprachen und Nationalitäten *(Germany, the Germans, German)*
- das erste Wort am Satzanfang und in Überschriften

Stumme Buchstaben
Manche Wörter enthalten Buchstaben, die du zwar schreibst, aber nicht sprichst:
- b   *lamb*
- c   *science*
- d   *sandwich*
- g   *design*
- h   *technology*
- i   *fruit*
- k   *(to) know, knife*
- l   *(to) walk, (to) talk*
- u   *guitar, building*
- t   *(to) listen*
- w   *(to) answer, wrong*

Verdoppelung der Endkonsonanten
(to) stop – stopping, stopped
(to) win – winning, winner

-y wird zu -ie
- im Plural: *a pony – three ponies*
- in der 3. Person Singular: *(to) tidy – he tidies*
- bei der Steigerung von Adjektiven: *busy – busier – busiest*, *easy – easier – easiest*

Buchstabenverbindungen
Merke dir häufige Buchstabenverbindungen bei der Schreibung englischer Wörter:
- -ee-   *(to) see, deep, (to) meet, street*
- -ea-   *beach, meat, pea*
- -igh- *sight, fight, right, night*
- -oo-   *book, good, look*
- -ous- *dangerous, nervous, famously*
- -tion *station, competition*

Kleine Unterschiede Deutsch–Englisch
Achte auf diese kleinen Unterschiede bei der Schreibung englischer Wörter:
- k wird zu c: Musik – *music*
- f wird zu ph: Foto – *photo*
- isch wird zu ic: elektrisch – *electric*
- el wird zu le: Titel – *title*, Artikel – *article*
- sch wird zu sh: britisch – *British*
- deutsches -e am Wortende entfällt: Lampe – *lamp*, Ende – *end*

one hundred and eighty-five

Wordbank

Wordbank 1: On the street

▶ Unit 1 | p. 21

*Excuse me, how do I get to …? /
Sorry, I'm lost. Could you tell me the way to …?*

Directions

Go straight on.   Turn left.   Turn right.   Take the second street on the left.

Go across the road.   Go along the river.   Go down the steps.   Go over the bridge.

Go past the cinema.   Go to the end of the street.   Go through the park.   Go up the hill.

Places

bus stop, cinema, hospital, ice rink, library, museum, shopping centre, supermarket, train station

block of flats   car park   office building   petrol station

roundabout   skyscraper   traffic lights   zebra crossing

Wordbank 2: Giving opinions

▶ Unit 1 | p. 22

- I think ...
- I would say that ...
- From my point of view ...
- In my opinion ...
- I (don't) agree with ...
- Personally ...
- I believe that ...
- If you ask me ...
- I'm not really a fan of ...

Words for 'good'	Words for 'bad'
amazing	awful
awesome	horrible
brilliant	lousy
cool	nasty
excellent	not my thing
fantastic	poor
fine	rubbish
great	shocking
perfect	terrible
wonderful	useless

one hundred and eighty-seven **187**

Wordbank

Wordbank 3: Describing clothes and accessories ▶ Unit 2 | p. 46

Materials *(Materialien)*

canvas *(Segeltuch)*   cotton *(Baumwolle)*   leather *(Leder)*   metal *(Metall)*

polyester *(Polyester)*   rubber *(Gummi)*   silk *(Seide)*   wool *(Wolle)*

Colours and patterns *(Farben und Muster)*

checked *(kariert)*   colourful *(farbenfroh)*   dark / light *(dunkel / hell)*   flowery *(geblümt)*

patterned *(gemustert)*   plain *(einfarbig)*   dotted *(gepunktet)*   striped *(gestreift)*

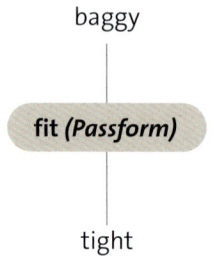  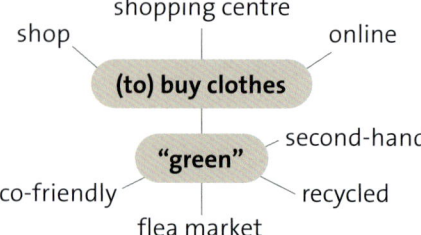

fit (Passform): baggy, tight

style: cool, casual, trendy, unusual, designer, sporty, vintage, smart

(to) buy clothes: shop, shopping centre, online

"green": eco-friendly, second-hand, recycled, flea market

Wordbank 4: Feelings

▶ Unit 2 | p. 54

all right / OK	in Ordnung
amazing	fantastisch, erstaunlich
brave	mutig
calm	ruhig, gelassen
cheerful	fröhlich
confident	selbstbewusst, sicher
content	zufrieden
creative	kreativ
energetic	energiegeladen, aktiv
excellent	hervorragend
excited	aufgeregt, gespannt
fantastic	fantastisch
fine	gut, prima
great	großartig
happy	froh, glücklich
motivated	motiviert
proud	stolz
relaxed	entspannt
strong	stark
surprised	überrascht
wonderful	wunderbar

angry	wütend, zornig
awful	schrecklich
bored	gelangweilt
disappointed	enttäuscht
embarrassed	peinlich berührt, verlegen
fed up	genervt, sauer
frustrated	frustriert
horrible	schrecklich
jealous	eifersüchtig
lonely	einsam
nasty	scheußlich
nervous	nervös
puzzled	verwirrt, ratlos
sad	traurig
scared	verängstigt
shocked	schockiert
stressed	gestresst
terrible	furchtbar
tired	müde
upset	verärgert, bestürzt
useless	nutzlos
worried	besorgt

Wordbank

Wordbank 5: Scary creatures

▶ Unit 3 | p. 78, 79

I know a scary story about a / an …
dragon, ghost, mermaid, merman, monster, vampire

demon

gargoyle

goblin

mummy

ogre

werewolf

witch

wizard

zombie

Wordbank 6: Sports

▶ Unit 3 | p. 83

I play ...
badminton, basketball, cricket, football, hockey, table tennis, tennis

handball

rugby

volleyball

I go ...
bowling, climbing, cycling, dancing, hiking, horse riding, paddleboarding, running, skateboarding, skiing, surfing, swimming, walking

canoeing

ice skating

rowing

I do ...
fitness, judo, trampolining, yoga

archery

athletics

boxing

scuba diving

gymnastics

karate

Wordbank

Wordbank 7: Nature

▶ Unit 3 | p. 84, 85

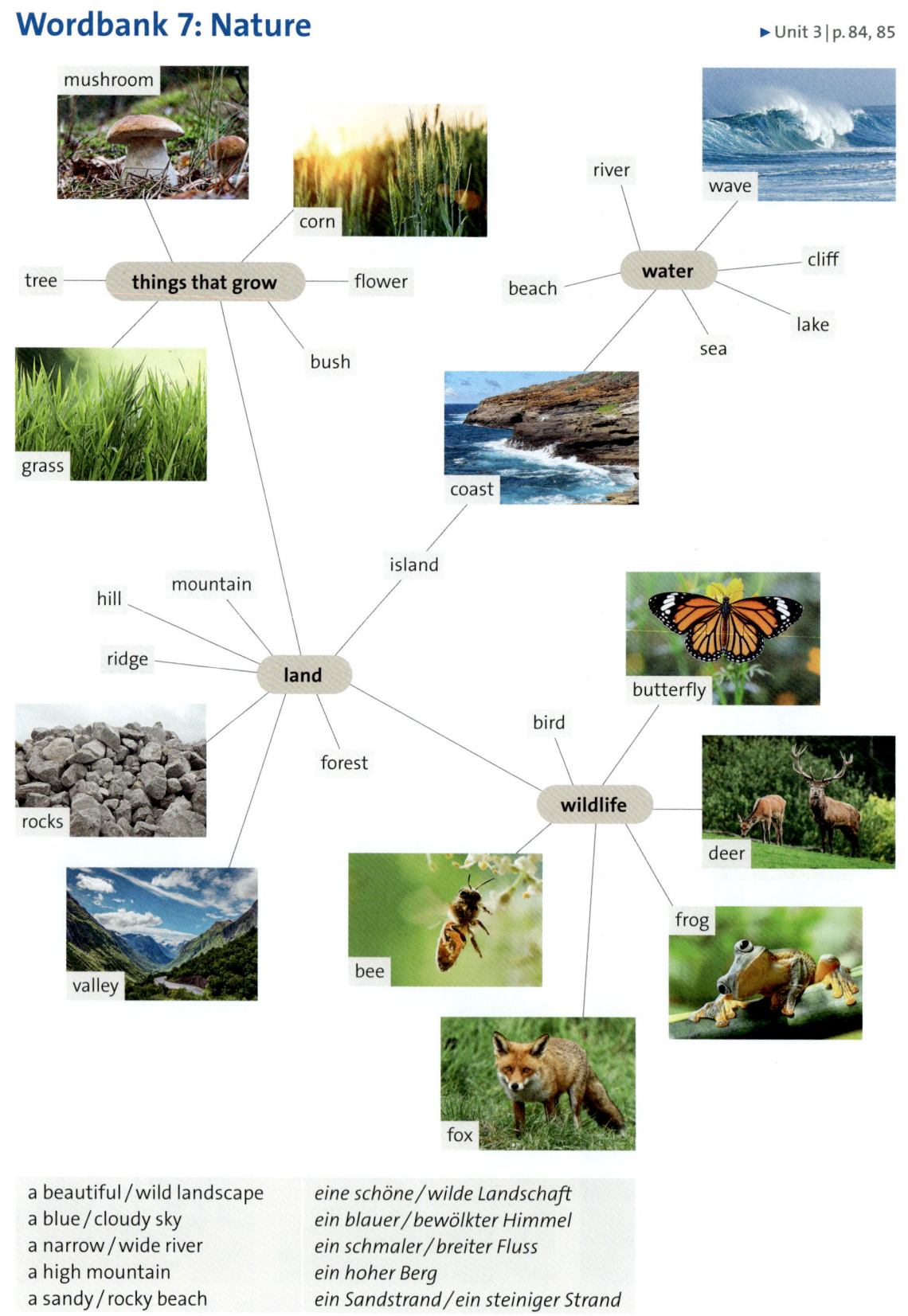

a beautiful / wild landscape	eine schöne / wilde Landschaft
a blue / cloudy sky	ein blauer / bewölkter Himmel
a narrow / wide river	ein schmaler / breiter Fluss
a high mountain	ein hoher Berg
a sandy / rocky beach	ein Sandstrand / ein steiniger Strand

Wordbank 8: Sights and places to visit

▶ Unit 4 | p. 107

In my area there is a/an ...
art gallery, castle, escape room, library, museum, opera, television tower, theatre, zoo

harbour

national park

old town

palace

theme park

tower

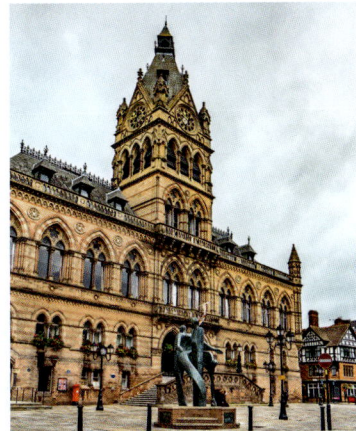
town hall

town / village square

waterfall

Wordbank

Wordbank 9: Tech instructions
▶ Unit 4 | p. 113

Show the order of instructions
First … / Second … / Third …
Then … / Next … / After that …
Finally…

Get started
(to) switch on / off a device
(to) charge a device / a laptop / a tablet
(to) check the connection
(to) connect to Wi-Fi
(to) enter / put in a password
(to) log on

Prepare
(to) choose / download an app / software / a program
(to) install an app / software / a program
(to) pair with another device
(to) set up a device

Use a device
(to) click on a link (with a mouse)
(to) press a key (on a keyboard)
(to) scroll up / down a page
(to) swipe a screen
(to) tap an icon
(to) use a search engine

Files, texts and videos
(to) add captions / music / text effects
(to) copy / cut / paste text
(to) edit a text / video / vlog
(to) save data / a file
(to) upload a file / photos / a video

Let's talk!

Hier findest du englische Sätze mit ihrer deutschen Übersetzung. Da jede Sprache anders funktioniert, ist eine wortwörtliche Übersetzung oft nicht möglich. Achte daher auf die kleinen Unterschiede.

1 Sich und andere vorstellen

Sich kennenlernen

	Hello, I'm … / Hi! I'm …	Hallo, ich bin …
	Hi, my name is … What's your name?	Hallo, ich heiße … Wie heißt du?
	How old are you?	Wie alt bist du?
	I'm … (years old). What about you?	Ich bin … (Jahre alt). Und du?
	Nice to meet you. – Nice to meet you too.	Freut mich, dich / euch / Sie kennenzulernen. – Freut mich auch.
	I'm from (Manchester in England).	Ich komme aus (Manchester in England).
	I grew up in (Inverness in Scotland).	Ich bin in (Inverness in Schottland) aufgewachsen.

Über Interessen und Dinge sprechen, die einem wichtig sind

Unit 1	What's your favourite book / film / …?	Was ist dein Lieblingsbuch / -film / …?
	What do you like to do in your free time?	Was machst du gerne in deiner Freizeit?
	What do(n't) you like / love?	Was magst / liebst du (nicht)?
	What kind of (music) do you like?	Welche Art von (Musik) magst du?
	I'm not really a fan of (history).	Ich bin nicht wirklich ein (Geschichts-)Fan.
	I think … is the best (film) ever.	Ich finde, dass … der beste (Film) überhaupt ist.
	I'm sorry, I think it's (boring).	Es tut mir leid, ich finde es / ihn (langweilig).
	Are you interested in (rap music)?	Interessiert dich (Rap)?
Unit 2	My favourite sport / … is … because it's …	Mein Lieblingssport / … ist …, weil es …
	I think that … is(n't) important, but (Omar) thinks …	Ich finde … (nicht) wichtig, aber (Omar) findet …
	(My family) is really important to me because …	(Meine Familie) ist mir sehr wichtig, weil …
	What's the most important thing to you?	Was ist dir am wichtigsten?
	… is very important to you – why is that?	… ist dir sehr wichtig – warum?
	Are / Is … important to you?	Sind / Ist dir … wichtig?
	(Saving our planet) is important because …	(Die Erde zu retten) ist wichtig, weil …
	I put (my family) first.	(Meine Familie) steht an erster Stelle.
Unit 3	Do you like … or do you prefer …?	Magst du … oder magst du … lieber?
	Which place / activity / … looks the most interesting?	Welche(r) Ort / Aktivität / … sieht am interessantesten aus?
	What are your hobbies and interests?	Was sind deine Hobbys und Interessen?
	How long have you played football / …?	Seit wann spielst du schon Fußball / …?

one hundred and ninety-five **195**

Let's talk!

Sich und andere beschreiben

Unit 2		She has (brown) eyes and (blond) hair.	Sie hat (braune) Augen und (blondes) Haar.
		I have curly / straight hair.	Ich habe lockiges / glattes Haar.
		My mum is (tall) and my dad is (short).	Meine Mutter ist (groß) und mein Vater ist (klein).
		The girl's (yellow tights) look really trendy.	(Die gelbe Strumpfhose) des Mädchens sieht sehr modisch aus.
		The (colourful T-shirt) looks amazing with the (plain white shorts).	(Das bunte T-Shirt) und (die einfarbigen weißen Shorts) sehen toll zusammen aus.
		Some people say she / he is (shy), but I think she / he is (cool).	Manche sagen, dass sie / er (schüchtern) ist, aber ich finde sie / ihn (cool).
		Sometimes (she) gets upset / angry / …	Manchmal ist (sie) aufgebracht / wütend / …

2 Sich verabreden und etwas planen

	What are we going to do this (weekend)?	Was machen wir am (Wochenende)?
	Are you doing anything (today)?	Machst du (heute) irgendetwas?
	What are you going to do on (Sunday) morning / afternoon / evening?	Was machst du am (Sonntag-)morgen / -nachmittag / -abend?
	(Saturday) would be best.	(Samstag) wäre am besten.
	Let's meet at (the station) / in (the park) at (7.30 p.m.).	Lass uns um (19.30 Uhr) am (Bahnhof) / im (Park) treffen.
	Sorry, I can't. I'm really busy.	Tut mir leid, da kann ich nicht. Ich bin sehr beschäftigt.
Unit 1	I can show you (the city) if you like.	Ich kann dir (die Stadt) zeigen, wenn du magst.
	Maybe we could (ride on the London Eye)?	Vielleicht könnten wir (mit dem London Eye fahren)?
	I'd love to (go there).	Ich würde sehr gerne (dorthin gehen).
	Sure, what's there?	Klar, was gibt es dort (zu sehen)?
	See you on (Saturday).	Wir sehen uns am (Samstag).
Unit 4	When are we going to edit the video?	Wann schneiden wir das Video?
	How / What about (later after dinner)?	Wie sieht es (später nach dem Abendessen) aus?
	Are you free?	Hast du Zeit?

3 Leben in der Stadt

Öffentliche Verkehrsmittel nutzen

	How much does (a bus ticket) cost?	Wie viel kostet (eine Busfahrkarte)?
Unit 1	This is our stop.	Das ist unsere Haltestelle.
	Do we have to change?	Müssen wir umsteigen?
	Do you need a ticket?	Brauchst du eine Fahrkarte?
	Mind the gap between the train and the platform.	Beachten Sie den Abstand zwischen Zug und Bahnsteig.
	Let's take (the tube) to …	Lass uns (die U-Bahn) nach / zu … nehmen.

one hundred and ninety-six

		We can take the bus / tram / ... from here.	Von hier können wir den Bus / die Straßenbahn / ... nehmen.
		How long does it take by taxi / bike / ...?	Wie lange dauert es mit dem Taxi / Fahrrad / ...?
		I usually travel by bus / train / ...	Normalerweise nutze ich den Bus / die Bahn / ...

Nach dem Weg fragen und Wege beschreiben

Unit 1	Go straight on / across / along / past / ...	Geh geradeaus / über / entlang / an ... vorbei / ...
	Turn left / right.	Biege links / rechts ab.
	If you go ..., you'll arrive at the ...	Wenn du ... gehst, kommst du an / am ... an.
	If you turn ..., you'll see a ...	Wenn du ... abbiegst, siehst du eine/n ...
	Take the first / second / ... road on the right / left.	Nimm die erste / zweite / ... Straße auf der rechten / linken Seite.
	Just follow (the river) that way and go past ...	Folge (dem Fluss) und gehe an/am ... vorbei.
	South / North / East / West from ...	Südlich / Nördlich / Östlich / Westlich von ...
	Only a few minutes' walk away from ...	Nur ein paar Minuten von / vom ... entfernt.

Essen gehen und in einem Restaurant bestellen

	Are you hungry?	Hast du Hunger?
	I'm really hungry. / No, I'm not hungry.	Ich bin echt hungrig. / Nein, ich habe keinen Hunger.
	My favourite dish is (pizza).	Mein Lieblingsgericht ist (Pizza).
	Would you like some more (water)?	Möchtest du / Möchten Sie noch etwas mehr (Wasser)?
	Enjoy your meal!	Guten Appetit!
Unit 1	(The Falafel) sound good.	(Die Falafel) hören sich lecker an.
	I'm allergic to ...	Ich bin gegen ... allergisch.
	Hi, are you ready to order?	Hi, mögt ihr / mögen Sie bestellen?
	What would you like to drink / eat?	Was möchtest du / möchten Sie trinken / essen?
	Could I have (a milkshake), please?	Könnte ich bitte (ein Milchshake) bekommen?
	I'd like (sparkling water), please.	Ich hätte gerne (Sprudelwasser).
	I'll have (a glass of tap water), please.	Ich bekomme (ein Glas Leitungswasser), bitte.
	Can I have it without (tomatoes)?	Könnte ich das / es ohne (Tomaten) haben / bekommen?
	Can you tell me what ... is?	Was ist ...?

4 Über Umwelt, Natur(schutz) und Nachhaltigkeit sprechen

Unit 2	I think it's interesting / surprising / terrible that ...	Ich finde es interessant / überraschend / schrecklich, dass ...
	Why don't we (recycle) ...?	Warum (recyceln) wir ... nicht?
	We can buy / repair / ... (old clothes).	Wir können (alte Kleidung) kaufen / reparieren / ...

Let's talk!

Unit 3	How important is nature to you?	Wie wichtig ist dir die Natur?
	Nature is important because it gives us food / clean air / …	Die Natur ist wichtig, weil sie uns Nahrung / frische Luft / … gibt.
	I like camping / hiking / … in nature.	Ich mag Campen / Wandern / … in der Natur.
	I don't like being in nature because (there are lots of insects).	Ich bin nicht gerne in der Natur, weil (es da viele Insekten gibt).

5 Miteinander reden

Über Probleme sprechen und Ratschläge erteilen

Unit 2	Could you help me, please?	Könntest du / Könnten Sie mir bitte helfen?
	What can I do? Please help!	Was kann / soll ich machen? Bitte hilf / helfen Sie mir.
	Should I …?	Sollte ich …?
	I'm really worried about …	Ich mache mir große Sorgen um …
	I feel that I must do something to help.	Ich habe das Gefühl, dass ich helfen sollte.
	The problem is that …	Das Problem ist, dass …
	I think you're right that …	Ich denke du hast recht damit, dass …
	You can (also) ask a teacher / a parent / …	Du kannst (auch) eine Lehrkraft / ein Elternteil / … fragen.
	You should / could talk to …	Du solltest / könntest mit … sprechen.
	I understand that you're unhappy / sad / disappointed / …	Ich verstehe, dass du unglücklich / traurig / enttäuscht / … bist.
	I think this is good / bad advice.	Ich finde das ist ein guter / schlechter Ratschlag.

Komplimente machen

Unit 2	I think you're funny / brave / …	Ich finde dich witzig / mutig / …
	I love your shoes / dress / …	Ich mag deine Schuhe / dein Kleid / …
	I want to tell you that you're great at football / an amazing friend / …	Ich wollte dir sagen, dass du sehr gut Fußball spielst / ein/e tolle/r Freund/in bist / …
	Thank you, that's nice of you.	Danke, das ist lieb / nett von dir.
	You're welcome!	Gern geschehen!

Einen Konflikt lösen und sich entschuldigen

Unit 3	I'm sorry, it was a bad idea to (take a different path).	Es tut mir leid, es war eine schlechte Idee, (einen anderen Weg zu nehmen).
	I'm sorry I forgot to (bring hiking boots).	Es tut mir leid, dass ich vergessen habe, (Wanderschuhe mitzubringen).
	I don't know why I thought that (was a good idea).	Ich weiß nicht, warum ich dachte, dass das (eine gute Idee wäre).
	That's OK.	Alles gut.
	Thank you for saying sorry.	Danke für deine Entschuldigung.
	Next time, you should …	Beim nächsten Mal solltest du …

Hilfe anbieten, erbitten und annehmen

Unit 4	I'd like to (use social media). But I don't know where to start.	Ich möchte gerne (soziale Medien nutzen). Aber ich weiß gar nicht, wo ich anfangen soll.
	I can help you if you like.	Ich kann dir helfen, wenn du magst.
	Could you / Can you help me (make an account)?	Könntest / Kannst du mir helfen, (einen Account einzurichten)?
	No problem.	Kein Problem.
	Would you like me to show you how to …?	Möchtest du, dass ich dir zeige, wie …?
	I'm OK, thanks.	Alles gut, danke. / Nein, danke.

6 Technologie im Alltag

Über Technologie und soziale Medien im Alltag sprechen

Unit 1	Is there (no) free Wi-Fi here?	Gibt es hier (kein) kostenloses WLAN?
Unit 4	I often / sometimes / never / … use (social media).	Ich nutze (soziale Medien) oft / manchmal / nie / …
	How often do you use (social media)?	Wie oft nutzt du (soziale Medien)?
	I'm (not) allowed to use (social media).	Ich darf (soziale Medien) (nicht) nutzen.
	I believe that (social media) is a positive / negative thing for teens because …	Ich denke, dass (soziale Medien) einen positiven / negativen Einfluss auf Jugendliche haben, weil …
	I think one of the problems with (social media) is that …	Ich denke, ein Problem der sozialen Medien ist, dass …
	I use social media / my phone / my smartwatch / … to …	Ich nutze soziale Medien / mein Smartphone / meine Smartwatch / …, um …
	I think it is(n't) a good idea to edit photos because …	Ich finde, es ist (k)eine gute Idee Fotos zu bearbeiten, weil …

Ein Telefongespräch führen

Unit 4	Hi, (Dylan). How are things?	Hi, (Dylan). Wie geht's?
	Are you free later?	Hast / Hättest du später Zeit?
	Can you say that again, please?	Kannst du das bitte nochmal wiederholen?
	Can you hear me now?	Kannst du mich jetzt hören?
	I can't hear you. You're breaking up.	Ich kann dich nicht hören. Die Verbindung bricht ab.
	Oh, one more thing.	Oh, eine Sache noch.
	Sorry, I have to go now.	Sorry, ich muss jetzt los.
	Bye. See you later / tomorrow.	Tschüss. Bis später / morgen.

7 Seine Meinung äußern und diskutieren

	I think that's true / false.	Ich glaube, das ist richtig / falsch.
	I'm sorry, I don't understand.	Es tut mir leid, das verstehe ich nicht.
	That's not a good idea.	Das ist keine gute Idee.
	I'm not really a fan of …	Ich bin nicht wirklich Fan von …

Let's talk!

	For me that isn't true.		Für mich ist das nicht so.
	That's a great idea!		Das ist eine sehr gute Idee!
Unit 2	I think (Omar's dad) is right / wrong because …		Ich glaube, (Omars Vater) hat recht / unrecht, weil …
	In my opinion, it's most important to …		Meiner Meinung nach ist es am wichtigsten, …
	If you ask me, I'd say that …		Wenn du mich fragst, würde ich sagen, dass …
	I don't agree with you (at all).		Ich stimme dir (ganz und gar) nicht zu.
	I (completely) disagree.		Ich stimme (überhaupt) nicht zu.
	Yes, you're so right.		Ja, du hast sowas von recht.
	That's a good point.		Das ist ein gutes Argument.
	I see it a bit differently.		Ich sehe das etwas anders.
	Just a minute, let me think.		Moment, lass mich nachdenken.

8 Feedback geben

	You can use more words or pictures.		Du kannst mehr Wörter oder Bilder verwenden.
	Your presentation was quite long / short.		Deine Präsentation war ziemlich lang / kurz.
	Please speak more loudly / clearly.		Sprich bitte ein bisschen lauter / deutlicher.
	Don't speak so fast, please.		Sprich bitte nicht so schnell.
	That was useful information.		Das waren nützliche Informationen.
	Your notes are really helpful.		Deine Notizen sind wirklich nützlich.
	Next time, check your spelling.		Prüfe deine Rechtschreibung beim nächsten Mal.
	Your presentation needs a better structure.		Deine Präsentation sollte besser strukturiert werden.
	You've done a great job!		Das hast du toll gemacht!
	The text on your slides was a bit small.		Der Text auf deinen Folien war etwas zu klein.
	You spoke loudly and clearly.		Du hast laut und deutlich gesprochen.
	I understood most of / some of what you said.		Ich habe das meiste / einiges von dem, was du gesagt hast, verstanden.
	You looked at your cards.		Du hast auf deine Karten geschaut.
	Please look at me / us more.		Schau mich / uns bitte öfter an.
	You smiled / didn't smile.		Du hast gelächelt / nicht gelächelt.
Unit 1	I thought (the tour) was interesting / easy / difficult / fun / …		Ich finde, (die Tour) war interessant / einfach / schwer / spaßig / …
	I liked (your post).		Ich mochte (deinen Post).
	The part about … was really funny.		Der Abschnitt über … war wirklich lustig.
	You made (two) spelling mistakes.		Du hast (zwei) Rechtschreibfehler gemacht.
Unit 3	You used lots of (adjectives).		Du hast viele (Adjektive) verwendet.
Unit 4	You gave some great reasons.		Du hast ein paar wichtige Gründe genannt.
	I really liked that you explained new words.		Es hat mir gut gefallen, dass du neue Wörter erklärt hast.

Classroom English

You and your teacher | Du und deine Lehrerin / dein Lehrer

Good morning, Mr / Mrs / Ms … (bis 12 Uhr)	Guten Morgen, Herr / Frau …
Good afternoon, Mr / Mrs / Ms … (ab 12 Uhr)	Guten Tag / Nachmittag, Herr / Frau …
Sorry, I'm late.	Entschuldigung, dass ich zu spät komme.
Can I open / close the window, please?	Kann ich bitte das Fenster öffnen / zumachen?
Can I go to the toilet, please?	Kann ich bitte zur Toilette gehen?

Homework and exercises | Hausaufgaben und Übungen

Sorry, I don't have my exercise book.	Es tut mir leid, ich habe mein Heft nicht dabei.
I don't understand this exercise.	Ich verstehe die Übung nicht.
I can't do number 3.	Ich kann Nummer 3 nicht lösen.
Sorry, I haven't finished.	Entschuldigung, ich bin noch nicht fertig.
I have … Is that right too?	Ich habe … Ist das auch richtig?
Sorry, I don't know.	Es tut mir leid, das weiß ich nicht.
What's for homework?	Was haben wir (als Hausaufgabe) auf?

You need help | Du brauchst Hilfe

Can you help me, please?	Können Sie / Kannst du mir bitte helfen?
What page is it, please?	Auf welcher Seite sind wir / steht das?
What's … in English / German?	Was heißt … auf Englisch / Deutsch?
Can you speak more loudly, please?	Können Sie / Kannst du bitte lauter sprechen?
Can I say it in German?	Kann ich das auf Deutsch sagen?
Can you write it on the board, please?	Können Sie das bitte an die Tafel schreiben?
Can you say / play that again, please?	Können Sie das bitte noch einmal sagen / abspielen?

Work with a partner | Partnerarbeit

Can I work with Julian?	Kann ich mit Julian arbeiten?
Can I use your (pen), please?	Kann ich bitte deinen (Stift) benutzen?
Yes, here you are.	Hier, bitte.
It's my / your turn.	Ich bin dran. / Du bist dran.
Let's make / draw a / an …	Lass uns ein / eine / einen … machen / zeichnen.
Let's act out the story / the dialogue.	Lass uns die Geschichte / den Dialog spielen.

What your teacher says | Was deine Lehrerin / dein Lehrer sagt

Let's start.	Lasst uns anfangen. / Los geht's.
Listen, please. / Quiet, please.	Hört bitte zu. / Ruhe bitte.
Open your books at page 24, please.	Schlagt bitte Seite 24 auf.
Do exercise 5 for homework, please.	Macht bitte Übung 5 als Hausaufgabe.
Write the correct words.	Schreibt die richtigen Wörter (auf).
Correct the false sentences.	Korrigiert die falschen Sätze.
Where's your book, Dana?	Wo ist dein Buch, Dana?
Try again!	Versuche es noch einmal.
That's all for today. You can go now.	Das ist alles für heute. Ihr könnt jetzt gehen.

two hundred and one

Alphabet, English sounds

The English alphabet

a	[eɪ]	h	[eɪtʃ]	o	[əʊ]	v	[viː]
b	[biː]	i	[aɪ]	p	[piː]	w	[ˈdʌbljuː]
c	[siː]	j	[dʒeɪ]	q	[kjuː]	x	[eks]
d	[diː]	k	[keɪ]	r	[ɑː]	y	[waɪ]
e	[iː]	l	[el]	s	[es]	z	[zed]
f	[ef]	m	[em]	t	[tiː]		
g	[dʒiː]	n	[en]	u	[juː]		

English sounds

> Die Lautschrift zeigt dir die Aussprache von Wörtern und Lauten *(sounds)*.

> Einige dieser Laute kommen im Deutschen nicht vor oder werden anders geschrieben. Sie sind hier mit einem Ausrufezeichen gekennzeichnet: ❗. Übe sie mit Hilfe der App.

[iː]	green, he, sea		[d]	day, window, good
[ɑː]	ask, class, car, park		[t]	ten, letter, at
❗ [ɔː]	or, ball, door, four, morning		[g]	go, again, bag
[uː]	ruler, blue, too, two, you		[k]	kitchen, car, back
[ɜː]	early, her, girl, work, T-shirt		[m]	man, remember, mum
[ɪ]	in, big, expensive		[n]	no, one, ten
[e]	yes, bed, again, breakfast	❗	[ŋ]	wrong, young, uncle, thanks
[æ]	animal, apple, black, cat		[l]	like, old, small
[ʌ]	mum, bus, colour		[r]	ruler, friend, sorry
[ɒ]	song, on, dog, what	❗	[w]	we, where, one
[ʊ]	book, good, put, bully		[j]	yes, you, uniform
[ə]	again, today, a sister		[f]	family, after, laugh
[i]	happy, monkey	❗	[v]	very, seven, have
[eɪ]	name, eight, play, great		[s]	six, poster, yes
[aɪ]	I, time, right, my	❗	[z]	zoo, quiz, his, music, please
[ɔɪ]	boy, toilet, noise		[ʃ]	she, station, English
[əʊ]	old, no, road, yellow	❗	[ʒ]	usually, revision, garage
[aʊ]	now, house		[tʃ]	chain, teacher, watch
[ɪə]	here, material, really, year	❗	[dʒ]	job, German, project, orange
[eə]	where, pair, share, their	❗	[θ]	thing, three, bathroom, north
[ʊə]	tour	❗	[ð]	the, weather, with
[b]	bike, table, verb		[h]	house, who, behind
[p]	pen, paper, shop		[x]	loch

English numbers

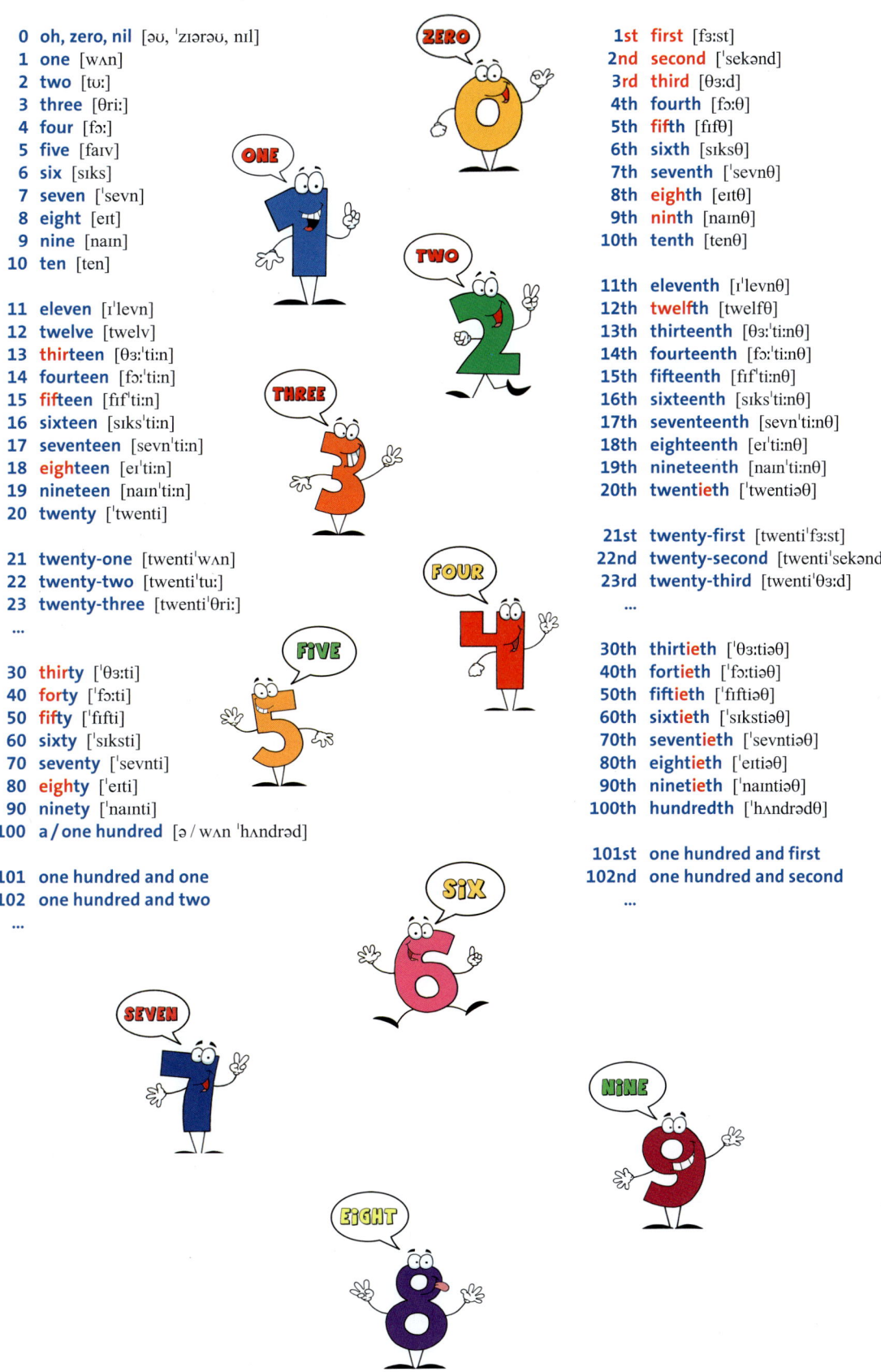

0	oh, zero, nil	[əʊ, ˈzɪərəʊ, nɪl]
1	one	[wʌn]
2	two	[tuː]
3	three	[θriː]
4	four	[fɔː]
5	five	[faɪv]
6	six	[sɪks]
7	seven	[ˈsevn]
8	eight	[eɪt]
9	nine	[naɪn]
10	ten	[ten]
11	eleven	[ɪˈlevn]
12	twelve	[twelv]
13	thirteen	[θɜːˈtiːn]
14	fourteen	[fɔːˈtiːn]
15	fifteen	[fɪfˈtiːn]
16	sixteen	[sɪksˈtiːn]
17	seventeen	[sevnˈtiːn]
18	eighteen	[eɪˈtiːn]
19	nineteen	[naɪnˈtiːn]
20	twenty	[ˈtwenti]
21	twenty-one	[twentiˈwʌn]
22	twenty-two	[twentiˈtuː]
23	twenty-three	[twentiˈθriː]
...		
30	thirty	[ˈθɜːti]
40	forty	[ˈfɔːti]
50	fifty	[ˈfɪfti]
60	sixty	[ˈsɪksti]
70	seventy	[ˈsevnti]
80	eighty	[ˈeɪti]
90	ninety	[ˈnaɪnti]
100	a / one hundred	[ə / wʌn ˈhʌndrəd]
101	one hundred and one	
102	one hundred and two	
...		

1st	first	[fɜːst]
2nd	second	[ˈsekənd]
3rd	third	[θɜːd]
4th	fourth	[fɔːθ]
5th	fifth	[fɪfθ]
6th	sixth	[sɪksθ]
7th	seventh	[ˈsevnθ]
8th	eighth	[eɪtθ]
9th	ninth	[naɪnθ]
10th	tenth	[tenθ]
11th	eleventh	[ɪˈlevnθ]
12th	twelfth	[twelfθ]
13th	thirteenth	[θɜːˈtiːnθ]
14th	fourteenth	[fɔːˈtiːnθ]
15th	fifteenth	[fɪfˈtiːnθ]
16th	sixteenth	[sɪksˈtiːnθ]
17th	seventeenth	[sevnˈtiːnθ]
18th	eighteenth	[eɪˈtiːnθ]
19th	nineteenth	[naɪnˈtiːnθ]
20th	twentieth	[ˈtwentiəθ]
21st	twenty-first	[twentiˈfɜːst]
22nd	twenty-second	[twentiˈsekənd]
23rd	twenty-third	[twentiˈθɜːd]
...		
30th	thirtieth	[ˈθɜːtiəθ]
40th	fortieth	[ˈfɔːtiəθ]
50th	fiftieth	[ˈfɪftiəθ]
60th	sixtieth	[ˈsɪkstiəθ]
70th	seventieth	[ˈsevntiəθ]
80th	eightieth	[ˈeɪtiəθ]
90th	ninetieth	[ˈnaɪntiəθ]
100th	hundredth	[ˈhʌndrədθ]
101st	one hundred and first	
102nd	one hundred and second	
...		

Vocabulary

Im *Vocabulary* findest du neue Wörter und Wendungen.
Sie stehen in der Reihenfolge, in der sie im Buch vorkommen.
Höre dir in der App jedes Wort genau an und sprich es nach.

Inhalt

	Seite
Hello!	205
Unit 1 London: City life	206
Merkboxen: *The royal family • care – (to) care – careful • -ful / -less • German "wenig, weniger, am wenigsten" • opposite • recent – recently • Irregular verbs*	
Unit 2 Manchester: Who we are	216
Merkboxen: *by • German "man" • they = he or she • möglich – wahrscheinlich – sicherlich • Reflexive pronouns • (to) keep, kept, kept • straight • point • Irregular verbs*	
Unit 3 Scotland: Adventure	225
Merkboxen: *Adjective: -ing – adverb: -ingly • German "seit" • before • Irregular verbs*	
Unit 4 Wales: Digital life	234
Merkboxen: *Possessive pronouns • (to) agree (zustimmen) • in touch with (in Kontakt / Verbindung mit) • "Möchtest du, dass ich ...?" – "Ich möchte, dass du ..." • (to) guess – guess • Irregular verbs*	
°**Unit 5 Two Irelands: Together**	242
Merkboxen: *Der Nordirlandkonflikt*	

Symbole und Abkürzungen

▶ p. 10 ▶ pp. 12/33	Die Seitenzahl in der linken Spalte zeigt dir, wo das Wort zum ersten Mal in diesem Buch vorkommt.
▶▶ taxi	Die doppelten Pfeile weisen auf ein Wort mit gleicher Bedeutung hin, das du bereits kennst.
cheap ◀▶ expensive	Das „Gegenteil"-Zeichen bedeutet: *cheap* ist das Gegenteil von *expensive*.
❗ the sea – das Meer, die See the lake – der See	Das ❗ bedeutet: Vorsicht, hier keinen Fehler machen!
German "wenig, weniger, am wenigsten"	In den Merkboxen findest du wichtige Hinweise zu den neuen Wörtern und Wendungen.

sb.	= *somebody* (jemand)	adj	= *adjective* (Adjektiv)
sth.	= *something* (etwas)	adv	= *adverb* (Adverb)
infml.	= *informal* (informell, umgangssprachlich)	conj	= *conjunction* (Konjunktion)
pl	= *plural* (Plural, Mehrzahlform)	prep	= *preposition* (Präposition)

Hinweise

- Seite 202 enthält eine Übersicht über die **Lautschriftzeichen** (English sounds).
- Tipps zum Vokabellernen findest du im **Skills file** auf S. 155–157.
- Die **Wordbanks** (S. 186–194) bieten dir nach wichtigen Themen gesammelte Stichwörter.
- **Let's talk** (S. 195–201) enthält Wendungen für wichtige Situationen, z. B. „Feedback geben".
- Eine **Liste mit unregelmäßigen Verben** findest du auf den Seiten 272–273, und eine Übersicht über **Continents, countries and regions** steht auf S. 280.
- Englische Wörter, die Wörtern im Deutschen ähnlich sind, findest du auf S. 274.
- Im **Dictionary** (S. 245–271) kannst du englische Wörter nachschlagen.

Hello!

Hello!

pp. 10/11

south [saʊθ]	der Süden; südlich; Süd-	
east [iːst]	der Osten; östlich; Ost-	
west [west]	der Westen; westlich; West-	

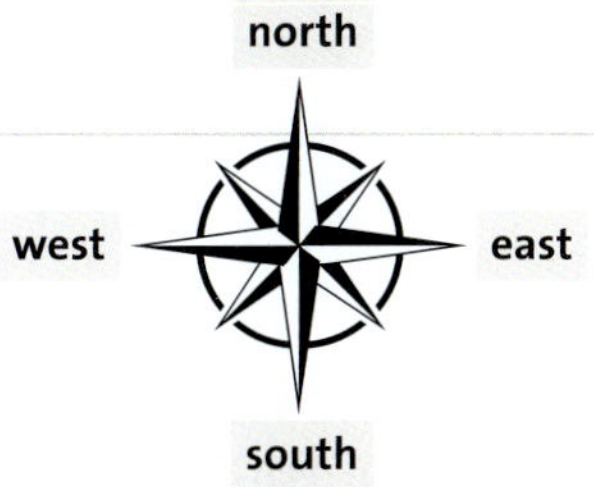

northern [ˈnɔːðən] — nördliche(r, s), Nord-

nouns: **north, east, south, west**
adj: **northern, eastern, southern, western**
❗ Aussprache:
south [saʊθ] – **southern** [ˈsʌðən]

republic [rɪˈpʌblɪk] — die Republik

❗ Betonung auf der 2. Silbe:
re**pub**lic [rɪˈpʌblɪk]

island [ˈaɪlənd] — die Insel

- **isle** [aɪl] *(kurz für **island**)* = die Insel, das Eiland
- **the British Isles** *(pl)* = die Britischen Inseln

Gaelic [ˈgeɪlɪk] — Gälisch *(Sprache)*

a language that many people in Scotland and Ireland speak

official [əˈfɪʃl] — offiziell

Is it true? What does the actor's **official** website say?
official language = die Amtssprache

pp. 12/13

bagpipes *(pl)* [ˈbægpaɪps] — der Dudelsack

❗ German: **Dudelsack spielen**
English: (to) **play the bagpipes**

bagpipes

lake [leɪk] — der See

❗ **the sea** – das Meer, d<u>ie</u> See
the lake – d<u>er</u> See
The word for **lake** in Scotland is **loch** [lɒx], [lɒk].

skyscraper [ˈskaɪskreɪpə] — der Wolkenkratzer

skyscrapers

mural [ˈmjʊərəl] — das Wandgemälde

a big picture on a wall or a building

boat [bəʊt] — das Boot; das Schiff

canal [kəˈnæl] — der Kanal

a canal / a boat

1 Vocabulary

foreground [ˈfɔːgraʊnd]	der Vordergrund	There is a woman in the **foreground**. In the **background**, you can see some mountains. 	
background [ˈbækgraʊnd]	der Hintergrund		

European Union (EU) [jʊərəpiːən ˈjuːniən]	die Europäische Union (EU)	noun: **Europe** [ˈjʊərəp] – adj: **European** [jʊərəˈpiːən]
vote [vəʊt]	die Abstimmung, das Votum	noun: **vote** – verb: (to) **vote** (**on** sth.) (wählen; abstimmen (über etwas))
		• (to) **have a vote** (**on** sth.) = abstimmen (über etwas)
		• (to) **vote for** sb./sth. = für jn./etwas stimmen
close (to) [kləʊs]	knapp; nahe (bei, an)	That was **close**! They nearly had an accident. The vote was very **close**. I don't like it when people stand too **close** to me. ❗ Aussprache: verb: (to) **close** (schließen) [kləʊz] – adj: **close** (knapp; nahe) [kləʊs]
(to) **remain** [rɪˈmeɪn]	(ver)bleiben	▶▶ (to) **stay**
result [rɪˈzʌlt]	das Ergebnis	**as a result** = folglich, demzufolge
(to) **join** sb./sth. [dʒɔɪn]	sich jm. anschließen; bei etwas mitmachen	• (to) **join a club** = in einen Klub eintreten • (to) **join a group** = sich einer Gruppe anschließen • (to) **join the EU** = EU-Mitglied werden

🔊 Unit 1 London: City life

▶ pp. 14/15

acrobat [ˈækrəbæt]	der Akrobat, die Akrobatin	❗ Betonung auf der 1. Silbe: **acrobat** [ˈækrəbæt]	
tower [ˈtaʊə]	der Turm	 a **tower**	
parliament [ˈpɑːləmənt]	das Parlament	❗ Aussprache: [ˈpɑːləmənt] – das **i** wird nicht gesprochen. **the Houses of Parliament** (pl) = das Parlamentsgebäude in London	
sculpture [ˈskʌlptʃə]	die Skulptur	❗ Betonung auf der 1. Silbe: **sculpture** [ˈskʌlptʃə]	
slide [slaɪd]	die Rutsche, die Rutschbahn	❗ **slide** = 1. die Rutsche, die Rutschbahn; 2. das Dia; die Folie (Präsentationssoftware) 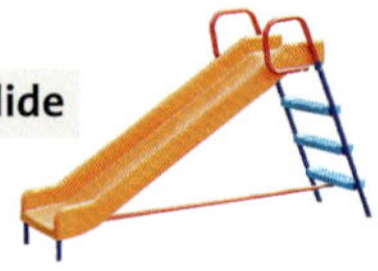 a **slide** noun: **slide** – verb: (to) **slide, slid, slid** (rutschen; schieben; gleiten (lassen))	

206 two hundred and six

tunnel [ˈtʌnl]	der Tunnel	❗ Aussprache: **tunnel** [ˈtʌnl]	
ride [raɪd]	die Fahrt; das Fahrgeschäft *(auf Volksfesten, in Vergnügungsparks)*	I don't want to go on that **ride**. It'll make me feel sick. noun: **ride** – verb: (to) **ride, rode, ridden**	
wheel [wiːl]	das Rad	**big wheel** = das Riesenrad noun: **wheel** – verb: (to) **wheel** (fahren; schieben; ziehen) I **wheeled** Grandpa up the hill.	
bank [bæŋk]	das (Fluss-)Ufer	❗ **bank** = 1. das (Fluss-)Ufer; 2. die Bank *(Geldinstitut)*	
stall [stɔːl]	der (Markt-)Stand, die Bude	*a stall*	

Topic 1

▶ p. 16	**out and about** [aʊt ənd əˈbaʊt]	unterwegs	When I'm in London, I'm **out and about** all the time. There's so much to do!
	because of [bɪˈkɒz əv]	wegen	We went home **because of** the rain. (= … **because** it was raining.)
	traffic [ˈtræfɪk]	der (Straßen-)Verkehr	There was a lot of **traffic**, so it took us an hour to drive home.
	Travelcard [ˈtrævlkɑːd]	die Ein- oder Mehrtagesfahrkarte *(in London)*	Don't buy single tickets! Save money and buy a **Travelcard**.
	the tube *(infml)* [tjuːb]	die Londoner U-Bahn	= the underground in London
	escalator [ˈeskəleɪtə]	die Rolltreppe	You should stand on the right on British **escalators**.
	Wi-Fi [ˈwaɪ faɪ]	das WLAN, die kabellose Datenübertragung	I want to look something up on the Internet. Is there no free **Wi-Fi** here?
	(to) mind sth. [maɪnd]	auf etwas achten, auf etwas aufpassen	• **Mind the gap.** = Achten Sie auf den Abstand zwischen Zug und Bahnsteigkante. • **Mind your head.** = Vorsicht, niedrige Decke! • **Mind the step.** = Vorsicht Stufe!
	gap [gæp]	die Lücke, der Abstand	Find the right words for the **gaps** in the text. I played the guitar as a kid and now, after a **gap** of ten years, I've started again.
	public [ˈpʌblɪk]	öffentlich	Are there any **public** toilets near here? **public transport** *(no pl)* = die öffentlichen Verkehrsmittel

two hundred and seven

1 Vocabulary

	tram [træm]	die Straßenbahn	*a tram*
	local [ˈləʊkl]	einheimisch, am/vom Ort	Do all your friends go to the **local** school? (= Gehen ... hier im Ort zur Schule?) **local train** = der Nahverkehrszug, die S-Bahn
▶ p. 17	**lift** [lɪft]	der Lift, der Aufzug, der Fahrstuhl	noun: **lift** – Do you want to walk up the stairs or take the **lift**? verb: (to) **lift sth.** – I can't **lift** this box. Can you help me? (etwas (hoch)heben)
	direct [dəˈrekt]	direkt, unmittelbar	**direct** ◀▶ **indirect** [ɪndəˈrekt] (indirekt)
	line [laɪn]	die (U-Bahn-)Linie, die (Zug-)Strecke	❗ **line** = 1. die Zeile; die Reihe; 2. die (U-Bahn-)Linie, die (Zug-)Strecke
	double [ˈdʌbl]	doppelt, Doppel-	**double-decker (bus)** = der Doppeldecker(bus) **double room** = das Doppelzimmer *(im Hotel)*
	(to) hire [ˈhaɪə]	mieten, leihen; *(Person:)* einstellen	verb: (to) **hire** – Let's **hire** a boat and have fun on the lake! noun: **hire** – There's a boat **hire** over there. (der Verleih, die Vermietung)
	all over London / all over the country	überall in London / überall im Land, in ganz London / im ganzen Land	**all over the country / the world** = everywhere in the country / the world
	cab [kæb]	das Taxi	▶▶ **taxi**
	cheap [tʃiːp]	billig, preiswert	**cheap** ◀▶ **expensive**

Topic 2

▶ p. 18	**form** [fɔːm]	die Form, die Art	noun: **form** – Which **form** of transport do you like best? (Welche Fortbewegungsart / Welche Art der Beförderung ...?) verb: (to) **form** – You can **form** a noun from the adjective "happy" and the ending "-ness". ((sich) formen, (sich) bilden)
	site [saɪt]	die Stelle, der Ort, die Stätte; *(kurz für website)* die Website	the **site** of the accident (die Unfallstelle) a **tourist site** = ein touristischer Ort
	golden [ˈgəʊldn]	golden, aus Gold	adj: **golden** – noun: **gold**
	young [jʌŋ]	jung	The youth centre is a place for **young** people. adj: **young** – noun: **youth** **young** ◀▶ **old**
	prince [prɪns]	der Prinz	

The royal family

royal [ˈrɔɪəl]	königlich		**prince** [prɪns]	der Prinz
king [kɪŋ]	der König		**princess** [prɪnˈses]	die Prinzessin
queen [kwiːn]	die Königin			

1

sight [saɪt]	die Sehenswürdigkeit	• Let's get away from the traditional tourist **sights**. (die Sehenswürdigkeiten)
		• The seagulls stole all the sandwiches … what a **sight**! (der Anblick)
		• I needed help, but there was no one **in sight**. (in Sicht(weite))
		! **sight** = 1. die Sehenswürdigkeit;
		          2. der Anblick;
		          3. die Sicht(weite)	

classic [ˈklæsɪk]	klassisch	adj: **classic** – noun: **classic** (der Klassiker)	
prime minister [praɪm ˈmɪnɪstə]	der Premierminister, die Premierministerin	The British **prime minister** lives at 10 Downing Street. **!** Betonung: **prime minister** [ˈmɪnɪstə]	
except (for) [ɪkˈsept]	außer, bis auf	In my family everyone is tall **except (for)** me.	
interested (in) [ˈɪntrəstɪd]	interessiert (an)	Are you **interested in** science? / Are you **interested in** learning more about science? Then join the Science Club. **!** (to) **be interested in sth.** = an etwas interessiert sein, sich für etwas interessieren (to) **be interesting** = interessant sein	
▶ p. 19 **type (of)** [taɪp]	die Art (von), die Sorte (von)	▶▶ kind (of), sort (of)	
(to) **push** [pʊʃ]	schieben, stoßen, schubsen	verb: (to) **push** – Push the door to open it. noun: **push** – Give the door a **push** to open it. (der Stoß, der Schubs)	
handle [ˈhændl]	der Griff, der Handgriff	noun: **handle** verb: (to) **handle sth.** (etwas handhaben, mit etwas umgehen) – It'll be interesting to see how they **handle** the situation.	a **door handle**
possible [ˈpɒsəbl]	möglich	• That's not **possible**. (= You can't do that. or That can't be true.) • We'll have to solve this problem **as soon as possible**. (so bald wie möglich) **possible** ◀ ▶ **impossible** [ɪmˈpɒsəbl] (unmöglich)	
condition [kənˈdɪʃn]	die Bedingung; der Zustand	It's too cold and too loud in this office. I can't work **in / under** these **conditions**. (bei / unter diesen Bedingungen)	
umbrella [ʌmˈbrelə]	der (Regen-)Schirm	an **umbrella**	
▶ p. 20 **St = Saint** [seɪnt]	St = Sankt		
central [ˈsentrəl]	zentral	**in central London** = in der Londoner Innenstadt / Stadtmitte adj: **central** – noun: **centre**	

1 Vocabulary

	pelican [ˈpelɪkən]	der Pelikan	*a pelican*
	(to) **tip** sb. [tɪp]	jm. Trinkgeld geben	verb: (to) **tip** (sb.) – Of course I'll **tip** our tour guide. noun: **tip** – I'll give her a generous **tip**. (das Trinkgeld)
▶ p. 21	**virtual** [ˈvɜːtʃuəl]	virtuell	❗ Betonung auf der 1. Silbe: **virtual** [ˈvɜːtʃuəl]
	road [rəʊd]	die Straße *(in oder zwischen Orten)*	❗ German: **in der** Hill Road / **in der** Park Street English: in Hill Road / in Park Street
	instead [ɪnˈsted]	stattdessen	I don't like chips. Can I have pasta **instead**? I'd like pasta **instead of** chips. (= anstelle von)
	roundabout [ˈraʊndəbaʊt]	der Kreisverkehr	*a roundabout*
	column [ˈkɒləm]	die Säule; die Spalte *(in Texten)*	*columns*
	guard [gɑːd]	der Wärter, die Wärterin; die Wache; der/die Sicherheitsbedienstete	noun: **guard** – The people in uniform are the king's **guards**. verb: (to) **guard sth.** – They **guard** the king's palace. (etwas schützen, bewachen) **Changing of the Guards** = die Wachablösung
	capsule [ˈkæpsjuːl]	die Kapsel; die Raumkapsel; die Kabine *(auf einem Riesenrad)*	*capsules* The **big wheel** in London is called "The London Eye".
	along the road [əˈlɒŋ]	die Straße entlang	❗ German: Geh **die Straße entlang**. English: Walk **along** the road.

Topic 3

▶ p. 22	**against** [əˈgenst]	gegen	Would you vote for or **against** Vanessa as head student?
	homeless [ˈhəʊmləs]	obdachlos	A **homeless** person doesn't have a home and often lives on the streets.

two hundred and ten

1

▶ p.23	(to) **cross** [krɒs]	kreuzen, überqueren	verb: (to) **cross** – Don't **cross** the road here. It's too dangerous. noun: **cross** (das Kreuz) – Put a **cross** (x) next to your favourite type of music.
	care [keə]	die Sorgfalt, die Vorsicht	

care – (to) care – careful

- **nouns**:

care	Choose your words **with care**. **Take care.** Can you **take care of** our dog next week?	mit Sorgfalt, sorgfältig Pass auf dich auf. sich kümmern um	**care** (n) = 1. die Sorgfalt, die Vorsicht; 2. die Versorgung, die Betreuung; die Pflege
carer	I think we will need a **carer** for Grandpa soon.	die Pflegekraft; der Betreuer, die Betreuerin	

- **verbs**:

(to) **care for sb.** (betreuen, pflegen; sich kümmern um; aufpassen auf)	Who is going to **care for** our dog when we're on holiday?	Wer kümmert sich um unseren Hund ...?
(to) **care about sth.** (wichtig nehmen)	I really **care about** animals. I don't **care about** money.	Tiere liegen mir sehr am Herzen. Geld ist mir nicht wichtig. / Geld ist mir egal.

- **adjective**:

careful (vorsichtig)	Be **careful** when you cross the road.	Sei vorsichtig, wenn du die Straße überquerst.

directions *(pl)* [dəˈrekʃnz]	die Wegbeschreibung(en)	❗ (to) **give directions** = den Weg beschreiben (to) **ask for directions** = nach dem Weg fragen
peace [piːs]	der Friede(n)	Will there ever be **peace** in the world? noun: **peace** – adj: **peaceful** (friedlich, friedfertig)

-ful / -less

careful	[ˈkeəfl]	vorsichtig	careless	[ˈkeələs]	unvorsichtig, leichtsinnig
colourful	[ˈkʌləfl]	farbenprächtig, bunt	cloudless	[ˈklaʊdləs]	wolkenlos
helpful	[ˈhelpfl]	hilfsbereit, hilfreich	colourless	[ˈkʌlələs]	farblos
peaceful	[ˈpiːsfl]	friedlich, friedfertig	endless	[ˈendləs]	endlos, unendlich
stressful	[ˈstresfl]	anstrengend, stressig	helpless	[ˈhelpləs]	hilflos
successful	[səkˈsesfl]	erfolgreich	homeless	[ˈhəʊmləs]	obdachlos
tasteful	[ˈteɪstfl]	geschmackvoll	tasteless	[ˈteɪstləs]	geschmacklos
useful	[ˈjuːsfl]	nützlich	useless	[ˈjuːsləs]	nutzlos, unnütz

goal [gəʊl]	das Ziel *(Absicht; Lebensziel)*; das Tor *(im Sport)*	What are your **goals** in life? What do you want to do when you finish school? Our team scored a **goal** in the last minute!
bike lane [ˈbaɪk leɪn]	der Radweg	▶▶ **cycle lane** **lane** = die Gasse
less [les]	weniger	This winter we had **less** snow than last winter. (= not as much snow as last winter) **less** ◀▶ **more**

1 Vocabulary

few [fjuː]	wenige	**!** **a few** = einige, ein paar – I talked to **a few** people at the party. **few** = (nur) wenige – Very **few** people came to the party. **few** ◄ ► many, a lot of

German "wenig, weniger, am wenigsten"			
1. mit dem <u>Plural von zählbaren Nomen</u>:	**few** cars / coins wenige Autos / Münzen	**fewer** cars / coins weniger Autos/Münzen	the **fewest** cars / coins die wenigsten Autos / Münzen
2. mit <u>nicht zählbaren Nomen</u>:	**little** traffic / money wenig Verkehr / Geld	**less** traffic / money weniger Verkehr / Geld	the **least** traffic / money der wenigste Verkehr / das wenigste Geld

air [eə]	die Luft	We all need **air** to breathe.
pollution [pəˈluːʃn]	die (Umwelt-)Verschmutzung	We have to stop water and air **pollution**.
(to) **lead** [liːd], **led, led** [led]	führen, leiten	verb: (to) **lead, led, led** – noun: *(person)* **leader**
(to) **make** sb. sth.	jn. zu etwas machen	• We **made Joe the new trainer** of our team. (... machten Joe zum neuen Trainer ...) • My grandparents came from Turkey and **made Germany their new home**. (... machten Deutschland zu ihrer neuen Heimat.)
▶ p. 24 **tap** [tæp]	der Wasserhahn	a **tap** **tap water** = das Leitungswasser
sparkling [ˈspɑːklɪŋ]	kohlensäurehaltig	**sparkling water** = der Sprudel
soft [sɒft]	weich; *(Stimme)* leise	This is my favourite shirt because it is so **soft**. **soft drink** = das alkoholfreie Getränk
mint [mɪnt]	die (Pfeffer-)Minze	I sometimes like to drink **mint** tea.
plate [pleɪt]	der Teller	Who is going to wash these **plates**?
chickpea [ˈtʃɪkpiː]	die Kichererbse	**chickpeas**
cucumber [ˈkjuːkʌmbə]	die Gurke *(Salatgurke)*	a **cucumber**
olive [ˈɒlɪv]	die Olive	**!** Betonung auf der 1. Silbe: **olive** [ˈɒlɪv]
sesame [ˈsesəmi]	der Sesam	**!** Aussprache: [ˈsesəmi] – mit scharfem **s** und [i] am Ende

two hundred and twelve

I'll have …	Ich nehme … *(beim Essen, z. B. im Restaurant)*	**I'll have** the chicken and some water, please.
(to) order [ˈɔːdə]	bestellen	verb: **(to) order** – Are you ready to **order**? noun: **order** – Can I take your **orders**? (… Ihre Bestellungen aufnehmen?)
waiter [ˈweɪtə], **waitress** [ˈweɪtrəs]	der Kellner, die Kellnerin	a **waiter** and two customers
▶ p. 25 **(to) introduce** sb. **to** sb./sth. [ˌɪntrəˈdjuːs]	jm. jn. / etwas vorstellen, jn. mit jm. / etwas bekanntmachen	Can you **introduce** me **to** your sister, John? verb: **(to) introduce** – noun: **introduction**
paragraph [ˈpærəɡrɑːf]	der (Text-)Abschnitt	Each **paragraph** in your text should start on a new line.

Story

▶ p. 26 **statue** [ˈstætʃuː]	die Statue	This is a famous **statue**.
gate [ɡeɪt]	das Tor	Who left the garden **gate** open?
right after school	gleich / direkt nach der Schule	• **right by the sea** = direkt am Meer • **right from the start** = gleich / direkt, von Anfang an • **right now / then** = genau jetzt / dann ❗ **right** = 1. richtig; 2. (nach) rechts; 3. (das) Recht; 4. gleich, direkt
▶ p. 27 **doorkeeper** [ˈdɔːkiːpə]	der Pförtner, die Pförtnerin	A **doorkeeper** guards the doors of a building, for example a big shop.
(to) shake [ʃeɪk], **shook** [ʃʊk], **shaken** [ˈʃeɪkən]	schütteln; zittern	Are you cold? You're **shaking**! • **(to) shake your head** = den Kopf schütteln • **(to) shake sb.'s hand** / (to) **shake sb. by the hand** = jm. die Hand schütteln / geben
towards [təˈwɔːdz]	nach, auf … zu, in Richtung (von)	Nick was running **towards** me. He looked very excited.
natural [ˈnætʃrəl]	natürlich, Natur-	**natural history** = die Naturkunde adj: **natural** – noun: **nature** [ˈneɪtʃə] (die Natur)
opposite [ˈɒpəzɪt]	gegenüber (von); gegenüberliegende(r, s)	The library is **opposite** the CD shop. (= is on the **opposite** side from the CD shop.)

opposite		
1. gegenüber (von)	**opposite** the bank / bike shop / …	gegenüber der Bank / vom Fahrradladen / …
2. gegenüberliegende(r, s)	on the **opposite** side / page / …	auf der gegenüberliegenden Seite / …
3. entgegengesetzt, gegensätzlich	in the **opposite** direction	in die entgegengesetzte Richtung
4. das Gegenteil	What's the **opposite** of "useful"?	… das Gegenteil von …

1 Vocabulary

	grass [grɑːs]	das Gras; der Rasen	*grass*
	(to) suggest [səˈdʒest]	vorschlagen	Tom **suggested** a visit to York. **!** *German:* **Tom schlug vor, nach York zu fahren.** *English:* **Tom suggested (that) we go to York.** *or* **Tom suggested going to York.** (*never:* Tom suggested to go …)
	(to) sigh [saɪ]	seufzen	verb: (to) **sigh** – "OK," she **sighed**. noun: **sigh** (der Seufzer) – "OK," she said with a **sigh**.
	(to) follow [ˈfɒləʊ]	(be)folgen; verfolgen	• Someone was **following** me on my way home. (folgen, verfolgen) • Always **follow** the rules, please. (befolgen)
	(to) hurry [ˈhʌri]	sich beeilen; eilen	verb: (to) **hurry** – It's late. We have to **hurry**. **Hurry up**! (Beeil dich!) noun: **hurry** (Eile) – We're **in a hurry**! (Wir sind in Eile. / Wir haben es eilig!)
▶ p. 28	**route** [ruːt]	die Route, der Weg	What's the fastest **route** from here to Dover?
	finally [ˈfaɪnəli]	schließlich, endlich	It was a long journey. We were very tired when we **finally** got home.
	clue [kluː]	der (Lösungs-)Hinweis; der Anhaltspunkt	• Nobody knows who killed the man. The police are still looking for **clues** in his flat. • I don't have a **clue**. / I have no **clue**. *(infml)* = Ich habe keine Ahnung. / Keine Ahnung.
	board [bɔːd]	die Tafel	It says on the information **board** that our train will be on time. **information board** = die Informationstafel
	path [pɑːθ]	der Weg, der Pfad	*a path*
	bench [bentʃ]	die Bank *(zum Sitzen)*	*a bench* — *a bank* — *river banks*

214 two hundred and fourteen

similar (to sb./sth.) [ˈsɪmələ]	(jm./einer Sache) ähnlich		Your new bike is **similar to** my brother's bike. (= The two bikes are nearly the same.)
(to) discuss [dɪˈskʌs]	diskutieren (über); besprechen		Mum and I **discussed** my problems with these maths exercises. She helped a lot! verb: (to) **discuss** – noun: **discussion** (die Diskussion)

Viewing

▶ p. 29	(to) make a difference	etwas bewirken, etwas ausmachen	Does voting **make a difference**? What do you think?
	(to) volunteer [vɒlənˈtɪə]	freiwillig/ehrenamtlich arbeiten *(unbezahlt)*	verb: (to) **volunteer** – I **volunteer** in a charity shop two afternoons a week. noun: **volunteer** (der/die Freiwillige; der/die ehrenamtliche Mitarbeiter/in) – I'm a **volunteer** and work in a charity shop (= I get no money for my work).
	community [kəˈmjuːnəti]	die Gemeinschaft, die Gemeinde	My favourite football club has a big **community** of fans all over Europe.
	(to) recognize [ˈrekəgnaɪz]	(wieder)erkennen	He has changed so much that I didn't **recognize** him.

Study skills

▶ p. 30	(to) search (for sth.) [sɜːtʃ]	(etwas) suchen; (nach etwas) suchen	verb: (to) **search (for)** – I **searched for** photos for my presentation on the Internet. noun: **search (for)** (die Suche (nach)) – It was a long **search**, but finally I found some nice pictures.
	recent [ˈriːsnt]	aktuell, jüngst	

recent – recently		
recent *(adj)*	**Recent** history shows … Here's a **recent** photo of me. He's changed a lot in **recent** years.	Die jüngere/jüngste Geschichte zeigt … … ein aktuelles Foto von mir. … in den letzten Jahren.
recently *(adv)*	I've started doing more sport **recently**.	in letzter Zeit, kürzlich, neuerdings

	government [ˈgʌvənmənt]	die Regierung	We'll vote for a new **government** soon.
	company [ˈkʌmpəni]	die Firma, die Gesellschaft	This **company** makes and sells special bikes. ❗ Betonung auf der 1. Silbe: **company** [ˈkʌmpəni]
	wax [wæks]	das Wachs	You need **wax** to make candles.
	figure [ˈfɪgə]	die Figur	❗ Betonung auf der 1. Silbe: **figure** [ˈfɪgə]
	regular [ˈregjələ]	regelmäßig; gewohnt, normal	adj: **regular** – Is "arrive" a **regular** verb? (regelmäßig) Mr Brown is not our **regular** maths teacher. (gewohnt, normal) adv: **regularly** – I do sport **regularly**. (regelmäßig)

two hundred and fifteen

2 Vocabulary

wash [wɒʃ]	die Wäsche, das (Sich-)Waschen		These T-shirts are dirty. They need a **wash**. How often do you give your hair a **wash**? verb: (to) **wash** – nouns: **washing** (die Wäsche(stücke)); **wash** (die Wäsche, das (Sich-)Waschen)
(to) copy ['kɒpi]	kopieren, abschreiben		verb: (to) **copy** – **Copy** these sentences and write the correct words in the gaps. noun: **copy** (die Kopie; das Exemplar) – I'll give you all **copies** of the text.

Irregular verbs

Infinitive	Simple past	Past participle		Infinitive	Simple past	Past participle	
(to) cost	cost	cost	kosten	(to) shake	shook	shaken	schütteln; zittern
(to) draw	drew	drawn	zeichnen	(to) slide	slid	slid	rutschen; schieben; gleiten (lassen)
(to) lead	led	led	führen, leiten	(to) write	wrote	written	schreiben

🔊 Unit 2 Manchester: Who we are

▶ pp. 44/45

hometown ['həʊmtaʊn]	die Heimatstadt		the town where you come from; the town that is your home
fashion ['fæʃn]	die Mode, die Fashion		I'd like to learn to design and make my own **fashion**. (= clothes that are cool and popular)
kindness ['kaɪndnəs]	die Güte, die Freundlichkeit		noun: **kindness** – adj: **kind**
reason ['riːzn]	der Grund, die Begründung		What could be **the reason why** Jill did this? (der Grund dafür, dass …) ❗ German: **aus** diesem Grund English: **for** this reason
(to) support [sə'pɔːt]	unterstützen		(to) give help to sb.; (to) be a fan of a sports team verb: (to) **support** – My parents always **support** my dreams and plans. nouns: • **support** (die Unterstützung) – My parents are a great **support**. • (person) **supporter** – I'm a Manchester United **supporter**.
disability [dɪsə'bɪləti]	die Behinderung		Ms Adu has a **disability**. She's in a wheelchair. noun: **disability** – adj: **disabled** [dɪs'eɪbld] ((körper)behindert)

Topic 1

▶ p. 46

by Omar		von Omar (geschrieben)

by

a text **by** Omar	ein Text / eine SMS von Omar (von Omar geschrieben)
a campsite **by** the river	ein Campingplatz am Fluss
(to) go **by** bus / **by** bike	mit dem Bus / dem Rad fahren
(to) pay **by** card	mit Karte bezahlen
(to) send sth. **by** email	etwas per E-Mail schicken

(to) **decide** [dɪˈsaɪd]	beschließen, sich entscheiden	• (to) **decide to do** sth. – We **decided to do** a project about clothes. • (to) **decide on** sth. – We can't **decide on** a name for our baby.	
attractive [əˈtræktɪv]	attraktiv	❗ Betonung auf der 2. Silbe: **attractive** [əˈtræktɪv]	
tight [taɪt]	knapp, eng (anliegend) *(Kleidung)*	adj: **tight** – This dress is too **tight**. I can't breathe. I need a bigger size. noun: **tights** *(pl)* – In winter I often wear **tights** with skirts or dresses. (die Strumpfhose)	
(to) **prefer** sth. **to** sth. [prɪˈfɜː]	etwas einer Sache vorziehen, etwas lieber tun / haben als etwas	• I **prefer** juice **to** cola. (= I like juice better than cola.) • What about a nice sandwich? – Well, I'**d prefer** (= I **would prefer**) a fruit salad. (Ich würde ... vorziehen.) ❗ *Simple past und -ing form* mit **-rr-**: **preferred, preferring**	
baggy [ˈbægi]	weit (geschnitten), sackig *(Kleidung)*	**baggy trousers** *(pl)* = die Schlabberhose *(weit geschnittene Hose)*	
skirt [skɜːt]	der Rock	a **skirt**	
light [laɪt]	hell; leicht	❗ **light** = **1.** hell; **2.** leicht; **3.** das Licht, die Lampe	
patterned [ˈpætənd]	gemustert	**pattern** = das *(wiederkehrende)* Muster, das Schema	
old-fashioned [ˌəʊld ˈfæʃənd]	altmodisch	**old-fashioned** ◀ ▶ **trendy / modern**	
plain [pleɪn]	einfach, schlicht; „ohne alles"	She wore a **plain** black dress, but it looked great. I think **plain** white bread is boring.	
style [staɪl]	der Stil; die Mode; die Art	(to) **be in style** = in Mode sein (to) **be out of style** = aus der Mode sein (to) **go out of style** = aus der Mode kommen	
▶ p. 47 **clothing** *(no pl)* [ˈkləʊðɪŋ]	die Kleidung	❗ *German:* ein Kleidungsstück *English:* **a piece of clothing** ❗ Das Wort **clothing** ist förmlicher als **clothes**.	
percentage [pəˈsentɪdʒ]	der Anteil, der Prozentsatz	What **percentage** of your pocket money do you spend on clothes?	
litre [ˈliːtə]	der Liter	**a one-litre bottle** = eine Einliterflasche ❗ *German:* **10 Liter** – *English:* **10 litres**	

two hundred and seventeen **217**

2 Vocabulary

about [əˈbaʊt]	ungefähr	We get up at **about** 9 o'clock on Sundays. ❗ **about** = 1. *(adv)* ungefähr; 　　　　　 2. *(prep)* von, über
material [məˈtɪərɪəl]	der Stoff; das Material	I have some nice **material** for a new dress. This could be **material** for a horror story!
bit [bɪt]	das Teil, das Stück(chen)	This is the hard **bit** of the task. ❗ **bit** = 1. das Teil, das Stück(chen); 　　　　2. **a bit** … = ein bisschen …, 　　　　　　　　　ein wenig …
cotton [ˈkɒtn]	die Baumwolle	**Cotton** and **silk** are natural materials. **Cotton** grows in fields, **silk** comes from insects called silkworms.
silk [sɪlk]	die Seide	
quick [kwɪk]	schnell	▶▶ **fast** adj: **quick** – I'm a **quick** worker. adv: **quickly** – I work **quickly**. **quick / fast** ◀▶ **slow**
brand [brænd]	die (Produkt-)Marke	This shop doesn't sell expensive **brands**, but their bikes are very good. What **brand** is your new bike?
(to) **reuse** [riːˈjuːz]	wiederverwenden	verb: (to) **reuse** [riːˈjuːz] – Don't put the box in the bin. **Reuse** it. noun: **reuse** [riːˈjuːs] – The **reuse** of materials saves a lot of money.
(to) **upcycle** [ˈʌpsaɪkl]	upcyceln *(gebrauchte Gegenstände als höherwertige Waren weiterverwenden)*	verbs: (to) **recycle** (recyceln, wiederverwerten) / (to) **upcycle** – nouns: **recycling / upcycling** (das Upcycling, die Weiternutzung gebrauchter Gegenstände als höherwertige Waren)
(to) **repair** [rɪˈpeə]	reparieren	verb: (to) **repair** – noun: **repair** (die Reparatur)
(to) **throw** [θrəʊ], **threw** [θruː], **thrown** [θrəʊn]	werfen	He **threw** the ball and it hit our neighbours' window. Don't **throw** these clothes away, take them to a charity shop!
(to) **produce** [prəˈdjuːs]	produzieren	verb: (to) **produce** – nouns: **product** (das Produkt); *(person)* **producer** (der/die Produzent/in) ❗ Betonung: (to) **produce** [prəˈdjuːs] – **pro**duct [ˈprɒdʌkt]

Topic 2

▶ p. 48	**friendship** [ˈfrendʃɪp]	die Freundschaft	Sue is my best friend. My **friendship** with Sue is very important to me. nouns: **friendship**; *(person)* **friend** – adj: **friendly**

218　two hundred and eighteen

you	man	❗ **you** = 1. du; ihr; Sie; 2. man

German "man"

you	**You** never know! How do **you** say that in English?	Man weiß nie! Wie sagt man das auf Englisch?
they	**They** say he's ill. In France **they** love cheese.	Man sagt, er sei krank / er ist krank. In Frankreich liebt man Käse.
people	**People** still don't know our product. I don't believe what **people** say about her.	Man kennt unser Produkt immer noch nicht. Ich glaube nicht, was man über sie sagt.

advice *(no pl)* [əd'vaɪs]	der Rat, der Ratschlag, die Ratschläge	❗ **advice** ist unzählbar: *German:* **Er gab mir einen Rat.** *English:* **He gave me some advice.** / **He gave me a piece of advice.** (*never:* He gave me an advice.) • Take my **advice**: Go and see a doctor. (Hör auf meinen Rat: …) • **advice column** = der Kummerkasten, die Ratgeber-Spalte (z. B. in Zeitschriften)
you **needn't** do it ['niːdnt]	du musst es nicht tun; du brauchst es nicht zu tun	I can do the exercise. You **needn't** help me. (= You don't have to help me.) ❗ Nicht verwechseln: You **needn't** help him. = … musst nicht … You **mustn't** help him. = … darfst nicht …
it **might** help … [maɪt]	es könnte … helfen, vielleicht hilft es …	That **might** be true, but I'm not sure. You **might** hate school, but you learn useful things there.
enemy ['enəmi]	der Feind, die Feindin	**friend** ◄ ► **enemy**
frenemy ['frenəmi]	der falsche Freund, die falsche Freundin	A **frenemy** is part friend, part enemy. Maybe this person was your friend, but is now your enemy.
(to) **be in love (with** sb.**)**	verliebt sein (in jn.)	(to) **fall in love (with** sb.**), fell, fallen** = sich verlieben (in jn.)
they	er/sie *(geschlechtsneutral)*	

they = he or she

A nice teacher will always help you if **they** can. = if he or she can

Not every student can talk to **their** parents about **their** problems. = his or her parents / problems

Our friend Chris doesn't identify as a man or a woman. We use the pronouns "**they / them / their**" for **them**.

(to) **identify** [aɪ'dentɪfaɪ]	(sich) identifizieren; erkennen	(to) **identify (yourself) (as)** = sich identifizieren (als); sich zu erkennen geben (als)
forever [fər'evə], **for ever**	für immer, ewig (lange)	• The accident changed her life **forever** / **for ever**. • I hope Simon arrives soon. We can't wait **forever** / **for ever**. **best friend forever (BFF)** *(infml)* = der beste Freund / die beste Freundin für immer
situation [sɪtʃu'eɪʃn]	die Situation	❗ Betonung auf der 3. Silbe: **situation** [sɪtʃu'eɪʃn]

two hundred and nineteen

2 Vocabulary

▶ p. 49	(to) **be nerdy** [ˈnɜːdi]	ein Nerd sein *(absonderlich, streberhaft)*	They say Jill **is nerdy**, but that's unfair. She's just not like everybody else, and I think she's really cool.
	(to) **say sorry to** sb.	sich bei jm. entschuldigen	That was so stupid of me. I really want to **say sorry to** all of you.
	(to) **trust** sb. [trʌst]	jm. vertrauen	verb: (to) **trust** – Be careful. You shouldn't **trust** everybody. noun: **trust** – Too much **trust** in others can be a problem. *(das Vertrauen)*
	strict [strɪkt]	streng	Some teachers aren't **strict** at all, and then we all do what we want during the lessons!
	(to) **be allowed to do** sth. [əˈlaʊd]	etwas tun dürfen	• We**'re not allowed to** eat in class. • Are you **allowed to** use dictionaries in your English tests? – No, dictionaries **are not allowed**. *(... sind nicht erlaubt)*
	(to) **have a crush (on** sb.**)** [krʌʃ]	in jn. verliebt sein	▶▶ (to) **be in love with** sb. **crush** = die Schwärmerei, das Verliebtsein; der Schwarm *(jd., in den/die man verliebt ist)*
	(to) **deal with** sth. [diːl], **dealt, dealt** [delt]	mit etwas klarkommen, mit etwas fertigwerden; mit etwas umgehen	Let's try and **deal with** this problem first and think about everything else later. When people at school bully you, you'll find it hard to **deal with** your school work.
▶ p. 50	**annoying** [əˈnɔɪɪŋ]	ärgerlich *(unangenehm)*	adj: **annoying** – I find it very **annoying** that the trains are always late. **annoyed** – I'm often **annoyed** about the trains. *(verärgert)* verb: (to) **annoy** sb. – It **annoys** me that the trains are always late. *(jn. ärgern)*
	he **may** find out ... [meɪ]	er findet vielleicht heraus, ...; er kann herausfinden, ...	This **may** not be such a good idea. *(... ist vielleicht keine so gute Idee.)*

möglich – wahrscheinlich – sicherlich

My parents	may might could should must	be at home now.	Meine Eltern	sind jetzt **vielleicht** zu Hause. **könnten** jetzt **(vielleicht)** zu Hause sein. **könnten** jetzt zu Hause sein. **sollten / müssten eigentlich** jetzt zu Hause sein. **müssen** jetzt zu Hause sein.

▶ p. 51	(to) **be / feel ashamed (of)** [əˈʃeɪmd]	sich schämen (für)	I'm really **ashamed of** the stupid things that I said. I'm so sorry!
	(to) **shout** [ʃaʊt]	rufen, schreien	verbs: (to) **shout** – "Leave me alone!" he **shouted**. (to) **shout at** sb. – Don't **shout at me**. *(jn. anschreien)* noun: **shout** – We heard angry **shouts** in the street. *(der Ruf, der Schrei)*
	probably [ˈprɒbəbli]	wahrscheinlich	You're **probably** right. = I'm quite sure you're right.

Topic 3

▶ p. 52 **confidence** [ˈkɒnfɪdəns]   das (Selbst-)Vertrauen, die Zuversicht   noun: **confidence** – adj: **confident**

Reflexive pronouns				
I	▶ **myself** [maɪˈself]	mir, mich	I'm trying to teach **myself** the guitar.
you	▶ **yourself** [jɔːˈself]	dir, dich	Be careful with that knife or **you** might cut **yourself**.
he	▶ **himself** [hɪmˈself]	sich	I didn't know if **he** was talking to me or to **himself**.
she	▶ **herself** [hɜːˈself]	sich	**My sister** should have more confidence in **herself**.
it	▶ **itself** [ɪtˈself]	sich	**The cat** fell off a tree and hurt **itself**.
we	▶ **ourselves** [aʊəˈselvz]	uns	Our team is great – **we** can be proud of **ourselves**!
you	▶ **yourselves** [jɔːˈselvz]	euch	**You** must believe in **yourselves**, kids!
they	▶ **themselves** [ðəmˈselvz]	sich	**Small children** can't look after **themselves**.

❗ Merk dir auch die Wendung **Enjoy yourselves.** = Viel Spaß! / Amüsiert euch gut!

microphone [ˈmaɪkrəfəʊn]   das Mikrofon

a microphone

❗ Betonung auf der 1. Silbe: microphone [ˈmaɪkrəfəʊn]

(to) switch sth. **on / off** [swɪtʃ ˈɒn], [swɪtʃ ˈɒf]   etwas einschalten / ausschalten   verb: **(to) switch** sth. **on / off** – Please **switch off** the lights when you leave the house.
noun: **switch** – I couldn't find the light **switch** in the dark. (der Schalter)

a light switch

▶ p. 53 **that's why**   deshalb, darum   Sam was alone. **That's why** she felt sad.

role model [ˈrəʊl mɒdl]   das Vorbild   a person that you like very much, and you try to be like them

certainly [ˈsɜːtnli]   sicher(lich), gewiss   This is **certainly** no easy job, but I'll do my best.

(to) keep (yourself) busy   sich beschäftigen, auf Trab bleiben

(to) keep, kept, kept		
1. (to) **keep**	Here's some tea to **keep** you warm. / Don't tell them. Let's **keep** it secret.	halten
	Can I **keep** your pencil? / **Keep** the change.	behalten
	Where do you **keep** vegetables? / We **keep** our biscuits in a tin.	aufbewahren
2. (to) **keep doing sth.**	I told him to stop, but he **kept hitting** me. / **Keep walking** till you get to the bridge.	etwas dauernd / immer wieder / immer weiter tun
3. (to) **keep sb. busy**	Here's a list of activities to **keep** the children **busy**.	jn. beschäftigen, auf Trab halten

penalty [ˈpenəlti]   der Strafstoß; der Elfmeter (Fußball)   (to) **miss a penalty** = einen Elfmeter verschießen *(nicht treffen)*

two hundred and twenty-one

2 Vocabulary

	nasty [ˈnɑːsti]	gemein, fies; schlimm, scheußlich	▶▶ **mean, not nice, really bad** It's really **nasty** to bully other students. Don't use plastic bags all the time! They're **nasty** for nature.
	whenever [wenˈevə]	wann (auch) immer	You can come and visit us **whenever** you like. Sit **wherever** there's space. (wo (auch) immer …) **Wherever** you go, take care! (Egal, wo(hin) …)
	poverty [ˈpɒvəti]	die Armut	noun: **poverty** – adj: **poor**
▶ p. 54	**(to) appear** [əˈpɪə]	erscheinen; auftauchen	• A funny picture **appeared** on the screen. (erscheinen) • Suddenly a man **appeared** behind the gate. (auftauchen) • He **appeared** to be very sad. (zu sein scheinen)
	(to) slouch [slaʊtʃ]	sich lümmeln, in krummer Haltung stehen / sitzen	verb: **(to) slouch** – noun: **slouch** (die krumme / schlaffe Haltung) When you **slouch** / stand or sit **in a slouch**, it can mean that you're not very confident.
▶ p. 55	**classmate** [ˈklɑːsmeɪt]	der Mitschüler, die Mitschülerin	The other students in your class are your **classmates**.
	compliment [ˈkɒmplɪmənt]	das Kompliment	❗ Betonung auf der 1. Silbe: **compliment** [ˈkɒmplɪmənt] (to) **pay** sb. **a compliment** = jm. ein Kompliment machen
	nervous [ˈnɜːvəs]	nervös, aufgeregt	❗ Betonung auf der 1. Silbe: **nervous** [ˈnɜːvəs]

Story

▶ p. 56	**conflict** [ˈkɒnflɪkt]	der Konflikt, die Auseinandersetzung, der Streit	❗ Betonung auf der 1. Silbe: **conflict** [ˈkɒnflɪkt]
	No way! [nəʊ ˈweɪ]	Auf keinen Fall!	Do you want green hair? – **No way!**
	Come on! [kʌm ˈɒn]	Komm(t) (schon)! Na los!	**Come on**, we're late! Get ready, or we'll miss our train!
	(to) admire [ədˈmaɪə]	bewundern	We stopped at the lake to **admire** the view.
	queue [kjuː]	die (Warte-)Schlange	noun: **queue** – verb: **(to) queue** (Schlange stehen, sich anstellen) a **queue**
▶ p. 57	**pitch** [pɪtʃ]	der Platz *(Sport)*, das Spielfeld	
	(to) ping [pɪŋ]	pingen *(elektronisch anklopfen)*	When your phone **pings**, it means that someone has sent you a message.

half-time [hɑːf ˈtaɪm]	die Halbzeit(pause)		❗ German: **in** der Halbzeit English: **at** half-time noun: **half**, pl **halves** = die Hälfte – **the first half** (Sport) = die erste Halbzeit adv: **half** – **half full, half empty** = halb voll, halb leer **half the time, half the money** = die Hälfte der Zeit, die Hälfte des Geldes **half an hour** = eine halbe Stunde
chance [tʃɑːns]	die Chance, die Gelegenheit		If you have the **chance**, you should visit the British Museum.
goalkeeper [ˈɡəʊlkiːpə]	der Torwart, die Torhüterin		
net [net]	das Netz (Sport)		a net — a goalkeeper
(to) cheer [tʃɪə]	jubeln, (Sportler/innen) anfeuern		Everyone **cheered** when Amy's team won the match.
additional [əˈdɪʃənl]	zusätzliche(r, s)		The job sounds interesting, but I'd like some **additional** information about the company. **additional time** = die Nachspielzeit (Fußball)
finger [ˈfɪŋɡə]	der Finger		You have ten **fingers** – five on each hand. **(to) cross your fingers** = die Daumen drücken / halten (jm. Glück / gutes Gelingen wünschen)
(to) clap (your hands) [klæp]	(in die Hände) klatschen		It was a great concert. At the end everyone **clapped** and cheered.
(to) call sb. **names**	jn. beschimpfen		What? Mike really **called you names** in front of all your friends? How nasty!
(to) tell sb. **(not) to do** sth.	jn. auffordern, etwas (nicht) zu tun; jm. sagen, dass er/sie etwas (nicht) tun soll		The teacher **told** the students **to be** quiet. How many times do I have to **tell** you **not to hit** your brother?
further [ˈfɜːðə]	weiter (entfernt)		**further (from)** ◄ ► **closer (to)** **further on** = (etwas) weiter entfernt
racist [ˈreɪsɪst]	der Rassist, die Rassistin; rassistisch		nouns: **racism** (der Rassismus); (person) **racist** adj: **racist** ❗ Betonung auf der 1. Silbe: **r**acist [ˈreɪsɪst], **r**acism [ˈreɪsɪzəm]
(to) pull [pʊl]	ziehen		verb: **(to) pull** – noun: **pull** (das Ziehen, der Ruck)
straight [streɪt]	direkt, gleich, geradewegs		

straight
1. (adj) **gerade**; (Haare) **glatt**
2. (adv) **direkt, gleich, geradewegs**

a **straight** road / a **straight** line
straight hair (not curly)
He looked **straight** at me as if he knew everything.
We went **straight** home / **straight** to the station.
We bought a takeaway pizza and ate it **straight** from the box.
Go **straight on** till you get to the bridge. (geradeaus weiter)

2 Vocabulary

▶ p. 58 | (to) **disagree** [dɪsəˈgriː] | nicht zustimmen, widersprechen | Sorry, but I **disagree** with you. (= I don't agree with you. I think you're wrong). (to) **agree** ◄ ► (to) **disagree**

(to) **interrupt** [ɪntəˈrʌpt] | unterbrechen | It's rude to **interrupt** people when they're talking.

pose [pəʊz] | die Pose, die Haltung | This yoga **pose** is sometimes called "the snake". **power pose** = die Machtpose

Viewing

▶ p. 59 | **coach** [kəʊtʃ] | der (Reise-)Bus

buses — a **coach**

tyre [ˈtaɪə] | der Reifen | My bike needs new **tyres**.

service station [ˈsɜːvɪs steɪʃn] | die Tankstelle; die (Autobahn-)Raststätte

a **service station**

Study skills

▶ p. 60 | **pineapple** [ˈpaɪnæpl] | die Ananas

a **pineapple**

savoury [ˈseɪvəri] | pikant, herzhaft | I'll have something **savoury** first, and then something sweet for dessert.

completely [kəmˈpliːtli] | völlig, absolut | verb: (to) **complete** – Please **complete** the list. (vervollständigen)
adj: **complete** – Is the list **complete** now? (vollständig, komplett)
adv: **completely** – My clothes needn't be **completely** new. I'm happy with second-hand clothes too.

point | das Argument, der Standpunkt

point				
(to) **make your point** Make your point.	ein Argument vorbringen Leg deinen Standpunkt dar. / Sag, wie du darüber denkst.		(to) **take a point** I take your point.	einen Standpunkt verstehen Ich verstehe, was du sagen willst. / Einverstanden.
That's a good point.	Das ist ein gutes Argument.			

Unit task

▶ p. 61 | (to) **argue (for / against** sth.) ['ɑːgjuː] | argumentieren; sich (für / gegen etwas) aussprechen | • (to) **argue an opinion** = eine Meinung vertreten
• (to) **argue (about)** = (sich) streiten (über / wegen)
verb: (to) **argue** –
noun: **argument** ['ɑːgjumənt] (das Argument; der Streit)

Irregular verbs

Infinitive	Simple past	Past participle		Infinitive	Simple past	Past participle	
(to) **become**	became	become	werden	(to) **keep**	kept	kept	(be)halten
(to) **deal with** [iː]	dealt [e]	dealt [e]	klarkommen / fertigwerden mit	(to) **read** [iː]	read [e]	read [e]	lesen
(to) **fall**	fell	fallen	fallen	(to) **say** [eɪ]	said [e]	said [e]	sagen
(to) **fight**	fought	fought	kämpfen	(to) **speak**	spoke	spoken	sprechen
(to) **hit**	hit	hit	treffen, schlagen, stoßen	(to) **throw**	threw	thrown	werfen

🔊 Unit 3 Scotland: Adventure

▶ pp. 74/75 | **kayak** ['kaɪæk] | der/das Kajak

kayaking = das Kajakfahren
kayaker = der/die Kajakfahrer/in

| **coast** [kəʊst] | die Küste | ❗ *German:* **an der Küste**
English: **on the coast** |

| (to) **carry** ['kæri] | tragen; bei sich haben; befördern | • Let me help you **carry** those bags! (tragen)
• You're not allowed to **carry** knives on a plane. (bei sich haben)
• This car can **carry** five people. (befördern) |

Topic 1

▶ p. 76 | **legend** ['ledʒənd] | die Legende, die Sage | ❗ Betonung auf der 1. Silbe: **legend** ['ledʒənd] |

| (to) **include** [ɪnˈkluːd] | (mit) einschließen | £80 – does that **include** breakfast?
Yes, it's for everything, **including** breakfast.
including = einschließlich, inklusive |

| **mermaid** ['mɜːmeɪd] | die Nixe, die Meerjungfrau | ❗ **mermaid** = die Nixe, die Meerjungfrau
merman, *pl* **mermen** = der Nix, der Wassermann, der Meermann |

| **creature** ['kriːtʃə] | das Geschöpf, das (Lebe-)Wesen | ❗ Betonung auf der 1. Silbe: **creature** ['kriːtʃə] |

two hundred and twenty-five

3 Vocabulary

mystery [ˈmɪstri]	das Geheimnis, das Rätsel	• It's a complete **mystery** why they suddenly have so much money. • Will we ever solve this **mystery**? (das Geheimnis lüften, das Rätsel lösen)
deep [diːp]	tief	a **deep** lake / **deep** snow
loving [ˈlʌvɪŋ]	liebevoll	

Adjective: *-ing* – adverb: *-ingly*

• adj: a **loving** family	– adv: He looked **lovingly** at his son.	liebevoll, mit viel Liebe
• adj: a **surprising** ending	– adv: They **surprisingly** discovered that … a **surprisingly** good result	überraschenderweise; überraschend
• adj: an **interesting** story	– adv: **Interestingly**, he didn't recognize me.	interessanterweise

(to) **seem (to be / do)** [siːm]	erscheinen; (zu sein / zu tun) scheinen	He **seems** sad. (erscheinen) He **seems to be** very sad. (scheint … zu sein)
unfortunately [ʌnˈfɔːtʃənətli]	unglücklicherweise, leider	**unfortunately** ◄ ► **fortunately** [ˈfɔːtʃənətli] (zum Glück, glücklicherweise)
definitely [ˈdefɪnətli]	auf jeden Fall; ganz bestimmt	The party is **definitely** on the 10th, not on the 17th. (= I'm sure the party is on the 10th.)

No way! | maybe | probably | certainly, surely | definitely

sonar [ˈsəʊnɑː]	Sonar-, das Sonargerät	**Sonar** equipment can help you to find things underwater with the help of sound. ❗ Betonung auf der 1. Silbe: **sonar** [ˈsəʊnɑː]
several [ˈsevrəl]	mehrere, einige	The shop has **several** bikes for under £400. ►► some, but not a lot
large [lɑːdʒ]	groß	Six brothers and sisters? What a **large** family! ❗ You don't use **large** to describe people. People are **tall** (groß), **big** (dick, schwer) or **great** (bedeutend, angesehen).
centimetre (= cm) [ˈsentɪmiːtə]	der Zentimeter	One hundred **centimetres** are one metre.
it says that …	es heißt (im Text), dass …	**It says here that** the artist lives in Spain now. (Hier steht, dass …)
(to) **hunt** [hʌnt]	jagen	verb: (to) **hunt** – nouns: **hunt** (die Jagd); *(person)* **hunter** (der/die Jäger/in)
eel [iːl]	der Aal	an **eel**
fake [feɪk]	falsch, gefälscht	This isn't real gold, it's only **fake**. Is this true? Or is it just **fake** news? adj: **fake** – noun: **fake** (der/das Fake, die Fälschung) – verb: (to) **fake sth.** (etwas faken, fälschen, vortäuschen)

	submarine [sʌbməˈriːn]	das U-Boot	*a submarine*
	catfish [ˈkætfɪʃ], *pl* **catfish**	der Wels *(Fisch)*	*a catfish*
	however [haʊˈevə]	allerdings, jedoch	She was born in France. She isn't French, **however**. (= But she isn't French.)
	therefore [ˈðeəfɔː]	daher, deshalb	Our teacher was sick. **Therefore**, school finished early. (= So school finished early.)
▶ p. 77	**waste** [weɪst]	die Verschwendung	noun: **waste** – This is a **waste** of time. I'm leaving. verb: (to) **waste** – I don't want to **waste** my time like this. (verschwenden)
	(to) **spot** sth. [spɒt]	etwas entdecken	verb: (to) **spot** – We went hiking on the coast, and dad **spotted** some sea lions. noun: **spot** – Our cat is black with some white **spots**. (der Fleck) This is my favourite **spot** in Wales. (die Stelle, der Punkt)
	(to) **translate** [trænsˈleɪt]	übersetzen	verb: (to) **translate** – You've **translated** this text really well. noun: **translation** [trænsˈleɪʃn] – This is a very good **translation** of the text. (die Übersetzung)
▶ p. 78	**witch** [wɪtʃ]	die Hexe	People believe she has magic powers. They seem to think she's a **witch**.
	soldier [ˈsəʊldʒə]	der Soldat, die Soldatin	*soldiers*
	careful [ˈkeəfl]	aufmerksam; sorgfältig	❗ **careful** = 1. vorsichtig – Be **careful**! 2. aufmerksam; sorgfältig – This text needs **careful** checking. adj: **careful** – adv: **carefully** = 1. vorsichtig – You should always drive **carefully**. 2. aufmerksam; sorgfältig – Read the text **carefully**.

two hundred and twenty-seven

3 Vocabulary

▶ p. 79	**piper** [ˈpaɪpə]	der Dudelsackspieler, die Dudelsackspielerin	a bagpipe player

Topic 2

▶ p. 80	**cliff** [klɪf]	die Klippe	**cliff jumping** = das Klippenspringen
▶ p. 81	**(to) ski** [skiː]	Ski laufen, Ski fahren	We love to **go skiing** in the mountains in winter.
	(to) pack [pæk]	packen, einpacken	(to) **pack** ◀ ▶ (to) **unpack** [ʌnˈpæk] (auspacken)
	adventurous [ədˈventʃərəs]	abenteuerlustig	adj: **adventurous** – nouns: **adventure**; *(person)* **adventurer** (der/die Abenteurer/in)
	(to) catch [kætʃ], **caught, caught** [kɔːt]	(ein)fangen; erwischen; einholen; nehmen *(z. B. einen Zug, einen Bus)*	• Our cat sometimes **catches** mice. (fangen) • If we hurry, we'll **catch** Joe. He has only just left! (einholen) • I want to **catch** the train at 12.55. (nehmen)
	tent [tent]	das Zelt	**tents** on a campsite
	twice [twaɪs]	zweimal	**once** = one time **twice** = two times
▶ p. 82	**skydiving** [ˈskaɪdaɪvɪŋ]	das Fallschirmspringen	**skydiving**
	for thirty years	seit 30 Jahren; 30 Jahre (lang)	❗ **for** = 1. für – a present **for** you 2. seit; … lang – We've lived here **for** 10 years. (seit zehn Jahren) She's been asleep **for hours**. (stundenlang; seit Stunden)
	outdoor activity [ˈaʊtdɔː]	die Outdoor-Aktivität; die Aktivität für draußen / im Freien	I like **outdoor activities** like hiking and cycling. adv: **outdoors** [aʊtˈdɔːz] – I like to be **outdoors**. (im Freien, draußen)
	motivation [məʊtɪˈveɪʃn]	die Motivation	noun: **motivation** – verb: (to) **motivate** [ˈməʊtɪveɪt] (motivieren)
	jungle [ˈdʒʌŋgl]	der Dschungel	It is very important to save the **jungles** and rainforests on our planet. **rainforest** = der Regenwald

volcano [vɒlˈkeɪnəʊ], pl **volcanoes** or **volcanos**	der Vulkan		a **volcano**
cave [keɪv]	die Höhle		a **cave**
wild [waɪld]	wild	On our safari we saw many **wild** animals. ❗ Aussprache: **wild** [waɪld]	
since 2010 [sɪns]	seit 2010	**since then** = seitdem	

German "seit"
- **since** + Zeitpunkt: **since** 2010 / last year / yesterday / six o'clock / …   We've had our dog **since 2018**.
- **for** + Zeitraum: **for** six years / a week / a long time / three hours / …   We've had our dog **for many years**.

(to) **take part (in)** [teɪk ˈpɑːt]	teilnehmen (an), mitmachen (bei)	More than 10,000 people **took part in** the Pride parade.
serious [ˈsɪəriəs]	ernst(haft)	adj: **serious** – • Jen is a very **serious** person. (ernst) • Are you **serious**? (Meinst du das ernst?) adv: **seriously** – • **Seriously**, horses can be dangerous. (im Ernst, ernsthaft) • I can't take this message **seriously**. (Ich kann … nicht ernst nehmen.)
(to) **scan** (a text **for** sth.) [skæn]	(einen Text) überfliegen, (einen Text) absuchen (nach etwas)	(to) read a text quickly, looking only for important information
specific [spəˈsɪfɪk]	bestimmte(r, s), spezielle(r, s); genau, präzise	• Any **specific** time when you need the car back? (bestimmte) • She gave us very **specific** instructions. (genau, präzise)
e.g. *(aus dem Lateinischen)* [iː ˈdʒiː]	z. B. (zum Beispiel)	❗ **e.g.** wird in geschriebenem Englisch benutzt. Wenn man spricht, sagt man **for example**.
▶ p. 83 **period (of time)** [ˈpɪəriəd]	der Zeitraum, die (Zeit-)Periode	I especially like the band's music from the **period** between 1990 and 2000.
primary school [ˈpraɪməri skuːl]	die Grundschule	In Britain children go to **primary school** from when they're 4 or 5 till when they're 10 or 11.
biography [baɪˈɒgrəfi], *(kurz auch:* **bio** [ˈbaɪəʊ])	die Biografie	❗ Betonung auf der 2. Silbe: bi**o**graphy [baɪˈɒgrəfi]

two hundred and twenty-nine   **229**

3 Vocabulary

	interest (in) [ˈɪntrəst]	das Interesse (an)	noun: **interest (in)** – Do you have an **interest in** skydiving? (= Are you interested …?) verb: (to) **interest** sb. (**in** sth.) – Can I **interest** you **in** our school magazine? (jn. (für etwas) interessieren) adj: **interesting** (interessant); **interested (in)** (interessiert (an)) – adv: **interestingly** (interessanterweise)

Topic 3

▶ p. 84	(to) **protect (from / against)** [prəˈtekt]	(be)schützen (vor)	An umbrella **protects** you **from** the rain.
	plant [plɑːnt]	die Pflanze	noun: **plant** – Which **plants** do you have in your garden? verb: (to) **plant** – What else would you like to **plant** in your garden? (pflanzen)
	landscape [ˈlændskeɪp]	die Landschaft; das Landschaftsbild	What a great **landscape**!
	countryside [ˈkʌntrisaɪd]	das Land *(ländliche Gegend)*, die Landschaft; die Natur	London is so busy! I'd prefer to live in the **countryside**. The **countryside** in Scotland is very beautiful. ❗ German: **auf** dem Land English: **in** the countryside
	deer [dɪə], *pl* **deer**	das Reh; der Hirsch	This is a big forest with lots of wild **deer**.
	(to) **adopt** [əˈdɒpt]	adoptieren	verb: (to) **adopt** – Come to our animal home and **adopt** an animal! noun: **adoption** [əˈdɒpʃn] – The **adoption** of animals is very easy. (die Adoption)
▶ p. 85	**Scots** [skɒts]	Schottisch *(Sprache)*; schottisch	**Scots** is similar to English. People in Scotland speak it. "wee" is a **Scots** word. It means "small".
	blueberry [ˈbluːbəri]	die Blaubeere, die Heidelbeere	
	heather [ˈheðə]	das Heidekraut	**heather** and **blueberries**

Story

▶ p. 86	**before** [bɪˈfɔː]	zuvor; vorher; schon einmal	Have you ever been to Scotland **before**?

before			
1. *(prep)* **vor**		**before** school / **before** lunch / …	**vor** der Schule / **vor** dem Mittagessen / …
2. *(conj)* **bevor**		**before** you read the text / **before** we eat / …	**bevor** du den Text liest / bevor wir essen / …
3. *(adv)* **vorher; schon einmal**		I've never been to Scotland **before**. I've seen this film **before**.	Ich war **vorher** noch nie in Schottland. Ich habe diesen Film **schon mal** gesehen.

whole [həʊl]	ganze(r, s)	I can't eat a **whole** pizza. Let's eat half a pizza each.	
trainer [ˈtreɪnə]	der Sportschuh	**trainer** = 1. der/die Trainer/in; 2. der Sportschuh	
halfway [hɑːfˈweɪ]	auf halbem Wege, halb(wegs)	You want to go back? Now? We're more than **halfway** there!	
view (of) [vjuː]	der (An-)Blick; die (Aus-)Sicht (auf)	From our hotel room we had a great **view of** the sea. noun: **view** – verb: (to) **view sth.** (sich etwas anschauen)	
▶ p. 87 **narrow** [ˈnærəʊ]	eng, schmal	This old bridge is so **narrow** that two cars can't cross it at the same time.	
ridge [rɪdʒ]	der Bergkamm, der Grat	Careful! The path on the **ridge** of the mountain is very narrow.	
valley [ˈvæli]	das Tal	There's a river in the **valley**.	
(to) cry [kraɪ]	weinen; rufen, schreien	❗ Schreibung: (to) **cry**, *simple past*: **cried** – The baby **cried** a lot. *but*: **crying** – He's **crying**. verb: (to) **cry** – noun: **cry** (der Schrei, der Ruf)	
height [haɪt]	die Höhe; die Größe *(bei Menschen)*	adj: **high** – noun: **height**	
eventually [ɪˈventʃuəli]	letztendlich, schließlich	If we don't protect our jungles and forests, we will **eventually** get big problems.	
(to) calm down [kɑːm ˈdaʊn]	sich beruhigen	adj: **calm** – verb: (to) **calm down** (sich beruhigen); (to) **calm sb. down** (jn. beruhigen)	
(to) walk / run / drive on	weitergehen / -laufen / -fahren	I don't want to stop here. Please let's walk **on**.	
(to) slip [slɪp]	(aus)rutschen	I **slipped** on the wet grass and fell down.	
rock [rɒk]	der Fels(en), der Stein	❗ Nicht verwechseln: *German* **der Rock** = skirt *English* **rock** = der Felsen noun: **rock** – adj: **rocky** (felsig, steinig)	
rescue [ˈreskjuː]	die Rettung	verb: (to) **rescue** (retten) – There was a fire at the old house. Firefighters **rescued** a man from the top floor. nouns: **rescue**; *(person)* **rescuer** – For the **rescuers**, it was quite a difficult and dangerous **rescue**.	

two hundred and thirty-one

3 Vocabulary

helicopter [ˈhelɪkɒptə]	der Hubschrauber	*a helicopter*
fault [fɔːlt]	der Fehler; die Schuld	I'm sorry about what happened, but it wasn't my **fault**. (… es war nicht meine Schuld.)
loose [luːs]	locker (sitzend), lose	❗ Aussprache und Schreibung: **loose** *(adj)* [luːs] locker (sitzend), lose (to) **lose** *(verb)* [luːz] verlieren
at last [ət ˈlɑːst]	schließlich, endlich	We stood at the bus stop for nearly an hour when the bus came **at last**.
(to) lower [ˈləʊə]	hinunterlassen, herunterlassen; sinken (lassen)	They **lowered** a box down the cliff to rescue the dog.
paramedic [pærəˈmedɪk]	der Rettungssanitäter, die Rettungssanitäterin	*paramedics — an ambulance*
rope [rəʊp]	das Seil	They used **ropes** to lower a box down the cliff.
▶ p. 88 **choice** [tʃɔɪs]	die (Aus-)Wahl; die Entscheidung	noun: **choice** – • Stay at school or find a job? You have the **choice**! / It's your **choice**! • I don't have a **choice** – I'll have to take a taxi. (Ich habe keine Wahl …) verb: (to) **choose**, **chose**, **chosen**; (to) **choose to do** sth. (sich entscheiden / beschließen, etwas zu tun) – I asked him some questions, but he **chose** not to answer them.
order [ˈɔːdə]	die Reihenfolge; die Ordnung	noun: **order** – Please put these pictures **in order** (in eine Reihenfolge) / **in the correct order** (in die richtige Reihenfolge). verb: (to) **order** (ordnen, anordnen) – Please **order** your ideas and give your text a better structure.
summary [ˈsʌməri]	die Zusammenfassung	For the **summary** of a text you only need the most important points, no details.
contrast [ˈkɒntrɑːst]	der Kontrast, der Gegensatz	noun: **contrast** [ˈkɒntrɑːst] – Coming home to London from Peru … what a **contrast**! verb: (to) **contrast** [kənˈtrɑːst] (vergleichen, (einander) gegenüberstellen) – Please **contrast** schools in Japan with your own school.
(to) make sure that …	sicherstellen, dass …; dafür sorgen, dass …	**Make sure that** all the lights are off when you leave the house.

Study skills

▶ p. 90 | **stormy** [ˈstɔːmi] | stürmisch | adj: **stormy** –
 noun: **storm** (der Sturm; das Gewitter)

(to) **sort** sth. [sɔːt] | etwas sortieren, (ein)ordnen |
- Please **sort** these words to make correct sentences. (= Put these words in the correct order to make sentences.)
- (to) **sort** sth. **(out)** *(infml)* (etwas in Ordnung bringen, regeln) – Can you help me to **sort out** my computer problems?

(to) **develop** [dɪˈveləp] | entwickeln; sich entwickeln | verb: (to) **develop** –
- She **develops** new apps. (entwickeln)
- Her business has **developed** well. (sich entwickeln)

noun: *(person)* **developer**

Unit task

▶ p. 91 | **fishing** [ˈfɪʃɪŋ] | das Fischen, das Angeln; die Fischerei | noun: **fish** –
 verb: (to) **fish** (fischen, angeln)

lifeguard [ˈlaɪfɡɑːd] | der Rettungsschwimmer, die Rettungsschwimmerin; der Bademeister, die Bademeisterin | The **lifeguards** at a beach watch people when they are swimming in the sea and help them if they are in danger.

digital [ˈdɪdʒɪtl] | digital | adj: **digital** – I have a **digital** camera.
 adv: **digitally** – I take all my photos **digitally**.
 ❗ Betonung auf der 1. Silbe: **digital(ly)** [ˈdɪdʒɪtl], [ˈdɪdʒɪtəli]

(to) **rewrite** [riːˈraɪt], **rewrote** [riːˈrəʊt], **rewritten** [riːˈrɪtn] | neu schreiben, umschreiben | Don't copy texts from the Internet. **Rewrite** them in your own words!

Irregular verbs

Infinitive	Simple past	Past participle		Infinitive	Simple past	Past participle	
(to) **begin**	began	begun	beginnen	(to) **know**	knew	known	wissen
(to) **bring**	brought	brought	(mit)bringen	(to) **pay**	paid	paid	(be)zahlen
(to) **catch**	caught	caught	(ein)fangen; erwischen	(to) **read** [iː]	read [e]	read [e]	lesen
(to) **choose**	chose	chosen	(aus)wählen	(to) **rewrite**	rewrote	rewritten	neu schreiben, umschreiben
(to) **drink**	drank	drunk	trinken	(to) **run**	ran	run	rennen
(to) **drive**	drove	driven	(Auto) fahren	(to) **say** [eɪ]	said [e]	said [e]	sagen
(to) **fight**	fought	fought	kämpfen	(to) **show**	showed	shown	zeigen
(to) **give**	gave	given	geben	(to) **sit**	sat	sat	sitzen
(to) **hit**	hit	hit	schlagen, treffen	(to) **teach**	taught	taught	lehren, unterrichten
(to) **hurt**	hurt	hurt	verletzen; wehtun	(to) **win**	won	won	gewinnen

4 Vocabulary

🔊 Unit 4 Wales: Digital life

▶ pp. 106/107	donkey ['dɒŋki]	der Esel	

a **donkey**

	national ['næʃnəl]	national	adj: **national, international** [ɪntə'næʃnəl] (international) – noun: **nation** ['neɪʃn] (die Nation)
	million ['mɪljən]	die Million	▶▶ 1,000,000 ❗ three **million** people – but: **millions** of people
	waterfall ['wɔːtəfɔːl]	der Wasserfall	

a **waterfall**

	coal [kəʊl]	die Kohle	

coal

	mining ['maɪnɪŋ]	der Bergbau	verb: (to) **mine** sth. (etwas abbauen, fördern (Bergbau)) – noun: **mine** (das Bergwerk)
	ship [ʃɪp]	das Schiff	

a **ship**

shipbuilding = der Schiffbau

	voice-over ['vɔɪs əʊvə]	das Voiceover (Filmkommentar, Off-Stimme)	When you hear a person talk or give information e.g. in a film, but you can't see them, that's a **voice-over**.

Topic 1

▶ p. 108	exchange [ɪksˈtʃeɪndʒ]	der Schüleraustausch; der Austausch, der Wechsel	• **exchange class** = die Schulklasse, die am Schüleraustausch teilnimmt • **exchange student / exchange partner** = der/die Austauschschüler/in, -partner/in noun: **exchange** – verb: (to) **exchange** (tauschen, austauschen)

234 two hundred and thirty-four

ours [ɑːz], [ˈaʊəz]		unserer, unsere, unseres	

Possessive pronouns

I	▶ **mine** [maɪn]	meine, meiner, meins	This isn't your bike. It's **mine**. (= It's my bike.)
you	▶ **yours** [jɔːz]	deine, deiner, deins; Ihrer, Ihre, Ihres	These aren't my shorts. Are they **yours**?
he	▶ **his** [hɪz]	seiner, seine, seins	Nick has a phone like that. So maybe it's **his**?
she	▶ **hers** [hɜːz]	ihrer, ihre, ihres	Lucie has two rulers. You can use one of **hers**.
it	▶ **its** [ɪts]	seiner, seine, seins; ihrer, ihre, ihres	*(Das Possessivpronomen zu "it" heißt "its", aber es wird kaum verwendet.)*
we	▶ **ours** [ɑːz], [ˈaʊəz]	unserer, unsere, unseres	Your house is really nice. **Ours** is smaller and older.
you	▶ **yours** [jɔːz]	eurer, eure, eures; Ihrer, Ihre, Ihres	Our bikes are over there. Where are **yours**?
they	▶ **theirs** [ðeəz]	ihrer, ihre, ihrs	This isn't the Millers' car. **Theirs** is blue.

❗ *Am Briefschluss:* **Yours, Jill** = Deine / Ihre / Eure Jill

(to) **edit** [ˈedɪt]	bearbeiten, editieren	(to) change a text / video to make it better
roller coaster [ˈrəʊlə kəʊstə]	die Achterbahn	*a roller coaster*
theme [θiːm]	das Thema	**theme park** = der Themenpark *(Freizeitpark m. Attraktionen zu einem bestimmten Thema)*
actually [ˈæktʃuəli]	tatsächlich; eigentlich	I'm not English, **actually**: I'm Scottish.
▶ p.109 **melody** [ˈmelədi]	die Melodie	❗ Betonung auf der 1. Silbe: **melody** [ˈmelədi]
rhythm [ˈrɪðəm]	der Rhythmus	The band was super, and everyone danced to the **rhythm** of their music.
instrument [ˈɪnstrəmənt]	das Instrument	**musical instrument** = das Musikinstrument ❗ Betonung auf der 1. Silbe: **instrument** [ˈɪnstrəmənt]
voice [vɔɪs]	die Stimme	You can sing very well. You have a great **voice**! **voice message** = die Sprachnachricht ❗ *German:* **mit** tiefer / hoher / leiser Stimme *English:* **in** a deep / high / soft voice

Topic 2

▶ p.110 **without** [wɪˈðaʊt]	ohne	**Without** clouds, there can't be rain. **with** ◀ ▶ **without**
cardigan [ˈkɑːdɪɡən]	die Strickjacke	*a cardigan* *an apron*
apron [ˈeɪprən]	die (Koch-)Schürze	

4 Vocabulary

	waistcoat [ˈweɪskəʊt]	die Weste	 a **waistcoat**
▶ p. 111	**gymnastics** [dʒɪmˈnæstɪks]	die Gymnastik, das Turnen	 *sport:* **gymnastics** [dʒɪmˈnæstɪks] – *person:* **gymnast** [ˈdʒɪmnæst] (der/die Turner/in)
	(to) **break up**	zerbrechen; zusammenbrechen *(Telefonverbindung)*	• The vase fell onto the ground and **broke up** into many pieces. • (to) **break up** *(e.g. for Christmas)* = (Schul- / Weihnachts-)Ferien bekommen • **You're breaking up.** = Die (Telefon-)Leitung bricht zusammen. / Das Netz geht weg. (= Ich kann dich nicht mehr hören.)
	How are things?	Wie geht's (so)?	I haven't seen you for a long time! **How are things** with you? (= How are you?)
▶ p. 112	(to) **install** [ɪnˈstɔːl]	installieren; einbauen	Don't **install** too many apps on your phone.
	(to) **charge** *(e.g. a phone)* [tʃɑːdʒ]	aufladen *(z. B. ein Telefon)*	Do you have to **charge** your phone every day? verb: (to) **charge** – noun: **charger** (das Ladegerät)
	(to) **connect (to / with)** [kəˈnekt]	(sich) verbinden (mit)	• The bridge **connects** the two parts of the city. (verbinden) • Can your phone **connect** to our Wi-Fi? (sich verbinden) verb: (to) **connect** – noun: **connection** [kəˈnekʃn] (die Verbindung) Something is wrong with our internet **connection** this morning. The train **connections** to the city centre are good.
	(to) **press** [pres]	drücken	"If you are phoning about tickets, **press** 1."
	(to) **tap** sth. [tæp]	tippen an / auf etwas; (leise) klopfen	verb: (to) **tap** – **Tap** an icon on the screen. noun: **tap** – Give that icon on the screen a little **tap**. (das (leise) Klopfen) (to) **tap your fingers** = mit den Fingern klopfen
	(to) **swipe** [swaɪp]	wischen *(auf Touchscreen)*; durchziehen, einlesen *(z. B. Kreditkarte)*	To view the next picture, **swipe** left. We had to **swipe** a card at the door to get into our hotel room. 

two hundred and thirty-six

device [dɪˈvaɪs]	das Gerät, der Apparat	A clock is a **device** that tells you the time.
key [ˈkiː]	der Schlüssel; die Taste	pressing a key on a keyboard ❗ **key** = 1. der Schlüssel; 2. die Taste *(auf einer Tastatur)* **keyboard** = die Tastatur
document [ˈdɒkjumənt]	das Dokument; die Textdatei	Finish your work and save your **document**. ❗ Betonung auf der 1. Silbe: **document** [ˈdɒkjumənt]
▶ p. 113 **watch** [wɒtʃ]	die Armbanduhr	a **watch** **smartwatch** = die Smartwatch
normally [ˈnɔːməli]	normalerweise	**Normally** we don't open on Saturdays.
(to) **mediate** [ˈmiːdieɪt]	vermitteln *(inhaltlich wiedergeben)*	verb: (to) **mediate** – noun: **mediation** [miːdiˈeɪʃn] (die Vermittlung, die Sprachmittlung)
exact [ɪɡˈzækt]	genau, exakt	adj: **exact** information / the **exact** opposite adv: **exactly** the same colour / What **exactly** do you mean?
(to) **set** sth. **up**	etwas einrichten; etwas aufbauen	It's not difficult to **set up** this smartwatch. I'd like to **set up** my own business.
(to) **agree to** sth.	in etwas einwilligen, einer Sache zustimmen	(to) **agree to do** sth. = einwilligen, etwas zu tun; sich bereit erklären, etwas zu tun

(to) agree (zustimmen)

1. (to) **agree to** sth.	in etwas einwilligen, einer Sache zustimmen	Did your parents **agree to** your plan?
2. (to) **agree to do** sth.	einwilligen, etwas zu tun; sich bereit erklären, etwas zu tun	Jonathan **agreed to make** breakfast.
3. (to) **agree with** sb. (to) **agree with** sth.	jm. zustimmen mit etwas einverstanden sein	I **agree with** Pia and Elias. Listen to Rashid and say if you **agree with** his opinion.
4. (to) **agree on** sth.	sich auf etwas einigen	We try to **agree on** one special activity every weekend.

terms *(pl)* [tɜːmz]	die (Vertrags-)Bedingungen, die Konditionen	"Please read the **terms** and conditions for using this website."
(to) **pair** sth. **(with** sth.**)** [peə]	etwas (mit etwas) koppeln *(z. B. Geräte)*	You can use Bluetooth to **pair** your phone with your smartwatch. verb: (to) **pair** – noun: **pair**
simple [ˈsɪmpl]	einfach	• These instructions are **simple**. (= easy to understand) • I didn't have much time, so I made a quick, **simple** meal. (= plain)

two hundred and thirty-seven

4 Vocabulary

Topic 3

▶ p. 114	**social media** *(pl)* [ˈsəʊʃl ˈmiːdiə]	die sozialen Medien	• **social** = sozial – Till some years ago this was a poor area with lots of **social** problems. • **media** *(pl)* = die Medien – Today it's so easy to use **media** like chat or email. ❗ *German:* **in** den sozialen Medien *English:* **on** social media
	(to) debate (sth.) [dɪˈbeɪt]	debattieren; diskutieren (über etwas)	verb: (to) **debate** (sth.) – Let's **debate** this. noun: **debate** (die Debatte) – Let's **hold / have a debate** about this. (eine Debatte führen)
	versus (**v** *or* **vs**) [ˈvɜːsəs]	gegen *(bei Wettkämpfen)*; gegenüber	What an exciting match: Manchester City **versus / vs / v** Manchester United!
	(to) subscribe to sth. [səbˈskraɪb]	etwas abonnieren	We **subscribe to** a daily newspaper. (= We pay money to get a paper every day.)
	channel [ˈtʃænl]	der Sender, der (TV-)Kanal	I watched an old film, but when the football match started, I changed **channels**. (= I switched to a different **channel**.) **the (English) Channel** = der Ärmelkanal
	(to) forward sth. **to** sb. [ˈfɔːwəd]	etwas an jn. weiterleiten; jm. etwas nachsenden	You didn't get John's email? I'll **forward** it **to** you.
	(to) keep / stay in touch (with) [tʌtʃ]	in Verbindung / Kontakt bleiben (mit)	

in touch with (in Kontakt / Verbindung mit)		
(to) **get in touch (with)**	If you come to York, **get in touch with** me.	(sich) in Verbindung setzen (mit), Kontakt aufnehmen (zu)
(to) **keep / stay in touch (with)**	When you move to Wales, let's **keep / stay in touch**.	in Verbindung / Kontakt bleiben (mit)
(to) **lose touch (with)**	When you move to Wales, let's not **lose touch**.	den Kontakt verlieren (zu)

	comment (about / on sth.) [ˈkɒment]	der Kommentar (über / zu etwas)	noun: **comment (about / on)** – Can you **make a comment on** recent events? (einen Kommentar abgeben) verb: (to) **comment (about / on** sth.) – Can you **comment on** recent events? ((etwas) kommentieren)
	(to) unfollow [ʌnˈfɒləʊ]	entfolgen *(auf sozialen Medien nicht mehr folgen)*	(to) stop following sb. on social media
	well-being [ˈwel biːɪŋ]	das Wohl(ergehen)	Look after your **well-being**. = Make sure you stay healthy and happy.
	diary [ˈdaɪəri]	der Kalender; das Tagebuch	Friday afternoon? OK. Let me put that in my **diary**. (der Kalender) (to) **keep a diary** (Tagebuch führen)
▶ p. 115	**(to) offer** [ˈɒfə]	bieten, anbieten	verb: (to) **offer** – noun: **offer** (das Angebot)
	Shall I …? [ʃæl], [ʃəl]	Soll ich …?	It's hot in here. **Shall I** open the window?
	profile [ˈprəʊfaɪl]	das Profil; die Beschreibung, das Portrait	❗ Betonung auf der 1. Silbe: **profile** [ˈprəʊfaɪl]

There you go.	Hier, bitte schön.; *(auch:)* Da hast du's! / Na siehst du!	• **There you go**, two veggie burgers. That's £5.60, please. (Hier, bitte schön.) • **There you go!** I told you it would look great. (Na siehst du!)
private [ˈpraɪvət]	privat; persönlich	❗ Betonung auf der 1. Silbe: **private** [ˈpraɪvət] **private** ◄ ► **public**
Would you like me to …?	Möchtest du, dass ich …?	**Would you like me to do** the shopping?

> **"Möchtest du, dass ich …?"** – „Ich möchte, dass du …"
>
> Im Deutschen benutzt du „**dass**"-Sätze, wenn du möchtest, dass **jemand etwas tut**:
> - Ich **möchte, dass du** den Geschirrspüler ausräumst.
> - **Möchtest du, dass ich** einkaufen gehe?
>
> Im Englischen darf auf **would like** und **want** nicht ein **"that"**-Satz folgen. Vergleiche:
> - I **want you to** empty the dishwasher. / I **would like you to** empty the dishwasher.
> - **Would you like me to** do the shopping?
>
> *Nie:* I want that you … / Would you like that I …?

▶ p. 116	**cyberbullying** [ˈsaɪbəbʊlɪŋ]	das Cybermobbing	using social media or messages to bully somebody
	a charity **which** helps …	eine Hilfsorganisation, die … hilft	❗ Das Relativpronomen **which** benutzt du nur für Dinge und Tiere: songs **which** I sing every day the cat **which** ate my sandwich
	statistic [stəˈtɪstɪk]	die statistische Tatsache, die statistische Größe	❗ Meist wird der Plural **statistics** verwendet: **Statistics** show that … = die Statistik zeigt … / die Statistiken zeigen, dass …
	one in five	eine/r von fünf(en); jede/r fünfte	**One in three** children in the UK have never climbed a tree. ❗ Auf **One in three kids / teens / cars / …** kann ein Verb im Plural oder im Singular folgen: **One in three kids have never climbed …** oder **One in three kids has never climbed …**
	victim [ˈvɪktɪm]	das Opfer	No one should become a **victim** of bullying.
	a boy / boys **who** …	ein Junge, der … / Jungen, die …	❗ Das Relativpronomen **who** benutzt du für Personen: I know a girl **who** has four sisters.
	(to) **let** [let], let, let	lassen	His parents **let** him go to Costa Rica. (= They allowed him to go …)
	(to) **invent** [ɪnˈvent]	erfinden	Did you know that Ada Lovelace **invented** computer programs over 170 years ago?
	emotional [ɪˈməʊʃənl]	emotional	adj: **emotional** – noun: **emotion** (die Emotion, das Gefühl) ❗ Betonung auf der 2. Silbe: **emotion** [ɪˈməʊʃn], **emotional** [ɪˈməʊʃənl]
▶ p. 117	**network** [ˈnetwɜːk]	das Netz(werk)	**social network** = das soziale Netzwerk

4 Vocabulary

Story

▶ p. 118

(to) **skim a text** [skɪm]	einen Text überfliegen (*um den Inhalt grob zu erfassen*)		(to) read a text quickly to find the main idea(s)
(to) **lie (to** sb.**)** [laɪ]	(jn. an)lügen		verb: (to) **lie** – Jo didn't tell the truth. She **lied to** us.
			noun: **lie** (die Lüge) – Jo didn't tell the truth. She told us **lies**.
			❗ (to) **lie, lied, lied** = lügen
			(to) **lie, lay, lain** = liegen
(to) **type (in)** [taɪp]	(ein)tippen		Please **type in** your name and password, then press "enter".
… as well as … [əz ˈwel]	sowohl … als auch …		❗ **as well** = auch
			as well as = sowohl … als auch
			I have a bike **as well as** a car.
			= I have a bike, and I have a car **as well**.
(to) **notice** [ˈnəʊtɪs]	(be)merken		verb: (to) **notice** – I didn't **notice** him because I was playing a video game.
			noun: **notice** (der Anschlag, die Bekanntmachung (*an einem Schwarzen Brett*))
			notice board = das Schwarze Brett, die Anschlagtafel
latest [ˈleɪtɪst]	neueste(r, s), aktuelle(r, s)		The band's **latest** album is their best, I think.
Who cares? [keəz]	Wen interessiert das? / Was soll's? / Na und?		• The neighbours won't like your outfit. – **Who cares?**
			• I wear what I want! **You shouldn't care** what other people think. (Es sollte einem egal sein, … / Man sollte nicht wichtig nehmen, …)

▶ p. 119

truth [truːθ]	die Wahrheit		noun: **truth** – adj: **true**
			(to) **tell the truth** ◀ ▶ (to) **tell lies**
			To tell the truth, I hate parties. (Ehrlich gesagt, …)
(to) **delete** [dɪˈliːt]	löschen		I **deleted** the message from my phone.
breath [breθ]	der Atem(zug)		(to) **take a deep breath** = tief durchatmen
			noun: **breath** [breθ]
			verb: (to) **breathe** [briːð]
(to) **guess** [ges]	(er)raten; annehmen, vermuten		Can you **guess** the right answer?
			I **guess** it's too late now.

(to) guess – guess

verb: (to) **guess**

1. raten, erraten
   Guess how old I am. / **Guess** what I did!
   Guess what! She's dating Sam! (Stell dir / Stellt euch (mal) vor! …)
2. annehmen, vermuten
   I guess I'll leave school next year. /
   I guess he's just shy. / **I guess** you're right.

noun: **guess**

Make / Have / Take a **guess**!
(Rate(t) mal!)

My **guess** is he'll leave school next year. (die Vermutung)

jealous (of) [ˈdʒeləs]	neidisch (auf); eifersüchtig		You get so much pocket money! I'm really **jealous**. She was **jealous** of her baby brother. She thought her parents loved him more.

	for once	ausnahmsweise; dieses eine Mal	Wow, Dave! You're always late, but now **for once** you've arrived on time!
▶ p. 120	**original** [əˈrɪdʒənl]	original, ursprünglich	adj: **original** – noun: **original** (das Original) **!** Betonung auf der 2. Silbe: ori**g**inal [əˈrɪdʒənl]
	tool [tuːl]	das Werkzeug; das (Hilfs-)Mittel	tools
	lighting [ˈlaɪtɪŋ]	die Beleuchtung	Good **lighting** in public spaces is important so that people feel safe at night.

Viewing

▶ p. 121	**series** [ˈsɪəriːz], *pl* **series**	die Serie, die Sendereihe	This is a great sci-fi **series** about creatures who live on a planet far away from earth.
	(to) sew [səʊ], **sewed** [səʊd], **sewn** [səʊn]	nähen	**!** Aussprache: **sew** [səʊ], **sewed** [səʊd], **sewn** [səʊn] I'd like to learn to **sew** and design and make my own fashion. a **sewing machine**
	skin [skɪn]	die Haut; die Schale (z. B. Banane)	No one should experience bullying because of their **skin** colour. There's a banana **skin** on the floor.
	headpiece [ˈhedpiːs]	der Kopfschmuck	a **headpiece**

Study skills

▶ p. 122	**(to) flow** [fləʊ]	fließen; strömen	verb: (to) **flow** – The water **flows** very fast here. noun: **flow** (der Fluss; der Strom) – • Don't try to swim against the **flow** of the water. • The village is happy about the growing **flow** of tourists.
	symbol [ˈsɪmbl]	das Symbol	A red rose is a **symbol** of love. (Symbol für …) **!** Betonung auf der 1. Silbe: **s**ymbol [ˈsɪmbl]
	abbreviation (of / for) [əbriːviˈeɪʃn]	die Abkürzung (für)	a short form of a word or phrase "e. g." is the **abbreviation of / for** "for example".

two hundred and forty-one

5 Vocabulary

habit [ˈhæbɪt]	die (An-)Gewohnheit		something that you do regularly Eating too many sweets is a bad **habit**.
(to) sum sth. **up** [sʌm ˈʌp]	etwas zusammenfassen		**To sum up, …** = Um (es) zusammenzufassen, … / Zusammenfassend kann man sagen, … verb: (to) **sum** sth. **up** – noun: **summary**
To begin with …	Zunächst (einmal) …; Anfangs …		▶▶ To start with … **To begin with / To start with**, I'd like to ask you all what you know about this topic.

Unit task

▶ p. 123	**image** [ˈɪmɪdʒ]	das Bild, die Abbildung	▶▶ a picture or a photo
	source [sɔːs]	die Quelle (z. B. Website, Text)	Where did you find this information? You always have to give your **source** or **sources**.

Irregular verbs

Infinitive	Simple past	Past participle		Infinitive	Simple past	Past participle	
(to) **cut**	cut	cut	schneiden	(to) **lie**	lay	lain	liegen
(to) **let**	let	let	lassen	(to) **sew**	sewed	sewn	nähen

🔊 °Unit 5 Two Irelands: Together

> Die Unit 5 ist keine Pflicht-Unit, daher sind die neuen Wörter alle mit einem Kringel (°) markiert. Wenn ihr die Unit bearbeitet, kannst du die neuen Wörter lernen, aber sie werden nicht in Band 4 vorausgesetzt.

▶ pp. 138/139	°**Catholic** [ˈkæθlɪk]	der Katholik, die Katholikin; katholisch	❗ Betonung auf der 1. Silbe: **Catholic** [ˈkæθlɪk]
	°**Protestant** [ˈprɒtɪstənt]	der Protestant, die Protestantin; protestantisch, evangelisch	❗ Betonung auf der 1. Silbe: **Protestant** [ˈprɒtɪstənt]
	°**the Troubles** (pl) [ˈtrʌblz]	der Nordirlandkonflikt (wörtlich: die Unruhen)	Der Nordirlandkonflikt war eine jahrzehntelange Phase bewaffneter Konflikte zwischen Katholiken und Protestanten zur Frage, ob Nordirland Teil des Vereinigten Königreiches bleiben sollte. Sie endete 1998 mit dem „Karfreitagsabkommen".
	°**checkpoint** [ˈtʃekpɔɪnt]	der Kontrollpunkt	a **checkpoint**
	°**bed and breakfast (B&B)** [bed ən ˈbrekfəst]	das Zimmer mit Frühstück; die Frühstückspension	We stayed at a nice **B&B** in York last year. **Bed and breakfast** can be quite expensive.
	°**(to) recommend** sth. **(to** sb.**)** [rekəˈmend]	(jm.) etwas empfehlen	Can you **recommend** a good bike shop?

242 two hundred and forty-two

5

Topic 1

▶ p. 140	°**abroad** [əˈbrɔːd]	im / ins Ausland	in or to another country
	°**passport** [ˈpɑːspɔːt]	der (Reise-)Pass	
	°**identity card** [aɪˈdentəti kɑːd] (= **ID card**)	der Personalausweis	
	°**age** [eɪdʒ]	das Alter, die Altersgruppe	**people of all ages** = Menschen aller Altersgruppen ❗ German: **im Alter von 12 (Jahren)** English: **at the age of 12**
	°**advanced** [ədˈvɑːnst]	fortgeschritten	What level is this dance class? – It's for **advanced** dancers. **advanced level** = high or difficult level
	°**accommodation** [əkɒməˈdeɪʃn]	die Unterkunft; die Wohnung, das (Fremden-)Zimmer	❗ **accommodation** ist unzählbar: German: Wir brauchen **eine** billige Unterkunft in Paris für drei Tage. English: We need **cheap accommodation** in Paris for three days. (*never:* an accommodation)
	°**kettle** [ˈketl]	der Wasserkocher *(elektrisch)*	*a* **kettle**
	°(**to**) **belong to** sb. / sth. [bɪˈlɒŋ]	jm. gehören / zu etwas gehören	Is this your bike? – No, it **belongs to** Jill.
▶ p. 141	°**twin beds** *(pl)* [ˈtwɪn bedz]	zwei einzelne Betten *(z. B. im Hotelzimmer)*	**twin room** = das Zweibettzimmer
	°**cooked breakfast** [kʊkt ˈbrekfəst]	ein warmes Frühstück, z. B. mit gebratenem Speck und Spiegeleiern	**full cooked breakfast** = *ein reichhaltiges warmes Frühstück mit allem, was dazugehört*
	°**guest** [gest]	der Gast	someone who visits someone else
	°**bath** [bɑːθ]	das Bad; die Badewanne	❗ German: **baden, ein Bad nehmen** English: (to) **have a bath** *or* (to) **take a bath**
	°**buffet** [ˈbʊfeɪ]	das Büfett	❗ Betonung auf der 1. Silbe: **buffet** [ˈbʊfeɪ]
	°**cereals** *(pl)* [ˈsɪəriəlz]	die Getreide- / Frühstücksflocken	**breakfast cereals**
	°**cold meat** [kəʊld ˈmiːt]	der (Braten- / Wurst-)Aufschnitt	❗ **meat** = 1. *unzählbar:* I don't eat **meat**. (Fleisch) 2. *zählbar:* **meats** = Fleischsorten **cold meats** = Aufschnittsorten

two hundred and forty-three **243**

5 Vocabulary

	°form [fɔːm]	das Formular	(to) **complete a form** = ein Formular ausfüllen ❗ **form** = **1.** die Form; **2.** das Formular

Topic 2

▶ p. 142	°(to) **divide (up) (into)** [dɪˈvaɪd]	aufteilen / einteilen (in)	The teacher **divided** the class **into** groups. Berlin **was divided** for many years. (… war geteilt / war eine geteilte Stadt …)
	°**construction** [kənˈstrʌkʃn]	der Bau; die Konstruktion	the ship's **construction** = the time when they built the ship

Story

▶ p. 144	°**aim** [eɪm]	das Ziel	What's the **aim** of this exercise? (= Why are we doing it? / What can we learn from it?)
	°**routine** [ruːˈtiːn]	die (Tanz-)Nummer, die Choreographie; die Routine	A dance **routine** is a series of different parts which form a longer dance.
	°**not … either** [ˈaɪðə]	auch nicht	I hate coffee and I **don't** like tea **either**.
	°**Good luck.** [ɡʊd ˈlʌk]	Viel Glück!	If you're lucky, you'll win. So – **good luck!** noun: **luck** (das Glück (die glückliche Fügung)) adj: **lucky** (Glücks-, glücklich)
	°(to) **do well**	es gut machen; gut abschneiden, erfolgreich sein	Joe **did well** in his maths test. My sister started a new business, and it's **doing** very **well**.
	°(to) **beat** [biːt], **beat, beaten** [ˈbiːtn]	schlagen, besiegen	I **beat** my brother at tennis last Sunday. (= I won and he lost.)
▶ p. 145	°(to) **perform** [pəˈfɔːm]	auftreten *(Künstler/in)*; aufführen	**Perform** the scene / dialogue for your class. The band first **performed** in the USA in 2014.
	°**flash** [flæʃ]	der Blitz *(Kamera)*; das Aufblitzen; das Blinklicht	noun: **flash** – verb: (to) **flash** (blinken, blitzen (mit); *(Telefon)* mit Blitz fotografieren)
	°(to) **confuse** [kənˈfjuːz]	verwirren; durcheinanderbringen	Now you've **confused** me. Is Jim your uncle or your cousin?
	°**judge** [dʒʌdʒ]	der Richter, die Richterin; das Jurymitglied	**judges**
▶ p. 146	°**purpose** [ˈpɜːpəs]	die Absicht; der Sinn, der Zweck	Did you do that **on purpose**? ❗ *German:* **mit** Absicht – *English:* **on** purpose on purpose ◀ ▶ by accident

Viewing

▶ p. 147	°**times** [taɪmz]	mal	Six **times** three is eighteen.
	°**spectacular** [spekˈtækjələ]	spektakulär, aufsehenerregend	❗ Betonung auf der 2. Silbe: spect**a**cular [spekˈtækjələ]

English – German Dictionary

Im *English-German Dictionary* kannst du nachschlagen, was ein Wort bedeutet oder wie es ausgesprochen wird.

Es werden folgende **Abkürzungen und Symbole** verwendet:

infml = informal (umgangssprachlich) *pl = plural* (Mehrzahl)
sb. = somebody (jemand) *sth. = something* (etwas)
jd. = jemand jm. = jemandem jn. = jemanden

° Mit diesem Kringel sind Wörter markiert, die nicht zum Lernwortschatz gehören.

Die **Fundstellenangaben** zeigen, wo ein Wort zum ersten Mal vorkommt.
Die Ziffern in Klammern bezeichnen Seitenzahlen.

1 = Lighthouse 1   2 = Lighthouse 2   3: 1 (16) = Lighthouse 3, Unit 1, Seite 16

A

a [ə] ein, eine 1 **once a month** einmal pro Monat 2
abbreviation (of / for) [əbriːviˈeɪʃn] die Abkürzung (für) 3: 4 (122)
°**able** [ˈeɪbl]: **be able to do sth.** etwas tun können, in der Lage sein, etwas zu tun
about [əˈbaʊt]:
1. ungefähr 3: 2 (47)
2. **out and about** unterwegs 3: 1 (16)
3. **about me / you /...** über mich / dich /... 1
What about you? Und du? / Was ist mit dir? 1 **How about ...?** Wie wäre es mit ...? 2 **What about a ...?** Wie wäre es mit einer / einem ...? 1
above [əˈbʌv] über, oberhalb (von); oben 2
°**abroad** [əˈbrɔːd] im / ins Ausland
accident [ˈæksɪdənt]:
1. der Unfall 2
2. der Zufall 2
by accident zufällig 2
°**accommodation** [əkɒməˈdeɪʃn] die Unterkunft; die Wohnung, das (Fremden-)Zimmer
account [əˈkaʊnt] das (Bank-)Konto; der Account 2
acoustic [əˈkuːstɪk] akustisch 2
acrobat [ˈækrəbæt] der / die Akrobat/in 3: 1 (14/15)
across [əˈkrɒs] über *(quer über)* 2
act [ækt]:
1. die Tat, die Handlung 2
2. handeln, sich verhalten 2
3. Theater spielen, schauspielern 2
act out aufführen, vorspielen 2
action [ˈækʃn] die Action *(z. B. Film)*; die Aktion, die Handlung 2
active [ˈæktɪv] aktiv 1
activist [ˈæktɪvɪst] der / die Aktivist/in 2
activity [ækˈtɪvəti] die Aktivität, die Tätigkeit 1
actor [ˈæktə] der / die Schauspieler/in 2
actually [ˈæktʃuəli] tatsächlich; eigentlich 3: 4 (108)
add [æd] hinzufügen; addieren 1
additional [əˈdɪʃnl] zusätzliche(r, s) 3: 2 (57)
additional time [əˈdɪʃnl taɪm] die Nachspielzeit *(Fußball)* 3: 2 (57)
address [əˈdres] die Adresse 1

admire [ədˈmaɪə] bewundern 3: 2 (56)
adopt [əˈdɒpt] adoptieren 3: 3 (84)
adoption [əˈdɒpʃn] die Adoption 3: 3 (84)
°**advanced** [ədˈvɑːnst] fortgeschritten
adventure [ədˈventʃə] das Abenteuer 2
adventurer [ədˈventʃərə] der / die Abenteurer/in 3: 3 (81)
adventurous [ədˈventʃərəs] abenteuerlustig 3: 3 (81)
advice *(no pl)* [ədˈvaɪs] der Rat, der Ratschlag, die Ratschläge 3: 2 (48)
give sb. advice jm. Rat geben 3: 2 (48)
take sb.'s advice Rat annehmen, auf jn. hören 3: 2 (48)
advice column [ədˈvaɪs kɒləm] der Kummerkasten, die Ratgeber-Spalte *(z. B. in Zeitschriften)* 3: 2 (48)
after [ˈɑːftə]:
1. **after (school)** nach (der Schule) 1
2. **after (you read)** nachdem (du liest) 1
afternoon [ɑːftəˈnuːn] der Nachmittag 1 **in the afternoon** nachmittags, am Nachmittag 1
again [əˈgen] wieder, noch einmal 1
against [əˈgenst] gegen 3: 1 (22)
°**age** [eɪdʒ] das Alter, die Altersgruppe **at the age of 12** im Alter von 12 (Jahren) **people of all ages** Menschen aller Altersgruppen
°**agency** [ˈeɪdʒənsi] die Agentur, die Organisation
agent [ˈeɪdʒənt] der / die Agent/in 2
ago [əˈgəʊ]: **a long time ago** vor langer Zeit 2
agree [əˈgriː] **agree (with sb. / sth.)** jm. zustimmen; mit etwas einverstanden sein 2 **agree on** sich einigen auf 2 **agree to do sth.** einwilligen, etwas zu tun; sich bereit erklären, etwas zu tun 3: 4 (113)
agree to sth. in etwas einwilligen, einer Sache zustimmen 3: 4 (113)
°**agreement** [əˈgriːmənt]:
1. die Zustimmung, die Übereinstimmung
2. das Abkommen, der Vertrag, die Einigung
Good Friday Agreement das Karfreitagsabkommen **reach an agreement** eine Vereinbarung treffen, eine Einigung erzielen

°**aim** [eɪm] das Ziel
air [eə] die Luft 3: 1 (23)
airport [ˈeəpɔːt] der Flughafen 2
alarm [əˈlɑːm] der Wecker; der Alarm; die Alarmanlage 2
album [ˈælbəm] das Album 3: 1 (18)
alien [ˈeɪliən]:
1. außerirdisch 2
2. der / die Außerirdische 2
all [ɔːl] alle(s) 1 **all over London / all over the country** überall in London / überall im Land, in ganz London / im ganzen Land 3: 1 (17) **all the family** die ganze Familie 2 **all the time** die ganze Zeit, ständig 2 **not ... at all** überhaupt nichts, gar nichts; überhaupt kein/e, gar kein/e 2
allergic (to) [əˈlɜːdʒɪk] allergisch (gegen) 1
allowed [əˈlaʊd] erlaubt 3: 2 (49) **be allowed to do sth.** etwas tun dürfen 3: 2 (49)
alone [əˈləʊn] allein 1
along the road [əˈlɒŋ] die Straße entlang 3: 1 (21)
°**aloud** [əˈlaʊd]: **read aloud** laut (vor)lesen
alphabet [ˈælfəbet] das Alphabet 1
already [ɔːlˈredi] schon 1
also [ˈɔːlsəʊ] auch 1
alternative [ɔːlˈtɜːnətɪv]:
1. die Alternative 2
2. alternativ 2
always [ˈɔːlweɪz] immer 1
am [æm]: **I'm (= I am)** ich bin 1
a.m. [eɪˈem]: **4 a.m.** 4 Uhr (früh)morgens 1 **9 a.m.** 9 Uhr vormittags 1
amazing [əˈmeɪzɪŋ] erstaunlich; großartig 1
ambulance [ˈæmbjələns] der Krankenwagen 2
an [ən] ein/e *(vor Vokalen)* 1
and [ən], [ənd] und 1
angry [ˈæŋgri] wütend 1 **angry at sb.** wütend auf jn. 2
animal [ˈænɪml] das Tier 1
animal charity [ˈænɪml tʃærəti] die wohltätige Organisation, die Tiere unterstützt 2
ankle [ˈæŋkl] der Knöchel, das Fußgelenk 2
announce [əˈnaʊns] verkünden, bekanntgeben; durchsagen 2

two hundred and forty-five **245**

Dictionary — English – German

announcement [əˈnaʊnsmənt]:
1. die Durchsage, die Ansage 2
2. die Bekanntgabe, die Ankündigung 2
annoy sb. [əˈnɔɪ] jn. ärgern 3: 2 (50)
annoyed [əˈnɔɪd] verärgert 3: 2 (50)
annoying [əˈnɔɪɪŋ] ärgerlich (unangenehm) 3: 2 (50)
°**anonymous** [əˈnɒnɪməs] anonym
another [əˈnʌðə] ein/e andere/r/s; noch ein/e 1
answer [ˈɑːnsə]:
1. die Antwort 1
2. (be)antworten 1
any [ˈeni] jede(r/s) (beliebige), jegliche(r/s) 2 **(at) any time** zu jeder Zeit, jederzeit 2 **Do you have any questions?** Habt ihr / Hast du (irgendwelche) Fragen? 1 **not (…) any more** nicht mehr 2 **there aren't any …** es gibt keine … 1
anybody [ˈenibɒdi] irgendjemand; jede/r (beliebige) 2 **Can you see anybody?** Kannst du (irgend-)jemanden sehen? 2 **not … anybody** niemand 2
anyone [ˈeniwʌn] irgendjemand; jede/r (beliebige) 2 **Can you see anyone?** Kannst du (irgend-)jemanden sehen? 2 **not … anyone** niemand 2
anything [ˈeniθɪŋ] (irgend)etwas; alles; egal, was 2 **Can you see anything?** Kannst du (irgend)etwas sehen? 2 **not … anything** nichts 2
anywhere [ˈeniweə] irgendwo(hin); überall 2 **Can I sit anywhere?** Kann ich mich irgendwo hinsetzen? 2 **not … anywhere** nirgendwo(hin) 2
apartment [əˈpɑːtmənt] (AE) die Wohnung 2
app [æp] die App 1
appear [əˈpɪə] erscheinen; auftauchen 3: 2 (54) **appear to be / do** zu sein / zu tun scheinen 3: 2 (54)
apple [ˈæpl] der Apfel 1
April [ˈeɪprəl] der April 1
apron [ˈeɪprən] die (Koch-)Schürze 3: 4 (110)
°**aqueduct** [ˈækwɪdʌkt] der / das Aquädukt (Brücke für eine Wasserleitung / einen Kanal)
architect [ˈɑːkɪtekt] der / die Architekt/in 2
are [ɑː] bist, sind, seid 1 **The books are £2.** Die Bücher kosten 2 Pfund. 2 **we / they are** wir/sie sind 1 **you are** du bist / ihr seid 1
area [ˈeəriə] die Gegend, der Bereich 2
argue [ˈɑːɡjuː]:
1. argumentieren 3: 2 (61) **argue an opinion** eine Meinung vertreten 3: 2 (61) **argue for / against sth.** sich für / gegen etwas aussprechen 3: 2 (61)
2. **argue (about)** (sich) streiten (über / wegen) 3: 2 (61)

argument [ˈɑːɡjumənt]:
1. das Argument 3: 2 (61)
2. der Streit 3: 2 (61)
arm [ɑːm] der Arm 2
°**army** [ˈɑːmi] die Armee
around … [əˈraʊnd] um (… herum), in … umher 2 **all around the globe** auf der ganzen Welt 2
arrival [əˈraɪvl] die Ankunft 2
arrive [əˈraɪv] ankommen 2
art [ɑːt] die Kunst 1
article [ˈɑːtɪkl] der Artikel 1
artist [ˈɑːtɪst] der / die Künstler/in 2
artistic [ɑːˈtɪstɪk] kunstvoll, künstlerisch 2
as [æz], [əz]:
1. als, während (Konjunktion) 2 **as if** als ob 2
2. als (Präposition) 1 **as the winner** als Gewinner/in 2
3. wie (Präposition) 2 **as well** auch 3: 4 (118) **(not) as good as** (nicht) so gut wie 2 **… as well as …** sowohl … als auch … 3: 4 (118)
ashamed [əˈʃeɪmd]: **be / feel ashamed (of)** sich schämen (für) 3: 2 (51)
ask [ɑːsk]:
1. fragen 1 **ask a question** eine Frage stellen 1
2. **ask sb. for sth.** jn. um etwas bitten 1 **ask sb. to do sth.** jn. bitten, etwas zu tun 1
asleep [əˈsliːp]: **be asleep** schlafen 1 **fall asleep** einschlafen 2
assembly [əˈsembli] die Schulversammlung 1
assistant [əˈsɪstənt]:
1. der/die Assistent/in 2
2. (= shop assistant) der / die Verkäufer/in 2
at [æt], [ət] an; in; bei; auf 1 **at 8 o'clock** um 8 Uhr 1 **at a place** an einem Ort 2 **at her mum's (house)** bei ihrer Mutter (zu Hause / daheim) 1 **at last** schließlich, endlich 3: 3 (87) **at least** wenigstens, zumindest 2 **at night** nachts, in der Nacht 2 **at the cinema** im Kino 1 **at the top (of)** oben, am oberen Ende (von); an der Spitze (von) 1 **at work** bei der Arbeit, am Arbeitsplatz 1 **be good at sth. / at doing sth.** etwas gut können; gut in etwas sein 1 **Open your books at page 10.** Schlagt eure Bücher auf Seite 10 auf. 1
ate [eɪt], [et] *siehe* eat
°**attack** [əˈtæk]:
1. angreifen
2. der Angriff
attention [əˈtenʃn] die Aufmerksamkeit 2 **get sb.'s attention** js. Aufmerksamkeit erregen, gewinnen 2 **keep sb.'s attention** js. Aufmerksamkeit aufrecht erhalten 2 **pay attention (to)** aufpassen (auf), aufmerksam sein; Beachtung schenken, zuhören 2
attractive [əˈtræktɪv] attraktiv 3: 2 (46)

audience [ˈɔːdiəns] die Zuschauer/innen, die Zuhörer/innen; das Publikum 2
audio [ˈɔːdiəʊ] Audio-, Ton- 2
August [ˈɔːɡəst] der August 1
aunt [ɑːnt] die Tante 1
autumn [ˈɔːtəm] der Herbst 1
°**avoid** [əˈvɔɪd] (ver)meiden; verhindern
awake [əˈweɪk] wach 2
away [əˈweɪ] weg, fort 1

B

baby [ˈbeɪbi] das Baby 2
babysat [ˈbeɪbisæt] *siehe* babysit
babysit [ˈbeɪbisɪt], babysat, babysat babysitten 2
babysitter [ˈbeɪbisɪtə] der / die Babysitter/in 2
babysitting [ˈbeɪbisɪtɪŋ] das Babysitten 2
back [bæk] zurück 1 **back at home** wieder zu Hause 1
background [ˈbækɡraʊnd] der Hintergrund 3: (12/13)
bad [bæd] schlecht; schlimm 1
badminton [ˈbædmɪntən] das Badminton, der Federball (Spiel) 1
bag [bæɡ] die Tasche 1
baggy [ˈbæɡi] weit (geschnitten), sackig (Kleidung) 3: 2 (46)
baggy trousers (pl) [ˈbæɡi ˈtraʊzəz]: die Schlabberhose (weit geschnittene Hose) 3: 2 (46)
bagpipes (pl) [ˈbæɡpaɪps] der Dudelsack 3: (12/13)
bake [beɪk] backen 1
baked beans (pl) [beɪkt ˈbiːnz] die weißen Bohnen in Tomatensoße 2
baker [ˈbeɪkə] der / die Bäcker/in 2
bakery [ˈbeɪkəri] die Bäckerei 2
baking powder [ˈbeɪkɪŋ paʊdə] das Backpulver 1
balcony [ˈbælkəni] der Balkon 1
ball [bɔːl] der Ball 1
balloon [bəˈluːn] der Ballon 1
banana [bəˈnɑːnə] die Banane 1
band [bænd] die Band, die Musikgruppe 1
bank [bæŋk]:
1. die Bank (Geldinstitut) 2
2. das (Fluss-)Ufer 3: 1 (14/15)
banker [ˈbæŋkə] der / die Banker/in 2
barbecue [ˈbɑːbɪkjuː] das Grillfest, das Grillen 1
bark (at sb.) [bɑːk] (jn. an)bellen 1
basketball [ˈbɑːskɪtbɔːl] der Basketball 1
°**bass** [beɪs] der Bass (Instrument; Stimmlage)
°**bath** [bɑːθ] das Bad; die Badewanne **have / take a bath** baden, ein Bad nehmen (in der Badewanne)
bathroom [ˈbɑːθruːm] das Bad(ezimmer) 1
be [biː], **was / were, been** sein 1 **I want to be a nurse.** Ich möchte Krankenpfleger/in werden. 2

beach [biːtʃ] der Strand 1 **on the beach** am Strand 1 **to the beach** zum Strand, an den Strand 1
bean [biːn] die Bohne 2
baked beans *(pl)* die weißen Bohnen in Tomatensoße 2
beast [biːst] das Tier; die Bestie; das Biest 2
°**beat** [biːt]:
1. *(Musik)* der Beat, der Rhythmus **drop the beat** den/einen Beat unter die Musik legen
2. **beat, beat, beaten** schlagen, besiegen
°**beaten** [ˈbiːtn] *siehe* beat **it cannot be beaten** es ist unschlagbar *(wörtlich: es kann nicht geschlagen/besiegt werden)*
beautiful [ˈbjuːtɪfl] wunderschön 2
beauty [ˈbjuːti] die Schönheit 2
became [bɪˈkeɪm] *siehe* become
because [bɪˈkɒz] weil 1
because of [bɪˈkɒz əv] wegen 3: 1 (16)
become [bɪˈkʌm], became, become werden 2
bed [bed] das Bett 1 **go to bed** ins Bett gehen 1
°**bed and breakfast (B&B)** [bed ən ˈbrekfəst] das Zimmer mit Frühstück; die Frühstückspension
bedroom [ˈbedruːm] das Schlafzimmer 1
beef [biːf] das Rindfleisch 2
been [biːn] *siehe* be
before [bɪˈfɔː]:
1. zuvor; vorher; schon einmal 3: 3 (86)
2. **before (school/the lesson)** vor (der Schule/der Unterrichtsstunde) 1
3. **before (you read)** bevor (du liest) 1
began [bɪˈɡæn] *siehe* begin
begin [bɪˈɡɪn], began, begun anfangen, beginnen 2 **To begin with ...** Zunächst (einmal) ...; Anfangs ... 3: 4 (122)
beginning [bɪˈɡɪnɪŋ] der Anfang 2
begun [bɪˈɡʌn] *siehe* begin
behind [bɪˈhaɪnd]:
1. hinter *(Präp.)* 1
2. dahinter *(Adv.)* 2
believe (in) [bɪˈliːv] glauben (an) 2
°**bell** [bel] die Klingel, die Glocke
°**belong to sb./sth.** [bɪˈlɒŋ] jm./zu etwas gehören
below [bɪˈləʊ] unter(halb von); unten 2
bench [bentʃ] die Bank *(zum Sitzen)* 3: 1 (28)
best [best] beste(r, s); am besten 1 **Best wishes** Viele Grüße *(Briefschluss)* 2 **like sth. best** etwas am liebsten mögen 2
best friend forever (BFF) [best frend fərˈevə] der/die beste Freund/in für immer 3: 2 (48)

better [ˈbetə] besser 2 **for better or (for) worse** was auch immer geschieht, in guten wie in schlechten Zeiten *(beim Ehegelöbnis)* 2 **Get better soon!** Gute Besserung! 2 **like sth. better** etwas lieber mögen 2
between [bɪˈtwiːn] zwischen 2
BFF (best friend forever) [biː ef ˈef] der/die beste Freund/in für immer 3: 2 (48)
big [bɪɡ]:
1. groß 1
2. schwer, dick *(Person)* 2
big wheel [bɪɡ ˈwiːl] das Riesenrad 3: 1 (14/15)
biggest [ˈbɪɡɪst] der/die/das größte; am größten 1
bike [baɪk] das Fahrrad 1
bike lane [baɪk leɪn] der Radweg 3: 1 (23)
bin [bɪn] der (Müll-)Eimer 1
bio [ˈbaɪəʊ] *siehe* biography
biography [baɪˈɒɡrəfi] *kurz auch* bio die Biografie 3: 3 (83)
biology [baɪˈɒlədʒi] die Biologie 1
bird [bɜːd] der Vogel 2
birthday [ˈbɜːθdeɪ] der Geburtstag 1 **Happy birthday!** Herzlichen Glückwunsch zum Geburtstag! 1 **My birthday is in April.** Ich habe im April Geburtstag. 1 **on my birthday** an meinem Geburtstag 1 **When's your birthday?** Wann hast du Geburtstag? 1
biscuit [ˈbɪskɪt] der Keks, das Plätzchen 2
bisexual [baɪˈsekʃuəl]:
1. bisexuell 2
2. der/die Bisexuelle 2
bit [bɪt] das Teil, das Stück(chen) 3: 2 (47) **a bit** ein bisschen, ein wenig 2
black [blæk] schwarz 1
blanket [ˈblæŋkɪt] die Decke *(zum Zudecken u. Ä.)* 2
blazer [ˈbleɪzə] der Blazer *(Jackett, oft Teil der Schuluniform)* 1
blew [bluː] *siehe* blow
blind [blaɪnd] blind 2
blog [blɒɡ]:
1. bloggen 3: 1 (25)
2. der/das Blog *(Internet-Tagebuch)* 3: 1 (25)
blond [blɒnd] blond 2
°**bloody** [ˈblʌdi] blutig, voller Blut
blow [bləʊ], blew, blown pusten, blasen; wehen 2 **blow sth. up** etwas aufblasen *(z. B. Ballon)* 2
blown [bləʊn] *siehe* blow
blue [bluː] blau 1
blueberry [ˈbluːbəri] die Blaubeere, die Heidelbeere 3: 3 (85)
°**blues** [bluːz] der Blues **sing the Blues** den Blues singen *(auch: traurig sein, Trübsal blasen)*
board [bɔːd] die Tafel 3: 1 (28) **information board** die Informationstafel 3: 1 (28)

boat [bəʊt] das Boot; das Schiff 3: (12/13)
body [ˈbɒdi] der Körper 2
boil [bɔɪl] kochen *(in Wasser)*; sieden 1
book [bʊk]:
1. das Buch 1
2. buchen; reservieren 2
booking [ˈbʊkɪŋ] die Buchung, die Reservierung 2
boot [buːt] der Stiefel 2
bored [bɔːd] gelangweilt 2 **be bored** sich langweilen 2 **I got bored** mir wurde langweilig 2 **I'm bored** mir ist langweilig 2
boring [ˈbɔːrɪŋ] langweilig 1
born [bɔːn]: **he was born** er wurde geboren 2
borrow [ˈbɒrəʊ] (aus)leihen, sich borgen 2
boss [bɒs] der Boss, der/die Chef/in 2
both [bəʊθ] beide 2 **both ... and ...** sowohl ... als auch ... 2
bottle [ˈbɒtl] die Flasche 2
bottom [ˈbɒtəm] das untere Ende 2
bought [bɔːt] *siehe* buy
bowl [bəʊl] die Schüssel, die Schale 2
bowling [ˈbəʊlɪŋ] das Bowling, das Kegeln 2
box [bɒks] die Box, der Kasten 2
box [bɒks] boxen 1
boxing [ˈbɒksɪŋ] das Boxen 1
boy [bɔɪ] der Junge 1
boyfriend [ˈbɔɪfrend] der (feste) Freund 2
braces *(pl)* [ˈbreɪsɪz] die Zahnspange, die Zahnklammer 2
°**bracket** [ˈbrækɪt] die Klammer
°**brae** [breɪ] der (steile) Hügel, der (Ab-)Hang *(schottisches Englisch)*
°**brainstorm** [ˈbreɪnstɔːm] Ideen (ungeordnet) sammeln
brand [brænd] die (Produkt-)Marke 3: 2 (47)
brave [breɪv] mutig 1
bravery [ˈbreɪvəri] der Mut, die Tapferkeit 2
bread [bred] das Brot 1
break [breɪk] die Pause 1
break [breɪk], broke, broken: **break sth.** etwas zerbrechen 1 **break the fast** das Fasten brechen 2 **break up** *(e. g. for Christmas)* Schulferien bekommen *(z. B. Weihnachtsferien)* 3: 4 (111) **You're breaking up.** Die (Telefon-)Leitung bricht zusammen./Das Netz geht weg. *(= Ich kann dich nicht mehr hören.)* 3: 4 (111)
breakfast [ˈbrekfəst] das Frühstück 1 °**cooked breakfast** ein warmes Frühstück, z. B. mit gebratenem Speck und Spiegeleiern °**full cooked breakfast** ein reichhaltiges warmes Frühstück mit allem, was dazugehört
breath [breθ] der Atem(zug) 3: 4 (119)
breathe (in/out) [briːð] (ein-/aus-) atmen 2
°**Brexit** [ˈbreksɪt] der Brexit *(Austritt des Vereinigten Königreiches aus der EU)*

Dictionary — English – German

bridge [brɪdʒ] die Brücke 2
bring [brɪŋ], **brought, brought** bringen, mitbringen 1
Britain [ˈbrɪtn] Großbritannien 1
British [ˈbrɪtɪʃ] britisch 1
British Isles (pl) [brɪtɪʃ ˈaɪlz] die Britischen Inseln 3: (10/11)
°**brochure** [ˈbrəʊʃə] die Broschüre, der Prospekt
broke [brəʊk] siehe break
broken [ˈbrəʊkən] siehe break
brother [ˈbrʌðə] der Bruder 1
brought [brɔːt] siehe bring
brown [braʊn] braun 1
browser [ˈbraʊzə] der Browser (Computerprogramm) 1
brunch [brʌntʃ] das Brunch 2
brush [brʌʃ]:
 1. die Bürste 1
 2. bürsten 1
 brush your teeth (sich) die Zähne putzen 1
°**buffet** [ˈbʊfeɪ] das Büfett
build [bɪld], **built, built** bauen 2
builder [ˈbɪldə] der / die Bauarbeiter/in 2
building [ˈbɪldɪŋ] das Gebäude 1
built [bɪlt] siehe build
bully [ˈbʊli]:
 1. der / die Mobber/in; der/die Tyrann/in 1
 2. tyrannisieren, mobben 1
burger [ˈbɜːgə] der Hamburger (Frikadelle) 1
bus [bʌs] der Bus 1 **by bus** mit dem Bus 1 **double-decker bus** der Doppeldeckerbus 3: 1 (17) **on the bus** im Bus 1
bus stop [ˈbʌs stɒp] die Bushaltestelle 1
business [ˈbɪznəs] das Geschäft, der Betrieb 2 **start a business** ein Geschäft aufmachen, einen Betrieb gründen / eröffnen 2
business card [ˈbɪznəs kɑːd] die Visitenkarte, die Geschäftskarte 2
business people [ˈbɪznəs piːpl] Plural von business person
business person [ˈbɪznəs pɜːsn], pl **business people** die Geschäftsperson 2
businessman [ˈbɪznəsmən], pl **businessmen** der Geschäftsmann 2
businessmen [ˈbɪznəsmən] Plural von businessman
businesswoman [ˈbɪznəswʊmən], pl **businesswomen** die Geschäftsfrau 2
businesswomen [ˈbɪznəswɪmɪn] Plural von businesswoman
busy [ˈbɪzi]:
 1. hektisch, belebt 1
 2. (viel)beschäftigt 1
 keep (yourself) busy sich beschäftigen, auf Trab bleiben 3: 2 (53)
 keep sb. busy jn. beschäftigen, auf Trab halten 3: 2 (53) **you're busy** du bist beschäftigt, du hast (viel) zu tun 1
but [bʌt], [bət] aber 1

butter [ˈbʌtə] die Butter 1
buy [baɪ], **bought, bought** kaufen 1
by [baɪ]:
 1. **by Omar** von Omar (geschrieben) 3: 2 (46)
 2. **by bus** mit dem Bus 1
 by email per E-Mail 3: 2 (46)
 pay by card mit Karte (be)zahlen (z. B. Bankkarte) 2
 3. **by the river** am Fluss 2
 by the sea am Meer, an der See 1
Bye. [baɪ] Tschüs. 1

C

cab [kæb] das Taxi 3: 1 (17)
°**caber** [ˈkeɪbə] der Baumstamm
cafe [ˈkæfeɪ] das Café 1
cake [keɪk] der Kuchen, die Torte 1
calendar [ˈkælɪndə] der Kalender 2
call [kɔːl]:
 1. nennen; rufen; anrufen 1
 call sb. names jn. beschimpfen 3: 2 (57) **be called** heißen 1
 2. der Ruf 1
 3. (kurz für phone call) der (Telefon-)Anruf 1
calm [kɑːm]:
 1. ruhig, besonnen 2
 2. **calm down** sich beruhigen 3: 3 (87)
 calm sb. down jn. beruhigen 3: 3 (87)
came [keɪm] siehe come
camera [ˈkæmərə] die Kamera 2
camping [ˈkæmpɪŋ] das Camping 3: 3 (85)
campsite [ˈkæmpsaɪt] der Campingplatz 2
can [kæn], [kən] können 1 **I can see ...** Ich kann ... sehen. 1
canal [kəˈnæl] der Kanal 3: (12/13)
candle [ˈkændl] die Kerze 2
can't [kɑːnt]: **I can't (= cannot) see ...** Ich kann ... nicht sehen. 1
canteen [kænˈtiːn] die Kantine, die (Schul-)Mensa 1
cap [kæp] die (Schirm-)Mütze, die Kappe 1
cape [keɪp] das Cape (Umhang) 2
capital [ˈkæpɪtl]:
 1. **capital (city)** die Hauptstadt 2
 2. **capital (letter)** der Großbuchstabe 2
capsule [ˈkæpsjuːl] die Kapsel; die Raumkapsel; die Kabine (auf einem Riesenrad) 3: 1 (21)
caption [ˈkæpʃn] die Bildunterschrift 2
car [kɑː] das Auto 1
car light [ˈkɑː laɪt] der Autoscheinwerfer 1
card [kɑːd]:
 1. die Karte 1
 playing card die Spielkarte 1
 2. die (Bank-/Kredit-)Karte 2
 pay by card mit Karte (be)zahlen (z. B. Bankkarte) 2
cardigan [ˈkɑːdɪgən] die Strickjacke 3: 4 (110)

care [keə]:
 1. **care about sth.** etwas wichtig nehmen 3: 1 (23)
 care for betreuen, pflegen; sich kümmern um; aufpassen auf 3: 1 (23) **I care about animals.** Tiere liegen mir am Herzen. 3: 1 (23)
 I don't care. Es ist mir egal. 3: 4 (118)
 Who cares? Wen interessiert das? / Was soll's? / Na und? 3: 4 (118)
 2. die Sorgfalt, die Vorsicht 3: 1 (23)
 Take care. Pass auf dich auf. 3: 1 (23)
 3. die Versorgung, die Betreuung; die Pflege 3: 1 (23)
 take care of sich kümmern um 3: 1 (23)
careful [ˈkeəfl]:
 1. vorsichtig 1
 2. aufmerksam; sorgfältig 3: 3 (78)
careless [ˈkeələs] leichtsinnig, unvorsichtig 3: 1 (23)
carer [ˈkeərə] die Pflegekraft; der / die Betreuer/in 3: 1 (23)
carnival [ˈkɑːnɪvl] der Karneval 2
carrot [ˈkærət] die Möhre, die Karotte 1
carry [ˈkæri] tragen; bei sich haben; befördern 3: 3 (74/75)
carton [ˈkɑːtn] der (Papp-)Karton; die Packung 2
cartoon [kɑːˈtuːn] der Zeichentrickfilm; der / das Comic; der Cartoon 2
case [keɪs] das Etui, der Behälter, der Kasten 1
cash [kæʃ] das Cash, das Bargeld 2 **pay (in) cash** bar bezahlen 2
cash machine [ˈkæʃ məʃiːn] der Geldautomat 2
castle [ˈkɑːsl] die Burg 2
cat [kæt] die Katze 1
catch [kætʃ], **caught, caught** (ein)fangen; erwischen; nehmen (z. B. Zug, Bus) 3: 3 (81)
catfish [ˈkætfɪʃ], pl **catfish** der Wels (Fisch) 3: 3 (76)
°**Catholic** [ˈkæθlɪk]:
 1. der / die Katholik/in
 2. katholisch
caught [kɔːt] siehe catch
cave [keɪv] die Höhle 3: 3 (82)
celebrate [ˈselɪbreɪt] feiern 2
celebration [selɪˈbreɪʃn] die Feier, das Fest 2
cent [sent] der Cent 1
centimetre (= cm) [ˈsentɪmiːtə] der Zentimeter 3: 3 (76)
central [ˈsentrəl] zentral 3: 1 (20)
centre [ˈsentə] das Zentrum; die Mitte 1
°**cereals** (pl) [ˈsɪəriəlz] die Getreide- / Frühstücksflocken
ceremony [ˈserəməni] die Feier, die Zeremonie 1
certainly [ˈsɜːtnli] sicher(lich), gewiss 3: 2 (53)
chain [tʃeɪn] die Kette 1
chair [tʃeə] der Stuhl 1

challenge [ˈtʃælɪndʒ]:
1. die Herausforderung 2
    take on a challenge eine Herausforderung annehmen, sich einer Herausforderung stellen 2
2. **challenge sb. (to sth.)** jn. (zu etwas) herausfordern 2

challenging [ˈtʃælɪndʒɪŋ] anspruchsvoll, (heraus)fordernd 2

champion [ˈtʃæmpiən] der/die Meister/in *(in einer Sportart)*, der Champion 3: 2 (53)

chance [tʃɑːns] die Chance, die Gelegenheit 3: 2 (57)

change [tʃeɪndʒ]:
1. sich umziehen *(die Kleidung wechseln)* 2
2. **change (into)** (sich) (ver)ändern (zu/in); wechseln; (sich) verwandeln (in), werden (zu) 2
    Changing of the Guards die Wachablösung 3: 1 (21)
    change (trains) umsteigen 2
3. die Veränderung, der Wechsel, die Verwandlung 2
4. das Wechselgeld 2

changing room [ˈtʃeɪndʒɪŋ ruːm] der Umkleideraum; die Anprobe *(im Geschäft)* 2

channel [ˈtʃænl] der Sender, der (TV-)Kanal 3: 4 (114) **the (English) Channel** der Ärmelkanal 3: 4 (114)

°**chant** [tʃɑːnt] singen *(Sprechgesänge)*

character [ˈkærəktə] der Charakter; die Figur *(aus einer Geschichte)* 2

charge (e.g. a phone) [tʃɑːdʒ] aufladen *(z. B. ein Telefon)* 3: 4 (112)

charger [ˈtʃɑːdʒə] das Ladegerät 3: 4 (112)

charity [ˈtʃærəti] die wohltätige Organisation 2 **animal charity** die wohltätige Organisation, die Tiere unterstützt 2

charity shop [ˈtʃærəti ʃɒp] *das Geschäft, das gespendete Waren für wohltätige Zwecke verkauft* 2

chat [tʃæt]:
1. **chat (with)** chatten (mit); sich unterhalten (mit) 2
2. die Unterhaltung; der Chat 2
    have a chat eine Unterhaltung führen, sich unterhalten 2

chatty [ˈtʃæti] gesprächig; geschwätzig 2

cheap [tʃiːp] billig, preiswert 3: 1 (17)

check [tʃek]:
1. die (Über-)Prüfung, die Kontrolle 1
2. (über)prüfen, kontrollieren 1
    check sb./sth. out *(infml)* sich jn./etwas anschauen, anhören; etwas ausprobieren 2

checklist [ˈtʃeklɪst] die Checkliste 2

°**checkout** [ˈtʃekaʊt] die Abreise, das Auschecken *(z. B. Hotel)*

°**checkpoint** [ˈtʃekpɔɪnt] der Kontrollpunkt

cheer [tʃɪə] jubeln, *(Sportler/innen)* anfeuern 3: 2 (57)

cheese [tʃiːz] der Käse 1

cheesy [ˈtʃiːzi] kitschig 2

chemical [ˈkemɪkl]:
1. chemisch 2
2. die Chemikalie 2

chicken [ˈtʃɪkɪn] das Huhn; das (Brat-)Hähnchen 1

chickpea [ˈtʃɪkpiː] die Kichererbse 3: 1 (24)

child [tʃaɪld], *pl* **children** das Kind 2

children [ˈtʃɪldrən] *Plural von* **child**

chips *(pl)* [tʃɪps] die Pommes frites 1
fish and chips der Fisch mit Pommes Frites 1

chocolate [ˈtʃɒklət]:
1. die Praline 2
2. die Schokolade 1
    hot chocolate Kakao, heiße (Trink-)Schokolade 1

choice [tʃɔɪs] die (Aus-)Wahl; die Entscheidung 3: 3 (88)

choose [tʃuːz], **chose**, **chosen** (aus)wählen 1 **choose to do sth.** sich entscheiden, beschließen etwas zu tun 3: 3 (88)

chore [tʃɔː] die (Haus-)Arbeit, die *(lästige)* Pflicht 2 **do chores** (Haus-)Arbeiten erledigen 2

chose [tʃəʊz] *siehe* **choose**

chosen [ˈtʃəʊzn] *siehe* **choose**

christening [ˈkrɪsnɪŋ] die Taufe 2

Christmas [ˈkrɪsməs] Weihnachten 1

Christmas Day [krɪsməs ˈdeɪ] der 1. Weihnachtstag (25.12.) 1

°**church** [tʃɜːtʃ] die Kirche 1

cinema [ˈsɪnəmə] das Kino 1
at the cinema im Kino 1

circle [ˈsɜːkl] der Kreis 1

circus [ˈsɜːkəs] der Zirkus 1

citizen [ˈsɪtɪzn] der/die (Staats-)Bürger/in 2

city [ˈsɪti] die (Groß-)Stadt 1

clap (your hands) [klæp] (in die Hände) klatschen 3: 2 (57)

class [klɑːs] die Klasse; der Unterricht; der Kurs 1 **in class** im Unterricht 1

class teacher [ˈklɑːs tiːtʃə] der/die Klassenlehrer/in 1

classic [ˈklæsɪk]:
1. der Klassiker 3: 1 (18)
2. klassisch 3: 1 (18)

classical [ˈklæsɪkl] klassisch 2

classical music [klæsɪkl ˈmjuːzɪk] klassische Musik 2

classmate [ˈklɑːsmeɪt] der/die Mitschüler/in 3: 2 (55)

classroom [ˈklɑːsruːm] das Klassenzimmer 1

clean [kliːn]:
1. sauber 1
2. sauber machen, putzen 1
    clean sth. up etwas aufräumen, sauber machen 1

clean-up [ˈkliːn ʌp] das Säubern, das Saubermachen 1

clean-up day [ˈkliːn ʌp deɪ] der Dreck-weg-Tag *(Aktionstag zum Müllsammeln)* 1

cleaner [ˈkliːnə] die Reinigungskraft 1

clear [klɪə] klar, deutlich 1

clever [ˈklevə] schlau, klug 1

click [klɪk]:
1. der Klick, das Klicken 2
2. **click (on)** klicken (auf), anklicken 2

cliff [klɪf] die Klippe 3: 3 (80)

cliff jumping [ˈklɪf dʒʌmpɪŋ] das Klippenspringen 3: 3 (80)

climb [klaɪm]:
1. der Aufstieg, die Klettertour; der Anstieg 2
2. klettern (auf) 2

climber [ˈklaɪmə] der Kletterer, die Kletterin 2

clock [klɒk] die (Wand-, Stand-, Turm-)Uhr 1

close [kləʊz] schließen, zumachen 1

close (to) [kləʊs] knapp; nahe (bei, an) 3: (12/13)

clothes *(pl)* [kləʊðz] die Kleidung, die Kleidungsstücke 1

clothes swap [ˈkləʊðz swɒp] der Kleidertausch, die Kleidertauschparty 1

clothing *(no pl)* [ˈkləʊðɪŋ] die Kleidung 3: 2 (47) **piece of clothing** das Kleidungsstück 3: 2 (47)

cloud [klaʊd] die Wolke 1

cloudless [ˈklaʊdləs] wolkenlos 3: 1 (23)

cloudy [ˈklaʊdi] wolkig, bewölkt 1

club [klʌb] der Klub, der Verein 1
school club die AG *(in der Schule)* 1

clue [kluː] der (Lösungs-)Hinweis; der Anhaltspunkt 3: 1 (28) **I don't have a clue./I have no clue.** *(infml)* Ich habe keine Ahnung./Keine Ahnung. 3: 1 (28)

coach [kəʊtʃ] der (Reise-)Bus 3: 2 (59)

coal [kəʊl] die Kohle 3: 4 (106/107)

coast [kəʊst] die Küste 3: 3 (74/75)

cocoa [ˈkəʊkəʊ] der Kakao 1

code [kəʊd]:
1. programmieren *(Computer)*; kodieren 1
2. der Code 1
3. die Vorwahl(nummer) 1

coding [ˈkəʊdɪŋ] das Programmieren 1

coffee [ˈkɒfi] der Kaffee 1

coin [kɔɪn] die Münze 2

cola [ˈkəʊlə] die Cola 1

cold [kəʊld]:
1. kalt 1
    be cold frieren 1
2. die Kälte 1
3. die Erkältung 1
    have a cold erkältet sein 1

°**cold meat** [kəʊld ˈmiːt] der (Braten-/Wurst-)Aufschnitt

collect [kəˈlekt] (ein)sammeln 1

collection [kəˈlekʃn] die Sammlung 2

°**Cologne** [kəˈləʊn] Köln

colour [ˈkʌlə] die Farbe 1 **What colour is …?** Welche Farbe hat …? 1

colourful [ˈkʌləfl] bunt, farbig 3: 1 (23)

colourless [ˈkʌlələs] farblos 3: 1 (23)

column [ˈkɒləm] die Säule; die Spalte *(in Texten)* 3: 1 (21) **advice column** der Kummerkasten, die Ratgeber-Spalte *(z. B. in Zeitschriften)* 3: 2 (48)

two hundred and forty-nine

Dictionary — English – German

°**comb (your hair)** [kəʊm] (sich die Haare) kämmen
come [kʌm], came, come:
1. (mit)kommen 1
   come off abgehen, sich lösen 2
   Come on! Komm(t) (schon)! Na los! 3: 2 (56) **come round (to sb.)** vorbeikommen, vorbeischauen (bei jm.) 2 **come up** (Sonne) aufgehen 1
2. **come true** wahr werden 2

comfortable [ˈkʌmftəbl] bequem, gemütlich 2
comic [ˈkɒmɪk] der Comic 1
comment (about/on sth.) [ˈkɒment]:
1. (etwas) kommentieren 3: 4 (114)
2. der Kommentar (über/zu etwas) 3: 4 (114) **make a comment** einen Kommentar abgeben 3: 4 (114)

°**common** [ˈkɒmən]: **have sth. in common** etwas gemeinsam haben
community [kəˈmjuːnəti] die Gemeinschaft, die Gemeinde 3: 1 (29)
company [ˈkʌmpəni] die Firma, die Gesellschaft 3: 1 (30)
°**compare** [kəmˈpeə] vergleichen
competition [kɒmpəˈtɪʃn] der Wettbewerb 1
°**competitor** [kəmˈpetɪtə] der/die Konkurrent/in (z. B. im Wettbewerb)
complete [kəmˈpliːt]:
1. vervollständigen 3: 2 (60)
2. vollständig, komplett 3: 2 (60)

completely [kəmˈpliːtli] völlig, absolut 3: 2 (60)
compliment [ˈkɒmplɪmənt] das Kompliment 3: 2 (55) **(to) pay sb. a compliment** jm. ein Kompliment machen 3: 2 (55)
computer [kəmˈpjuːtə] der Computer 1
computing [kəmˈpjuːtɪŋ] die Informatik 1
concert [ˈkɒnsət] das Konzert 2
condition [kənˈdɪʃn] die Bedingung; der Zustand 3: 1 (19) **conditions** (pl) die Bedingungen, die Verhältnisse 3: 1 (19)
confidence [ˈkɒnfɪdəns] das (Selbst-)Vertrauen, die Zuversicht 3: 2 (52)
confident [ˈkɒnfɪdənt] (selbst)sicher; zuversichtlich 2
conflict [ˈkɒnflɪkt] der Konflikt, die Auseinandersetzung, der Streit 3: 2 (56)
°**confuse** [kənˈfjuːz] verwirren; durcheinanderbringen
connect (to/with) [kəˈnekt] (sich) verbinden (mit) 3: 4 (112)
connection [kəˈnekʃn] die Verbindung 3: 4 (112)
console [kənˈsəʊl] die Konsole 1
°**construction** [kənˈstrʌkʃn] der Bau; die Konstruktion
contact [ˈkɒntækt]:
1. der Kontakt 2
2. **contact sb.** Kontakt aufnehmen mit jm., sich in Verbindung setzen mit jm. 2

continue [kənˈtɪnjuː] fortfahren, weitermachen, (sich) fortsetzen, weitergehen 1 **continue to do sth.** etwas weiterhin tun, (mit) etwas weitermachen, fortfahren 1
contrast [kənˈtrɑːst] vergleichen, (einander) gegenüberstellen 3: 3 (88)
contrast [ˈkɒntrɑːst] der Kontrast, der Gegensatz 3: 3 (88)
°**conversation** [kɒnvəˈseɪʃn] das Gespräch
cook [kʊk]:
1. kochen 1
2. der Koch, die Köchin 1

°**cooked breakfast** [kʊkt ˈbrekfəst] ein warmes Frühstück, z. B. mit gebratenem Speck und Spiegeleiern **full cooked breakfast** ein reichhaltiges warmes Frühstück mit allem, was dazugehört
cooking [ˈkʊkɪŋ]:
1. das Kochen 1
2. das (gekochte) Essen 1

cool [kuːl] cool 1
copy [ˈkɒpi]:
1. die Kopie; das Exemplar 3: 1 (30)
2. kopieren, abschreiben 3: 1 (30)

correct [kəˈrekt]:
1. korrekt 2
2. korrigieren 2

corridor [ˈkɒrɪdɔː] der Korridor 1
cosplay [ˈkɒspleɪ] das Cosplay (Sichverkleiden als eine Figur z. B. aus einem Manga) 3: 4 (121)
cost [kɒst]:
1. die Kosten; der Preis 1
2. **cost, cost, cost** kosten 1

costume [ˈkɒstjuːm] das Kostüm, die Verkleidung 2
cotton [ˈkɒtn] die Baumwolle 3: 2 (47)
cough [kɒf]:
1. der Husten 2
2. husten 2

could [kʊd]:
1. **I could …** Ich konnte … 2
2. **Could I …?** Könnte ich …? 2

°**count** [kaʊnt] zählen
country [ˈkʌntri] das Land, (auch:) die ländliche Gegend 1
countryside [ˈkʌntrisaɪd] das Land (ländliche Gegend), die Landschaft; die Natur 3: 3 (84)
course [kɔːs]:
1. der Kurs 2
2. **main course** das Hauptgericht 1

cousin [ˈkʌzn] der Cousin, die Cousine 1
°**cover** [ˈkʌvə]:
1. bedecken
2. der (Buch-)Umschlag, die (Schutz-)Hülle, die Verpackung

cow [kaʊ] die Kuh 2
crazy [ˈkreɪzi] verrückt 2 **crazy about sth.** wild auf etwas, versessen auf etwas 2
cream [kriːm] die Sahne 1
create [kriˈeɪt] (er)schaffen, erstellen 2
creative [kriˈeɪtɪv] kreativ 2

°**creative commons** [krieɪtɪv ˈkɒmənz] „das schöpferische Gemeingut" (gemeinnützige Organisation, die das einfache Verbreiten von Nutzungsrechten zum Ziel hat)
creativity [kriːeɪˈtɪvəti] die Kreativität 2
creature [ˈkriːtʃə] das Geschöpf, das (Lebe-)Wesen 3: 3 (76)
cricket [ˈkrɪkɪt] das Kricket (Mannschaftssportart) 1
cross [krɒs]:
1. das Kreuz 3: 1 (23)
2. kreuzen, überqueren 3: 1 (23) **cross your fingers** die Daumen drücken/halten (jm. Glück/gutes Gelingen wünschen) 3: 2 (57)

°**crown** [kraʊn] die Krone
crush [krʌʃ]:
1. die Schwärmerei, das Verliebtsein 3: 2 (49) **have a crush (on sb.)** in jn. verliebt sein 3: 2 (49)
2. der Schwarm (jd., in den/die man verliebt ist) 3: 2 (49)

cry [kraɪ]:
1. der Schrei, der Ruf 3: 3 (87)
2. weinen; rufen, schreien 3: 3 (87)

cucumber [ˈkjuːkʌmbə] die Gurke (Salatgurke) 3: 1 (24)
culture [ˈkʌltʃə] die Kultur 1
°**cup** [kʌp]: **World Cup** die Weltmeisterschaft
cupcake [ˈkʌpkeɪk] der Cupcake (kleiner Muffin-ähnlicher Kuchen) 2
curious (about) [ˈkjʊəriəs] neugierig (auf) 2
curl [kɜːl] die Locke 2
curly [ˈkɜːli] lockig 2
curry [ˈkʌri] das Curry (Gewürz und auch Gericht) 1
cushion [ˈkʊʃn] das Kissen 1
custard [ˈkʌstəd] der Custard (Vanillesoße) 1
customer [ˈkʌstəmə] der Kunde, die Kundin 2
cut [kʌt]:
1. der Schnitt 2
2. **cut, cut, cut** schneiden 2 ausschneiden 3: 4 (123) **cut sth. out** etwas ausschneiden; etwas weglassen, auf etwas verzichten 2

cute [kjuːt] niedlich, süß 1
cyberbullying [ˈsaɪbəbʊliɪŋ] das Cybermobbing 3: 4 (116)
cycle [ˈsaɪkl] Rad fahren 1
cycle lane [ˈsaɪkl leɪn] der Radweg 3: 1 (23)
cycling [ˈsaɪklɪŋ] das Radfahren 1
°**Cymru** [ˈkʌmri] Name für Wales auf Walisisch

D

dad [dæd] der Papa, der Vati 1
dance [dɑːns]:
1. tanzen 1
2. der Tanz 1
   do a dance einen Tanz tanzen 1

dancer [ˈdɑːnsə] der/die Tänzer/in 1
dancing [ˈdɑːnsɪŋ] das Tanzen 1
danger [ˈdeɪndʒə] die Gefahr 2
dangerous [ˈdeɪndʒərəs] gefährlich 2
dare [deə]:
 1. wagen, sich trauen 2
 2. die Mutprobe 2
  for a dare als Mutprobe 2
dark [dɑːk]:
 1. dunkel 2
 2. das Dunkel, die Dunkelheit 2
darkness [ˈdɑːknəs] die Dunkelheit 2
date [deɪt]:
 1. das Datum 1
  birthday date das Datum des Geburtstags 1
 2. die Verabredung, das Date *(auch die Person, mit der man ausgeht)* 2
 3. **date sb.** mit jm. gehen, eine Beziehung haben 2
daughter [ˈdɔːtə] die Tochter 1
day [deɪ] der Tag 1 **work long days** lange arbeiten, lange Arbeitstage haben 1
dead [ded] tot 1 **My phone is dead.** Mein Telefon-Akku ist leer. 3: 1 (26)
deal with [ˈdiːl wɪð], **dealt, dealt** klarkommen mit, fertigwerden mit, umgehen mit 3: 2 (49)
dealt [delt] *siehe* **deal with**
dear [dɪə]: **Dear ...** Liebe/r ... 1
 °**be dear to sb.** jm. lieb (und teuer) sein *(jm. sehr wichtig sein)*
debate [dɪˈbeɪt]:
 1. debattieren 3: 4 (114)
 2. die Debatte 3: 4 (114)
  hold/have a debate eine Debatte führen 3: 4 (114)
December [dɪˈsembə] der Dezember 1
decide [dɪˈsaɪd] beschließen, sich entscheiden 3: 2 (46) **decide on sth.** etwas beschließen, sich für etwas entscheiden 3: 2 (46) **decide to do sth.** beschließen, sich entscheiden etwas zu tun 3: 2 (46)
decorate [ˈdekəreɪt] dekorieren, schmücken 1
decoration [dekəˈreɪʃn] die Dekoration, der Schmuck, die Verzierung 1
deep [diːp] tief 3: 3 (76)
deer [dɪə], *pl* **deer** das Reh; der Hirsch 3: 3 (84)
definitely [ˈdefɪnətli] auf jeden Fall; ganz bestimmt 3: 3 (76)
°**definition** [defɪˈnɪʃn] die Definition
degree [dɪˈɡriː] das/der Grad 1
delete [dɪˈliːt] löschen 3: 4 (119)
delicious [dɪˈlɪʃəs] köstlich, lecker 1
°**department** [dɪˈpɑːtmənt] die Abteilung
°**department store** [dɪˈpɑːtmənt stɔː] das Kaufhaus
dependent (on) [dɪˈpendənt] abhängig (von), angewiesen (auf) 2
describe [dɪˈskraɪb] beschreiben 1
description [dɪˈskrɪpʃn] die Beschreibung 1

design [dɪˈzaɪn]:
 1. die Gestaltung, das Design 1
 2. entwerfen, gestalten 2
design and technology [dɪzaɪn ən tekˈnɒlədʒi] das Werken, der Werkunterricht 1
designer [dɪˈzaɪnə] der/die Designer/in 2
desk [desk]:
 1. der Schreibtisch 1
 2. der Schalter *(z. B. Verkaufs-, Postschalter)* 3: 1 (27)
dessert [dɪˈzɜːt] die Nachspeise, das Dessert 1 **for dessert** zum/als Nachtisch 1
destination [destɪˈneɪʃn] das Ziel, der Bestimmungsort 2
°**detail** [ˈdiːteɪl] das Detail, die Einzelheit
develop [dɪˈveləp] entwickeln; sich entwickeln 3: 3 (90)
developer [dɪˈveləpə] der/die Entwickler/in *(z. B. f. Software)* 3: 3 (90)
device [dɪˈvaɪs] das Gerät, der Apparat 3: 4 (112)
°**Dia Duit!** [dʒɪə ˈxɔɪtʃ] Hallo! *(irisches Gälisch; wörtlich: Gott sei mit dir/euch/Ihnen!)*
°**dialogue** [ˈdaɪəlɒɡ] der Dialog
diary [ˈdaɪəri] der Kalender; das Tagebuch 3: 4 (114) **keep a diary** Tagebuch führen 3: 4 (114)
dictionary [ˈdɪkʃənri] das Wörterbuch, das *(alphabetische)* Wörterverzeichnis 2
did [dɪd] *siehe* **do** **they didn't go ...** (= **did not**) sie gingen nicht/sie sind nicht gegangen 2
difference [ˈdɪfrəns] der Unterschied 1 **make a difference** etwas bewirken, etwas ausmachen 3: 1 (29)
different (to) [ˈdɪfrənt] verschieden; anders (als) 1
difficult [ˈdɪfɪkəlt] schwierig, schwer 1
dig [dɪɡ], **dug, dug** graben 1
digital [ˈdɪdʒɪtl] digital 3: 3 (91)
dining room [ˈdaɪnɪŋ ruːm] das Esszimmer 1
dinner [ˈdɪnə] das Abendessen 1 **for dinner** zum Abendessen 1
dip [dɪp] der Dip 3: 1 (24)
direct [dəˈrekt] direkt, unmittelbar 3: 1 (17)
directions *(pl)* [dəˈrekʃnz] Wegbeschreibung(en) 3: 1 (23) **ask for directions** nach dem Weg fragen 3: 1 (23) **give directions** den Weg beschreiben 3: 1 (23)
dirty [ˈdɜːti] schmutzig 1
disability [dɪsəˈbɪləti] die Behinderung 3: 2 (44/45)
disabled [dɪsˈeɪbld] (körper)behindert 3: 2 (44/45)
disagree [dɪsəˈɡriː] nicht zustimmen, widersprechen 3: 2 (58)
disappoint sb. [dɪsəˈpɔɪnt] jn. enttäuschen 2

disappointed (in/with) [dɪsəˈpɔɪntɪd] enttäuscht (von) 2
disappointing [dɪsəˈpɔɪntɪŋ] enttäuschend 2
disappointment [dɪsəˈpɔɪntmənt] die Enttäuschung 2
°**disaster** [dɪˈzɑːstə] die Katastrophe, das Unglück
disco [ˈdɪskəʊ] die Disco 2
discover [dɪˈskʌvə] entdecken 2
discuss [dɪˈskʌs] diskutieren (über); besprechen 3: 1 (28)
discussion [dɪˈskʌʃn] die Diskussion 3: 1 (28)
dish [dɪʃ] das Gericht *(Mahlzeit)* 1 **main dish** das Hauptgericht 1
dishwasher [ˈdɪʃwɒʃə] die Geschirrspülmaschine 2
disorganized [dɪsˈɔːɡənaɪzd] schlecht organisiert, chaotisch 2
°**ditch sth.** [dɪtʃ] *(infml)* etwas über Bord werfen
°**divide (up) (into)** [dɪˈvaɪd] auf-/einteilen (in)
DNA [diː en ˈeɪ] die DNA *(Erbanlagen)* 3: 3 (76)
do [duː], **did, done** machen, tun 1 **do your homework** Hausaufgaben machen 1
doctor (Dr) [ˈdɒktə] der Arzt, die Ärztin 2
document [ˈdɒkjumənt] das Dokument; die Textdatei 3: 4 (112)
dog [dɒɡ] der Hund 1 **walk the dog** mit dem Hund rausgehen, mit dem Hund Gassi gehen 2
dog walker [ˈdɒɡ wɔːkə] der/die Hundeausführer/in 2
dog walking [ˈdɒɡ wɔːkɪŋ] Hunde ausführen 2
dolphin [ˈdɒlfɪn] der Delfin 2
done [dʌn] *siehe* **do** **Well done. Gut gemacht!** 1
donkey [ˈdɒŋki] der Esel 3: 4 (106/107)
donut [ˈdəʊnʌt] der Donut *(ringförmiges Gebäck aus Hefeteig)* 2
door [dɔː] die Tür 1
doorkeeper [ˈdɔːkiːpə] der/die Pförtner/in 3: 1 (27)
double [ˈdʌbl] doppelt, Doppel- 3: 1 (17)
double-decker (bus) [dʌbl ˈdekə] der Doppeldecker(bus) 3: 1 (17)
double room [dʌbl ˈruːm] das Doppelzimmer 3: 1 (17)
down [daʊn] hinunter, herunter 1 **down a hill** einen Hügel hinunter, herunter 2
download [ˈdaʊnləʊd]:
 1. der/das Download 3: 3 (87)
 2. herunterladen 3: 3 (87)
downstairs [daʊnˈsteəz] (nach) unten *(die Treppe hinunter)* 2
dragon [ˈdræɡən] der Drache 2
drama [ˈdrɑːmə] das Schauspiel, die darstellende Kunst 1
dramatic [drəˈmætɪk] dramatisch 2
drank [dræŋk] *siehe* **drink**
draw [drɔː], **drew, drawn** zeichnen 1
drawing [ˈdrɔːɪŋ] das Zeichnen 1

two hundred and fifty-one

Dictionary — English – German

drawn [drɔːn] *siehe* draw
dream [driːm]:
 1. der Traum 1
 2. **dream (of / about sth.)** träumen (von etwas) 1
dress [dres]:
 1. sich kleiden, sich anziehen 2
  get dressed sich anziehen 1
 2. das Kleid 2
  wedding dress das Hochzeitskleid 2
drew [druː] *siehe* draw
drink [drɪŋk]:
 1. das Getränk 1
 2. **drink, drank, drunk** trinken 1
drive [draɪv], **drove, driven** *(mit dem Auto)* fahren 2
driven [ˈdrɪvn] *siehe* drive
driver [ˈdraɪvə] der / die Fahrer/in 2
drone [drəʊn] die Drohne 1
°**drop the beat** [drɒp ðə ˈbiːt] den / einen Beat unter die Musik legen
drove [drəʊv] *siehe* drive
°**drummer** [ˈdrʌmə] der / die Trommler/in
drunk [drʌŋk] *siehe* drink
°**dug** [dʌɡ] *siehe* dig
duke [djuːk] der Herzog 1
dungeon [ˈdʌndʒən] der Kerker, das Verlies *(in einer Burg)* 2
during [ˈdjʊərɪŋ] während *(Präposition)* 2

E

each [iːtʃ] jede(r, s) (einzelne), jeweils 1
each other [iːtʃ ˈʌðə] einander, sich (gegenseitig) 2
ear [ɪə] das Ohr 2
earlier [ˈɜːliə] vorhin; vorher, früher 3: 1 (27)
early [ˈɜːli] früh 2
earn [ɜːn] verdienen *(Geld)* 2
earth [ɜːθ] die Erde 2
east [iːst] der Osten; östlich; Ost- 3: (10/11)
eastern [ˈiːstən] östliche(r, s), Ost- 3: (10/11)
easy [ˈiːzi] einfach, leicht 2
eat [iːt], **ate, eaten** essen; fressen 1
eaten [ˈiːtn] *siehe* eat
edit [ˈedɪt] bearbeiten, editieren 3: 4 (108)
eel [iːl] der Aal 3: 3 (76)
effect (on) [ɪˈfekt] die (Aus-)Wirkung (auf), der Einfluss (auf); der Effekt 2
effective [ɪˈfektɪv] effektiv, wirksam 2
e.g. [iː ˈdʒiː] *(aus dem Lateinischen)* z. B. (zum Beispiel) 3: 3 (82)
egg [eg] das Ei 1
eight [eɪt] acht 1
eighteen [eɪˈtiːn] achtzehn 1
eighty [ˈeɪti] achtzig 1
°**either** [ˈaɪðə]: **not … either** auch nicht
electric [ɪˈlektrɪk] elektrisch, Elektro- 1
electro [ɪˈlektrəʊ] der Electro, die Elektromusik 2
electronic [ɪlekˈtrɒnɪk] elektronisch 2

electronics *(pl)* [ɪlekˈtrɒnɪks] die Elektronik; die elektronischen Geräte 2
elephant [ˈelɪfənt] der Elefant 1
eleven [ɪˈlevən] elf 1
else [els]: **everybody / everyone else** alle anderen; jede/r andere 2 **no one else** niemand anders, niemand sonst 2 **somebody / someone else** jemand anders 2 **What else?** Was sonst noch? 2
email [ˈiːmeɪl]:
 1. die E-Mail 3: 2 (46)
 2. **email sb.** jm. mailen, eine E-Mail schicken 3: 2 (46)
embarrass sb. [ɪmˈbærəs] jn. in Verlegenheit bringen, jm. peinlich sein 2
embarrassed [ɪmˈbærəst] verlegen, peinlich berührt 2 **be / feel embarrassed** peinlich berührt sein 2
embarrassing [ɪmˈbærəsɪŋ] peinlich 2
emoji [ɪˈməʊdʒi] das Emoji 3: 4 (115)
emotion [ɪˈməʊʃn] die Emotion, das Gefühl 3: 4 (116)
emotional [ɪˈməʊʃənl] emotional 3: 4 (116)
empty [ˈempti]:
 1. leer 2
 2. leeren 2
end [end]:
 1. enden; beenden 1
 2. das Ende, der Schluss 1
  at the end (of) am Ende (von) 1
  in the end schließlich; zum Schluss 1
ending [ˈendɪŋ] die Endung; das Ende *(Text, Geschichte)* 2
endless [ˈendləs] endlos 3: 1 (23)
enemy [ˈenəmi] der / die Feind/in 3: 2 (48)
energetic [enəˈdʒetɪk] aktiv, tatkräftig, energiegeladen 2
energy [ˈenədʒi] die Energie 2
England [ˈɪŋglənd] England 1
English [ˈɪŋglɪʃ] Englisch; englisch 1
enjoy [ɪnˈdʒɔɪ] genießen 1 **enjoy doing sth.** es genießen, etwas zu tun 1 **Enjoy yourselves.** Viel Spaß! Amüsiert euch gut! 3: 2 (52) **Enjoy!** Viel Vergnügen! / Guten Appetit! 1
enough [ɪˈnʌf] genug 1
equipment *(no pl)* [ɪˈkwɪpmənt] die Ausrüstung 2
°**erm** [ɜːm] äh *(Verlegenheitslaut)*
escalator [ˈeskəleɪtə] die Rolltreppe 3: 1 (16)
especially [ɪˈspeʃəli] insbesondere 2
estate [ɪˈsteɪt] die Wohnsiedlung; das Gewerbegebiet 1
EU (= European Union) [iː ˈjuː] die EU (Europäische Union) 3: (12/13)
euro [ˈjʊərəʊ], *pl* **euros** der Euro 1
European Union [jʊərəpiːən ˈjuːnɪən] die Europäische Union 3: (12/13)
even [ˈiːvn] sogar, selbst 2 **even if** selbst wenn, sogar wenn 2 **not even** nicht einmal 2

evening [ˈiːvnɪŋ] der Abend 1
 in the evening abends, am Abend 1
event [ɪˈvent] das Ereignis 2
eventually [ɪˈventʃuəli] letztendlich, schließlich 3: 3 (87)
ever [ˈevə] jemals, schon einmal 2
 for ever für immer, ewig (lange) 3: 2 (48) **the best son ever** der beste Sohn überhaupt / der beste Sohn, den man sich wünschen kann 1
every [ˈevri] jede(r, s) 1 **every 30 minutes** alle 30 Minuten 1
everybody [ˈevribɒdi] jeder; alle 1
everyone [ˈevriwʌn] jeder, alle 1
everything [ˈevriθɪŋ] alles 2
everywhere [ˈevriweə] überall(hin) 1
exact [ɪɡˈzækt] genau, exakt 3: 4 (113)
example [ɪɡˈzɑːmpl] das Beispiel 1
 for example zum Beispiel 1
except (for) [ɪkˈsept] außer, bis auf 3: 1 (18)
exchange [ɪksˈtʃeɪndʒ]:
 1. der Schüleraustausch; der Austausch, der Wechsel 3: 4 (108)
 2. tauschen, austauschen 3: 4 (108)
exchange class [ɪksˈtʃeɪndʒ klɑːs] die Schulklasse, die am Schüleraustausch teilnimmt 3: 4 (108)
exchange partner [ɪksˈtʃeɪndʒ pɑːtnə] der / die Austauschpartner/in 3: 4 (108)
exchange student [ɪksˈtʃeɪndʒ stjuːdnt] der / die Austauschschüler/in 3: 4 (108)
excited [ɪkˈsaɪtɪd] aufgeregt, gespannt 2
exciting [ɪkˈsaɪtɪŋ] aufregend 2
Excuse me, … [ɪksˈkjuːz miː] Entschuldigung, … / Entschuldigen Sie, … 1
exercise [ˈeksəsaɪz] die Übung, die Aufgabe 1
exercise book [ˈeksəsaɪz bʊk] das Schulheft, das Übungsheft 1
°**expect** [ɪkˈspekt] erwarten
expensive [ɪkˈspensɪv] teuer 1
experience [ɪkˈspɪərɪəns]:
 1. die Erfahrung; das Erlebnis 2
 2. **experience sth.** etwas erfahren; erleben 2
°**experiment** [ɪkˈsperɪmənt] das Experiment
explain sth. to sb. [ɪkˈspleɪn] jm. etwas erklären 1
explanation [ekspləˈneɪʃn] die Erklärung 2
extra [ˈekstrə] Extra-, zusätzliche(r, s) 2
eye [aɪ] das Auge 2

F

face [feɪs]:
 1. das Gesicht 2
 2. **face sb./sth.** jm. / einer Sache ins Gesicht / ins Auge sehen, jm. / einer Sache entgegentreten 2
fact [fækt] die Tatsache 2 **in fact** tatsächlich, in Wirklichkeit, genau genommen 2
fair [feə] fair 2
fair play [feə ˈpleɪ] das Fair Play 3: 2 (44/45)

fake [feɪk]:
1. falsch, gefälscht 3: 3 (76)
2. der/das Fake, die Fälschung 3: 3 (76)
3. **fake sth.** etwas faken, fälschen, vortäuschen 3: 3 (76)

falafel [fəˈlæfl] die/das Falafel 3: 1 (24)

fall [fɔːl], **fell, fallen** fallen; hinfallen 2 **fall asleep** einschlafen 2 **fall off** herunterfallen 2

fallen [ˈfɔːlən] *siehe* **fall**

false [fɔːls] falsch, unrichtig 2

false friend [ˌfɔːls ˈfrend] der „falsche Freund" (Übersetzungsfalle) 2

fame [feɪm] der Ruhm 2

family [ˈfæməli] die Familie 1

family name [ˈfæməli neɪm] der Familienname, der Nachname 1

famous (for) [ˈfeɪməs] berühmt (für, wegen) 2

fan [fæn] der Fan 1

far [fɑː] weit (entfernt) 2 **so far** bis jetzt, bis hierher 2

farm [fɑːm] der Bauernhof, die Farm 2

fashion [ˈfæʃn] die Mode, die Fashion 3: 2 (44/45)

fast [fɑːst] schnell 1

fast [fɑːst]:
1. fasten 2
2. das Fasten, die Fastenzeit 2 **break the fast** das Fasten brechen 2

fast fashion [ˌfɑːst ˈfæʃn] die Fast Fashion („schnelle Mode", die zu niedrigen Preisen verkauft und nur kurz getragen wird) 3: 2 (47)

father [ˈfɑːðə] der Vater 2

fault [fɔːlt] der Fehler; die Schuld 3: 3 (87)

favourite [ˈfeɪvərɪt]:
1. Lieblings- 1
2. der Liebling, der/die Favorit/in 1

February [ˈfebruəri] der Februar 1

fed [fed] *siehe* **feed**

feed [fiːd], **fed, fed** füttern; ernähren 2

feedback *(no pl)* [ˈfiːdbæk] das Feedback *(Rückmeldung)* 1

feel [fiːl], **felt, felt** sich fühlen; fühlen 1 **feel sorry for sb.** Mitleid haben mit jm. 1

feeling [ˈfiːlɪŋ] das Gefühl 2

feet [fiːt] *Plural von* **foot**

fell [fel] *siehe* **fall**

felt [felt] *siehe* **feel**

ferry [ˈferi] die Fähre 2

festival [ˈfestɪvl] das Fest(ival) 2

few [fjuː] wenige 3: 1 (23) **a few** ein paar, einige 2 **in the last few weeks** in den letzten paar Wochen 2

field [fiːld] das Feld; die Weide 1 **in the field** auf der Weide 1

fifteen [fɪfˈtiːn] fünfzehn 1

fifty [ˈfɪfti] fünfzig 1

fight [faɪt]:
1. der Kampf 2
2. der Streit 2 **have a fight/fights (over/about sth.)** Streit haben (um/wegen etwas) 2
3. **fight, fought, fought** kämpfen, bekämpfen 2

fighter [ˈfaɪtə] der/die Kämpfer/in 2

figure [ˈfɪɡə] die Figur 3: 1 (30)

file [faɪl] die Datei; der Ordner, die Liste 1

film [fɪlm]:
1. der Film 1
2. **film sth.** etwas filmen 3: 1 (21)

filter [ˈfɪltə]:
1. der Filter 3: 4 (120)
2. filtern 3: 4 (120)

finally [ˈfaɪnəli] schließlich, endlich 3: 1 (28)

find [faɪnd], **found, found** finden 1 **find out (about)** herausfinden; sich informieren (über) 1

fine [faɪn] **I'm fine.** Mir geht es gut. 1

finger [ˈfɪŋɡə] der Finger 3: 2 (57) **tap your fingers** mit den Fingern klopfen 3: 4 (112)

finish [ˈfɪnɪʃ]:
1. das Ende, das Ziel *(z. B. beim Sport)* 2
2. enden; beenden, zu Ende machen 2

fire [ˈfaɪə] das Feuer 2

fire engine [ˈfaɪər endʒɪn] das Feuerwehrauto 2

firefighter [ˈfaɪəfaɪtə] der Feuerwehrmann, die Feuerwehrfrau 2

firework [ˈfaɪəwɜːk] der Feuerwerkskörper 2 **fireworks** *(pl)* das Feuerwerk 2

first [fɜːst]:
1. erste(r, s) 1
2. zuerst, als Erstes 1 **at first** zuerst, am Anfang 1

first name [ˈfɜːst neɪm] der Vorname 1

fish [fɪʃ]:
1. fischen, angeln 3: 3 (91)
2. *pl* **fish** der Fisch 1

fish and chip shop [fɪʃ ən ˈtʃɪp ʃɒp] die Imbissstube, die Fisch mit Pommes Frites verkauft 1

fishing [ˈfɪʃɪŋ] das Fischen, das Angeln; die Fischerei 3: 3 (91)

fit [fɪt] fit 2

°**fit** [fɪt] passen (zu)

fitness [ˈfɪtnəs] die Fitness 2

five [faɪv] fünf 1

flag [flæɡ] die Fahne, die Flagge 2

flamenco [fləˈmeŋkəʊ] der Flamenco *(Tanz)* 2

°**flash** [flæʃ]:
1. der Blitz *(Kamera)*; das Aufblitzen; das Blinklicht
2. blinken, blitzen (mit); *(Telefon)* mit Blitz fotografieren

flat [flæt] die Wohnung 1

flew [fluː] *siehe* **fly**

floor [flɔː]:
1. der Fußboden 1
2. die Etage, der Stock, das Stockwerk 1

flour [ˈflaʊə] das Mehl 1

flow [fləʊ]:
1. der Fluss; der Strom 3: 4 (122)
2. fließen; strömen 3: 4 (122)

flower [ˈflaʊə] die Blume; die Blüte 2

flowerpot [ˈflaʊəpɒt] der Blumentopf 2

flown [fləʊn] *siehe* **fly**

fly [flaɪ], **flew, flown** fliegen 1

°**focus (on)** [ˈfəʊkəs] sich konzentrieren (auf)

fold [fəʊld] falten 2 °**fold sth. over** etwas umknicken, umfalten

follow [ˈfɒləʊ] (be)folgen; verfolgen 3: 1 (27)

follower [ˈfɒləʊə] der Follower 3: 4 (117)

food [fuːd] das Essen, das Lebensmittel; das Futter 1

foot [fʊt], *pl* **feet:**
1. der Fuß *(Körperteil)* 2
2. der Fuß *(Längenmaß; ca. 30 cm)* 2

football [ˈfʊtbɔːl] der Fußball 1

footballer [ˈfʊtbɔːlə] der/die Fußballspieler/in 1

for [fɔː] für 1 **for 30 seconds** für 30 Sekunden, 30 Sekunden lang 1 **for 30 years** 30 Jahre (lang); seit 30 Jahren 3: 3 (82) **for a dare** als Mutprobe 2 **for a long time** seit langem; lange *(für eine lange Zeit)* 2 **for hours** seit Stunden, stundenlang 2 **for once** ausnahmsweise, dieses eine Mal 3: 4 (119) **for the first time** zum ersten Mal 2 **it's for free** es ist kostenlos, es kostet nichts 2 **What's for homework?** Was haben wir als Hausaufgabe(n) auf? 1 **What's for lunch?** Was gibt es zum Mittagessen? 1

foreground [ˈfɔːɡraʊnd] der Vordergrund 3: (12/13)

forest [ˈfɒrɪst] der Wald 2

forever, for ever [fərˈevə] für immer, ewig (lange) 3: 2 (48) **best friend forever (BFF)** der/die beste Freund/in für immer 3: 2 (48)

forget [fəˈɡet], **forgot, forgotten** vergessen 2

forgot [fəˈɡɒt] *siehe* **forget**

forgotten [fəˈɡɒtn] *siehe* **forget**

fork [fɔːk] die Gabel 1

form [fɔːm]:
1. (sich) formen, (sich) bilden 3: 1 (18)
2. die Form, die Art 3: 1 (18) **form of transport** die Fortbewegungsart, die Art der Beförderung 3: 1 (18)
°3. das Formular
°**complete a form** ein Formular ausfüllen

°**format** [ˈfɔːmæt] formatieren

fortunately [ˈfɔːtʃənətli] zum Glück, glücklicherweise 3: 3 (76)

forty [ˈfɔːti] vierzig 1

forward [ˈfɔːwəd]:
1. **forward sth. to sb.** etwas an jn. weiterleiten; jm. etwas nachsenden 3: 4 (114)
2. **look forward to doing sth.** sich darauf freuen, etwas zu tun 2 **look forward to sth.** sich auf etwas freuen 2

fought [fɔːt] *siehe* **fight**

found [faʊnd] *siehe* **find**

°**fountain** [ˈfaʊntən]:
1. der (Spring-/Trink-)Brunnen **memorial fountain** der Gedenkbrunnen
2. die Quelle

Dictionary — English – German

four [fɔː] vier 1
fourteen [fɔːˈtiːn] vierzehn 1
free [friː]:
  1. frei 1
    free time die Freizeit, die freie Zeit 1 **Are you free after school?** Hast du nach der Schule Zeit? 1
  2. kostenlos 1
    it's (for) free es ist kostenlos, es kostet nichts 2
°**freeze** [friːz]**, froze, frozen** erstarren
°**freeze-frame** [ˈfriːz freɪm] das Standbild *(Film)*
frenemy [ˈfrenəmi] der/die falsche Freund/in 3: 2 (48)
Friday [ˈfraɪdeɪ], [ˈfraɪdi] der Freitag 1
fried [fraɪd] frittiert, gebraten 1
friend [frend] der/die Freund/in 1
  best friend forever (BFF) der/die beste Freund/in für immer 3: 2 (48)
  make friends Freunde/-innen finden 2
friendly [ˈfrendli] freundlich, nett 1
friendship [ˈfrendʃɪp] die Freundschaft 3: 2 (48)
°**frighten** [ˈfraɪtn] Angst einjagen, verängstigen; erschrecken
from [frɒm] von, aus 1 **Where are you from?** Wo kommst du her? 1
front [frʌnt] **in front of** vor 1
°**froze** [frəʊz] *siehe* **freeze**
°**frozen** [ˈfrəʊzn] *siehe* **freeze**
fruit [fruːt] das Obst 1
fry [fraɪ] braten; frittieren 1
full [fʊl]:
  1. voll 1
    full of … voller … 2
  2. satt 2
    I'm full. Ich bin satt/voll bis obenhin. 2
fun [fʌn] der Spaß 1 **be fun** Spaß machen; lustig sein 1 **have fun** Spaß haben 1
fun run [ˈfʌn rʌn] der Volkslauf *(z. B. zum Geldsammeln für wohltätige Zwecke)* 2
funny [ˈfʌni]:
  1. seltsam 1
  2. witzig, lustig 1
    What's funny about …? Was ist lustig an …? 1
further [ˈfɜːðə] weiter (entfernt) 3: 2 (57)
future [ˈfjuːtʃə]:
  1. die Zukunft 2
  2. zukünftige(r, s) 2

G

Gaelic [ˈɡeɪlɪk] Gälisch *(Sprache)* 3: (10/11)
°**gallery** [ˈɡæləri] die Galerie
game [ɡeɪm]:
  1. das Spiel 1
  2. Computerspiele spielen 2
gamer [ˈɡeɪmə] der/die Gamer/in *(Computerspieler/in)* 2
gaming [ˈɡeɪmɪŋ] das Gaming *(Spielen am Computer)* 2

gap [ɡæp] die Lücke, der Abstand 3: 1 (16)
garage [ˈɡærɑːʒ] die Garage 1
garden [ˈɡɑːdn] der Garten 1
gate [ɡeɪt] das Tor 3: 1 (26)
gave [ɡeɪv] *siehe* **give**
gay [ɡeɪ]:
  1. der Schwule 2
  2. schwul 2
°**general** [ˈdʒenrəl] allgemein
generous [ˈdʒenərəs] großzügig 2
geography [dʒiˈɒɡrəfi] die Geografie, die Erdkunde 1
German [ˈdʒɜːmən] deutsch; Deutsch; der/die Deutsche 1
Germany [ˈdʒɜːməni] Deutschland 1
get [ɡet]**, got, got:**
  1. bekommen 1
    get sth. (sich etwas) holen/besorgen 1
  2. werden 1
    Get better / well soon! Gute Besserung! / Werde bald gesund! 2
    get dressed sich anziehen 1
    get ready (for) sich fertig machen (für), sich vorbereiten (auf) 2
    get warm warm werden 1
  3. **get (to)** gelangen, (hin)kommen (nach) 2 **get in touch (with)** (sich) in Verbindung setzen (mit), Kontakt aufnehmen (zu) 3: 4 (114), **get off a train / bus** aus einem Zug/Bus aussteigen 2 **get off your bike / your horse** vom Fahrrad/vom Pferd absteigen 2 **get on a train / bus** in einen Zug/Bus einsteigen 2 **get up** aufstehen 1
°**4. get sth.** etwas verstehen, mitbekommen
    °**Don't get me wrong.** Versteh(t) mich nicht falsch.
ghost [ɡəʊst] der Geist, das Gespenst 2
ghost tour [ˈɡəʊst tʊə] die Geistertour *(Stadtführung mit gruseligen Themen/Elementen)* 2
gift [ɡɪft] das Geschenk, die Gabe; das Talent 2
gift shop [ˈɡɪft ʃɒp] der Geschenk(artikel)laden, der Souvenirladen 2
girl [ɡɜːl] das Mädchen 1
girlfriend [ˈɡɜːlfrend] die (feste) Freundin 2
give [ɡɪv]**, gave, given** geben 1
given [ˈɡɪvn] *siehe* **give**
glasses *(pl)* [ˈɡlɑːsɪz] die Brille 2
global [ˈɡləʊbl] global, weltweit 2
globe [ɡləʊb] der Globus; die Kugel 2
  across the globe auf der ganzen Welt 2 **all (a)round the globe** auf der ganzen Welt 2
glove [ɡlʌv] der Handschuh 2
glue [ɡluː] der Kleber, der Klebstoff 1
glue stick [ˈɡluː stɪk] der Klebestift 1

go [ɡəʊ]**, went, gone:**
  1. gehen, fahren 1
    go down (Sonne) untergehen 2
    go out rausgehen, weggehen; ausgehen 3: 2 (48) **How's it going?** *(infml)* Wie geht's? / Wie läuft's? 2 **I must go.** Ich muss Schluss machen. *(am Telefon/Briefschluss)* 1 **There you go.** Hier, bitte schön.; *(auch:)* Da hast du's! / Na siehst du! 3: 4 (115) °**it goes bong** es macht *bong*
  2. werden 1
    go green grün / umweltfreundlich werden 1
  3. **I'm going to …** ich werde … *(Plan, Vorhaben)* 2
goal [ɡəʊl] das Ziel *(Absicht, Lebensziel)*; das Tor *(im Sport)* 3: 1 (23)
goalkeeper [ˈɡəʊlkiːpə] der Torwart, die Torhüterin 3: 2 (57)
goat [ɡəʊt] die Ziege 2
god [ɡɒd] der Gott 2
gold [ɡəʊld]:
  1. das Gold 1
  2. goldfarben 1
golden [ˈɡəʊldn] golden, aus Gold 3: 1 (18)
gone [ɡɒn] *siehe* **go**   **be gone** weg sein 2
good [ɡʊd]:
  1. gut 1
    be good at sth. gut in etwas sein 1
    be good with … gut umgehen können mit … 1 **too much of a good thing** zu viel des Guten 2
  2. brav 1
°**Good Friday** [ɡʊd ˈfraɪdeɪ], [ɡʊd ˈfraɪdi] der Karfreitag
°**Good Friday Agreement** [ɡʊd fraɪdeɪ əˈɡriːmənt] das Karfreitagsabkommen
Goodbye. [ɡʊdˈbaɪ] Auf Wiedersehen! 1
got [ɡɒt] *siehe* **get**
government [ˈɡʌvənmənt] die Regierung 3: 1 (30)
graffiti [ɡrəˈfiːti] das Graffiti 3: 1 (14/15)
gram (g) [ɡræm] das Gramm 1
granddaughter [ˈɡrændɔːtə] die Enkelin 1
grandma [ˈɡrænmɑː] die Oma 1
grandpa [ˈɡrænpɑː] der Opa 1
grandparents *(pl)* [ˈɡrænpeərənts] die Großeltern 1
grandson [ˈɡrænsʌn] der Enkel 1
grass [ɡrɑːs] das Gras; der Rasen 3: 1 (27)
great [ɡreɪt]:
  1. großartig, toll 1
  2. groß *(bedeutend, angesehen)* 3: 3 (76)
Great Britain [ɡreɪt ˈbrɪtn] Großbritannien 1
green [ɡriːn]:
  1. grün 1
  2. umweltbewusst 1
    go green grün / umweltfreundlich werden 1
grew [ɡruː] *siehe* **grow**

grey [greɪ] grau 1
ground [graʊnd] der (Erd-)Boden 1
ground floor [graʊnd ˈflɔː]
das Erdgeschoss 1
group [gruːp] die Gruppe 1
grow [grəʊ], **grew, grown** wachsen 2
grow up aufwachsen; erwachsen werden 2
°**grown** [grəʊn] *siehe* **grow**
guard [gɑːd]:
1. der/die Wärter/in; die Wache; der/die Sicherheitsbedienstete 3:1 (21) **Changing of the Guards** die Wachablösung 3:1 (21)
2. **guard sth.** etwas schützen, bewachen 3:1 (21)
guess [ges]:
1. die Vermutung 3:4 (119)
2. (er)raten; annehmen, vermuten 3:4 (119) **Guess what!** Stell dir/Stellt euch (mal) vor! 3:4 (119) **I guess …** Ich glaube …, Ich nehme an … 3:4 (119)
°**guest** [gest] der Gast
guide [gaɪd]:
1. führen, leiten 1
2. (*kurz für* **tour guide**) der/die Reiseleiter/in; der/die Fremdenführer/in 1
guide dog [ˈgaɪd dɒg] der Blindenhund 1
guitar [gɪˈtɑː] die Gitarre 1
guys [gaɪz] (*pl, infml*) Leute (*als Anrede verwendet*) 1
gymnast [ˈdʒɪmnæst] der/die Turner/in 3:4 (111)
gymnastics [dʒɪmˈnæstɪks] die Gymnastik, das Turnen 3:4 (111)

H

habit [ˈhæbɪt] die (An-)Gewohnheit 3:4 (122)
had [hæd] *siehe* **have**
hair [heə] das Haar, die Haare 2
hairdresser [ˈheədresə] der/die Friseur/in 2
hairdresser's [ˈheədresəz] der Friseursalon 2
half [hɑːf]:
1. halbe(r, s) 3:2 (57) **half an hour** eine halbe Stunde 3:2 (57) **half full** halb voll 3:2 (57) **half past 6** halb 7 2 **half the time/half the money** die Hälfte der Zeit/des Geldes 3:2 (57)
2. *pl* **halves** die Hälfte; (*Fußball*) die Halbzeit 3:2 (57)
half-time [hɑːf ˈtaɪm] die Halbzeit(pause) 3:2 (57)
halfway [hɑːfˈweɪ] auf halbem Wege, halb(wegs) 3:3 (86)
hall [hɔːl]:
1. der Flur, die Diele 1
2. die Halle, der Saal 1 **sports hall** die Sporthalle 1
halloumi [həˈluːmi] der Halloumi (*Käse*) 3:1 (24)
Halloween [hæləʊˈiːn] (das) Halloween (*der Abend des 31. Oktober*) 2

°**Halò!** [ˈhʌləʊ] Hallo! (*schottisches Gälisch*)
halves [hɑːvz] *Plural von* **half**
ham [hæm] der Schinken 1
hamster [ˈhæmstə] der Hamster 1
hand [hænd] die Hand 1 **shake sb.'s hand / shake sb. by the hand** jm. die Hand schütteln/geben 3:1 (27)
handle [ˈhændl]:
1. der Griff, der Handgriff 3:1 (19)
2. **handle sth.** mit etwas umgehen, etwas handhaben 3:1 (19)
hang out [hæŋ ˈaʊt]**, hung, hung** rumhängen, abhängen 2
happen (to sb.) [ˈhæpən] (jm.) geschehen, passieren 1
happiness [ˈhæpɪnəs] das Glück, die Zufriedenheit 2
happy [ˈhæpi] glücklich, froh 1 **Happy birthday!** Herzlichen Glückwunsch zum Geburtstag! 1
hard [hɑːd] schwer, schwierig; hart 1 **think hard** scharf nachdenken 1
hard-working [hɑːd ˈwɜːkɪŋ] fleißig 1
has [hæz], [həz]: **he / she / it has** er/sie/es hat 1
hashtag [ˈhæʃtæg] das/der Hashtag 3:4 (118)
hat [hæt] der Hut, die Mütze 1
hate [heɪt]:
1. hassen 1
2. der Hass 1
have [hæv]**, had, had** haben 1 **have (food)** (Nahrung/etwas) essen; (*im Restaurant:*) nehmen 2 **have to do sth.** etwas tun müssen 2 **I have to go.** Ich muss Schluss machen. (*am Telefon/Briefschluss*) 2 **I'll have …** Ich nehme … (*beim Essen, z. B. im Restaurant*) 3:1 (24)
he [hiː] er 1 **he's** (= **he is**) er ist 1
head [hed] der Kopf 1 **shake your head** den Kopf schütteln 3:1 (27)
head student [hed ˈstjuːdnt] der/die Schulsprecher/in; der/die Vertrauensschüler/in 2
headache [ˈhedeɪk] Kopfschmerzen 2 **have a headache** Kopfschmerzen haben 2
heading [ˈhedɪŋ] die Überschrift 1
headphones (*pl*) [ˈhedfəʊnz] der Kopfhörer 1
headpiece [ˈhedpiːs] der Kopfschmuck 3:4 (121)
health [helθ] die Gesundheit 1 **in sickness or in health** wenn man krank oder gesund ist 2
healthy [ˈhelθi] gesund 1
hear [hɪə]**, heard, heard** hören 1
heard [hɜːd] *siehe* **hear**
°**heart** [hɑːt] das Herz **break sb.'s heart** jm. das Herz brechen
heather [ˈheðə] das Heidekraut 3:3 (85)
height [haɪt] die Höhe; die Größe (*bei Menschen*) 3:3 (87)
helicopter [ˈhelɪkɒptə] der Hubschrauber 3:3 (87)
Hello. [həˈləʊ] Hallo. 1 **Hello everybody!** Hallo allerseits! 1

helmet [ˈhelmɪt] der Helm 2
help [help]:
1. helfen 1
2. die Hilfe 1
helpful [ˈhelpfl] hilfsbereit; hilfreich, nützlich 1
helpless [ˈhelpləs] hilflos 3:1 (23)
henna [ˈhenə] die/das Henna 2
her [hɜː], [hə]:
1. sie; ihr (*zu „she"*) 1 **like her** wie sie 1
2. **her friends** ihre Freunde/Freundinnen 1
here [hɪə] hier; hierher 1 **Here you are.** Bitte schön. / Hier, bitte. 1
hero [ˈhɪərəʊ], *pl* **heroes** der/die Held/in
hers [hɜːz] ihrer, ihre, ihres (*zu „she"*) 3:4 (108)
herself [hɜːˈself] sich (selbst) (*zu „she"*) 3:2 (52)
Hi. [haɪ] Hallo. 1
high [haɪ] hoch 2
°**Highlands** [ˈhaɪləndz]: **the Highlands** (*pl*) das schottische Hochland
highlight [ˈhaɪlaɪt]:
1. das Highlight (Höhepunkt) 1
2. hervorheben, markieren, unterstreichen 1
hike [haɪk] wandern 1
hiker [ˈhaɪkə] der Wanderer, die Wanderin 3:3 (86)
hiking [ˈhaɪkɪŋ] das Wandern 1
hill [hɪl] der Hügel 2
him [hɪm] ihm, ihn (*zu „he"*) 1
himself [hɪmˈself] sich (selbst) (*zu „he"*) 3:2 (52)
hire [ˈhaɪə]:
1. der Verleih, die Vermietung 3:1 (17)
2. mieten, leihen; (*Person:*) einstellen 3:1 (17)
his [hɪz]:
1. seiner, seine, seins (*zu „he"*) 3:4 (108)
2. **his room** sein Zimmer 1
history [ˈhɪstri] die Geschichte (*vergangene Zeiten*) 1
hit [hɪt]**, hit, hit**:
1. schlagen 2
2. stoßen gegen, zusammenstoßen mit; treffen auf 2
hobby [ˈhɒbi] das Hobby 1
hockey [ˈhɒki] das Hockey 1
holiday [ˈhɒlədeɪ] der Urlaub 1 **holidays** (*pl*) die Ferien 1 **on holiday** im/in den Urlaub 1
home [həʊm]:
1. das Heim, das Zuhause 1 **at home** zu Hause 1
2. nach Hause 1 **go home** nach Hause gehen 1
homeless [ˈhəʊmləs] obdachlos 3:1 (22)
hometown [ˈhəʊmtaʊn] die Heimatstadt 3:2 (44/45)
homework [ˈhəʊmwɜːk] die Hausaufgabe(n) 1 **do your homework** Hausaufgaben machen 1 **What's for homework?** Was haben wir als Hausaufgabe(n) auf? 1

two hundred and fifty-five 255

Dictionary — English – German

honey [ˈhʌni] der Honig 1
hope [həʊp]:
1. hoffen 2
2. die Hoffnung 2
hopeful [ˈhəʊpfl] zuversichtlich, hoffnungsvoll 3: 3 (82)
°**horn** [hɔːn] die Hupe (Auto); das Horn
horoscope [ˈhɒrəskəʊp] das Horoskop 2
horrible [ˈhɒrəbl] schrecklich 1
horse [hɔːs] das Pferd 1
hospital [ˈhɒspɪtl] das Krankenhaus 1
hostel [ˈhɒstl] das Hostel (günstige Unterkunft für Reisende) 2
hot [hɒt] heiß, warm 1
hot chocolate [hɒt ˈtʃɒklət] der Kakao, die heiße (Trink-)Schokolade 1
hot dog [ˈhɒt dɒg] der/das Hotdog (heißes Würstchen in einem Brötchen) 1
hot meal [hɒt ˈmiːl] die warme Mahlzeit 1
hotel [həʊˈtel] das Hotel 2
hour [ˈaʊə] die Stunde 1 **a two-hour class** ein zweistündiger Kurs 2 **per hour** pro Stunde 1
house [haʊs] das Haus 1
house-warming (party) [ˈhaʊs wɔːmɪŋ] die Einzugsfeier 2
how [haʊ] wie 1 **How about ... ?** Wie wäre es mit ... ? 2 **How are you?** Wie geht's? / Wie geht es dir / euch / Ihnen? 1 **How much is / are ...?** Was (Wie viel) kostet / kosten ...? 2
however [haʊˈevə] allerdings, jedoch 3: 3 (76)
hug [hʌg]:
1. die Umarmung 2
2. **hug (sb.)** (jn.) umarmen; einander umarmen 2
hummus [ˈhʊməs] der/das Hummus 3: 1 (24)
hundred [ˈhʌndrəd]: **a / one hundred** (ein)hundert 1
hung [hʌŋ] siehe hang out
hungry [ˈhʌŋgri] hungrig 1 **I'm hungry.** Ich habe Hunger. 1
hunt [hʌnt]:
1. jagen 3: 3 (76)
2. die Jagd 3: 3 (76)
hunter [ˈhʌntə] der/die Jäger/in 3: 3 (76)
hurry [ˈhʌri]:
1. sich beeilen; eilen 3: 1 (27) **Hurry up!** Beeil dich! / Beeilt euch! 3: 1 (27)
2. die Eile 3: 1 (27) **in a hurry** in Eile 3: 1 (27)
hurt [hɜːt], hurt, hurt verletzen; wehtun 2 **be hurt** verletzt sein 2 **get hurt** sich verletzen; verletzt werden 2
husband [ˈhʌzbənd] der Ehemann 1

I

I [aɪ] ich 1 **I'm (= I am)** ich bin 1
ice cream [aɪs ˈkriːm] das (Speise-)Eis 2
ice rink [ˈaɪs rɪŋk] die Schlittschuhbahn 1
icing [ˈaɪsɪŋ] die Glasur, der Zuckerguss 1
icing sugar [ˈaɪsɪŋ ʃʊgə] der Puderzucker 1
icon [ˈaɪkɒn] das Icon (Symbol auf einem Bildschirm) 3: 4 (112)
°**ID card** [aɪ ˈdi kɑːd] (kurz für identity card) der Personalausweis
idea [aɪˈdɪə] die Idee 1
identify [aɪˈdentɪfaɪ] (sich) identifizieren; erkennen 3: 2 (48) **identify (yourself) (as)** sich identifizieren (als); sich zu erkennen geben (als) 3: 2 (48)
°**identity card** [aɪˈdentəti kɑːd] der Personalausweis
if [ɪf]:
1. wenn, falls 1 **even if** selbst wenn, sogar wenn 2 **What if ...?** Was wäre, wenn ...? 1
2. ob 1 **as if** als ob 2
ill [ɪl] krank 1
illness [ˈɪlnəs] die Krankheit 1
image [ˈɪmɪdʒ] das Bild, die Abbildung 3: 4 (123)
imaginative [ɪˈmædʒɪnətɪv] fantasievoll, einfallsreich, kreativ 2
imagine sth. [ɪˈmædʒɪn] sich etwas vorstellen 2 **imagine being / doing sth.** sich vorstellen, etwas zu sein / etwas zu tun 2
impatient [ɪmˈpeɪʃnt] ungeduldig 2
important [ɪmˈpɔːtnt] wichtig 1 **What's important to you in a friend?** Was ist dir an/bei einem Freund/einer Freundin wichtig? 2
impossible [ɪmˈpɒsəbl] unmöglich 3: 2 (19)
°**impress** [ɪmˈpres] beeindrucken
°**improve** [ɪmˈpruːv] verbessern; sich verbessern
in [ɪn] in; auf 1 **in a place** an einem Ort 2 **in English** auf Englisch 1 **in the afternoon** nachmittags, am Nachmittag 1 **in the country** auf dem Land 1 **in the evening** abends, am Abend 1 **in the field** auf der Weide 1 **in the morning** morgens, am Morgen 1 **in the picture** auf dem Bild 1 **in town** in der Stadt 1 **one in five** eine/r von fünf(en); jede/r fünfte 3: 4 (116) **What's important to you in a friend?** Was ist dir an/bei einem Freund/einer Freundin wichtig? 2 °**in the sky** am Himmel
include [ɪnˈkluːd] (mit) einschließen 3: 3 (76)
including [ɪnˈkluːdɪŋ] einschließlich, inklusive 3: 3 (76)
independent (of / from) [ɪndɪˈpendənt] unabhängig (von) 2
indirect [ɪndəˈrekt] indirekt 3: 1 (17)
°**indoor** [ˈɪndɔː] im Haus / Gebäude, drinnen stattfindend
influencer [ˈɪnfluənsə] der/die Influencer/in 2
information [ɪnfəˈmeɪʃn] die Information(en) 1 **visitor information centre** die Touristeninformation, das Fremdenverkehrsbüro 1
information board [ɪnfəˈmeɪʃn bɔːd] die Informationstafel 3: 1 (28)
insect [ˈɪnsekt] das Insekt 2
inside [ɪnˈsaɪd]:
1. (dr)innen; nach (dr)innen (Adv.) 1
2. innerhalb (von) (Präp.) 1 **inside the house** im Haus 1
install [ɪnˈstɔːl] installieren; einbauen 3: 4 (112)
instead [ɪnˈsted] stattdessen 3: 1 (21)
instead of [ɪnˈsted əv] anstatt, anstelle von 3: 1 (21)
instruction [ɪnˈstrʌkʃn] die Anweisung 1
°**instructor** [ɪnˈstrʌktə] der/die Lehrer/in, der/die Ausbilder/in
instrument [ˈɪnstrəmənt] das Instrument 3: 4 (109)
°**interactive** [ɪntərˈæktɪv] interaktiv
interest [ˈɪntrəst]:
1. **interest (in)** das Interesse (an) 3: 3 (83)
2. **interest sb. (in sth.)** jn. (für etwas) interessieren 3: 3 (83)
interested (in) [ˈɪntrəstɪd] interessiert (an) 3: 1 (18)
interesting [ˈɪntrəstɪŋ] interessant 1
interestingly [ˈɪntrəstɪŋli] interessanterweise (Adv.) 3: 3 (76)
international [ɪntəˈnæʃnəl] international 3: 4 (106/107)
internet [ˈɪntənet] das Internet 1
interrupt [ɪntəˈrʌpt] unterbrechen 3: 2 (58)
interview [ˈɪntəvjuː]:
1. befragen, interviewen 3: 2 (44/45)
2. das Interview 3: 2 (44/45)
into [ˈɪntu], [ˈɪntə] in (... hinein) 2
intolerant (of) [ɪnˈtɒlərənt] intolerant (gegenüber) 2
intro [ˈɪntrəʊ] (kurz für introduction) die Einführung, die Einleitung 3: 4 (122)
introduce sb. to sb. / sth. [ɪntrəˈdjuːs] jm. / etwas vorstellen, jn. mit jm. / etwas bekanntmachen 3: 1 (25)
introduction [ɪntrəˈdʌkʃn] die Einführung, die Einleitung 1
invent [ɪnˈvent] erfinden 3: 4 (116)
invitation (to) [ɪnvɪˈteɪʃn] die Einladung (zu, nach) 1
invite (to) [ɪnˈvaɪt] einladen (zu, nach) 2
Ireland [ˈaɪələnd] Irland 3: (10/11)
is [ɪz] (er/sie/es) ist 1 **he isn't (= is not)** er ist nicht 1 **he's (= he is)** er ist 1 **The football is £3.** Der Fußball kostet 3 Pfund. 2
island [ˈaɪlənd] die Insel 3: (10/11)
isle [aɪl] die Insel, das Eiland (kurz für „island") 3: (10/11) **British Isles** (pl) die Britischen Inseln 3: (10/11)

it [ɪt] es 1 **it's (= it is)** es ist *(bei Sachen und Tieren auch:* er ist; sie ist*)* 1
its [ɪts]:
1. sein / seine, ihr / ihre *(besitzanzeigend: Dinge und Tiere)* 1
2. seiner, seine, seins; ihrer, ihre, ihres *(zu „it")* 3: 4 (108)

itself [ɪtˈself] sich (selbst) (zu „*it*") 3: 2 (52)

J

jacket [ˈdʒækɪt] die Jacke; das Jackett 2
rain jacket die Regenjacke 2
January [ˈdʒænjuəri] der Januar 1
jar [dʒɑː] das Glas(gefäß) 2
jealous (of) [ˈdʒeləs] neidisch (auf); eifersüchtig 3: 4 (119)
jeans *(pl)* [dʒiːnz] die Jeans(hose) 2
jelly [ˈdʒeli] das Gelee; der Wackelpudding 1
°**jewels** *(pl)* [ˈdʒuːəlz] die Juwelen
jigsaw (puzzle) [ˈdʒɪɡsɔː] das Puzzle 1
job [dʒɒb] der Job, die (Arbeits-)Stelle; die Aufgabe 2
join sb. / sth. [dʒɔɪn] sich jm. anschließen; bei etwas mitmachen 3: (12/13) **join a club** in einen Klub eintreten 3: (12/13) **join a group** sich einer Gruppe anschließen 3: (12/13) **join the EU** EU-Mitglied werden 3: (12/13)
joke [dʒəʊk]:
1. der Witz, der Scherz 2
2. Witze machen, scherzen 2 **You're joking!** Du machst wohl Witze! 2

joker [ˈdʒəʊkə] der Witzbold, der Joker 2
journey [ˈdʒɜːni]:
1. die Reise, die Fahrt; der Weg 1
°2. reisen

°**judge** [dʒʌdʒ] der / die Richter/in; das Jurymitglied
judo [ˈdʒuːdəʊ] das Judo 3: 4 (106/107) **do judo** Judo machen 3: 4 (106/107)
juggle [ˈdʒʌɡl] jonglieren 1
juice [dʒuːs] der Saft 2
July [dʒuˈlaɪ] der Juli 1
jump [dʒʌmp]:
1. springen 2
2. der Sprung, das Hindernis 2

June [dʒuːn] der Juni 1
jungle [ˈdʒʌŋɡl] der Dschungel 3: 3 (82)
just [dʒʌst]:
1. nur, bloß; einfach 1
2. gerade (eben) 2

K

karaoke [kæriˈəʊki] das Karaoke 1
karate [kəˈrɑːti] das Karate 2
kayak [ˈkaɪæk] der / das Kajak 3: 3 (74/75)
kayaker [ˈkaɪækə] der / die Kajakfahrer/in 3: 3 (74/75)
kayaking [ˈkaɪækɪŋ] das Kajakfahren 3: 3 (74/75)

kebab [kɪˈbæb] der Kebab 1
keep [kiːp], **kept, kept**:
1. halten; behalten; aufbewahren 2 **keep (yourself) busy** sich beschäftigen, auf Trab bleiben 3: 2 (53) **keep in touch (with)** in Verbindung / Kontakt bleiben (mit) 3: 4 (114) **keep sb. busy** jn. beschäftigen, auf Trab halten 3: 2 (53)
2. **keep doing sth.** etwas dauernd / immer wieder tun 2 **keep going** (immer) weiter gehen 2

kept [kept] *siehe* **keep**
°**kettle** [ˈketl] der Wasserkocher (elektrisch)
key [kiː]:
1. der Schlüssel; Schlüssel- 2
2. die Taste *(auf einer Tastatur)* 3: 4 (112)

key ring [ˈkiː rɪŋ] das Schlüsselbund, der Schlüsselring 3: 1 (28)
keyboard [ˈkiːbɔːd] die Tastatur 3: 4 (112)
keyword [ˈkiːwɜːd] das Stichwort, das Schlagwort 2
kibbeh *(pl)* [ˈkɪbiː] die Kibbeh *(orientalische Hackbällchen mit Bulgur)* 3: 1 (24)
kid [kɪd] das Kind, der / die Jugendliche 1
kill [kɪl] töten 2
killer [ˈkɪlə] der / die Mörder/in 2
kilometre (km) [ˈkɪləmiːtə] der Kilometer 1
kind [kaɪnd] nett, freundlich 1
kind (of) [kaɪnd] die Art (von), die Sorte (von) 1
kindness [ˈkaɪndnəs] die Güte, die Freundlichkeit 3: 2 (44/45)
king [kɪŋ] der König 3: 1 (18)
Kingdom [ˈkɪŋdəm]: **the United Kingdom (the UK)** das Vereinigte Königreich 1
kiosk [ˈkiːɒsk] der Kiosk, die Verkaufsbude, der Verkaufsstand 1
kitchen [ˈkɪtʃɪn] die Küche 1
knew [njuː] *siehe* **know**
knife [naɪf], *pl* **knives** das Messer 1
°**knight** [naɪt] der Ritter 1
knit [nɪt] stricken 2
knives [naɪvz] *Plural von* **knife**
knock [nɒk]:
1. der Stoß, der Schlag, das Klopfen 2
2. stoßen, klopfen 2 **knock at** (an)klopfen (an) *(z. B. Tür)* 2 **knock sth. over** etwas umstoßen 2

know [nəʊ], **knew, known** wissen; kennen 1 **know sb. / sth. by …** jn. /etwas erkennen an … 2 **you know** nämlich, weißt du 3: 1 (27)
known [nəʊn] *siehe* **know**

L

°**label** [ˈleɪbl] das Etikett *(auch: wenn man abgestempelt wird)*
°**laddie** [ˈlædi] der Junge *(schottisches Englisch)*
lain [leɪn] *siehe* **lie**

lake [leɪk] der See 3: (12/13)
lamb [læm] das Lamm(fleisch) 2
lamp [læmp] die Lampe 1
land [lænd]:
1. das Land *(Grund und Boden)* 2
2. landen 2

landscape [ˈlændskeɪp] die Landschaft; das Landschaftsbild 3: 3 (84)
lane [leɪn] die Gasse 3: 1 (23) **bike lane** der Radweg 3: 1 (23) **cycle lane** der Radweg 3: 1 (23)
language [ˈlæŋɡwɪdʒ] die Sprache 1
large [lɑːdʒ] groß 3: 3 (76)
°**lassie** [ˈlæsi] das Mädchen *(schottisches Englisch)*
last [lɑːst] letzte(r,s); als letztes 2 **last week / month / year** die letzte / vorige Woche, der letzte / vorige Monat, das letzte / vorige Jahr 2 **at last** schließlich, endlich 3: 3 (87)
late [leɪt] (zu) spät 1 **I'm late.** Ich habe mich verspätet.
later [ˈleɪtə] später 1 **Speak later.** Tschüs. / Bis später. 1
latest [ˈleɪtɪst] neueste(r, s), aktuelle(r, s) 3: 4 (118)
laugh [lɑːf]:
1. das Lachen 2
2. **laugh (at)** lachen (über) 2 **laugh at sb.** jn. auslachen 2 **laugh out loud** laut auf-/loslachen 2

lay [leɪ] *siehe* **lie**
lazy [ˈleɪzi] faul 2
lead [liːd], **led, led** führen, leiten 3: 1 (23)
leader [ˈliːdə] der / die Leiter/in; der / die (An-)Führer/in 3: 1 (23)
learn [lɜːn] lernen 1
least [liːst] (der / die /das) wenigste, am wenigsten 3: 1 (23) **at least** wenigstens, zumindest 2
leave [liːv], **left, left** lassen; verlassen; zurücklassen 2 **leave sb. alone** jn. allein lassen; jn. in Ruhe lassen 2
led [led] *siehe* **lead**
left [left] *siehe* **leave**
left [left] links; nach links 2 **on the left** auf der linken Seite 2 **to the left of …** links von … 2
leg [leɡ] das Bein 2
legend [ˈledʒənd] die Legende, die Sage 3: 3 (76)
lemon [ˈlemən] die Zitrone 1
lemonade [leməˈneɪd] die Limonade 1
lesbian [ˈlezbiən]:
1. lesbisch 2
2. die Lesbe 2

less [les] weniger 3: 1 (23)
lesson [ˈlesn] die (Unterrichts-)Stunde 1
let [let], **let, let** lassen 3: 4 (116) **let's (= let us)** lass(t) uns 1
letter [ˈletə]:
1. der Brief 1
2. der Buchstabe 1

level [ˈlevl] der Grad, die Stufe; das Niveau, die Ebene 2
LGBTQ [el dʒi bi ti ˈkjuː] LGBTQ 2
library [ˈlaɪbrəri] die Bücherei, die Bibliothek 1

Dictionary — English – German

lie [laɪ]:
1. die Lüge 3: 4 (118)
   tell a lie / lies lügen 3: 4 (118)
2. **lie (to sb.)** (jn. an)lügen 3: 4 (118)

lie [laɪ], **lay, lain** liegen 1
2. liegen 3: 4 (118)

life [laɪf], *pl* **lives** das Leben 2

°**life skills** *(pl)* [ˈlaɪf skɪlz] die Alltagskompetenzen, die lebenswichtigen Fertigkeiten

lifeguard [ˈlaɪfɡɑːd] der / die Rettungsschwimmer/in; der / die Bademeister/in 3: 3 (91)

lift [lɪft]:
1. heben, hochheben 3: 1 (17)
2. der Lift, der Aufzug, der Fahrstuhl 3: 1 (17)

light [laɪt]:
1. hell 3: 2 (46)
2. leicht 3: 2 (46)

light [laɪt] das Licht; die Lampe 1
car light der Autoscheinwerfer 1

lighting [ˈlaɪtɪŋ] die Beleuchtung 3: 4 (120)

like [laɪk]:
1. mögen 1
   I'd (= I would) like … Ich hätte gern … / Ich möchte … 1 **I'd (= I would) like to meet …** Ich würde mich gerne mit … treffen. 1 **Would you like me to make …?** Möchtest du, dass ich … mache? 3: 4 (115)
2. liken *(in sozialen Netzwerken positiv bewerten)* 3: 4 (118)
3. der Like *(positive Rückmeldung / „Gefällt mir" in sozialen Netzwerken)* 3: 4 (114)

like [laɪk] wie; wie zum Beispiel 1 **like this** so, auf diese Art 1 **a story like this** so / solch eine Geschichte 1 **something like that** so etwas 2 **What's … like?** Wie ist …? / Wie sieht … aus? 1

line [laɪn]:
1. die Reihe 1
2. die Zeile 1
3. die (U-Bahn-)Linie, die (Zug-)Strecke 3: 1 (17)

link [lɪŋk]:
1. die Verbindung; der Link 2
2. **link (to / with)** verbinden (mit) 2

lion [ˈlaɪən] der Löwe 1

list [lɪst]:
1. die Liste 1
2. (auf)listen 1

listen [ˈlɪsn] zuhören 1 **listen to sth.** sich etwas anhören 1

listener [ˈlɪsənə] der / die Zuhörer/in 3: 2 (53)

litre [ˈliːtə] der Liter 3: 2 (47) **a one-litre bottle** eine Einliterflasche 3: 2 (47)

little [ˈlɪtl]:
1. klein 1
2. **a little** ein wenig, ein bisschen 1

live [lɪv] leben, wohnen 1

lives [laɪvz] Plural von **life**

living [ˈlɪvɪŋ] lebendig, lebend 3: 3 (76)

living room [ˈlɪvɪŋ ruːm] das Wohnzimmer 1

lizard [ˈlɪzəd] die Eidechse 1

local [ˈləʊkl] einheimisch, am / vom Ort 3: 1 (16)

local train [ˌləʊkl ˈtreɪn] der Nahverkehrszug, die S-Bahn 3: 1 (16)

loch [lɒx] der See *schottisches Wort für „lake"* 3: (12/13)

lock [lɒk]:
1. das Schloss *(Türschloss)* 2
2. abschließen *(z. B. Tür)* 2
   be locked out ausgesperrt sein 2

long [lɒŋ] lang 1 **(for) a long time** lange, (für) eine lange Zeit 1 **work long days** lange arbeiten, lange Arbeitstage haben 1

look [lʊk]:
1. aussehen 1
2. sehen, schauen 1
   look after sich kümmern um; aufpassen auf 1 **look at sb. / sth.** jn. anschauen; sich etwas anschauen 1 **look for** suchen; Ausschau halten nach 2 **look forward to doing sth.** sich darauf freuen, etwas zu tun 2 **look forward to sth.** sich auf etwas freuen 2 **look sth. up** etwas nachschlagen, nachschauen 1
3. der Look, das Aussehen 2 **looks** *(pl)* das Aussehen 2
4. der Blick 3: 1 (14/15) **have / take a (good) look at sth.** sich etwas (gut) anschauen 3: 1 (14/15)

loose [luːs] locker (sitzend), lose 3: 3 (87)

lose [luːz], **lost, lost** verlieren 2 **lose touch (with)** den Kontakt verlieren (zu) 3: 4 (114)

°**loss** [lɒs] der Verlust **loss of life** Verluste an Menschenleben

lost [lɒst] *siehe* **lose Are you lost?** Hast du dich verlaufen / verirrt? 1

lot [lɒt]:
1. **a lot (of) / lots (of)** viel/e 1
2. **a lot** sehr 1

loud [laʊd] laut 1 **laugh out loud** laut auf- / loslachen 2

love [lʌv]:
1. der Liebling 1
2. die Liebe 1
   be in love (with sb.) verliebt sein (in jn.) 3: 2 (48) **fall in love (with sb.)** sich verlieben (in jn.) 3: 2 (48)
3. lieben, sehr mögen 1
   I'd (= I would) love … Ich hätte liebend gern … / Ich möchte liebend gern … 1 **I'd (= I would) love to meet ….** Ich würde mich liebend gerne mit … treffen. 1

loving [ˈlʌvɪŋ] liebevoll 3: 3 (76)

lower [ˈləʊə] hinunterlassen, herunterlassen; sinken (lassen) 3: 3 (87)

°**luck** [lʌk]: **Good luck.** Viel Glück!

luckily [ˈlʌkɪli] glücklicherweise 2

lucky [ˈlʌki] Glücks-, glücklich 1 **be lucky** Glück haben 1

lucky number [ˌlʌki ˈnʌmbə] die Glückszahl 1

lunch [lʌntʃ] das Mittagessen 1 **What's for lunch?** Was gibt es zum Mittagessen? 1

lunchtime [ˈlʌntʃtaɪm] die Mittagszeit 1 **at lunchtime** zur Mittagszeit 1

lyrics *(pl)* [ˈlɪrɪks] der Liedtext 2

M

machine [məˈʃiːn] der Automat, die Maschine 2 **ticket machine** der Fahrkartenautomat 2

made [meɪd] *siehe* **make**

mag [mæɡ] *siehe* **magazine**

magazine [ˌmæɡəˈziːn], *infml auch* **mag** die Zeitschrift 2

magic [ˈmædʒɪk]:
1. magisch 1
2. die Zauberei 1
   do magic zaubern 1

magic set [ˈmædʒɪk set] der Zauberkasten 1

magic trick [ˌmædʒɪk ˈtrɪk] der Zaubertrick 1

main [meɪn] Haupt-, wichtigste(r, s) 1 **main course / dish** das Hauptgericht 1

make [meɪk], **made, made** machen, herstellen 1 **make (money)** (Geld) verdienen 2 **make friends** Freunde / -innen finden 2 **make sb. do sth.** jn. dazu bringen, etwas zu tun 2 **make sb. sth.** jn. zu etwas machen 3: 1 (23) **make sb. / sth. into** jn. / etwas machen zu 3: 3 (82) **make sure that …** sicherstellen, dass …; dafür sorgen, dass … 3: 3 (88) °**make sth. up** etwas bilden, ausmachen

make-up [ˈmeɪk ʌp] das Make-up 2

man [mæn], *pl* **men** der Mann 1

manage sth. [ˈmænɪdʒ] etwas verwalten, regeln, leiten 2

manager [ˈmænɪdʒə] der / die Manager/in 2

manga [ˈmæŋɡə] der / das Manga *(Comic aus Japan)* 3: 4 (121)

mango [ˈmæŋɡəʊ], *pl* **mangoes** die Mango 3: 1 (24)

many [ˈmeni] viele 1 **how many? wie viele?** 1

map [mæp] die Landkarte, der Stadtplan 1

March [mɑːtʃ] der März 1

marina [məˈriːnə] der Jachthafen 1

mark [mɑːk]:
1. die (Schul-)Note, die Zensur 2
2. die Markierung; das Zeichen 2
3. kennzeichnen, markieren 2

market [ˈmɑːkɪt] der Markt 1

married (to) [ˈmærid] verheiratet (mit) 1 **get married (to sb.)** (jn.) heiraten 2

marry [ˈmæri] heiraten 2

mask [mɑːsk] die Maske 1

°**match** [mætʃ] (passend) zusammenfügen **match to** zuordnen

match [mætʃ] das Spiel, der Wettkampf 1

material [məˈtɪəriəl] der Stoff; das Material 3: 2 (47)

maths [mæθs] die Mathe(matik) 1

May [meɪ] der Mai 1

may [meɪ]:
1. dürfen 2
   May I ...? Darf ich ...? 2 °**May the best team win!** Möge das beste Team gewinnen!
2. he may find out ... er findet vielleicht heraus; er kann herausfinden 3: 2 (50)

maybe [ˈmeɪbi] vielleicht 1

me [miː]:
1. mich; mir 1
2. **It's me.** Ich bin's. 1
   Not me! Ich nicht! (= Ich bin / war / habe / ... es / das nicht!) 1

meal [miːl] die Mahlzeit, das Essen 1 **hot meal** die warme Mahlzeit 1

mean [miːn] gemein, fies 1

mean [miːn], **meant, meant** bedeuten; sagen wollen 1 °**mean to do sth.** etwas mit Absicht tun, etwas tun wollen

meaning [ˈmiːnɪŋ] die Bedeutung 1

°**meant** [ment] siehe **mean**

meat [miːt] das Fleisch 1

meatball [ˈmiːtbɔːl] das Fleischbällchen 3: 1 (24)

mechanic [mɪˈkænɪk] der / die Mechaniker/in 2

media (pl) [ˈmiːdɪə] die Medien 3: 4 (114)

mediate [ˈmiːdɪeɪt] vermitteln (inhaltlich wiedergeben) 3: 4 (113)

mediation [miːdiˈeɪʃn] die Vermittlung, die Sprachmittlung 3: 4 (113)

meet [miːt], **met, met** kennenlernen; (sich) treffen 1 **Nice to meet you.** Freut mich, dich / euch / Sie kennenzulernen. 1

meeting [ˈmiːtɪŋ] das Meeting (Treffen, Zusammenkunft) 2

melody [ˈmelədi] die Melodie 3: 4 (109)

melon [ˈmelən] die Melone 1

member [ˈmembə] das Mitglied 2

°**memorial (to sb./sth.)** [məˈmɔːrɪəl] das Denkmal (für jn. / etwas), die Gedenkstätte

°**memorial fountain** [məˈmɔːrɪə fauntənl] der Gedenkbrunnen

°**memorize sth.** [ˈmeməraɪz] sich etwas einprägen, sich etwas merken

men [men] Plural von **man**

menu [ˈmenjuː] die Speisekarte 1

mermaid [ˈmɜːmeɪd] die Nixe, die Meerjungfrau 3: 3 (76)

merman [ˈmɜːmən], pl **mermen** der Nix, der Wassermann, der Meermann 3: 3 (76)

mess [mes] das Chaos, die Unordnung 1

message [ˈmesɪdʒ]:
1. die Nachricht, die Mitteilung 1
2. die Botschaft 3: 1 (25)

messy [ˈmesi] unordentlich 1

met [met] siehe **meet**

metal [ˈmetl]:
1. das Metall 2
2. Metall-, aus Metall 2

metre [ˈmiːtə] der Meter 1

mice [maɪs] Plural von **mouse**

microphone [ˈmaɪkrəfəʊn] das Mikrofon 3: 2 (52)

middle [ˈmɪdl] die Mitte 2 **in the middle (of)** in der Mitte (von) 2

might [maɪt]: **it might help ...** es könnte ... helfen, vielleicht hilft es ... 3: 2 (48)

mile [maɪl] die Meile (ca. 1,6 km) 1

miles per hour (mph) [maɪlz pər ˈaʊə] Meilen pro Stunde 1 **at 30 miles per hour** mit 30 Meilen pro Stunde 1

°**military** [ˈmɪlətri] militärisch

milk [mɪlk] die Milch 1

milkshake [ˈmɪlkʃeɪk] der Milchshake 3: 1 (24)

°**millennium** [mɪˈlenɪəm] das Jahrtausend

millilitre (ml) [ˈmɪlɪliːtə] der Milliliter 1

million [ˈmɪljən] die Million 3: 4 (106/107)

mind map [ˈmaɪnd mæp] die Gedankenkarte, das Wörternetz, die / das Mindmap 1

mind sth. [maɪnd]:
1. auf etwas achten, auf etwas aufpassen 3: 1 (16) **Mind the gap.** Achten Sie auf den Abstand zwischen Zug und Bahnsteigkante. 3: 1 (16) **Mind the step.** Vorsicht Stufe! 3: 1 (16) **Mind your head.** Vorsicht, niedrige Decke! 3: 1 (16)
2. **I don't mind doing sth.** Es macht mir nichts aus, etwas zu tun. 2

mine [maɪn] meine, meiner, meins 3: 4 (108)

mine [maɪn]:
1. das Bergwerk 3: 4 (106/107)
2. **mine sth.** etwas abbauen, fördern (Bergbau) 3: 4 (106/107)

mini [ˈmɪni] Mini- 1

mini-drone [ˈmɪni drəʊn] die Minidrohne 1

mining [ˈmaɪnɪŋ] der Bergbau 3: 4 (106/107)

mint [mɪnt] die (Pfeffer-)Minze 3: 1 (24)

minute [ˈmɪnɪt] die Minute 1 **Just a minute.** Einen Moment. / Moment mal. 3: 2 (61) **Wait a minute.** Warte mal. / Einen Moment. 2

mirror [ˈmɪrə] der Spiegel 1

miss [mɪs]:
1. vermissen 2
2. verpassen 2
   miss a penalty einen Elfmeter verschießen (= nicht treffen) 3: 2 (53)
3. versäumen, auslassen 2

missing [ˈmɪsɪŋ] vermisst 1

mistake [mɪˈsteɪk] der Fehler 2 **by mistake** aus Versehen; versehentlich 2

mix [mɪks] (ver)mischen 1 °**mix sth. up** etwas (durcheinander)mischen

mixture [ˈmɪkstʃə] die Mischung 1

°**model** [ˈmɒdl] das Modell

modern [ˈmɒdn] modern 1

moment [ˈməʊmənt] der Moment 1 **at the moment** im Moment, zurzeit 1

Monday [ˈmʌndeɪ], [ˈmʌndi] der Montag 1

money [ˈmʌni] das Geld 1 **pocket money** das Taschengeld 2

monkey [ˈmʌŋki] der Affe 1

monster [ˈmɒnstə] das Monster 3: 3 (76)

month [mʌnθ] der Monat 1

moon [muːn] der Mond 2

more [mɔː] mehr, weitere 1 **three more** noch drei, drei weitere 1

morning [ˈmɔːnɪŋ] der Morgen 1 **in the morning** morgens, am Morgen 1

mosque [mɒsk] die Moschee 2

most [məʊst] die meisten, am meisten 1 **most schools** die meisten Schulen 1

mother [ˈmʌðə] die Mutter 2

motivate [ˈməʊtɪveɪt] motivieren 3: 3 (82)

motivation [məʊtɪˈveɪʃn] die Motivation 3: 3 (82)

mountain [ˈmaʊntən] der Berg 2

mouse [maʊs], pl **mice** die Maus 1

move [muːv]:
1. (sich) bewegen 1
2. **move (to)** (um)ziehen (nach) 2

Mr Lee [ˈmɪstə] Herr Lee 1

Mrs Lee [ˈmɪsɪz] Frau Lee (Anrede für verheiratete Frauen) 1

Ms Lee [mɪz] Frau Lee 1

much [mʌtʃ] viel; sehr 1 **How much is/are ...?** Was (Wie viel) kostet / kosten ...? 2 **Thank you very much.** Vielen Dank. / Danke vielmals. 1 **too much of a good thing** zu viel des Guten

multicultural [mʌltiˈkʌltʃərəl] multikulturell 2

mum [mʌm] die Mama, die Mutti 1

mural [ˈmjʊərəl] das Wandgemälde 3: (12/13)

museum [mjuˈziːəm] das Museum 1

music [ˈmjuːzɪk] die Musik 1 **classical music** klassische Musik 2

musical [ˈmjuːzɪkl]:
1. das Musical 2
2. musikalisch, Musik- 2

musical instrument [mjuːzɪkl ˈɪnstrəmənt] das Musikinstrument 3: 4 (109)

musician [mjuˈzɪʃn] der / die Musiker/in 2

Muslim [ˈmʊzlɪm]:
1. muslimisch 2
2. der / die Muslim/Muslima 2
   practising Muslim der / die praktizierende Muslim / Muslima (gläubig) 2

must [mʌst] müssen 1 **I must go.** Ich muss Schluss machen. (am Telefon / Briefschluss) 1

mustn't do [ˈmʌsnt] nicht tun dürfen 2

my [maɪ] mein/e 1

myself [maɪˈself] mich / mir (selbst) 3: 2 (52)

mystery [ˈmɪstri] das Geheimnis, das Rätsel 3: 3 (76)

Dictionary — English – German

N

name [neɪm]:
1. der Name 1
call sb. names jn. beschimpfen 3: 2 (57) **family name** der Familienname, der Nachname 1 **first name** der Vorname 1 **What's your name?** Wie heißt du? 1
2. (be)nennen 3: 3 (76)

narrow [ˈnærəʊ] eng, schmal 3: 3 (87)
nasty [ˈnɑːsti] gemein, fies; schlimm, scheußlich 3: 2 (53)
nation [ˈneɪʃn] die Nation 3: 4 (106/107)
national [ˈnæʃnəl] national 3: 4 (106/107)
natural [ˈnætʃrəl] natürlich, Natur- 3: 1 (27)
natural history [nætʃrəl ˈhɪstri] die Naturkunde 3: 1 (27)
nature [ˈneɪtʃə] die Natur 3: 1 (27)
near [nɪə] nahe (bei), in der Nähe von 1
nearly [ˈnɪəli] fast 2
neck [nek] der Hals, der Nacken 2
need [niːd] brauchen 1 **need to do sth.** etwas tun müssen 1 **you needn't do it** du musst es nicht tun; du brauchst es nicht zu tun 3: 2 (48)
negative [ˈnegətɪv] negativ 2
neighbour [ˈneɪbə] der/die Nachbar/in 1
neighbourhood [ˈneɪbəhʊd] die Nachbarschaft, die Gegend, das Viertel 1
nerdy [ˈnɜːdi]: **be nerdy** ein Nerd sein (absonderlich, streberhaft) 3: 2 (49)
nervous [ˈnɜːvəs] nervös, aufgeregt 3: 2 (55)
nest [nest] das Nest 1
net [net] das Netz (Sport) 3: 2 (57)
network [ˈnetwɜːk] das Netz(werk) 3: 4 (117) **social network** das soziale Netzwerk 3: 4 (117)
never [ˈnevə] nie, niemals 1
new [njuː] neu 1
news [njuːz] die Nachrichten 1
newsagent [ˈnjuːzeɪdʒənt] der/die Zeitungshändler/in 2
newsagent's [ˈnjuːzeɪdʒənts] der Zeitschriftenladen, der Zeitungskiosk 2
newspaper [ˈnjuːspeɪpə] die (Tages-)Zeitung 1
next [nekst]:
1. nächste(r, s) 1
the next day am nächsten Tag 1
2. Next, ... Als Nächstes ... 1

next to [ˈnekst tə] neben 1
nice [naɪs] nett, schön 1
night [naɪt] die Nacht 2 **at night** nachts, in der Nacht 2
nine [naɪn] neun 1
nineteen [naɪnˈtiːn] neunzehn 1
ninety [ˈnaɪnti] neunzig 1
no [nəʊ]:
1. nein 1
2. kein/e; verboten 1

no one [ˈnəʊ wʌn] niemand 2
nobody [ˈnəʊbədi] niemand 1
noise [nɔɪz] das Geräusch; der Lärm 1
noodles (pl) [ˈnuːdlz] die Nudeln 1
normal [ˈnɔːml] normal 2
normally [ˈnɔːməli] normalerweise 3: 4 (113)
north [nɔːθ] der Norden; nördlich; Nord- 1
north-east [nɔːθˈiːst] der Nordosten, nordöstlich; Nordost- 1
north-west [nɔːθˈwest] der Nordwesten, nordwestlich; Nordwest- 1
northern [ˈnɔːðən] nördliche(r, s), Nord- 3: (10/11)
nose [nəʊz] die Nase 2
not [nɒt] nicht 1 **I'm not a boy.** Ich bin kein Junge. 1
note [nəʊt] die Notiz; der kurze Brief 1 **make notes** (sich) Notizen machen (zur Vorbereitung) 1 **take notes** (sich) Notizen machen (beim Lesen oder Zuhören) 2 °**sticky note** die Haftnotiz, der Klebezettel
nothing [ˈnʌθɪŋ] nichts 2
notice [ˈnəʊtɪs]:
1. (be)merken 3: 4 (118)
2. der Anschlag, die Bekanntmachung (an einem Schwarzen Brett) 3: 4 (118)

notice board [ˈnəʊtɪs bɔːd] das Schwarze Brett, die Anschlagtafel 3: 4 (118)
November [nəʊˈvembə] der November 1
now [naʊ] nun, jetzt 1
nowhere [ˈnəʊweə] nirgendwo(hin) 2
number [ˈnʌmbə] die Zahl, die Ziffer, die Nummer 1
nurse [nɜːs] der/die Krankenpfleger/in 2

O

object [ˈɒbdʒɪkt] das Objekt, der Gegenstand 2
o'clock [əˈklɒk]: **at 8 o'clock** um 8 Uhr 1
October [ɒkˈtəʊbə] der Oktober 1
of [ɒv], [əv] von 1 **a bottle of water** eine Flasche Wasser 2 **bags of rubbish** Tüten/Säcke mit/voller Müll 1 **the first of April (1st April)** der erste April 1
of course [əv ˈkɔːs] natürlich, selbstverständlich 1
off [ɒf]:
1. weg von; hinunter von 2
come off abgehen, sich lösen 2
fall off herunterfallen 2 get off (a train/bus) aussteigen (aus einem Zug/Bus) 2 get off your bike/your horse vom Fahrrad/vom Pferd absteigen 2 run off weglaufen 3: 3 (87)
2. be off aus sein (ausgeschaltet sein) 2

offer [ˈɒfə]:
1. (an)bieten 3: 4 (115)
2. das Angebot 3: 4 (115)

office [ˈɒfɪs] das Büro 2
officer [ˈɒfɪsə] der Beamte, die Beamtin 2
official [əˈfɪʃl] offiziell 3: (10/11)
official language [əfɪʃl ˈlæŋgwɪdʒ] die Amtssprache 3: (10/11)
often [ˈɒfn], [ˈɒftən] oft 1

oh [əʊ] Null (im gesprochenen Englisch) 1
oil [ɔɪl] das Öl 1
OK [əʊˈkeɪ]: **I'm OK.** Es geht mir gut. 1
old [əʊld] alt 1 **How old are you?** Wie alt bist du? 1
old-fashioned [əʊld ˈfæʃənd] altmodisch 3: 2 (46)
olive [ˈɒlɪv] die Olive 3: 1 (24)
on [ɒn]:
1. auf 1
on holiday im/in den Urlaub 1
on Monday am Montag 1
on Mondays an jedem Montag, montags 1 **on my birthday** an meinem Geburtstag 1 **on the beach** am Strand 1 **on the bus** im Bus 1 **on the phone** am Telefon 1 **get on (a train/bus)** einsteigen (in einen Zug/Bus) 2
2. **be on** gezeigt werden (Kino, Fernsehen), stattfinden, „laufen"; an sein (eingeschaltet sein) 2 **What's on?** Was läuft?/Was findet statt? (Kino, Theater) 2
3. **walk/run/drive on** weitergehen/-laufen/-fahren 3: 3 (87)

once [wʌns]:
1. einmal 2
for once ausnahmsweise, dieses eine Mal 3: 4 (119)
°2. einst, (früher) einmal

one [wʌn]:
1. eins 1
one way eine Strecke (= ohne Rückfahrt/Rückflug) 2 one-way ticket die einfache Fahrkarte (= ohne Rückfahrt) 2
2. the last one der/die/das Letzte 2

onion [ˈʌnjən] die Zwiebel 1
online [ɒnˈlaɪn] online, Online- 1
only [ˈəʊnli] nur, bloß; erst 1
onto the table [ˈɒntu], [ˈɒntə] auf den Tisch 2
open [ˈəʊpən]:
1. öffnen; aufschlagen (Buch) 1
°2. sich öffnen, aufgehen
°3. offen, geöffnet

opinion [əˈpɪnjən] die Meinung 1 **in my opinion** meiner Meinung nach 1
opposite [ˈɒpəzɪt]:
1. das Gegenteil 2
2. gegensätzlich, entgegengesetzt 2
3. gegenüberliegende(r, s) 3: 1 (27)
4. gegenüber (von) 3: 1 (27)

or [ɔː] oder; sonst 1
orange [ˈɒrɪndʒ]:
1. orange(farben) 1
2. die Orange 1

orbit [ˈɔːbɪt] der Orbit (Umlaufbahn z. B. eines Satelliten) 3: 1 (14/15)
order [ˈɔːdə]:
1. ordnen, anordnen 3: 3 (88)
2. die Reihenfolge; die Ordnung 3: 3 (88) **in order** in eine(r) Reihenfolge 3: 3 (88) **in the correct order** in der richtigen Reihenfolge, in die richtige Reihenfolge 3: 3 (88)

order [ˈɔːdə]:
1. die Bestellung 3: 1 (24)
2. **order sth.** etwas bestellen 3: 1 (24)

organization [ɔːgənaɪˈzeɪʃn] die Organisation 2

organize [ˈɔːgənaɪz] organisieren 2

organized [ˈɔːgənaɪzd]: **be (well-)organized** gut organisiert sein, alles voll im Griff haben 2

original [əˈrɪdʒənl]:
1. das Original 3: 4 (120)
2. original, ursprünglich 3: 4 (120)

other [ˈʌðə] andere(r, s) 1 **each other** einander, sich (gegenseitig) 2 **the others** die anderen 1

our [ˈaʊə] unser/e 1

ours [ɑːz], [ˈaʊəz] unserer, unsere, unseres 3: 4 (108)

ourselves [aʊəˈselvz] uns (selbst) 3: 2 (52)

out (of ...) [aʊt]:
1. **out** heraus, hinaus, nach draußen 2 **out and about** unterwegs 3: 1 (16) **go out** rausgehen, weggehen; ausgehen 3: 2 (48)
2. **out of ...** aus ... (heraus/hinaus) 2

outdoor [ˈaʊtdɔː] Outdoor- 1

outdoor activity [ˈaʊtdɔː ækˈtɪvəti] die Outdoor-Aktivität; die Aktivität für draußen/im Freien 3: 3 (82)

outdoors [aʊtˈdɔːz] im Freien, draußen 3: 3 (82)

outfit [ˈaʊtfɪt] das Outfit 3: 2 (46)

outside [aʊtˈsaɪd]:
1. draußen; nach draußen (Adv.) 1
2. außerhalb (von) (Präp.) 1 **outside the house** außerhalb des Hauses 1

oven [ˈʌvn] der Backofen 1

over [ˈəʊvə]:
1. über (räumlich) 1 **over here** hier herüber; hier drüben 1 **over there** da drüben, dort drüben 1 **all over London/all over the country** überall in London/überall im Land, in ganz London/im ganzen Land 3: 1 (17)
2. **over 50** über/mehr als 50 1

own [əʊn]: **my own room** mein/ein eigenes Zimmer 1

P

pack [pæk] packen, einpacken 3: 3 (81)

packet [ˈpækɪt] die Packung, das Päckchen 1

°**paddleboarding** [ˈpædlbɔːdɪŋ] das Stehpaddeln, Paddleboardfahren

page (p.) [peɪdʒ] die (Buch-/Heft-)Seite 1

paid [peɪd] siehe **pay**

°**pain** [peɪn] der Schmerz; die Plage

paint [peɪnt]:
1. die Farbe, der Lack 2
2. (an)malen; lackieren, (an)streichen 2

pair [peə]:
1. das Paar 2
2. **pair sth. (with sth.)** etwas (mit etwas) koppeln (z. B. Geräte) 3: 4 (113)

palace [ˈpæləs] der Palast, das Schloss 1

pancake [ˈpænkeɪk] der Pfannkuchen 2

paper [ˈpeɪpə]:
1. die (Tages-)Zeitung 1
2. das Papier 1 **piece of paper** das Stück Papier, der Zettel 1

parade [pəˈreɪd] die Parade, der Umzug 2

paragraph [ˈpærəgrɑːf] der (Text-)Abschnitt 3: 1 (25)

°**parallel** [ˈpærəlel] parallel, Parallel-

paramedic [pærəˈmedɪk] der/die Rettungssanitäter/in 3: 3 (87)

parents (pl) [ˈpeərənts] die Eltern 1

park [pɑːk] der Park 1

parkour [pɑːˈkʊə] der Parkour (akrobatischer Hindernislauf in der Stadt) 1

parliament [ˈpɑːləmənt] das Parlament 3: 1 (14/15) **the Houses of Parliament** (pl) das Parlamentsgebäude in London 3: 1 (14/15)

parrot [ˈpærət] der Papagei 1

part (of) [pɑːt] der Teil (von) 1 **take part (in)** teilnehmen (an), mitmachen (bei) 3: 3 (82)

partner [ˈpɑːtnə] der/die Partner/in 1

party [ˈpɑːti] die Party 1

passive [ˈpæsɪv] passiv 1

°**passport** [ˈpɑːspɔːt] der (Reise-)Pass

past [pɑːst]:
1. die Vergangenheit 2
2. vergangene(r, s) 2

past [pɑːst]:
1. vorbei, vorüber (Adv.) 3: 2 (59)
2. vorbei an, vorüber an (Präp.) 2
3. nach (bei Uhrzeitangaben) 2 **half past 6** halb 7 2 **quarter past 7** viertel nach 7 2

pasta [ˈpæstə] die Pasta (italienische Bezeichnung für Teigwaren) 1

path [pɑːθ] der Weg, der Pfad 3: 1 (28)

patient [ˈpeɪʃnt] geduldig 2

pattern [ˈpætən] das (wiederkehrende) Muster, das Schema 3: 2 (46)

patterned [ˈpætənd] gemustert 3: 2 (46)

°**pause** [pɔːz] die Pause

pay (for sth.) [peɪ], **paid, paid** zahlen; (etwas) bezahlen 1 **pay attention (to)** aufpassen (auf), aufmerksam sein; Beachtung schenken, zuhören 2 **pay by card** mit Karte (be)zahlen (z. B. Bankkarte) 2

PE (= physical education) [piː ˈiː] der (Schul-)Sport 1

pea [piː] die Erbse 1

peace [piːs] der Friede(n) 3: 1 (23)

peaceful [ˈpiːsfl] friedlich, friedfertig 3: 1 (23)

pelican [ˈpelɪkən] der Pelikan 3: 1 (20)

pen [pen] der Kugelschreiber, der Stift; der Füller 1

penalty [ˈpenəlti] der Strafstoß; der Elfmeter (Fußball) 3: 2 (53)

pence [pens] Plural von **penny**

pencil [ˈpensl] der Bleistift 1

pencil case [ˈpensl keɪs] das Federmäppchen 1

pencil sharpener [ˈpensl ʃɑːpnə] der Bleistift(an)spitzer 1

penny (p) [ˈpeni] der Penny (kleinste britische Münze) 1

people (pl) [ˈpiːpl]:
1. die Leute, die Menschen 1
2. man 3: 2 (48)

pepper [ˈpepə]:
1. der Pfeffer 1
2. die Paprika, die Peperoni 1

per [pɜː], [pə] pro 1 **miles per hour (mph)** Meilen pro Stunde 1

per cent (%) [pəˈsent] das Prozent 2

percentage [pəˈsentɪdʒ] der Anteil, der Prozentsatz 3: 2 (47)

perfect [ˈpɜːfɪkt] perfekt 1

perfectly (still) [ˈpɜːfɪktli] ganz/völlig (still) 1

°**perform** [pəˈfɔːm] auftreten (Künstler/in); aufführen

period (of time) [ˈpɪəriəd] der Zeitraum, die (Zeit-)Periode 3: 3 (83)

person [ˈpɜːsn] die Person 1

personal [ˈpɜːsənl] persönlich 2

personality [pɜːsəˈnæləti] die Persönlichkeit; der Charakter 2

pet [pet] das (Haus-)Tier 1

phone [fəʊn]:
1. anrufen; telefonieren 1
2. das Handy, das Telefon 1 **on the phone** am Telefon 1

phone call [ˈfəʊn kɔːl] der (Telefon-)Anruf 1

phone number [ˈfəʊn nʌmbə] die Telefonnummer 1

photo [ˈfəʊtəʊ] das Foto 1 **in the photo** auf dem Foto 1 **take photos** Fotos machen 1

photograph [ˈfəʊtəgrɑːf]:
1. das Foto 2
2. fotografieren 2

photographer [fəˈtɒgrəfə] der/die Fotograf/in 1

photography [fəˈtɒgrəfi] die Fotografie (Hobby), das Fotografieren 2

phrase [freɪz] die Ausdruck, die (Rede-)Wendung 1

physical education (PE) [fɪzɪkl edʒuˈkeɪʃn] der (Schul-)Sport 1

pick [pɪk] pflücken; (aus)wählen, aussuchen 2 **pick sth. up** etwas aufheben (vom Boden), etwas hochheben 2

picker [ˈpɪkə] die Greifzange (z. B. für Müll); der/die Pflücker/in 2

picnic [ˈpɪknɪk] das Picknick 1 **have a picnic** ein Picknick machen 1

picture [ˈpɪktʃə] das Bild 1

piece [piːs] das Stück, der/das Teil 1 **piece of paper** das Stück Papier 1

pier [pɪə] der Pier, die Seebrücke 1

pig [pɪg] das Schwein 2

piggy bank [ˈpɪgi bæŋk] das Sparschwein 2

pineapple [ˈpaɪnæpl] die Ananas 3: 2 (60)

ping [pɪŋ] pingen (elektronisch anklopfen) 3: 2 (57)

pink [pɪŋk] rosa 1

two hundred and sixty-one **261**

Dictionary — English – German

piper [ˈpaɪpə] der/die Dudelsack-spieler/in 3: 3 (79)
°**piping** [ˈpaɪpɪŋ] das Dudelsackspielen
pitch [pɪtʃ] der Platz *(Sport)*, das Spielfeld 3: 2 (57)
pizza [ˈpiːtsə] die Pizza 2
place [pleɪs] der Ort, der Platz 1
  at/in a place an einem Ort 2
  take place stattfinden 2
plain [pleɪn] einfach, schlicht; „ohne alles" 3: 2 (46)
plan [plæn]:
  1. der Plan 1
  2. planen 1
    plan to do sth. planen, etwas zu tun 1
plane [pleɪn] das Flugzeug 2
planet [ˈplænɪt] der Planet 2
plant [plɑːnt]:
  1. die Pflanze 3: 3 (84)
  2. pflanzen 3: 3 (84)
plastic [ˈplæstɪk] das Plastik, der Kunststoff 2
plate [pleɪt] der Teller 3: 1 (24)
platform [ˈplætfɔːm] der Bahnsteig 2
  at platform 4 auf Gleis 4 2
play [pleɪ]:
  1. das Spiel 3: 2 (44/45)
  2. spielen 1
player [ˈpleɪə] der/die Spieler/in 1
playing card [ˈpleɪɪŋ kɑːd] die Spielkarte 1
playlist [ˈpleɪlɪst] die Playlist 1
please [pliːz] bitte 1
p.m. [piːˈem]: **4 p.m.** 4 Uhr nachmittags, 16 Uhr 1 **9 p.m.** 9 Uhr abends, 21 Uhr 1
pocket [ˈpɒkɪt] die Tasche *(an Kleidungsstücken)* 2
pocket money [ˈpɒkɪt mʌni] das Taschengeld 2
podcast [ˈpɒdkɑːst] der Podcast *(Audiodatei zum Herunterladen aus dem Internet)* 2
poem [ˈpəʊɪm] das Gedicht 2
point [pɔɪnt]:
  1. der Punkt 2
    point in time der Zeitpunkt 3: 3 (83)
  2. das Komma *(Dezimalzeichen)* 1
    1.6 (one point six) 1,6 (eins Komma sechs) 1
  3. das Argument, der Standpunkt 3: 2 (60) **I take your point.** Ich verstehe, was du sagen willst. 3: 2 (60) **make a/your point** ein Argument vortragen/vorbringen 3: 2 (60) **Make your point.** Leg deinen Standpunkt dar. / Sag, wie du darüber denkst. 3: 2 (60) **take a point** einen Standpunkt verstehen 3: 2 (60) **That's a good point.** Das ist ein gutes Argument. 3: 2 (60)
°**point (at/to)** [pɔɪnt] zeigen, deuten (auf)
police *(pl)* [pəˈliːs] die Polizei 2
police officer [pəˈliːs ɒfɪsə] der Polizeibeamte, die Polizeibeamtin 2
polite [pəˈlaɪt] höflich 1
pollution [pəˈluːʃn] die (Umwelt-)Verschmutzung 3: 1 (23)

polyester [pɒliˈestə] der Polyester 3: 2 (47)
pony [ˈpəʊni] das Pony 3: 3 (81)
pool [puːl] das Pool(billiard) 1
pool [puːl] *(kurz für swimming pool)* das Schwimmbad 2
poor [pɔː], [pʊə] arm 2 **Poor George!** Der arme George! / Armer George! 2
pop (music) [ˈpɒp mjuːzɪk] der Pop, die Popmusik 2
popcorn [ˈpɒpkɔːn] das Popcorn 1
popular (with) [ˈpɒpjələ] beliebt, populär (bei) 2
pork [pɔːk] das Schweinefleisch 2
pose [pəʊz] die Pose, die Haltung 3: 2 (58) **power pose** die Machtpose 3: 2 (58)
positive [ˈpɒzətɪv] positiv 2
possible [ˈpɒsəbl] möglich 3: 1 (19)
post [pəʊst]:
  1. der Post *(Teil eines Blogs)* 1
  2. posten *(im Internet veröffentlichen)* 1
  3. die Post *(Briefe etc.)* 3: 2 (48)
postbox [ˈpəʊstbɒks] der Briefkasten 3: 2 (48)
postcard [ˈpəʊstkɑːd] die Postkarte 2
poster [ˈpəʊstə] das Poster 1
pot [pɒt] der Topf; die Kanne *(z. B. Tee-, Kaffeekanne)* 2
potato [pəˈteɪtəʊ], *pl* **potatoes** die Kartoffel 1
pound (£) [paʊnd] das Pfund *(britische Währung)* 2
poverty [ˈpɒvəti] die Armut 3: 2 (53)
powder [ˈpaʊdə] das Pulver 1
power [ˈpaʊə] die Kraft, die Macht, die Energie; der (elektrische) Strom 2
power pose [ˈpaʊə pəʊz] die Machtpose 3: 2 (58)
practical [ˈpræktɪkl] praktisch 2
  play a practical joke on sb. jm. einen Streich spielen 2
practice [ˈpræktɪs] die Übung(en) 1
practise [ˈpræktɪs] üben 1 **a practising Muslim** ein/e praktizierende/r Muslim/Muslima *(gläubig)* 2
practising doctor der praktizierende Arzt, die praktizierende Ärztin *(seinen/ihren Beruf ausübend)* 2
pray [preɪ] beten 2
prayer [preə] das Gebet 2
prediction [prɪˈdɪkʃn] die Vorhersage, die Voraussage 2
prefer sth. to sth. [prɪˈfɜː] etwas einer Sache vorziehen, etwas lieber tun/haben als etwas 3: 2 (46) **I'd prefer ...** Ich würde ... vorziehen. 3: 2 (46)
preparation [prepəˈreɪʃn] die Vorbereitung; die Zubereitung 2
prepare (for) [prɪˈpeə] vorbereiten, zubereiten; sich vorbereiten (auf) 2
present [ˈpreznt] das Geschenk 1
  wedding present das Hochzeitsgeschenk 2
present sth. (to sb.) [prɪˈzent] (jm.) etwas präsentieren, vorstellen 1

presentation [preznˈteɪʃn] das Referat, die Präsentation 1 **give a presentation** ein Referat halten 1
presenter [prɪˈzentə] der/die Moderator/in 2
press [pres] drücken 3: 4 (112)
°**pretty** [ˈprɪti]:
  1. hübsch
  2. **pretty busy/old/cool/...** ziemlich hektisch/alt/cool/...
price [praɪs] der (Kauf-)Preis 2
pride [praɪd] der Stolz 2
primary school [ˈpraɪməri skuːl] die Grundschule 3: 3 (83)
prime minister [praɪm ˈmɪnɪstə] der/die Premierminister/in 3: 1 (18)
prince [prɪns] der Prinz 3: 1 (18)
princess [prɪnˈses] die Prinzessin 3: 1 (18)
°**print** [prɪnt] drucken **print sth. out** etwas ausdrucken
°**prison** [ˈprɪzn] das Gefängnis
private [ˈpraɪvət] privat; persönlich 3: 4 (115)
prize [praɪz] der Preis, der Gewinn 1
prize ceremony [ˈpraɪz serəməni] die Preisverleihung 1
probably [ˈprɒbəbli] wahrscheinlich 3: 2 (51)
problem [ˈprɒbləm] das Problem 1
produce [prəˈdjuːs] produzieren 3: 2 (47)
producer [prəˈdjuːsə] der/die Produzent/in 3: 2 (47)
product [ˈprɒdʌkt] das Produkt 3: 2 (47)
professional [prəˈfeʃənl]:
  1. professionell, Profi- 2
  2. *(infml auch pro)* der Fachmann, die Fachfrau, der Profi 2
profile [ˈprəʊfaɪl] das Profil; die Beschreibung, das Portrait 3: 4 (115)
program [ˈprəʊɡræm]:
  1. das (Computer-)Programm 2
  2. programmieren 2
programme [ˈprəʊɡræm] das (Fernseh-)Programm, die Sendung 2
programmer [ˈprəʊɡræmə] der/die Programmierer/in 2
project [ˈprɒdʒekt] das Projekt 1
promise [ˈprɒmɪs]:
  1. versprechen 2
  2. das Versprechen 2
    keep a promise ein Versprechen halten 2
pronounce [prəˈnaʊns] aussprechen 2
pronunciation [prənʌnsiˈeɪʃn] die Aussprache 2
°**prop** [prɒp] die Requisite
protect (from/against) [prəˈtekt] (be)schützen (vor) 3: 3 (84)
°**protest** [ˈprəʊtest] der Protest, die (Protest-)Demonstration
°**Protestant** [ˈprɒtɪstənt]:
  1. der/die Protestant/in
  2. protestantisch, evangelisch
proud (of) [praʊd] stolz (auf) 2
public [ˈpʌblɪk] öffentlich 3: 1 (16)

public transport *(no pl)* [pʌblɪk ˈtrænspɔːt] die öffentlichen Verkehrsmittel 3: 1 (16)
pull [pʊl]:
1. ziehen 3: 2 (57)
2. das Ziehen, der Ruck 3: 2 (57)

purple [ˈpɜːpl] violett, lila 1
°**purpose** [ˈpɜːpəs] die Absicht; der Sinn, der Zweck
push [pʊʃ]:
1. der Stoß, der Schubs 3: 1 (19)
2. schieben, stoßen, schubsen 3: 1 (19)

put [pʊt], **put, put** *(etwas wohin)* tun, legen, stellen, stecken 1 **put sth. on** etwas anziehen *(Kleidung)*, aufsetzen *(z. B. Hut, Brille)* 2 **put your hand / hands up** die Hand / die Hände hochstrecken 1
puzzle [ˈpʌzl] das Rätsel 1
puzzled [ˈpʌzld]:
1. verwundert 2
2. verdutzt, ratlos 3: 2 (48)

Q

quarter [ˈkwɔːtə] das Viertel 2
quarter past 7 viertel nach 7 2
quarter to 7 viertel vor 7 2
queen [kwiːn] die Königin 3: 1 (18)
queer [kwɪə] queer *(= durch den Ausdruck der sexuellen Orientierung oder geschlechtlichen Identität von der gesellschaftlichen Norm abweichend)* 2
question [ˈkwestʃən] die Frage 1
ask a question eine Frage stellen 1
queue [kjuː]:
1. die (Warte-)Schlange 3: 2 (56)
2. Schlange stehen, sich anstellen *(in einer Warteschlage)* 3: 2 (56)

quick [kwɪk] schnell 3: 2 (47)
quiet [ˈkwaɪət] ruhig, still, leise 1
quite [kwaɪt] ziemlich, ganz 1
quiz [kwɪz], *pl* **quizzes** das Quiz, das Ratespiel; der Test 1 **do a quiz** ein Quiz / ein Ratespiel / einen Test machen 1
quizzes [ˈkwɪzɪz] *Plural von* **quiz**

R

rabbit [ˈræbɪt] das Kaninchen 1
racism [ˈreɪsɪzəm] der Rassismus 3: 2 (57)
racist [ˈreɪsɪst]:
1. der / die Rassist/in 3: 2 (57)
2. rassistisch 3: 2 (57)

radio [ˈreɪdiəʊ] das Radio 3: 2 (52)
°**rafting** [ˈrɑːftɪŋ] das Rafting *(Schlauchbootfahren auf Flüssen)*
rain [reɪn]:
1. regnen 1
2. der Regen 1

rain jacket [ˈreɪn dʒækɪt] die Regenjacke 2
rainbow [ˈreɪnbəʊ] der Regenbogen 2
rainforest [ˈreɪnfɒrɪst] der Regenwald 3: 3 (82)
°**rainstorm** [ˈreɪnstɔːm] der heftige Regenguss, der Gewitterschauer

rainy [ˈreɪni] regnerisch 1
ran [ræn] *siehe* **run**
rap [ræp]:
1. der Rap 2
2. rappen 2

rare [reə] selten *(Adj.)* 1
rarely [ˈreəli] selten *(Adv.)* 1
rate sth. [reɪt] etwas bewerten, beurteilen 2
rating [ˈreɪtɪŋ] die Bewertung, die Beurteilung 2
ravioli [ræviˈəʊli] die Ravioli 2
read [red] *siehe* **read**
read [riːd], **read, read** lesen 1
°**read out** (laut) vorlesen
reader [ˈriːdə] der / die Leser/in 1
ready [ˈredi] fertig, bereit 1 **get ready (for)** sich fertig machen (für), sich vorbereiten (auf) 2
real [rɪəl] echt, wirklich 2
really [ˈriːəli], [ˈrɪəli] wirklich 1
reason [ˈriːzn] der Grund, die Begründung 3: 2 (44/45) **for this reason** aus diesem Grund 3: 2 (44/45) **the reason why ...** der Grund dafür, dass ... 3: 2 (44/45)
receipt [rɪˈsiːt] der (Kauf-)Beleg, die Quittung, der Kassenzettel 2
recent [ˈriːsnt] aktuell, jüngst 3: 1 (30) **in recent years** in den letzten Jahren 3: 1 (30)
recently [ˈriːsntli] in letzter Zeit, kürzlich, neuerdings 3: 1 (30)
recipe [ˈresəpi] das (Koch-)Rezept 1
recipe book [ˈresəpi bʊk] das Kochbuch 1
recognize [ˈrekəgnaɪz] (wieder)erkennen 3: 1 (29)
°**recommend sth. (to sb.)** [rekəˈmend] (jm.) etwas empfehlen
record [rɪˈkɔːd] aufnehmen, aufzeichnen; dokumentieren, verzeichnen 2
recording [rɪˈkɔːdɪŋ] die Aufnahme 2
recycle [riːˈsaɪkl] recyceln, wiederverwerten 3: 1 (23)
recycling [rɪˈsaɪklɪŋ] das Recycling 3: 1 (23)
red [red] rot 1
regular [ˈregjələ] regelmäßig; gewohnt, normal 3: 1 (30)
relax [rɪˈlæks] sich entspannen 2
reliable [rɪˈlaɪəbl] verlässlich, zuverlässig 2
remain [rɪˈmeɪn] (ver)bleiben 3: (12/13)
remember [rɪˈmembə]:
1. daran denken, nicht vergessen 1 **remember to do sth.** daran denken, etwas zu tun 1
2. sich erinnern an 1 **remember doing sth.** sich daran erinnern, etwas getan zu haben 1

repair [rɪˈpeə]:
1. die Reparatur 3: 2 (47)
2. reparieren 3: 2 (47)

repeat [rɪˈpiːt] wiederholen 2
republic [rɪˈpʌblɪk] die Republik 3: (10/11)

°**republican** [rɪˈpʌblɪkən] republikanisch
rescue [ˈreskjuː]:
1. retten 3: 3 (87)
2. die Rettung 3: 3 (87)

rescuer [ˈreskjuːə] der / die Retter/in 3: 3 (87)
research [rɪˈsɜːtʃ]:
1. erforschen, untersuchen, recherchieren 1
2. die Forschung(en), die Recherche(n) 1 **do research** recherchieren 1

respect [rɪˈspekt]:
1. der Respekt 2
2. respektieren, achten 2

rest [rest]:
1. ruhen; sich ausruhen 1
2. die Ruhe, die Pause, die Erholung 1 **take a rest** Pause machen 1
3. der Rest 1

restaurant [ˈrestrɒnt] das Restaurant 1
result [rɪˈzʌlt] das Ergebnis 3: (12/13) **as a result** folglich, demzufolge 3: (12/13)
return [rɪˈtɜːn]:
1. zurückkehren, zurückkommen 2
2. die Rückkehr 2
3. **return ticket** (kurz auch: **return**) die (Hin- und) Rückfahrkarte 2

reuse [riːˈjuːz] wiederverwenden 3: 2 (47)
reuse [riːˈjuːs] die Wiederverwendung 3: 2 (47)
°**review** [rɪˈvjuː] der Bericht, die Rezension *(kritische Besprechung)*
°**revision** [rɪˈvɪʒn] die Wiederholung *(von Lernstoff)*
rewrite [riːˈraɪt], **rewrote, rewritten** neu schreiben, umschreiben 3: 3 (91)
rewritten [riːˈrɪtn] *siehe* **rewrite**
rewrote [riːˈrəʊt] *siehe* **rewrite**
°**rhino** *(infml)* [ˈraɪnəʊ], *pl* **rhinos** Nashorn
rhythm [ˈrɪðəm] der Rhythmus 3: 4 (109)
rice [raɪs] der Reis 1
ridden [ˈrɪdn] *siehe* **ride**
ride [raɪd]:
1. die Fahrt; das Fahrgeschäft *(auf Volksfesten, in Vergnügungsparks)* 3: 1 (14/15)
2. **ride, rode, ridden** reiten; fahren *(z. B. Fahrrad)* 1 **ride a bike** mit dem Fahrrad fahren 1 **ride (a horse)** (ein Pferd) reiten 2

ridge [rɪdʒ] der Bergkamm, der Grat 3: 3 (87)
right [raɪt]:
1. richtig *(Adj.)* 1 **be right** Recht haben 1
2. *(adv.)* genau, gerade, direkt 3: 1 (26) **right after school** gleich / direkt nach der Schule 3: 1 (26) **right by the sea** direkt am Meer 3: 1 (26) **right from the start** gleich / direkt von Anfang an 3: 1 (26) **right now** genau / gerade jetzt 3: 1 (26) **right then** genau / gerade dann 3: 1 (26)

Dictionary — English – German

right [raɪt] rechts; nach rechts 2 **on the right** rechts, auf der rechten Seite 2 **to the right of ...** rechts von ... 2
ring [rɪŋ] der Ring 1 **key ring** das Schlüsselbund, der Schlüsselring 3: 1 (28) **wedding ring** der Ehering 2
river [ˈrɪvə] der Fluss 2
road [rəʊd] die Straße *(in oder zwischen Orten)* 3: 1 (21)
road trip [ˈrəʊd trɪp] die Autoreise 3: 3 (89)
robot [ˈrəʊbɒt] der Roboter 1
rock [rɒk]:
 1. der Rock *(Rockmusik)* 2
 2. der Fels(en), der Stein 3: 3 (87)
rocky [ˈrɒki] felsig, steinig 3: 3 (87)
rode [rəʊd] *siehe* **ride**
role [rəʊl] die Rolle *(Film, Theater)* 2
role model [ˈrəʊl mɒdl] das Vorbild 3: 2 (53)
role-play [ˈrəʊlpleɪ]:
 1. das Rollenspiel 2
 2. **role-play sth.** etwas in einem Rollenspiel darstellen 2
roller coaster [ˈrəʊlə kəʊstə] die Achterbahn 3: 4 (108)
romantic [rəʊˈmæntɪk] romantisch 2
room [ruːm] der Raum, das Zimmer 1 **double room** das Doppelzimmer 3: 1 (17) °**twin room** das Zweibettzimmer
rope [rəʊp] das Seil 3: 3 (87)
round [raʊnd]:
 1. rund *(Adj.)* 2
 2. **round ...** um (... herum), in ... umher 2 **all round the globe** auf der ganzen Welt 2
 3. **come round (to)** vorbeikommen, vorbeischauen (bei) 2
roundabout [ˈraʊndəbaʊt] der Kreisverkehr 3: 1 (21)
route [ruːt] die Route, der Weg 3: 1 (28)
°**routine** [ruːˈtiːn] die (Tanz-)Nummer, die Choreographie; die Routine
royal [ˈrɔɪəl] königlich 3: 1 (18)
rubber [ˈrʌbə] das Radiergummi 1
rubbish [ˈrʌbɪʃ] der (Haus-)Müll, der Abfall 1
rucksack [ˈrʌksæk] der Rucksack 1
rude [ruːd] unhöflich, frech 1
rugby [ˈrʌɡbi] das Rugby *(Ballsportart)* 3: 4 (106/107)
°**ruins** *(pl)* [ˈruːɪnz] die Ruine
rule [ruːl]:
 1. die Herrschaft 2
 2. herrschen (über) 2
rule [ruːl] die Regel 2
ruler [ˈruːlə] das Lineal 1
run [rʌn]:
 1. der Lauf, das Rennen 2 **fun run** der Volkslauf *(z. B. zum Geldsammeln für wohltätige Zwecke)* 2
 2. **run, ran, run** rennen, laufen 1
running [ˈrʌnɪŋ] das Laufen *(Sport)* 1

S

sad [sæd] traurig 1
safe [seɪf] sicher *(gefahrlos)* 2
safety [ˈseɪfti] die Sicherheit 2
said [sed] *siehe* **say**
°**sailor** [ˈseɪlə] der/die Seefahrer/in; der Matrose, die Matrosin
Saint (= St) [seɪnt] Sankt (St) 3: 1 (20)
salad [ˈsæləd] der Salat *(als Gericht oder Beilage)* 1
salt [sɔːlt] das Salz 1
same [seɪm]: **the same** gleich; derselbe / dieselbe / dasselbe; dieselben 1
sandwich [ˈsænwɪtʃ], [ˈsænwɪdʒ] das Sandwich 1
sang [sæŋ] *siehe* **sing**
°**sank** [sæŋk] *siehe* **sink**
sari [ˈsɑːri] der Sari *(Kleid / Gewand indischer Frauen)* 2
sat [sæt] *siehe* **sit**
Saturday [ˈsætədeɪ], [ˈsætədi] der Samstag 1
sauce [sɔːs] die Soße 1
sausage [ˈsɒsɪdʒ] das (Brat-, Bock-)Würstchen, die Wurst 1
save [seɪv]:
 1. retten 2
 2. sparen 2
 3. sichern *(Daten)* 2
savings *(pl)* [ˈseɪvɪŋz] die Ersparnisse 2
savings account [ˈseɪvɪŋz əkaʊnt] das Sparkonto 2
savoury [ˈseɪvəri] pikant, herzhaft 3: 2 (60)
saw [sɔː] *siehe* **see**
say [seɪ], **said, said** sagen 1 **say sorry to sb.** sich bei jm. entschuldigen 3: 2 (49) **it says that ...** es heißt (im Text), dass ... 3: 3 (76)
scan (a text for sth.) [skæn] (einen Text) überfliegen, (einen Text) absuchen (nach etwas) 3: 3 (82)
scare sb. [skeə] jn. erschrecken, jm. Angst machen 2
scared [skeəd]: **be scared (of)** Angst haben (vor) 1
scarf [skɑːf], *pl* **scarves** Schal 2
scarves [skɑːvz] *Plural von* **scarf**
scary [ˈskeəri] unheimlich, beängstigend, gruselig 2
°**scene** [siːn] die Szene
school [skuːl] die Schule 1 **at school** in der Schule 1
school club [ˈskuːl klʌb] die AG *(in der Schule)* 1
school uniform [skuːl ˈjuːnɪfɔːm] die Schuluniform 1
sci-fi [ˈsaɪ faɪ] *siehe* **science fiction**
science [ˈsaɪəns] die Naturwissenschaft 1
science fiction [saɪəns ˈfɪkʃn] *infml* auch **sci-fi** die Sciencefiction 2
scientist [ˈsaɪəntɪst] der/die (Natur-)Wissenschaftler/in 2
scooter [ˈskuːtə] der (Tret-)Roller 1

score [skɔː]:
 1. der Spiel-/Punktestand; der *(im Spiel / Sport erzielte)* Punkt 2
 2. *(einen Punkt / ein Tor / einen Treffer)* erzielen 2
Scotland [ˈskɒtlənd] Schottland 3: (10/11)
Scots [skɒts] Schottisch *(Sprache)*; schottisch 3: 3 (85)
scream [skriːm]:
 1. der Schrei 2
 2. schreien 2
screen [skriːn] der Bildschirm; die Leinwand *(Kino)* 2
screenshot [ˈskriːnʃɒt] der Screenshot *(Abbildung dessen, was auf einem Bildschirm zu sehen ist)* 3: 4 (113)
sculpture [ˈskʌlptʃə] die Skulptur 3: 1 (14/15)
sea [siː] das Meer, die See 1 **by the sea** am Meer, an der See 1
sea level [ˈsiː levl] der Meeresspiegel 2
seagull [ˈsiːɡʌl] die Möwe 1
search (for) [sɜːtʃ]:
 1. die Suche (nach) 3: 1 (30)
 2. **search (for sth.)** (etwas) suchen; (nach etwas) suchen 3: 1 (30)
season [ˈsiːzn] die Jahreszeit; die Saison 1
seat [siːt] der (Sitz-)Platz 2 **take a seat** Platz nehmen 2
second [ˈsekənd] die Sekunde 1 **for 30 seconds** für 30 Sekunden, 30 Sekunden lang 1
second (= 2nd) [ˈsekənd] zweite(r, s) 1
second-hand [sekənd ˈhænd] second-hand *(gebraucht, aus zweiter Hand)* 2
second-hand shop [sekənd hænd ˈʃɒp] der Secondhandladen 2
secondary school [ˈsekəndri skuːl] die weiterführende Schule 1
secret [ˈsiːkrət]:
 1. geheim 1
 2. das Geheimnis 1
see [siː], **saw, seen** sehen 1 **see sb.** zu jm. gehen, jn. aufsuchen 2 **See you soon.** Bis bald! 1 **See you.** Bis dann. / Tschüs. 1 **go and see sb. / go to see sb. (about sth.)** jn. besuchen (gehen / fahren); jn. (wegen etwas) aufsuchen 2
seem (to be / do) [siːm] erscheinen; (zu sein / zu tun) scheinen 3: 3 (76)
seen [siːn] *siehe* **see**
sell [sel], **sold, sold** verkaufen 2
send [send], **sent, sent** senden, schicken 1
sent [sent] *siehe* **send**
sentence [ˈsentəns] der Satz 1
September [sepˈtembə] der September 1
series [ˈsɪəriːz], *pl* **series** die Serie, die Sendereihe 3: 4 (121)
serious [ˈsɪəriəs] ernst(haft) 3: 3 (82) **Are you serious?** Meinst du das ernst? 3: 3 (82)

264 two hundred and sixty-four

seriously [ˈsɪəriəsli]: **Seriously, ...** Im Ernst, ... / Ernsthaft, ... *(Adv.)* 3: 3 (82) **take sth. seriously** etwas ernst nehmen 3: 3 (82)
service station [ˈsɜːvɪs steɪʃn] die Tankstelle; die (Autobahn-)Raststätte 3: 2 (59)
sesame [ˈsesəmi] der Sesam 3: 1 (24)
set [set], set, set stellen, legen, setzen 2 **set sth. up** etwas einrichten; etwas aufbauen 3: 4 (113) **set the alarm** (sich) den / einen Wecker stellen 2 **set the table** den Tisch decken 2
seven [ˈsevn] sieben 1
seventeen [sevnˈtiːn] siebzehn 1
seventy [ˈsevnti] siebzig 1
several [ˈsevrəl] mehrere, einige 3: 3 (76)
sew [səʊ], sewed, sewn nähen 3: 4 (121)
sewing machine [ˈsəʊɪŋ məʃiːn] die Nähmaschine 3: 4 (121)
sewn [səʊn] *siehe* sew
shake [ʃeɪk], shook, shaken schütteln; zittern 3: 1 (27) **shake sb.'s hand / shake sb. by the hand** jm. die Hand schütteln / geben 3: 1 (27) **shake your head** den Kopf schütteln 3: 1 (27)
shaken [ˈʃeɪkən] *siehe* shake
Shall I ...? [ʃæl], [ʃəl] Soll ich ...? 3: 4 (115)
shame [ʃeɪm]: **a shame** schade; eine Schande 1
share [ʃeə]:
1. der (An-)Teil 1
2. teilen 1
sharpener [ˈʃɑːpnə] der Anspitzer 1
she [ʃiː] sie *(weibliche Person)* 1 **she's (= she is)** sie ist 1
sheep [ʃiːp], *pl* sheep das Schaf 2
shelf [ʃelf], *pl* shelves das Regal(brett) 1
shelves [ʃelvz] *Plural von* shelf
ship [ʃɪp] das Schiff 3: 4 (106/107)
shipbuilding [ˈʃɪpbɪldɪŋ] der Schiffbau 3: 4 (106/107)
shirt [ʃɜːt] das Shirt, das Hemd 2
shock [ʃɒk]:
1. der Schock 2
2. **shock sb.** jn. schockieren 2
shocked [ʃɒkt] schockiert 2
shocking [ˈʃɒkɪŋ] schockierend 2
shoe [ʃuː] der Schuh 1
shook [ʃʊk] *siehe* shake
shop [ʃɒp]:
1. das Geschäft, der Laden 1 **be at the shops** Einkäufe erledigen 1
2. (ein)kaufen, „shoppen" 2 **shop for sth.** etwas kaufen (gehen) 2
shop assistant [ˈʃɒp əsɪstənt] der / die Verkäufer/in 1
shopper [ˈʃɒpə] der Kunde, die Kundin; der/die Einkäufer/in 2
shopping [ˈʃɒpɪŋ] das Einkaufen; Einkäufe 1 **do the shopping** die Einkäufe erledigen, einkaufen gehen 1 **go shopping** einkaufen gehen 1

shopping centre [ˈʃɒpɪŋ sentə] das Einkaufszentrum 1
shopping list [ˈʃɒpɪŋ lɪst] die Einkaufsliste 1
short [ʃɔːt]:
1. kurz 1
2. klein *(Person; Körpergröße)* 1
shorts *(pl)* [ʃɔːts] die kurze Hose, die Shorts 2
should [ʃʊd]: **it should ...** es sollte ... 2
shout [ʃaʊt]:
1. der Ruf, der Schrei 3: 2 (51)
2. rufen, schreien 3: 2 (51) **shout at sb.** jn. anschreien 3: 2 (51)
show [ʃəʊ]:
1. die Show, die Aufführung; die Ausstellung 1
2. show, showed, shown zeigen 1
shower [ˈʃaʊə] die Dusche 1 **have a shower** (sich) duschen 1
shown [ʃəʊn] *siehe* show
shy [ʃaɪ] scheu, schüchtern 2
sick [sɪk] krank 2 **be sick** sich übergeben 2 **I feel sick.** Mir ist schlecht 2
sickness [ˈsɪknəs] die Krankheit 2 **in sickness or in health** wenn man krank oder gesund ist 2
side [saɪd] die Seite *(z. B. Straßenseite)* 2
sigh [saɪ]:
1. seufzen 3: 1 (27)
2. der Seufzer 3: 1 (27)
sight [saɪt]:
1. die Sehenswürdigkeit 3: 1 (18)
2. der Anblick; die Sicht(weite) 3: 1 (18)
sightseeing [ˈsaɪtsiːɪŋ] das Sightseeing *(Besichtigung von Sehenswürdigkeiten)* 3: 3 (89)
sign [saɪn] das Zeichen; das Schild 2
silence [ˈsaɪləns] die Stille; das Schweigen 2
silent [ˈsaɪlənt] still, lautlos 2 **fall / go silent** still werden, verstummen 2
silk [sɪlk] die Seide 3: 2 (47)
silver [ˈsɪlvə]:
1. das Silber 1
2. silberfarben 1
similar (to sb. / sth.) [ˈsɪmələ] *(jm. / einer Sache)* ähnlich 3: 1 (28)
simple [ˈsɪmpl] einfach 3: 4 (113)
since [sɪns]: **since 2010** seit 2010 3: 3 (82) **since then** seitdem 3: 3 (82)
sing [sɪŋ], sang, sung singen 1
singer [ˈsɪŋə] der / die Sänger/in 1
singing [ˈsɪŋɪŋ] das Singen 1
single [ˈsɪŋgl] Einzel-, einzeln(e, r, s) 2
single ticket [sɪŋgl ˈtɪkɪt] die einfache Fahrkarte (= ohne Rückfahrt) 2
°**sink** [sɪŋk], sank, sunk sinken
sister [ˈsɪstə] die Schwester 1
sit [sɪt], sat, sat sitzen; sich setzen 1 **sit down** sich hinsetzen 1
site [saɪt] die Stelle, der Ort, die Stätte 3: 1 (18) *(kurz für website)* die Website 3: 1 (18)
situation [sɪtʃuˈeɪʃn] die Situation 3: 2 (48)
six [sɪks] sechs 1
sixteen [sɪksˈtiːn] sechzehn 1
sixty [ˈsɪksti] sechzig 1

size [saɪz] die Größe 2 **What size do you take?** Welche Größe hast du? 2
skateboard [ˈskeɪtbɔːd]:
1. das Skateboard 1
2. Skateboard fahren 1
skateboarder [ˈskeɪtbɔːdə] der / die Skateboardfahrer/in 2
skateboarding [ˈskeɪtbɔːdɪŋ] das Skateboardfahren 1
skatepark [ˈskeɪtpɑːk] der Skatepark 1
°**sketchbook** [ˈsketʃbʊk] das Skizzenbuch
ski [skiː] Ski laufen, Ski fahren 3: 3 (81) **go skiing** Skilaufen gehen 3: 3 (81)
skill [skɪl] die Fähigkeit, die Fertigkeit 1 °**life skills** die Alltagskompetenzen, die lebenswichtigen Fertigkeiten °**study skills** die Lerntechniken
skim a text [skɪm] einen Text überfliegen *(um den Inhalt grob zu erfassen)* 3: 4 (118)
skin [skɪn] die Haut; die Schale *(z. B. Banane)* 3: 4 (121)
skirt [skɜːt] der Rock 3: 2 (46)
°**sky** [skaɪ] der Himmel **in the sky** am Himmel
skydiving [ˈskaɪdaɪvɪŋ] das Fallschirmspringen 3: 3 (82)
skyscraper [ˈskaɪskreɪpə] der Wolkenkratzer 3: (12/13)
sleep [sliːp]:
1. der Schlaf 1
2. sleep, slept, slept schlafen 1 **sleep late** lange schlafen 2
°**sleepy** [ˈsliːpi] müde, schläfrig, verschlafen
slept [slept] *siehe* sleep
slid [slɪd] *siehe* slide
slide [slaɪd]:
1. das Dia; die Folie *(Präsentationssoftware)* 2
2. die Rutsche, die Rutschbahn 3: 1 (14/15)
3. slide, slid, slid schieben, rutschen; gleiten (lassen) 3: 1 (14/15)
slide show [ˈslaɪd ʃəʊ] die Slideshow, die Bildschirmpräsentation 1
slip [slɪp] (aus)rutschen 3: 3 (87)
slippers *(pl)* [slɪpə] die Hausschuhe 2
slouch [slaʊtʃ]:
1. die krumme / schlaffe Haltung 3: 2 (54)
2. sich lümmeln, in krummer Haltung stehen / sitzen 3: 2 (54)
slow [sləʊ] langsam 1
small [smɔːl] klein 1
smart [smɑːt]:
1. schick 1
2. intelligent, clever 1
smartwatch [ˈsmɑːtwɒtʃ] die Smartwatch 3: 4 (113)
smell [smel]:
1. der Geruch; der Gestank 1
2. riechen; schlecht riechen 1
smile [smaɪl]:
1. das Lächeln 1
2. lächeln 1 **smile at sb.** jn. anlächeln 1
smiley [ˈsmaɪli] das Smiley 2

two hundred and sixty-five

Dictionary — English – German

snack [snæk] der Snack, die kleine Mahlzeit 1
snake [sneɪk] die Schlange 1
snow [snəʊ]:
1. der Schnee 1
2. schneien 1
snowboarding [ˈsnəʊbɔːdɪŋ] das Snowboardfahren 3: 3 (81)
snowy [ˈsnəʊi] schneebedeckt; verschneit 1
so [səʊ]:
1. so 1
   so good so gut 1
2. also, daher 1
3. **so (that)** sodass 1
4. He said so. Das hat er gesagt. 2
   I don't think so. Das glaube/denke ich nicht. 2 I hope so. Das hoffe ich. 2 I think so. Ich glaube/denke ja. 2 If so, ... Wenn ja, ... 2
so far [səʊ ˈfɑː] bis jetzt, bis hierher 2
sociable [ˈsəʊʃəbl] kontaktfreudig, gesellig 2
social [ˈsəʊʃl] sozial 3: 4 (114)
social media [səʊʃl ˈmiːdiə] die sozialen Medien 3: 4 (114) **on social media** in den sozialen Medien 3: 4 (114)
social network [səʊʃl ˈnetwɜːk] das soziale Netzwerk 3: 4 (117)
sofa [ˈsəʊfə] das Sofa 1
soft [sɒft] weich; (Stimme) leise 3: 1 (24) **in a soft voice** mit leiser Stimme 3: 1 (24)
soft drink [ˈsɒft drɪŋk] das alkoholfreie Getränk 3: 1 (24)
software [ˈsɒftweə] die Software 1
sold [səʊld] siehe **sell**
soldier [ˈsəʊldʒə] der/die Soldat/in 3: 3 (78)
solution (to a problem) [səˈluːʃn] die Lösung (eines Problems) 2
solve [sɒlv] lösen (Rätsel, Problem), lüften (Geheimnis) 2
some [sʌm], [səm] einige, ein paar; etwas, ein wenig 1
somebody [ˈsʌmbədi] jemand 1
someone [ˈsʌmwʌn] jemand 1
something [ˈsʌmθɪŋ] etwas 1
sometimes [ˈsʌmtaɪmz] manchmal 1
somewhere [ˈsʌmweə] irgendwo(hin) 2
son [sʌn] der Sohn 1
sonar [ˈsəʊnɑː] Sonar-, das Sonargerät 3: 3 (76)
song [sɒŋ] das Lied 1
soon [suːn] bald 1
sorry [ˈsɒri]: **Sorry./I'm sorry.** Tut mir leid./Entschuldigung. 1 **be/feel sorry for sb.** Mitleid haben mit jm. 1 **I'm/I feel sorry for him.** Er tut mir leid. 1 **say sorry to sb.** sich bei jm. entschuldigen 3: 2 (49)
sort (of) [sɔːt] die Art (von) 1
sort sth. [sɔːt] etwas sortieren, (ein-)ordnen 3: 3 (90) **sort sth. out** (infml) etwas in Ordnung bringen, regeln 3: 3 (90)
sound [saʊnd]:
1. der Laut; das Geräusch; der Klang 2
2. klingen (sich gut/... anhören) 2

soup [suːp] die Suppe 2
source [sɔːs] die Quelle (z. B. Website, Text) 3: 4 (123)
south [saʊθ] der Süden; südlich; Süd- 3: (10/11)
south-east [saʊθˈiːst] der Südosten, südöstlich; Südost- 3: (10/11)
south-west [saʊθˈwest] der Südwesten; südwestlich; Südwest- 3: (10/11)
southern [ˈsʌðən] südliche(r, s), Süd- 3: (10/11)
souvenir [suːvəˈnɪə] das Souvenir 3: 1 (19)
space [speɪs] der Raum, der Platz; der Weltraum 2
°**spaceship** [ˈspeɪsʃɪp] das Raumschiff
spaghetti [spəˈgeti] die Spaghetti 1
sparkling [ˈspɑːklɪŋ] kohlensäurehaltig 3: 1 (24)
sparkling water [spɑːklɪŋ ˈwɔːtə] der Sprudel 3: 1 (24)
speak (to) [spiːk], **spoke, spoken** sprechen (mit) 1 **Speak later.** Tschüs./Bis später. 1
speaking [ˈspiːkɪŋ] das Sprechen 1
special [ˈspeʃl] besondere(r, s) 1
special effects (pl) [speʃl ɪˈfekts] die Special Effects (in Filmen) 2
specific [spəˈsɪfɪk] bestimmte(r, s), spezielle(r, s); genau, präzise 3: 3 (82)
°**spectacular** [spekˈtækjələ] spektakulär, aufsehenerregend
°**speech bubble** [ˈspiːtʃ bʌbl] die Sprechblase
spell [spel] buchstabieren 1
spellchecker [ˈspeltʃekə] der Spellchecker (Programm zur Rechtschreibüberprüfung) 3: 3 (91)
spelling [ˈspelɪŋ] die Schreibweise, die Rechtschreibung 1
spend [spend], **spent, spent: spend money (on ...)** Geld ausgeben (für ...) 2 **spend time** Zeit verbringen 2
spent [spent] siehe **spend**
spice [spaɪs] das Gewürz 1
spicy [ˈspaɪsi] würzig 1
°**split** [splɪt], **split, split** (sich) (auf-)teilen, sich (auf)spalten **split in two** sich in zwei Teile aufspalten
spoke [spəʊk] siehe **speak**
spoken [ˈspəʊkən] siehe **speak**
spoon [spuːn] der Löffel 1
sport [spɔːt] der Sport; die Sportart 1
sports hall [ˈspɔːts hɔːl] die Sporthalle 1
sportspeople [ˈspɔːtspiːpl] Plural von **sportsperson**
sportsperson [ˈspɔːtspɜːsn], pl **sportspeople** der/die Sportler/in 2
sporty [ˈspɔːti] sportlich 2
spot [spɒt]:
1. die Stelle, der Punkt; der Fleck 3: 3 (77)
2. **spot sth.** etwas entdecken 3: 3 (77)
spotlight [ˈspɒtlaɪt] das Spotlight, der Scheinwerfer; die Aufmerksamkeit 2 **in/under the spotlight** im Rampenlicht, im Blickpunkt des Interesses 2 **turn the spotlight on sb./sth.** den Scheinwerfer/die Aufmerksamkeit auf jn./etwas richten 2

spring [sprɪŋ] der Frühling 1
square [skweə]:
1. der Platz (in der Stadt) 2
2. rechteckig 2
St = Saint [seɪnt] St = Sankt 3: 1 (20)
stadium [ˈsteɪdiəm] das Stadion 1
stairs (pl) [steəz] die Treppe; die (Treppen-)Stufen 2
stall [stɔːl] der (Markt-)Stand, die Bude 3: 1 (14/15)
stand [stænd], **stood, stood** stehen; sich (hin)stellen 1 **stand up** (auf)stehen 1
star [stɑː]:
1. der Stern 2
2. der (Film-/Pop-)Star 1
star sign [ˈstɑː saɪn] das Sternzeichen 2
start [stɑːt]:
1. der Anfang, der Start 1
2. beginnen, anfangen (mit) 1 **start a business** ein Geschäft aufmachen, einen Betrieb gründen/eröffnen 2 **To start with ...** Zunächst (einmal) ...; Anfangs ... 3: 4 (122)
°**state** [steɪt] der Zustand
°**statement** [ˈsteɪtmənt] die Aussage, der Aussagesatz
station [ˈsteɪʃn] der Bahnhof 1
statistic [stəˈtɪstɪk] die statistische Tatsache, die statistische Größe 3: 4 (116) **statistics** (pl) die Statistik(en) 3: 4 (116)
statue [ˈstætʃuː] die Statue 3: 1 (26)
stay [steɪ]:
1. der Aufenthalt 2
2. bleiben; übernachten 2 **stay in touch (with)** in Verbindung/Kontakt bleiben (mit) 3: 4 (114) **stay up** aufbleiben (nicht ins Bett gehen) 2
steal [stiːl], **stole, stolen** stehlen, rauben 2
step [step] die Stufe; der Schritt 1
stepbrother [ˈstepbrʌðə] der Stiefbruder 1
stepdad [ˈstepdæd] der Stiefvater 1
stepdaughter [ˈstepdɔːtə] die Stieftochter 1
stepfather [ˈstepfɑːðə] der Stiefvater 1
stepmother [ˈstepmʌðə] die Stiefmutter 1
stepmum [ˈstepmʌm] die Stiefmutter 1
stepsister [ˈstepsɪstə] die Stiefschwester 1
stepson [ˈstepsʌn] der Stiefsohn 1
°**stick** [stɪk], **stuck, stuck** kleben; stecken; (haften) bleiben
°**sticky note** [stɪki ˈnəʊt] die Haftnotiz, der Klebezettel
still [stɪl] (immer) noch; trotzdem 1
stir [stɜː] (um)rühren 1
stir-fry [ˈstɜː fraɪ]:
1. das Gericht aus kurz angebratenen Zutaten, z. B. kleinen Stücken Fleisch, Fisch und/oder Gemüse 1
2. (Gemüse- oder Fleischstücke) unter Rühren scharf anbraten 1
stole [stəʊl] siehe **steal**
stolen [ˈstəʊlən] siehe **steal**

stood [stʊd] *siehe* **stand**
stop [stɒp]:
1. (an)halten; stoppen; aufhören (mit) 1
2. der Halt, der Haltepunkt; die Unterbrechung 1
bus stop die Bushaltestelle 1
°**store** [stɔː] das Geschäft
storm [stɔːm] der Sturm; das Gewitter 3: 3 (90)
stormy [ˈstɔːmi] stürmisch 3: 3 (90)
story [ˈstɔːri] die Geschichte *(Erzählung)* 1
storyteller [ˈstɔːri telə] der/die (Geschichten-)Erzähler/in 2
straight [streɪt]:
1. gerade; *(Haare)* glatt 2
2. direkt, gleich, geradewegs 3: 2 (57)
straight on geradeaus (weiter) 2
strange [streɪndʒ] seltsam, sonderbar 2
stranger [ˈstreɪndʒə] der/die Fremde 2
strawberry [ˈstrɔːbəri] die Erdbeere 1
street [striːt] die Straße *(in Ortschaften)* 1
street dance [ˈstriːt dɑːns] der Streetdance *(Tanzstil)* 1
street music [ˈstriːt mjuːzɪk] die Straßenmusik 1
street musician [ˈstriːt mjuzɪʃn] der/die Straßenmusiker/in 2
strength [streŋθ] die Stärke, die Kraft 2
stress [stres]:
1. der Stress 2
2. **stress sb.** jn. stressen, (über)belasten 2
stressed (out) [strest] gestresst 2
stressful [ˈstresfl] stressig 3: 1 (23)
strict [strɪkt] streng 3: 2 (49)
strong [strɒŋ] stark 2
structure [ˈstrʌktʃə]:
1. die Struktur 2
2. strukturieren, aufbauen 2
°**stuck** [stʌk] *siehe* **stick** **be stuck** festsitzen, festhängen, stecken bleiben
student [ˈstjuːdnt] der/die Schüler/in; der/die Student/in 1
studio [ˈstjuːdiəʊ] das Studio 1
study [ˈstʌdi] studieren; lernen *(z. B. für Prüfungen)* 2
°**study skills** *(pl)* [ˈstʌdi skɪlz] die Lerntechniken
stupid [ˈstjuːpɪd] dumm, blöd; albern 1
style [staɪl] der Stil; die Mode; die Art 3: 2 (46) **(be/go) out of style** aus der Mode (sein/kommen) 3: 2 (46) **(be) in style** in Mode (sein) 3: 2 (46)
subject [ˈsʌbdʒɪkt] das (Schul-)Fach 1
submarine [sʌbməˈriːn] das U-Boot 3: 3 (76)
subscribe to sth. [səbˈskraɪb] etwas abonnieren 3: 4 (114)
success [səkˈses] der Erfolg 2
successful [səkˈsesfl] erfolgreich 2
such (a) [sʌtʃ] so(lch) (ein/e) 2
sudden [ˈsʌdn] plötzliche(r, s) 3: 3 (79)
suddenly [ˈsʌdənli] plötzlich, auf einmal 2
sugar [ˈʃʊgə] der Zucker 1

suggest [səˈdʒest] vorschlagen 3: 1 (27)
suit [suːt] der (Herren-)Anzug; das (Damen-)Kostüm 2
sum sth. up [sʌm ˈʌp] etwas zusammenfassen 3: 4 (122) **To sum up, ...** Um (es) zusammenzufassen, ... / Zusammenfassend kann man sagen, ... 3: 4 (122)
summary [ˈsʌməri] die Zusammenfassung 3: 3 (88)
summer [ˈsʌmə] der Sommer 1
sun [sʌn] die Sonne 1
sunbathe [ˈsʌnbeɪð] sonnenbaden 2
Sunday [ˈsʌndeɪ], [ˈsʌndi] der Sonntag 1
sung [sʌŋ] *siehe* **sing**
sunglasses *(pl)* [ˈsʌnglɑːsɪz] die Sonnenbrille 2
°**sunk** [sʌŋk] *siehe* **sink**
sunny [ˈsʌni] sonnig 1 **It's sunny.** Die Sonne scheint. 1
sunrise [ˈsʌnraɪz] der Sonnenaufgang 2
sunset [ˈsʌnset] der Sonnenuntergang 2
super [ˈsuːpə] super 2
superhero [ˈsuːpəhɪərəʊ], *pl* **superheroes** der/die Superheld/in 1
supermarket [ˈsuːpəmɑːkɪt] der Supermarkt 1
superpower [ˈsuːpəpaʊə] die Superkraft 2
support [səˈpɔːt]:
1. unterstützen 3: 2 (44/45)
2. die Unterstützung 3: 2 (44/45)
supporter [səˈpɔːtə] der/die Anhänger/in, der Fan 3: 2 (44/45)
sure [ʃʊə], [ʃɔː] sicher 1 **make sure that ...** sicherstellen, dass ...; dafür sorgen, dass ... 3: 3 (88)
surf [sɜːf] surfen 2
surfing [ˈsɜːfɪŋ] das Surfing 1
surprise [səˈpraɪz]:
1. überraschen 2
2. die Überraschung 2
surprised [səˈpraɪzd] überrascht 1
surprisingly [səˈpraɪzɪŋli] überraschenderweise, überraschend *(Adv.)* 3: 3 (76)
°**Sutmae!** [səˈmaɪ] Hallo, wie geht es dir/euch/Ihnen? *(walisisches Gälisch)*
swam [swæm] *siehe* **swim**
swap [swɒp]:
1. tauschen 1
2. der Tausch 1
clothes swap der Kleidertausch, die Kleidertauschparty 1
sweatshirt [ˈswetʃɜːt] das Sweatshirt 1
sweet [swiːt]:
1. süß 1
2. das Bonbon 1
sweets *(pl)* [swiːts] die Süßigkeiten 1
swim [swɪm], **swam, swum** schwimmen 1
swimmer [ˈswɪmə] der/die Schwimmer/in 1
swimming [ˈswɪmɪŋ] das Schwimmen 1

swimming pool [ˈswɪmɪŋ puːl] das Schwimmbad 2
swimsuit [ˈswɪmsuːt] der Badeanzug 2
swipe [swaɪp] wischen *(auf Touchscreen)*; durchziehen, einlesen *(z. B. Kreditkarte)* 3: 4 (112)
switch [swɪtʃ]:
1. der Schalter 3: 2 (52)
2. **switch sth. on/off** etwas einschalten/ausschalten 3: 2 (52)
swum [swʌm] *siehe* **swim**
symbol [ˈsɪmbl] das Symbol 3: 4 (122)
°**synagogue** [ˈsɪnəgɒg] die Synagoge

T

T-shirt [ˈtiː ʃɜːt] das T-Shirt 1
table [ˈteɪbl]:
1. der Tisch 1
set the table den Tisch decken 2
°2. die Tabelle
table tennis [ˈteɪbl tenɪs] das Tischtennis 1
tablespoon [ˈteɪblspuːn] der Esslöffel 1
tablet [ˈtæblət] das Tablet (Tablet-PC) 3: 4 (111)
take [teɪk], **took, taken**:
1. dauern, *(Zeit)* brauchen, in Anspruch nehmen 1
2. (mit)nehmen; bringen 1
take notes sich Notizen machen 2 **take out the rubbish** den Müll rausbringen 2 **take part (in)** teilnehmen (an), mitmachen (bei) 3: 3 (82) **take photos** Fotos machen 1 **take place** stattfinden 2 **take sb.'s advice** js. Rat annehmen, auf jn. hören 3: 2 (48) **take sth. off** etwas ausziehen *(Kleidung)*, ablegen *(Hut, Brille)* 2 **take sth. seriously** etwas ernst nehmen 3: 3 (82)
taken [ˈteɪkn] *siehe* **take**
talk [tɔːk]:
1. das Gespräch; die Rede, der Vortrag
2. **talk (to)** sprechen, reden (mit) 1 **talk about** sprechen, reden über 1
tall [tɔːl] groß *(Person)*; hoch *(Gebäude)* 2
tap [tæp]:
1. der Wasserhahn 3: 1 (24)
2. das (leise) Klopfen 3: 4 (112)
3. **tap sth.** tippen an/auf etwas; (leise) klopfen 3: 4 (112) **tap your fingers** mit den Fingern klopfen 3: 4 (112)
tap water [ˈtæp wɔːtə] das Leitungswasser 3: 1 (24)
°**task** [tɑːsk] die Aufgabe **do a task** eine Aufgabe machen
taste [teɪst]:
1. der Geschmack 2
2. schmecken; kosten, probieren 2
tasteful [ˈteɪstfl] geschmackvoll 3: 1 (23)
tasteless [ˈteɪstləs] geschmacklos 3: 1 (23)
°**tattoo** [təˈtuː] der (Große) Zapfenstreich *(Konzert beim Militär)*
taught [tɔːt] *siehe* **teach**

Dictionary English – German

taxi [ˈtæksi] das Taxi 2
tea [tiː] der Tee 1
teach [tiːtʃ], taught, taught lehren, unterrichten 1 **teach sb. to do sth.** jm. beibringen, etwas zu tun 1
teacher [ˈtiːtʃə] der/die Lehrer/in 1
team [tiːm] das Team, die Mannschaft 2
teamwork [ˈtiːmwɜːk] das Teamwork, die Zusammenarbeit 2
teapot [ˈtiːpɒt] die Teekanne 2
teaspoon [ˈtiːspuːn] der Teelöffel 1
tech [tek] siehe **technology**
tech people [ˈtek piːpl] Plural von **tech person**
tech person [ˈtek pɜːsn] (infml), pl **tech people** der/die Techniker/in; die technisch begabte Person 2
technology [tekˈnɒlədʒi], infml auch **tech** die Technik, der Technikunterricht; die Technologie 1
teen [tiːn] der Teenager 3: 1 (30)
teenager [ˈtiːneɪdʒə] der Teenager 3: 4 (116)
teeth [tiːθ] Plural von **tooth** **brush your teeth** (sich) die Zähne putzen 1
tell [tel], told, told erzählen, sagen 1 **tell sb. (not) to do sth.** jn. auffordern, etwas (nicht) zu tun; jm. sagen, dass er/sie etwas (nicht) tun soll 3: 2 (57)
ten [ten] zehn 1
ten thousand [ten ˈθaʊznd] zehntausend (10 000) 2
tennis [ˈtenɪs] das Tennis 1
tent [tent] das Zelt 3: 3 (81)
terms (pl) [tɜːmz] die (Vertrags-)Bedingungen, die Konditionen 3: 4 (113)
terrarium [teˈreəriəm] das Terrarium 1
terrible [ˈterəbl] schrecklich, fürchterlich 2
test [test]:
 1. testen 1
 2. der Test; die Klassenarbeit 1
text [tekst]:
 1. der Text 1
 2. die SMS 1
 3. **text sb.** jm. eine SMS schicken 1
than [ðən]: **louder / older than ...** lauter / älter als ... 2
thank sb. [θæŋk] sich bei jm. bedanken 2
thank you [ˈθæŋk juː] danke (schön) 1 **Thank you very much.** Vielen Dank. / Danke vielmals. 1
thanks [θæŋks] danke (schön) 1
that [ðæt]:
 1. das (dort) 1
  that's (= that is) das (da) ist 1
 2. der, die, das (Relativpronomen) 1
  things that I can use Dinge, die ich gebrauchen / benutzen kann 1
 3. dass (leitet einen Nebensatz ein) 2
  he thought that ... er dachte, dass ... 2 **so that** sodass 1
the [ðə] der, die, das 1
theatre [ˈθɪətə] das Theater 2
their [ðeə] ihr/e (Plural) 1
them [ðem], [ðəm] sie, ihnen 1

theme [θiːm] das Thema 3: 4 (108)
theme park [ˈθiːm pɑːk] der Themenpark (Freizeitpark mit Attraktionen zu einem bestimmten Thema) 3: 4 (108)
themselves [ðəmˈselvz] sich (selbst) (zu „they") 3: 2 (52)
then [ðen] dann, danach 1
there [ðeə] da, dort; dahin, dorthin 1
 there are es sind ... / es gibt ... 1
 there's (= there is) es ist ... / es gibt ... 1
therefore [ˈðeəfɔː] daher, deshalb 3: 3 (76)
these [ðiːz] diese (hier) 1 **These are my friends.** Das hier sind meine Freunde / Freundinnen. 1
they [ðeɪ]:
 1. sie (Plural)
  they're (= they are) sie sind 1
 2. man 3: 2 (48)
 3. er/sie (geschlechtsneutral) 3: 2 (48)
thing [θɪŋ] das Ding, die Sache 1 **How are things?** Wie geht's (so)? 3: 4 (111)
think [θɪŋk], thought, thought denken, meinen, glauben 1 **think about** nachdenken über; denken über, halten von 2 **think of sb. / sth.** an jn. / etwas denken 2 **think of sth.** sich etwas überlegen, ausdenken 2 **I think ...** Ich denke / meine / glaube / finde, ... 1
third (3rd) [θɜːd] dritte(r, s) 1
thirsty [ˈθɜːsti]: **be thirsty** durstig sein, Durst haben 2
thirteen [θɜːˈtiːn] dreizehn 1
thirty [ˈθɜːti] dreißig 1
this [ðɪs] dies; diese(r, s) 1 **this morning / afternoon / evening** heute Morgen / Nachmittag / Abend 2
those [ðəʊz] die dort, jene (dort) 1
thought [θɔːt] siehe **think**
thousand [ˈθaʊznd] tausend 2
three [θriː] drei 1
threw [θruː] siehe **throw**
through [θruː] durch 2
throw [θrəʊ], threw, thrown werfen 3: 2 (47) **throw sth. away** etwas wegwerfen 3: 2 (47)
thrown [θrəʊn] siehe **throw**
Thursday [ˈθɜːzdeɪ], [ˈθɜːzdi] der Donnerstag 1
ticket [ˈtɪkɪt] die Eintrittskarte, die Fahrkarte, das Ticket 1 **one-way ticket** die einfache Fahrkarte (= ohne Rückfahrt) 2 **single ticket** die einfache Fahrkarte (= ohne Rückfahrt) 2
ticket machine [ˈtɪkɪt məʃiːn] der Fahrkartenautomat 2
tidy [ˈtaɪdi]:
 1. ordentlich 1
 2. aufräumen 1
tie [taɪ] die Krawatte 1
tight [taɪt] knapp, eng (anliegend) (Kleidung) 3: 2 (46)
tights (pl) [taɪts] die Strumpfhose 3: 2 (46)
till [tɪl] bis 2 **not ... till** erst, wenn ... 2

time [taɪm]:
 1. die Zeit; die Uhrzeit 1
  (for) a long time lange, (für) eine lange Zeit 1 **all the time** die ganze Zeit, ständig 2 **have a great / good time** (viel) Spaß haben, sich vergnügen 2 **on time** pünktlich 2 **What time is it?** Wie spät ist es? 2 **What's the time?** Wie spät ist es? 1
 2. das Mal 2
  for the first time zum ersten Mal 2 **lots of times** viele Male, oft 2 **three times** dreimal 2
°**timeline** [ˈtaɪmlaɪn] die Zeitachse, die Chronik
timer [taɪmə] der Timer (elektronischer Zeitmesser) 2
°**times** [taɪmz] mal
timetable [ˈtaɪmteɪbl] der Stundenplan 1
tin [tɪn] die Dose, die Büchse 2
tip [tɪp]:
 1. der Tipp 1
 2. das Trinkgeld 3: 1 (20)
 3. **tip sb.** jm. Trinkgeld geben 3: 1 (20)
tired [ˈtaɪəd] müde 1
title [ˈtaɪtl] der Titel, die Überschrift 1
to [tu], [tə]:
 1. zu, nach 1
  the answer to the question die Antwort auf die Frage 1
 2. bis 1
  (from) A to Z (von) A bis Z 1
 3. (um) zu 1
  how to do sth. wie man etwas tut / tun kann / tun soll 1 **things to eat** Dinge zum Essen 1
 4. vor (bei Uhrzeitangaben) 2
  quarter to 7 viertel vor 7 2
today [təˈdeɪ] heute 1
together [təˈgeðə] zusammen 1
toilet [ˈtɔɪlət] die Toilette 1
told [təʊld] siehe **tell**
tolerant (of) [ˈtɒlərənt] tolerant (gegenüber) 2
tomato [təˈmɑːtəʊ], pl **tomatoes** die Tomate 1
tomato sauce [təˈmɑːtəʊ sɔːs] die Tomatensoße 1
tomorrow [təˈmɒrəʊ] morgen 2
tonight [təˈnaɪt] heute Nacht, heute Abend 2
too [tuː]:
 1. auch 1
  from York too auch aus York 1
 2. too slow zu langsam 1
took [tʊk] siehe **take**
tool [tuːl] das Werkzeug; das (Hilfs-)Mittel 3: 4 (120)
tooth [tuːθ], pl **teeth** der Zahn 1
top [tɒp] die Spitze, das obere Ende 1 **at the top (of)** oben, am oberen Ende (von); an der Spitze (von) 1 **the top six films** die sechs besten Filme 1
top floor [tɒp ˈflɔː] das Dach- / Obergeschoss, das oberste Stockwerk, die oberste Etage 1
topic [ˈtɒpɪk] das Thema 1

touch [tʌtʃ]:
1. anfassen, berühren 2
2. die Berührung 2
3. Kontakt, Verbindung 3: 4 (114) **get in touch (with)** (sich) in Verbindung setzen (mit), Kontakt aufnehmen (zu) 3: 4 (114) **in touch with** in Kontakt mit 3: 4 (114) **keep / stay in touch (with)** in Verbindung / Kontakt bleiben (mit) 3: 4 (114) **lose touch (with sb. / sth.)** den Kontakt (zu jm. / etwas) verlieren 3: 4 (114)

tour (of) [tʊə] die Tour, die Reise, der Rundgang / die Rundfahrt (durch) 1

tour guide ['tʊə gaɪd] der / die Reiseleiter/in; der / die Fremdenführer/in 1

tourist ['tʊərɪst] der / die Tourist/in 1

towards [tə'wɔːdz] nach, auf ... zu, in Richtung (von) 3: 1 (27)

tower ['taʊə] der Turm 3: 1 (14/15)

town [taʊn] die Stadt 1

town centre [taʊn 'sentə] das Stadtzentrum 1

toy [tɔɪ] das Spielzeug 1

tradition [trə'dɪʃn] die Tradition 1

traditional [trə'dɪʃənl] traditionell 1

traffic ['træfɪk] der (Straßen-)Verkehr 3: 1 (16)

trailer ['treɪlə] der Trailer (Filmvorschau) 2

train [treɪn] der Zug, die Eisenbahn 1 **local train** der Nahverkehrszug, die S-Bahn 3: 1 (16)

train driver ['treɪn draɪvə] der / die Lokomotivführer/in 2

train sb. [treɪn] jn. trainieren; ausbilden 2

train station ['treɪn steɪʃn] der Bahnhof 1

trainer ['treɪnə]:
1. der / die Trainer/in 1
2. der Sportschuh 3: 3 (86)

training ['treɪnɪŋ] das Training 1

tram [træm] die Straßenbahn 3: 1 (16)

trampoline ['træmpəliːn] das Trampolin 1

trampolining ['træmpəliːnɪŋ] das Trampolinspringen / -turnen 1

transgender [trænz'dʒendə] transgender 2

translate [træns'leɪt] übersetzen 3: 3 (77)

translation [træns'leɪʃn] die Übersetzung 3: 3 (77)

transport (no pl) ['trænspɔːt] das Fortbewegungsmittel; die Beförderung 2 **form of transport** die Fortbewegungsart, die Art der Beförderung 3: 1 (18) **public transport** die öffentlichen Verkehrsmittel 3: 1 (16)

travel ['trævl]:
1. das Reisen 1
2. reisen, fahren 1

Travelcard ['trævlkɑːd] die Ein- oder Mehrtagesfahrkarte (London) 3: 1 (16)

treat ['triːt]:
1. der Hochgenuss, das besondere Vergnügen; die (besondere) Leckerei 2
2. **treat sb. (to sth.)** jn. (zu etwas) einladen 2

tree [triː] der Baum 1

trendy ['trendi] modisch, trendy, „angesagt" 3: 2 (46)

trick [trɪk] der Trick, das Kunststück 1

trifle ['traɪfl] das Trifle (britischer Nachtisch) 1

trip [trɪp] der Ausflug; die Reise 2 **class trip** der Klassenausflug 2 **school trip** der Schulausflug 2

troll [trəʊl] der Troll (Provokateur/in in Online-Medien) 3: 4 (122)

trophy ['trəʊfi] die Trophäe; der Pokal 2

trouble ['trʌbl] der Ärger, Schwierigkeiten 1 **be in trouble** Ärger haben, in Schwierigkeiten sein 1 °**the Troubles** (pl) der Nordirlandkonflikt (wörtlich: die Unruhen)

trousers (pl) ['traʊzəz] die Hose 2 **baggy trousers** die Schlabberhose (weit geschnittene Hose) 3: 2 (46)

true [truː] wahr, richtig 1 **come true** wahr werden 2

trust [trʌst]:
1. das Vertrauen 3: 2 (49)
2. **trust sb.** jm. vertrauen 3: 2 (49)

truth [truːθ] die Wahrheit 3: 4 (119) **tell the truth** die Wahrheit sagen 3: 4 (119) **To tell the truth, ...** Ehrlich gesagt, ... 3: 4 (119)

try [traɪ]:
1. der Versuch 2
2. versuchen, (aus)probieren 2 **try sth. on** etwas anprobieren (Kleidung) 2 **try to do sth.** versuchen, etwas zu tun 2

tube [tjuːb] (infml) die Londoner U-Bahn 3: 1 (16)

Tuesday ['tjuːzdeɪ], ['tjuːzdi] der Dienstag 1

tunnel ['tʌnl] der Tunnel 3: 1 (14/15)

turn [tɜːn]:
1. (sich) (um)drehen 1 **Turn it upside down.** Dreh / Stell es auf den Kopf. 1 **turn right / left** (nach) rechts / links abbiegen 2 **turn sth. (over)** etwas umdrehen 1 °**turn sth. up** etwas laut(er) stellen 2
2. **it is sb.'s turn (to do sth.)** jd. ist dran / an der Reihe (etwas zu tun) 1 **take turns / take it in turns (to do sth.)** sich abwechseln; sich dabei abwechseln, etwas zu tun 1 **When is (it) my turn (to do sth.)?** Wann bin ich dran / an der Reihe (etwas zu tun)? 1

TV [tiːˈviː] der Fernseher; das Fernsehen 1

twelfth (12th) [twelfθ] zwölfte(r, s) 1

twelve [twelv] zwölf 1

twenty ['twenti] zwanzig 1

twice [twaɪs] zweimal 3: 3 (81)

°**twin beds** (pl) ['twɪn bedz] zwei einzelne Betten (z. B. im Hotelzimmer)

°**twin room** [twɪn 'ruːm] das Zweibettzimmer

two [tuː] zwei 1

type (in) [taɪp] (ein)tippen 3: 4 (118)

type (of) [taɪp] die Art (von), die Sorte (von) 3: 1 (19)

tyre ['taɪə] der Reifen 3: 2 (59)

U

°**Ugh!** [ɜː] Bah!

UK (= United Kingdom) [juː ˈkeɪ] das Vereinigte Königreich (Großbritannien und Nordirland) 1

umbrella [ʌm'brelə] der (Regen-)Schirm 3: 1 (19)

uncle ['ʌŋkl] der Onkel 1

uncomfortable [ʌn'kʌmftəbl] unbequem, ungemütlich 2

uncool [ʌn'kuːl] uncool 2

under ['ʌndə] unter 1

underground ['ʌndəɡraʊnd] die U-Bahn 1

underground [ʌndə'ɡraʊnd] unterirdisch, unter der Erde 2

°**underlined** [ʌndə'laɪnd] unterstrichen

understand [ʌndə'stænd], **understood, understood** verstehen 1

°**understood** [ʌndə'stʊd] siehe **understand**

underwater [ʌndə'wɔːtə] unter Wasser, Unterwasser- 2

unfair [ʌn'feə] unfair 2

unfollow [ʌn'fɒləʊ] entfolgen (auf sozialen Medien nicht mehr folgen) 3: 4 (114)

unfortunately [ʌn'fɔːtʃənətli] unglücklicherweise, leider 3: 3 (76)

unfriendly [ʌn'frendli] unfreundlich 1

unhappiness [ʌn'hæpinəs] die Unzufriedenheit, die Traurigkeit 2

unhappy [ʌn'hæpi] unglücklich, unzufrieden 2

unhealthy [ʌn'helθi] ungesund 2

unhelpful [ʌn'helpfl] wenig hilfreich 2

uniform ['juːnɪfɔːm] die Uniform 1

unit ['juːnɪt] die Unit (Lerneinheit) 1

United Kingdom (UK) [juˌnaɪtɪd 'kɪŋdəm] das Vereinigte Königreich (Großbritannien und Nordirland) 1

unkind [ʌn'kaɪnd] unfreundlich, herzlos 2

unknown [ʌn'nəʊn] unbekannt 3: 3 (81)

unlock [ʌn'lɒk] aufschließen, entsperren 2

unlucky [ʌn'lʌki]: **be unlucky** Pech haben 3: 2 (57)

unpack [ʌn'pæk] auspacken 3: 3 (81)

unsafe [ʌn'seɪf] unsicher 3: 4 (115)

untidy [ʌn'taɪdi] unordentlich 2

until [ən'tɪl] bis (zeitlich) 2 **not ... until** erst, wenn ... 2

up [ʌp] hinauf, hoch 1 **up a hill** einen Hügel hinauf, hoch 2

Dictionary — English – German

upcycle [ˈʌpsaɪkl] upcyceln *(gebrauchte Gegenstände als höherwertige Waren weiterverwenden)* 3: 2 (47)
upcycling [ˈʌpsaɪklɪŋ] das Upcycling *(Weiternutzung gebrauchter Gegenstände als höherwertige Waren)* 3: 2 (47)
upload [ʌpˈləʊd]:
1. der / das Upload 3: 1 (29)
2. uploaden, hochladen 3: 1 (29)
upset [ʌpˈset]:
1. bestürzt; aufgebracht, verärgert 2
2. **upset sb.**, upset, upset jn. erschüttern; jn. aufregen, ärgern, 2
upside down [ˌʌpsaɪd ˈdaʊn] verkehrt herum, auf dem Kopf 1
upstairs [ʌpˈsteəz] (nach) oben *(die Treppe hinauf)* 2
us [ʌs], [əs] uns 1
use [juːz] benutzen, verwenden 1
useful [ˈjuːsfl] nützlich, hilfreich 1
useless [ˈjuːsləs] nutzlos 3: 1 (23)
user [ˈjuːzə] der / die (Be-)Nutzer/in 1
usually [ˈjuːʒuəli] normalerweise, meistens 1

V

vacuum [ˈvækjuəm] Staub saugen 2
vacuum cleaner [ˈvækjuəm kliːnə] der Staubsauger 2
valley [ˈvæli] das Tal 3: 3 (87)
vampire [ˈvæmpaɪə] der Vampir 2
vanilla [vəˈnɪlə] die Vanille 1
vegan [ˈviːɡən]:
1. der / die Veganer/in 1
2. vegan 1
vegetables *(pl)* [ˈvedʒtəblz] das / die Gemüse 1
vegetarian [ˌvedʒəˈteəriən], *infml auch* **veggie**:
1. der / die Vegetarier/in 1
2. vegetarisch 1
veggie [ˈvedʒi] *siehe* **vegetarian**
versus (v; vs) [ˈvɜːsəs] gegen *(bei Wettkämpfen)*; gegenüber 3: 4 (114)
very [ˈveri] sehr 1
vet [vet] der Tierarzt, die Tierärztin 1
victim [ˈvɪktɪm] das Opfer 3: 4 (116)
video [ˈvɪdiəʊ] das Video; Video- 1
view [vjuː]:
1. **view (of)** der (An-)Blick; die (Aus-)Sicht (auf) 3: 3 (86)
2. **view sth.** sich etwas anschauen 3: 3 (86)
°**viewing** [ˈvjuːɪŋ] das Fernsehen, das Betrachten *(von DVDs, Filmen usw.)*
village [ˈvɪlɪdʒ] das Dorf 1
virtual [ˈvɜːtʃuəl] virtuell 3: 1 (21)
visit [ˈvɪzɪt]:
1. der Besuch 1
2. besuchen 1
visitor [ˈvɪzɪtə] der / die Besucher/in; der Gast 1
visitor information centre [ˈvɪzɪtə ɪnfəˈmeɪʃn sentə] die Touristeninformation, das Fremdenverkehrsbüro 1

visual [ˈvɪʒuəl] visuell, optisch 2
vlog [vlɒɡ]:
1. der / das Vlog *(Video-Blog)* 3: 4 (122)
2. ein/en Vlog führen 3: 4 (122)
vlogger [ˈvlɒɡə] der / die Vlogger/in *(Video-Blogger/in)* 3: 4 (122)
vocab [ˈvəʊkæb] *siehe* **vocabulary**
vocabulary [vəˈkæbjələri], *infml auch* **vocab** der Wortschatz, das Vokabular; das Vokabelverzeichnis 1
voice [vɔɪs] die Stimme 3: 4 (109)
voice message [ˈvɔɪs mesɪdʒ] die Sprachnachricht 3: 4 (109)
voice-over [ˈvɔɪs əʊvə] das Voiceover *(Filmkommentar, Off-Stimme)* 3: 4 (106/107)
voicemail [ˈvɔɪsmeɪl] die / das Voicemail 3: 1 (26)
volcano [vɒlˈkeɪnəʊ], *pl* **volcanoes** *or* **volcanos** der Vulkan 3: 3 (82)
volunteer [ˌvɒlənˈtɪə]:
1. der / die Freiwillige; der / die ehrenamtliche Mitarbeiter/in 3: 1 (29)
2. freiwillig / ehrenamtlich arbeiten *(unbezahlt)* 3: 1 (29)
vote [vəʊt]:
1. die Abstimmung, das Votum 3: (12/13)
have a vote (on) abstimmen (über) 3: (12/13)
2. **vote (on)** wählen; abstimmen (über) 3: (12/13)
vote for sb. / sth. für jn. / etwas stimmen 3: (12/13)

W

waistcoat [ˈweɪskəʊt] die Weste 3: 4 (110)
wait (for) [weɪt] warten (auf) 2 **Wait a minute.** Warte mal. / Einen Moment. 2 **I can't wait!** Ich kann es kaum erwarten! 2
waiter [ˈweɪtə] der Kellner 3: 1 (24)
waitress [ˈweɪtrəs] die Kellnerin 3: 1 (24)
Wales [weɪlz] Wales 3: (10/11)
walk [wɔːk]:
1. der Spaziergang 1
2. (zu Fuß) gehen, wandern 1 **walk around** umhergehen (in) 2 **walk the dog** mit dem Hund rausgehen, mit dem Hund Gassi gehen 2
walking [ˈwɔːkɪŋ] das Wandern 1
walking boot [ˈwɔːkɪŋ buːt] der Wanderstiefel 2
wall [wɔːl] die Wand, die Mauer 1 **on the wall** an der Wand; an die Wand 1
want [wɒnt] wollen 1 **want sb. to do sth.** wollen, dass jd. etwas tut 3: 4 (115) **want to do sth.** etwas tun wollen 1
wanted [ˈwɒntɪd] gesucht; polizeilich gesucht 2
war [wɔː] der Krieg 2
wardrobe [ˈwɔːdrəʊb] der Kleiderschrank 1

warm [wɔːm] warm 1
was [wɒz], [wəz] *siehe* **be**
wash [wɒʃ]:
1. (sich) waschen 2
2. die Wäsche, das (Sich-)Waschen 3: 1 (30)
washing [ˈwɒʃɪŋ] die Wäsche 2 **do the washing** die Wäsche erledigen, Wäsche waschen 2
waste [weɪst]:
1. verschwenden 3: 3 (77)
2. die Verschwendung 3: 3 (77)
watch [wɒtʃ] die Armbanduhr 3: 4 (113)
watch (sth.) [wɒtʃ] (sich etwas) anschauen; (etwas) beobachten 1
water [ˈwɔːtə] das Wasser 1
waterfall [ˈwɔːtəfɔːl] der Wasserfall 3: 4 (106/107)
watermelon [ˈwɔːtəmelən] die Wassermelone 1
wave (to sb.) [weɪv] (jm. zu)winken 1
wax [wæks] das Wachs 3: 1 (30)
way [weɪ]:
1. der Weg 1 **one-way ticket** die einfache Fahrkarte (= ohne Rückfahrt) 2
2. die Art und Weise 1 **(in) this way** auf diese Art / Weise 1 **in different ways** unterschiedlich *(Adv.)*, auf unterschiedliche Art / Weise 1 **No way!** Auf keinen Fall! 3: 2 (56)
3. die Richtung 2 **that way** da entlang, in jene(r) Richtung 2 **the wrong way** (in) die falsche Richtung 2 **this way** hier entlang, in diese(r) Richtung 2
we [wiː] wir 1 **we're (= we are)** wir sind 1
wear [weə], **wore, worn** tragen, anhaben *(Kleidung)* 1
weather [ˈweðə] das Wetter, die Witterung 1
website [ˈwebsaɪt] die Website 1
wedding [ˈwedɪŋ] die Hochzeit 2
wedding dress [ˈwedɪŋ dres] das Hochzeitskleid 2
wedding present [ˈwedɪŋ preznt] das Hochzeitsgeschenk 2
wedding ring [ˈwedɪŋ rɪŋ] der Ehering 2
Wednesday [ˈwenzdeɪ], [ˈwenzdi] der Mittwoch 1
°**wee** [wiː] klein *(schottisches Englisch)*
week [wiːk] die Woche 1
weekday [ˈwiːkdeɪ] der Werktag, der Wochentag 1
weekend [ˌwiːkˈend] das Wochenende 1 **at the weekend** am Wochenende 1
weird [wɪəd] seltsam, komisch 1
welcome [ˈwelkəm]:
1. **Welcome to …** Willkommen in / an … 1
2. **You're welcome.** Bitte, gern geschehen. / Nichts zu danken. 1

well [wel]:
1. gut *(Adv.)* 1
   Well done. Gut gemacht! 1 ... **as well as ...** sowohl ... als auch ...
   3: 4 (118) **as well** auch 3: 4 (118)
   °**do well** es gut machen; gut abschneiden, erfolgreich sein
2. gesund 2
   Get well soon! Gute Besserung! 2
3. **Well, ...** Nun, ... / Also, ... / Na ja, ... 1

well-being [ˈwel biːɪŋ] das Wohl(ergehen) 3: 4 (114)
went [went] *siehe* **go**
were [wɜː], [wə] *siehe* **be**
west [west] der Westen; westlich; West- 3: (10/11)
western [ˈwestən] westliche(r, s), West- 3: (10/11)
wet [wet] nass 3: 3 (95)
what [wɒt]:
1. was 1
2. welche(r, s) 1
   What about a ... ? Wie wäre es mit einer / einem ... ? 1 **What about you?** Und du? / Was ist mit dir? 1
   What's your name? Wie heißt du? 1

wheel [wiːl]:
1. fahren; schieben; ziehen 3: 1 (14/15)
2. das Rad 3: 1 (14/15)
   big wheel das Riesenrad 3: 1 (14/15)

wheelchair [ˈwiːltʃeə] der Rollstuhl 1
when [wen]:
1. wann 1
2. wenn *(zeitlich)* 1
3. als *(zeitlich)* 1

whenever [wenˈevə] wann (auch) immer 3: 2 (53)
where [weə] wo; wohin 1 **Where are you from?** Wo kommst du her? 1
wherever [weərˈevə] wo / wohin (auch) immer; egal, wo(hin) 3: 2 (53)
which [wɪtʃ]:
1. welche(r, s) 1
   Which clubs ...? Welche AGs ...? 1
2. der, die, das; die *(Relativpronomen)* 3: 4 (116) **a charity which helps ...** eine Hilfsorganisation, die ... hilft 3: 4 (116)

while [waɪl] während 2
white [waɪt] weiß 1
who [huː]:
1. wer 1
2. wen; wem 2
3. der, die *(Relativpronomen)* 3: 4 (116) **a boy / boys who ...** ein Junge, der ... / Jungen, die ... 3: 4 (116)

whole [həʊl] ganze(r, s) 3: 3 (86)
why [waɪ] warum 1 **that's why** deshalb, darum 3: 2 (53) **the reason why ...** der Grund dafür, dass ... 3: 2 (44/45)
Wi-Fi [ˈwaɪ faɪ] das WLAN, die kabellose Datenübertragung 3: 1 (16)
wife [waɪf], *pl* **wives** die (Ehe-)Frau 2
wild [waɪld] wild 3: 3 (82)
will [wɪl]: **I'll (= I will) be ...** ich werde ... sein 2

win [wɪn]:
1. der Sieg 3: 1 (25)
2. **win, won, won** gewinnen 1

wind [wɪnd] der Wind 1
window [ˈwɪndəʊ] das Fenster 1
windsurfing [ˈwɪndsɜːfɪŋ] das Windsurfing 1
windy [ˈwɪndi] windig 1
winner [ˈwɪnə] der / die Gewinner/in; der / die Sieger/in 1
winter [ˈwɪntə] der Winter 1
wish [wɪʃ]:
1. (sich) wünschen 2
2. der Wunsch 2
   Best wishes Viele Grüße *(Briefschluss)* 2 **make a wish** sich etwas wünschen 2

witch [wɪtʃ] die Hexe 3: 3 (78)
with [wɪð]:
1. mit 1
2. bei 1

without [wɪˈðaʊt] ohne 3: 4 (110)
wives [waɪvz] *Plural von* **wife**
wok [wɒk] der Wok *(chinesischer Kochtopf)* 1
woman [ˈwʊmən], *pl* **women** die Frau 1
women [ˈwɪmɪn] *Plural von* **woman**
won [wʌn] *siehe* **win**
wonderful [ˈwʌndəfl] wunderbar 2
won't [wəʊnt]: **they won't (= will not) believe ...** sie werden ... nicht glauben 2
word [wɜːd] das Wort 1 **words (of a song)** *(pl)* der (Song-)Text 2
°**wordbank** [ˈwɜːdbæŋk] die Wortbank *(Sammlung von Wörtern zu einem Thema)*
wore [wɔː] *siehe* **wear**
work [wɜːk]:
1. die Arbeit 1
   at work bei der Arbeit, am Arbeitsplatz 1
2. arbeiten; funktionieren 1
   work long days lange arbeiten, lange Arbeitstage haben 1 **work sth. out** etwas herausfinden, etwas erarbeiten, etwas verstehen 2
   °**work on sth.** an etwas arbeiten

worker [ˈwɜːkə] der / die Arbeiter/in; die Arbeitskraft 3: 4 (79)
world [wɜːld] die Welt 2 **the best place in the world** der beste Ort der Welt / auf der Welt 2
°**World Cup** [wɜːld ˈkʌp] die Weltmeisterschaft
world-famous [wɜːld ˈfeɪməs] weltberühmt 3: 1 (20)
worn [wɔːn] *siehe* **wear**
worried (about) [ˈwʌrid] beunruhigt, besorgt (wegen) 2
worry [ˈwʌri]:
1. die Sorge 2
2. **worry (about)** sich Sorgen machen (wegen, um) 2 **worry sb.** jn. beunruhigen 2 **Don't worry.** Mach dir keine Sorgen. 2

worse [wɜːs] schlechter, schlimmer 2 **for better or (for) worse** was auch immer geschieht, in guten wie in schlechten Zeiten *(beim Ehegelöbnis)* 2
worst [wɜːst] der / die / das schlechteste, schlimmste; am schlechtesten, am schlimmsten 2
°**worth** [wɜːθ] wert **It is / was worth it.** Das ist / war es wert.
would [wʊd]: **Would you like me to make ...?** Möchtest du, dass ich ... mache? 3: 4 (115) **I'd (= I would) like / love ...** Ich hätte (liebend) gern ... / Ich möchte (liebend gern)... 1 **I'd love / like to meet ....** Ich würde mich (liebend) gerne mit ... treffen. 1
write [raɪt], **wrote, written** schreiben 1 **write sth. down** etwas aufschreiben 3: 1 (30)
writer [ˈraɪtə] der / die Autor/in; der / die Verfasser/in
written [ˈrɪtn] *siehe* **write**
wrong [rɒŋ] falsch 1 **be wrong** Unrecht haben 1 **Something is wrong.** Irgendetwas ist nicht in Ordnung. / Irgendetwas stimmt nicht. 2 **What's wrong?** Was ist los? / Was / Wo ist das Problem? 2
wrote [rəʊt] *siehe* **write**

Y

°**Yay!** [jeɪ] *(infml)* Hurra!
year [jɪə] das Jahr; der Jahrgang 1
yellow [ˈjeləʊ] gelb 1
yes [jes] ja 1
yesterday [ˈjestədeɪ] gestern 2
yet [jet]: **... yet?** ... schon ...? 2
not ... yet noch nicht ... 2
yoga [ˈjəʊgə] das Yoga 1
yoghurt [ˈjɒgət] der Joghurt 2
you [ju], [jə]:
1. man 3: 2 (48)
2. du; dich; dir; ihr; euch; Sie; Ihnen 1
   you're (= you are) du bist; ihr seid; Sie sind 1

young [jʌŋ] jung 3: 1 (18)
your [jɔː], [jə] dein/e; euer / eure; Ihr/e 1
yours [jɔːz] deine, deiner, deins; eurer, eure, eures; Ihrer, Ihre, Ihres *(zu „you")* 3: 4 (108) **Yours, Jill** Deine / Ihre / Eure Jill *(am Briefschluss)* 3: 4 (108)
yourself [jəˈself] du / dir / dich (selbst) 2
yourselves [jɔːˈselvz] ihr / euch (selbst) 3: 2 (52) **Enjoy yourselves.** Viel Spaß! Amüsiert euch gut! 3: 2 (52)
youth [juːθ] die Jugend; der Jugendliche
youth centre [ˈjuːθ sentə] das Jugendzentrum 1

Z

zip [zɪp] *(kurz für zip wire)* die Seilrutsche 2
zip wire [ˈzɪp waɪə] die Seilrutsche 2
zoo [zuː] der Zoo 1

Irregular verbs

infinitive	simple past	past participle	
(to) babysit	babysat	babysat	babysitten
(to) be	was / were	been	sein
(to) beat	beat	beaten	schlagen, besiegen
(to) become	became	become	werden
(to) begin	began	begun	anfangen, beginnen
(to) blow	blew [uː]	blown	pusten, blasen; wehen
(to) break	broke	broken	zerbrechen
(to) bring	brought	brought	(mit)bringen
(to) build [ɪ]	built [ɪ]	built [ɪ]	bauen
(to) buy	bought	bought	kaufen
(to) catch	caught [ɔː]	caught [ɔː]	(ein)fangen; erwischen
(to) choose	chose	chosen	(aus)wählen
(to) come	came	come	(mit)kommen
(to) cost	cost	cost	kosten
(to) cut	cut	cut	(aus)schneiden
(to) deal with [iː]	dealt [e]	dealt [e]	klarkommen (mit), fertigwerden (mit)
(to) do	did	done [ʌ]	tun, machen
(to) draw	drew	drawn	zeichnen
(to) drink	drank	drunk	trinken
(to) drive [aɪ]	drove [əʊ]	driven [ɪ]	fahren
(to) eat [iː]	ate [et, eɪt]	eaten [iː]	essen; fressen
(to) fall	fell	fallen	(hin)fallen
(to) feed	fed	fed	füttern; ernähren
(to) feel	felt	felt	fühlen, sich fühlen
(to) fight	fought	fought	(be)kämpfen
(to) find	found	found	finden
(to) fly	flew	flown	fliegen
(to) forget	forgot	forgotten	vergessen
(to) get	got	got	bekommen; (sich etw.) holen; werden
(to) give [ɪ]	gave	given [ɪ]	geben
(to) go	went	gone	gehen, fahren
(to) grow (up)	grew (up)	grown (up)	(auf)wachsen
(to) hang out	hung out [ʌ]	hung out	rumhängen, abhängen
(to) have	had	had	haben; etw. essen
(to) hear [ɪə]	heard [ɜː]	heard	hören
(to) hit	hit	hit	treffen auf, schlagen, stoßen gegen
(to) hurt	hurt	hurt	verletzen; wehtun
(to) keep	kept	kept	(be)halten; aufbewahren
(to) know [nəʊ]	knew [njuː]	known [nəʊn]	wissen; kennen
(to) lead [iː]	led [e]	led [e]	führen, leiten
(to) leave	left	left	lassen, zurücklassen, verlassen
(to) let	let	let	lassen
(to) lie	lay	lain	liegen
(to) lose [uː]	lost	lost	verlieren
(to) make	made	made	machen, herstellen
(to) mean	meant	meant	bedeuten, meinen
(to) meet	met	met	treffen; (sich) treffen

infinitive	simple past	past participle	
(to) pay	paid	paid	(be)zahlen
(to) put	put	put	legen, stellen, stecken
(to) read [iː]	read [e]	read [e]	lesen
(to) rewrite	rewrote	rewritten	neu schreiben, umschreiben
(to) ride [aɪ]	rode	ridden [ɪ]	reiten; *(Rad)* fahren
(to) run	ran	run	rennen, laufen
(to) say	said [sed]	said [sed]	sagen
(to) see	saw	seen	sehen
(to) sell	sold	sold	verkaufen
(to) send	sent	sent	senden, schicken
(to) set	set	set	stellen, legen, setzen
(to) sew [əʊ]	sewed [əʊ]	sewn [əʊ]	nähen
(to) shake	shook	shaken	schütteln; zittern
(to) show	showed	shown	zeigen
(to) sing	sang	sung	singen
(to) sink	sank	sunk	sinken
(to) sit	sat	sat	sitzen; sich setzen
(to) sleep	slept	slept	schlafen
(to) slide	slid	slid	rutschen; schieben; gleiten (lassen)
(to) speak [iː]	spoke	spoken	sprechen
(to) spend	spent	spent	*(Geld)* ausgeben, *(Zeit)* verbringen
(to) split	split	split	(sich) (auf)teilen, sich (auf)spalten
(to) stand	stood	stood	stehen; sich (hin)stellen
(to) steal	stole	stolen	stehlen, rauben
(to) stick	stuck	stuck	kleben; stecken
(to) swim	swam	swum	schwimmen
(to) take	took	taken	(mit)nehmen; bringen; dauern
(to) teach	taught	taught	lehren, unterrichten
(to) tell	told	told	sagen; erzählen, berichten
(to) think	thought	thought	denken, glauben, meinen
(to) throw	threw [uː]	thrown	werfen
(to) understand	understood	understood	verstehen
(to) upset	upset	upset	jn. erschüttern; jn. aufregen, ärgern
(to) wear [eə]	wore [ɔː]	worn [ɔː]	tragen, anhaben *(Kleidung)*
(to) win	won [ʌ]	won [ʌ]	gewinnen
(to) write [aɪ]	wrote	written [ɪ]	schreiben

Du kannst die unregelmäßigen Verben in Gruppen einteilen, damit das Lernen leichter wird:
- Alle drei Formen sind gleich *(chicken verbs)*: *put, put, put* – das klingt wie gackernde Hühner
- Zwei Formen sind gleich:
  1 *(echo verbs)*: z. B. *bring, brought, brought*   2 *(sandwich verbs)*: *become, became, become*
- Alle drei Formen sind verschieden: Da gibt es z. B. die *cat verbs*, bei denen der Klang der drei Formen an das Miau einer Katze erinnert: *sing, sang, sung*
  Wenn du diese Formen in ähnlichen Zweiergruppen lernst, kannst du sie besser behalten:
  be, was, been – see, saw, seen oder *break, broke, broken – speak, spoke, spoken*
Finde zu jeder Gruppe weitere Beispiele in der Übersicht auf diesen beiden Seiten. ▶ p. 81 | Ex 2b)

Ähnliche Wörter im Englischen und Deutschen

Viele englische Wörter ähneln deutschen Wörtern: *a cowboy* = ein Cowboy
Beachte aber die Unterschiede 1–3!

(1) Nomen werden im Deutschen großgeschrieben, aber im Englischen klein.
(2) Manche Wörter haben im Deutschen andere Endungen, aber einen ähnlichen Stamm, z. B. planen – *(to) plan*.
(3) Oft unterscheidet sich die Aussprache. Höre dir die blau markierten Wörter in der App an und sprich sie nach.

🔊 active / activity
address
allergic (to)
alphabet
alternative
anonymous
April
article
August
balcony
ball
banana
barbecue
bass
biology
blues
bowling
Brexit
(to) bring
British
browser
bus
butter
cafe
camera
card
character
chocolate
circus
class
classroom
clever
club
coffee
comic
computer
console
cool
corridor
cost / (to) cost
cousin
creative
crown
culture
curry

dance / (to) dance
December
decoration
definition
detail
dialogue
drama
drink / (to) drink
electric
elephant
end / (to) end
England / English
experiment
family
February
film
(to) find
fish
football
friend / friendly
gallery
garage
garden
gold
group
guest
hamster
happy
hello
highlight
horn
house
hungry
idea
information
insect
January
jewels
July
June
karaoke
kebab
kilometre (km)
kiosk
lamp

market
maths
melon
milk
millilitre
minute
modern
moment
museum
music
name
negative
November
number
object
October
online
open
orange
parallel
partner
pasta
pause
perfect
person
photo
picnic
plan / (to) plan
pool
post
poster
problem
project
pronoun
rafting
respect
restaurant
ring
robot
room
rucksack
salad
sandwich
sauce
scene

school
(to) send
September
shopping centre
silver
(to) sink
skateboard
smart
sofa
software
song
sport
star
stop
story
student
summer
supermarket
surfing
sweatshirt
(to) swim
synagogue
test / (to) test
text / (to) text
title
toilet
tomato
top
tourist
tradition
trainer
trick
uniform
vanilla
vegan
vegetarian / veggie
video
warm
website
wind
winner
winter
word
yoghurt
zoo

Typical tasks

Typical tasks	Häufige Arbeitsanweisungen
Act out the conversation / song / story.	Führt das Gespräch / das Lied / die Geschichte vor.
Add more ideas / points / ...	Füge weitere Ideen / Punkte / ... hinzu.
Answer the questions / partner B's questions.	Beantworte die Fragen / Partner Bs Fragen.
Brainstorm ideas.	Sammle spontane Einfälle / Gedanken.
Check the spelling / your answers / ideas (with a partner).	Überprüfe deine Rechtschreibung / Antworten / Ideen (mit einem/r Partner/-in).
Choose the correct answer / word.	Wähle die richtige Antwort / das richtige Wort aus.
Collect ideas / words / phrases / information.	Sammle Ideen / Wörter / Ausdrücke / Informationen.
Compare the pictures / your answers / ideas / ...	Vergleiche die Bilder / deine Antworten / Ideen / ...
Complete the table / list / sentences / conversation / ...	Vervollständige die Tabelle / Liste / Sätze / Unterhaltung / ...
Copy the table / list / notes.	Schreibe die Tabelle / die Liste / Notizen ab.
Correct the false / wrong sentences / answers.	Berichtige die falschen Sätze / Antworten.
Describe the picture / your room / ...	Beschreibe das Bild / dein Zimmer / ...
Discuss with a partner.	Diskutiere mit einem/r Partner/-in.
Explain what ... means.	Erkläre was ... bedeutet.
Find the answers / the correct / right / wrong words / information / images / ...	Finde die Antworten / die richtigen / falschen Wörter / Informationen / Bilder / ...
Find reasons for and against ...	Finde Gründe, die für und gegen ... sprechen.
Finish the sentences.	Vervollständige die Sätze.
Give advice / feedback.	Gib Ratschläge / Rückmeldung.
Give reasons.	Begründe (deine Antwort).
Give your opinion.	Sag / Äußere deine Meinung.
Have a conversation with (two partners).	Unterhalte dich mit (zwei Partner/-innen).
Listen and check / practise / repeat / guess / take notes.	Höre zu und überprüfe / übe / wiederhole / rate / mache Notizen.
Look at the photos / pictures / map / title.	Sieh dir die Fotos / Bilder / Karte / die Überschrift an.
Make groups (of six / ... students).	Bildet Gruppen (zu je sechs / ... Schüler/-innen).
Make sentences / notes / lists / a mind map.	Fertige Sätze / Notizen / Listen / eine Mindmap an.
Match the sentence parts / the words to ...	Verbinde die Satzhälften / die Wörter mit ...
Put the sentences / dialogue in the correct order.	Bringe die Sätze / den Dialog in die richtige Reihenfolge.
Read the conversation / text / story / article.	Lies den Dialog / Text / die Geschichte / den Artikel.
Swap cards / roles.	Tauscht die Karten / die Rollen.
Take notes (about ...).	Mache dir Notizen (zu ...).
Take turns.	Wechselt euch ab.
Talk to a partner / in groups.	Sprich mit einem/r Partner/-in / deiner Gruppe.
Tell your partner / the class.	Erzähle es deinem Partner / deiner Partnerin / der Klasse.
Think of (reasons for) ...	Überlege dir (Gründe für) ...
True, false or not in the text?	Richtig, falsch oder nicht im Text?
Use your notes / the words in a) / keywords / the information (in the table).	Benutze deine Notizen / die Wörter aus Aufgabe a) / Stichworte / die Informationen (aus der Tabelle).
Watch part 1 / scene 1 / all the film / the video.	Sieh dir Teil 1 / Szene 1 / den ganzen Film / das Video an.
Work alone / in pairs / in groups.	Arbeite allein / in Partnerarbeit / in Gruppen.
Work out the meaning of (the words).	Finde die Bedeutung (der Wörter) heraus.
Write the correct answers / sentences / questions.	Schreibe die richtigen Antworten / Sätze / Fragen (auf).
Write a short description / a blog post / an ending to the story ...	Schreibe eine kurze Beschreibung / einen Blogeintrag / ein Ende für die Geschichte ...

Quellenverzeichnis

Titelbild
Cornelsen/li.: Shutterstock.com/Ron Ellis/courtesy of Transport for London; Personen: Chocolate Films; Hintergrund re.: stock.adobe.com/anatoliycherkas

Illustrationen
Cornelsen/Harald Ardeias: S. 17 (Illus); S. 24 oben re.; S. 25 oben li.; S. 32; S. 48 unten re.; S. 50 unten; S. 52 unten re., unten li.; S. 55 unten re.; S. 56 unten re., unten li.; S. 57 unten re.; S. 62, A–F; S. 70 oben re.; S. 72 oben re., Mitte re.; S. 73; S. 77 unten; S. 79, 1–6; S. 84; S. 86; S. 87; S. 88 Mitte re.; S. 92, A u. B; S. 101 un.; S. 102; S. 112 un.; S. 133; S. 135; S. 141 unten re.; S. 166; S. 186; **Cornelsen/Carlos Borrell Eiköter:** Umschlagseite hinten (U3): Karte; S. 26 oben; **Cornelsen/Inhouse/Josephine Bienert-Köhler:** S. 99; S. 105; S. 151 unten re., Mitte re.; S. 164; S. 190; **Cornelsen/Chellie Carroll:** S. 129; S. 131; **Cornelsen/Inhouse/Melina Frick:** S. 36 Karte; **Cornelsen/Irina Zinner:** S. 170–175; S. 177; S. 180; S. 181; S. 183; S. 195; S. 197; S. 199; S. 200; S. 201

Abbildungen
Umschlagseite vorne (U2): oben: Siehe S. 14, S. 16, S. 26; **S. 1** oben: Siehe S. 30, S. 31, S. 32; **S. 4** Shutterstock.com/S-F; **S. 5** stock.adobe.com/Kaspars; **S. 6** Shutterstock.com/Fotimageon; **S. 7** stock.adobe.com/Tomas Marek; **S. 8** Shutterstock.com/John McGreevy; **S. 10** Kompass: Shutterstock.com/Aldiki Gustiyan; Flaggen: Shutterstock.com/SLdesign; Karte: stock.adobe.com/lesniewski; **S. 11** Cornelsen/Chocolate Films; **S. 12** A: stock.adobe.com/Patryk Kosmider; C: stock.adobe.com/zgphotography; B: mauritius images/David Ball; **S. 13** F: stock.adobe.com/coward_lion; D: stock.adobe.com/Tomas Marek; E: mauritius images/Prisma; **S. 14** C: stock.adobe.com/sborisov; Ali: Cornelsen/Chocolate Films; A: mauritius images/alamy stock photo/dov makabaw; B: mauritius images/Novarc Images; Lily: Cornelsen/Anja Poehlmann; **S. 15** F: stock.adobe.com/Photocreo Bednarek; E: dpa Picture-Alliance/robertharding; D: Panther Media GmbH/Lucy Clark; **S. 16** A: stock.adobe.com/Wei Huang/IWei; B: mauritius images/Rene Meyer; unten re.: mauritius images/Simon Belcher; C: Shutterstock.com/sirtravelalot; oben re.: Cornelsen/Personen: Chocolate Films, Hintergrund: stock.adobe.com/vhoke; **S. 17** Fahrrad: stock.adobe.com/Tomas Marek; Taxi: mauritius images/Hans-Peter Merten; roter Bus: Shutterstock.com/S-F; **S. 18** C: stock.adobe.com/Юлия Клюева; A: Imago Stock&People GmbH/Jeff Greenberg; B: mauritius images/alamy stock photo/Scott Sim; **S. 19** Cornelsen/Chocolate Films; **S. 20** oben re.: stock.adobe.com/Liliya Trott; unten li.: stock.adobe.com/Nicola; **S. 21** oben re.: Cornelsen/Chocolate Films; Mi.re: Anja Poehlmann; unten re.: Anja Poehlmann; **S. 22** unten re.: stock.adobe.com/Cultura Allies; unten li.: stock.adobe.com/Eddie Cloud; **S. 23** oben re.: stock.adobe.com/CHRIS COOK/Piranhi; unten re.: mauritius images/alamy stock photo/Dmytro Zinkevych; Mitte re.: SDG wheel: courtesy of the UNITED NATIONS/Department of Global Communications (https://www.un.org/sustainabledevelopment/ The content of this publication has not been approved by the United Nations and does not reflect the views of the United Nations or its officials or Member States.); **S. 24** Bread: stock.adobe.com/anaumenko; Chicken: stock.adobe.com/CassianoCorreia; Halloumi: stock.adobe.com/Esin Deniz; Hummus: stock.adobe.com/fudio; Falafel: stock.adobe.com/Luc.Pro; Kibbeh: stock.adobe.com/Thiago Santos; Spicy sausages: stock.adobe.com/Wirestock Creators/Ismail Kassem; **S. 25** unten re.: stock.adobe.com/AntonioDiaz; **S. 26** Harrods: stock.adobe.com/Richie Chan; unten re.: mauritius images/Steve Vidler; **S. 27** oben re.: mauritius images/Loop Images; unten re.: mauritius images/Steve Vidler; unten li.: Cornelsen/Personen: Chocolate Films, Hintergrund: mauritius images/alamy stock photo/Fotomaton; **S. 28** Cornelsen/Chocolate Films; **S. 29** Digital Learning Ass. Ltd.; **S. 30** unten re.: ImagoStock&People GmbH/Mark Beto; oben re.: Cornelsen/Laptop: Shutterstock.com/Passatic, Bildschirm-Illustration: Shutterstock.com/I000s_pixels; **S. 33** Mitte re.: stock.adobe.com/pxl.store; icon Bahn: Shutterstock.com/Vector FX; icon Person: Shutterstock/Dyek Marina; **S. 34** oben li.: Shutterstock.com/Damir Khabirov; Mitte re.: Shutterstock.com/paulaphoto; **S. 35** Cornelsen/Anja Poehlmann; **S. 36** oben re.: Cornelsen/Chocolate Films; **S. 37** unten li.: mauritius images/alamy stock photo/Alex Segre; Mitte li.: mauritius images/alamy stock photo/Vickie Flores; unten re.: mauritius images/Vantage; oben re.: Shutterstock.com/Monkey Business Images; **S. 38** mauritius images/Steve Vidler; **S. 39** stock.adobe.com/Richie Chan; **S. 40** C: stock.adobe.com/Denis Feldmann; D: stock.adobe.com/I-Wei Huang; B: stock.adobe.com/Mistervlad; A: Imago Stock&People GmbH/Loop Images/Peter Noyce; **S. 42** unten re.: stock.adobe.com/peopleimages.com/Kobus Louw; Mitte re.: Imago Stock&People GmbH/robertharding/CharlesBowman; **S. 43** stock.adobe.com/Maksym; **S. 44** Mitte re.: stock.adobe.com/Nicola; links: Cornelsen/Chocolate Films; rechts: Cornelsen/Chocolate Films; Mitte: Shutterstock.com/Monkey Business Images; **S. 45** Mitte re.: stock.adobe.com/Kaspars; rechts: Cornelsen/Chocolate Films; links: Cornelsen/Chocolate Films; Mitte li.: Shutterstock.com/Spotmatik Ltd; **S. 46** 3: Imago Stock & People GmbH/Addictive Stock/Adalberto Rodriguez; 2: mauritius images/Cavan Images; 1: mauritius images/Mariano Gaspar; **S. 47** oben re.: stock.adobe.com; **S. 48** oben re.: Cornelsen/Chocolate Films; **S. 49** mitte li.: Shutterstock.com/Yefym Turkin; **S. 50** oben re.: Cornelsen/Chocolate Films; **S. 51** unten re.: Shutterstock.com/LightField Studios; **S. 52** oben re.: Shutterstock.com/sitthiphong; **S. 53** Shutterstock.com/Ververidis Vasilis; **S. 54** unten re.: Digital Learning Ass. Ltd.; Mitte re.: mauritius images/alamy stock photo/Jeffrey Mayer; oben re.: Person li. im Bild: Chocolate Films, Rest des Bildes: Shutterstock.com/sitthiphong; **S. 55** oben re.: Shutterstock.com/sitthiphong; **S. 56** Mitte re.: Shutterstock.com; oben re.: Shutterstock.com; Fußball: Shutterstock.com/Great_Kit;

Basketball: Shutterstock.com/Great_Kit; Controller: Shutterstock.com/Hasebalcon; oben mi.: Shutterstock.com/Illizium; schwimmen: Shutterstock.com/Makkuro GL; Skateboard: Shutterstock.com/my_design; Würfel: Shutterstock.com/popicon; Karten: Shutterstock.com/popicon; Bowling: Shutterstock.com/popicon; Tischtennisschläger: Shutterstock.com/popicon; Puzzle: Shutterstock.com/popicon; oben li.: Shutterstock.com/VectorSun58; **S. 57** unten li.: Cornelsen/Chocolate Films; oben li.: Shutterstock.com/Alexsey t17; unten li.: Shutterstock.com/JosepPerianes; oben li.: Shutterstock.com/Yefym Turkin; **S. 58** unten re.: Cornelsen/Chocolate Films; unten li.: Shutterstock.com/Alexsey t17; **S. 59** unten: Interfilm Berlin Management; 2: Interfilm Berlin Management; oben: Interfilm Berlin Management; 3.: Interfilm Berlin Management; **S. 60** A: Shutterstock.com/Marian Fil; B: Shutterstock.com/Khosro; C: Shutterstock.com/Max Topchii; D: Shutterstock.com/DiversityStudio; E: stock.adobe.com/Jelena Ivanovic; **S. 61** Shutterstock.com/VH-studio; S.63 Shutterstock.com/tommaso79; **S. 64** 3: Shutterstock.com/chomplearn; 1: Shutterstock.com/Daniel Hoz; 2: Shutterstock.com/Gleb Usovich; 4: Shutterstock.com/Kaentian Street; **S. 65** Cornelsen/Personen: Chocolate Films, Hintergrund: Shutterstock.com/Ian Reay; **S. 66** unten mi.: Bridgeman Images/SSPL/Manchester Daily Express; oben re.: Cornelsen/Chocolate Films; unten re.: dpa Picture-Alliance/Photoshot/PYMCA/Peter J Walsh; **S. 67** unten re.: Imago Stock & People GmbH/Avalon/Mike Gray; unten mi.: Imago Stock & People GmbH/ZUMA Press/Joel Goodman; unten li.: mauritius images/alamy stock photo/Rob Watkins; oben re.: mauritius images/alamy stock photo/Simon Newbury; **S. 68** oben re.: stock.adobe.com; A: mauritius images/robertharding; B: stock.adobe.com/David Matthew Lyons; C: mauritius images/alamy stock photo/CBW; D: mauritius images/alamy stock photo/Matthew Wilkinson; **S. 69** unten re.: Shutterstock.com/Phil Halfmann; **S. 70** unten re.: stock.adobe.com/irissca; **S. 74** A: stock.adobe.com/Sergii Figurnyi; B: mauritius images/alamy stock photo/Nicola Campbell; C: stock.adobe.com/moofushi; oben links: Cornelsen/Chocolate Films; **S. 75** D: stock.adobe.com/Fun Altitude; E: stock.adobe.com/Apostolis Giontzis; F: mauritius images/Destinations; Mitte links: stock.adobe.com/Richie Chan; **S. 76** Imago Stock & People GmbH/imagebroker/Roland Marske; **S. 77** oben re.: CartoonStock/Mike Turner; **S. 78** oben re.: stock.adobe.com/G3D Studio; Mitte re.: Cornelsen/Personen: Chocolate Films, Hintergrund: stock.adobe.com/avtk; **S. 80** 1: stock.adobe.com/www.QuincyDein.com/EpicStockMedia; 2: mauritius images/alamy stock photo/Iain Lowson; 3: mauritius images/alamy stock photo/Euan Cherry; 4: mauritius images/alamy stock photo/Ken Jack; 5: stock.adobe.com/Duncan Andison; 6: stock.adobe.com/Ellis Travel Photography/Matthew Williams; **S. 81** Cornelsen/Chocolate Films; **S. 82** 1: Aldo Kane; 2: Shutterstock.com/Dario Verdugo; 3: Shutterstock.com/HPH Image Library; **S. 85** oben li.: stock.adobe.com/Andris Tkachenko; oben Mi.: Shutterstock.com/DGreenPhoto; **S. 88** oben re.: Cornelsen/Chocolate Films; **S. 89** Digital Learning Ass. Ltd.; **S. 92** oben re.: stock.adobe.com/Calming Presence; oben li.: stock.adobe.com/davidionut; **S. 93** 1: stock.adobe.com/fongleon356; 2: stock.adobe.com/AdobeTim82; 3: stock.adobe.com/Pawel Gubernat; 4: stock.adobe.com/alexandrum01; oben re.: Shutterstock.com/eurobanks; **S. 94** A: Shutterstock.com/Helen Hotson; B: stock.adobe.com/Magdalena Bujak; **S. 95** mauritius images/alamy stock photo/stephanie hager; **S. 96** oben li.: stock.adobe.com/lisa_h; Mitte re.: mauritius images/alamy stock photo/Martin Thomas Photography; oben re.: Shutterstock.com/Superlime; unten li.: Shutterstock.com/TTstudio; **S. 97** Mitte li.: stock.adobe.com/cornfield/Frank Cornfield; oben re.: mauritius images/alamy stock photo/Ryan Morrison; unten re.: mauritius images/alamy stock photo/Stan Proudlock; Mitte: Shutterstock.com/Claudio Divizia; **S. 98** unten re.: stock.adobe.com/design/exclusive; oben re.: Cornelsen/Chocolate Films; oben li.: Shutterstock.com/Marti Bug Catcher; **S. 99** oben re.: mauritius images/Roger parkes/Alamy/Alamy Stock Photos; Mitte: Shutterstock.com/Moving Moment; **S. 100** dpa Picture-Alliance/Benedikt von Imhoff; **S. 101** oben re.: mauritius images/alamy stock photo/Philip Hills; Mitte li.: mauritius images/robertharding; **S. 104** Mitte re.: mauritius images/alamy stock photo/GFC Collection; oben re.: Shutterstock.com/Lukassek; **S. 106** A: mauritius images/alamy stock photo/StockimoNews/Lancashire Images; C: stock.adobe.com/Sebastien; B: Shutterstock.com/Richard Whitcombe; oben li.: Cornelsen/Chocolate Films; **S. 107** D: stock.adobe.com/wavebreak3; E: stock.adobe.com/Alexey Fedorenko; **S. 108** unten li.: Cornelsen/Chocolate Films; Mitte re.: StockFood GmbH/Look/Pompe, Ingolf; **S. 109** stock.adobe.com/Richard Whitcombe; **S. 110** Digital Learning Ass. Ltd.; **S. 111** Cornelsen/Chocolate Films; **S. 112** oben re.: Cornelsen/Chocolate Films; unten mitte: Shutterstock.com; **S. 113** oben re.: mauritius images/Westend61; **S. 114** unten re.: stock.adobe.com/Soloviova Liudmyla; oben re.: Shutterstock.com; Emojis: Shutterstock.com/Yefym Turkin; **S. 115** A: stock.adobe.com/Adobe Systems; B: stock.adobe.com/Adobe Systems; C: stock.adobe.com/4luck; D: Shutterstock.com; E: Shutterstock.com; F: Shutterstock.com/Cosmic_Design; oben re.: Cornelsen/Chocolate Films; unten re.: Cornelsen/Chocolate Films; **S. 116** Shutterstock.com/LightField Studios; **S. 117** Mitte re.: Shutterstock.com/Auttapol Sangsub; unten re.: Shutterstock.com/stockfour; **S. 118** Mitte li.: Cornelsen/Chocolate Films; Emojis: Shutterstock.com/Yefym Turkin; unten li.: Cornelsen/Person re.: Chocolate Films, Wagen + Hintergrund: mauritius images/PHILIP SMITH/Alamy; **S. 119** unten mi.: stock.adobe.com/Krakenimages; oben mi.: Cornelsen/Chocolate Films; unten re.: Cornelsen/Chocolate Films; oben links: Cornelsen/Chocolate Films; Emojis: Shutterstock.com/Yefym Turkin; oben re.: Cornelsen/Person: Chocolate Films, Hintergrund: Shutterstock.com/muroPhotographer; **S. 120** a : Shutterstock.com/daddy.icon; b: Shutterstock.com/koblizeek; c: Shutterstock.com/Dreamerdesign; d: Shutterstock.com/Leremy; f: Shutterstock.com/Rawpixel Ltd.; e: Shutterstock.com/sore88;

Quellenverzeichnis

S. 121 Mitte re.: Digital Learning Ass. Ltd.; oben re.: Shutterstock.com/gritsalak karalak; **S. 122** stock.adobe.com/Krakenimages.com; **S. 123** stock.adobe.com/Tyler Olson; **S. 124** oben re.: stock.adobe.com/Colin & Linda McKie; unten re.: stock.adobe.com/JoeE Jackson; Mitte li.: Shutterstock.com/Tomas Marek; **S. 125** Mitte re.: stock.adobe.com/Krakenimages.com; Mitte: Cornelsen/Chocolate Films; Mitte li.: Shutterstock.com/Yefym Turkin; **S. 126** A: Shutterstock.com/Santorines; B: Shutterstock.com/Stu Porter; C: Shutterstock.com/gowithstock; D: Shutterstock.com/Vtmila; E: Shutterstock.com/TeodorLazarev; **S. 127** Shutterstock.com/Terelyuk; **S. 128** oben re.: Cornelsen/Chocolate Films; **S. 131** Shutterstock.com/AndreyUG; **S. 132** unten Mitte: stock.adobe.com/David; unten re.: stock.adobe.com/Eddie Cloud; unten li.: stock.adobe.com/postywood1; **S. 136** Shutterstock.com/Sutipond Somnam; **S. 137** unten re.: Cornelsen/Chocolate Films; unten Mi.: Cornelsen/Chocolate Films; unten re.: Shutterstock.com/Cosmic_Design; unten li.: Shutterstock.com/Cosmic_Design; **S. 138** A: Imago Stock & People GmbH/VWPics/Sergix Reboredo; B: stock.adobe.com/aitormmfoto; C: mauritius images/Matthias Graben; mitte li.: Cornelsen/Chocolate Films; **S. 139** oben re.: Cornelsen/Chocolate Films; D: mauritius images/DP RF; E: mauritius images/alamy stock photo/Striking Images – Tourism Ireland; F: mauritius images/Rene Mattes; **S. 140** Mitte re.: stock.adobe.com/master1305; oben Mi.: stock.adobe.com/stellamc; oben re.: stock.adobe.com/Steven Heap; **S. 141** oben re.: stock.adobe.com/BCFC; **S. 142** 1: mauritius images/Loop Images/Extramural Activity; 2: mauritius images/SagaPhoto; 3: stock.adobe.com/hunterbliss; 4: mauritius images/alamy stock photo/Jane Sweeney; 5: mauritius images/John Warburton-Lee; **S. 143** Cornelsen/Person: Chocolate Films, Hintergrund: stock.adobe.com/zephyr_p; **S. 144** Cornelsen/Personen: Chocolate Films, Hintergrund: Shutterstock.com/hxdbzxy; **S. 145** oben re.: Cornelsen/Person: Chocolate Films, Hintergrund: Shutterstock.com/Rocksweeper; **S. 146** mauritius images/Maskot; **S. 147** Interfilm Berlin Management; **S. 148** A: stock.adobe.com/Cultura Creative; B: stock.adobe.com/Denis Mamin; C: Shutterstock.com/ Monkey Business Images; D: stock.adobe.com/Slawomir Fajer; E: stock.adobe.com/Kaset Chukittipong; **S. 149** unten re.: Shutterstock.com/Ajmoc; oben re.: Shutterstock.com/alphaspirit.it; **S. 150** unten li.: Bridgeman Images/ Look and Learn; English; Mitte re.: mauritius images/Glasshouse; oben re.: mauritius images/Image Source; **S. 151** oben re.: Cornelsen/Chocolate Films; **S. 152** Shutterstock.com/Duncan Andison; **S. 153** Cornelsen/Chocolate Films; **S. 156** stock.adobe.com/Maayan; **S. 157** Ungermeyer; **S. 158** Shutterstock.com/IIIerlok_xolms; **S. 165** Shutterstock.com/Iakov Filimonov; **S. 168** Shutterstock.com/fizkes; **S. 185** Shutterstock.com/Laurie Barr; **S. 186** traffic light: stock.adobe.com/alice_photo; block of flats: stock.adobe.com/DZIEN.PL/ODJECHANY/bzy; skyscraper: stock.adobe.com/Rich Lindie; car park: stock.adobe.com/Sai Chan/Zoe; roundabout: stock.adobe.com/ Sampajano- Anizza; petrol station: stock.adobe.com/Wendell Franks/Carolyn Franks; office building: stock.adobe.com/william87; oben re.: Shutterstock.com/Barbara Sauder; zebra crossing: Shutterstock.com/Claudio Divizia; **S. 187** Mitte li.: stock.adobe.com; unten re.: stock.adobe.com; oben: mauritius images/Maskot; **S. 188** patterned: stock.adobe.com/Dmitry Naumov; wool: stock.adobe.com/Kapawtord; light: Shutterstock.com/Africa Studio; polyester: Shutterstock.com/Anastasiia Horova; cotton: Shutterstock.com/Gemenacom; checked: Shutterstock.com/hidesy; leather: Shutterstock.com/In Green; silk: Shutterstock.com/Jag_cz; metal: Shutterstock.com/Jan Dix; rubber: Shutterstock.com/Nataliia K; flowery: Shutterstock.com/NJMSTOCK; dotted: Shutterstock.com/pornpawit; canvas: Shutterstock.com/Preto Perola; plain: Shutterstock.com/RooftopStudioBangkok; dark: Shutterstock.com/RooftopStudioBangkok; striped: Shutterstock.com/Sandratsky Dmitriy; colourful: Shutterstock.com/VLADIMIR VK; **S. 189** oben: stock.adobe.com/Maryna; Emojis: Shutterstock.com/Yefym Turkin; **S. 191** judo: stock.adobe.com/Iakov Filimonov/JackF; ice skating: stock.adobe.com/petunyia; gymnastics: Shutterstock.com/BearFotos; handball: Shutterstock.com/Focus and Blur; athletics: Shutterstock.com/Jacob LundShutterstock/Jacob Lund; scuba diving: Shutterstock.com/Jukkis; canoeing: Shutterstock.com/Kzenon; volleyball: Shutterstock.com/Monkey Business Images; boxing: Shutterstock.com/PeopleImages.com - Yuri A; archery: Shutterstock.com/VicVic Liu; rowing: Shutterstock.com/videoTD; rugby: Shutterstock.com/wavebreakmedia; **S. 192** coast: stock.adobe.com/Gordon Fahey; wave: stock.adobe.com/NorthShoreSurfPhotos; rocks: stock.adobe.com/pamela_d_mcadams; valley: stock.adobe.com/Tomasz Zajda; corn: Shutterstock.com/ABCDstock; butterfly: Shutterstock.com/CHAINFOTO24; frog: Shutterstock.com/Dinda Yulianto; bee: Shutterstock.com/Feng Lu; deer: Shutterstock.com/Radek Karko; mushroom: Shutterstock.com/romvo; fox: Shutterstock.com/Sandra Standbridge; grass: Shutterstock.com/SHUTTER TOP; **S. 193** theme park: stock.adobe.com/cceliaphoto; town hall: stock.adobe.com/Leonid Andronov; palace: stock.adobe.com/M. Schoenfeld; waterfall: stock.adobe.com/M·H; national park: stock.adobe.com/MICHAEL HEWARD/Michael Conrad; harbour: stock.adobe.com/motorradcbr; tower: stock.adobe.com/Ralf; old town: stock.adobe.com/Sina Ettmer; town/village square: stock.adobe.com/WernerHilpert; **S. 194** Icons von: Shutterstock.com/Arafat Uddin; Shutterstock.com/Great_Kit; stock.adobe.com/anisa; stock.adobe.com/atScene; stock.adobe.com/Dilip; stock.adobe.com/iconin Ja; stock.adobe.com/KR Studio; stock.adobe.com/manstock007; stock.adobe.com/martialred; stock.adobe.com/North; stock.adobe.com/yoyonpujiono; **S. 203** Shutterstock.com/HitToon; **S. 205** skyscrapers: stock.adobe.com/Elnur Amikishiyev; unten re.: stock.adobe.com/EMrpize; bagpipes: stock.adobe.com/mipan; **S. 206** mitte: stock.adobe.com/Elena Duvernay/Elenarts; unten rechts: stock.adobe.com/Jongruk Anudachakul/lightsecond; oben re.: stock.adobe.com/serkat Photography; **S. 207** oben re.:

Shutterstock.com/Adam Wasilewski; Mitte re.: Shutterstock.com/Sonyaudina; **S. 208** stock.adobe.com/ Leonid Andronov; **S. 209** unten: stock.adobe.com/jantima14; Mitte re.: Shutterstock.com/Karramba Production; **S. 210** a roundabout: stock.adobe.com/Harald Schindler; columns: stock.adobe.com/milavas; Pelican: stock.adobe.com/petrsalinger; columns: stock.adobe.com/TimurD; **S. 212** a tap: stock.adobe.com/Alex Mit; chickpeas: stock.adobe.com/Diana Taliun; cucumber: stock.adobe.com/sommai; plates: Shutterstock.com/Africa Studio; mint: Shutterstock.com/Valentina Proskurina; **S. 213** gate: Shutterstock.com/Dim Dimich; Mitte re.: Shutterstock.com/Patra.K; oben re.: Shutterstock.com/worradirek; **S. 214** grass: stock.adobe.com/andreusK; a path: stock.adobe.com/Creaturart; a bank: Shutterstock.com/MicroOne; a bench: Shutterstock.com/ OHishiapply; river banks: Shutterstock.com/Zoa.Arts; **S. 217** Mitte re.: stock.adobe.com/ArtFamily; skirt: stock.adobe.com/Tarzhanova; **S. 218** stock.adobe.com/ photoguns; **S. 221** microphone: stock.adobe.com/Hayati Kayhan; a light switch: stock.adobe.com/Matthew Gilbert; **S. 222** unten re.: stock.adobe.com/Olga Yastremska, New Africa; Mitte re.: Shutterstock.com/StoryTime Studio; **S. 223** Shutterstock.com/wavebreakmedia; **S. 224** service station: Shutterstock.com/arsa35; pineapple: Shutterstock.com/BookyBuggy; tyres: Shutterstock.com/Chonlawut; a coach: Shutterstock.com/Nerthuz; buses: Shutterstock.com/Syda Productions; **S. 225** Shutterstock.com/Popartic; **S. 226** stock.adobe.com/dwi; **S. 227** a catfish: stock.adobe.com/voren1; a submarine: Shutterstock.com/pixel creator; soldiers: Shutterstock.com/sirtravelalot; **S. 228** skydiving: stock.adobe.com/2happy; tents: stock.adobe.com/Enrico Ferraresi; **S. 229** volcano: stock.adobe.com/Xanthius; cave: Shutterstock.com/rogelson; **S. 230** unten re.: stock.adobe.com/evgeniya; Mitte re.: stock.adobe.com/ photobboy/Pawel Pajor; **S. 231** oben re.: stock.adobe.com/David Peperkamp; Mitte re.: Shutterstock.com/ Denis Belitsky; **S. 232** oben re.: Shutterstock.com/lynx_v; Mitte re.: Shutterstock.com/Sapann Design; **S. 233** Shutterstock.com/Dan Thornberg; **S. 234** Mitte: stock.adobe.com/evegenesis; Mitte re.: Shutterstock.com/ Apolinariy; unten re.: Shutterstock.com/Federico Rostagno; oben re.: Shutterstock.com/photomaster; **S. 235** a cardigan: stock.adobe.com/Olga; an apron: stock.adobe.com/Olga Yastremska, New Africa; Mitte re.: stock.adobe.com/Юлия Дружкова ; **S. 236** unten re.: stock.adobe.com/pcruciatti; a waistcoat: stock.adobe.com/ Tarzhanova; gymnastics: Shutterstock.com/Anna Aybetova; **S. 237** oben re.: stock.adobe.com/fotomaximum; Mitte re.: Shutterstock.com/New Africa; **S. 241** Mitte re.: stock.adobe.com/Africa Studio; unten re.: stock.adobe.com/ Olga Yastremska, New Africa; oben re.: Shutterstock.com/Arthito; **S. 242** stock.adobe.com/Rudzhan; **S. 243** oben re.: Shutterstock.com/Animaflora PicsStock; Mitte: Shutterstock.com/Vydrin; unten re.: Shutterstock.com/Yulia Davidovich; **S. 244** Shutterstock.com/banderlog.

Textquellen
S. 36: *All in this together:* Zaina / *https://www.museumoflondon.org.uk/discover/languages-london*
S. 128–131: *Rescued* (first chapter): Christina de la Mare, Cornelsen 2024

Datenquellen
S. 36: Die Karte basiert auf Daten (Census 2021) des Office for National Statistics in London, *https://www.ons.gov.uk/datasets/TS024/editions/2021/versions/1#version-history* (Zugriff: 16.08.2023)
S. 116: Die statistischen Daten in Text A basieren auf Informationen von *https://cybercrew.uk/blog/cyberbullying-statistics-uk/* (Zugriff: 09.11.2023) und *https://www.mayoclinic.org/healthy-lifestyle/tween-and-teen-health/in-depth/teens-and-social-media-use/art-20474437#:~:text=Social%20media%20is%20a%20big,media%20 use%20have%20on%20teens%3F* (Zugriff: 09.11.2023)

Liedquellen
S. 66: *Station Approach* by Elbow: Salvation Music Ltd. / Neue Welt Musikverlag GmbH, Hamburg. Text: Guy Edward John Garvey / Richard Barry Jupp / Craig Lee Potter / Mark Ellis Potter / Peter James Turner
S. 67: *Manchester* by The Beautiful South: Paul David Heaton / David Ricardo Rotheray
S. 85: *The Braes of Balquhidder:* Cornelsen (gemeinfrei) / Scottish folk song by Scottish poet Robert Tannahill (1774–1810), first published in Robert Archibald Smith's Scottish Minstrel (1821–24)
S. 98: *Auld Lang Syne:* Cornelsen (gemeinfrei) / Robert Burns (auf der Basis der Ballade *Old Long Syne*, publiziert 1711 von James Watson), publiziert 1800 in Playford's Original Scotch Tunes

Continents, countries and regions

continent / country / region	adjective	person	people
Afghanistan [æfˈgænɪstɑːn] *Afghanistan*	Afghan [ˈæfgæn]	an Afghan	the Afghans
Albania [ælˈbeɪnɪə] *Albanien*	Albanian [ælˈbeɪnɪən]	an Albanian	the Albanians
America [əˈmerɪkə] *Amerika*	American	an American	the Americans
Asia [ˈeɪʒə] *Asien*	Asian [ˈeɪʒn]	an Asian	the Asians
Austria [ˈɒstrɪə] *Österreich*	Austrian [ˈɒstrɪən]	an Austrian	the Austrians
Bangladesh [bæŋgləˈdeʃ] *Bangladesch*	Bangladeshi [bæŋgləˈdeʃi]	a Bangladeshi	the Bangladeshis
Caribbean [kærɪˈbiːən] *die Karibik*	Caribbean	a Carib [ˈkærɪb]	the Caribs
China [ˈtʃaɪnə] *China*	Chinese [tʃaɪˈniːz]	a Chinese	the Chinese
Cuba [ˈkjuːbə] *Kuba*	Cuban	a Cuban	the Cubans
Czechia, the Czech Republic [tʃek rɪˈpʌblɪk] *Tschechien, die Tschechische Republik*	Czech [tʃek]	a Czech	the Czechs
Denmark [ˈdenmɑːk] *Dänemark*	Danish [ˈdeɪnɪʃ]	a Dane [deɪn]	the Danes
England [ˈɪŋglənd] *England*	English [ˈɪŋglɪʃ]	an Englishman / -woman	the English
Europe [ˈjʊərəp] *Europa*	European [ˌjʊərəˈpiːən]	a European	the Europeans
France [frɑːns] *Frankreich*	French [frentʃ]	a Frenchman / -woman	the French
Germany [ˈdʒɜːməni] *Deutschland*	German [ˈdʒɜːmən]	a German	the Germans
Great Britain [ˈbrɪtn] *Großbritannien*	British [ˈbrɪtɪʃ]	a Briton [ˈbrɪtn]	the British
India [ˈɪndɪə] *Indien*	Indian [ˈɪndɪən]	an Indian	the Indians
Ireland [ˈaɪələnd] *Irland*	Irish [ˈaɪrɪʃ]	an Irishman / -woman	the Irish
Italy [ˈɪtəli] *Italien*	Italian [ɪˈtælɪən]	an Italian	the Italians
Jamaica [dʒəˈmeɪkə] *Jamaika*	Jamaican [dʒəˈmeɪkən]	a Jamaican	the Jamaicans
Japan [dʒəˈpæn] *Japan*	Japanese [dʒæpəˈniːz]	a Japanese	the Japanese
Kenya [ˈkenjə] *Kenia*	Kenyan [ˈkenjən]	a Kenyan	the Kenyans
Latin America [latɪn əˈmerɪkə] *Lateinamerika*	Latin American [latɪn əˈmerɪkən]	a Latin American	the Latin Americans
Lebanon [ˈlebənən] *der Libanon*	Lebanese [lebəˈniːz]	a Lebanese	the Lebanese
Lithuania [lɪθjuˈeɪnɪə] *Litauen*	Lithuanian [lɪθjuˈeɪnɪən]	a Lithuanian	the Lithuanians
Mexico [ˈmeksɪkəʊ] *Mexiko*	Mexican [ˈmeksɪkən]	a Mexican	the Mexicans
Nepal [nəˈpɔːl] *Nepal*	Nepalese [nepəˈliːz]	a Nepalese	the Nepalese
the Netherlands [ˈneðələndz] *die Niederlande, Holland*	Dutch [dʌtʃ]	a Dutchman / -woman	the Dutch
Nigeria [naɪˈdʒɪərɪə] *Nigeria*	Nigerian	a Nigerian	the Nigerians
Pakistan [pɑːkɪˈstɑːn] *Pakistan*	Pakistani [pɑːkɪˈstɑːni]	a Pakistani	the Pakistanis
Poland [ˈpəʊlənd] *Polen*	Polish [ˈpəʊlɪʃ]	a Pole [pəʊl]	the Poles
Portugal [ˈpɔːtʃʊgl] *Portugal*	Portuguese [pɔːtʃʊˈgiːz]	a Portuguese	the Portuguese
Puerto Rico [pwɜːtə ˈriːkəʊ] *Puerto Rico*	Puerto Rican	a Puerto Rican	the Puerto Ricans
Russia [ˈrʌʃə] *Russland*	Russian [ˈrʌʃn]	a Russian	the Russians
Scotland [ˈskɒtlənd] *Schottland*	Scottish [ˈskɒtɪʃ]	a Scot [skɒt]	the Scots
South Africa [saʊθ ˈæfrɪkə] *Südafrika*	South African	a South African	the South Africans
South America [saʊθ əˈmerɪkə] *Südamerika*	South American [saʊθ əˈmerɪkən]	a South American	the South Americans
Spain [speɪn] *Spanien*	Spanish [ˈspænɪʃ]	Spaniard [ˈspænjəd]	the Spanish / the Spaniards
Turkey [ˈtɜːki]; Türkiye *die Türkei*	Turkish [ˈtɜːkɪʃ]	a Turk [tɜːk]	the Turks
the United Kingdom (the UK) [juˌnaɪtɪd ˈkɪŋdəm, ˌjuːˈkeɪ] *das Vereinigte Königreich*	British [ˈbrɪtɪʃ]	a Briton [ˈbrɪtn]	the British
Ukraine [juːˈkreɪn] *die Ukraine*	Ukrainian	a Ukrainian	the Ukrainians
Wales [weɪlz] *Wales*	Welsh [welʃ]	a Welshman / -woman	the Welsh

Lösungsbeispiele

Hinweis

Lösungen zu geschlossenen Aufgaben finden Sie auf den Unitseiten, direkt bei den Aufgaben. Auf sehr umfangreiche Lösungen sowie auf Lösungsbeispiele zu halboffenen Aufgaben wird von der Unitseite hierher in den Anhang verwiesen. Zu komplett individuellen Lösungen gibt es keine Muster.

Hello! Where we're from

▶ 10, Ex 1 c) **Lösungsbeispiel**

country	capital	☒ more information
England	London	GB's biggest country, 57 million people
Wales	Cardiff	smallest country, 3 million people, 10 million sheep
Scotland	Edinburgh	big country, in the north, 790 islands, 5 ½ million people
Northern Ireland	Belfast	in north of Ireland, 2 million people, from 1922 separated from the south, and still part of the UK
Ireland	Dublin	the Republic of Ireland, in the south, 5 million people, until 1921 part of the UK, became independent in 1922, has its own government

▶ 11, Ex 2 b) **Lösung**

Pearl London: in the south-east of England
Omar Manchester: in the north-west of England
Grace Inverness: in the north of Scotland
Dylan Llandudno: in the north of Wales
Jack Belfast: in the east of Northern Ireland
Orla Limerick: in the west of the Republic of Ireland

▶ 12, Ex 3 a) **Lösungsbeispiel**

A In the foreground I can see a river or the sea and behind it there's a wall. In the middle of the picture there's an old church. Next to the church on the left there's a big green tree. On the right of the picture there are some small old houses. There's a red house and two green ones. In the background there's a blue sky with big white clouds.

B In the foreground there's a man. The man is wearing traditional clothes and a black hat with a feather on it. He's playing the bagpipes. In the background I can see the walls of an old building and a loch/lake.

C In this picture I can see a city with lots of skyscapers and modern buildings. The skyscrapers are very high and they have many windows. In the foreground there are some smaller buildings.

D In the middle of the picture there's a very big castle. In front of it there's an old bridge over a river. On the right of the picture there's a white boat on the river. In the background on the right there are mountains. On the left of the picture there's a small park with a place to sit down.

E In the picture there's a house with a big mural on it. In the middle of the mural there is a ship/boat. On the left of the mural there are two men. One of the men is wearing a suit and the other one is wearing a sailor's uniform. On the right of the mural there's a young boy with a newspaper with bad news on the first page.

F This picture shows a canal. In the middle of the picture there's a long boat on the canal. On the left and on the right of the picture there are more boats. The boat in the foreground on the right is red, blue and yellow. On the sides of the canal I can see trees. In the background there are some old red buildings and a bridge.

Lösungsbeispiele

▶ 12, Ex 3 c) **Lösungsbeispiel**
1 C old buildings and modern skyscrapers; exciting city: a lot to do and to see
2 F lots of canals; had a lot of industry, they used boats to transport things; some people now live on boats
3 B lake = loch; Loch Ness: famous for monster; beautiful, you can hear bagpipes: very Scottish
4 D pretty, by the sea; Wales = 'castle capital' of world; 600 castles
5 E murals and street art everywhere; mural of the Titanic that hit an iceberg
6 A a lot of rain so it's green everywhere; past: poor country, but different today, big businesses; Limerick: old castles, festivals, music, friendly people

Unit 1 London: City Life

▶ 14, Ex 1 a) **Lösungsbeispiel**
A In the foreground I can see an acrobat. He's dancing. A lot of people are watching and clapping.
B I can see a street with houses in different colours. I can see a black, a blue and a yellow house. A lot of people are walking on the street and it looks like there are a lot of shops.
C I can see a river and a bridge. On the left there's a big house with a big tower. The tower has a clock.
D In the foreground I can see a tower. It looks funny because there's a lot of red metal around it. In the background I can see the blue sky and some clouds.
E I can see a tunnel with lots of murals and graffiti. It looks like art because a lot of people are looking at the walls.
F There's a big wheel on the right. In the middle I can see a river and boats and in the background there's a bridge.

▶ 14, Ex 1 c) **Lösungsbeispiel**
Big Ben L *(at the Houses of Parliament)*
London Eye L *(big wheel by the river)*
South Bank A *(musicians, dancers, acrobats on the street)*
Leake Street Tunnel A *(biggest graffiti walls in London)*
Orbit Slide L *(tallest sculpture in Britain, fast rides)*,
Camden Market A *(hundreds of little shops, food stalls)*

▶ 16, Ex 1 c) **Lösung**
1 True.
2 False: It's two stops to Camden Town.
3 False: It's direct from here.
4 True.
5 True.
6 True.
7 False: The train will soon be here.
8 False: There is an announcement about the gap and the platform.

▶ 17, Ex 3 a), b)
▶ 38, Ex 3 a), b) **Lösungsbeispiel**
B: How long does it take by bus? – **A:** 16 min.
B: How long does it take by tube? – **A:** 7 min.
B: How much is the journey by bus? – **A:** It's free for kids.
B: How much is the journey by tube? – **A:** 90p.
B: How much is the journey if they walk? – **A:** It's free.

Lösungsbeispiele

A: How long does it take by taxi? – B: 6 min.
A: How long does it take by bike? – B: 13–17 min.
A: How long does it take if they walk? – B: 36 min.
A: How much is the journey by taxi? – B: £10.
A: How much is the journey by bike? – B: £1.65 for 30 min.

▶ 17, Ex 3 c) **Lösungsbeispiel**
the fastest taxi • **the slowest** walk • **the cheapest** walk, bus for kids • **the most expensive** taxi • **the greenest** bike, walk • **the healthiest** walk • **the most fun** bus, bike

▶ 18, Ex 1 a) **Lösungsbeispiel**
Tours *boat tours, film tours,* walking tours, (open-top) bus tours, Segway tours, guided tours …
Themes Buckingham Palace tour, 'London by night' bus tour, sightseeing tour, Harry Potter tour, …

▶ 20, Ex 5 a)
▶ 38, Ex 5 a) **Lösungsbeispiel** (Partner B's answers)
1 a street art tour
2 you will walk / you will travel on foot
3 street art / graffiti artists
4 It's free, but you can tip the guide.
5 Text or call.
6 There are two tours. / You can eat at a restaurant afterwards.

▶ 20, Ex 5 b)
▶ 38, Ex 5 b) **Lösungsbeispiel** (Partner A's answers)
1 an afternoon tea tour
2 by bus
3 the top sights (London Eye, Buckingham Palace, Houses of Parliament …)
4 It's £25 per person.
5 Online or from their kiosk.
6 You can enjoy sandwiches, cakes and tea. / There's an audio guide.

▶ 20, Ex 6 **Lösungsbeispiel**

Guide	Here we are in St James's Park. It's not the biggest park in London, but I think it's the most beautiful.
Mum	Was hat er/sie gesagt?
You	Er/Sie hat gesagt, dass *das nicht der größte Park in London ist, aber der schönste.*
Mum	OK, aber kannst du fragen, was der größte Park in London ist?
You	Excuse me, my mum has a question: *What's the biggest park in London?*
Guide	Great question! Well, the biggest park in central London is Hyde Park. In fact, over 40 % of London is green space!
You	Er/Sie hat gesagt, *dass der größte Park in London der Hyde Park ist. Mehr als 40 % von London sind Grünflächen!*
Guide	Now, if you look over the Blue Bridge, you'll see Buckingham Palace. It has 775 rooms.
Mum	Was sagt er/sie über den Palast?
You	*Der Palast hat 775 Räume.*
Mum	Ach ja. Und kannst du fragen, was das für Vögel sind?
You	My mum has another question: *What are those birds?*
Guide	Oh yes! We're lucky to see those birds! They're pelicans and they're very rare. Aren't they beautiful?
You	*Er/Sie sagt, dass das Pelikane sind, sie sind sehr selten. Und er/sie fragt, ob du sie nicht auch schön findest.*

Lösungsbeispiele

▶ 22, Ex 1 a), c) Lösungsbeispiel

for	against
exciting places, lots of things to do, easy to get around, public transport	*traffic,* noise, rubbish, dirty, bad air, expensive
born here, good things to eat, hip-hop beats, cool people, graffiti, favourite place	smells, crowds, grey clouds, graffiti

▶ 23, Ex 3 a) Lösungsbeispiel

More ...	Less/Fewer ...
bike lanes, clean transport, green energy, green spaces and parks, lakes, recycling, second-hand shops, trees	*air pollution,* plastic, rubbish, traffic
☒ more ideas:	
green roofs, pedestrian areas, gardens, bikes	noise cars

▶ 24, Ex 5 Lösungsbeispiel

Waiter Are you ready to order? What would you like to drink?
You   Could I have a mint tea, please?
Waiter And to eat?
You   Can you tell me *what hummus is*?
Waiter It's a dip. You make it from chickpeas.
You   Could I have that please?
Waiter Anything else?
You   Could I have some falafel too, please?
Waiter So for drinks, that's 5 and for food, that's *7 and 11*. Thank you.
You   Thanks.

▶ 26, Ex 2 Lösung
Ali's flat
Knightsbridge (tube station)
Harrods (department store)
Hyde Park
the Lido (Hyde Park's swimming area)
the Lido Cafe
Princess Diana's Memorial Fountain
Peter Pan Statue

Lösungsbeispiele

▶ 28, Ex 3a)   **Lösungsbeispiel**

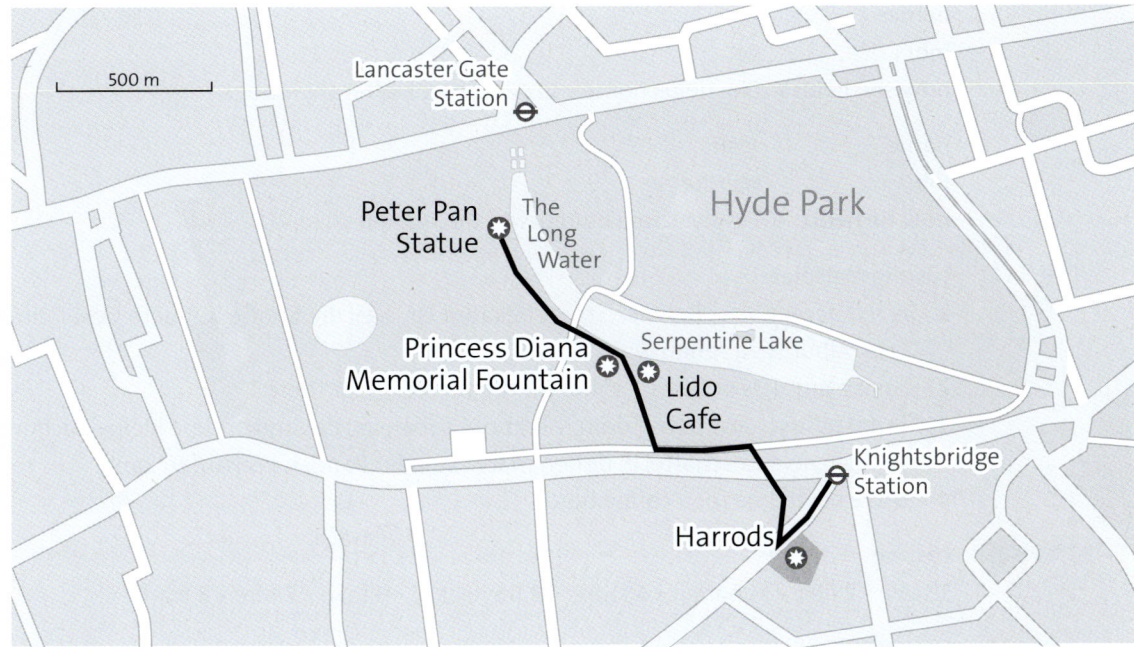

First, they took the tube to Knightsbridge Station. Then they went to Harrods, from there they went to Hyde Park and to the Lido Cafe. After that they went past Princess Diana's Memorial Fountain and finally they got to the Peter Pan Statue.

▶ 28, Ex 3 b)   **Lösungsbeispiel**

place	clue
at Ali's flat	Lily sent photos from Harrods.
Knightsbridge	This is the nearest tube station to Harrods.
Harrods	The doorkeeper remembered Lily – she asked for directions to Hyde Park.
Hyde Park	Ali knows Lily misses the sea and beach in Brighton. Maybe she wanted to swim in the lake (at the Lido) in Hyde Park.
The Lido	The woman behind the desk told them to try the cafe.
The Lido Cafe	Pearl saw Lily's sunglasses – so she was here.
Princess Diana's Memorial Fountain	Pearl remembered that Lily's mum loved Princess Diana. An old lady remembered Lily and gave her directions to Lancaster Gate Station.
Peter Pan Statue	The old lady said they should go past the statue.

▶ 28, Ex 4 c)   **Lösung**

information board die Informationstafel • **path** der Weg, der Pfad • **key ring** der Schlüsselbund, der Schlüsselring • **park bench** die Parkbank

▶ 28, Ex 4 d)   **Lösungsbeispiel**

The story ends in an exciting way.
We want to know if Ali finds Lily before something bad happens.
We want to know if Pearl gets to them in time.
The ending shows how much the friends want to find Lily.

285

Lösungsbeispiele

▶ 29, Ex 2 b) **Lösungsbeispiel**

name:	Jade
job:	vet
how she helps:	She helps homeless people look after their dogs.

name:	Josh
job:	hairdresser
how he helps:	He gives free haircuts to the homeless.

▶ 32, Ex 2 **Lösungsbeispiel**

1 *Sie hat gesagt, dass* Berwick Street bekannt ist, weil die Straße auf dem Cover eines berühmten Oasis-Albums zu sehen war.
2 Can we buy CDs or band T-shirts (in the market) over there?
3 *Sie hat gesagt, dass* es auf dem Markt nur Lebensmittel und andere kleine Sachen gibt. Aber es gibt hier viele Geschäfte, in denen man CDs oder Bandshirts kaufen kann.
4 Do we have time for a coffee here?

▶ 33, Ex 3 a) **Lösung**

1 tube • 2 line • 3 change • 4 stops • 5 Travelcard • 6 take • 7 hire • 8 traffic

▶ 33, Ex 3 b) **Lösungsbeispiel**

A: *It's a nice day. Do you want to go to* St James's Park?
B: *Sure, let's* take the Northern line. It takes 22 minutes and it's direct.
A: *I don't really want to* take the tube *because* it's so busy. *Why don't we* walk? *We can* talk while we walk. It takes 55 minutes and it's 2.7 miles from here.
B: *That's a good idea, and it's* healthy.
A: *Great, let's go!*

▶ 34, Ex 5 **Lösungsbeispiel**

Hi, everybody! I want to tell you about my life in Dortmund. Dortmund is a big city in west Germany. Dortmund is famous for its football team. There are some great things about my city, like a big park, great places to go shopping and a nice zoo. But there are also some problems, like lots of traffic, air pollution and expensive cost of living. What's your city like? I'm looking forward to reading about it in the comments.

▶ 35, Ex 6 b) **Lösungsbeispiel**

Hey, Sunita! *You won't believe what happened today! I went to* the graffiti tunnel with Ali and I saw some amazing art. I brought my paper and pencils to draw some ideas. Ali had to go outside for a bit and I drew a sunset on the beach. Then a boy called Zach came and said he liked my picture. He wants to teach me how to paint on the wall next week. Isn't that cool?

▶ 35, Ex 6 c) **Lösungsbeispiel**

Lily wasn't sure if her picture was good enough. It was just an idea. She was surprised when Ali and Zach said, 'It's a good picture'. She was even more surprised when Zach asked if she wanted to paint it on the tunnel.

▶ 35, Ex 7 **Lösungsbeispiel**

keywords	websites	notes
London + The British Museum	1. https://www.britishmuseum.org	place: … near Central London; tickets: £0; open: 10 a.m.–5 p.m. daily; fun facts: The British Museum has a big collection of art and historical objects such as the Rosetta Stone and Egyptian mummies.

Lösungsbeispiele

▶ 42, MP 6   **Lösung**
1. What time did you get up? – At 7.
2. Did you do anything interesting or exciting at school? – Yes, we had a science experiment in the lab, and it was really fun.
3. Did you eat something nice for lunch? – Yes, I had my favourite pizza.
4. What did you do after school? – I went to the library and then I played football with my friends.
5. Did you have a lot of homework? – No, not really.
6. When did you go to bed? – At about 11.

Unit 2 Manchester: Who we are

▶ 44, Ex 1 b)   **Lösungsbeispiel**

	Omar	reasons
1	his family	They *always support him*.
2	his hometown Manchester	The people are friendly, and it has beautiful canals and a fantastic football team.
3	football	It's the best game ever.
4	his best friend Trent	Trent also loves football and he's really funny.
5	fair play	Fair play is important in football and other sports. It isn't OK when players are mean.
6	clothes and fashion	It's important for Omar to look good.
	Rosie	**reasons**
1	her health	She *has a disability* and can't walk well.
2	her family and friends	Her family and friends help her and they see her, not just her disability.
3	kindness	Some people aren't kind to her, that hurts. Everything is better if people are kind to each other.
4	saving the planet	It's the future.
5	clothes	She likes to try out different styles.
6	her phone	She needs it because sometimes she falls and has to call somebody, also for writing messages to her friends.

▶ 44, Ex 1 c)   **Lösungsbeispiel**

Omar's *family is important to him because they always* support him. Manchester is important to him because the people are friendly, and it has beautiful canals and a fantastic football team. Football is important to him because it's the best game ever. His best friend Trent is important because he loves football too. Clothes are important to Omar because it's important to him how he looks.

Rosie's health is important to her because she has a disability and can't walk well. Her friends and family are important because they don't see her disability, they help her, but don't treat her differently. That's also why kindness is important to her, some people are unkind to her and that hurts. Her phone is important to Rosie because she uses it to write messages to her friends. And she needs her phone to call for help.

Lösungsbeispiele

▶ 46, Ex 2 **Lösungsbeispiel**
- *I'd like to buy* a new dress because I am invited to a wedding.
- *I'd like to shop at* ... or at a shop called ..., they have nice dresses.
- It should be smart and trendy, I think red or colourful would be nice.

▶ 47, Ex 3 c) **Lösungsbeispiel**

I think it's terrible that we produce so many new clothes and that we recycle only 1% of them. *We can buy* clothes from recycled materials or buy second-hand. *Why don't we* take good care of our clothes and repair them instead of always buying new ones?

▶ 48, Ex 1 b) **Lösungsbeispiel**

Liebe Redaktion,
ich habe gerade in meinem Englischbuch etwas über eine Schülerzeitung gelesen. Es geht um eine neue Kolumne. Manchmal haben wir alle ja mal ein Problem. Jetzt kann man dieser Zeitung von Problemen berichten und dann eine Antwort mit einer Idee, wie man das Problem lösen könnte, erhalten. Das geht auch anonym, ohne dass man den Namen oder die Klasse angibt. Vielleicht könnten wir so etwas auch in unserer Schule starten, um Hilfe bei unseren Problemen zu bekommen.
Liebe Grüße

▶ 48, Ex 2 c) **Lösungsbeispiel**

1 'Puzzled friend' *doesn't know if they can trust their friend.*
2 'Angry student' isn't happy because they *always have to be back at 6 o'clock.*
3 'Shy student' *doesn't know if they should tell the girl that they have a crush on her.*
4 'BFF' thinks they *should do something to help their friend.*

▶ 50, Ex 5 b) **Lösung**

They think it's difficult to give advice because they have to think about all the possible situations.

▶ 50, Ex 5 c) **Lösung**

1 false: Her sister had a crush on one of her friends.
2 false: Her friend got a/another girlfriend.
3 true
4 true
5 false: Omar thinks that would be terrible.

▶ 50, Ex 5 d) **Lösungsbeispiel**

I think 'Shy student' might get a good answer and the girl might tell them that she likes them too. Then they could be more than friends. It may also happen that the girl doesn't like 'Shy student' back, that could be bad for their friendship then.

▶ 51, Ex 6 b) **Lösungsbeispiel**

I think both answers are very good advice. I like it that the Hey! Advice column tells the student that they can also ask teachers or their parents for help, that's very important. In the second advice they also tell the student to try to tell their parents about their feelings and not shout, I think that's very good advice.

▶ 51, Ex 6 c) **Lösungsbeispiel**

- *You should call your friend's dad* and tell him that you're worried. You should also do nice things with your friend so that she doesn't think about her difficult situation so much. Then she may feel more ready to talk about her feelings.
- *You shouldn't get angry* or think that your parents make you stay at home because they're mean to you. They just care for you. You should tell them that you understand that they're worried.

Lösungsbeispiele

▶51, Ex 7 a) **Lösungsbeispiel**
(Answer to Letter 1)
Dear student,
Thank you for your letter. We understand why you're upset. We think you shouldn't be afraid to talk to your friend. You should tell them it made you feel bad. You should ask why they say things like this. But we think you shouldn't end the friendship.
Best wishes, the Hey! Advice column

▶53, Ex 4 b) **Lösung**
Marcus Rashford is famous for being
1 a champion footballer,
2 an activist who helps poor children to get free meals,
3 the writer of two books about confidence.

▶54, Ex 5 a) **Lösungsbeispiel**
I think the dancers feel very brave and happy. They must be a bit nervous too because they are dancing in front of many other people in not so normal places for dancing.

▶54, Ex 5 c) **Lösungsbeispiel**
I really liked the video, it made me feel confident and it made me think that I shouldn't care about what others think and that I should do what I like.

▶54, Ex 6 a) **Lösungsbeispiel**
I feel more confident when I wear my favourite clothes • when I'm with my best friend • when I do yoga • when I put on nice make-up • when I spend time with my family • when I buy new clothes • when I have a good day

▶54, Ex 6 b) **Lösungsbeispiel**

You should …	You shouldn't …
stand up straight speak clearly and loudly feel free to repeat yourself wear clothes that make you feel good smile	*slouch* shout interrupt others apologize / say sorry for being you

▶56, Ex 2 **Lösungsbeispiel**
The main characters are Omar and his best friend Trent.
They support different football teams. Omar supports Manchester City and Trent supports Manchester United.
The other characters are Omar's sister and dad and Trent's cousin Ollie.
Omar's sister and dad support Manchester City and Ollie supports Manchester United.
The conflict is between Omar, his sister and dad and Ollie, Trent's cousin.
It happens because Manchester City wins and Manchester United fans get angry. When Omar and his family want to leave, Ollie calls them racist names.

▶58, Ex 5 a) **Lösungsbeispiel**
Omar's dad tells Omar and his sister to not look at the nasty fans and keep walking. When Ollie pushes him, Omar's dad tries to pull Omar away to keep him safe.

▶58, Ex 5 b) **Lösungsbeispiel**
I think Omar's dad is right because he doesn't want to get into a dangerous situation when he's there with his children. He could also ask other people to help or call the police.

Lösungsbeispiele

▶ 58, Ex 6 a)   **Lösungsbeispiel**
Trent was really shocked when his cousin pushed Omar's dad, but also scared so he took a moment to think how to answer Omar's question. He decided that he should be brave and help his friend. He said: 'Of course I'm your friend. Ollie, please stop saying racist things to my friend and his family. And say sorry for pushing Omar's dad!' Ollie didn't know that Omar and Trent were friends. He said that he made a mistake and that he was sorry.

▶ 59, Ex 1   **Lösungsbeispiel**
1 They're going to an international football match.
2 He has an English flag because he's supporting the English national team.
3 There are English football fans on the coach.
4 The car breaks down and they ask for a ride on the coach.
5 There's a conflict between David's dad and the fans on the coach so he doesn't want to join them.

▶ 59, Ex 3   **Lösungsbeispiel**
1 I think that David's dad was already very stressed from the situation: he was in a different country, there was a problem with the car and the fans were loud. Maybe one of the fans said something nasty to him.
2 David saw that the fans hurt his dad so he changed his mind and helped him.
3 I think it was a really good film, it shows the problems of kids who want to break rules and have fun, but it also shows that bad things can happen, that the rules of our parents are not always bad for us and that they only want the best for their children. *I liked the part when* they sang the same song again that they were singing in the beginning.

▶ 62, Ex 1 a)   **Lösungsbeispiel**
My family is most important to me because they're always there for me, and so are my friends. I also really enjoy travelling. My room is my safe space for me. My phone and sport are not that important to me. (F – E – C – D – A – B)

▶ 62, Ex 1 c)   **Lösungsbeispiel**
Ethan   Home (D) – He feels safe and happy there. He loves to go home and see his dog, play some music and relax.
Hafsa   Hockey team (A) – They have played together for a long time, so they know each other really well. She can talk to the people in her team about everything.
Ryan   Grandparents (F) – His parents work late, so he spends a lot of time with his grandparents. They always listen to him.
Laura   Travel (C) – She learns so much when she goes to different countries. It never gets boring for her.

▶ 62, Ex 2 b)   **Lösungsbeispiel**
I'm going to wear the outfit that I bought when I was in a second hand shop with my mum. It's a dress with two colours and it was just 5 euros. The material is cotton. I think my outfit will look very cute.

▶ 63, Ex 3 b)   **Lösungsbeispiel**
Hi Aya,
I understand that you feel worried and sad because you can't come to Zoe's party. I think you should ask your parents again. Try to tell them how important this party is to you and that you can do your homework in the morning. If you do that, maybe they will say you can come!

Lösungsbeispiele

▶63, Ex 4 **Lösungsbeispiel**
Lieber Ole,
ich habe gerade in einer englischen Schulzeitung über einen Jungen gelesen, der das gleiche Problem hat wie du: Sein bester Freund hat eine neue Freundin und er kann nicht mehr so viel Zeit mit ihm verbringen. *Das Zeitungsteam rät ihm,* seinem Freund zu erklären, wie er sich fühlt. *Er soll* dabei ruhig bleiben. *Vielleicht* könnt ihr euch auf eine spezielle Aktivität einigen, die ihr jede Woche nur zu zweit macht?
Schöne Grüße …

▶64, Ex 5 a) **Lösungsbeispiel**
The girl in picture 2 looks confident. She's smiling and standing up straight.
The boy in picture 3 doesn't look confident. He looks nervous. He isn't looking up and he's slouching.

▶64, Ex 5 b) **Lösungsbeispiel**
I feel most confident when I'm with my friends because when I'm with them, I can be myself. They're never unfair or mean. That makes me feel comfortable.

▶64, Ex 6 a) **Lösungsbeispiel**
If you ask me, dogs are the best because you can play games with them!
I think chocolate is better than cheese because it's sweet.
I would say that football is better than basketball because you can play it anywhere.
If you ask me, computers are better than phones because they're bigger.
I think snow is better than the sun because you can go skiing.

▶64, Ex 6 b) **Lösungsbeispiel**
I don't agree with Jack at all because dogs are loud.
In my opinion, cheese is better than chocolate because it's not so sweet.
In my opinion, phones are better than computers because you can take them everywhere.

▶64, Ex 6 c) **Lösungsbeispiel**
In my opinion, bikes are better than cars because they're better for your health.
In my opinion, books are better than TV shows because you can read them anywhere and you don't need a TV to read them.
I think Sundays are better than Saturdays because it's a day for relaxing.
I think old-fashioned clothes are better than modern clothes because they're made from better material.

▶65, Ex 7 c) **Lösungsbeispiel**
I don't think that Omar wanted to upset Rosie. I think he thought he would help her by giving her something to do where she can sit down and doesn't have to stand.

▶70, Ch 1 **Lösungsbeispiel**
Nia has the shortest trousers.
Her hair is shorter *than* Ada's *hair.*
Max has the shortest hair.
Max has the longest trousers.
Nia's trousers are darker than Ada's.
Max has the darkest trousers.
Max's trousers are baggier than Nia's trousers.
…

▶71, MP 3 a) **Lösungsbeispiel**
feelings   *upset,* puzzled, embarrassed, angry, shy, sad …
personality   *helpful,* nerdy, uncool, strict, nice, clever, positive, funny, interesting, chatty, fun, quiet, …

291

Lösungsbeispiele

▶ 72, MP 6 a) Lösungsbeispiel
1. *You should go on a talk show.*
2. She should go on a talk show.
3. You shouldn't go into the garden.
4. You shouldn't worry: you can run much faster with four legs.
5. You should take them to the doctor's.
6. You should move to another house.

Unit 3 Scotland: Adventure

▶ 74, Ex 1 a) Lösungsbeispiel
- Scotland is (in) the north of the UK.
- Capital: Edinburgh
- Biggest city: Glasgow
- People speak English and Scottish Gaelic.
- Bagpipes are a traditional Scottish instrument.
- 'Loch' is Scottish for 'lake'.
- Loch Ness near Inverness is famous for its monster (Nessie).
- Kilts are part of traditional Scottish clothing.

▶ 74, Ex 1 c) Lösungsbeispiel

Place or activity	Grace	Rhona
Edinburgh	the castle is cool; many shops are expensive for tourists; they sell mainly kilts and tartan things	aunt and uncle live there; it sounds really exciting there won't be much shopping on the school trip
Inverness	lives in Inverness, it's cool likes cycling by the river	likes cycling by the river too
Loch Ness	doesn't believe in a monster	hopes to see the monster
Eilean Donan Castle	(no information)	loves castles; hopes to see the ghost that lives in the castle
Kayaking	can't wait to go kayaking; thinks it will be great	thinks kayaking looks easy; is a good swimmer
Ben Nevis	is looking forward to hiking in the mountains; hiked up Ben Nevis before and thought it was fun	thinks that hiking up Ben Nevis won't be easy (because it's the highest mountain in the UK)

▶ 76, Ex 1 c)
▶ 100, Ex 1 c) Lösungsbeispiel
Partner A Scientists found some big creatures in the loch, but they didn't find Nessie.
Partner B Scientists found no monsters or catfish in Loch Ness, but they found many eels. Another scientist said that eels can't be that big.

▶ 76, Ex 1 d)
▶ 100, Ex 1 d) Lösungsbeispiel
Partner A *The main idea of my article is that* there's something big in the loch, but nobody knows what it is. It says that there are two famous pictures of the monster. Scientists used special sonar equipment, but didn't find Nessie. They only discovered other large living creatures.

Partner B *The main idea of my article is that* Nessie might be a very large eel, but nobody knows. It says that scientists have found no monsters or catfish in the loch, but they found many eels. Another scientist argues that eels can't be that large.

▶ 77, Ex 2 b) **Lösungsbeispiel**

In my opinion, it's just a legend. I think people saw something in the loch, but they didn't know what it was. Because they couldn't explain what they saw, they told a story about a monster.

▶ 77, Ex 3
▶ 101, Ex 3

Lösungsbeispiel

Hi Grace!
Thanks for your message about the Loch Ness monster! I want to tell you about a German legend.
A young woman called Loreley was very in love with a young knight. They wanted to get married and on their wedding day Loreley waited for her knight on a high cliff. She waited there for a long, long time, but the knight didn't come. It broke her heart.
From this day on, Lorely sat on the cliff every day. She brushed her long golden hair and cried and sang sad songs with her beautiful voice. Every time sailors passed the cliffs in their boats, they looked up at Loreley and listened to her songs. Because they only had eyes for Loreley, their ships hit the dangerous rocks and sank.
Love,
Smilla

▶ 78, Ex 4 c) **Lösungsbeispiele**

1 ghost was a Spanish soldier, he stayed in the castle in 1719, wanted to help a group of Scottish Catholics to kill the king, the king's soldiers destroyed the castle and killed everyone
2 ghost wears old-fashioned clothes and looks sad
3 ghost walks around the castle, carries his head under his arm
4 ghost is called 'Carlos'

▶ 80, Ex 1 a) **Lösungsbeispiel**

Picture	Sport	Where you do this sport
1	*cliff jumping*	*by the sea*
2	rafting	on a river, on the sea
3	paddleboarding	on the sea, on a lake, on a river
4	snowboarding	in the mountains, on snow
5	hiking	in the mountains, in the countryside
6	skiing	in the mountains, on snow

▶ 80, Ex 1 b) **Lösungsbeispiel**

Rhona is worried because she gets nervous when she has to try new things.

▶ 80, Ex 1 c) **Lösungsbeispiel**

Grace has tried hiking, paddle boarding and skiing (on fake snow). *She hasn't tried* snow-boarding.
Rhona has tried snowboarding. *She hasn't tried* hiking, paddle boarding and skiing.

▶ 81, Ex 2 b) **Lösung**

Verbs with three different parts:
be, was, been • *see, saw,* seen • *fly, flew,* flown • *show, showed,* shown • *draw, drew,* drawn • *wear, wore,* worn • *break, broke,* broken • *speak, spoke,* spoken • *drive, drove,* driven • *give, gave,* given • *shake, shook,* shaken • *take, took,* taken • *ride, rode,* ridden • *write, wrote,* written

Lösungsbeispiele

Echo verbs:
buy, bought, bought • *bring, brought,* brought • *fight, fought,* fought • *think, thought,* thought • *keep, kept,* kept • *sleep, slept,* slept • *say, said,* said • *read, read,* read • *make, made,* made • *pay, paid,* paid • *sit, sat,* sat • *have, had,* had

Sandwich verbs:
become, became, become • *come, came,* come • *run, ran,* run

Cat verbs:
drink, drank, drunk • *swim, swam,* swum • *sing, sang,* sung • *begin, began,* begun

Chicken verbs:
put, put, put • *cut, cut,* cut • *cost, cost,* cost • *hit, hit,* hit • *hurt, hurt,* hurt • *set, set,* set

▶ 81, Ex 3   **Lösung**
1. Have you packed *your rain jacket*?
2. *Yes, I have.* I have just done *that*.
3. Have you remembered *your water bottle*?
4. *Yes, I have.* I've already put *it in my rucksack*.
5. Has Ms McKenzie called *us yet*?
6. *No, she hasn't.* But I've already finished *my packing*.
7. *You're so organized*! Have you ever forgotten *anything*?
8. *No, I haven't.* I've never forgotten *anything*.

▶ 81, Ex 4 a)   **Lösungsbeispiel**
Have you ever caught a fish?
Have you ever gone to the mountains?
Have you ever climbed a tree?
Have you ever jumped from a cliff?
Have you ever ridden a pony?
Have you ever gone on a zip wire?
Have you ever slept in a tent?
Have you ever slept under the stars?
Have you ever swum in a lake or river?

▶ 82, Ex 5 a)   **Lösungsbeispiel**
I think he's brave because he does dangerous activities like climbing mountains.
I think he's fit and sporty because he does many adventure sports.
I think he's clever because he needs to plan adventures really well.

▶ 82, Ex 5 b)   **Lösungsbeispiel**
The biography is about the adventurer Aldo Kane, his life, outdoor experiences and skills and what's important to him (in his job).

▶ 82, Ex 5 c)   **Lösungsbeispiel**
He has done mountain climbing and skydiving.
He has travelled through the jungles (of South America).
He has climbed into an active volcano, swum through underwater caves and run away from angry wild animals.
He has taken part in adventure programmes on TV.
He has helped with safety on TV programmes and film sets.
He has written a book about his adventures.

Lösungsbeispiele

▶ 83, Ex 7 — **Lösungsbeispiel**
1 *How long have you been awake today? – For four hours. What about you?*
2 *How long have you had your favourite T-shirt? – For five years.*
3 *How long have you known me? – Since kindergarten.*
4 *How long have you liked your favourite singer? – Since I was a kid.*
5 *How long have you lived in your city? – For ten years now.*

▶ 84, Ex 1 b) — **Lösungsbeispiel**
- **landscapes** *countryside, island*, mountains, hill, forest, river, coast, …
- **wild animals** *deer, dolphin,* fox, bear, butterfly, rabbit, seagull, …
- **things in nature** *tree, path,* flower, plant, grass …
- **farm animals** *chicken, goat,* sheep, cow, cat, dog …

▶ 85, Ex 2 c) — **Lösung**
1 true
2 true
3 false – 'to the braes'
4 false – 'of the hills and sky and nature'

▶ 85, Ex 2 d) — **Lösung**
- **landscapes** braes, mountain, sky
- **wild animals** deer, rabbit
- **things in nature** blueberries, heather, flower, fountain

▶ 88, Ex 2 — **Lösungsbeispiel**
1 *Grace helped* Rhona when she hurt her ankle, *but she* wanted to take the dangerous path.
2 *Rhona used* the app on her phone to find out where they were, *but she* wore trainers instead of walking boots.

▶ 88, Ex 3 — **Lösungsbeispiel**

order	summary	contrast	result
then	*in the end*	*but*	*so*
later	*eventually*	*however*	*therefore*
soon	*finally*		

▶ 88, Ex 5 a) — **Lösungsbeispiel**
Grace *I'm sorry, it was a bad idea to* take the different path.
Rhona *I'm sorry I forgot to* tell you that I'm afraid of heights.
That's OK. / Thank you for saying sorry.

▶ 92, Ex 1 — **Lösungsbeispiel**
I'd like to visit Edinburgh Castle. I'm really interested in castles and history. It's cheaper than Edinburgh Zoo. I don't want to go to the zoo because I have already been there.

▶ 93, Ex 4 — **Lösungsbeispiel**
Hi Mark, I want to tell you about Rüdiger Nehberg. He was born in 1935. He was an adventurer and activist. He lived in Hamburg where he worked as a baker. Then, he became more interested in travel and adventure. He travelled to so many countries, often with no water, food or other things he needed. He worked to support people all over the world for many years. He won a prize for his work.

Lösungsbeispiele

▶ 94, Ex 5 **Lösungsbeispiel**
Dear Michelle,
I'm camping in Scotland at the moment. We're in the Scottish Highlands. The landscape is beautiful. It's so quiet here. Sometimes I can hear the birds singing and I can see far away from the top of the mountain. I can see lots of beautiful mountains and lochs. Yesterday I went hiking and saw a beautiful sunset. I like it here because it's quiet and relaxing and the nature is beautiful.
Best wishes, ...

▶ 94, Ex 6 **Lösung**
- **who** two boys – James and Hussein; James – nervous; Hussein – brave
- **why** want to see the monster
- **when** last summer
- **where** on Loch Ness, Scotland
- **what** school trip • big storm • lights on the boat stop working • James thinks he sees a big animal in the water, but it's very dark ...

▶ 95, Ex 7 c) **Lösungsbeispiel**
1 bad choice because they should focus on the boat at all times
2 bad choice because all of their things should be in the dry bag
3 bad choice because there were rocks under the boat
4 good choice because the instructor is there to help

Unit 4 Wales: Digital life

▶ 106, Ex 1 a) **Lösungsbeispiel**
Wales is in the west of the UK. Wales is the smallest country in Britain.
People speak English and Welsh. Welsh is an official language.
The capital is Cardiff, it's in the south of Wales.
Llandudno is in the north of Wales by the sea. It has a nice beach with a pier and donkeys.
There are many castles in Wales (about 600). One of them is called Conwy Castle (it's near Llandudno).
There are about ten million sheep in Wales. Wales uses green energy. The national sport is rugby.

▶ 107, Ex 2 b) **Lösungsbeispiel**
A *Owen* speaks Welsh at home with his parents, he learned Welsh as a child. He plays table tennis and sings in the choir. Owen prefers to meet friends in real life.
Dylan is in the school's rugby team; he's always on social media.
Both are from Cymru (Wales), they live in Llandundo. They are in class 9A at Prince of Wales School. They learn Welsh at school, they are proud of their country.
B *Llandundo* is a popular tourist destination. It's a small town by the sea, there are a beach and a pier. There are lots of things to do in Llandundo: you can ride donkeys on the beach, go swimming, buy souvenirs, play lots of different sports. You can even ride the tram up the hill to see the highest mountain in Wales, Snowdon.
Wales: Cymru means Wales in Welsh. The flag of Wales has a red dragon and a green and white background. There are lots of stories and legends about dragons and castles. Rugby is the Welsh national sport. People love singing in Wales. Wales was famous for coal mining, but now has green energy and lots of tech industries and great internet. There are many sheep, about three times more sheep than people! Prince William is the Prince of Wales. A waterfall in Wales is home to the Batcave in one of the Batman films. You can visit it for free.

Lösungsbeispiele

▶109, Ex 4 a) **Lösungsbeispiel**
Places: Cardiff, Conwy, Llandundo, Brecon Beacons, Aberystwyth, GreenWood theme park, …
Activities: ride donkeys on the beach, go swimming, do sports (e.g. rugby), ride the tram up the hill, visit a castle / a city / a beach / a pier, go shopping, …

▶109, Ex 4 b) **Lösungsbeispiel**
Hi, Dylan, thank you for the song! I think it's great. *I'm looking forward to the visit* in Wales. I'd like to visit some old castles because I love legends about castles and dragons. I really want to see the Batcave because Batman is my favourite superhero. And I hope we can go shopping and buy some souvenirs.

▶110, Ex 1 b) **Lösung**
1 They're acting in a TV show. • **2** He's going to miss TV most. • **3** *individuelle Lösungen*

▶110, Ex 1 c) **Lösungsbeispiel**
I was surprised that …
… there's no electricity or gas.
… there's no bathroom in the house.
… the men have to walk to work.
… they don't go to the shops, but the shops come to them.
… they make presents themselves.
… men meet up to sing.

▶110, Ex 1 d) **Lösungsbeispiel**
1 *Women and girls wore cardigans, dresses, aprons,* boots. *Men and boys wore waistcoats,* caps, shorts (boys), trousers (men), shirts.
2 They didn't have a bathroom, they washed in the kitchen. They used a fire to heat water. There were no washing machines, they washed their clothes by hand.
3 They walked everywhere because there was no car or bus. The men walked to work for 1 ½ hours.
4 A shop with food came to their houses, they got eggs from chickens. They cooked on a fire in the kitchen (and made cakes and biscuits).
5 They sang at church (the men) and at home, and they played games.
6 They used candles and oil lamps.

▶111, Ex 2 a) **Lösungsbeispiel**
do sports • play football, tennis, basketball, hockey • play the guitar • play chess, card games, video games • dance • watch a film, videos • go to the cinema • hang out with friends • use the computer, social media • read a book, a magazine, a comic

▶112, Ex 4 c) **Lösung**
A cut the parts that we don't need
B add captions
C check the edited video
D save the video
E install an editing app
F add music
G upload the video to the app

▶113, Ex 6 a)
▶132, Ex 6 a) **Lösungsbeispiel**
1 *Zuerst musst du* die Smartwatch vollständig aufladen.
2 Dann musst du die richtige App für dein Handy installieren.
3 Schalte die Smartwatch an.
4 Berühre den Bildschirm, um zu beginnen. Wähle die Sprache.
5 Starte die App auf deinem Handy.

Lösungsbeispiele

▶113, Ex 6 b) **Lösungsbeispiel**
▶132, Ex 6 b)
6 *Als Nächstes musst du* die Uhr einrichten.
7 Du musst die allgemeinen Geschäftsbedingungen lesen und ihnen zustimmen.
8 Tippe auf den Namen deiner Uhr in der App auf dem Handy.
9 Verbinde nun dein Handy mit der Uhr. Dafür musst du „Verbinden" antippen.
10 Und jetzt verbinde noch die Smartwatch mit dem WLAN.

▶113, Ex 7 **Lösungsbeispiel**
1 Press the 'Print screen' key on your keyboard.
2 Copy your screenshot into an app as a new picture.
3 Click on the picture with your mouse.
4 Click on 'Format picture'.
5 Edit the screenshot.
6 Save the picture.

▶114, Ex 2 b) **Lösungsbeispiel**
• *I think* Zenn *is more useful because you can* use it to talk to other teens about your problems.
• *I think* Clok *is more useful because* it helps you to stay healthy and fit.
• *I think both apps are* useful because you can use them for two different things.

▶115, Ex 3 b) **Lösung**
Dylan *is helping* Owen *to* set up a social media account.

▶115, Ex 3 c) **Lösung**
asking for help: Could you …? • Can you …?
offering help: I can help you if you like. • Shall I …? • Would you like me to …?

▶116, Ex 5 b) **Lösungsbeispiel**
Text A has facts, is an article from a news website called Llandudno Times.
Text B has opinions, seems to be a post on social media.

▶116, Ex 5 c) **Lösungsbeispiel**
1 (A) '*Ditch The Label* is a charity … It has researched how …'
2 (B) 'I hate … I can't believe …'
3 (A) '97% of teenagers …'
4 (B) 'We must stop …'; 'Social media is the worst thing EVER …'
5 (B) 'The person that invented social media wanted all teens to be mean …'
6 (A) 'However, there's good news too …'

▶117, Ex 8 a) **Lösungsbeispiel**
▶137, Ex 8 a)
Partner A *I believe that social media is a good thing for teens because* they can keep in touch with their friends and learn about what's going on in their lives. It also lets them share important information and just have fun. For teens who are shy or who don't know many people with the same interests, social media can be a good way to make connections.
Partner B *I think one of the problems with social media is that* it can be used for bullying. Many teenagers experience cyberbullying and it can be really difficult to do something about it because many teenagers don't tell anybody about the messages they see. Another problem is that it's very easy to lie about who you are on social media. Some people act as somebody else on social media and that can be dangerous.

▶118, Ex 1 a) **Lösungsbeispiel**
I think that Dylan is going to post photos on social media that don't look like him.
I think that Owen is going to post a different photo of Dylan.
Maybe the story is about how on social media you can act as if you were somebody you are not.

Lösungsbeispiele

▶ 124, Ex 1 b) **Lösungsbeispiel**
1 false – You can't drive up to the castle.
2 false – Only one castle has a cafe.
3 true
4 false – Castell Dinas Brân is free / the cheapest.
5 true
6 true

▶ 125, Ex 2 **Lösungsbeispiel**
1 *I wrote that it's* a small town by the sea and that it's very pretty.
2 *I wrote that we* will watch a rugby game on Saturday because your parents are big rugby fans.
3 *I'm* excited about the match.
4 *I wrote that we* went to the pier and ate ice cream. After that we went to the beach and played with your dog.

▶ 126, Ex 4 c) **Lösungsbeispiel**
My experience with social media is mostly positive because I'm really careful which information I share online. *I had a bad experience when* somebody posted a bad photo of me and everybody in my school saw it.

▶ 126, Ex 5 c) **Lösungsbeispiel**
1 Elsa – It's bad advice because online dates aren't always bad.
2 Marie – It's bad advice because there are real reviews too / not everything on the internet is fake.
3 Oskar – It's bad advice because buying things online can be safe, you just have to be careful.
4 Hadi – It's good advice because it tells you to be careful and not to believe everything you see.

▶ 126, Ex 5 d) **Lösungsbeispiel**
Some people on social media don't believe that nature must be protected. They post fake facts and hope that people who read the fake facts will believe them. When you read fake facts all the time it can become difficult to know what the truth is.

▶ 132, MP 1 **Lösung**

City	Where	About the city	Sights	Other information
Cardiff	south Wales	capital of Wales, biggest city in Wales	Cardiff Castle, Principality Stadium (rugby matches), Millennium Centre (concerts)	
Swansea	south-west Wales	second biggest Welsh city, modern city	Carreg Cennen Castle	many parks, beautiful beaches
Wrexham	north-east Wales	very old city	Pontcysyllte Aqueduct (you can go across with a boat)	Wrexham's football club was bought by two Hollywood actors (and became famous)

Lösungsbeispiele

▶ 135, Ch 1 **Lösung**
1 *Dylan and Owen* are going to be late.
2 *Oh no! Owen's phone* is going to fall.
3 *Owen's parents* aren't going to be happy.
4 *Owen* is going to be sick.
5 *It* isn't going to rain.
6 *Dylan* isn't going to win.

▶ 135, MP 4 **Lösungsbeispiel**
A Hi, how are things?
B Great, thanks.
A Can we meet up to practice our presentation?
B Yes, sure. How about …
A Sorry, I can't hear you. You're breaking up.
B How about tomorrow afternoon at 2 o'clock?
A Yes, that's fine. Oh, one more thing: Could we meet at your house? My …
B Can you say that again, please?
A Can we meet at your house? My mum is meeting some friends at our house tomorrow.
B Yes, no problem. Sorry, I have to go now. Bye!
A Bye!

▶ 135, MP 5 **Lösungsbeispiel**
Switch on/off the lights.
Turn on/off the TV.
Open/close the windows / the doors.
Lock the doors.
Start the coffee machine.
Play some music.
Tell me the time.
Look up …
Set an alarm for … / Set a timer for …

▶ 136, MP 7 **Lösungsbeispiel**
1 *A smartphone is a device which you can use to* call or text people or to go on the internet.
2 *A YouTuber is a* person who uploads videos to their video channel.
3 *A smartwatch is a* device that helps you with your fitness and well-being.
4 A video channel is a page which has lots of videos on it.
5 A developer is a person who programs websites or apps.

▶ 136, Ch 2 **Lösungsbeispiel**
This is something that you can use to play music, so only you can hear it. (**headphones**)
This is something that you use to write/type words on your computer. (**a keyboard**)
This is something that you can use to click on things on your computer screen. (**a mouse**)
This is something that shows what was on your computer screen after you have closed it. (**a screenshot**)
This is an app on which you can watch many interesting/funny short videos. (**my favourite site**)
This is a person who posts pictures of cool outfits and talks about fashion and upcycling on their social media accounts. (**my favourite influencer**)

Unit 5 Two Irelands: Together

▶138, Ex 1 a) **Lösungsbeispiel**

Northern Ireland is part of the UK. The capital of Northern Ireland is Belfast.
Ireland is an independent country. The capital of Ireland is Dublin.
Before 1922 Ireland was part of the UK. But after a lot of fighting the Republic of Ireland became independent and Northern Ireland stayed in the UK.

▶138, Ex 1 b) **Lösungsbeispiel**

	city	problems in the past	favourite places
Jack	*Belfast*	fighting and bombs checkpoints 'the Troubles' conflicts/fighting between Protestants and Catholics	River Lagan Giant's Causeway
Orla	Limerick	Ireland was one big country before the English took over the island. Some people (mostly Catholics) want the two countries to become one again; others (mostly Protestants) want Northern Ireland to stay part of the UK.	Limerick (castle, shops, river) Dublin (the capital city, live music, St Patrick's Day Parade)

▶139, Ex 1 d) **Lösungsbeispiel**

A *Belfast: a sculpture in the city centre*
B Giant's Causeway: sunrise/sunset
C Belfast: street art at one of the old checkpoints
D Limerick: sunrise/sunset over a lake
E Dublin: live music in a pub
F Dublin: St Patrick's Day Parade

▶140, Ex 2 c) **Lösungsbeispiel**

1 They want to stay for three nights.
2 They're going to travel by bus.
3 They're going to stay at a B&B.
4 They want two/twin beds, their own bathroom, Wi-Fi, a kettle and a vegetarian cooked breakfast.

▶140, Ex 2 d) **Lösungsbeispiel**

Northern Ireland is part of the UK, they use British money. But Orla doesn't need a passport to go there because the Republic of Ireland and the UK have a travel agreement.

▶141, Ex 3 a), b)
▶152, Ex 3 a), b)

Lösung

a) **Partner B's answers:** The Beyond B&B
1 £85 • 2 yes • 3 yes • 4 yes • 5 yes • 6 yes • 7 in the centre of Belfast, vegetarian breakfast option available

b) **Partner A's answers:** Ivy House B&B
1 £95 • 2 yes • 3 yes • 4 yes • 5 no • 6 no • 7 free water bottles in every room, living room with TV, books and games, breakfast buffet, garden

Lösungsbeispiele

▶ 141, Ex 3 c) **Lösungsbeispiel**
The Beyond B&B is better for Orla and her mum because it's cheaper, there's a kettle in the room and there's a cooked breakfast with vegetarian alternatives.

▶ 143, Ex 2 b) **Lösungsbeispiel**
Orla and her mum are going to do the black cab tour in the morning. Orla is going to spend the afternoon with Jack. He's going to show her around Belfast.

▶ 143, Ex 2 c) **Lösungsbeispiel**

Belfast Castle	Orla doesn't want to see it, there are a lot of castles (back home) in Limerick
Peace Walls tour	Orla thinks there may be sad stories; later she says that it actually sounds fun.
Market	There's music, Orla loves music.
Shopping	Orla hates shopping for clothes.

▶ 143, Ex 3 **Lösungsbeispiel**
1 We'd like one room with a double bed and a second room with twin beds for our two sons.
2 We'd prefer rooms that aren't on the ground floor. But we'll have many bags. Is there a lift?
3 One of our sons is vegan. Can you offer vegan breakfast alternatives?

▶ 143, Ex 4 a) **Lösungsbeispiel**
– Belfast is the capital city of Northern Ireland. Northern Ireland is part of the UK.
– If you're Irish you don't need a passport to go to Belfast / Northern Ireland even if it is not part of the EU because there's an agreement between the Republic of Ireland and the UK. You pay in £.
– There are many things to do: you can visit Belfast Castle / St George's Market / the Murals / …, do a black cab tour to learn more about Belfast's history and the Troubles, …
– The Titanic was built in Belfast.
– You can do a day trip to the Giant's Causeway.

▶ 143, Ex 4 b) **Lösungsbeispiel**
Hi, …! Yes, Belfast is a great place to visit!
I can really recommend these sights and activities: Go and see the Murals because you can really learn a lot about Irish history there. And then there's the Titanic Belfast museum, you must go there because you loved the film so much! And then there's St George's Market, a great place for shopping and listening to local street music.
I hope you have a great time! …

▶ 144, Ex 1 a) **Lösungsbeispiel**
I think the story is about the dance competition.
In the first picture, Orla looks surprised to see Jack and Jack looks annoyed to see Orla.
In the second and third picture you can see Orla and Jack dancing.
Orla and Jack both dance in the competition.

▶ 144, Ex 1 b) **Lösungsbeispiel**
The main competitors are

Jack	very good dancer, nearly got top marks, first after first routine, from Belfast
Declan	third place after first routine, mean, did well in the freestyle category, from Belfast
Quinn	is in the top four, from Dublin
Orla	good dancer, confident that she's going to beat Jack, second place after first routine, needs to beat Jack, Declan and Quinn to get in the first three and beat Jack to win, performed perfectly until she was distracted by the audience, from Dublin

Lösungsbeispiele

▶ 147, Ex 3 b) **Lösungsbeispiel**

First Tina 2 talked to Tina's parents and took their tablets and threw food at them.
Then she went out to the dance class and did her own dance.
When Tina found Tina 2, they argued and fought, then danced together. Finally Tina 2 went away.

▶ 147, Ex 4 a) **Lösungsbeispiel**

She helped her to be more confident / less shy.
She helped her to talk to the boy / make friends.
She helped her to get on better with her parents.

▶ 148, Ex 1 **Lösungsbeispiel**

Es gibt viele Unterschiede zwischen Irland und Nordirland: z. B. bezahlt man in Irland mit Euro. Weil Nordirland zum Vereinigten Königreich gehört, wird dort hingegen mit Pfund bezahlt. Irland ist in der EU, während Nordirland, wie der Rest des Vereinigten Königreichs, nicht in der EU ist. In beiden Ländern wird Englisch gesprochen und Tee getrunken.
In Irland zeigen Verkehrsschilder Kilometer an, während in Nordirland Meilen verwendet werden. In beiden Ländern fährt man auf der linken Seite, aber Vorsicht, viele Straßen sind nur breit genug für ein Auto!
Viele Menschen in beiden Ländern sind sportbegeistert. Fußball ist überall beliebt, aber Gaelic Football ist in Irland beliebter als in Nordirland. Es unterscheidet sich vom gewöhnlichen Fußball: es gibt 15 Spieler pro Team und es ist eine Mischung aus Fußball, Rugby und Basketball.
Die irische Flagge ist grün, weiß und orange. In Nordirland sieht man die Flagge des Vereinigten Königreichs – den Union Jack, der rot, weiß und blau ist.

▶ 148, Ex 2 c) **Lösungsbeispiel**

A *Bay View hotel, good morning. How* can I help you?
B *Hello, I need* a room for tonight, please.
A How many people is it for?
B It's for me and my friend.
A A room for two... Would you like a double bed or twin beds?
B Twin beds would be great. We'll arrive around 11.15. Would that be alright?
A 11.15 is fine. You can pay when you get here.
B Thank you! See you later.

▶ 149, Ex 3 b) **Lösungsbeispiel**

I *visited** the Giant's Causeway near Belfast *when I was on holiday* and I want to share my experience with you.
The place is so beautiful and the views are amazing. We had a great *tour guide* who knew a lot of *interesting* facts and the best part is that the tour was free!
Unfortunately, there were a lot of people and it was very windy and cold, so make sure to wear warm clothes. Also, the cafe there is a bit *expensive*.
I had a great time and I think you should visit the Giant's Causeway if you can handle the crowd and cool weather – *5 stars from me*.

(*Die *kursiven* Begriffe sind aus Ex 3a), S. 149 wiederverwendet.)

Methodisch-didaktisches Glossar

Acrostic (Akrostichon) — Das Akrostichon (griechisch *akros*: Spitze, *stichos*: Vers) ist eine Versform, bei der die Zeilenanfänge hintereinander gelesen einen Sinn, z.B. einen Namen oder einen Satz, ergeben. Dies können Buchstaben bei reinen Wortfolgen oder Worte bei Versfolgen sein.

Im Unterricht wird meist folgende vereinfachte Form eingesetzt: Die Buchstaben eines Wortes werden senkrecht untereinandergeschrieben. Jeder Buchstabe kommt auch in einem anderen Wort vor (häufig als Anfangsbuchstabe), diese Wörter werden waagerecht um das senkrechte Startwort angeordnet.

Alphabet game — Die S spielen das *Alphabet game* in Kleingruppen à vier bis fünf S. Ein/-e S schreibt das Alphabet auf einen Zettel. Allen Gruppen wird das Thema genannt, dann beginnen sie gleichzeitig, zu jedem Buchstaben ein zum Thema passendes Wort aufzuschreiben.

Variante 1: L stoppt die Gruppen nach einer vorgegebenen Zeit (z.B. zwei Minuten).

Variante 2: Die Gruppe, die als Erstes zu jedem Buchstaben ein Wort gefunden hat, ruft: „Stopp!" Da es besonders schwer ist, Begriffe mit den Buchstaben k, q und x zu finden, sollten sie besonders für Variante 2 ausgeklammert werden. Es kann aber vereinbart werden, dass sie Extrapunkte liefern.

Auswertung: Die Vokabeln können gemeinsam, z.B. an der Tafel, gesammelt werden, um eine Vokabelliste zu einem Thema zu erstellen. Alternativ kann eine Gruppe ihre Liste kurz vorstellen und die anderen ergänzen sie. Um den Wettbewerbsfaktor und die Aufmerksamkeit beim Vergleichen zu erhöhen, kann außerdem die Regel aufgestellt werden, dass Gruppen nur dann einen Punkt für ein Wort erhalten, wenn keine andere Gruppe dieses Wort benutzt hat.

Antwortkärtchen — ▶ Right/wrong cards

Appointments — Die kooperative Lernform *Appointments* ist eine gesteuerte Form von wechselnder PA in vier Phasen:
1. Die S schreiben drei vorgegebene Uhrzeiten in eine Tabelle. Dann gehen sie zu drei Mit-S, bitten jeweils um ein *Appointment* (*Can we meet at 1/2/3 o'clock?*) und tragen die Namen der Mit-S bei der entsprechenden Uhrzeit in ihrer Tabelle ein.
2. Im zweiten Schritt bearbeiten die S die Aufgabenstellung zunächst für sich und halten ihre Antwort in der Tabelle fest.
3. Auf das Signal der L (*It's 1/2/3 o'clock.*) gehen die S zum jeweiligen *Appointment* mit ihrem Mit-S, befragen ihn/sie und notieren die Antwort in der Tabelle.
4. In der letzten Phase berichten die S im Plenum über ihre Umfrageergebnisse.

Thema	Me: ___	1 o'clock Name: ___	2 o'clock Name: ___	3 o'clock Name: ___
Frage 1				
Frage 2				
Frage 3				

Arbeitsanweisung, Aufgabenstellung — ▶ Klären der Arbeitsanweisung (AA)

Bang — **Vorbereitung:** L bereitet Buchstabenkarten mit je einem Anfangsbuchstaben vor. Dabei sollten häufige (Anfangs-)Buchstaben öfter genutzt werden, seltene hingegen weniger bzw. gar nicht. Alternativ kann auch ein Buchstabenzufallsgenerator aus dem Internet genutzt werden.

Vor Spielbeginn stellt L einen Timer mit einer den S unbekannten Zeit ein. (Tipp: Zeit immer unterschiedlich wählen.)

Glossar

L gibt eine Kategorie vor (z. B. *pets / something you can eat / something green / ...*). Die S bekommen nun der Reihe nach einen zufälligen Buchstaben gezeigt und müssen ein Wort nennen, welches mit diesem Buchstaben beginnt. Wenn der Timer abläuft, scheidet der/die S aus, der/die gerade an der Reihe war, ein Wort zu nennen.

Das Spiel ist beendet, wenn a) alle S ausgeschieden und nur noch ein/-e S übrig ist, b) eine von L vorab festgelegte Zeit bzw. Rundenzahl erreicht ist.

Das Spiel eignet sich insbesondere, um den Wortschatz eines Themenbereichs zu wiederholen.

Erweiterung (für Einstiegsphase): Die S erhalten vor Spielbeginn (leere) Karten. Das Spiel wird wie beschrieben durchgeführt. Hat ein/-e S ein Wort genannt, wird dieses auf der Karte notiert. Am Spielende werden die Karten getauscht (z. B. eins nach links weitergegeben). Die S müssen nun versuchen, die Karten in der Stunde loszuwerden, indem sie einen Beitrag mit dem Wort auf der Karte leisten. Wurde das Wort auf der Karte genannt, darf die Karte abgegeben oder zerstört werden.

Bewegtes Lernen

Insbesondere die Ausweitung von Ganztagsschulen führt dazu, dass S länger im Unterricht sitzen und sich weniger bewegen. Neben gesundheitlichen Auswirkungen ist dies auch aus lernpsychologischer Sicht nicht förderlich für den Lernprozess. Der Faktor Bewegung verhilft S u. a. durch die Verknüpfung beider Hirnhälften, ihre Aufnahme- und Konzentrationsfähigkeit zu erhalten bzw. wiederherzustellen.

Im Sinne eines effektiven Fremdsprachenlernens sollten Bewegungselemente daher ein integrativer Bestandteil des Unterrichts sein. Dazu zählen neben dem Prinzip der ▶ Total Physical Response, bei dem Formulierungen in der Zielsprache mit passenden Bewegungen assoziiert werden, auch kooperative Lernformen (z. B. ▶ Bus stop), bei denen dem Aspekt Bewegung in einem inhaltlichen Kontext Rechnung getragen wird.

Binnendifferenziertes Arbeiten

Heterogene Lerngruppen erfordern einen individualisierten Unterricht, in dem differenziert auf lernstärkere sowie lernschwächere S eingegangen wird. Das Potenzial lernstärkerer S kann z. B. genutzt werden, indem sie aufstehen, sobald sie eine Aufgabe fertig bearbeitet haben. S, die sich mit der Aufgabe schwertun, können sich melden und von den stehenden S Unterstützung holen (*students as experts*). Dieses Vorgehen gewährleistet einen weitestgehend ruhigen Arbeitsablauf.

Da es in vielen Situationen nicht nötig ist, allen S der Lerngruppe Differenzierungshilfen zu geben, bietet es sich oftmals an, diese verdeckt zu geben (▶ Optional help). Je nach Gegebenheiten im Unterrichtsraum können Hilfen z. B. auf ein verdecktes Flipchart geschrieben oder kopiert in Briefumschläge gelegt werden, die sich die S an ihren Tisch holen und nach Gebrauch wieder zurücklegen.

Blitzlichtrunde

Die Methode der Blitzlichtrunde ermöglicht es allen S, eine kurze, persönliche Stellungnahme zu einem bestimmten Impuls (z. B. Fragen, Themen, Zitate) mündlich abzugeben. Dabei strukturieren die S ihre Gedanken in jeweils nur einem Satz und äußern diesen einzeln nacheinander (meist im Sitzkreis). Die Beiträge der S werden nicht gewertet oder kommentiert. Die Einsatzmöglichkeiten der Methode umfassen den Einstieg in ein neues Thema, als Ritual für die Stundeneröffnung (z. B. Rückmeldungen oder Austausch zum letzten Lernstoff) oder für Evaluationen (z. B. als Reflexion für Gruppenarbeiten oder zu Aufgabenstellungen).

Brainstorming

Brainstorming ist eine Methode, bei der durch freies Assoziieren möglichst viele – auch ungewöhnliche und zunächst scheinbar abwegige – Ideen und/oder Lösungsmöglichkeiten zu einem bestimmten Thema gefunden werden sollen. In der ersten Phase werden Ideen gesammelt, erweitert, kombiniert und schriftlich festgehalten. In der zweiten Phase stehen das Kommentieren und die Bewertung der einzelnen Ideen im Mittelpunkt, um zu einer Entscheidung zu gelangen. Verschiedene Techniken können beim Brainstorming zum Einsatz kommen:

- Listensystem: Alle Ideen werden untereinander aufgelistet; dabei bekommt jede Idee eine eigene Zeile. Wichtige Ideen werden dann unterstrichen und ggf. nach Wichtigkeit nummeriert, unwichtige gestrichen.
- Mindmap: Das Thema wird in der Mitte des Blattes festgehalten. Dann werden Oberbegriffe, die zu diesem Thema passen, mithilfe von Hauptästen hinzugefügt. Schließlich kommen Ideen, die zu den Oberbegriffen passen, auf Nebenäste. Die Mindmap erfordert bereits bei der Erstellung eine Strukturierung.

Glossar

- *Wh*-Fragen: *Who? What? When? Where? Why?* Diese Fragewörter werden in eine Tabelle geschrieben. Die Ideen zur jeweiligen Frage werden darunter festgehalten.

Buddy book   Das *Buddy book* ist ein kleines Buch mit acht bzw. 16 Seiten. Die S können es selbst herstellen, denn es kann in wenigen Schritten aus einem DIN-A4-Blatt gebastelt werden. Als kompakter, selbst gemachter Lernbegleiter wird es unter anderem eingesetzt als Notizbuch zu einem Thema, ähnlich wie Karteikarten zum Vokabellernen, sowie als Gedankenstütze für einen Vortrag oder als Medium zur Reflexion von Lernfortschritten. Bastelanleitungen finden sich leicht online.

Bus stop (Lerntempoduett)   Die Methode des Lerntempoduetts ermöglicht es den S, gemäß ihrer individuellen Arbeitsgeschwindigkeit zu arbeiten und ihre Arbeitsergebnisse eigenverantwortlich in PA zu kontrollieren. S, die eine Aufgabe fertig bearbeitet haben, stehen auf. Sobald ein zweiter S aufsteht, kontrollieren sie die Aufgabe im ▸ Partner check.

Vorteil: Es arbeiten nicht immer dieselben S (Freunde/Freundinnen, Tischnachbarn/-nachbarinnen) zusammen und schnellere S müssen nicht warten, bis alle Mit-S die Aufgabe gelöst haben und diese im Plenum ausgewertet wird.

In gestuften Übungsarrangements bietet sich auch die erweiterte Form *Bus stop* an. Dabei ist es nicht das Ziel, alle Aufgaben zeitlich zu schaffen, sondern je nach individuellem Lernstand das eigene Pensum zu erledigen (Ermöglichen zieldifferenten Arbeitens). Um jederzeit auf diese kooperative Lernform zurückgreifen zu können, empfiehlt es sich, dass L im Klassenraum – z.B. in den vier Raumecken – Schilder mit dem Symbol einer Bushaltestelle anbringt, die entsprechend durchnummeriert sind (A–D oder 1–4). Hierfür kann L die ▸ KV Extra: Bus stop nutzen. Die Schilder können für alle Fächer genutzt werden. Ablauf:

1. Die S bearbeiten die erste Aufgabe ihrer Wahl in EA.
2. Wenn ein/-e S fertig ist, begibt er/sie sich zum jeweiligen *Bus stop* im Klassenraum und wartet auf eine/-n Mit-S, der/die dieselbe Aufgabe bearbeitet hat. Um evtl. Wartezeiten zu überbrücken, kann L dort kleinere (spielerische) Aufgaben mit hohem Aufforderungscharakter bereitlegen. Die S besprechen ihre Ergebnisse in PA. Um zu gewährleisten, dass der Austausch auf Englisch stattfindet, kann L im Vorfeld Redemittel zur Verfügung stellen. Alternativ (z.B. wenn keine Schilder zur Verfügung stehen) kann die Methode auch durchgeführt werden, indem S, die fertig sind, aufstehen und durch vorher vereinbarte Handzeichen, z.B. das Hochhalten von Fingern (ein Finger: Aufgabe 1 etc.) eine/-n Mit-S finden, der/die dieselbe Aufgabe bearbeitet hat und für die PA bereit ist.
3. Nach erfolgtem Lösungsvergleich begeben sich die S wieder an ihre Plätze und arbeiten an der nächsten Aufgabe weiter. Die Kontrolle erfolgt am nächsten *Bus stop*, i.d.R. mit einem/einer anderen Mit-S, der/die ebenfalls die Aufgabe schon bearbeitet hat. Eine abschließende Kontrolle aller Aufgaben im Zusammenhang kann schließlich im Plenum oder mithilfe eines Lösungsblattes erfolgen und durch eine Reflexion der Methode ergänzt werden.

Buzz group (Murmelgruppe)   Die *Buzz group* ist eine variabel einsetzbare Methodik, um S zu eigenen Stellungnahmen anzuregen oder Verständnisfragen zu klären.
1. L bittet S, mit den Nachbarn/Nachbarinnen spontane Kleingruppen zu bilden und sich in den nächsten (z.B. zwei) Minuten leise über die Frage / das Thema zu unterhalten.
2. L sorgt wieder für Ruhe (akustisches Signal) und animiert einige Gruppen dazu, die Klasse kurz über die Inhalte ihres Gesprächs zu informieren.

Tipp: Bei schwierigeren Themen ist es sinnvoll, Moderationskarten bereitzustellen, um offene Fragen an Pinnwänden auszuhängen und damit weiterzuarbeiten.

Buzz reading (Lesegemurmel)   Das *Buzz reading* dient dazu, den Redeanteil aller S zu erhöhen und Sprachhemmungen abzubauen. Alle S lesen einen bekannten Text gleichzeitig und leise murmelnd vor sich hin. Die Methode kann flexibel im Unterricht eingesetzt werden. Es empfiehlt sich, diese Phase kurzzuhalten und sie z.B. zur Vorbereitung auf einen Lesevortrag einzusetzen. In Kombination mit dem ▸ Mitleseverfahren trägt diese Methode besonders zur Festigung von Aussprache und Intonation bei.

Glossar

Chain game

Den meisten S ist das *Chain game* sicher als „Ich packe meinen Koffer …" bekannt. Bei diesem einfachen Spiel fügt jede/-r S der „Kette" ein neues Glied hinzu. Die Regeln lassen sich dabei variieren, sodass der Schwierigkeitsgrad an die Leistungsstärke der S angepasst werden kann. So kann z. B. festgelegt werden, ob das zuvor Genannte komplett wiederholt werden muss oder ob der letzte Teil ausreicht. Das *Chain game* kann unterschiedlich eingesetzt werden; es lässt sich als Buchstabierspiel, Wort- oder Satzkette und auch als *Story chain* spielen. Häufig wird das *Chain game* zum Festigen oder Wiederholen von Vokabular verwendet.

Beispiel: Ein/-e S oder L beginnt mit dem Einstiegssatz *My town has a shop …* Der/Die nächste S wiederholt den Satz und fügt hinzu: *My town has a shop and a library …* Der/Die wiederum nächste S wiederholt erneut den kompletten Satz und ergänzt ihn: *My town has a shop, a library and an ice rink …* So wird das Spiel entsprechend fortgesetzt. Die Klasse passt auf, ob alles richtig gemacht wird. Sagt ein/-e S etwas Falsches oder kommt nicht weiter, gibt er/sie z. B. ein Pfand ab.

Continue my story

Nach Vorgabe eines spannenden/interessanten Einstiegssatzes erstellen die S mündlich eine fortlaufende Geschichte, wobei die S nacheinander einen semantisch passenden Satz zur Geschichte ergänzen.

Correcting circle (Schreibkonferenz)

Bei der Methode *Correcting circle* (auch *Peer correction*) handelt es sich um die gegenseitige Textkorrektur und Hilfe der S untereinander. Diese Form des Feedbacks ist für manche S weniger einschüchternd als die Fehlerkorrektur durch L. Die Methode eignet sich besonders für die Arbeit in Kleingruppen. Es sollte ein Kriterienkatalog für die Textkorrektur vorliegen, der vorher gemeinsam erarbeitet werden kann. Ablauf:

1. Jede/-r S erhält ein spezielles Gebiet (z. B. *content, structure, spelling, tenses, word order*).
2. Die S geben ihre Texte reihum weiter und nehmen Korrekturen zu ihrem Gebiet vor, bis der Text wieder bei seinem Verfasser / seiner Verfasserin angekommen ist.
3. Zum Abschluss fertigen die S eine Reinschrift des eigenen Textes an.

L sammelt nach dem Zufallsprinzip einige Ergebnisse zur Bewertung ein. Im Sinne des selbstständigen Lernens kann vereinbart werden, dass S eine DOs-and-DON'Ts-Liste anlegen, die in der Klassenarbeit verwendet werden darf. Dies hilft S bei der Selbstkorrektur und motiviert, an den eigenen Fehlern zu arbeiten.

Cue cards

Cue cards sind Kärtchen, die S als Impuls bzw. als Gedankenstütze während des freien Sprechens nutzen können. Sie bieten die Möglichkeit, die Sprechfertigkeit der S gelenkt zu trainieren und so das längere freie Sprechen einzuüben. Zudem kann L sie lernschwächeren S als Hilfsmittel für *Speaking activities* zur Verfügung stellen. *Cue cards* können sowohl Arbeitsaufträge als auch Redemittel oder kleine Zeichnungen abbilden. Sie eignen sich für das dialogische Sprechen ebenso wie für das Üben von Prüfungssituationen oder von Präsentationen. Eine Möglichkeit, *Cue cards* dafür einzusetzen, ist die folgende:

Um sich Notizen für Präsentationen zu machen, hilft es besonders schwachen S, sich vorher ihren Text zu überlegen. Die S knicken von einem Blatt ca. 1/3 des Rands ab. Dann schreiben sie den Text für ihre Präsentation o. Ä. auf die breitere Seite und schreiben schließlich die wichtigsten Stichworte aus ihrem Text auf den Rand. Bei der Präsentation sollten die S nach Möglichkeit die Seite mit den Stichworten benutzen. Wenn sie jedoch ihren Text vergessen, können sie die Seite mit dem ausgeschriebenen Text kurz zu Hilfe nehmen.

Daumenabfrage

▶ Thumbs up

Democratic vote

Davon ausgehend, dass bei Gruppenarbeiten häufig die Frage aufkommt, welches Gruppenmitglied das Ergebnis präsentiert, stellt die *Democratic vote* ein Zufallsprinzip zur Auswahl eines/einer S aus einer Gruppe dar. Um möglichst alle S in den Arbeitsprozess einzubinden, sollte erst am Ende der Arbeitsphase ein/-e S bestimmt werden, der/die das Ergebnis vorstellt. Dazu stellen sich alle Gruppenmitglieder in einem Kreis auf und zeigen auf ein Signal hin auf eine/-n S der Gruppe. Auf den die meisten oder die wenigsten Finger zeigen, trägt das Ergebnis vor. Damit sich jedoch die S nicht schon vorher eine/-n Mit-S aussuchen, sollte regelmäßig zwischen beiden Varianten gewechselt werden.

Glossar

Didaktische Folge — Für den effektiven Spracherwerb ist es bei der Einführung von neuem Wortschatz wichtig, die didaktische Folge zu beachten. Dabei ist die Reihenfolge der Fertigkeiten, die im Zusammenhang mit einem neuen Lexem gefordert sind, genau festgelegt:

1. Hören: Die S hören ein neues Wort mehrfach (Sprachvorbild L oder Audio).
2. Sprechen: Die S sprechen das neue Wort mehrfach nach (▶ Lautschulung).
3. Lesen: Die S sehen das Schriftbild und lesen das neue Lexem.
4. Schreiben: Erst in diesem Schritt produzieren die S das neue Wort schriftlich.

Mit zunehmendem Lernstand können S in verstärktem Maße, vor allem in der Textarbeit, auf erworbene Erschließungstechniken zurückgreifen.

Discussion fan — Der *Discussion fan* (Redemittelfächer) bietet ein hilfreiches und übersichtliches ▶ Scaffolding, welches in Diskussionen und anderen *Speaking activities* eingesetzt werden kann, um die S mit wichtigen Redemitteln zu versorgen.

Die S nutzen die ▶ Discussion tickets als *Discussion fan*, indem sie die einzelnen Tickets mit einer Musterbeutelklammer zu einem beweglichen Fächer zusammenheften. Alternativ können die Tickets auch an einer Seite gelocht und mit einer Schnur zusammengebunden werden.

Discussion tickets — Die S erhalten vor einer *Speaking activity* (z. B. *discussion, role play*) jeweils drei bis vier *discussion tickets*, mit denen sie während der Diskussion für jede Äußerung bezahlen. Dadurch müssen alle S mindestens drei- bis viermal reden, dürfen aber auch nicht mehr beitragen, sodass die Diskussion gleichmäßig von allen getragen wird.

Variante: Die *Discussion tickets* können auch bestimmte Redemittel enthalten, die von den S an passenden Stellen in der *Speaking activity* verwendet werden müssen. Sie können auch Angaben für den Diskussionsprozess enthalten, die im Laufe der Diskussion befolgt werden müssen (z. B. *In the course of the discussion ask one of the students in your group for his/her opinion. / In the course of the discussion use the following phrase: I see what you mean but …*).
Tipp: Die *Discussion tickets* können hervorragend als ▶ Discussion fan wiederverwendet werden.

Dossier — Die S sammeln ihre kreativen Beiträge, wie z. B. illustrierte Texte, selbst verfasste Gedichte oder Poster, in einem Dossier. Zusammen mit ihren Selbsteinschätzungsbögen kann daraus zum Schuljahresende eine Präsentationsmappe erstellt werden, die ein umfangreiches Bild der Sprachkompetenz der S bietet.

Double circle (Doppelter Stuhlkreis, Kugellager) — Die kooperative Lernform *Double circle* ist eine Form von wechselnder PA, die sich zum Üben von Diskussionsstrategien eignet. Sie ermöglicht einen hohen Sprachumsatz bei niedriger Hemmschwelle zur aktiven Teilnahme. Ablauf:

1. Die S sitzen (oder stehen) sich in einem Innen- und einem Außenkreis gegenüber. Sie diskutieren ein vorgegebenes Thema oder eine Fragestellung mit ihrem Gegenüber und machen sich ggf. Notizen.
2. Auf ein (akustisches) Signal von L hin bewegen sich entweder die S im Innen- oder im Außenkreis um einige Plätze weiter, damit neue Paarungen entstehen. L bestimmt sowohl die Länge der Gesprächszeit als auch die Anzahl der weiterzurückenden Plätze.
3. In einem zweiten Durchgang berichten sich die S über das Gehörte, wobei die Partner/-innen jeweils korrigieren und ergänzen. So sind die S zum aktiven Zuhören gezwungen.

Als Variante bietet es sich an, Innen- und Außenkreis verschiedene Themen oder Fragestellungen zu geben, die sich die S gegenseitig erklären oder beantworten.

Early finisher — *Early-finisher*-Aufgaben sind für besonders lernstarke S, die schneller als andere S die im Unterricht gestellten Aufgaben fertigstellen. Diese S können zur Zeitüberbrückung zusätzliche Aufgaben bearbeiten, die zum ▶ Binnendifferenzierten Arbeiten und zur Kreativität beitragen.

Glossar

English corner — Die *English corner* ist eine Pinnwand bzw. ein Teil einer Pinnwand im Klassenzimmer, die ganz dem Fach Englisch vorbehalten ist. In der *English corner* werden z. B. Unterrichtsergebnisse (Texte, Poster etc.) ausgestellt. Der Bereich wird von den S grafisch-visuell gestaltet, sodass er leicht erkennbar ist. Zum einen ergibt sich hierdurch die Möglichkeit, z. B. an Elternabenden oder sonstigen Schulveranstaltungen die Unterrichtsprodukte zu veröffentlichen. Zum anderen können in der *English corner* weitere Lernangebote für ▸ Early finishers dargeboten werden.

Im Sinne des ▸ Binnendifferenzierten Arbeitens können zudem lernstärkere S die ausgestellten Produkte korrigieren bzw. den Mit-S nach vorgegebenen Kriterien ▸ Feedback geben.

English folder — Für den Englischunterricht eignen sich am besten schmale Ringordner. So können die S die Blätter in den verschiedenen Teilen einheften, ohne dabei alle Seiten herausnehmen zu müssen.
Eine mögliche Unterteilung ist:
- *Exercises* (für alle Übungen zur Festigung der Kompetenzen)
- *Looking at language* (der Merkteil für sprachliche Strukturen)
- *Vocab file* (für Wortschatz)
- *My tasks* (für eigene Texte, Geschichten, … ▸ Dossier)

English-only-Karte — Die *English-only*-Karte ist ein nützliches Hilfsmittel, um S einen Anreiz zu geben, Hemmungen zu überwinden und in GA mit den Mit-S Englisch zu sprechen. Zu Beginn einer einsprachigen Arbeitsphase wird ein Symbol (z. B. eine Karte mit *Union Jack*) an Tafel oder (Pinn-)Wand geheftet. Die *English-only*-Karte fungiert dann wie ein „Schwarzer Peter": Wer Deutsch spricht, erhält diese Karte und darf sie erst abgeben, wenn ein/-e andere/-r S Deutsch spricht. Wer bei Beendigung der Arbeitsphase die Karte besitzt, muss eine kleine Pflicht erfüllen, wie z. B. einen Zungenbrecher oder Limerick vortragen oder einen spontanen Kurzvortrag (z. B. *My life as a chair*) halten.

Evaluationszielscheibe — Die Evaluationszielscheibe ist für nahezu alle Feedbackthemen einsetzbar. Zum Zwecke der Rückmeldung über Unterricht, Präsentationen u. Ä. erhält jede/-r S von L eine vorbereitete Zielscheibe. Vor dem Ausfüllen wird die Form der vorzunehmenden Markierung auf der Zielscheibe (innen = trifft voll zu, außen = trifft nicht zu) besprochen. Die Markierung kann mit Filzstiften oder Klebepunkten erfolgen. Die Zielscheibe kann in mehrere Bereiche (empfohlen: Quadranten), die wiederum bestimmten thematisch-inhaltlichen Schwerpunkten entsprechen, aufgeteilt werden.

Die Auswertung der Zielscheiben sollte unmittelbar erfolgen. Die S lesen ihre Ergebnisse vor. Diese werden auf eine große Zielscheibe übertragen. Dadurch entstehen reichlich Anlässe zur Diskussion/Auseinandersetzung mit dem Thema.

Alternative: L stellt eine große Zielscheibe zur Verfügung, die von allen S markiert wird. Nachteil: S neigen dazu, sich an Eintragungen ihrer Vorgänger/-innen zu orientieren.

Faltgeschichte — Bei der Reihum-, Fortsetzungs-, Ketten- oder Faltgeschichte gibt L einen Satzanfang vor (z. B. TA), welchen die S auf einem A4-Blatt vervollständigen. Dann geben die S das Blatt mit dem vervollständigten Satz an den/die nächste/-n S weiter. Diese/-r ergänzt einen weiteren Satz zur Geschichte und faltet das Blatt so, dass nur noch der neuste Satz zu sehen ist. Dann wird das Blatt erneut weitergegeben und das Vorgehen wiederholt. Ggf. kann L den Schreibprozess mithilfe von Textvorgaben steuern und die S mit zusätzlichem ▸ Scaffolding (z. B. *linking words, useful words and phrases*) unterstützen. L sagt die letzten 1–3 Sätze an, damit die S ein Ende für die Geschichten finden können.

Die Faltgeschichte ist beendet, wenn alle Blätter einmal die Klasse durchlaufen haben oder alternativ wenn eine bestimmte Anzahl vorab festgelegter Weitergaben (z. B. 7–10) erfolgt ist. Die S lesen dann die Geschichten (im Plenum) vor.

Feedback — Die Durchführung von Feedbackphasen ist von grundlegender Bedeutung für die Entwicklung von methodischen Kompetenzen wie beispielsweise Vortragstechniken. Als Grundlage werden im Vorfeld klare Kriterien definiert, an denen sich das Feedback orientiert. Folgende Regeln sollten dabei beachtet werden:

Glossar

1. Das Feedback wird so konkret wie möglich formuliert. Dabei werden immer zuerst positive Dinge genannt, bevor in einer zweiten Runde optimierungswürdige Aspekte angeführt werden – am besten mit Handlungsalternativen.
2. Zunächst hat der/die Präsentierende Gelegenheit, sich zu äußern, danach die übrigen S und zuletzt ergänzt L.
3. Wer ein Feedback gibt, sollte versuchen, das Gesehene zu beschreiben, anstatt zu bewerten. Dabei redet man den Angesprochenen am besten direkt an (also 2. Person, nicht 3.), wobei Meinungen in der Ich-Form vorgetragen werden sollten.

Die Person, die das Feedback erhält, sollte zuhören und es vermeiden, sich zu verteidigen. Letztlich geht es darum, sich selbst durch die Kritik der anderen zu verbessern. Hierzu ist es auch sinnvoll, die Rückmeldungen in einer Art DOs-and-DON'Ts-Liste zu notieren.

Film dice Den Zahlen 1–6 eines Würfels werden Satzanfänge zugeordnet, mit deren Hilfe die S den Film oder Filmausschnitt kommentieren. Alternativ basteln die S einen Würfel, auf dem die Satzanfänge stehen. Die Methode ist in PA oder in Vierergruppen möglich. Falls ein/-e S einen Satzanfang ein zweites Mal würfelt, muss der Wurf wiederholt werden.

Fishbowl discussion Bei der *Fishbowl discussion* handelt es sich um eine dynamische Diskussionsform, die eine Mischung aus Podiumsdiskussion und Diskussion im Plenum darstellt. In einem Innenkreis sitzend tauschen fünf S ihre Argumente aus, während die übrigen S im Außenkreis sitzend oder stehend die Diskussion beobachten. Ein Stuhl im Innenkreis ist frei. Auf diesen kann sich jederzeit ein/-e Beobachter/-in aus dem Außenkreis setzen, um selbst aktiv an der Diskussion teilzunehmen. Nach seinem/ihrem Beitrag kehrt diese/-r S wieder in den Außenkreis zurück und der/die nächste Beobachter/-in kann teilnehmen. Auf diese Weise können auch stillere S ihre Sprechhemmungen abbauen, da sie sich zunächst als Beobachter/-in in die Diskussion einfinden können, bevor sie selbst aktiv werden. Gleichzeitig haben sie die Sicherheit, dass sie jederzeit wieder in ihre Beobachtungsrolle im Außenkreis zurückkehren können.

Vor Beginn der Diskussion sollte bestimmt werden, welche Positionen (Ansichten) die fünf S im Innenkreis in der Diskussion einnehmen; ggf. werden Rollenkarten verteilt. Die S im Außenkreis beobachten den inhaltlichen und formalen Verlauf. Über gezielte und differenzierte Beobachtungsaufträge (z. B. Verwendung von Redemitteln, Beitragshäufigkeit, Gesprächsverhalten, Argumentationstiefe, Sprechlautstärke) kann anschließend der Diskussionsverlauf reflektiert werden.

Five-finger brainstorming Das *Five-finger brainstorming* intendiert eine begrenzte Sammlung von Informationen zu einem Thema bzw. Sachverhalt. Wie beim ▶Brainstorming werden zunächst freie Assoziationen zum Thema gebildet, allerdings mit der Herausforderung, diese auf fünf (Haupt-)Aspekte zu reduzieren bzw. präzisieren. Die S zeichnen dazu ihre eigene Hand auf ein Blatt Papier und notieren in jedem Finger einen Aspekt zur vorgegebenen Frage- oder Themenstellung. Einsatzort ist insbesondere die Einstiegsphase zur Reaktivierung oder zur Sammlung des Wortschatzes als Grundlage für den weiteren Ablauf der Unterrichtsstunde (z. B. die Sammlung von Vor- und Nachteilen für eine sich anschließende Diskussion oder die Sammlung von eigenen Interessen für eine folgende kurze Minipräsentation).

Five-minute teacher Bei dieser Methode übernimmt ein/-e S für eine kurze Zeit die Rolle von L. Sie eignet sich besonders für das Vergleichen geschlossener Aufgaben oder für immer wiederkehrende Situationen, wie z. B. die Begrüßung und mögliche Stundenrituale. Der *Five-minute teacher* nimmt selbstständig Mit-S dran, vergleicht ihre Lösungen und gibt eine Rückmeldung dazu.

Die S sollten besonders zu Beginn dieser Methode das notwendige ▶Scaffolding bekommen, welches am besten als Poster im Klassenraum angebracht wird. Für das Vergleichen von Aufgaben bietet sich als ▶Scaffolding an: *Who wants to do the next task? / I think that is right. / I think that is wrong.*

Flashcards Flashcards sind Bildkarten, die den S helfen, das Laut- bzw. Schriftbild eines Wortes nachhaltig mit seiner Bedeutung zu verknüpfen. Sie nutzen den auditiven und visuellen Lernkanal parallel (*Dual Code Theory*), wenn ihnen ein Wort mit dem entsprechenden Bild präsentiert wird und damit im Gehirn verknüpft werden kann. Als Applikationen an der Tafel eignen sich Flashcards auch zur schüleraktivierenden Wortschatzarbeit, z. B. indem in einer Reorganisationsphase die Bilder den entsprechenden Wörtern zugeordnet werden.

Glossar

Four corners — Die vier Ecken des Klassenzimmers werden einer bestimmten Position zu einem Thema zugeordnet und es werden dort Symbole oder gut lesbare schriftliche Statements aufgehängt. Dann trägt L die Frage oder das Problem vor. Nach einer kurzen Nachdenkphase ruft L *Corner!*, woraufhin die S sich einer der vier Positionen zuordnen. Die S in den einzelnen Ecken sollen Ihre Meinungen oder Begründungen in kleinen Gruppen oder zu zweit zusammentragen. Zum Schluss werden die Meinungen auch im Plenum vorgestellt.

Variante: Die vier Ecken werden mit den Buchstaben A, B, C und D (oder 1, 2, 3, 4) versehen. L liest jeweils vier verschiedene Optionen vor, für die die S sich durch Zuordnung zu einer Ecke entscheiden müssen. Da diese Aufgabe auch Hörverstehen und Konzentration fordert, sollten die Optionen zweimal vorgelesen werden, ehe L *Corner!* ruft und eine Entscheidung erforderlich ist. Nach jedem Durchgang erfragt L Begründungen oder Details von einzelnen S.

Beispiel: *What type of holiday would you choose?* (A) *Camping at the seaside*, (B) *a luxury hotel in the mountains*, (C) *a cycling tour staying in B&Bs*, (D) *a city-trip staying in a youth hostel?*

Freeze-frame (Standbildmethode) — Die S erfassen Facetten von textlichen Figurenkonstellationen auf darstellerische Weise. In Gruppen tauschen sich die S zunächst über die darzustellende Situation aus, dann werden Rollen verteilt. Der/Die „Baumeister/-in" bringt die „Modelle" in ein zuvor abgesprochenes Standbild und schöpft körperlich-räumliche Ausdrucksmöglichkeiten aus: Abstände zueinander, Körperhaltung, Gestik und Mimik spiegeln die Situation im Text auf intensive Weise wider. Beim Ausruf *Freeze!* verharren die Modelle regungslos. Jetzt können zusätzliche Fotos aus verschiedenen Perspektiven gemacht werden.

Als Auswertung bietet sich eine kurze Erläuterung der jeweiligen Gruppe an, es erscheint jedoch oft didaktisch sinnvoller, wenn die anderen Gruppen den *Freeze frame* zunächst mithilfe von Leitfragen interpretieren: *How are the characters presented? What can we tell about their relationships?* Ein Abgleich mit den Intentionen der präsentierenden Gruppe ist ratsam, um herauszuarbeiten, an welchen Stellen Ideen der Gruppe nicht verständlich waren. Diese kreative und körperbezogene Methode bringt Abwechslung in die oftmals einseitig kognitive Interpretationsarbeit.

Fruit salad — Die S sitzen im Stuhlkreis, ein/-e S steht in der Mitte. L nennt jedem/jeder S eine Obstsorte, wobei jede Obstsorte mehrfach genannt werden sollte. Wenn nun der/die S in der Mitte eine Obstsorte nennt, tauschen alle S, die diese Sorte haben, schnell die Plätze. Wenn *Fruit salad!* gerufen wird, tauschen alle S schnell die Plätze. Der/Die S in der Mitte versucht nun auch, einen Platz zu bekommen. Der/Die S ohne Sitzplatz bleibt nun in der Mitte und das Spiel beginnt erneut.

Das Spiel kann thematisch verändert werden, indem z. B. *hobbies, subjects* genannt werden.

Gallery walk (Galeriespaziergang) — Die kooperative Lernform *Gallery walk* bietet eine gute Möglichkeit, Arbeitsergebnisse zu präsentieren und zu diskutieren. Ablauf:
- Die S sind in EA oder GA zu einem Arbeitsergebnis gelangt (z. B. Text, Bild, Poster), das im Raum ausgestellt wird.
- Die S gehen einzeln oder in Gruppen im Uhrzeigersinn von Station zu Station und schauen sich die Ergebnisse der anderen an.

Wenn alle S alle Arbeitsergebnisse gesehen haben, präsentieren sie entweder nacheinander ihre Eindrücke oder besprechen sie gemeinsam in der Klasse.

Als Variante der GA bietet es sich an, die S neu aufzuteilen. In jeder neuen Gruppe sollte jeweils ein/-e S aus den ursprünglichen Gruppen sein. Wer aus der neuen Gruppe an dem ausliegenden Produkt mitgewirkt hat, präsentiert es den anderen. Die Gruppen wechseln im Uhrzeigersinn so lange die Tische, bis jede/-r S jedes Gruppenergebnis einmal erklärt bekommen hat und das eigene Gruppenprodukt einmal erklären musste.

Get-up game — Ein/-e freiwillige/-r S steht mit dem Rücken zur Tafel vor der Klasse. L schreibt eine Aussage an die Tafel. Alle S, auf die diese Aussage zutrifft, stehen auf. Der/Die S vor der Klasse kann nun mit Hilfe des Stellens von Fragen und Hilfestellungen aus der Klasse die Aussage an der Tafel erraten.

Glossar

Give me five Bei dieser Art des ▶Brainstormings nennen die S fünf Begriffe zu einem vorgegebenen Themenbereich (z. B. *Give me five outdoor activities / sports / emotions / ...*). L kann dabei die Aufforderung *Give me five ...* an fünf unterschiedliche S oder an eine/-n einzelne/-n S richten. Um einen Sprechanlass unter den S zu schaffen, können sich die S auch in Kleingruppen gegenseitig dazu auffordern, fünf Begriffe zu einem Themenbereich zu nennen.

Alternativ besteht die Möglichkeit, die S in zwei oder mehreren Gruppen gegeneinander antreten zu lassen, in dem S aus den Gruppen auf Zeit jeweils fünf Begriffe nennen bzw. aufschreiben. Wer zuerst fünf Begriffe nennt, erhält einen Punkt. Die Gruppe mit den meisten Punkten gewinnt.

Unter anderem eignet sich *Give me five* hervorragend für die Reaktivierung von Wortschatz.

Grammatikwiederholung Die Grammatikwiederholung im kompetenzorientierten Fremdsprachenunterricht sollte nicht isoliert erfolgen, sondern stets mit einem inhaltlichen Fokus in einen für die S bedeutungsvollen, authentischen Kontext eingebettet sein (*task-based learning*). Hierfür eignen sich unter anderem die nachstehend gelisteten Methoden, welche hier in erster Linie kommunikativ ausgerichtet sind:

1. Swap cards:
Swap cards eignen sich auch optimal zur Wiederholung der Zeitformen. Hierfür erhalten die S Karten mit Sätzen oder Verben, die in eine andere Zeitform (z. B. *simple present – simple past*) oder innerhalb einer Zeitform in eine andere Person (z. B. *1. Ps. Sg. – 3. Ps. Sg.*) umgewandelt werden können. Die Aktivität wird dann wie im Eintrag zu ▶Swap cards beschrieben durchgeführt.

2. Find someone who:
Die S erhalten eine KV mit max. fünf Aktivitäten (z. B. *weekend activities, holiday plans, future plans* etc.). Die S gehen dann im Klassenraum herum und erfragen die Aktivitäten der anderen S (▶Milling around). Je nach Zeitpunkt und Art der Aktivität können so durch das Erfragen verschiedene Zeitformen wiederholt und geübt werden (z. B. *simple past, present perfect, going to-future*). Ziel ist es, für möglichst viele der auf der KV angegebenen Aktivitäten jeweils eine/-n S zu finden und einzutragen. Gewonnen hat, wer für jede der Aktivitäten eine/-n S eingetragen hat.

Auswertung: Die Ergebnisse können im Plenum präsentiert werden. Dabei achtet L auf die richtige Verwendung der Zeitform.

Gruppenbildung Eine Einteilung der S in Gruppen kann mithilfe folgender Methoden erfolgen:

1. Methoden mit gelenktem Zufall: L bereitet Elemente vor, die zusammen ein Ganzes ergeben. Dies können z. B. Puzzleteile sein, die ein Bild ergeben, oder Wortkarten, die einem Oberbegriff zugeordnet werden können. Die S ziehen ein solches Element und finden sich in den jeweils entsprechenden Gruppen zusammen.
2. Gruppen können durch Auszählen, Würfeln oder nach dem *Line-up*-Verfahren gebildet werden. Bei diesem stellen sich S in der aufsteigenden Reihenfolge ihrer Geburtstage oder Hausnummern auf. L zählt dann die benötigten Gruppen ab, z. B. die ersten drei S, die gemeinsam eine Gruppe bilden, etc.
3. L teilt Gruppen ein und gibt die Namen der Gruppenmitglieder bekannt. Dabei sollten Leistungsniveau, Arbeitstempo und Sozialverhalten der S berücksichtigt werden.

Gucklochmethode Bei dieser Methode der Bildpräsentation schneidet L aus einem Blatt Papier ein Loch aus und legt das Blatt auf eine Abbildung (Foto, Stadtplan etc.) die L z. B. per Dokumentenkamera präsentiert. Anschließend fährt L mit dem Blatt über die Abbildung, sodass die S immer einen anderen kleinen Ausschnitt mit Details des Bildes sehen. L fragt, worum es sich bei der Abbildung handeln könnte. Die S spekulieren, bis L schließlich das ganze Bild präsentiert.

Die Methode lässt sich auch digital mithilfe von Präsentationsprogrammen anwenden, wobei über das Bild eine halbtransparente Folie bzw. Füllung gelegt wird, aus der mithilfe eines Zeichentools ein Guckloch eingefügt wird.

Glossar

Herringbone technique — Diese Technik fungiert als *graphic organizer* und ermöglicht es den S, Informationen aus einem Text (in der Regel zu den fünf *wh*-Fragen und *how*) in übersichtlicher Form zusammenzufassen. Zu diesem Zweck zeichnen die S eine schematische Fischgräte mit sechs Abzweigungen für die Fragewörter in ihr Heft und notieren dazu die entsprechenden Informationen.

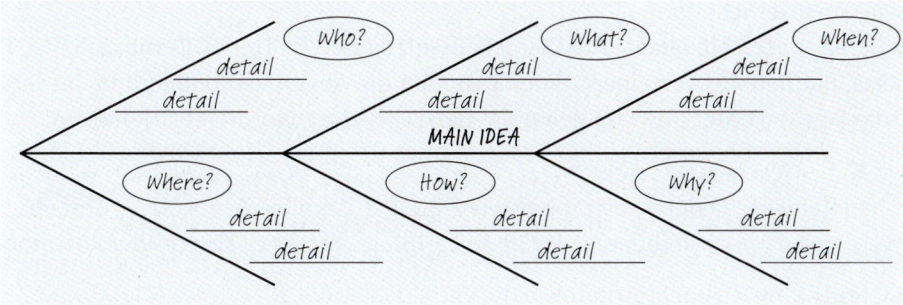

Hot seat — *Hot seat* ist eine Methode, bei der ein/-e S von den Mit-S auf einem *hot seat* befragt wird oder er/sie ihre (kontroverse) Meinung wiedergeben. Auf diese Weise können zuvor erarbeitete Unterrichtsinhalte zur Diskussion gestellt bzw. genutzt werden.

Variante: L stellt fünf Stühle vor der Klasse auf. Vier Stühle werden von S besetzt. Jeweils zwei vertreten denselben Standpunkt (z. B. *We like the film because … / We don't like it because …*). Der freie Stuhl kann von Mit-S, die die Diskussion verfolgen, belegt werden, um fehlende Gesichtspunkte zu ergänzen.

Ideenregen — Ähnlich wie beim ▶ Brainstorming geht es beim Ideenregen darum, durch freies Assoziieren möglichst viele Ideen und/oder Wörter zu einem bestimmten Thema zu finden. In einer Wortsammlung werden die Wörter bzw. Ideen, wie Regentropfen, beliebig, d. h. ohne bestimmtes System, an der Tafel angeordnet. Zur Visualisierung des „Ideenregens" kann über den Wörtern eine Wolke gezeichnet werden.

Info-gap activity — Bei der *Info-gap activity* handelt es sich um eine kooperative Lernform, die den aktiven Umsatz der Fremdsprache erfordert und schult. Den S fehlen Informationen zum Lösen einer Aufgabe, die ihren Partnern/Partnerinnen vorliegen und die sie durch gegenseitiges Befragen herausfinden. Es empfiehlt sich PA in einem festen Team (*Partner A, Partner B*).

Für die Durchführung müssen den S die Informationen und die zu füllenden Lücken vorliegen (Kopiervorlage, Arbeitsblatt, Tabelle im SB etc.). Es ist sinnvoll, den S eine Zeitvorgabe für die Bearbeitung zu geben. Eine Auswertung der Ergebnisse kann zunächst mit einem anderen S-Paar und anschließend im Plenum erfolgen.

Jigsaw (Gruppenpuzzle) — Als *Jigsaw* wird eine arbeitsteilige Gruppenarbeit in zwei Phasen bezeichnet.

Phase 1: Die S bilden Expertengruppen (Gruppe A, B, C etc.), innerhalb derer jedem Gruppenmitglied eine Nummer zugeteilt wird (1, 2, 3 etc.). Alle S einer Expertengruppe (A1, A2, A3 etc.) bearbeiten innerhalb einer vorgegebenen Zeitspanne dieselbe Aufgabe in EA. Anschließend diskutieren die S ihre Arbeitsergebnisse und halten die wichtigsten Informationen fest. Bei Abschluss der 1. Phase verfügen somit alle Mitglieder der Expertengruppe über dieselben Informationen.

Phase 2: Es werden nun Querschnittsgruppen gebildet, in denen alle S mit derselben Nummer zu einer neuen Gruppe zusammenkommen (A1, B1, C1 etc.). Die S berichten den neuen Gruppenmitgliedern über die Ergebnisse ihrer Expertenrunde und beantworten Fragen. Alle S machen sich hierbei Notizen, sodass sie abschließend in der Lage sind, die Ergebnisse sowohl in ihrer Stammgruppe als auch ggf. im Plenum zu präsentieren.

Kimspiel — Die auf Rudyard Kiplings Romanfigur *Kim* basierenden Kimspiele werden zur Wahrnehmungs- und Gedächtnisschulung eingesetzt.

Kimspiele werden nach den verschiedenen Sinneswahrnehmungen eingeteilt. Zusätzlich zu Sehen, Hören, Riechen, Schmecken, Tasten zählen auch Gleichgewicht, Warm-/Kaltwahrnehmung und Schmerzempfinden dazu. Beispiele für Kimspiele:

Glossar

Seh-Kim: (Sehen)
- Ein/-e S verlässt das Klassenzimmer, die anderen S ändern/vertauschen ein Detail im Klassenzimmer (Tausch von Kleidungsstücken, Sitzplätzen, Brillen etc.). Der/Die S wird wieder ins Klassenzimmer gebeten und stellt fest, was verändert wurde.

Nasen-Kim: (Geruchssinn)
- L bereitet verschiedene Düfte/Gerüche wie z. B. geschnittenes Gemüse, Säfte, Essig, Schokolade, Käse, Blumen etc. vor. Einem/Einer S werden die Augen verbunden und die verschiedenen Dinge zum Riechen unter die Nase gehalten. Der/Die S errät, worum es sich handelt.

Mund-Kim: (Geschmackssinn)
- L bereitet verschiedene Kostproben wie z. B. Obst, Gemüse, Schokolade, Brot etc. vor. Einem/Einer S werden die Augen verbunden. Er/Sie soll erraten, worum es sich bei der Kostprobe handelt.

Gedächtnis-Kim: (Gedächtnis)
- L bereitet ein Tablett mit verschiedenen kleinen Gegenständen vor. L oder ein/-e S präsentiert die Gegenstände, sodass sich die anderen S diese einprägen können. Nach ein paar Sekunden werden die Gegenstände mit einem Tuch verdeckt. Die S zählen dann die Gegenstände möglichst vollständig auf.

Tast-Kim: (Tastsinn)
- L bereitet Gegenstände vor, die hinter einem Tuch platziert werden. Die S erraten durch Tasten die Gegenstände hinter dem Tuch.

Klären der Arbeitsanweisung (AA)

Für das Klären von Arbeitsanweisungen (AA) gibt es unterschiedliche Möglichkeiten. Im Hinblick auf selbstständiges Arbeiten sollten S möglichst früh dazu befähigt werden, AA ohne Hilfe der L zu erschließen. Damit S sich aktiv mit der AA auseinandersetzen, empfiehlt sich folgendes Vorgehen:

1. Stilles Lesen der AA
2. Verständnisklärung in PA
3. Erklärung der AA durch eine/-n S im Klassenverband
4. Bestätigung und/oder Korrektur durch L

Andere Möglichkeiten sind:

5. L demonstriert die Vorgehensweise (ggf. mit einem/einer S) anhand von Gesten, einem Produkt oder Beispielen.
6. Die AA wird gemeinsam im Plenum gelesen und erläutert.

Kugellager ▶ Double circle

Lautschulung Für die Lautschulung bieten sich verschiedene Techniken an:
1. **Chorsprechen:** Es bietet besonders zurückhaltenden S eine gute Übungsmöglichkeit und erzeugt einen hohen Sprachumsatz, da alle S gleichzeitig sprechen. L spricht jeweils vor und gibt dann ein Zeichen (z. B. Gestik: Hand ans Ohr halten), auf das hin die S nachsprechen.
2. **Nachsprechen im Teilchor:** L teilt Gruppen ein (z. B. Tischgruppen, Sitzreihen, Jungen/Mädchen), die auf das Signal hin nachsprechen. Diese Methode dient dazu, Fehler genauer zu lokalisieren.
3. **Einzelsprechen:** Dies bietet die Möglichkeit, eine individuelle Korrektur durchführen zu können.

Nachsprechen sollte generell abwechslungsreich gestaltet werden – durch Lautstärke, Geschwindigkeit, verstellte Stimme (like a parrot, like a computer). Neben der Lautschulung von einzelnen Wörtern können auch ganze Sätze nachgesprochen werden, um das Intonationsmuster der Fremdsprache zu üben.

Lernen an Stationen Bei dieser Form des offenen Unterrichts wird der Lernstoff auf mehrere Stationen aufgeteilt, die die S eigenständig in ihrem Tempo nach ihren Interessen bearbeiten. Normalerweise gibt es Pflichtstationen und Wahlstationen, die zu einem übergeordneten Thema gehören, aber unterschiedliche Schwerpunkte setzen. Sie sprechen durch verschiedene Materialien, Medien, Sozialformen und Aufgabenarten möglichst alle Lerntypen an. Diese handlungsorientierte Methode bietet sich zur differenzierten Vertiefung von Wissen oder im fächerübergreifenden Unterricht besonders an.

Glossar

Lerntempoduett ▶ Bus stop

Leseacht Die Methode Leseacht ermöglicht den S ein kooperatives Erschließen eines Sachtextes, indem sie sich den Text absatzweise abwechselnd vorlesen und sich beim Erfassen des Textinhaltes gegenseitig unterstützen können. Dabei werden zwei Stühle so aufgestellt, dass die S in entgegengesetzte Richtungen blicken. Mit der „20-cm-Stimme" klappt der verbale Austausch untereinander, ohne Mit-S zu stören.

Lesegemurmel ▶ Buzz reading

Lesetechniken Die Leseintention legt fest, wie tief die S in einen Text eindringen müssen, um die gewünschten Informationen zu erhalten. Die S müssen lernen, dass die Tiefe des Textverständnisses eng an die gestellten Aufgaben gebunden ist, und abhängig davon eine passende Lesetechnik auswählen und anwenden. Für L bedeutet dies, sorgfältig zu prüfen, welche Intention die Aufgaben zum Leseverstehen haben und welche Leseleistungen die S zur Lösung jeweils erbringen müssen.

Die folgenden Lesetechniken eignen sich für unterschiedliche Aufgabenstellungen. Als überfliegende Lesetechniken stehen sie dem vollständigen Lesen eines Textes, dem *Reading for detail*, gegenüber:

Skimming: Das *Skimming* stellt eine erste, oberflächliche Beschäftigung mit dem Text dar. S überfliegen Überschriften, Fotos/Zeichnungen oder die Aufmachung des Textes. Dies gibt ihnen z. B. Aufschluss über das Thema oder den möglichen Inhalt und zeigt, ob der Text für sie interessant ist oder ihnen zum Lösen einer Aufgabe nützt.

Speed reading: Beim *Speed reading* geht es darum, einen Text zu überfliegen, einen groben Eindruck zu gewinnen und nach *key words* zu suchen. *Speed reading* bedeutet, mit einem Blick mehr Wörter zu erfassen als gewöhnlich, um eine höhere Lesegeschwindigkeit zu erreichen (siehe auch ausführlicher Eintrag zum ▶ Speed Reading).

Scanning: Das *Scanning* ist eine suchende Lesetechnik, die auf Schlüsselwörter und -gedanken ausgerichtet ist. Dabei gehen die S von einer Frage oder Aufgabe aus und überfliegen den Text, bis sie die gesuchte Information gefunden haben. Auch hier ist es nicht das Ziel, den Inhalt des gesamten Textes oder jedes unbekannte Wort zu verstehen.

Weitere Lesetechniken: *Reading between* und *Reading beyond the lines* beziehen sich auf Verstehensprozesse beim Lesen von Texten, die über die reine Informationsentnahme hinausgehen.

Unter *Reading between the lines* versteht man die Fähigkeit des/der Lesenden, die gegebenen Informationen zu interpretieren und so Antworten auf Fragen zu finden. Beispiele hierfür sind das Antizipieren des Ausgangs oder das Ziehen von Schlüssen. Mögliche Fragen des *Reading between the lines* sind z. B.: *Why did …? • What do you think about …? • Can you explain …? • How was this similar to …?*

Beim *Reading beyond the lines* stellt der/die Lesende Zusammenhänge zwischen dem Gelesenen und dem eigenen Vorwissen her, um Antworten auf Fragen zu finden. Um dieses vertiefte Verständnis zu erreichen, muss der/die Lesende in der Lage sein, zu vergleichen, zu generalisieren, zu beurteilen oder das Gelesene weiterzuentwickeln. Beispiele für Fragen auf dieser Ebene sind: *How would you …? • Do you agree …? • What would have happened if …? • How might …? • What effect does …? • If you were … what would you …?*

***Line-up*-Verfahren** ▶ Gruppenbildung

Market-place activity (Marktplatz) Bei der kooperativen Lernform *Market-place activity* sprechen die S mit verschiedenen Partnern/Partnerinnen über ein vorgegebenes Thema. Ablauf:

1. Die S bewegen sich frei im Klassenraum. L stellt eine Aufgabe, die S in einem vorgegebenen Zeitrahmen bearbeiten. Dieser kann durch ein akustisches Signal, wie z. B. das Abspielen und Anhalten von Musik, begrenzt werden.
2. Auf das vereinbarte Signal hin bleiben die S stehen und tun sich mit dem/der vor ihnen stehenden zusammen. Die Partner/-innen tauschen sich über das Thema bzw. die Aufgabe aus. Je nach Aufgabenart machen sich die S Notizen.

Glossar

3. Auf das erneute Signal durch L wechseln die S ihren Partner / ihre Partnerin, sodass sie in einem begrenzten Zeitraum mit möglichst vielen S sprechen.
4. Die Ergebnisse können in einem anschließenden Unterrichtsgespräch ausgewertet werden.

Die *Market-place activity* ist eine Form des ▶ Milling around.

Mediation (Sprachmittlung) — Dies ist eine Vermittlungsstrategie zwischen Gesprächspartnern und -partnerinnen, die sich nicht direkt sprachlich verständigen können. Im Englischunterricht bedeutet dies die zusammenfassende, paraphrasierende Wiedergabe eines Hör- oder Lesetextes in der jeweils anderen Sprache. Bei der *Mediation* werden von dem/der Sprachmittelnden sowohl rezeptive Kompetenzen (einen Ausgangstext zu verstehen) als auch produktive Kompetenzen (einen Ausgangstext in der anderen Sprache wiederzugeben) und häufig interkulturelle Kenntnisse verlangt.

L kann den S zur Unterstützung folgende Leitregeln geben:
- Keine Wort-für-Wort-Übersetzung!
- Freie Wiedergabe der wichtigsten Informationen!
- Nicht alle Details wiedergeben!

Meinungsbarometer — Im Gruppenraum wird eine Linie gezogen, die beiden Eckpunkte werden mit 0 % und 100 % markiert, alternativ mit der Farbe Rot für Ablehnung und Grün für Zustimmung. L erläutert, dass die beiden Eckpunkte für *I fully agree* bzw. *I totally disagree* stehen, dass aber auch Zwischenpositionen möglich sind. L (oder S) liest dann *statements*, Meinungen oder Ideen vor, die S positionieren sich entlang der Linie je nach Grad der Zustimmung. Wenn alle Position bezogen haben, kann L Begründungen von einzelnen S erfragen. Danach kann noch ein weiterer Durchgang erfolgen, um festzustellen, ob S aufgrund der Äußerungen ihre Meinung geändert haben. Diese Möglichkeit sorgt außerdem für mehr Aufmerksamkeit während der Besprechung.

Variante 1: Statt den Grad der Zustimmung zu zeigen, ordnen die S sich einem von drei Bereichen im Klassenzimmer zu, die für *agree*, *disagree* und *unsure* stehen.
Variante 2: Ebenso können in den vier Ecken des Klassenzimmers Schilder mit *strongly agree*, *agree*, *disagree*, *strongly disagree* aufgehängt werden und die S beziehen dort jeweils Stellung.
Variante 3: Der Raum kann auch einfach in zwei Hälften für *yes* und *no* eingeteilt werden.

Egal in welcher Variante sollten die S ihre Meinungen im Anschluss begründen.

Meldekette — Die Meldekette dient der Förderung der S-Interaktion. Sie ist in Plenumsphasen universell einsetzbar, z. B. zur Auswertung von Ergebnissen oder zur Besprechung von Aufgaben. Die S rufen sich gegenseitig auf, wobei jede/-r S einen Satz oder eine Antwort nennt. L greift nur bei Bedarf korrigierend ein.

Menschen-Domino — Das Menschen-Domino ist eine gute Methode für ein *Warm-up* zu Stundenbeginn, bei dem z. B. Zeitformen wiederholt und geübt werden können. Jede/-r S erhält eine Dominokarte mit Motiven bzw. Informationen. Dazu schreibt L ein oder zwei passende Fragen an, die die zu übende Zeitform vorgeben. Beispiel für Aktivitäten im *simple present*: *What do you usually do on Saturdays?* Die S versuchen dann, im ▶ Milling around ihren Partner / ihre Partnerin zu finden, indem sie sich gegenseitig die Fragen stellen und sie mit den Motiven ihrer Karte beantworten, z. B. S1: *What do you usually do on Saturdays?* S2: *I usually do arts and drama. And you?* S1: *I usually go running and trampolining.* S2: *We aren't partners. Good bye.* Wenn sich Partner/-innen finden, laufen sie zusammen herum, bis sie weitere Partner/-innen finden (jede/-r S hat je zwei). Am Ende sollte eine Schlange entstehen.

Menschen-Memo — L legt ein Oberthema fest, z. B. Verben, Tiere, Körperteile. Es ist für die S einfacher, wenn ihnen die Begriffe vorgegeben werden und sie sich keine ausdenken müssen. Dazu können die Wörter auch auf Karteikarten ausgeteilt werden.

Zwei S werden ausgewählt und verlassen den Raum, um anschließend die einzelnen Paare zu erraten. Während die zwei S draußen warten, suchen sich die anderen S eine/-n Partner/-in und überlegen sich eine passende Bewegung. Anschließend kommen die zwei „Ratekinder" wieder herein. Die zwei ratenden S spielen nun gegeneinander und suchen jeweils zwei S aus, die ihr Wort nennen und die Bewegung vormachen. Wurde ein Paar zusammen „aufgedeckt", stellt es sich hinter das „Ratekind", das dann noch einmal raten darf. Wurden alle Paare erraten, ist das Spiel vorbei.

Glossar

Differenzierungsmöglichkeiten:
- Es wird nur eine bestimmte Zeit gespielt und nicht, bis alle Paare gefunden wurden.
- Es können Beispielbegriffe genutzt werden.
- Es kann in Teams geraten werden.

Metakognition Metakognition bedeutet, dass S über ihr Lernen nachdenken, Strategien und Methoden reflektieren und daraus die für sie geeigneten Lernstrategien ableiten. Bereits zu Beginn des Sprachenlernens ist es wichtig, dass S hinterfragen, warum sie in einer Lernsituation so vorgehen, wie sie es tun. Die Erkenntnis dieses Prozesses soll den S helfen, das Sprachenlernen bewusst zu erlernen.

Milling around Bei dieser Methode bewegen die S sich innerhalb einer vorgegebenen Zeitspanne frei im Klassenraum und begeben sich wieder auf ihren Platz, sobald sie die relevanten Informationen erfragt haben. Die Auswertung erfolgt im Plenum (▶ Market-place activity).

Mindmap Eine Mindmap dient den S als „Gedankenkarte". Sie ordnen darin ihre Ideen übersichtlich an, wobei Zusammengehöriges beieinandersteht, alle Ideen vernetzt werden können und Farben sowie Zeichnungen Wichtiges hervorheben. Mindmaps können individuell und in der Gruppe erstellt werden und eignen sich als Anregung für mündliche und schriftliche Äußerungen. Mögliches Vorgehen:

1. Die Ideen werden zuerst ungeordnet gesammelt (z. B. auf Kärtchen).
2. Im zweiten Schritt werden Oberbegriffe für die Ideen gefunden (z. B. auf farbigen Kärtchen).
3. Im letzten Schritt visualisieren die S diese Grundlagen systematisch in einer Mindmap.

Mini saga Die S schreiben zu einem bestimmten Thema eine Geschichte, wobei die exakte Wortzahl von 50 erreicht werden muss. Aufgrund der begrenzten Wortzahl setzen sich die S lexikalisch, textlich und inhaltlich aktiv mit der Geschichte auseinander (z. B. *Write a mini saga about your best school day so far.*).

Mitleseverfahren Beim Mitleseverfahren hören die S während des Lesens eines neuen Textes diesen zugleich. Die Aktivierung des visuellen und des auditiven Kanals (Mehrkanallernen) ermöglicht eine enge Verknüpfung von Laut- und Schriftbild, sodass unbekannte Lexeme nachhaltiger verarbeitet werden können. Das Mitleseverfahren ist didaktisch dem Leseverstehen zugeordnet, da die primäre Sprachaufnahme über die Textvorlage erfolgt. Das laute Lesen dient der Ausspracheschulung und nicht dem Leseverstehen, da durch die Konzentration auf die phonologische Oberfläche das Erfassen des Textinhalts erschwert wird. Als Faustregel gilt: Das laute Lesen sollte immer erst eingesetzt werden, nachdem ein Text bereits inhaltlich erarbeitet worden und unbekannter Wortschatz erschlossen worden ist.

Mnemotechniken Unter dem Begriff Mnemotechniken werden verschiedene Methoden des Gedächtnistrainings zusammengefasst. Im Fremdsprachenunterricht eingesetzt, helfen sie S, sich Worte und Informationen über die Schritte des Rekodierens, Assoziierens und schließlich des Abrufens besser einprägen zu können. Häufig verwendete Mnemotechniken sind das ▶ Akrostichon, das Finden von Ersatzwörtern, das Einprägen von Merkversen, die Assoziation von Begriffen/Schriftbild und Bildkarten (▶ Flashcards) und das Memospiel.

Mothering *Mothering* beschreibt ein Korrekturverhalten von L, das mit dem Korrekturverhalten der Mutter bzw. der Eltern beim Mutterspracherwerb vergleichbar ist. Fehlerhafte Aussagen der S werden dabei z. B. durch Wiederholung, übertriebene Intonation oder übertrieben langsames Sprechtempo korrigiert.

Never have I ever Die Übung eignet sich für das spielerische Wiederholen und Festigen des *present perfect*. Ein/-e S berichtet dabei von einer Aktivität, die er/sie noch nie gemacht hat und folgt dabei dem Muster *Never have I ever …* (z. B. *Never have I ever climbed a tree.*). Alle S, die die Aktivität schon einmal durchgeführt haben, stehen auf. Eine/-r der stehenden S kann nun in einem Satz, unter Anwendung des *present perfect* und ggf. Verwendung eines Signalworts (z. B. *already, once, lots of times* etc.) von der Aktivität berichten. Dann ist diese/-r S an der Reihe einen Satz mit *Never have I ever …* zu bilden. Auf diese Weise wird das Spiel fortgesetzt.

Spielende: Das Spiel oder eine Spielrunde endet, wenn eine Aktivität erraten wird, die noch niemand aus der Klasse durchgeführt hat.

Glossar

Alternative: Bei Spielbeginn haben alle S fünf Leben (symbolisiert durch fünf nach oben gehaltene Finger). Ein/-e S bildet einen Satz mit *Never have I ever ...* (z. B. *Never have I ever tried skiing*.) Alle S, die die genannte Aktivität bereits gemacht haben, verlieren ein Leben und müssen einen Finger nach unten klappen. Dann ist der/die nächste S an der Reihe einen Satz nach dem o. g. Muster zu bilden. Ziel ist es, bis zum Spielende möglichst viele Finger oben zu behalten. Es gewinnt der/die S, der/die nach einem Durchlauf noch die meisten Finger oben hat.

Im Gegensatz zur ersten Variante liegt hier der Fokus mehr auf den Aktivitäten, die noch nicht gemacht wurden.

Note-making Das Anfertigen von Notizen ist eine Methodenkompetenz, die auch im Alltag bedeutsam ist. Das *Note-making* ist für die S eine wichtige Fertigkeit zum Generieren und Organisieren von Informationen und Ideen. Die dazu notwendigen Arbeitsschritte reichen vom Sammeln, Sichten und Ordnen der Notizen bis zum Überarbeiten und Anwenden von Stichworten, Themen etc. Für das Ordnen von Notizen eignet sich auch eine ▶ Mindmap.

Note-taking Das *Note-taking* ist eine Strategie des Hörverstehens. Wenn möglich, versuchen die S zunächst, aus Titel oder Überschrift und ggf. aus Fotos, Bildern oder Grafiken erste Informationen über den Hörtext abzuleiten. Sie stellen sich darauf ein und bauen inhaltliche Erwartungen auf. Während des Hörens machen sie sich Notizen. Diese dienen ihnen dazu, wichtige *key words* oder Ideen aus dem Hörtext festzuhalten. Grundlegendes in Form von Stichpunkten aufzuschreiben, ermöglicht nicht nur einen besseren Zugang zu einem Text, sondern den Zugriff auf das Notierte an späterer Stelle. Insgesamt wird dadurch das Lernen effektiver.

L kann folgende Tipps geben:
- Höre auf das, was gesagt wird und wie es gesagt wird.
- Halte einen Stift bereit und schreibe mit. Nicht jedes Wort ist wichtig.
- Nutze Abkürzungen und Symbole beim Notieren (z. B. Sternchen, Ausrufezeichen, Fragezeichen).

Achte auf Schlüsselwörter und -sätze, besonders solche, die wiederholt werden.

Numbered heads together Diese kooperative Lernform ermöglicht eine hohe Schüleraktivierung, da die S, die das Gruppenergebnis präsentieren, per Zufallsprinzip ausgewählt werden und somit jede/-r S Verantwortung für das Gruppenergebnis übernehmen muss. Zunächst bildet L Gruppen (▶ Gruppenbildung). Innerhalb dieser Gruppen erhält jede/-r S eine Zahl (abhängig von der Gruppengröße). L (oder auch eine der Gruppen) stellt nun eine Aufgabe, die die Gruppen gemeinsam bewältigen. Das Startsignal für die Beratungsphase ist *Numbered heads together*! Nach Ablauf einer zuvor festgelegten Zeit beendet L die Beratung und wählt durch Nennung einer Zahl die Person aus, die aufsteht und für die Gruppe antwortet. Pro richtiger Antwort erhält die Gruppe einen Punkt.

Die einzelnen Gruppen können unterschiedliche, aber auch dieselben Aufgaben bearbeiten. Um bei identischen Aufgaben zu verhindern, dass die ausgewählten S mit derselben Zahl die Antworten der anderen Gruppe mithören, verlassen sie zunächst den Klassenraum.

One-minute presentation Eine *One-minute presentation* ist ein Minireferat, in dem einzelne S die Klasse über ein zuvor besprochenes/gewähltes Thema informieren. Der Vortrag erfolgt möglichst frei. Der Zeitrahmen von ca. einer Minute dient zur Beschränkung auf wesentliche Punkte (kann aber bei Bedarf beliebig variiert und z. B. auch auf zwei Minuten ausgeweitet werden: ▶ Two-minute talk). Gleichzeitig ermöglicht die Zeitbeschränkung das Halten von mehreren Vorträgen, ohne dass es für die zuhörenden S langweilig wird.

In fortgeschritteneren Lerngruppen achten die S auf eine kurze Anmoderation und geeignete Überleitungen zwischen den vorgetragenen Aspekten.

Optional help Bei der *Optional help* handelt es sich um eine Form der Differenzierung (▶ Binnendifferenziertes Arbeiten), bei der die S individuell bei Bedarf eine zusätzliche Lernhilfe verwenden können. Dies kann z. B. ein Hilfsblatt sein, das auf dem Pult bereitliegt und dort eingesehen oder mitgenommen werden kann. Es kann zudem eine zusätzliche Hilfe auf den Arbeitsmaterialien sein. Ideal ist es, wenn die *Optional help* zunächst nicht für S sichtbar ist (z. B. als umgeknickter Wort-/Lösungspool am unteren Blattrand) und sie nur dann darauf zurückgreifen, wenn sie Hilfe benötigen.

Glossar

Partner check Die Methode des *Partner check* ist eine Form der ▶ Peer correction. Sie fördert einerseits die Eigenverantwortung der S für ihre Lernergebnisse und ermöglicht andererseits eine breite Aktivierung der S und einen hohen Sprachumsatz. Auch kann damit in gestuften Aufgabenstellungen den unterschiedlichen Lerntempi der S Rechnung getragen werden, z. B. mithilfe der Methode ▶ Bus stop. Beim *Partner check* tauschen sich die S nach Bearbeitung einer Aufgabe bzw. eines Aufgabenteils mündlich zu den Ergebnissen aus und korrigieren mögliche Fehler. Dieses Vorgehen gibt besonders lernschwächeren S zusätzliche Sicherheit für die anschließende Auswertung im Plenum und ist schnell und flexibel einsetzbar.

Partnerpuzzle Das Partnerpuzzle ist eine Variante des ▶ Jigsaw mit dem Unterschied, dass bei dieser Aktivität insgesamt vier S (A, B, C, D) in unterschiedlichen Schritten kooperativ miteinander arbeiten. So erhalten die S-Paare A+B sowie C+D jeweils eine andere Aufgabe, die zunächst von allen S alleine bearbeitet wird. Anschließend tauschen sich die S-Paare A+B sowie C+D, die die identische Aufgabe hatten, untereinander aus. In der letzten Phase informieren sich S-Paare A+C und B+D gegenseitig über die Inhalte ihrer Aufgaben und nehmen so nach der Rolle des Lernenden die des Lehrenden ein.

Partner talk Die Methode des *Partner talk* ist eine einfache Methode, die sich an vielen Stellen des Lernprozesses einsetzen lässt und die dazu dient, Schüleraktivität und Sprechzeit der Lernenden zu erhöhen. S tauschen sich dabei kurz (oft sind ein bis zwei Minuten ausreichend) zu zweit über einen vorgegebenen Sprechanlass (bestimmte Fragestellung, Vorerfahrungen etc.) aus. Die Fragestellungen sollten – wenn nicht im SB enthalten – an der Tafel oder auf Folie festgehalten werden, damit S darauf zurückgreifen können. In lernschwächeren Gruppen sollte L zusätzlich einige situationsbezogene Redemittel anbieten.

Peer correction ▶ Correcting circle

Phasen des Schreibprozesses Zur nachhaltigen Schreibförderung sollten S bei der Textproduktion grundsätzlich folgende drei Phasen durchlaufen:

1. Entwerfen (▶ Brainstorming): Die S sammeln Ideen, z. B. in einer Mindmap oder bei einem ▶ stummen Schreibgespräch.
2. Schreiben: Die S verfassen auf dieser Grundlage einen ersten Entwurf. Dieser sollte entweder von L oder in höheren Klassenstufen durch Mit-S, z. B. in Form eines ▶ Correcting circle, korrigiert werden.
3. Überarbeiten: Auf der Grundlage der Korrekturanmerkungen fertigen die S eine Reinschrift an. Im Sinne einer Differenzierung (▶ Binnendifferenziertes Arbeiten) ist es oftmals hilfreich oder sogar notwendig, entsprechende Schreibhilfen oder Sprachmuster bereitzustellen.

Picture dictation Die S malen bzw. zeichnen nach den genauen Anweisungen von L ein Bild (z. B. *In the middle of the picture there is a big house* …). Alternativ kann auch ein/-e S die Rolle von L übernehmen und Bildanweisungen geben.

Picture duet Bei einem *Picture duet* beschreiben die S einander in PA ein vorgegebenes Bild, indem sie jeweils abwechselnd einen Satz dazu formulieren. (L kann eine Mindestzahl an Sätzen pro Bild und S vorgeben.)

Placemat Bei einer *Placemat activity* sitzen vier oder fünf S um ein Blatt Papier (DIN A3 oder DIN A4), das in einen Schreibbereich pro S sowie einen zusätzlichen Bereich für die Gruppe in der Blattmitte eingeteilt ist.

1. *Placemat* in Gruppen à vier S: 2. *Placemat* in Gruppen à fünf S:

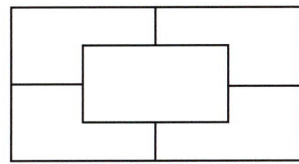 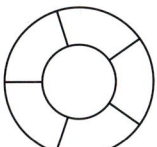

Zu Beginn der Gruppenarbeit schreibt jede/-r S zunächst seine Ideen in den eigenen Schreibbereich. Anschließend wird die *Placemat* so lange gedreht, bis jedes Gruppenmitglied die Ideen der anderen S kommentieren und zudem die Kommentare der anderen zu den eigenen Ideen lesen konnte. Um zu verdeutlichen, wer welche Kommentare verfasst hat, sollten die S verschiedenfarbige Stifte verwenden.

Glossar

Im nächsten Schritt diskutiert die Gruppe die notierten Gedanken und schreibt die wichtigsten Punkte oder Argumente in die Mitte der *Placemat*. Auch kontroverse Positionen sollten dabei aufgenommen werden. Abschließend werden die Ergebnisse im Plenum ausgewertet.

Der Zeitbedarf variiert je nach Komplexität des Themas von zehn bis 30 Minuten. Die Vorgabe eines Zeitlimits für die einzelnen Phasen kann sinnvoll sein.

Pro-und-Kontra-Debatte

Eine Debatte ist eine genau geregelte Diskussion. Ziel einer Debatte ist es, zu einer Entscheidung in einer Streitfrage / bei einer Problemstellung zu kommen. Dabei stehen sich klar abgegrenzte Pro- und Kontra-Positionen gegenüber, denen sich die S zuordnen. Zur Untermauerung ihrer jeweiligen Positionen suchen die S in ihren Gruppen nach Gründen, Argumenten und Beispielen, um diese zu belegen. Falls gewünscht kann L die jeweiligen Gruppen auf eine Größe von drei bis fünf S beschränken.

Ein/-e Moderator/-in (*chairperson*) leitet die Debatte, überwacht die Einhaltung der Reihenfolge, ruft ggf. zur Ordnung und überwacht die festgelegte Redezeit für die einzelnen Gruppen (diese Rolle kann ggf. auch von L übernommen werden). Die an der Debatte nicht direkt beteiligten S agieren als Beobachtende. Sie erhalten Beobachtungsaufgaben, stellen Fragen an die beiden Gruppen und stimmen am Ende darüber ab, welche Gruppe überzeugender argumentiert hat. Die Sitzordnung muss ggf. umorganisiert werden.

Die Debatte folgt festen Regeln:
1. Der/Die Moderator/-in eröffnet die Debatte, indem er/sie das Problem vorstellt und die Regeln erklärt.
2. Die erste Gruppe (Pro-Gruppe) stellt ihren Standpunkt dar.
3. Die zweite Gruppe (Kontra-Gruppe) stellt ihren Standpunkt dar.
4. Die Gruppen befragen sich gegenseitig zu ihren Positionen und auch die Beobachtenden können nun Fragen an die Gruppen richten. Mögliche Regeln zur Steuerung: Wenn Beobachtende etwas sagen wollen, müssen sie die Hand heben. Wenn sie direkt etwas entgegnen wollen, müssen sie beide Hände heben. Die Redner/-innen beziehen sich auf die Vorredner/-innen, signalisieren Zustimmung oder Ablehnung und nennen ihr Argument, das sie durch ein Beispiel untermauern.
5. Jede Gruppe fasst ihre Argumente noch einmal abschließend zusammen.
6. Die Beobachtenden stimmen über die Argumente/Standpunkte ab und der/die Moderator/-in beendet die Debatte.

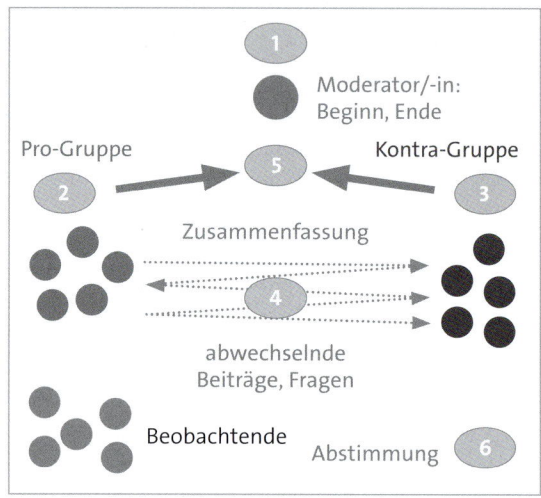

Pyramidendiskussion

Die Pyramidendiskussion (wachsende Gruppe) ist eine Methode, bei der S ein Thema zunächst in Einzel-, dann in Partner- und schließlich in Gruppenarbeit bearbeiten, um sich darüber zu informieren und aus vielen Perspektiven die zentralsten Ideen, Aspekte und Meinungen dazu in der Diskussion zu ermitteln. Die Erarbeitung, bei der die Auseinandersetzung mit Thema und Sprache durch die stetig wachsende Gruppe immer intensiver wird, erfolgt in folgenden Schritten:

1. Die Aufgabe wird von den S in EA erarbeitet. S machen sich Notizen zum Thema und halten eine vorgegebene Anzahl an Vorschlägen am besten ranglistenartig fest.
2. L gibt nach vorgegebener Zeit ein Signal zum Bilden von Paaren und die Aufgabe wird in PA fortgeführt. Die Partner/-innen müssen ihre Listen vergleichen und in der Diskussion eine neue Liste mit gleicher Anzahl an Aspekten erstellen.
3. Nach erneutem Signal finden sich Vierergruppen zusammen, die wiederum ihre Listen vergleichen und auf die anfangs festgelegte Anzahl vereinheitlichen und priorisieren.

Glossar

4. Nach Ablauf der festgelegten Zeit bilden sich Achtergruppen, in denen der Vorgang wiederholt und durch Priorisierung und Abwägen die endgültige Liste erstellt wird.
5. Die Gruppen oder L wählen je eine/-n Sprecher/-in, der/die das Ergebnis im Plenum vorstellt. In erneuter Diskussion kann sich auch noch im Plenum auf ein Klassenergebnis geeinigt werden.
6. Zum Abschluss wird die Methode im Plenum reflektiert.

Question pot Die Methode des *Question pot* eignet sich besonders gut zur Sicherung des Hör-/Sehverstehens von Filmen oder des Leseverstehens von längeren (fiktionalen) Texten. In einem Gefäß sammelt L Fragen oder (*True-/False-*)Aussagen zu einem gezeigten Film oder einem Lesetext auf Papierstreifen. Anschließend ziehen die S einen Streifen, beantworten die Frage oder sagen, ob die Aussage richtig oder falsch ist. Wird die Methode zur Sicherung des Hör-/Sehverstehens eingesetzt, so sollten sich die Aufgaben nicht nur auf das Gesagte, sondern besonders auch auf Gesehenes beziehen. Die Fragen und Aussagen können je nach Leistungsstand der Klasse entweder von L vorgegeben oder von (lernstärkeren) S formuliert werden.

Read-and-look-up technique Diese Lesetechnik dient der Förderung des freien Sprechens und bildet für die S einen behutsamen Übergang zwischen dem Ablesen und Vortragen von Texten, Informationen und Inhalten. Der/Die präsentierende S hält die Vorlage in den Händen und liest sich einen (Teil-)Satz still durch, bevor er/sie die Klasse oder den/die Partner/-in anschaut und den Satz aus dem Gedächtnis wiedergibt. Dabei ist es wichtig, dass S erst dann spricht, wenn er/sie Blickkontakt hergestellt hat. Diese Technik bereitet den freien Vortrag bzw. die Präsentation (auch mithilfe von Stichwortzetteln) vor und hilft unsicheren S, Inhalte vor dem Plenum darzustellen.

L kann die *Read-and-look-up technique* zunächst anhand eines beliebigen Textes demonstrieren. Die S üben danach mit geeigneten kurzen Texten, wobei die zuhörenden Partner-/innen darauf achten, dass nicht abgelesen, sondern vor dem Sprechen Blickkontakt hergestellt wird.

Reading circle Beim *Reading circle* lesen alle S denselben Text oder dieselben Texte (z. B. S-Produkte), wobei jede/-r S eine andere Rolle übernehmen oder sich auf einen bestimmten Aspekt des Textes konzentrieren kann. Die S schreiben dazu jeweils Informationen, Aussagen oder Assoziationen auf ein Blatt, das anschließend ausgelegt oder bei dem Text aufgehängt wird. Sie gehen herum, lesen die Beiträge der anderen S und tragen ihre Kommentare dazu ein. Die Eindrücke der S werden anschließend im Plenum diskutiert.

Reading club (Reciprocal/Guided reading) Der *Reading club* ist eine kooperative Lernform, bei der die Erschließung eines Textes in Vierergruppen arbeitsteilig in verschiedenen Rollen erfolgt. Pro Kapitel/Abschnitt etc. übernimmt jede/-r S im Wechsel eine der folgenden Aufgaben:

Der *Clarifier* klärt unbekannten Wortschatz (schlägt diesen nach) und erklärt den Mit-S die neuen Begriffe.

Der *Summarizer* fasst die Inhalte des Abschnitts zusammen und beantwortet die 5 *Wh*-Fragen (*Who? What? When? Where? Why?*).

Wenn der Lesetext Illustrationen zu mehreren Abschnitten enthält, kann statt des *Summarizer* alternativ auch ein *Describer* eingesetzt werden, der/die die Bilder beschreibt und daraus Rückschlüsse auf den Handlungsverlauf zieht.

Der *Questioner* formuliert Fragen an den Text, die von den Mit-S beantwortet werden.

Der *Predictor* stellt anhand des bisherigen Inhalts Hypothesen zum weiteren Verlauf der Handlung an. Nach jedem Textabschnitt tauschen die S ihre Arbeitsergebnisse aus und rotieren für den nächsten Abschnitt in der Aufgabenverteilung. Durch die arbeitsteilige Vorgehensweise werden metakognitive Textverarbeitungsstrategien gezielt und effektiv angebahnt; zugleich herrscht ein hohes Maß an Kommunikation und Sprachumsatz. Die S müssen an die Methode des *Reading club* (*Reciprocal reading*) schrittweise herangeführt werden. Dazu können entsprechende *Role cards* mit Hinweisen zur jeweiligen Aufgabe hilfreich sein.

Glossar

Reading log
(Lesetagebuch)

Ein *Reading log* dient als Unterstützung beim Lesen einer Ganzschrift (Lektüre) oder von längeren Texten. Der Text wird dabei in entsprechende Abschnitte aufgeteilt, z. B. Kapitel oder Sinneinheiten. Zu diesen Abschnitten gibt L Aufgaben und Arbeitsaufträge – im besten Fall bereits als *Reading log*-Heftchen zusammengestellt – vor, die die S nach dem Lesen des entsprechenden Teils bearbeiten.

Kernbereiche eines *Reading log* sind grundlegende Informationen zu den fünf *Wh*-Fragen *Who? When? Where? What? Why?* sowie eine kurze Inhaltsangabe des jeweiligen Kapitels. Eine vertiefende Charakterisierung der Protagonist/-innen kann den S dabei helfen, ein tieferes Verständnis für die Handlungszusammenhänge und -motive zu erlangen.

Zusätzlich kann ein Lesetagebuch den S Raum geben, um vor dem Lesen des Abschnitts jeweils ihre Erwartungen zu notieren; diese werden dann anschließend mit den Leseerfahrungen verglichen und können am Ende so eine Bewertung des gelesenen Buchs/Texts unterstützen.

Für L bietet sich der Vorteil, dass durch den Einsatz eines *Reading log* besser kontrolliert werden kann, ob die S die Lektüre tatsächlich lesen oder nicht.

Right/wrong cards
(Antwortkärtchen)

Der Einsatz von *Right/wrong cards* eignet sich besonders zur Überprüfung von Aussagen zum Textverständnis. Die Karten können sowohl zur Lese- als auch Hörverstehenskontrolle eingesetzt werden. Ihr Einsatz ermöglicht eine valide Erfassung des Detailverständnisses und erfordert dabei keine eigene Sprachproduktion der S.

L stellt den S Karten aus farbigem Karton zur Verfügung (alternativ auch farbige Gegenstände, z. B. Stifte). Es wird vereinbart, dass grün für *right* und rot für *wrong* sowie ggf. blau für *not in the text* steht. Nachdem L eine Aussage zum Text vorgelesen hat, halten die S auf Kommando eine Karte in die Höhe. L erhält auf diese Weise auf einen Blick eine breite Rückmeldung darüber, ob der jeweilige Textinhalt von den S verstanden wurde. Wenn sich hier größere Abweichungen zeigen, sollte L dies zum Anlass nehmen, einen erneuten Lese-/Hörauftrag zu stellen, um das gesuchte Detail zu erfassen (selektives Lese-/Hörverstehen).

Das synchrone Ausführen auf Kommando ist wichtig, damit sich unsichere S nicht an ihren Mit-S orientieren. Wenn die Methode mehrfach eingesetzt wurde, können lernstärkere S die L-Rolle übernehmen.

Role-play

Role-plays dienen der Förderung des freien Sprechens und Reagierens in klar umrissenen Gesprächssituationen. Die S schlüpfen in die Rolle einer anderen Person und orientieren sich bei der Ausgestaltung an den Rollenvorgaben bzw. füllen ein vorgegebenes Dialoggerüst mit eigenen Ideen. Dürfen leistungsschwächere bzw. unsichere S Notizen zu Hilfe nehmen, sollte L die ▶ Read-and-look-up technique einsetzen und darauf achten, dass S nicht „am Blatt kleben", um das freie Sprechen zu schulen.

Für die Präsentation ist es vorteilhaft, einen Tisch zwischen die Klasse und die Präsentierenden zu stellen, um somit v. a. für verunsicherte S einen „geschützten Raum" zu schaffen. Bei relativ frei zu gestaltenden *Role-plays* sollte vor der Einübung auf jeden Fall eine Kontrolle und Korrektur stattfinden, um ein Einschleifen von fehlerhaften Sprachmustern zu verhindern.

Running competition

Die Methode *Running competition* ist eine Form der *Whole-class activity* mit Wettbewerbscharakter. Sie vereint das Festigen von Vokabeln oder Strukturen mit Bewegung und kommt daher insbesondere jüngeren S sehr entgegen. Ablauf:

L platziert eine Liste (z. B. mit unregelmäßigen Verben, wobei die Anzahl der Hälfte der Klassengröße entspricht) auf dem Pult, ohne dass sie für die S von ihrem Platz aus einzusehen ist. Die Klasse wird in zwei Gruppen eingeteilt und jeder Gruppe wird eine Tafelseite zugeteilt.

Die Teams legen fest, in welcher Reihenfolge die S „aktiv" werden (am besten von vorne nach hinten). Pro Gruppe geht ein/-e S zum Pult und schaut nach, welches Verb dort steht. Er oder sie bildet die entsprechende unregelmäßige Form des simple past und schreibt sie an die Tafelseite seines Teams. Ähnlich wie bei einem Staffellauf kehrt S möglichst schnell zu seiner Gruppe zurück und übergibt die Kreide an den/die Nächste/-n in der Reihe. Dabei darf weder gerannt noch dürfen Hinweise von den nicht agierenden S gegeben werden. Die Gruppe, die als erste die Liste abgearbeitet hat, bekommt einen Punkt.

Glossar

Im Anschluss erhält jede Gruppe die Möglichkeit, ihre Ergebnisse zu verbessern. Dabei sollte L die Zahl der S, die verbessernd eingreifen dürfen, sowie die zur Verfügung stehende Zeit begrenzen (z. B. zwei Minuten). Die festgelegten S kommen an die Tafel und greifen korrigierend in das Ergebnis ein. Es folgt eine Auswertung im Plenum, bei der pro richtige Form ein Punkt vergeben wird. Die Gruppe mit den meisten Punkten hat gewonnen.

Diese Form der Wiederholung und Festigung von sprachlichen Mitteln ist auf zahlreiche Inhalte, wie z. B. Vokabeln, Adjektive, Steigerungsformen und Wortfelder, übertragbar.

Scaffolding — Das *Scaffolding* ist eine Form der Hilfestellung. Dabei gibt L den S Grundgerüste mit Wortelementen vor, mit denen sie einen Text konstruieren, z. B. *My name is … There is/are … in my bag*. Solche Wortgerüste können sowohl für alle Lernenden einer Gruppe gegeben werden oder als individuelle Differenzierung für lernschwächere S.

Scenic play (Szenisches Spielen) — Durch die Methode des *Scenic play* werden kognitive Fähigkeiten, emotionale und körperliche Ausdruckskräfte sowie manuelle und künstlerische Fertigkeiten der S entwickelt und geschult. Das szenische Spielen von Geschichten bettet die Fremdsprache in einen Kontext ein, an dem die S selbst mit allen Sinnen beteiligt sind. L sollte vorher mit den S besprechen, was für das Nachspielen benötigt wird, und dann die Rollen verteilen. Benötigte Requisiten können oft als Zeichnungen an der Tafel dargestellt werden oder es finden Gegenstände aus dem Klassenraum Verwendung.

Schreibgespräch — Ein Schreibgespräch ist eine schriftliche Form der Kommunikation, bei der zwei S in Stillarbeit auf einem Blatt und mit nur einem Stift einen Dialog führen. Beide S schreiben abwechselnd und in Reaktion auf den vorherigen Beitrag ihre Gedanken auf, wobei sie einander nicht beobachten dürfen. Es entsteht somit ein Text, in dem sich beide Partner/Partnerinnen intensiv und konzentriert mit den Gedanken des/der anderen auseinandersetzen und der im Anschluss mündlich diskutiert und kommentiert werden kann.

Schreibkonferenz — ▶ Correcting circle

Semantisierung — Neuer Wortschatz sollte grundsätzlich nicht isoliert, sondern stets im Zusammenhang eingeführt werden. Hierbei bieten sich verschiedene Verfahrensweisen an:

1. Deiktische Semantisierungstechniken: Hierunter versteht man bildhafte, nonverbale Verfahren, die sich besonders in der Orientierungsstufe eignen. Zum Einsatz kommen:
   - Realia: Realgegenstände eignen sich vorrangig zur anschaulichen Vermittlung konkreter Begriffe. Geht es z. B. um das Wort *pencil case*, so hält L ein Federmäppchen hoch und sagt: *This is a pencil case*. Wort und Bedeutung können so nachhaltig miteinander verknüpft werden.
   - Flashcards: ▶ Flashcards
   - *Vocab file*: ▶ Vokabelarbeit
   - Mimik, Gestik, Demonstration: Lebendiges Handeln der L kann den S die Bedeutung entsprechender Lexeme nachhaltig vermitteln. Dies kann geschehen durch:
     a) Mimik: L demonstriert ein Wort mithilfe des entsprechenden Gesichtsausdrucks, z. B. *angry, happy, sad*. Dies kann auch verbal unterstützt werden, z. B. *angry*: *Hey, stop that!*
     b) Gestik: Wenn es um das Wort *first* geht, streckt L den Daumen nach oben und sagt: *It's the first morning in London*.
     c) Demonstration: Das Verb *open* wird eindeutig demonstriert, indem L das Fenster öffnet und dabei sagt: *Let's open the window*. Noch lernwirksamer ist es, wenn dazu das gegenteilige Lexem *close* demonstriert und eingeführt wird: *Now let's close the window*.

2. Verbaldefinitorische Semantisierungstechniken: Mit zunehmendem Lernstand spielen verbaldefinitorische Semantisierungstechniken in der Zielsprache eine stärkere Rolle. Den S sollten alle zur Semantisierung herangezogenen Wortschatzelemente bekannt sein. Zum Einsatz kommen:
   - Ganzheitliche Verfahren: Verwendung des Wortes in einem typischen Kontext: *We wash our hands with soap and water*.

Glossar

- Logische Bezüge: Einführung eines Lexems durch:
  a) Definition: *A dog is an animal with four legs and a tail. It barks.*
  b) Rule of three (Dreisatz): *A man has a mouth, a bird has a beak, ...*
  c) Part – whole (Rückschluss vom Ganzen aufs Einzelne): *a week = seven days*

- Lexikalische Bezüge: Einführung eines Lexems mithilfe von:
  a) Synonymen: *shop – store*
  b) Antonymen: *young ≠ old*
  c) Über-/Unterordnung: *Dogs, cats and rabbits are pets.*
  d) Herleitung: *happy – happiness*

- Der Rückgriff auf die Muttersprache sollte nur sehr selten erfolgen. In einigen Ausnahmefällen kann dieser allerdings hilfreich sein:
- um auf orthografische Ähnlichkeiten aufmerksam zu machen: *theatre – Theater*
- um phonetische Ähnlichkeiten hervorzuheben: *shoe – Schuh*
- wenn die fremdsprachliche Erklärung sehr umständlich wäre (z. B. *although*)

3. Erschließungstechniken: Mit zunehmendem Lernstand sollten wichtige Erschließungstechniken (Kontext, Vorwissen aus der Fremdsprache, Ähnlichkeiten im Schrift- oder Lautbild zur Muttersprache etc.) trainiert werden. Ein neues Wort sollte v. a. dann semantisiert werden, wenn
   a) es sich um ein Schlüsselwort für das Textverständnis handelt,
   b) eine hohe Diskrepanz zwischen Laut- und Schriftbild besteht, die Aussprachefehler bewirken kann,
   c) es nicht aus dem Kontext oder auf andere Weise erschließbar ist.

Situativer Wortschatz, der keine zentrale Bedeutung für das Textverständnis hat, muss nicht semantisiert werden. Den S wird auf diese Weise verdeutlicht, dass sie einen Text auch dann verstehen können, wenn sie nicht jedes einzelne Wort kennen (= Training der Toleranz im Umgang mit „Verständnislücken").

Seven letters — Die S wählen sieben Buchstaben des Alphabets und nutzen sie als Anfangsbuchstaben für das Schreiben von Wörtern zu einem bestimmten Thema. Anschließend wird aus diesen Wörtern ein zusammenhängender Text geschrieben.

Simon says — Beim Spiel *Simon says* geht es um eine ▶ Total Physical Response (TPR). Ein/-e S oder L steht vor der Klasse, fordert die Lernenden auf, eine Aktion durchzuführen, und führt diese direkt vor. Sagt S/L dabei vor der Aktion *Simon says*, so sollen die Lernenden die Aktion nachahmen. Sagt S dies nicht, dürfen die Lernenden sie nicht nachahmen. Lernende, die dies trotzdem tun, scheiden für diese Runde aus. Beispiel: L: *Simon says jump.* (S hüpfen.) L: *Sit.* (Lernende bleiben stehen.)

Small talk — Innerhalb des *Small talk* äußern sich die S zu verschiedenen interessanten, persönlichen und aktuellen Themen im Plenum. Dabei werden die S-Antworten immer wieder erneut von L aufgegriffen und vertieft, an weitere Mit-S weitergegeben bzw. ausführlicher behandelt.

Snowball-Verfahren — Die S arbeiten zunächst paarweise und diskutieren ein Thema, stellen ein Schreibprodukt vor o. Ä. Beide müssen sich innerhalb einer vorgegebenen Zeit auf eine Meinung, eine Idee, ein Schreibprodukt etc. einigen. Dann diskutieren zwei S-Paare miteinander und müssen sich wiederum einigen. Im nächsten Schritt diskutieren zwei Viererteams und müssen sich wieder einig werden. Zuletzt erfolgt der Austausch der Meinungen oder Ergebnisse im Plenum.

Speed dating — Diese Methode entspricht im Prinzip der Idee des ▶ Double circle mit dem Unterschied, dass die S nicht in einem Kreis, sondern in zwei sich anschauenden Linien interagieren.

Speed reading — Um das *Scanning* zu üben bzw. um zu lernen, dass man auch dem Layout bzw. der grafischen Gestaltung grundlegende Informationen entnehmen kann, bietet sich das *Speed-reading*-Verfahren an. Die S arbeiten individuell. L erklärt, dass sie in einem Wettbewerb stehen und die erforderlichen Informationen (drei bis vier Fragen werden an Tafel notiert) so schnell wie möglich finden sollen. Alle S beginnen auf ein Signal hin, gleichzeitig zu lesen. Wer alle Antworten gefunden hat, lehnt sich zurück bzw. gibt ein Handzeichen, sodass L erkennt, wer schon fertig ist und den schnellsten S ermitteln kann.

Glossar

Alternativ blendet L einen gut lesbaren, überschaubaren Text über Smartboard oder Beamer für kurze Zeit ein. Die S nennen die Hauptaussage und/oder möglichst viele Details und tauschen sich darüber im Plenum aus. Die kurze Lesephase kann mehrmals wiederholt werden.

Split viewing — L teilt das Plenum in zwei Gruppen ein. Die eine Hälfte sieht und hört das Video, die andere Gruppe hört nur den Soundtrack, da diese S sich zur Rückwand drehen. L erklärt, dass die sehende Gruppe nach dem *viewing* den anderen die Handlung erklären muss und dass die hörende Gruppe spekulieren soll, was geschieht bzw. sich Fragen überlegt. Nach dem Anschauen des Videoclips beginnen zunächst die „Hörenden" mit dem Austausch von Ideen, dann erklären oder ergänzen die „Sehenden", was genau passiert ist. Für den Austausch bietet sich im Sinne der Erhöhung der individuellen Sprechzeit PA an.

Variante: Man kann durch die Verwendung von Kopfhörern die Klasse auch in reine „Sehende" und „Hörende" einteilen. Die „Hörenden" drehen sich wie oben einfach um. Die „Sehenden" blockieren den Soundtrack durch das Hören von Musik und sehen das Video nur. Bei dieser Variante haben beide Gruppen ein Informationsdefizit und können sich über die Bedeutungen, die sie entweder aus dem Gesehenen oder aus dem Gehörten erschlossen haben, vergleichen.

Sprachmittlung — ▶ Mediation

Standbildmethode — ▶ Freeze-frame

Stimmungsbarometer — Diese Methode wird i. d. R. zu Beginn oder zum Abschluss einer Gruppenarbeit angewandt, um die anfängliche bzw. abschließende Stimmungslage der Mitglieder zu erfassen und zu veranschaulichen. Die moderierende Person stellt hierzu ein Plakat bereit, auf welchem z. B. eine Sonne, Nebel und Gewitterwolken abgebildet sind. Die Gruppenmitglieder erhalten die Gelegenheit, je einen Punkt neben diejenige Abbildung zu kleben bzw. zeichnen, die ihrer Stimmung am ehesten entspricht. Das entstandene Stimmungsbild dient der Gruppe als Diskussionsgrundlage und sofern die Methode regelmäßig durchgeführt wird, kann eine langfristige Entwicklung der Gruppenstimmung protokolliert werden.

Students as experts — ▶ Binnendifferenziertes Arbeiten

Stummer Impuls — Ein stummer Impuls kann ein Bild, ein Gegenstand oder ein angeschriebenes Wort bzw. mehrere Wörter sein. L gibt den stummen Impuls, ohne zu sprechen, und wartet auf die Äußerungen der S. So kann beispielsweise ein neues Thema gut eingeleitet werden, zu dem die S schon erste Ideen äußern.

Stummes Schreibgespräch — Hierbei kommunizieren zwei oder mehrere S schriftlich und bei absolutem Schweigen miteinander. Die S geben ein Blatt herum und jede/-r von ihnen schreibt nacheinander eine These zu einem Thema, eine Antwort auf eine Frage, einen Kommentar o. Ä. auf und gibt das Blatt dann weiter. Der/Die Nächste schreibt eine Ergänzung oder eine neue Stellungnahme dazu, die wichtig für das Thema ist. Auch Schlagworte, Zeichnungen oder Symbole sind erlaubt.

Auf diese Weise lassen sich Ideen und Antworten zu einem Thema entwickeln, Beziehungen aufbauen und vertiefen sowie ein Gedankenaustausch entwickeln. Falls die Ergebnisse im Plenum präsentiert werden sollen, bietet es sich an, dass die beteiligten S sich auf eine festgelegte Anzahl von Ideen oder Thesen einigen, die ihnen am wichtigsten oder prägnantesten erscheinen.

Variante: Es besteht auch die Möglichkeit, dass jede/-r S auf einem eigenen Blatt anfängt und die Blätter reihum zur Kommentierung weitergegeben werden. Wenn am Ende alle jedes Blatt kommentiert haben, lesen alle die Kommentare auf ihrem eigenen Blatt.

Swap cards — Bei der Methode *Swap cards* bewegen sich die S im Raum. Dabei haben sie eine Karte mit einer Frage, einer Wendung, Wortschatz etc. in der Hand. Nach einem akustischen Signal durch L finden die S mithilfe einer ▶ Market-place activity einen Partner / eine Partnerin. Dann bearbeiten sie die Aufgaben (S1 fragt S2, S2 fragt S1). Die Karten werden getauscht und die Lernenden suchen sich neue Partner/-innen. Um einen zügigen Verlauf zu gewährleisten, werden die Lernenden darauf hingewiesen, immer eine/-n Mit-S in ihrer unmittelbaren Nähe zu wählen. Die *Swap cards* eignen sich auch optimal zur ▶ Grammatikwiederholung.

Glossar

Szenisches Spielen	▶ Scenic play
Think-Pair-Share	Diese kooperative Lernform dient den S dazu, von einer individuellen zu einer gemeinsamen Lösung zu gelangen. Ablauf:

1. EA: Die S denken allein über die Aufgabenstellung nach und machen sich ggf. Notizen.
2. PA: Zwei S besprechen ihre Notizen und kommen zu einer gemeinsamen Lösung.
3. GA: Zwei Paare bilden eine Vierergruppe, die gemeinsam ihre Lösungen bespricht. Eine andere Möglichkeit ist, dass die Paare ihre Lösungen im Plenum vorstellen.

L sollte für jeden Arbeitsschritt ein Zeitlimit setzen.

Three truths, two lies Die S formulieren Sätze, z. B. über ein Bild oder einen Text. Dabei achten sie darauf, mindestens zwei inhaltlich falsche Sätze zu bilden. Die Anzahl an falschen und richtigen Sätzen kann von L variiert werden, sollte aber immer klar vorgegeben sein.

Es empfiehlt sich, diese Sätze aufschreiben zu lassen, da es den S oft schwerfällt, sich die falschen Sätze zu merken. Anschließend können die Sätze im Plenum vorgestellt werden und die Klasse rät, welche Sätze falsch sind.

Thumbs up (Daumenabfrage) Bei dieser Feedbackmethode geben alle S auf Zeichen von L hin mit geschlossenen Augen mit ihrem Daumen eine i. d. R. dreistufige Wertung (*thumbs up* – "neutral" – *down*) zu einer Fragestellung ab (z. B. *Were you able to understand the text/presentation?*). Wenn alle ihre Wertung abgegeben haben, bittet L die S, die Augen wieder zu öffnen und sich die Bewertungen der Klasse anzusehen. Wer möchte, darf sich zu seiner eigenen Bewertung anschließend verbal äußern (z. B. begründen, warum die Bewertung so abgegeben wurde). Auf diese Weise lassen sich Auswertungsprozesse effektiv nonverbal und unter Einbeziehung aller S initiieren.

Ticket vote Die Methode des *Ticket vote* dient dazu, eine Einschätzung der Lerngruppe zu einem Film zu erhalten. Zu diesem Zweck erhält jede/-r S eine (imaginäre) Eintrittskarte, die nach dem Sehen in vorbereitete Schachteln geworfen wird. Die Schachteln können zwei (+, –) oder drei (+, 0, –) Kategorien haben. Das Ergebnis kann als Grundlage zu einer Diskussion über den Film dienen, die z. B. als ▶ Hot seat organisiert werden kann.

Total Physical Response (TPR) Das Konzept der *Total Physical Response* (TPR) beruht auf der Einbeziehung von Körpersprache und Bewegung, um das Hörverstehen der S zu fördern. *TPR* spricht in besonderem Maße S mit Sprechhemmungen oder geringem Sprachinventar an, die mithilfe der Methode die Fremdsprache handelnd umsetzen und so Erfolgserlebnisse erzielen.

Die S reagieren auf eine Anweisung der L oder einem anderen S nonverbal, indem sie diese in Bewegung umsetzen. Die Anweisungen sollten z. B. durch Gestik oder den Einsatz von Realgegenständen verständlich gemacht werden. Durch mehrfache Wiederholung kann die Behaltensleistung gesteigert werden, indem Handlung und Sprache nachhaltig miteinander verknüpft werden.

Two-minute talk ▶ One-minute presentation

Two stars and a wish Diese Feedbackmethode birgt einen hohen Grad an Wertschätzung und sprachlicher Würdigung, da grundsätzlich die erbrachte Leistung mit mehr Positiva im Vordergrund steht. Es werden zunächst zwei positive Aspekte benannt (= *stars*) und anschließend ein Optimierungswunsch (= *wish*).

Uniform day Um zu erfahren, wie sich das Tragen einer Uniform anfühlen kann, lohnt es sich, einen *Uniform day* durchzuführen. Hierzu spricht sich die Klasse auf Englisch ab, was sie am *Uniform day* anziehen kann, z. B. eine schwarze Hose und ein weißes T-Shirt, wobei das Ziel ist, eine einheitliche Kleidungsfarbe jeweils für ein Oberteil und ein Unterteil zu finden. Es lohnt sich, die S darauf hinzuweisen, dass die Kleidung möglichst schick/gepflegt sein sollte. Gleichzeitig wird darauf hingewiesen, dass keine neue Kleidung gekauft werden soll. Ob eine Krawatte getragen wird, sollte im Einzelfall entschieden werden.

Glossar

Der *Uniform day* sollte an einem Tag sein, an dem auch Englischunterricht stattfindet. So können Klassenfotos in Uniform gemacht und die Eindrücke gemeinsam reflektiert werden. Es bietet sich hier z. B. an, über die Gefühle zu sprechen, die man beim Tragen der Uniform hat. Da sich diese Gefühle oft von Unsicherheit (zu Hause) zu Freude (in der Schule) verwandeln, lohnt es sich auch, die S reflektieren zu lassen, wie sie sich vor der Schule gefühlt haben. Die authentischste Uniform kann gekürt werden, um den Mut der S zu belohnen, die besonders schicke Kleidung tragen. Es sollte hierbei jedoch unbedingt sensibel auf das soziale Gefüge in der Klasse geachtet werden.

Vokabelarbeit Die S sollten möglichst früh damit beginnen, sich eine Vokabelsammlung anzulegen. Dies kann z. B. mithilfe eines Vokabelhefts oder eines selbst angelegten *Vocab files* geschehen, in das die S auch kleine Bilder und Skizzen zur Verdeutlichung der Bedeutung einfügen. Neues Vokabular übertragen die S von der ▶ Vokabeltafel sofort in ihre Vokabelsammlung. Für bestimmte Wortgruppen bzw. thematischen Wortschatz empfiehlt es sich zusätzlich, *Wordwebs* ähnlich einer ▶ Mindmap anzulegen. Dabei sammeln die S Vokabeln, die sie durch Verbinden in Beziehung zueinander setzen bzw. thematisch gruppieren. Die *Wordwebs* können dem *Vocab file* hinzugefügt werden.

Vokabelrennen Für das Spiel *Vokabelrennen* bilden die S zunächst Kleingruppen. Die S einer Gruppe spielen gegeneinander. L bestimmt, welche Gruppe beginnt und gibt dieser Gruppe eine Vokabel. Der/Die S aus der Gruppe, der/die die Vokabel am schnellsten errät, darf sich zum nächsten Tisch bewegen. Dort tritt S nun gegen die S dieser Gruppe an. Wieder wird eine Vokabel erfragt und nur der/die schnellste S darf zur nächsten Tischgruppe weitergehen. Dies wird wiederholt, bis ein/-e S wieder am Ursprungstisch ankommt.

Vokabeltafel Wird mithilfe einer Tafel gelehrt, bietet es sich an, eine feste Tafelseite für Vokabeln zu reservieren, die die S immer abschreiben, sobald L dort neue Vokabeln anschreibt. Beim Semantisieren von Wortschatz (▶ Semantisierung) sollte L stets die Übersetzung mit anschreiben, die die S dann ebenfalls übertragen.

Voting finger ▶ Democratic vote

Wachsende Gruppe ▶ Pyramidendiskussion

Who is it? Bei diesem Spiel sitzt ein/-e freiwillige/-r S mit dem Rücken zur Tafel. Ein/-e S oder L schreibt den Namen einer berühmten Person an die Tafel. Der/die freiwillige S stellt Fragen, die von der Klasse mit *yes*/*no* beantwortet werden können. Der/die S versucht, über die Antworten die Person zu erraten. Alternative: Die S können in zwei (oder mehr) Teams gegeneinander antreten. Dabei darf pro Team eine Frage pro Runde gestellt werden. Es gewinnt das Team, in welchem die Person zuerst erraten wird.

Word memo Der Wortschatz (einzelne Wörter, Wortgruppen) wird senkrecht an der Tafel notiert und nacheinander im Chor gesprochen. Nach jedem Chorsprechen wird ein Wort / eine Wortgruppe von der Tafel gewischt. Die abgewischten Wörter werden jedoch beim Chorsprechen weiterhin (auswendig) mit aufgesagt. Am Ende ist der gesamte Wortschatz von der Tafel gewischt worden und wird komplett auswendig (nacheinander) im Chor gesprochen. Zusätzlich kann der verwendete Wortschatz anschließend im Kontext versprachlicht werden (z. B. indem Beispiele oder Definitionen genannt werden).

Words in the air Bei der Methode *Words in the air* arbeiten die S in PA. Sie schreiben ein Wort in die Luft, das der Partner / die Partnerin erraten soll. Es empfiehlt sich, den zu verwendenden Wortschatz einzuschränken, sodass das Raten leichter fällt und der richtige Wortschatz geübt wird.

Diese Aktivität eignet sich besonders gut als *Warm-up* und zur Vokabelwiederholung. Sie kann mit weiteren Bewegungen verknüpft werden, wenn der/die ratende S das Wort z. B. nachspielen oder mit einer Aktivität verknüpfen soll.

Word race Die Klasse wird in zwei Gruppen geteilt, die an je einer Tafelseite eine Schlange bilden. L gibt ein Thema vor. Die S schreiben so viele Begriffe wie möglich an die Tafel. Bei großen Klassen können auch mehr Gruppen gebildet werden, die die Begriffe auf einem A3-Blatt notieren.
Auswertung: Von beiden/mehreren Gruppen verwendete Wörter geben einen Punkt. Wörter, die nur eine der Gruppen hat, geben zwei Punkte. Gewonnen hat die Gruppe mit den meisten Punkten.

Glossar

World Cafe — Bei dieser Methode gibt es je nach Themen in der Klasse mehrere Gruppentische, die wahlweise mit Flipchartbögen, Packpapier und Stiften ausgestattet sind. Das jeweilige Thema der Gruppe steht in der Mitte der Bögen. Ein/-e S fungiert als *host* (Gastgeber/-in), d. h., S moderiert die Diskussion und verbleibt bei dem Wechsel der anderen Gruppenmitglieder am Tisch, um die nächste Gruppe über die bisherigen Ergebnisse zu informieren und den weiteren Prozess zu moderieren.

Der *host* stellt das Thema vor, die anderen Gruppenmitglieder haben nun Zeit, nachzudenken, zu diskutieren und anschließend ihre Überlegungen auf die Bögen zu schreiben. Diese dienen nun im weiteren Verlauf als Diskussionsgrundlage. Der *host* hält ggf. weitere Ergebnisse fest. Auf ein Signal der L wechseln die Gäste den Tisch und werden an dem neuen Tisch vom *host* über die bisherigen Ergebnisse informiert. Nun beginnt der oben beschriebene Ablauf erneut. Zum Abschluss der Diskussionsrunden kehren die S an ihren Ausgangstisch zurück, tauschen ihre Erfahrungen aus und berichten dem Plenum von den Ergebnissen ihrer Gruppe.

Worterschließungstechniken — Um sich Wörter in der Fremdsprache ohne die Hilfe von L zu erschließen, können sich die S verschiedener Techniken, die ihnen aus der Muttersprache geläufig sind, bedienen. So können sie Wörter aus dem Kontext erschließen, sich Bedeutungen aus der Wortzusammensetzung herleiten oder über eine phonologische oder grafische Ähnlichkeit des Wortes in der Muttersprache auf die Bedeutung schließen.

Wortschatzsemantisierung — ▶ Semantisierung

Zählen in der Gruppe — Ziel dieses kooperativen Spiels ist es, bis zu einer bestimmten Zahl zu zählen, die von L festlegt wird. Diese Zahl sollte nicht zu hoch sein, also etwa 20–25. Das Zählen erfolgt nach folgenden Regeln:
1. Die S dürfen sich nicht austauschen oder vorher absprechen. Dazu kann vereinbart werden, dass sie die Augen schließen.
2. Jede/-r S darf zählen.
3. Es darf immer nur eine Zahl genannt werden, d. h., kein/-e Mitspieler/-in darf zwei aufeinanderfolgende Zahlen nennen. Erst nachdem ein/-e andere/-r S dran war, darf man erneut mitzählen.
4. Wenn zwei S gleichzeitig eine Zahl nennen, muss die Gruppe vorn vorne mit dem Zählen beginnen.

Zufallsgenerator — Mithilfe dieser Methode kann L nach Zufallskriterien S auswählen, die eine Aufgabe, ein Projekt o. Ä. präsentieren sollen. Zu diesem Zweck stehen zunächst alle S auf und L nennt ein Kriterium. Falls S dieses erfüllen, setzen sie sich hin. Die Person, die am Ende noch steht, präsentiert die Aufgabe.

Tipp: Um zu verhindern, dass sich am Ende alle S setzen können, wählt L Sätze mit Superlativen (z. B. *The youngest / the tallest / ...*).

Bus stop — Extra

Where we're from   0.1

1 VIEWING The United Kingdom and Ireland

a) BEFORE YOU WATCH Look at the map in your book, p. 10, and complete the table:

Which countries make up …	
1 Great Britain (GB)?	England, _____ and _____
2 the island of Ireland?	_____ and _____
3 the United Kingdom (UK)?	_____, _____, _____ and _____

b) Watch part 1 of the video. Check your answers from **a)**.

c) Make a group of five students. Each one in your group picks one country.

d) Watch the video again and write the name of the country and the capital in the table. Then watch again and check. ☒ Watch part 2 and write more information for your country.

country	capital	☒ more information
England		

e) Present your results in the group.

- My country is …
- The capital is …
- … is the biggest / smallest country.
- It has … million[1] people.
- The country lies in the north / south of …

f) Complete the information for the other countries.

[1] million *Million(en)*

1 SWAP CARDS Verbs 1.1A

a) **PREPARATION** Cut out the swap cards. Decide which tense you want to practise (e.g. *simple past*).

b) **INSTRUCTION** Every student gets one card. Show your card to another student. They have to make a sentence with the correct verb form.

Lighthouse 3 | Lehrkräftefassung Plus
Illustrationen: Cornelsen/Karen Donnelly

1 SWAP CARDS Verbs 1.1B

a) PREPARATION Cut out the swap cards. Decide which tense you want to practise (e.g. *simple past*).

b) INTSTRUCTION Every student gets one card. Show your card to another student. They have to make a sentence with the correct verb form.

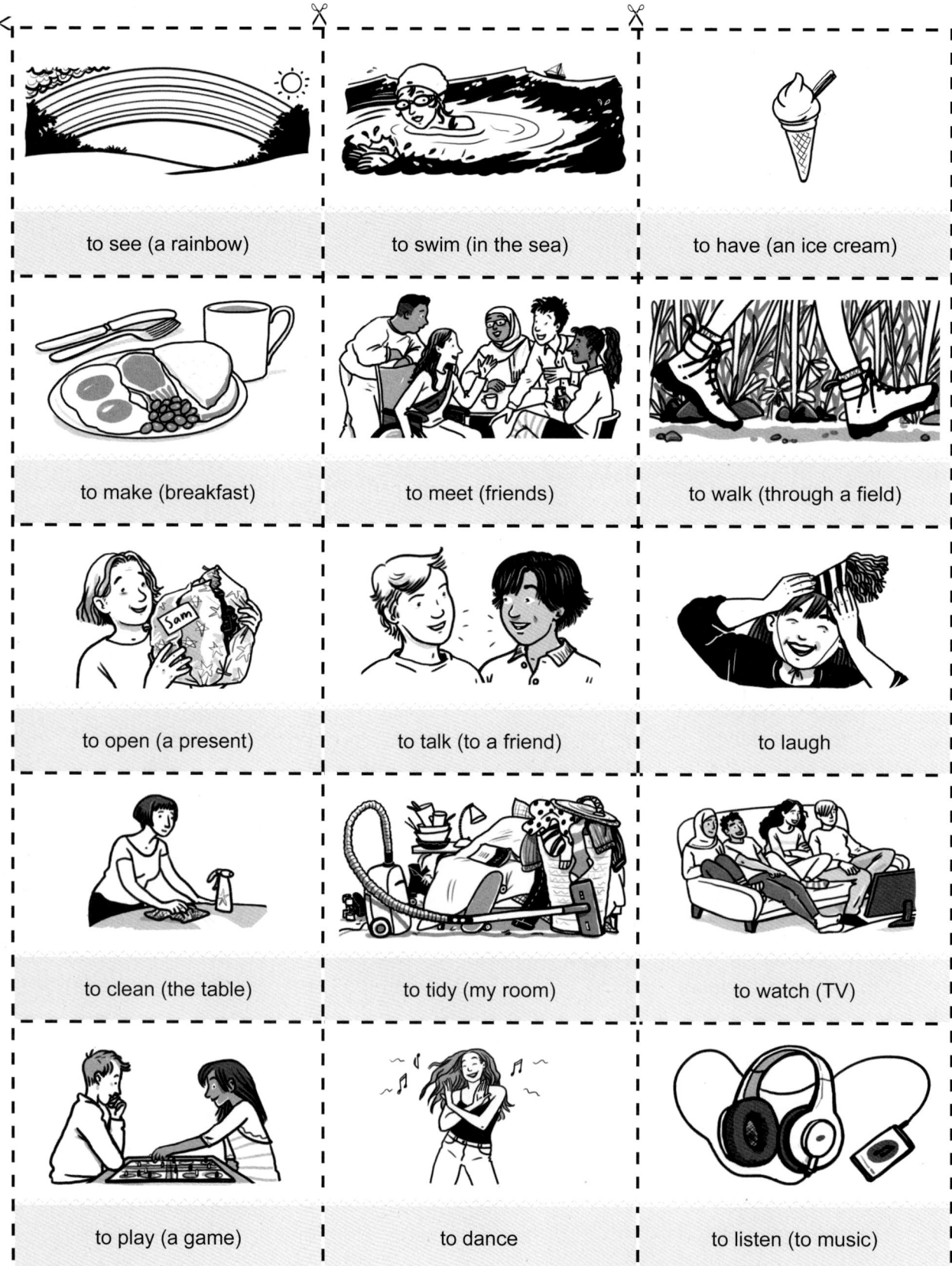

to see (a rainbow)	to swim (in the sea)	to have (an ice cream)
to make (breakfast)	to meet (friends)	to walk (through a field)
to open (a present)	to talk (to a friend)	to laugh
to clean (the table)	to tidy (my room)	to watch (TV)
to play (a game)	to dance	to listen (to music)

Lighthouse 3 | Lehrkräftefassung Plus
Illustrationen: Cornelsen/Karen Donnelly

1 GAME Quiz-quiz-swap   1.2

PREPARATION Cut out the cards according to the number of students in the class. The students can use the empty cards for their own ideas.

bring	buy	eat
travel	visit	go
walk	buy	spend
stay	meet	see
_____	_____	_____
_____	_____	_____
_____	_____	_____
_____	_____	_____

Lighthouse 3 | Lehrkräftefassung Plus

1 MY TASK My virtual tour   1.3A

a) Plan a walking tour of London with your partner. Look at the map on the next page and choose a start and an end. Start at Trafalgar Square, the London Eye, the Tower of London or Buckingham Palace.

> Go straight on / across / along / past / …
> Take the first / second / … street on the left / right.
> If you go / turn …, you'll arrive at the … / you'll see a …

_____

_____

_____

_____

_____

_____

_____

_____

_____

_____

_____

b) Do another pair's tour. Use a map or virtual tour app and follow the directions. Which famous places do you 'see' on the tour?

_____

_____

_____

c) Give feedback on the tour.

> I thought the tour was clever / difficult / easy / fun / interesting / …

> I liked seeing the …

Lighthouse 3 | Lehrkräftefassung Plus

1 MY TASK London Map — 1.3B

Look at this map of London and choose a start and an end for your walking tour. Start at Trafalgar Square, the London Eye, the Tower of London or Buckingham Palace.

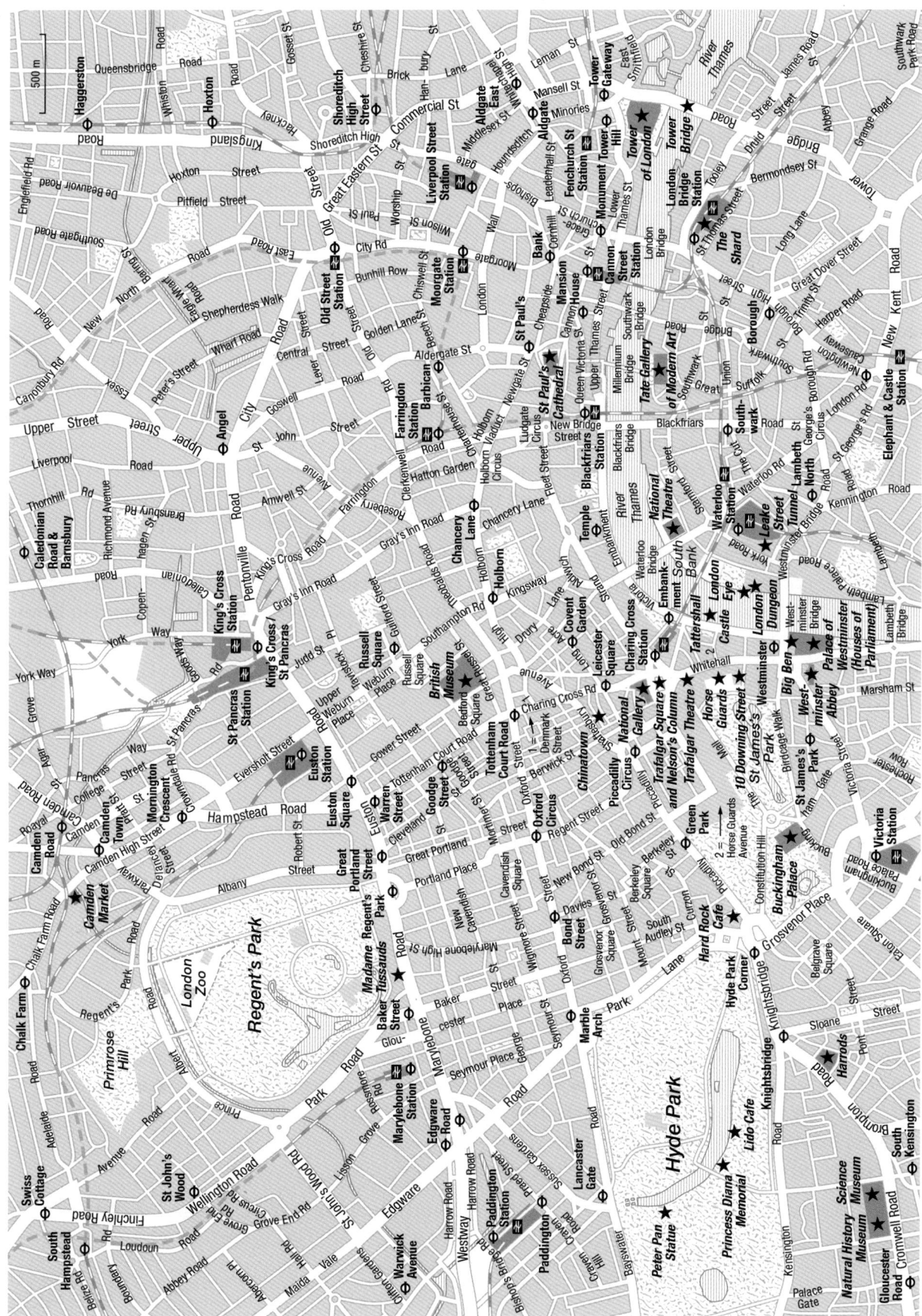

1 Checkpoint answers   1.4A

1 LISTENING London rock tour (1)

I can understand and share information about London.

a) 1 C • 2 B • 3 D • 4 E • 5 A   (5 points)

b) 1 false (three London sites)   (5 points)
2 false (a few minutes' walk away)
3 true
4 false (only until 1964)
5 true

2 MEDIATION London rock tour (2)

Guide:	So, this is Berwick Street. Lots of people will know this street because a photo of it was on the cover of a famous album by the band Oasis.	(8 points)
Dad:	Was hat sie gesagt?	
You:	Sie hat gesagt, dass (1) **Berwick Street bekannt ist, weil die Straße auf dem Cover eines berühmten Oasis-Albums zu sehen war.**	
Dad:	Ach so, danke! Da drüben ist ein Markt. Kannst du fragen, ob wir dort CDs oder T-Shirts kaufen können?	
You:	Excuse me. My dad has a question about the market over there: (2) **Can we buy CDs or band T-shirts (in the market) over there?**	
Guide:	The market only sells food and some other small things. But don't worry, there are lots of shops here where you can buy CDs or band T-shirts.	
You:	Sie hat gesagt, dass (3) **es auf dem Markt nur Lebensmittel und andere kleine Sachen gibt. Aber es gibt hier viele Geschäfte, in denen man CDs oder Bandshirts kaufen kann.**	
Dad:	OK. Und kannst du fragen, ob wir Zeit haben, hier noch einen Kaffee zu trinken?	
You:	My dad has another question: (4) **Do we have time for a coffee here?**	

(Für jede korrekte Antwort gibt es zwei Punkte.)

18–16	15–12	11–9	8–0

3 WORDS Let's go to the South Bank

I can talk about transport in London.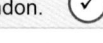

a) **extra words:** public • direct   (8 points)

1 tube	3 change	5 Travelcard	7 hire
2 line	4 stops	6 take	8 traffic

b) SPEAKING (Lösungsbeispiel)   (6 points)

A: It's a nice day. Do you want to go to **St James's Park**?
B: Sure, let's **take the Northern line. It takes 22 minutes and it's direct**.
A: I don't really want to **take the tube because it's so busy**. Why don't we **walk**? We can **talk while we walk. It takes 55 minutes and it's 2.7 miles from here**.
B: That's a good idea, and it's **healthy**.
A: Great, let's go!

(Es sind sind mehr als 4–6 Sätze pro Dialog möglich. Für jeden korrekten Satz gibt es einen Punkt)

14–12	11–10	9–7	6–0

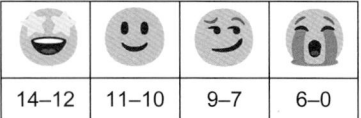

Lighthouse 3 | Lehrkräftefassung Plus
Smileys: Shutterstock.com/Yefym Turkin

1 Checkpoint answers — 1.4B

4 LANGUAGE Ideas for a day in London

I can plan a tour (conditional sentences type 1). ✓

a) 1 f • 2 a • 3 e • 4 c • 5 d • 6 b   (6 points)

b)
1. go / 'll stay
2. stop / 'll see
3. isn't / 'll find
4. don't go / 'll have
5. 'll see / visit
6. won't get / travel

(6 points)

| 12–11 | 10–8 | 7–6 | 5–0 |

5 WRITING Hanna's blog

I can describe life in cities and in my area. ✓

(Lösungsbeispiel) Hi, everybody! I want to tell you about my life in Dortmund. Dortmund is a big city in west Germany. Dortmund is famous for its football team. There are some great things about my city, like a big park, great places to go shopping and a nice zoo. But there are also some problems, like lots of traffic, air pollution and expensive cost of living. What's your city like? I'm looking forward to reading about it in the comments.   (6 points)

(Es sind mehr als 6 Sätze möglich. Für jeden korrekten Satz gibt es einen Punkt.)

| 6 | 5–4 | 3 | 2–0 |

6 READING At Leake Street Tunnel

I can follow and discuss the events in a story. ✓

a) 3 • 5 • 2 • 1 • 4 • 6   (6 points)

b) (Lösungsbeispiel)   (6 points)

Hey, Sunita! You won't believe what happened today! I went to the graffiti tunnel with Ali and I saw some amazing art. I brought my paper and pencils to draw some ideas. Ali had to go outside for a bit and I drew a sunset on the beach. Then a boy called Zach came and said he liked my picture. He wants to teach me how to paint on the wall next week. Isn't that cool?

(Es sind mehr als 6 Sätze möglich. Für jeden korrekten Satz gibt es einen Punkt.)

c) (Lösungsbeispiel)   (6 points)

Lily wasn't sure if her picture was good enough. It was just an idea. She was surprised when Ali and Zach said, 'It's a good picture'. She was even more surprised when Zach asked if she wanted to paint it on the tunnel.

(Es sind mehr als 6 Sätze möglich. Für jeden korrekten Satz gibt es einen Punkt.)

| 18–16 | 15–12 | 11–9 | 8–0 |

7 STUDY SKILLS London on a rainy day

I can do online research. ✓

(6 points)

keywords	websites	notes
London + The British Museum	1. https://www.britishmuseum.org	place: … near Central London; tickets: £0; open: 10 a.m.–5 p.m. daily; fun facts: The British Museum has a big collection of art and historical objects such as the Rosetta Stone and Egyptian mummies.

(Es kann mehr als eine Sehenswürdigkeit recherchiert werden. Für jede Sehenswürdigkeit gibt es 6 Punkte.)

| 6 | 5–4 | 3 | 2–0 |

Lighthouse 3 | Lehrkräftefassung Plus
Smileys: Shutterstock.com/Yefym Turkin

2 Letters to the advice column   2.1

1 READING Letters to the advice column

a) BEFORE YOU READ What problems do you think the letters on p. 49 will be about?

friends, _____

b) Read the letters (1–4) on p. 49. Match them to the correct headings (A–D).

A Problems with parents ☐   C Frenemies ☐
B Worried about a friend ☐   D Student in love ☐

c) Read the letters again and correct the sentences.

1 'Puzzled friend' thinks their friend was just joking.

_____

2 'Angry student' isn't happy because they mustn't go out.

_____

3 'Shy student' finds it hard to talk to the girl in their class.

_____

4 'BFF' thinks they can't do anything about their friend's situation.

_____

2 LOOKING AT LANGUAGE *must, mustn't, (don't) have to, needn't, (not) be allowed to*

Look at the examples from the letters on p. 49. Then answer the questions.

> 1 I **have to** be back at 6 o'clock when I go out.
> 2 I feel that I **must** do something to help.
> 3 And I **mustn't** be late.
> 4 I'**m not allowed to** do anything!
> 5 I **don't have to** be funny or interesting.
> 6 She says that I **needn't** worry.

Which of the underlined verbs or phrases mean …

1 *(ich) muss?* _____

2 *(ich) darf nicht?* _____

3 *(ich) muss nicht* or *(ich) brauche nicht?* _____

Lighthouse 3 | Lehrkräftefassung Plus

2 Giving feedback 2.2

Part 1: Feedback on your partner's letter of advice

a) Read your partner's letter and the checklist below.

b) Tick and write comments. Underline any problems in your partner's letter. Use different colours.

	😃	🙂	😉	comments/notes
Does the letter start with a greeting and is it addressed to someone (with a nickname)?				
Does the letter name the problem it wants to solve?				
Does your partner use *should* and *shouldn't*? How many times?				
Is the advice useful?				
Does the letter end with a greeting and your partner's name or 'Your advice column'?				
Can you find any grammar or spelling mistakes? Correct them.				

Part 2: Feedback on a group's discussion

Listen to the group's discussion. Tick and write comments. Then give feedback.

	😃	🙂	😉	comments/notes
People are speaking loudly and clearly.				
The people who are speaking are looking at each other.				
The group is using at least ____ opinion phrases.				
The group is using at least ____ phrases to disagree.				
The group is using at least ____ phrases to agree.				
People gave good reasons for their opinion.				
The group found a good compromise in the end.				

Lighthouse 3 | Lehrkräftefassung Plus
Smileys: Shutterstock.com/Yefym Turkin

2 Discussion tickets — 2.3

1 Have a discussion

Cut out the discussion tickets.

I think that …	In my opinion, …
opinion	opinion
If you ask me, …	I believe that …
opinion	opinion
I would say that …	I see it a bit differently.
opinion	disagreeing
I don't think that's true.	I don't agree with you at all.
disagreeing	disagreeing
That's a good point.	Yes, you're so right.
agreeing	agreeing
I completely agree.	I see your point, but have you thought of …?
agreeing	☒ introducing a new point

Lighthouse 3 | Lehrkräftefassung Plus

2 Mei's podcast / A quiz for Green Clothes Day

2.4

1 LISTENING Mei's podcast

a) What's important to you? Put the pictures (A–F) in order. Then tell a partner. Say why.

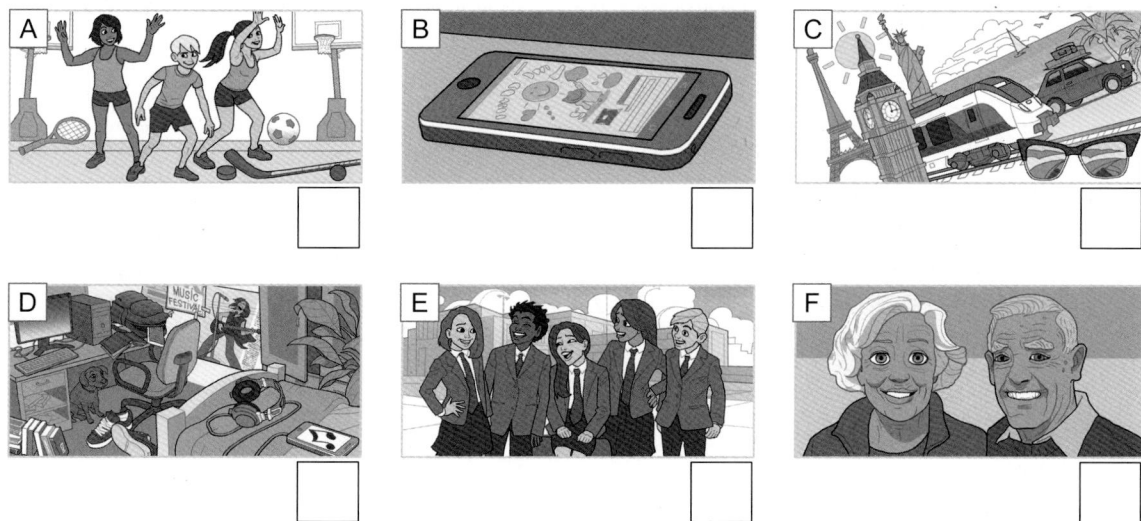

b) Listen to the podcast. What's important to the students?
Choose the correct picture (A–F) for each person. There are two extra pictures.

	Ethan	Hafsa	Ryan	Laura
picture				
reason				

c) Listen again. Write the reason why this is important to them.

2 WORDS A quiz for Green Clothes Day

Do the quiz. What's the word in the grey boxes?

When you wear second-hand clothes, you R ☐ ☐ ☐ ☐ (1) them.

You don't need to buy new clothes. You can also ☐ W ☐ ☐ ☐ (2) clothes with a friend!

It's a natural material for clothes: ☐ ☐ T ☐ ☐ ☐ (3)

To keep our seas free from plastic, don't wear too many ☐ O ☐ ☐ ☐ ☐ (4) clothes.

Old-fashioned clothes can look trendy and A ☐ ☐ ☐ ☐ ☐ V ☐ (5)!

You can use old M ☐ ☐ ☐ ☐ ☐ ☐ (6) to make new clothes.

There's a problem with your jacket? Don't buy a new one, ☐ ☐ ☐ P ☐ ☐ ☐ (7) it!

Lighthouse 3 | Lehrkräftefassung Plus
Illustrationen: Cornelsen/Harald Ardeias

2 Checkpoint answers 2.5A

1 LISTENING Mei's podcast

I can explain what's important to me. ✓

a) (Lösungsbeispiel) My family is most important to me because they're always there for me, and so are my friends. I also really enjoy travelling. My room is my safe space for me. My phone and sport are not that important to me. (F • E • C • D • A • B) (6 points)

b) + c) (8 points)

	Ethan	Hafsa	Ryan	Laura
picture	home – D	hockey team – A	grandparents – F	travel – C
reason	He feels safe and happy there. He loves to go home and see his dog, play some music and relax.	They have played together for a long time, so they know each other really well. She can talk to the people in her team about everything.	His parents work late, so he spends a lot of time with his grandparents. They always listen to him.	She learns so much when she goes to different countries. It never gets boring for her.

(Für jede korrekte Antwort in b) und c) gibt es jeweils einen Punkt.)

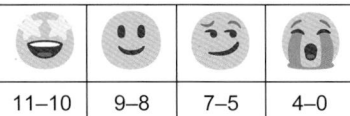

| 14–12 | 11–10 | 9–7 | 6–0 |

2 A quiz for Green Clothes Day

I can talk about fashion. ✓

a) WORDS 1 reuse   3 cotton   5 attractive   7 repair   (7 points)
          2 swap   4 polyester   6 material   **green boxes:** upcycle

b) SPEAKING (4 points)

(Lösungsbeispiel) I'm going to wear the outfit that I bought when I was in a second hand shop with my mum. It's a dress with two colours and it was just 5 euros. The material is cotton. I think my outfit will look very cute.

(Es sind mehr als 4 Sätze möglich. Für jeden korrekten Satz gibt es einen Punkt.)

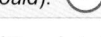

| 11–10 | 9–8 | 7–5 | 4–0 |

3 Aya's problem

I can give advice (mustn't, have to, needn't, not be allowed to, should). ✓

a) LANGUAGE 1 B • 2 C • 3 A • 4 B • 5 C (5 points)

b) WRITING (4 points)

(Lösungsbeispiel) Hi Aya, I understand that you feel worried and sad because you can't come to Zoe's party. I think you should ask your parents again. Try to tell them how important this party is to you and that you can do your homework in the morning. If you do that, maybe they will say you can come!

(Es sind mehr als 4 Sätze möglich. Für jeden korrekten Satz gibt es einen Punkt.)

4 MEDIATION Ole's problem

(8 points)

(Lösungsbeispiel) Lieber Ole, ich habe gerade in einer englischen Schulzeitung über einen Jungen gelesen, der das gleiche Problem hat wie du: **Sein bester Freund hat eine neue Freundin und er kann nicht mehr so viel Zeit mit ihm verbringen.** Das Zeitungsteam rät ihm, **seinem Freund zu erklären, wie er sich fühlt.** Er soll **dabei ruhig bleiben.** Vielleicht **könnt ihr euch auf eine spezielle Aktivität einigen, die ihr jede Woche nur zu zweit macht?** Schöne Grüße …

(Für jede korrekte Antwort gibt es zwei Punkte.)

| 17–15 | 14–12 | 11–8 | 7–0 |

Lighthouse 3 | Lehrkräftefassung Plus
Smileys: Shutterstock.com/Yefym Turkin

2 Checkpoint answers — 2.5B

5 SPEAKING Looking and feeling confident

I can talk about confidence. ✓

a) (Lösungsbeispiel) (5 points)
The girl in picture 2 looks confident. She's smiling and standing up straight. The boy in picture 3 doesn't look confident. He looks nervous. He isn't looking up and he's slouching.
(Es sind mehr als 5 Sätze möglich. Für jeden korrekten Satz gibt es einen Punkt.)

b) (Lösungsbeispiel) (3 points)
I feel most confident when I'm with my friends because when I'm with them, I can be myself. They're never unfair or mean. That makes me feel comfortable.
(Es sind mehr als 3 Sätze möglich. Für jeden korrekten Satz gibt es einen Punkt.)

c) siehe a) und b)

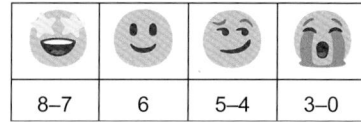

| 8–7 | 6 | 5–4 | 3–0 |

6 STUDY SKILLS An online profile

I can give and explain my opinion. ✓

a) (Lösungsbeispiel) (5 points)
If you ask me, dogs are the best because you can play games with them! **I think** chocolate is better than cheese because it's sweet. **I would say that** football is better than basketball because you can play it anywhere. **If you ask me,** computers are better than phones because they're bigger. **I think** snow is better than the sun because you can go skiing.

b) (Lösungsbeispiel) (3 points)
I don't agree with Jack at all because dogs are loud. In my opinion, cheese is better than chocolate because it's not so sweet. In my opinion, phones are better than computers because you can take them everywhere.
(Es sind mehr als 3 Sätze möglich. Für jeden korrekten Satz gibt es einen Punkt.)

c) (Lösungsbeispiel) (4 points)
In my opinion, bikes are better than cars because they're better for your health. In my opinion, books are better than TV shows because you can read them anywhere and you don't need a TV to read them. I think Sundays are better than Saturdays because it's a day for relaxing. I think old-fashioned clothes are better than modern clothes because they're made from better material.
(Für jeden korrekten Satz gibt es einen Punkt.)

| 12–11 | 10–8 | 7–6 | 5–0 |

7 READING The school fashion show

I can discuss a conflict in a story. ✓

a) 1 C • 2 D • 3 F • 4 A • 5 E (**extra heading:** B) (5 points)

b) 1 green fashion show   4 disability / as disabled (5 points)
2 take notes   5 doesn't want to
3 she doesn't want to be part of the show

c) (Lösungsbeispiel) (2 points)
I don't think that Omar wanted to upset Rosie. I think he thought he would help her by giving her something to do where she can sit down and doesn't have to stand.
(Es sind mehr als 2 Sätze möglich. Für jeden korrekten Satz gibt es einen Punkt.)

| 12–11 | 10–8 | 7–6 | 5–0 |

Lighthouse 3 | Lehrkräftefassung Plus
Smileys: Shutterstock.com/Yefym Turkin

3 My scary creature   3.1

1 Create a ghost or another scary creature.

a) Draw a ghost or another scary creature in the box below.

[drawing box]

b) Think of a good name: _____

c) Describe what your creature looks like, what it does and how it does it.

_____
_____
_____
_____
_____

d) What's your creature's story?

_____
_____
_____
_____
_____
_____

More help

– **What does your creature look like?**
My creature is big / small / colourless / … •
It has many / few / no ears / eyes / legs / … •
Its head is big / small / … •
The hair is …

– **What does it wear?**
It wears no / many / just one / a pair of / …
red / blue / pink / colourful / dark / strange clothes / skirt(s) / shoe(s) / shirt(s) …
(▶ Wordbank 5, p. 190)

– **Use adjectives:**
long – short • big / large – small • scary • friendly • sweet

– **Use activities for your creature:**
scare • eat • fight • play

– **How your creature acts:**
loudly • clearly • quietly • happily • sadly

More help

Once there was a … •
… lived in … •
… really liked … •
One day there was a … •
The … was never seen again, but today you can still hear / see …

Lighthouse 3 | Lehrkräftefassung Plus

3 Adventure sports   3.2

🔊 **1 LISTENING** An adventure trip

a) BEFORE YOU LISTEN Look at the pictures and complete columns **A** and **B** of the table. You can use an online dictionary.

🔊 b) Grace and Rhona are on the coach to the adventure centre. Listen and write why Rhona is worried.

_____

🔊 c) Listen again. Which activities have Grace and Rhona tried? Put ✓ or ✗ in column **C**.
☒ Take notes of the additional information on each activity in column **C**.

Pictures 1–6 from page 80	A Sport	B Where you do this sport	C Which activities have Grace and Rhona tried? (✓) And which not (✗)?
1	_____	_____ _____	Grace: ___ | Rhona: ___ ☒ _____ _____
2	_____	_____ _____	Grace: ___ | Rhona: ___ ☒ _____ _____
3	_____	_____ _____	Grace: ___ | Rhona: ___ ☒ _____ _____
4	_____	_____ _____	Grace: ___ | Rhona: ___ ☒ _____ _____
5	_____	_____ _____	Grace: ___ | Rhona: ___ ☒ _____ _____
6	_____	_____ _____	Grace: ___ | Rhona: ___ ☒ _____ _____

3 Chant   3.3

🔊 1 LISTENING Irregular verbs chant

a) Verbs with three different parts: Listen, repeat and write the past participles.

- be, was, _____
- fly, flew, _____
- draw, drew, _____
- see, saw, _____
- show, showed, _____
- wear, wore, _____

- break, broke, _____
- drive, drove, _____
- shake, shook, _____
- speak, spoke, _____
- give, gave, _____
- take, took, _____

- ride, rode, _____
- write, wrote, _____

b) Echo verbs: Listen, repeat and write the past participles.

- buy, bought, _____
- fight, fought, _____
- keep, kept, _____
- bring, brought, _____
- think, thought, _____
- sleep, slept, _____

- say, said, _____
- make, made, _____
- sit, sat, _____
- read, read, _____
- pay, paid, _____
- have, had, _____

c) Sandwich verbs: Listen, repeat and write the past participles.

- become, became, _____
- come, came, _____
- run, ran, _____

d) Cat verbs: Listen, repeat and write the past participles.

- drink, drank, _____
- sing, sang, _____
- swim, swam, _____
- begin, began, _____

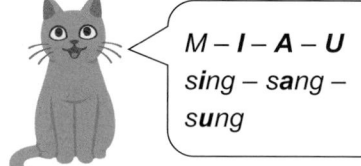

M – I – A – U
sing – sang – sung

e) Chicken verbs: Listen, repeat and write the past participles.

- put, put, _____
- cost, cost, _____
- cut, cut, _____
- hit, hit, _____

put, put, put

- hurt, hurt, _____
- set, set, _____

3 Checkpoint answers 3.4A

1 SPEAKING A day in Edinburgh

I can talk about Scotland.

(4 points)

(Lösungsbeispiel)
I'd like to visit Edinburgh Castle. I'm really interested in castles and history. It's cheaper than Edinburgh Zoo. I don't want to go to the zoo because I have already been there.

(Es sind mehr als 4 Sätze möglich. Für jeden korrekten Satz gibt es einen Punkt.)

2 LISTENING Grace's story

I can understand stories and legends (adverbs of manner).

a) B (1 point)

b) 1 small village   4 year on the day of the battle   (6 points)
   2 300   5 alone and wears tartan and looks sad
   3 soldiers   6 16th

c) LANGUAGE   (6 points)
   1 suddenly   4 slowly
   2 loudly   5 sadly
   3 fast   6 carefully

3 The adventure centre website

I can talk about adventures and interests (present perfect with *for* and *since*).

a) LANGUAGE (5 points)
   1 for
   2 since
   3 for
   4 since
   5 for

b) WORDS (4 points)
   1 cliff   2 stormy   3 pack   4 outdoor

4 MEDIATION A German adventurer (8 points)

(Lösungsbeispiel)
Hi Mark,
I want to tell you about **Rüdiger Nehberg. He was born in 1935. He was an adventurer and activist. He lived in Hamburg where he worked as a baker. Then he became more interested in travel and adventure. He travelled to so many countries, often with no water, food or other things he needed. He worked to support people all over the world for many years. He won a prize for his work.**

(Es sind mehr als 8 Sätze möglich. Für jeden korrekten Satz gibt es einen Punkt.)

Lighthouse 3 | Lehrkräftefassung Plus
Smileys: Shutterstock.com/Yefym Turkin

3 Checkpoint answers 3.4B

5 WRITING A message to a friend

I can talk about nature.

(8 points)

(Lösungsbeispiel)
Dear Michelle,
I'm camping in Scotland at the moment. We're in the Scottish Highlands. The landscape is beautiful. It's so quiet here. Sometimes I can hear the birds singing and I can see far away from the top of the mountain. I can see lots of beautiful mountains and lochs. Yesterday I went hiking and saw a beautiful sunset. I like it here because it's quiet and relaxing and the nature is beautiful.
Best wishes, …

(Es sind mehr als 8 Sätze möglich. Für jeden korrekten Satz gibt es einen Punkt.)

8–7	6	5–4	3–0

6 STUDY SKILLS Ahmed's story

I can structure ideas for a story.

(8 points)

(Lösungsbeispiel)
- **who:** two boys – James and Hussein; James – nervous; Hussein – brave
- **why:** want to see the monster
- **when:** last summer
- **where:** on Loch Ness, Scotland
- **what:** school trip; big storm; lights on the boat stop working; James thinks he sees a big animal in the water, but it's very dark …

(Für jede korrekt zugeordnete Idee gibt es einen Punkt.

8–7	6	5–4	3–0

7 READING Kayaking on the river

I can discuss good and bad choices in a story.

a) C   (1 point)

b) 1 Grace   (4 points)
2 Rhona
3 Rhona
4 Grace

c) 1 bad choice because they should focus on the boat at all times   (4 points)
2 bad choice because all of their things should be in the dry bag
3 bad choice because there were rocks under the boat
4 good choice because the instructor is there to help

9–8	7–6	5	4–0

Lighthouse 3 | Lehrkräftefassung Plus
Smileys: Shutterstock.com/Yefym Turkin

4 Wales 4.1A

1 WALK AROUND What do you know about Wales?

a) Walk around the room and ask these questions. Write down the answer and the name of the student.

Find someone who knows …	answer	name of the student
… the capital:		
… the highest mountain:		
… the most popular animal:		
… the languages:		

Do you know …?

Yes, I do. It's …

Sorry, I don't know the answer.

b) Present your results to the class.

… knows the capital / highest mountain / … of Wales. It's / They're …

2 READING & SPEAKING An online quiz about Wales

Dylan and Owen have made an online quiz about Wales for the German students.
Do you know or can you guess any of the answers? Circle your answers.

	Dylan and Owen's quiz about Wales			check
1	What's the Welsh word for Wales? **A** Ffrwyt **B** Afon **C** Cymru			
2	Who is the Prince of Wales? Prince … **A** Harry **B** William **C** George			
3	What's on the Welsh flag? **A** a red lion **B** a red dragon **C** a red sheep			
4	What's the national sport in Wales? **A** rugby **B** football **C** judo			
5	How many million sheep live in Wales? **A** two **B** five **C** ten			
6	What superhero has a large cave behind a waterfall in Wales? **A** Spiderman **B** Superman **C** Batman			
7	What was Wales famous for in the past? **A** fishing **B** coal mining **C** shipbuilding			

4 Wales 4.1B

3 LISTENING Dylan and Owen's voice-over

a) The two boys are recording a voice-over for a video for the exchange class.
Listen and check your quiz answers (4.1A).

b) Listen again and take notes. **Partner A:** Listen for information about Dylan and Owen.
Partner B: Listen for information about Llandudno and Wales. Then swap your information.

information about Dylan and Owen	information about Llandudno and Wales

Dylan / Owen learns / plays / uses …

In Llandudno / Wales there is …
You can …

c) What places in your area would you show exchange students? Make a mind map.

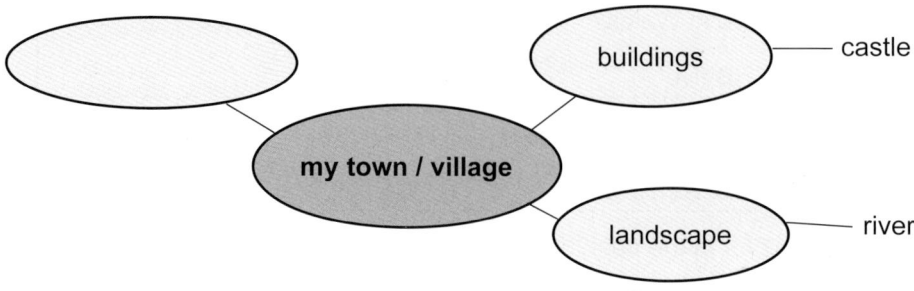

Lighthouse 3 | Lehrkräftefassung Plus

4 Three Welsh cities 4.2

1 READING Three Welsh cities

a) BEFORE YOU READ Find the three cities on the map on the last page of your book and complete the first column of the table.

City	Where	About the city	Sights	Other information
Cardiff	south Wales			
Swansea				
Wrexham				

b) Read about the three cities and complete the rest of the table.

Cardiff is the biggest city in Wales and its capital. In the city centre Cardiff Castle is popular. Watch rugby matches in the Principality Stadium and go to concerts in the amazing modern Millennium Centre by the water.

Swansea is the second biggest Welsh city. It's a modern city with many parks. You can also have a picnic on one of the beautiful beaches just outside the city or visit the romantic Carreg Cennen Castle.

Wrexham is a very old city. Its most famous sight is the Pontcysyllte Aqueduct. You can go across it in a boat. Wrexham's football club became famous when two Hollywood actors bought it.

4 How to edit a video   4.3

1 LISTENING How to edit a video

a) BEFORE YOU LISTEN Do you ever make and edit videos? What or who do you film? Tell a partner.

> I sometimes / often / … make videos on my computer / …

> I film …

> I edit videos because …

b) Dylan and Owen are going to edit their video for the exchange class.
Cut out the pictures (A–G) and the instructions in the boxes.
Listen to Dylan's instructions and put the pictures in the correct order.

c) Listen again and check. Then match the instructions to the correct pictures.

d) Start a page in your VOCAB FILE for instructions. Glue the pictures and phrases.

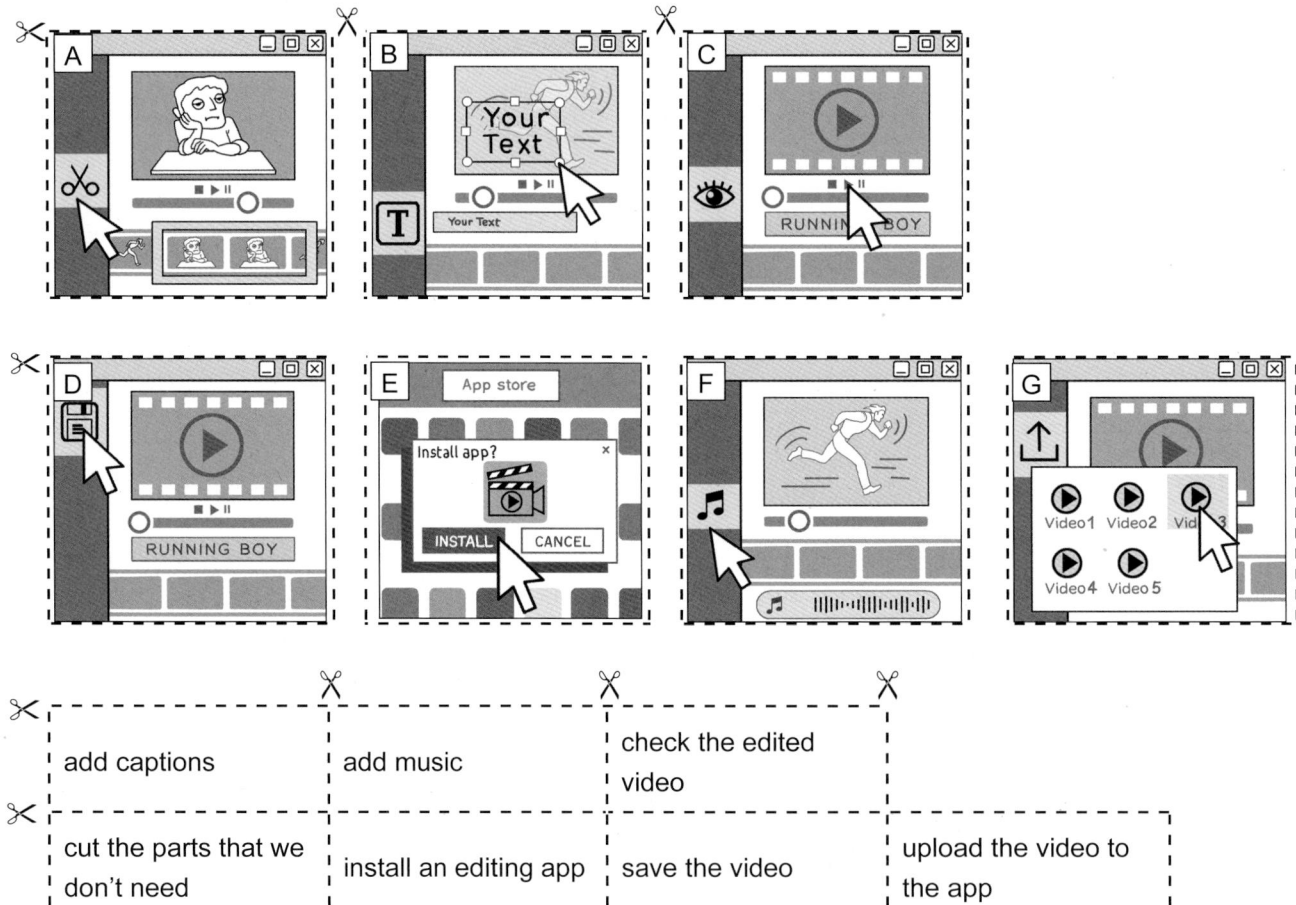

add captions | add music | check the edited video

cut the parts that we don't need | install an editing app | save the video | upload the video to the app

4 Checkpoint answers 4.4A

1 READING A poster about Wales

I can understand information about Wales. ✓

a) B (1 point)

b) 1 false (You can't drive up to the castle.) (6 points)
2 false (Only one castle has a cafe.)
3 true
4 false (Castell Dinas Brân is free / the cheapest.)
5 true
6 true

😃	🙂	😏	😮
7–6	5	4	3–0

2 MEDIATION An email from Saskia

I can talk about Wales. ✓

1 I wrote that it's **a small town by the sea and that it's very pretty.** (4 points)
2 I wrote that we **will watch a rugby game on Saturday because your parents are big rugby fans.**
3 I'm **excited about the match.**
4 I wrote that we **went to the pier and ate ice cream. After that we went to the beach and played with your dog.**

😃	🙂	😏	😮
4	3	2	1–0

3 WORDS Helping a neighbour

I can give simple instructions. ✓

1 B (8 points)
2 A
3 A
4 C
5 B
6 A
7 C
8 B

😃	🙂	😏	😮
8–7	6	5–4	3–0

Lighthouse 3 | Lehrkräftefassung Plus
Smileys: Shutterstock.com/Yefym Turkin

4 Checkpoint answers 4.4B

4 LANGUAGE Life online – positive or negative?

I can talk about the good and bad sides of social media. ✓

a) 1 which   3 which   5 who   7 who   (7 points)
   2 who   4 which   6 which

b) 1 ☹   3 ☹   5 ☺   7 ☺   (7 points)
   2 ☺   4 ☺   6 ☹

c) SPEAKING (Lösungsbeispiel) (2 points)

My experience with social media is mostly positive because I'm really careful which information I share online. I had a bad experience when somebody posted a bad photo of me and everybody in my school saw it.

(Es sind mehr als 2 Sätze möglich. Für jeden korrekten Satz gibt es einen Punkt.)

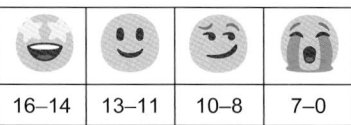

| 16–14 | 13–11 | 10–8 | 7–0 |

5 LISTENING Fake or real?

I can talk about truth and lies on social media. ✓

a) 1 E   2 B   3 A   4 D   (4 points)

b) 1 Elsa's grandma fell in love with a man who only wanted **her money**. (4 points)
   2 The 'lion' near Berlin really was a **wild pig**.
   3 The food at the restaurant in France was **expensive** and bad.
   4 Oskar's dad bought some things which never **arrived**.

c) 1 Elsa – It's bad advice because online dates aren't always bad. (4 points)
   2 Marie – It's bad advice because there are real reviews too / not everything on the internet is fake.
   3 Oskar – It's bad advice because buying things online can be safe, you just have to be careful.
   4 Hadi – It's good advice because it tells you to be careful and not to believe everything you see.

d) SPEAKING (Lösungsbeispiel) (3 points)

Some people on social media don't believe that nature must be protected. They post fake facts and hope that people who read the fake facts will believe them. When you read fake facts all the time it can become difficult to know what the truth is.

(Es sind mehr als 3 Sätze möglich. Für jeden korrekten Satz gibt es einen Punkt.)

| 15–13 | 12–10 | 9–7 | 6–0 |

6 STUDY SKILLS Describing a word that you forgot

I can make a talk flow. ✓

a) 1 C   2 B   3 E   4 F   5 A   6 D   (6 points)

b) SPEAKING (Lösungsbeispiel) (3 points)

It's a place where you can live and it's part of a bigger house. (flat)

(Für jeden korrekten Satz gibt es einen Punkt.)

7 STUDY SKILLS Learning Welsh online (5 points)

a) 1 E   2 C   3 A   4 B   5 D

b) siehe a)

c) (individuelle Lösungen)

| 14–12 | 11–10 | 9–7 | 6–0 |

Lighthouse 3 | Lehrkräftefassung Plus
Smileys: Shutterstock.com/Yefym Turkin

5 Belfast sights   5.1

An email about Belfast sights

a) Collect information about interesting sights and activities in Belfast (see book pages 138–139, 142–143 and 153).

Belfast sights

b) Imagine you've visited Belfast. Answer your friend's message and recommend at least three sights or activities. Say why you recommend them.

```
Hi, _____! Yes, Belfast is a great place to visit! I can recommend these sights and
activities:
1 _____ because _____
   _____.
2 _____ because _____
   _____.
3 _____ because _____
   _____.
I hope you have a great time! …
```

c) Check your email. Then swap with a partner and check their email. Give feedback:

Does the email include at least three sights or activities? _____

Do they sound interesting? _____

d) Correct or rewrite your message.

```
Hi, _____! Yes, Belfast is a great place to visit! I can recommend these sights and
activities:
1 _____ because _____
   _____.
2 _____ because _____
   _____.
3 _____ because _____
   _____.
I hope you have a great time! …
```

Lighthouse 3 | Lehrkräftefassung Plus

5 Checkpoint answers 5.2

1 MEDIATION Two countries

I can talk about Ireland and Northern Ireland. ✓

(Lösungsbeispiel) (11 points)

Es gibt viele Unterschiede zwischen Irland und Nordirland: z. B. bezahlt man in Irland mit Euro. Weil Nordirland zum Vereinigten Königreich gehört, wird dort hingegen mit Pfund bezahlt. Irland ist in der EU, während Nordirland, wie der Rest des Vereinigten Königreichs, nicht in der EU ist. In beiden Ländern wird Englisch gesprochen und Tee getrunken.

In Irland zeigen Verkehrsschilder Kilometer an, während in Nordirland Meilen verwendet werden. In beiden Ländern fährt man auf der linken Seite, aber Vorsicht, viele Straßen sind nur breit genug für ein Auto!

Viele Menschen in beiden Ländern sind sportbegeistert. Fußball ist überall beliebt, aber Gaelic Football ist in Irland beliebter als in Nordirland. Es unterscheidet sich vom gewöhnlichen Fußball: Es gibt 15 Spieler pro Team und es ist eine Mischung aus Fußball, Rugby und Basketball.

Die irische Flagge ist grün, weiß und orange. In Nordirland sieht man die Flagge des Vereinigten Königreichs – den Union Jack, der rot, weiß und blau ist.

(Es sind mehr als 11 Sätze möglich. Für jeden korrekten Satz gibt es einen Punkt.)

11–10	9–8	7–5	4–0

2 LISTENING & SPEAKING Phoning a hotel

I can plan and talk about a trip. ✓

a) 1 C • 2 D • 3 E • 4 B • 5 A (5 points)

b) 1 H • 2 J • 3 H • 4 J • 5 J • 6 H • 7 H • 8 H (8 points)

c) SPEAKING (Lösungsbeispiel) (4 points)

A: Bay View hotel, good morning. How can I help you?
B: Hello, I need a room for tonight, please.
A: How many people is it for?
B: It's for me and my friend.
A: A room for two … Would you like a double bed or twin beds?
B: Twin beds would be great. We'll arrive around 11.15. Would that be alright?
A: 11.15 is fine. You can pay when you get here.
B: Thank you! See you later.

(Es sind mehr als 4 Austausche (A–B) möglich. Für jeden korrekten Austausch gibt es einen Punkt.)

17–15	14–12	11–8	7–0

3 READING & WRITING Online reviews

I can talk and write about Belfast. ✓

a) 1 F (with her cousins)   3 T   5 F (not many people) (6 points)
   2 F (by car)   4 F (liked)   6 N

b) (Lösungsbeispiel) (13 points)

I **visited** the Giant's Causeway near Belfast **when I was on holiday** and I want to share my experience with you.

The place is so beautiful and the views are amazing. We had a great **tour guide** who knew a lot of **interesting** facts and the best part was that the tour was free!

Unfortunately, there were a lot of people and it was very windy and cold, so make sure to wear warm clothes. Also, the cafe there is a bit **expensive**.

I had a great time and I think you should visit the Giant's Causeway if you can handle the crowd and cool weather – **5 stars from me.**

*(Es sind mehr als 6 Sätze möglich. Für jeden korrekten Satz gibt es einen Punkt und für alle aus a) verwendeten **words & phrases** einen weiteren.)*

19–17	16–13	12–9	8–0

Lighthouse 3 | Lehrkräftefassung Plus
Smileys: Shutterstock.com/Yefym Turkin